The Routledge Handbook on the Israeli–Palestinian Conflict

The Israeli–Palestinian conflict is one of the most prominent issues in world politics today. Few other subjects have dominated the world's headlines and have attracted such attention from policy-makers, the academic community, political analysts, and the world's media.

The Routledge Handbook on the Israeli–Palestinian Conflict offers a comprehensive and accessible overview of the most contentious and protracted political issues in the Middle East. Bringing together a range of top experts from Israel, Palestine, Europe, and North America, the *Handbook* tackles a range of topics, including:

- the historical background to the conflict
- peace efforts
- domestic politics
- critical issues such as settlements, borders, Jerusalem and refugees
- the role of outside players such as the Arab states, the USA, and the EU.

This *Handbook* provides the reader with an understanding of the complexity of the issues that need to be addressed in order to resolve the conflict and a detailed examination of the varied interests of the actors involved. In-depth analysis is supplemented by a chronology of the conflict, key documents, and a range of maps.

The contributors are all leading authorities in their field and have published extensively on the Israeli–Palestinian conflict/peace process. Many have played a leading role in various Track II initiatives accompanying the peace process.

Joel Peters is Professor of Government and International Affairs in the School of Public and International Affairs at Virginia Tech, USA. His research interests cover Israeli security and foreign policy and the Israeli–Palestinian process. He is the co-author (with Sharon Pardo) of *Uneasy Neighbors: Israel and the European Union*.

David Newman is Dean of the Faculty of Humanities and Social Sciences at Ben-Gurion University, Israel. Originally a geographer, he founded the Department of Politics and Government at Ben-Gurion. He is chief editor of the peer-reviewed journal *Geopolitics*. His work focuses on territorial dimensions of ethnic conflict with a particular focus on the contemporary significance and functions of borders.

The Routledge Handbook on the Israeli–Palestinian Conflict

Edited by Joel Peters and David Newman

Routledge
Taylor & Francis Group

LONDON AND NEW YORK

First published 2013
by Routledge
2 Park Square, Milton Park, Abingdon, Oxfordshire OX14 4RN

Simultaneously published in the USA and Canada
by Routledge
711 Third Avenue, New York, NY 10017

First issued in paperback 2015

Routledge is an imprint of the Taylor & Francis Group, an informa business

British Library Cataloguing in Publication Data
A catalogue record for this book is available from the British Library

Library of Congress Cataloging in Publication Data
The Routledge handbook on the Israeli–Palestinian conflict / edited by Joel
Peters and David Newman.
    p. cm.
Includes bibliographical references and index.
1. Arab–Israeli conflict. I. Peters, Joel. II. Newman, David, 1956–
DS119.7.R679 2012
956.04—dc23

2012021777

ISBN 13: 978-1-138-92537-3 (pbk)
ISBN 13: 978-0-415-77862-6 (hbk)

Typeset in Bembo
by Book Now Ltd, London

Contents

Contents

Illustrations

Figures

Tables

Maps

Illustrations

Contributors

Arie Arnon is Professor in the Department of Economics, Ben-Gurion University. Since 2005 he has headed the Program on Economics and Society at the Van Leer Institute, Jerusalem. His areas of research include macroeconomics, monetary theory, the Israeli labor market, and the history of economic thought. He is the author of *Monetary Theory and Policy from Hume and Smith to Wicksell: Money, Credit and the Economy* (Cambridge University Press, 2011). He coordinates the Israeli side in the Aix Group, a think tank where Israeli, Palestinian, and international experts discuss various economic aspects of the current situation, as well as the areas of cooperation when a permanent peace agreement is reached (see www.aixgroup.org).

Rex Brynen is Professor of Political Science at McGill University and coordinator of Palestinian Refugee Research Net (www.prrn.org). He is the author, editor, or co-editor of nine books on various aspects of Middle East politics, among them *Palestinian Refugees: Challenges of Repatriation and Development* (I. B. Tauris/IDRC, 2007, co-edited with Roula el-Rifai) and *A Very Political Economy: Peacebuilding and Foreign Aid in the West Bank and Gaza* (United States Institute for Peace Press, 2000).

Naomi Chazan is Professor Emerita of Political Science at the Hebrew University of Jerusalem and is currently the Dean of the School of Government and Society at the Academic College of Tel Aviv–Yaffo. She is the author of numerous books and articles on comparative politics, African politics, the Palestinian–Israeli conflict, Israeli politics, and women and politics. She has been active in the Israeli peace and civil society organizations for decades. After three terms as a Member of the Knesset, she served as the president of the New Israel Fund, the largest organization supporting progressive causes in Israel.

Michael Dumper is Professor in Middle East Politics, University of Exeter. He is author of *The Future of the Palestinian Refugees: Towards Equity and Peace* (Lynne Rienner, 2007), *The Politics of Sacred Space: The Old City of Jerusalem and the Middle East Conflict, 1967–2000* (Lynne Rienner, 2001), and *The Politics of Jerusalem Since 1967* (Columbia University Press, 1997), editor of *Palestinian Refugee Repatriation: Global Perspectives* (Routledge, 2006), and joint editor of *International Law and the Israel–Palestinian Conflict* (Routledge, 2010). Professor Dumper is currently researching on comparative perspectives on exile and displacement and is also an investigator for the five-year Economic and Social Research Council (UK) project entitled *Conflict in Cities and the Contested State* (www.conflictincities.org).

Laura Zittrain Eisenberg is Full Teaching Professor in the History Department at Carnegie Mellon University, where she specializes in modern Middle East history. She is the author of *My Enemy's Enemy: Lebanon in the Early Zionist Imagination, 1900–1948* (Wayne State University Press, 1994) and, with Neil Caplan, *Negotiating Arab–Israeli Peace: Patterns, Problems, Possibilities* (Indiana University Press, 2010). She has published numerous articles and book chapters on Israel and Lebanon and on the Arab–Israel conflict and peace process and served as consultant for *PeaceMaker*, a video game simulating Palestinian–Israeli interactions (www. peacemakergame.com).

Robert O. Freedman is Peggy Meyerhoff Pearlstone Professor of Political Science Emeritus at Baltimore Hebrew University and Visiting Professor of Political Science at Johns Hopkins University, where he teaches courses in the Arab–Israeli conflict and in Russian foreign policy. Among his publications are *Russia, Iran and the Nuclear Question: The Putin Record* (US Army War College, 2007), *Contemporary Israel* (Westview Press, 2010), and *Israel and the United States* (Westview Press, 2012).

Galia Golan is Professor at the Lauder School of Government, Diplomacy and Strategy of the Interdisciplinary Center, Herzliya, and founder/Chair of the MA Program on Diplomacy and Conflict Studies. Formerly she was Darwin Professor and Head of the Department of Political Science at the Hebrew University of Jerusalem. She is the author of nine books, most recently *Israel and Palestine: Peace Plans and Proposals from Oslo to Disengagement* (Markus Wiener, 2007), along with "Globalization, Non-State Actors, and the Transformation of Conflict," in Bruce Dayton and Louis Kreisberg (eds), *Conflict Transformation and Peacebuilding* (Routledge, 2007). She is an associate editor of the *International Feminist Journal of Politics*.

Rosemary Hollis is Professor of Middle East Policy Studies and Director of the Olive Tree Scholarship Programme at City University, London. Her research focuses on British, European, and US involvement in the Middle East. She was Director of Research (2005–8) and Head of the Middle East Programme (1995–2005) at Chatham House, and before that at the Royal United Services Institute (1990–95). During the 1980s she was a lecturer at George Washington University in Washington, D.C., where she gained her PhD. She also holds a BA in History and an MA in War Studies from the King's College London.

Khaled Hroub teaches contemporary Middle East politics and history at the University of Cambridge, where he obtained his Ph.D. He is the author of *Hamas: A Beginner's Guide* (Pluto Press, 2010) and *Hamas: Political Thought and Practice* (Institute for Palestine Studies, 2000) and editor of *Political Islam: Context vs Ideology* (Saqi Books, 2011) and *Religious Broadcasting in the Middle East* (Columbia University Press, 2012). In Arabic he has published a current affairs account, *Fragility of Ideology and Might of Politics* (Beirut, 2010) and a book on the Arab Spring entitled *In Praise of Revolution* (2012). He hosted a weekly book review show on the Al-Jazeera channel from 2000 to 2006.

Amal Jamal is Senior Lecturer at the Political Science Department of Tel Aviv University, Director of the Political Communication Graduate Program and Co-Chair of the International Graduate Program in Political Science. He served three years as the Chair of the Political Science Department and serves currently as the General Director of I'lam: Media Center for Arab Palestinians in Israel. He has published extensively on Palestinian and Israeli politics in leading international journals. His recent books are *Arab Minority Nationalism in Israel: The Politics of Indigeneity* (Routledge, 2011), *The Arab Public Sphere in Israel: Media Space and Cultural Resistance* (Indiana University Press, 2009), *The Palestinian National Movement: Politics of Contention,*

1967–2005 (Indiana University Press, 2005), and *Media Politics and Democracy in Palestine* (Sussex Academic Press, 2005).

Ahmad Samih Khalidi is Senior Associate Member of St Antony's College, Oxford. He is editor-in-chief of the Arabic-language edition of the quarterly *Journal of Palestine Studies* and has written widely on Middle Eastern political and strategic affairs in both English and Arabic. His books (co-written with Hussein Agha) include *Syria and Iran: Rivalry and Cooperation* (Chatham House, 1995), *Track-2 Diplomacy: Lessons from the Middle East* (with S. Feldman and Z. Schiff, MIT Press, 2003), and *A Framework for a Palestinian National Security Doctrine* (Chatham House, 2006).

P. R. Kumaraswamy has taught since September 1999 at the School of International Studies, Jawaharlal Nehru University, New Delhi, where he has been researching and writing on various aspects of the Middle East. Between 1991 and 1999 he was a research fellow at the Harry S. Truman Research Institute for the Advancement of Peace at the Hebrew University of Jerusalem. Among his publications are *India's Israel Policy* (Columbia University Press, 2010) and *Historical Dictionary of the Arab–Israeli Conflict* (Scarecrow Press, 2006). Professor Kumaraswamy runs the virtual Middle East Institute, New Delhi (www.mei.org.in), and serves as its Honorary Director.

Yehezkel Landau is Faculty Associate in Interfaith Relations at Hartford Seminary in Connecticut, where he directs an interfaith training program, "Building Abrahamic Partnerships." His work has been in the fields of interfaith education and Jewish–Arab peacemaking. During the 1980s he directed the Oz veShalom-Netivot Shalom religious peace movement in Israel. He was co-founder in 1991 and co-director until 2003 of the Open House Center for Jewish–Arab Coexistence and Reconciliation in Ramle, Israel. His publications include (as co-editor) *Voices from Jerusalem: Jews and Christians Reflect on the Holy Land* (Paulist Press, 1992) and a research report entitled *Healing the Holy Land: Interreligious Peacebuilding in Israel/Palestine* (United States Institute of Peace Press, 2003; www.usip.org/files/resources/pwks51.pdf).

Steve Lutes is Director of Middle East and North Africa Affairs at the US Chamber of Commerce, where he is specifically responsible for managing the US–Iraq Business Initiative. He was previously a senior legislative affairs specialist in the International Trade Administration at the US Department of Commerce. Earlier in his career, he held a variety of positions in the US House of Representatives, including Chief of Staff and Legislative Director. Lutes earned his bachelor's degree from Indiana University and is currently pursuing a Masters in Public and International Affairs at Virginia Tech. He is a regular contributor to the *Diplomatic Courier*, a global affairs magazine based in Washington, DC.

Rami Nasrallah is the founder and Chairman of the International Peace and Cooperation Center (IPCC), a policy urban research center based in East Jerusalem. Dr Nasrallah received his doctorate degree in Urban Planning from TU Delft, Netherlands. From 2003 to 2007 he was a Research Associate with the "Conflict in Cities" project at the University of Cambridge Faculty of Architecture and History of Art. He is co-author of a number of publications: *The Jerusalem Urban Fabric* (IPCC, 2003), *Cities of Collision* (Birkhauser, 2006), *Successful Jerusalem* (IPCC, 2007), *Is a Viable Democratic Palestine Possible? Future Scenarios for Palestine* (Floersheimer Institute, 2007), and *Divided Cities in Transition* (IPCC, 2003), in which he contributed to urban studies and the political/social transformation of Palestinian society.

David Newman is Dean of the Faculty of Humanities and Social Sciences at Ben-Gurion University and editor of the international journal *Geopolitics*. A political geographer, he was educated in the UK at the universities of London and Durham. His work focuses on the territorial dimensions of ethnic conflict and an analysis of the contemporary significance of borders in a globalized world.

Magnus Norell is an Adjunct Scholar at the Washington Institute for Near East Policy in Washington, D.C., and a Senior Research Fellow at the Swedish Institute of International Affairs in Stockholm. He has extensive experience in Middle Eastern studies, primarily concerning conflict research, terrorism studies, and security policies in the Middle East region. He has a background as an analyst with the Swedish Secret Service and Swedish Military Intelligence. He has lectured at the Swedish National Defence College, where he developed courses on terrorism studies, and the US Marine Corps Staff and Command College in Quantico, Virginia. He has published widely and is a commentator in the media on current affairs in the Middle East and Central Asia.

Nigel Parsons is Senior Lecturer in Politics at Massey University, New Zealand. His research focuses on Palestinian institutions. Funded by a grant from the Royal Society of New Zealand, he is currently researching Israeli population management understood through the Foucauldian concept of "biopolitics," plus the institutional responses of the Palestinian Authority. He is the author of *The Politics of the Palestinian Authority: From Oslo to al-Aqsa* (Routledge, 2005).

Joel Peters is Professor of Government and International Affairs in the School of Public and International Affairs at Virginia Tech. He was previously a founder member of the Department of Politics and Government and the founding director of the Centre for the Study of European Politics and Society at Ben-Gurion University. He is the author (with Sharon Pardo) of *Uneasy Neighbors: Israel and the European Union* (Lexington Books, 2010) and *Israel and the European Union: A Documentary History* (Lexington Books, 2011), as well as of numerous articles and chapters in books on the Arab–Israeli conflict, and the editor of *The European Union and the Arab Spring: Promoting Democracy and Human Rights in the Middle East* (Lexington Books, 2012).

Paul Scham is Professor of Israel Studies at the University of Maryland and Executive Director of the University's Gildenhorn Institute for Israel Studies. He is co-editor (with Walid Salem and Benjamin Pogrund) of *Shared Histories* (Left Coast Press, 2006), which explores the role of Israeli and Palestinian historical narratives in the conflict, and of a forthcoming book, *Shared Narratives*. From 1996 to 2002 he coordinated Israeli–Palestinian joint research projects at the Truman Institute for Peace of the Hebrew University. He has published articles on various aspects of the Israeli–Palestinian peace process and since 2010 has been managing editor of the *Israel Studies Review*.

Michael Schulz is Associate Professor in Peace and Development Research at the School of Global Studies at the University of Gothenburg, Sweden. His most recent publications are "Palestine," in Joel Peters (ed.), *The European Union and the Arab Spring* (Lexington Books, 2012), "Palestinian Public Willingness to Compromise: Torn between Hope and Violence," in the *Journal of Security Dialogue*, and "The Role of Civil Society in Regional Governance in the Middle East," in Valeria Bello, Cristiano Bee, and David Armstrong (eds), *Civil Society and International Governance* (Routledge, 2010).

Kirsten E. Schulze is Senior Lecturer in International History at the London School of Economics. She is the author of *The Arab–Israeli conflict* (Longman 1999, 2008), *The Jews of Lebanon: Between Coexistence and Conflict* (Sussex Academic Press, 2001, 2008), and *Israel's Covert Diplomacy in Lebanon* (Palgrave Macmillan, 1998). She has also written articles on the Arab–Israeli conflict, the Israeli–Palestinian peace process, the Al-Aqsa *Intifada*, the Lebanese civil war, post-civil war reconstruction and reconciliation, the Jews of Lebanon, and Israeli–Maronite connections.

Colin Shindler is Emeritus Professor and Pears Senior Research Fellow at the School of Oriental and African Studies, University of London. He is founding chairman of the European Association of Israel Studies. His most recent book is *Israel and the European Left: Between Solidarity and Delegitimization* (Continuum, 2012). An updated second edition of his *History of Modern Israel* will be published by Cambridge University Press at the end of 2012.

Steven L. Spiegel is Professor of Political Science at the University of California, Los Angeles. Among other publications, he is co-author of *The Peace Puzzle: America's Quest for Arab–Israeli Peace, 1989–2011* (Cornell University Press, 2012) and *World Politics in a New Era* (Wadsworth, 2003) and author of *The Other Arab–Israeli Conflict: Making America's Middle East Policy, from Truman to Reagan* (Chicago University Press, 1986). He is working on a book on American–Israeli relations. Professor Spiegel serves as Director of the Center for Middle East Development at UCLA and is the editor of its series for Routledge on Middle East security and cooperation. He also provides assistance to Middle East programs at the Institute on Global Conflict and Cooperation of the University of California, San Diego.

Gerald M. Steinberg is a Professor in the Department of Political Science at Bar Ilan University, Israel, and is the founder of the Program on Conflict Management and Negotiation. He research focuses on diplomacy, military strategy and arms control, and human rights as a form of soft power. He has worked with international organizations such as NATO, the UN University, OSCE, and SIPRI and is president of NGO Monitor, a Jerusalem-based research organization. Among his academic publications are "Examining Israel's NPT Exceptionality," *Non-Proliferation Review*, 13 (2006): 117–41; "The Centrality of Confidence Building Measures: Lessons from the Middle East," in A. Schnabel and D. Carment (eds), *Conflict Prevention* (Lexington Books, 2004); and "The Politics of NGOs, Human Rights and the Arab–Israel Conflict," *Israel Studies*, 16 (2011): 24–54.

Julie Trottier holds a research chair with the Centre national de la recherche scientifique, France. She was previously a lecturer at the University of Newcastle and Senior Research Fellow at the University of Oxford, UK, and a post-doc researcher at McGill University, Canada. She is the author of *Hydropolitics in the West Bank and Gaza Strip* (PASSIA, 1999) and, with Paul Slack, co-editor of *Managing Water Resources: Past and Present* (Oxford University Press, 2004). Her forthcoming book, *The Problem with Water*, will be published by I. B. Tauris.

Dov Waxman is Associate Professor of Political Science at Baruch College and the Graduate Center of the City University of New York (CUNY). He has published widely on the Arab–Israeli conflict, Israeli politics, and US foreign policy towards the Middle East. He is the author of *The Pursuit of Peace and the Crisis of Israeli Identity: Defending/Defining the Nation* (Palgrave Macmillan, 2006) and (with Ilan Peleg) *Israel's Palestinians: The Conflict Within* (Cambridge University Press, 2011). He is on the board of directors of the Association for Israel Studies and was previously associate editor of the journal *Israel Studies Forum*.

Acknowledgements

Chapter 11 "Territory and Borders" is reprinted with permission and modifications:

Newman, David. 2012. 'Borders and Conflict Resolution', *A Companion to Border Studies*, first edition. Edited by Thomas M. Wilson and Hastings Donnan. Blackwell Publishing Ltd. Pp. 249–265.

Chapter 22 "Gush Emunium and the settler movement" is reprinted with permission and modifications:

Newman, David. 2005. 'From "hitnachalut" to "hitnatkut": The Impact of Gush Emunim and the Settlement Movement on Israeli Society', *Israel Studies*, Vol 10 (3), 192–224.

Maps on pages 459, 460, 461, 462 and 463 reprinted with permission of the Foundation for Middle East Peace.

Introduction

Understanding the Israeli–Palestinian conflict

Joel Peters

Without question, the Israeli–Palestinian conflict has been one of the most bitter and pro-tracted of modern times. Its continuation is seen as a threat to global security, and its resolution is viewed by global leaders as a strategic priority crucial to long-term peace and stability in the Middle East.

Efforts to resolve the conflict have featured prominently on the global agenda since its out-set. Leaders of the international community have expended considerable time and energy try-ing to bridge the differences between Israel and the Palestinians. The United Nations has spent more time discussing this issue than any other international conflict. The region is awash in peace plans and envoys on peace missions. American presidents have hosted summits, placing their personal prestige on the line. The international community has committed considerable financial resources to providing support for the Palestinian refugees, to developing Palestinian civil society, and to building the institutions needed for Palestinian self-government and state-hood. Despite these many and varied efforts, the Israeli–Palestinian conflict persists, with little prospect of an end in sight.

The history and issues surrounding any international conflict can be variously interpreted, depending on narrative and perspective. Rarely (if ever) do the dynamics of a conflict point to an objective or shared understanding, and the Israeli–Palestinian conflict is no exception. It has been marked by a number of pivotal moments subject to competing narratives, explanations, and justifications. These narratives feed into Israeli and Palestinian notions of history, self-identity, and perceived ideas about the motivations and goals of the other side (see chapter 3, by Paul Scham).

The oft-cited phrase "One land, two peoples" captures the essence of the conflict. For many, the Israeli–Palestinian conflict is a struggle of national identity, of two peoples and two nationalist movements (Zionist and Palestinian) located in the same territorial space. Framing it as a territorial dispute has led to a narrative of ownership and dispossession, with each side denying the rights, claims, and legitimacy of the other.

The notion of partition, first mooted by the 1937 Peel Commission and enshrined in the 1947 UN partition plan and the 2003 Road Map, has had a chequered history. In 1946 the British government handed its Mandate for Palestine over to the United Nations and, after considering various options, the UN General Assembly opted for partition. Resolution 181 of

29 November 1947 called for the creation of two separate states – one Jewish, one Arab – and for the internationalization of the city of Jerusalem. The immediate result of the vote was an intensification of violence between the Arab and Jewish communities in Palestine. Following Britain's withdrawal and Israel's declaration of independence on 14 May 1948, the violence turned into interstate war between the new State of Israel and the armies of the neighboring Arab states. The fighting came to an end in early 1949, with Israel signing armistice agreements with Egypt, Jordan, Lebanon, and Syria. No peace accords were discussed or signed.

By the end of the war, Israel had increased its territory by 21 percent in relation to the boundaries set out by the UN partition plan. By contrast, the Palestinians had lost any hope of an independent state – Jordan took control of the West Bank and Egypt the Gaza Strip. Above all, the war gave rise to the Palestinian refugee question. Close to three-quarters of a million Palestinians became refugees in the Arab world, having fled during the fighting or been driven out of their homes.

The 1948 war is a defining moment in the history of the Israeli–Palestinian conflict. The history of the war and its accompanying narratives continue to influence the politics of the peace process. For Israel, the 1948 war is depicted as a heroic struggle for survival, wherein the outnumbered forces of the Haganah (pre-state Jewish army) overcame overwhelming odds to defeat the combined forces of the Arab world intent on strangling the nascent Jewish state. That narrative has been challenged in recent years by a new wave of Israeli historians (see chapter 4, by Kirsten Schulze), but the discourse of vulnerability, annihilation, and Arab rejection of Israel's legitimacy are recurring themes in Israeli thinking on the conflict. For Palestinians, the 1948 war marks the start of their exile. Referred to as *al-Nakba* (the Catastrophe), the war is a symbol of Palestinian dispossession, displacement, and loss, individually and collectively, and of deliberate expulsion.

The outcome and consequences of the 1948 war plunged the Middle East into a cycle of conflict: a further five Arab–Israeli wars (the 1956 Suez Crisis, the Six Day/June War of 1967, the Yom Kippur/October War of 1973, and the Lebanon wars of 1982 and 2006); the eruption of two Palestinian *Intifadas*, in 1987 and 2000; a history of terrorism and political violence; and periodic cross-border clashes, military raids, and incursions. For the better part of the next three decades, however, the Israeli–Palestinian conflict and the Palestinian issue became submerged within the wider context of Israeli–Arab rivalry and the broader politics of the Cold War. The question of Palestinian national rights fell largely by the wayside. The outbreak of the Six Day/June War in 1967 escalated as a result of friction along the Israeli–Syrian border and had little to do with Palestinian rights. Indeed, UN Security Council Resolution 242, drawn up in the aftermath of the war and the cornerstone of the Israeli–Palestinian peace process, fails to mention the question of Palestinian national rights and makes reference to the Palestinians only within the context of "achieving a just settlement to the refugee problem." Instead, the resolution focuses on both the rights of all states in the region to live within secure and recognized borders and the return of territories captured by Israel in the war in exchange for peace.

The impact of the June 1967 war on the Israeli–Palestinian conflict cannot be overstated. Israel's dramatic victory created a new set of geopolitical and demographic realities. With the capture of the West Bank from Jordan and the Gaza Strip from Egypt, Israel now controlled all the territory allocated for both the Jewish and the Palestinian state under the terms of the 1947 UN partition plan. Jerusalem, divided after the 1948 war, became reunified. Israel immediately expanded the municipal boundaries of the city and applied Israeli law to East Jerusalem too (see chapter 10, by Michael Dumper). Significantly, a further million Palestinians now came under direct Israeli military rule.

The outcome of the war had far-reaching consequences for the internal social and political dynamics of both Israel and the Arab world, many of which are still felt today. For the Arab world, it was a humiliating defeat and a reminder of its weakness in the face of Israel's military power. For Israel, the feeling of being encircled and the threat of annihilation so prevalent before the war were replaced by a new sense of confidence and strength.

Israel's capture of the West Bank provided it with important strategic depth. It was widely celebrated in Israel and gave birth to Gush Emunim (Bloc of the Faithful) and the Israeli settler movement (see chapter 22, by David Newman). For many Israelis, especially those from the right-wing and religious spectrum of society, the West Bank is part of the Greater Land of Israel, the biblical lands of Judea (in the south) and Samaria (in the north), to which the Jewish people have historic right and claim. The electoral victory of Menachem Begin and the Likud Party in 1997 gave impetus to the settler movement and to the sustained growth of Israeli settlement-building in the West Bank and Gaza. The West Bank were no longer regarded by the Israeli government as just a "good," as territory to be bartered and returned in exchange for peace. Instead, Judea and Samaria, as the region came to be termed, was considered an integral part of the territory of the State of Israel. Today over 300,000 Israelis live in settlements in the West Bank, a testament to the influence of the settler movement to dictate policy. This has occurred in spite of the opposition of the international community, which has denounced Israeli settlement-building as illegal under international law. The future of the settlements has become a key issue in the peace process, impacting critically on discussions on the future geographic contours and territorial dimensions of a Palestinian state.

The post-1967 period did not lack for diplomatic initiatives (see chapter 7, by Laura Eisenberg). These efforts were, however, directed primarily at resolving the wider Arab–Israeli conflict and not at the question of Palestinian self-determination and statehood. In 1977, the Egyptian President, Anwar Sadat, broke ranks with the Arab world to make peace with Israel. The 1978 Camp David Accords and the 1979 Israeli–Egyptian peace treaty contained provisions for talks on autonomy for the Palestinians in the West Bank. Those talks quickly foundered. The Palestinians lacked representation in the diplomatic initiatives during this period – diplomacy was concerned more about the status of the West Bank than with the Palestinians. Israel refused to talk to the PLO, which it saw as a terrorist organization bent solely on Israel's destruction, and received the full backing of the United States in this stance. Instead, Israel sought – with little success – to develop an alternative locally based Palestinian leadership from the Occupied Territories, and looked upon King Hussein of Jordan as its main interlocutor.

The question of Palestinian self-determination and statehood slowly reemerged in the 1970s to take centre-stage on the global agenda. The PLO was steadily garnering international support, especially from Third World states, which identified the Palestinian cause with their own post-colonial struggles for independence. In 1974, the PLO was granted observer status in the United Nations and Yasser Arafat was invited to address the General Assembly. The European Community (EC) added its voice in support of Palestinian national self-determination with the issuing of the Venice Declaration in April 1980, though the Europeans fell short of explicitly calling for Palestinian statehood. Significantly, the nine member states of the EC called for the inclusion of the PLO in any future peace talks. But Europe exerted little influence in effecting diplomatic progress or in determining events on the ground (see chapter 28, by Rosemary Hollis).

At the beginning of December 1987, an Israeli truck collided with a car in Gaza, killing all four passengers. This accident triggered an unprecedented wave of demonstrations, starting first in Gaza and quickly spreading to East Jerusalem and the West Bank. The outbreak of the *Intifada* (literally, a "shaking off") marks the next significant transition in the Israeli–Palestinian conflict. Guided primarily by an emerging grassroots leadership rather than by the exiled political leadership of the PLO, the *Intifada* was a campaign of civil disobedience and popular resistance to the Israeli occupation. It is most notable for the widespread and active support it received from all sectors of Palestinian society (see chapter 5, by Rami Nasrallah). The *intifada* succeeded in directing international attention to the conditions of Israel's occupation of the West Bank and Gaza. Moreover, it highlighted the fact that Israeli rule and occupation, disingenuously portrayed by Israel as benign and even beneficial to Palestinian society, was not sustainable in the long run. The *Intifada* led many Israelis to consider a process of physical, if not emotional, disengagement from the West Bank and Gaza. The demand for separation from the Palestinians gained increasing traction within Israeli society following the collapse of the peace process at the end of 2000 and the outbreak of the Second, al-Aqsa, *Intifada* (see chapter 16, by Gerald Steinberg).

The end of the Cold War, the 1991 Gulf War, and the convening of the Madrid Conference in November 1991 combined to create a political dynamic that culminated in the dramatic breakthrough between Israel and the PLO and the signing of the Declaration of Principles on 13 September 1993. With the handshake on the White House lawn, Israel and the Palestinians had seemingly put their troubled history behind them and were about to enter a new era of mutual recognition, reconciliation, and peace. Yasser Arafat and the PLO leadership, long demonized, had now seemingly become Israel's partner for peace. The Oslo Accords comprised a set of interim measures designed to transfer land and authority to the Palestinians, paving the way for the eventual end of Israeli occupation and the signing of a full peace treaty. Critical issues such as the future of Jerusalem, borders, settlements, water, and refugees (termed "final-status issues") were to be negotiated at the end of the process. The Declaration of Principles was followed by a further set of agreements (the Gaza–Jericho Agreement, the Oslo II Accord, and the Wye Memorandum) leading to the return to Gaza and the West Bank of Yasser Arafat and the PLO leadership, the creation of the Palestinian Authority, and the holding of elections to the newly created Palestinian Legislative Council (see chapter 8, by Galia Golan).

The Oslo process was not without its detractors. The historic compromise lauded by many was seen by some as a threat to core values and interests. In Israel, Yitzhak Rabin was vilified for reaching out to the PLO and for his willingness to give back the West Bank and Gaza. Ultimately, this readiness to compromise cost Rabin his life. On 4 November 1995, he was assassinated by a lone right-wing Jewish fanatic, Yigal Amir, incited by the groundswell of hatred that had been building up. The interim stages of the Oslo process were designed to allow Israelis and Palestinians to build confidence and trust. But the implementation of the Oslo Accords was fraught with difficulties. The Oslo process lacked sufficient mechanisms to ensure compliance by the parties and demanded a defined, shared goal. Commitments were not fulfilled, deadlines were ignored, and agreements were renegotiated. Israeli settlement-building continued unabated, and even increased in intensity. Life for Palestinians involved economic hardship, restrictions on movement, roadblocks, and security closures. Israelis lived under the ever-present fear of terrorist attacks and bus bombings. Above all, Israeli and Palestinian leaders failed to engage and prepare their respective publics for the hard choices and compromises needed for peace, especially on the question of Jerusalem and the refugees.

By the time the Israelis and Palestinians met at Camp David in July 2000 to discuss final-status issues, they were skeptical of each other's commitment to peace. The idea behind the Camp David summit was ill-conceived and the meeting itself badly planned. The decision to hold the meeting was driven more by the political timetables of the Israeli Prime Minister, Ehud Barak, and US President Bill Clinton than by the belief that the two parties were ready to conclude a final settlement. The discussions at Camp David, notable only for the symbolic spectacle of the two sides discussing final-status issues together for the first time, achieved nothing of lasting substance. The long-term importance of the summit, however, lies in the conflicting accounts that emerged to explain its failure (see chapter 6, by Joel Peters).

At the conclusion of the summit, Israel presented an account that became the dominant and unchallenged narrative within both Israeli society and the American political establishment. Yasser Arafat was cast as the villain of the story. According to Israel's version of events, Ehud Barak made an unprecedented and generous territorial offer to the Palestinians which they rejected. Arafat, uninterested in making peace with Israel, failed to offer any counterproposals of his own. It was the question of Jerusalem that dominated discussions at Camp David; the refugee issue was barely mentioned. However, Israeli leaders intimated to the Israeli public that it was Palestinian intransigence over the right of return that led to the summit's collapse. Palestinian advocacy of the right of return was portrayed within Israel as a demographic-political weapon aimed at subverting the Jewish state. Israelis from across the political spectrum were of one mind that, by raising the issue of the right of return, the Palestinians had demonstrated they were not yet reconciled to the idea of coexistence. The "no partner" narrative severely undercut the voice of the Israeli peace movement (see chapter 23, by Naomi Chazan) and has had a stranglehold on Israeli discourse on the peace process for the past twelve years.

In a parallel vein, the Palestinians considered Israel's proposals unsatisfactory, if not dangerous. In their eyes Israel was interested only in restructuring the nature of the occupation, with the Palestinian Authority acting as its enforcer. They saw the Camp David summit as high-wire diplomacy aimed at pressuring them to reach a quick agreement, lowering their expectations, and increasing the political and symbolic costs if they did not. These fears were confirmed by the finger-pointing and "blame game" that occurred immediately following the summit's collapse.

Shortly after the failure of the Camp David summit, the Second (al-Aqsa) *Intifada* erupted, triggered by Ariel Sharon's visit to the Temple Mount/Haram al-Sharif at the end of September. The outbreak of a second Palestinian uprising hinted at deeper underlying causes: pent-up frustration and disenchantment with the Oslo process, economic hardship resulting from Israeli security measures, and a growing mistrust of Israel. In Israeli eyes, however, the outbreak of violence merely confirmed that Arafat was not a true partner for peace. They were certain that Arafat had made a strategic decision in the aftermath of Camp David to pressure Israel through a campaign of terror alongside the diplomatic-political route. For Israel, the return to violence was evidence that the Palestinians had not abandoned the armed struggle to promote their national goals.

The al-Aqsa *Intifada* left Israelis and Palestinians bitterly divided. Cooperative ventures and dialogue between Israeli and Palestinian civil society, which had flourished during the Oslo years, quickly evaporated. Strategies of peace and coexistence were replaced by confrontation, containment, and separation. Violence on a scale heretofore unwitnessed took root. In a period of four years, successive terrorist attacks on civilian targets led to over 1,000 Israeli deaths. In response, Israel resorted to overwhelming military force to suppress the uprising, destroying Palestinian infrastructure and leaving more than 5,000 Palestinians dead and scores more wounded.

While Israel and the Palestinians moved further apart, paradoxically, support for the two-state solution solidified. With the adoption of the 2003 Road Map, the promotion of a Palestinian state became the cornerstone of international policy and part of Israeli discourse on the conflict. Within Israel, this support arose more from a desire for separation from the Palestinians than from a genuine acceptance of the legitimacy of their national aspirations. Successive Israeli governments over the past decade have endorsed the two-state solution with varying degrees of enthusiasm and sincerity.

Israel's withdrawal from Gaza in the summer of 2005 offered a glimmer of hope. Supporters of the Gaza disengagement plan saw it as an opportunity to kick-start the moribund peace process. Skeptics, on the other hand, saw it as a cynical and calculated ploy by Ariel Sharon to tighten Israel's grip on the West Bank (see chapter 17, by Joel Peters). The Gaza disengagement led only to further violence and to the rise of Hamas. The latter's replacing of Fatah as the governing authority in Gaza has resulted both in the physical separation of Gaza from the West Bank and the outside world and in the bifurcation of Palestinian politics and society.

In recent years, statements by the international community have contained an equal measure of urgency and frustration at the inability of the Israelis and Palestinians to resolve their conflict. President Obama made its resolution a top priority of his administration, calling for an immediate settlement freeze and for the two sides to negotiate – to little effect. Despite his efforts, Israel and the Palestinians have become even more entrenched in their positions, their leaders lacking the political will and courage to make the compromises necessary for peace.

With the rise of popular support for Hamas and the demand for the right of return, the majority of Israelis see themselves as engaged in a struggle for survival. It is not a return to the 1967 boundaries that is at stake, but unresolved issues dating back to 1948. Palestinians see Israel's support for Palestinian statehood as mere rhetoric. They claim that Israel's continued expansion of the settlements and expropriation of land undermines the viability of any future Palestinian state and argue that Israel is offering little more than the bantustanization or cantonization of Palestinian lands.

Partition, a solution first mooted in 1937, is no longer seen by many on either side as a viable solution to the conflict. Ideas are beginning to circulate that address the rights of Israelis and Palestinians outside a territorial framing. But it remains to be seen if they are real alternatives to the two-state solution that has held stage for the past seventy-five years.

* * *

The Israeli–Palestinian conflict has, understandably, spawned a vast literature: competing histories of the wars and peace efforts; personal memoirs; journalists' accounts; ideas produced by think tanks and various Track II initiatives; reports by NGOs and international organizations; online blogs; and detailed analysis of different issues (such as settlements, borders, water, Jerusalem, refugees) and conflicting descriptions of the motivations of the actors (domestic and international). This literature can be overwhelming and confusing to the reader and student of the Middle East and international relations.

This book comprises a set of thirty essays on the Israeli–Palestinian conflict. It does not offer a detailed history of the conflict or of diplomatic efforts aimed at reaching a solution. Instead, we identify six broad themes that provide a comprehensive overview of the issues, the motivations of the various actors, and the dynamics underlying the conflict.

The book opens with two essays, by Colin Schindler and Ahmad Khalidi, which detail the early origins and aims of the Zionist and Palestinian national movements. The next section addresses the competing narratives surrounding the conflict. Paul Scham in his chapter offers an overview of those narratives, while essays by Kirsten Schulze (1948 war), Joel Peters (Camp David summit), and Rami Nasrallah (Palestinian *Intifadas*) look at the debates and meanings ascribed to three specific historical junctures which have affected both Israeli and Palestinian discourses on the conflict and continue to impact on the politics of the peace process. The various diplomatic initiatives are the subject of the third section of the book. Laura Zittrain Eisenberg covers the period through to 1993, while Galia Golan continues the story from the signing of the Oslo Accords in September 1993 through to the present day.

The Oslo process identified a number of final-status issues to be discussed at the end of process. Rex Brynen discusses the ideas put forward to resolve the Palestinian refugee question, Mick Dumper writes on the status of Jerusalem, Julie Trottier on water, and David Newman on the question of borders. Five other issues are covered in this section. Arie Arnon addresses the economic aspects of the conflict and various ideas on the nature of economic relations between Israel and the Palestinians. The question of terrorism and political violence, a recurring theme that has dominated the headlines throughout the conflict, is the subject of the chapter by Magnus Norell. As Yehezkel Landau notes, the conflict over Israel/Palestine is not, at its core, a religious conflict. However, religion, with its powerful symbols and loyalties, is fundamental to the identities of both Arabs and Jews, and religious traditions that sanctify territory and history are invoked to justify nationalistic claims, even for those who do not define themselves as traditionally observant. As discussed earlier, the demand for separation and disengagement has become a powerful theme in Israeli discourse on the conflict, the emergence of which is explored in Gerald Steinberg's essay. This demand for separation led to Israel's unilateral withdrawal from Gaza in the summer of 2005. The chapter by Joel Peters offers an analysis of the motives for and consequences of the Gaza disengagement. Hopes that the latter would revive the peace process failed to materialize. Instead, Gaza has become separated from the West Bank, governed by Hamas, and isolated from the world.

A vast array of actors, both domestic and international, have influenced the course of the Israeli–Palestinian conflict. The next section consists of five essays looking at the influence and role of domestic forces within Palestinian and Israeli society. Nigel Parsons looks at the critical role played by the PLO and its leadership of the Palestinian national movement. The Oslo Accords led to the return of the PLO leadership to the West Bank and Gaza and to the creation of the Palestinian Authority (PA) as the governing structure to replace Israel. Parsons follows up his essay on the PLO with an analysis of the PA. The majority of Palestinians quickly lost faith in the PA, seeing it increasingly as corrupt or powerless. Michael Schulz provides an analysis of the role played by civil society organizations in Palestinian life and discusses the change in scope, activity, and outreach of those organizations before, during, and after the Oslo process. For many years, the PLO dominated Palestinian political life. That position of hegemony has been challenged in recent years by the rise of popular support for Hamas. Khaled Hroub describes milestones in Hamas's historical and intellectual development and the political challenges it faces. He pays particular attention to the tension between utopian and ideological ideals driven by religious aspirations within the movement, as well as to the political realities which have compelled Hamas to consider relaxing its ideology and adopting more pragmatic positions.

Israeli society is deeply divided over the possibility of peace with the Palestinians and the future status of the West Bank. Peace movements have been an integral part of the Israeli political landscape since the inception of the Israeli–Palestinian conflict. Naomi Chazan tracks the development of extra-governmental peace activities in Israel since 1967. The essay maps the constituent groups, discusses the dynamics, and assesses the impact of the Israeli peace movement over time. The West Bank holds a particular religious significance for many Israelis as it forms part of the Greater Land of Israel, the biblical lands of Judea (in the south) and Samaria (in the north), to which the Jewish people have a historic claim. This has led to the steady growth of Israeli settlements in the West Bank since 1967. David Newman's essay assesses the impact of the settler movement on Israeli society and how the settlers have influenced Israeli policy on the peace process.

The final section of the book covers the role and interests of various international actors in resolving the Israeli–Palestinian conflict. Steve Spiegel discusses the changing positions and influence of the United States from the Truman administration through to the present day. Robert Freedman addresses the role of first the Soviet Union and then Russia. This is followed by an essay by Rosemary Hollis on the position of the European Union and its role in the Israeli–Palestinian peace process. P. R. Kumaraswamy looks at the way in which the Palestinians have sought and received political, economic, diplomatic, and, at times, military support from their Arab friends. He also shows how Arab rulers have occasionally exploited the Palestinian issue to further their own interests and to delegitimize their rivals.

In recent years, scholars, experts, and policy-makers have increasingly recognized the role, both positive and negative, that diaspora groups can play in violent ethno-national conflict. To understand fully the dynamics of the Israeli–Palestinian conflict, it is essential to take this extra-territorial dimension into account. For many Jews and Palestinians living outside Israel, the West Bank, the Gaza Strip, and East Jerusalem, the conflict, though far away, is the focus of their political activity. The book concludes with a chapter by Dov Waxman in which he discusses the role of the Jewish diaspora – in particular, the American Jewish community – and its impact on the dynamics of the conflict.

The authors of these essays are leading authorities in their field, and all have published extensively in their subject and on the Israeli–Palestinian conflict/peace process as a whole. Many have played a leading role in various Track II initiatives accompanying the peace process. The essays do not share a common position on the conflict or its resolution and should be read as stand-alone pieces. No strict editorial guidelines have been imposed on the authors, beyond asking them to be critical in their analysis, to desist, as far as possible, from apportioning blame, and to refrain from engaging in policy advocacy.

In recent years discussion of the Israeli–Palestinian conflict has become increasingly polarized, a sort of dialogue of the deaf. It is the hope that this book might in some small way lend itself to the emergence of a more constructive conversation.

Part I
Competing nationalisms

1

The origins of Zionism

Colin Shindler

Introduction

Zionism grew out of the French revolutionary tradition and the Jewish and European enlightenments – with the Bible as a cultural and historical backdrop. It was a progeny of early nineteenth-century European nationalism – when nationalism belonged to the left rather than the right. In part, it took as the paradigm the national revolutionary movements that arose in post-Napoleonic Europe which sought their independence from the great empires that were restored after Waterloo. There was a cross-fertilization between movements, spawning an internationalism which appealed to the Jewish sense of universalism. As early as 1792, an international army, fighting for the French revolutionary forces, had defeated the Prussians at Valmy and at Jemappes.

In the 1850s, the Polish national poet Adam Mickiewicz proposed the establishment of a Jewish Legion which would liberate Palestine. The common slogan of these movements, 'For your victory and ours', symbolized this internationalism and the struggle of small peoples to secure their independence. It was painted on the banner which Soviet dissidents raised in Red Square following the USSR's invasion of Czechoslovakia in 1968.[1] This grew out of the first phase of the French Revolution, epitomized by Mirabeau and the Constituent Assembly in 1789. Other Zionists looked to the later radical phase of Robespierre, St Just and Danton. The Jacobin legacy became their guiding light, the rationalist Jewish philosopher Baruch Spinoza their enlightened guide.

In addition, the advent of modernity in the nineteenth century had fragmented Jewish identity. What was the best synthesis of modernity and rationalism and the traditions of the Jewish past? Both in an individual and in a communal sense, Jews occupied different positions along the spectrum of accommodation. Some, in countries such as Hungary, rebuilt the ghetto walls and ignored the revolutionary wind. In Austria and Germany, some initiated a reformed Judaism and others a modern orthodoxy. In liberal England, some converted to Christianity to advance their entry into accepted society. Benjamin Disraeli, remarkably, became British Prime Minister. Despite his membership of the Church of England, he significantly described himself to Queen Victoria as the blank page between the Hebrew Bible and the New Testament. Jewishness, therefore, in nineteenth-century Europe had a different meaning for different people. It was not surprising that, like Jewish identity, Zionism, when it officially emerged under the stewardship of Theodor Herzl in 1897, was never a monolithic entity.

Different Zionisms

Many Zionists on the left believed fervently in Marxism – and, indeed, some prayed for the arrival of the Red Army in Palestine in the early days of the October revolution. The early Labor Zionists in the decade before the First World War regarded themselves as the Zionist wing of the international revolutionary movement. In 1924, David Ben-Gurion gave a eulogy following the demise of Lenin. By 1945, Hashomer Hatzair, a Marxist Zionist movement, had authorized the translation of Stalin's writings into Hebrew. Indeed, there were concerns on the US Republican right in 1948 that Israel would willingly fall into the Soviet orbit as a Jewish socialist state.

At the other end of the political spectrum, there were nationalist intellectuals such as Abba Achimeir, who idealized Mussolini – before the advent of fascist Italy's anti-Jewish laws. His weekly column in *Doar Hayom* was entitled 'From the Notebook of a Fascist'. Poets such as Uri Zvi Greenberg in Palestine mirrored the ideological swing from left to right of European intellectuals such as Robert Michels in the 1920s. On the other hand, liberal conservatives such as Vladimir Jabotinsky, the founder of the Revisionist Zionist movement, preached the virtues of nineteenth-century romantic nationalism, the Italian Risorgimento and the example of Garibaldi. A radical follower of his, Menachem Begin, believed in the doctrine of military Zionism and revolt against the British presence in Palestine. Avraham Stern disagreed with both Jabotinsky and Begin and looked to the example of Irish republicanism – he even translated parts of P. S. O'Hegarty's *The Victory of Sinn Fein* into Hebrew. Stern and his followers, known pejoratively as 'the Stern Gang', followed the approach of the Russian Narodnaya Volya organization, which advocated the assassination of key political and military figures.

Religious Zionists originally did not follow the redemptionist approach of their twenty-first-century successors and elevate messianism to a political level. They concentrated on the more practical aspects of how to live a religious life in Palestine and took little notice of the actual borders of a future Jewish state. Indeed, Hapoel Hamizrachi, the movement of religious labour pioneers, voted for partition of the Land of Israel into two states – one Jewish, the other Palestinian Arab – in 1947. Religious Zionists further distinguished themselves from the ultra-orthodox, who believed that Zionism was a heresy. The Zionists, they argued, had intervened, perhaps deflecting divine designs, and forced God's hand. The messiah would come only when God ordained it and would establish a truly Jewish state.

Zionism therefore has many faces; there are in reality a multitude of Zionist ideologies. Its complexity contrasts with the reductionism propagated in the megaphone war between Israelis and Palestinians over the origins of the conflict. A monochrome depiction of the conflict necessarily either satanizes Zionism or idealizes it.

The failure of emancipation

Jewish religious culture has for millennia believed in the eventual return of the Jews to Zion. Down the centuries, Diaspora Judaism and Jewish communal life emphasized the centrality of Jerusalem and the Land of Israel. In times of adversity, there was a deep desire for deliverance from oppression and a heightening of the sense that the Jews were in exile. Such wishful thinking was translated into a concrete political movement only in the age of rationalism and the nation-state in the nineteenth century. It was, however, buttressed previously by the Protestant

Reformation and Cromwell's English Republic, as well as by critical thinkers such as Spinoza, Voltaire, Herder, Mendelssohn, Kant and Rousseau. When the legions of the French Revolution battered down the ghetto walls in many European cities and ended the old order, Jews flooded out to embrace the bright future of emancipation. However, the French Revolution liberated the Jews in keeping with its own internal logic, according to theory and not to the reality in which the Jews found themselves. As Max Nordau commented in his speech to the first Zionist Congress in 1897 a century later:

> The philosophy of Rousseau and the encyclopaedists had led to a declaration of human rights. Then with this declaration, the strict logic of men of the Great Revolution deduced Jewish emancipation. They formulated a regular equation: Every man is born with certain rights; the Jews are human beings, consequently the Jews are born to all the rights of man. In this manner the emancipation of the Jews was pronounced, not through a fraternal feeling for the Jews, but because logic demanded it. Popular sentiment rebelled, but the philosophy of the Revolution decreed that principles must be placed higher than sentiments. Allow me an expression which implies no ingratitude. The men of 1792 emancipated us only for the sake of principle.[2]

Nordau's somewhat sorrowful commentary reflected the end of a century of dashed hopes. The liberation of the Jews was held aloft as a mark of the new liberalism – opposition to anti-Jewish discrimination was a revolutionary badge of honour. Yet there were conditions. In the Constituent Assembly, Count Stanislaus de Clermont-Tonnerre declared in December 1789:

> Everything must be refused to the Jews as a nation; everything must be granted to them as individuals. They must be citizens. It is claimed that they do not wish to be citizens. Let them say so and let them be banished; there cannot be a nation within a nation.[3]

This approach continued when Robespierre and the Jacobins took power and when Bonaparte crowned himself Emperor of the French. The new France would be mono-national, a nation, free of ethnicity – Jewish Frenchmen were welcome, but not French Jews. If theory did not accommodate the Jews, it was easier to make the Jews accommodate theory. Many Jews obliged and attempted to project themselves as no different from other members of society. However, by the end of the nineteenth century, even the most assimilated Jew found himself the target of anti-Semitic innuendo. In the British Parliament, Disraeli's Jewish origins were invoked by his opponents. As Lady Palmerston so succinctly observed in 1868: 'We are all dreadfully disgusted at the prospect of having a Jew for our prime minister.' Dislike of Jews was linked to opposition to British imperialism in the late Victorian era. J. A. Hobson, the well-known economist, argued that the Boer War had been instigated by international Jewish bankers and East End Jews made good, such as Barney Barnato. The non-Jewish Cecil Rhodes became 'Rhodes-stein'. Neither did it matter that the vast majority of Jews were impoverished; the widespread feeling was that 'the Jews are our misfortune'. An early Russian Zionist, Moses Leib Lilienblum, commented in 1883 on this all-pervading sense of the Jewish predicament:

> The opponents of nationalism see us as uncompromising nationalists, with a nationalist God and a nationalist Torah; the nationalists see us as cosmopolitans, whose homeland is wherever we happen to be well off. Religious gentiles say that we are devoid of any faith, and the freethinkers among them say that we are orthodox and believe in all kinds of nonsense; the liberals say we are conservative and the conservatives call us liberal. Some bureaucrats

and writers see us as the root of anarchy, insurrection and revolt, and the anarchists say we are capitalists, the bearers of the biblical civilization, which is, in their view, based on slavery and parasitism. Officialdom accuses us of circumventing the laws of the land – that is, of course, the laws directed specifically against us . . . Musicians like Richard Wagner charge us with destroying the beauty and purity of music. Even our merits are turned into shortcomings: "Few Jews are murderers", they say, "because Jews are cowards." This, however, does not prevent them from accusing us of murdering Christian children.[4]

The emancipation of the Jews had fragmented Jewish identity, but it had also multiplied the number of anti-Jewish stereotypes in an age of rising judeophobia – a Jew for all seasons.

The Jews of the Rhineland

The defeat of Napoleon led to attempts in Europe to reverse the emancipatory ethos of the revolution. With Prussia now in control of the Rhineland, Jews were forced out of numerous professions if they maintained their fidelity to Judaism. Many, such as Marx's father, converted to Protestantism to gain access to a professional life and to enter Prussian society. Regardless of the sincerity of the renunciation of their Jewishness, the opprobrium still hovered in the air. In the Rhineland, many Jewish intellectuals, such Heinrich Heine and Ludwig Borne, found themselves floating between identities.

The nation-state characterized the age and the mode of its governance offered several distinct choices. France, for example, took the best part of a century to decide between the autocratic monarchy of the Bourbons, the constitutional monarchy of the House of Orleans, the imperialism of the Bonapartes and the dream of Republicanism. The plight of working people in an age of industrial revolution began to be an issue. All this moved many Jews to embrace socialism as a means of repairing the world and, in so doing, liberating them from an epoch of discrimination. Some saw it as a means of escaping Jewishness into an egalitarian universalism. Such views dovetailed very well with Clermont-Tonnerre's approach to Jewish emancipation.

In his articles on the Jewish question, Marx projected a negative view of Judaism and, by extension, all those who adhered to it. In an anonymous article for the *New York Daily Tribune* in 1856, he had spoken of 'the freemasonry of the Jews which has existed in all ages'.[5] Marx's private remarks on figures such as Ferdinand Lassalle and Edouard Bernstein were marred by anti-Jewish commentary. Significantly, the hostility of both Marx and Engels towards Jews was also directed at Moses Hess, a one-time colleague. Hess had renounced Marx's belief that the actions of humankind could be placed in a scientific framework. As Isaiah Berlin commented:

Hess believed that social equality was desirable because it was just, not because it was inevitable; nor was justice to be identified with whatever was bound, in any case, to emerge from the womb of time. All kinds of bad and irrational conditions had been produced before now, and persisted. Nothing was to be accepted merely because it had occurred – but solely because it was objectively good.[6]

Hess, unlike Marx, had been given a traditional Jewish education by his grandfather. In his first book, although then distant from familial roots, he described himself as a follower of Spinoza rather than Hegel. Following the year of revolutions in Europe in 1848, he noted that anti-Semitism was on the rise and concluded that a state of the Jews in Palestine was the socialist solution to the Jewish problem. The reunification of Italy in 1861 catalysed the writing of his well-known book *Rome and Jerusalem*.

The tsars and the Jews

In Eastern Europe where the Jewish masses were concentrated, the situation of the Jews was far worse and the conditions distinctly primeval. The autocratic rule of the Romanov tsars had been relatively unimpaired by the new ideas circulating in Western Europe in the early nineteenth century. Under Catherine the Great, Russia had embarked on new imperial conquests and had benefited territorially from the successive partitions of Poland. Russia had therefore acquired a large population of traditional, unassimilated, poor Jews. In order to cope with this unwanted mass of humanity, Catherine initiated the Pale of Settlement, an area which traversed parts of Lithuania, Latvia, Ukraine, Moldova and Belarus. The objective was to ensure that its Jewish population did not enter Russia and thereby did not compete economically. The hemming in of the Jews in this swathe of territory was partly relieved by allowing them to reside in the new land on the Black Sea conquered from the Turks. Here, discriminatory legislation which affected Jews was lightly applied. Jews flooded in to dwell in the new seaport of cosmopolitan Odessa.

During the first part of the nineteenth century, the dead hand of tsarism lay heavily on the shoulders of Russian Jews. Child soldiers were enlisted in the army and were often not heard from again. If they did emerge after twenty-five years' service, they were often too old for marriage or a new profession and too estranged from their background and community. During the reign of Nicholas I, a raft of new laws were introduced and old ones reinvigorated, with the aim of decreasing the empire's Jewish population through conversion, assimilation and emigration. While cementing a profound hatred for tsarism, it also stimulated Jewish exploration of possible solutions to their collective plight. Alexander II, the 'Tsar-Liberator', started his reign with progressive rulings such as the freeing of the serfs. Some of his father's draconian laws were moderated, and generally there was a liberal climate of hope in the future. The reforms led to a flowering of Jewish culture in particular, manifested in publications in three languages – Russian, Yiddish and Hebrew. Up until the 1860s, Hebrew had been the language of the prayerbook and religious tracts; now it appeared as a living language in its own right.

This phenomenon had its origins in the development of the Haskalah, the Jewish Enlightenment in Russia in the early part of the nineteenth century. Non-religious publications in Hebrew were written by Yitzhak Dov Levinsohn, Avraham Mapu and Yehuda Leib Gordon long before the regime of Alexander II. They were influenced by the cultural awakening in Europe known as the *Wissenschaft des Judentums* – the science of Judaism. This framed Jewishness in more than purely religious terms and regarded it as being an inherently broad reflection of Jewish civilization –languages, literature, history, poetry – as well as of Judaism itself. Thus Heinrich Graetz wrote the first history of the Jews in the mid-nineteenth century – a Jewish history rather than a Judaic history.

While the Haskalah heavily influenced Western European Jewry, the progress of such ideas was much slower in Eastern Europe. The Haskalah was opposed not only by the tsarist authorities but also by rabbinical ones, whose authority was implicitly being challenged. Thus, when Napoleon's legions invaded Russia in 1812, Shneur Zalman of Lyady, one of the founders of Hasidism, refused to endorse the French because he feared the influence of the revolution. It was better to remain with the tsars and their oppression than to risk change.

The Hebrew awakening

Yet such ideas did begin to permeate the Jewish communities of imperial Russia. They were often carried by the sons of the well-to-do who sent their offspring to study in Germany. The idea of the Jews as carriers of an ethnic culture coincided with the evolution of the Jews into a people in the modern sense in the closeted territory of the Pale of Settlement. There was also a reaction by younger Jews against communal and rabbinical leaders for their lack of an active response to tsarist oppression. The ideas of the Berlin Haskalah pervaded the walls of the religious seminaries of Lithuania. Some members of these *yeshivot* began to leave the world of Jewish learning, don European clothes, shave off their beards and seek their destiny elsewhere – whether in the New World or within the revolutionary cause. All of these political and spiritual threads came together during the time of Alexander II's reforms. In 1856 the first Hebrew monthly, *Ha-Maggid*, appeared in eastern Prussia. The first Hebrew paper in Russia, *Ha-Melitz*, was published in Odessa four years later. Both were obliged to revamp biblical Hebrew and to modernize it for everyday usage.

Peretz Smolenskin provides a typical example of such a tortuous odyssey. He had lost a brother to the Tsar's army, left the *yeshiva* and settled in Odessa. In 1868, he founded *Ha-Shachar* in Vienna, and this emerged as the leading literary publication in the evolving modern Hebrew language. Smolenskin's passion for language and literature laid the foundations of a cultural nationalism.

In 1881, the Russian revolutionary movement the Narodnaya Volya finally succeeded in assassinating Alexander II after several failed attempts. The upshot of this was an outbreak of pogroms, unleashed indirectly by the vengeful, fearful, conservative new Tsar Alexander III in cities such as Yelizavetgrad, Kiev and Balta. It was 'Jewish exploitation', rather than the rioters themselves, that was deemed to be the cause of the killings. This presaged the introduction in May 1882 by the worried tsarist authorities of the May Laws, which restricted the Jews to certain territories and launched a quota for their attendance at schools and institutes of higher education. Jews were prohibited from trading on Sundays and on Christian holidays, as well as being forced to settle outside major towns. They were held responsible, in effect, for the actions of the Narodnaya Volya and thereby made the scapegoat for the movement's actions. In one sense, this could have been predicted, but what shocked many Russian Jews was not the action of the tsarist authorities, but the apparent public indifference of the Russian intelligentsia and revolutionary movement in general to the killing of several hundred Jews. The hope of the Narodnaya Volya was that the anger of the masses against the Jews would prove to be the blue touchpaper that would ignite a broader revolt against tsarism. For the most part, the pogroms created a sense of unease within the revolutionary movement, but they viewed this as a minor and temporary episode in the greater struggle. However, for the Jews in the revolutionary movement, this was a moment of truth – where did their allegiance lie? With the glory of the revolution or the cause of their persecuted people? All Jews were affected by the rash of pogroms, yet many accepted the silence of the movement in the hope that the ultimate triumph of the revolution would liberate them from their misery. There were others who turned away from the *Narodniki* – and also renounced acculturation and assimilation – and duly embraced Zionism.

The first Zionists

The assassination of the Tsar and the introduction of the May Laws concentrated minds. The Jews were unwanted. Cultural nationalists such as Smolenskin and Russifiers such as Leon Pinsker overnight dropped their former allegiances and embraced the idea of a territorial solution to the Jewish problem outside Russia. Some returned to Jewishness, but in the sense of a national identity, not primarily a religious one. Chaim Hisin, one of the first Zionist immigrants to Palestine, wrote in his diary:

The recent pogroms have violently awakened the complacent Jews from their sweet slumbers. Until now, I was uninterested in my origin. I saw myself as a faithful son of Russia which was to me my raison d'être and the very air that I breathed. Each new discovery by a Russian scientist, every classical literary work, every victory of the Russian Empire would fill my heart with pride. I wanted to devote my whole strength to the good of my homeland, and happily do my duty. Suddenly they come and show us the door and openly declare that we are free to leave for the West.[7]

At the beginning of 1882, Jewish students formed a group called 'BILU'. This was the Hebrew acronym for a quotation from the Book of Isaiah: 'O House of Jacob, come and let us go'. The first group of fourteen immigrants reached Jaffa in July 1882.

The deteriorating situation under the reactionary Alexander III produced a plethora of solutions to the Jewish problem – from national-cultural autonomy to conversion to Russian orthodoxy. Many focused on the quest for a Jewish homeland – and more than a score of Zions were located in countries as far apart as Alaska and Ecuador, Tasmania and Angola. Palestine, a backwater in the Ottoman Empire, however, was magically attractive. It was the key to the past and held a vision of the future. It was here that the destruction of Jerusalem would be reversed and where the earthly city would merge with the heavenly one of the Jewish imagination.

Many Zionists were former seminary students who had located themselves in Odessa. Philosophers such as Ahad Ha'am attracted an intellectual following with his ideas about the creation of a spiritual centre in Palestine which would reinvigorate the Jewish world. Poets such as Chaim Nachman Bialik and journalists such as Nachum Sokolov began to write in modern Hebrew and thereby revive a slumbering language. Young students such as Chaim Weizmann and Leo Motzkin were attracted to Ahad Ha'am's standard and soon became involved in the first Zionist groupings. By the 1890s, there was a real sense of idealism. As Ahad Ha'am remarked, 'The Jew is both optimist and pessimist; but his pessimism has reference to the present, his optimism to the future. This was true of the Prophets, and it is true of the people of the Prophets.' Yet such fervour was characterized by a paucity of adherents. Most Jews preferred to emigrate to the United States and Western Europe. Others believed that their mission in life was to work in the revolutionary movement in Russia.

In Central Europe, rising anti-Semitism forced many who were acculturated and assimilated to confront their predicament as Jews. This was especially true of the Jewish bourgeoisie in Habsburg Vienna. The journalist and playwright Theodor Herzl embarked on a slow, gradualist journey away from liberal Prussian nationalism, stopping off to consider conversion to Christianity and socialism as solutions. Herzl's arrival at a Zionist answer was coloured by a Jewish illiteracy, little Jewish background, and a lack of contact with the embryonic Zionist groups in Eastern Europe. His views and his writings were influenced by utopian authors of the time. His famous booklet *Der Judenstaat* translated in English more accurately as 'The State of the Jews' than as the conventional 'The Jewish State'. Ahad Ha'am remarked that there was a profound difference between a Jewish state – and all that it implied – and a state of the Jews like any other state. For Herzl, the new Israel would be Vienna by the Mediterranean. German would be the primary language and Hebrew utilized only by the clerics. The Academy would be modelled on the French example. The Eastern Europeans, embedded in tradition and Jewish culture, were astonished and infuriated. Yet Herzl's showmanship and political acumen brought Zionism to a mass Jewish audience and placed it on the international stage. Attempts to convince Jewish philanthropists, communal leaders and rabbis all failed gloriously before he embarked on establishing the Zionist Organization, based on a democratic representation of the people.

Herzl's attempts to secure an international charter as well his many diplomatic initiatives in the corridors of European power floundered. His early death at the age of forty-four, however, was mourned by many Jews across Europe, who sat *shiva* – the customary seven days of mourning – as if he was a member of their own family. Herzl's political Zionism was taken up and developed by central figures such as Weizmann and Jabotinsky, but the movement he had founded became factionalized into parties which espoused different understandings of Zionist ideology. In 1897, the year of the first Zionist Congress, everyone was a General Zionist. By the 1930s, the non-party General Zionists had also become a party – and had even split into two opposing factions.

The ideological fervour and determined effort of political and practical Zionism eventually led to the establishment of Israel in May 1948.

The end of Zionism?

Did Zionism therefore conclude its mission in 1948? Many argue that this is indeed the case and espouse a post-Zionist position. By the 1950s, Ben-Gurion began to argue that the title 'Zionist' now embraced entirely different things among which there was no connection, and to speak of Zionism per se had no real meaning. This was a long way from the idea that a Zionist was someone who immigrated to Israel, participated in the construction of the country and attempted to forge a just society. A Zionist could now be someone who decided to remain in his country of domicile – a supporter of the Zionist idea in the diaspora. Zionism thus became confused with a pro-Zionism and a pro-Israelism. When it became apparent that the Jews of America and Western Europe would not immigrate en masse, the hinterland of strong emotional diaspora support was cultivated by Ben-Gurion and his successors in order to buttress the policies of the government of the day, but in so doing it blurred the understanding of Zionism.

Indeed, such 'Zionization' was not welcomed by all diaspora Jews. Whereas a majority probably saw themselves as 'pro-Israel', not all identified to the extent of labelling themselves as 'Zionists'. Many, indeed, regarded themselves, in the original understanding of the term, as non-Zionists.

Moreover, Zionist public relations and Israeli public reality are not the same thing. Did new immigrants from the former Soviet Union move to Israel in the 1990s for Zionist reasons – or simply to seek a better life? There was the precedent of Jewish communists who were pushed out of Iraq in 1950 and forced to settle against their will in Israel.

From an opposite direction, European opponents of Israel today who wish to delegitimize the Zionist experiment often equate Zionism solely with the West Bank settlers. The adherents of the Israeli peace camp, on the other hand, are referred to as 'Israelis', yet organizations such as Peace Now do not disavow Zionism. In one sense, this desire was born partly of a continuation of a predominantly English evaluation of the Jewish situation. As Richard Crossman commented in 1946, the Englishman 'thinks of Zionism as something synthetic and unnatural' and as 'the product of high powered American propaganda.'[8]

Today some Israelis argue that Zionism did not cease to exist with the establishment of the state of Israel. A revolutionary phase certainly did end in 1948, but this was succeeded by a post-revolutionary Zionism whose task is to correct the distortions that have occurred along the way, including finding a solution to the conflict with the Palestinians. They point out that, as long as the conflict with the Palestinians persists, Zionism has not succeeded in establishing a stable national entity and that the ultimate Zionist success will be the founding of a Palestinian state. Still others remark that the *raison d'être* of Zionism was also to found a just Jewish society, to turn Israel into Zion. There is thus no agreement on what Zionism is or is not – or, indeed, whether it actually exists. Six decades after the establishment of the State of Israel, the meaning of Zionism is still open to a plethora of interpretations.

Notes

1   Shindler (2006), pp. 74–9.
2   Max Nordau, 'Speech to the First Zionist Congress', *The New Palestine*, 26 January 1923.
3   Mahler (1971), p. 32.
4   Moses Leib Lilienblum, *The Future of Our People* (1883), in Arthur Hertzberg (ed.), *The Zionist Idea: A Historical Analysis and Reader* (Philadelphia: Jewish Publication Society, 1997), p. 173.
5   Karl Marx, *New York Daily Tribune*, 4 January 1856.
6   Berlin (1979), p. 213.
7   Chaim Hisin, 'Mi yoman ehad ha Biluim' (From the 'Diary of One of the Bilu Members'), Tel Aviv, 1925, quoted in *Encyclopaedia Judaica*, vol. 4 (Jerusalem, 1972) p. 998.
8   Richard Crossman, *Palestine Mission* (London: Hamish Hamilton, 1947) p. 34.

References and further reading

Ahad Ha'am (1962) *Nationalism and the Jewish Ethic: Basic Writings of Ahad Ha'am* (New York: Schocken Books).
Avineri, Shlomo (1981) *The Making of Modern Zionism* (London: Basic Books).
Berlin, Isaiah (1979) 'The Life and Opinions of Moses Hess', in Henry Hardy (ed.), *Against the Current: Essays in the History of Ideas* (London: Hogarth Press), pp. 213–51.
Dieckhoff, Alain (2003) *The Invention of a Nation: Zionist Thought and the Making of Modern Israel* (London: Hurst).
Halpern, Ben (1969) *The Idea of the Jewish State* (2nd ed., Cambridge, MA: Harvard University Press).
Hertzberg, Arthur (1997) *The Zionist Idea: A Historical Analysis and Reader* (Philadelphia: Jewish Publication Society).
Laqueur, Walter (2003) *The History of Zionism* (London: Schocken Books).
Mahler, Raphael (1971) *A History of Modern Jewry 1780–1815* (London: Schocken Books).
Shimoni, Gideon (1995) *The Zionist Ideology* (Waltham, MA: Brandeis University Press).
Shindler, Colin (2006) *The Triumph of Military Zionism: Nationalism and the Origins of the Israeli Right* (London: I. B. Tauris).
Shindler, Colin (2007) *What Do Zionists Believe?* (London: Granta Books).

2

The Palestinian national movement

From self-rule to statehood

Ahmad Samih Khalidi

Over the span of a hundred years or so, from the late nineteenth century to the early twenty-first, the Palestinian national movement has been woven of many strands – a patchwork of various ideological and political influences, social and religious impulses, and proactive and reactive forces taking shape and evolving with the passage of different circumstances and under the impact of varying local and international conditions.

The attempt to pinpoint a specific beginning may be as fruitless as it is uninstructive. As with most modern nationalisms and their Middle Eastern variants, the national movement that emerged from the soil of Arab Palestine did not begin to take tangible political form until the turn of the twentieth century. This is not to deny a strong pre-existing sense of locale or territorial belonging, or that of a broader, if amorphous 'Palestinian' persona or identity – particularly among the educated and politically conscious elite. But this persona was also complex and multilayered, its varied threads comprising anti-Turkish Arabism, 'Modernist' Ottomanism, Islamist reformist tendencies, and pan–Arab and Greater Syrian nationalism – all with a different weight and impact at different times.

These sometimes contesting and at other times converging forces provided the underlay for other later influences. Indeed, it is arguable whether there is any one real 'movement' that can be ascribed to the Palestinian Arab population until well after the defeat of the Ottoman Empire in the First World War and the dramatic emergence of a new external twin threat – that of Zionism and its eventual sponsor, the British Mandate.

The subsequent development and direction of the Palestinian national movement has been addressed elsewhere repeatedly and at length. Rather than provide yet another narrative, the main body of this essay will focus on a number of specific and related themes in respect of Palestinian *political* demands and aspirations that run through the period until the end of the British Mandate. The emphasis will be less on *who* the Palestinians are (were) and more on what did the Arab population of Palestine – or those who claimed to speak on their behalf – *wanted*.

As will be seen, Palestinian political demands emerged slowly after the First World War, fired essentially by the notion of self-determination for the prevailing Arab majority and freedom from foreign rule. This took on an ever shifting and expanding aspect, from the relatively modest call for self-rule under the British Mandate to the demand for full independence and statehood by the late 1940s, culminating in the abortive experiment of the All Palestine Government in October 1948. In a short postscript, the final part of this essay will touch upon the emergence of the contemporary (post-1948) Palestinian movement and its eventual move away from full 'liberation' back to the notion of sovereign statehood – albeit in only part of the Palestinian national patrimony.

Home-rule to national government

The intertwined challenges of emergent Zionism and British Mandatory rule (armed with the mission of establishing a 'homeland for the Jewish people', as ordained by the 1917 Balfour Declaration and subsequently endorsed by the League of Nations) elicited an evolving if amorphous and multifaceted political resistance. The Palestinian Arabs' postwar efforts at articulating their demands were largely uncoordinated and scattered. They took the form of petitions, memoranda directed at the new British conquerors, and an increasingly vocal press campaign led by the more active and educated urban sectors of society, the effective if self-appointed representatives of the Arab population of Palestine at the time.

While local Arab awareness of Zionism and protests against its associated manifestations of land settlement and immigration preceded the First World War, a number of new themes emerged with the defeat of the Turks and the prospects of a new regional and global order fired by Allied promises to the Arabs (and other peoples) of independence and self-determination. A prominent such theme was to assert the primacy of the Arab-Muslim historic claim to Palestine and to decry the denial of the Arab majority's political rights in favour of the small Jewish minority as implicit in the Balfour Declaration.[1] But manifest right from the start was the demand for some form of freedom to self-government – variously termed 'home rule' (*hukumah ahliyyah*), 'self-rule' (*hukum dhati*) or 'national government' (*hukumah wataniyyah*).

As early as 1918, a petition from one of the numerous Muslim–Christian Associations that sprang up after the war in the first attempts at local representation expressed the fear that the native Arab majority's aspirations would be ignored, and it called for the Arabs to be given a say in determining their future:

> Palestine is Arab, inhabited by over three million Muslims and Christians, whereas the national [Arabic: *wataniyeen*] Jews number no more than twenty thousand of whom around half are settlers (who have become Arabs) ... How is it thus conceivable that the minority should be granted self-rule and that Palestine should be considered their homeland? ... We have also taken note of the official declaration made by the great powers of Britain and France ... whose message is that the object of these two aforementioned powers is the final liberation of those peoples who have been oppressed by the Turks and the establishment of home rule and interests based on the authority on the free choice of their national citizens. And as we are the nationals, the owners of this land, we call upon you not to make any decision regarding the fate of Palestine before consulting us in the belief that the state of Great Britain that saved us from the Turks will not hand us over to the Jews.[2]

The appeal is noteworthy in its territorial designation of 'Palestine' as the locus of the demand for home rule without a clear definition of its borders, but implicitly including all the lands then designated as such by the British military authorities. But, while the sense of injustice and grievance at the terms of the Balfour Declaration was widespread both inside and outside Palestine, the demand for home or self-rule was at apparent odds with the strong pan-Arab and pan-Syrian sentiments that emerged at roughly the same time from the Hashemite-led revolt against the Turks. However, pan-Syrian Palestinian sentiment (which maintained a residual hold on significant sectors of educated Palestinian opinion for some time to come) was largely contingent on the fortunes of the Hashemite thrust for Arab independence in the Levant. With the French colonial defeat of Feisal's experiment in Damascus in summer 1920, the Palestinian Arabs began to talk more explicitly of their local political and territorial demands centring on Palestine itself.

The Third Palestinian Arab Congress in December 1920 comprised a broad selection of Palestinian notables and public personalities and marked a distinct new phase in the development of a national movement that supplanted the religiously based Muslim–Christian Associations. In a more refined version of 'home rule', the Congress upgraded its demands for Great Britain to agree to a

> *national government accountable to a parliamentary assembly* whose members are to be elected by the Arabic-speaking peoples who were living in Palestine until the beginning of the [First World] War, in fulfillment of its lofty principles that it seeks to implement in Arabic-speaking Iraq and Transjordan, and as a reinforcement of the deep seated goodwill between it and the entire Arab nation.[3]

If Iraq and Transjordan and other 'formerly subjugated peoples' were worthy of 'a national government', there could be no good reason to deny this to the Palestinian Arabs. This was shortly followed up with the call for a new constitution that 'allows the people to run their own internal affairs with the help of the supporting [British] state', and that includes 'full religious freedoms and equality [for Arabs and Jews] to be guaranteed in a manner that cannot be revoked or changed by any Palestinian parliament' as well as – what is possibly the first Palestinian claim to a national armed force – 'a land force to be designated to a national gendarmerie that would thus save the British treasury large amounts of money'.[4]

But the demands for a 'national government' were caught in a trap. The Palestinian Arabs adamantly refused to participate in any form of government, premised on the terms of the Balfour Declaration, that required the establishment of a Jewish national home – as offered by the British. For their part, the British refused to deal with any Palestinian national *political* demands until the terms of the Mandate (and thus the Balfour Declaration) had been accepted. This set up a vicious circle that irked both sides.[5]

After an outbreak of Arab–Jewish violence in 1920 and 1921, and in partial appeasement of Arab concerns, the British opted to offer the Arabs a measure of *religious* rather than *political* authority, centring on the newly appointed mufti of Jerusalem, Haj Amin al-Husseini, and the Supreme Muslim Council of which he was made head. Husseini's British-aided entry into national politics eventually swept him into the position of leader of the Palestinian national movement and combined spiritual and political leader of the Palestinians for the next two decades. The mufti's growing role helped to infuse Palestinian politics with an Islamist hue that was to carry over into the post-1948 era.

Towards 'independence'

As the British Mandate took hold after 1922, the first glimmerings of a change in the Palestinian demands began to appear. In appealing to the 'civilized world', and in what seemed to be a step up from the demand for self-rule or national government, the Palestine Delegation called on the League of Nations to 'recognize the *independence* [emphasis added] of Palestine, the same as her sister states, in accordance with the pledges given to the Arabs and in the interest of the Covenant of the League and of justice and peace'.[6]

The exact lexicon of Palestinian Arab demands was not always consistent; self-rule and self-government were often conflated, confused or otherwise merged with the notion of parliamentary rule and, latterly, 'independence', with no clear distinction between them. The evolution of these demands was also a reflection of the manner in which Zionist national goals were perceived and how they were being implemented on the ground, separately or under perceived British sponsorship. But the theme of independence began to take firmer grip after the late 1920s, and in particular after the 1929 riots over the Wailing Wall. As the Arabs' immediate attention was drawn towards combating Jewish claims to contested religious sites, and against Zionist immigration and land sales, the desire for 'independence' was reflected in the programmes of the new political parties that sought to capture Palestinian aspirations and which now began to dominate the Palestinian political landscape.

The 'Arab Independence Party' (also known as the Istiqlalists), founded in 1932, included a number of well-known Palestinian and Arab political personalities and figures. It called for the establishment of 'Arab parliamentary rule in Palestine' and described its beliefs as '(a) The total independence of all the Arab countries. (b) The Arab countries are an integral whole that brooks no division. (c) Palestine is an Arab land and is a natural part of Syria.'[7] This territorial equivocation between 'independence' and 'Arab unity' is seemingly contradictory. Yet, for the pan-Arab Istiqlalists (and other pan-Arabists), there was no such contradiction, based on the assumption that *all* the Arab lands should eventually be united under independent Arab rule. For the Istiqlalists, the struggle for 'independence' was necessarily directed against the British, who formed the main impediment to such a goal.

Other parties had other ideas. The escalating conflict with the Zionist movement produced a number of currents vying for Palestinian representation and leadership. One such current, led by the Jerusalemite Nashashibi family, coalesced under the rubric of the National Defense Party (NDP). Its December 1934 founding document sought 'independence for Palestine in such a manner that ensures that it will have Arab sovereignty, and the non-recognition of any international conventions that lead to any form of foreign control or external influence, or any political or administrative situation that derogates from such independence'.[8]

A major rival to the NDP (and the Istiqlalists) was the Arab Palestinian Party (APP), established by Haj Amin al-Husseini's nephew and right-hand man, Jamal Husseini, in March 1935. The APP echoed the programme of the NDP in calling for 'the independence of Palestine' and added an explicit demand for an end to the Mandate as part of its basic constitution. The APP also called for 'safeguarding Palestine's Arab character and combating the establishment of a national home for the Jews' and, in a clear signal of its pan-Arab sympathies, declared that its goals comprised 'binding Palestine to the Arab states in a totally independent pan-national political union'. Other minor political parties, such as the small Nablus-based National Bloc Party (NBP) and the Arab Palestinian Reform Party (APRP), established in Jerusalem by Hussein Khalidi, also took varying and nuanced positions on the balance between national independence and pan-Arabism. But the call for 'independence' was a common and central theme to all the main parties.[9]

Whereas they largely failed to develop into effective mass popular organizations, these emerging political parties nonetheless jointly represented the various shades of the Palestinian national movement at the time. The collective call for independence was a natural reaction to the Arab majority's concern that it would become a minority under Zionist rule mixed with pan-Arab aspirations and a more localized demand for self-government. Faced with conflicting demands, the British began to refine the notion of a Legislative Council and sought to provide the Arabs with a political outlet via a limited form of self-rule, but without any readiness on their part to meet crucial Arab demands on a halt to land sales to the Jews and Jewish immigration.

By the late 1930s the political situation in Palestine was heading towards deadlock and escalating violence, partly in response to the failure of the British Legislative Council's proposals and partly on account of developments in Syria, where the national movement had just successfully renegotiated the terms of the French Mandate after a series of strikes and demonstrations. In the context of the Palestinians' primary concerns regarding the pace of Jewish immigration and land acquisition, together with their broader fears of national dispossession, the climate was combustible. The result was the general strike leading to the Arab revolt of 1936–9.

Independence to statehood

As a series of local strikes gathered pace and transformed into a general strike in early 1936, animated and encouraged by the Istiqlalists and fired by the example of armed resistance offered by Izz ad-Din al-Qassam (the Islamist Syrian preacher who led an abortive armed rebellion against the British and became a subsequent nationalist and Islamist icon), the most notable development on the Palestinian political front was the establishment of the Arab Higher Committee (AHC), made up of the five main Palestinian political parties, other smaller groupings and a number of leading independent figures, with Haj Amin al-Husseini as its president (he also retained his post as head of the Supreme Muslim Council). The AHC thus took on the role of political representative of the Palestinian Arabs and the body speaking on their behalf.

The call for independence appeared clearly in the AHC's Memorandum submitted to the Royal (Peel) Commission regarding its recommendations for partition in July 1937. In expressing its adamant opposition to the notion of partition, the AHC urged the British government to recognize that the

> only solution compatible with justice and a true desire for peace in the land must be based on the following principles (1) the recognition of the right of the Arabs to complete independence in their own land; (2) the cessation of the experiment of the Jewish National Home; (3) the cessation of the of the British Mandate and its replacement by a treaty similar to treaties existing between Britain and Iraq, Britain and Egypt and between France and Syria, *creating in Palestine a sovereign state* [emphasis added]; (4) the immediate cessation of all Jewish immigration and of land sales to Jews pending the negotiation and conclusion of the treaty.[10]

Most striking, however, is the clear reference to a '*sovereign state*' in a new reformulation of Palestinian political demands that stressed statehood as a strategic objective. But the political momentum appears to have been lost against the backdrop of continued large-scale Arab–Jewish strife in Palestine and harsh British repression of the Arab revolt. In late 1937, the mufti escaped British arrest and went into exile, and the AHC was riven with splits and divisions. Meanwhile, the British government began to search increasingly desperately for a solution as the situation in Europe darkened. In early 1938, the British convened the St James's Conference in London, attended by Palestinian representatives. More significantly, there were delegations from Egypt, Iraq, Saudi Arabia, Yemen and Transjordan, thus marking the first stage of the process whereby the ultimate say on Palestine gradually shifted away from the Palestinian national movement and towards the Arab states.

The British White Paper of May 1939 set a cap on Jewish immigration, limited land sales, and effectively reneged on the Balfour Declaration. Its most important clause, however, called for the establishment, 'within ten years, of *an independent Palestinian state* [emphasis added] in such treaty relations with the United Kingdom' and in which 'Arabs and Jews share in government in such a way as to ensure that the essential interests of each community are safeguarded'.[11] Despite the far-reaching nature of this proposal, it was rejected by both the Arab states and the AHC, mostly on the grounds that independence, as offered, was contingent on Jewish consent. The AHC also objected to the fact that the trajectory to independence was reversible if the British authorities deemed this necessary.[12] It was, of course, vehemently opposed by the Zionist movement, as it seemed to block the path to a Jewish state, the primary Zionist strategic objective.

The White Paper was eventually overtaken by the outbreak of the Second World War only a few months later. The political/diplomatic process in Palestine was largely suspended for the duration of the conflict (although Jewish terrorist activities against the British and Arabs escalated). Meanwhile, the AHC had been dispersed and effectively disbanded, and the Palestinian cause came increasingly to be determined by the positions and actions of the Arab states.

Between the establishment of the Arab League in 1945 and the 1947 UN partition plan, the Arab states unequivocally adopted the Palestinian demands for a fully independent state. Arab efforts to head off partition at the UN took their most elaborate form in a detailed blueprint for a unitary Palestinian state that was put to the 1946 London Conference convened by the British as a last-ditch attempt to resolve the Palestine problem. The plan called for a transitional Arab–Jewish government, made up of four Arab and three Jewish ministers appointed by the British High Commissioner, to prepare for the election of an Arab–Jewish 'Founding Council'. This would draft a constitution for the new state on the following basis: 1) that the state of Palestine would be a unitary state; 2) that it would have a democratic constitution and an elected parliament; and 3) that the constitution would offer guarantees of the sanctity and preservation of the Holy places and freedom of access and worship to them as currently existed.

The Arab plan also included citizenship for all those who had been legal residents of Palestine for the previous ten years, the use of Hebrew as an official second language, a maximum of 30 per cent of parliamentary seats for the Jewish population, a ban on further Jewish immigration, curtailed land sales, and any changes to the guarantees and rights of the Jewish population to be ratified by a majority of the Jewish members of parliament.[13]

Speaking on behalf of a newly reconstituted (by the Arab League) AHC, the mufti welcomed Arab support for 'independence and national sovereignty' but suggested that the plan needed to be modified, as it was unduly generous to the Jewish minority, whose numbers did not warrant a 3:4 ratio of participation in government.[14] Effectively, however, the plan represented the most advanced Arab–Palestinian version of an independent Palestinian state pre-1948. But this new formulation was largely academic. Since the 1942 Biltmore programme, the Zionist movement had already made clear its intention to establish a Jewish state and was in no mood to consider anything less in Palestine. And the international community, spearheaded by the USA, was heading rapidly towards partition.

All Palestine Government

As the Arab states took command of the Palestine issue after 1945, the Palestinian cause became increasingly subject to inter-Arab rivalries, primarily between Egypt and Transjordan, but with Iraq and Syria as other major players. Consequently, the Palestinians (and the AHC) lost much of their autonomy and control over their political fate. For his part, the mufti sought to manoeuvre between the competing Arab powers, leaning largely on Egypt to thwart Transjordanian ambitions and to prevent King Abdullah of Jordan (with whom he had relations of mutual enmity and profound suspicion) from annexing any part of Palestine to his kingdom.

Britain's announcement in September 1947 that it was going to withdraw from Palestine prompted the mufti to call upon the Arab League to set up a Palestinian government-in-exile, but to no avail. This demand was to be repeated and rejected several times between late 1947 and May 1948, as were the mufti's calls for the appointment of Palestinian military governors or even a loan to cover AHC expenses. Palestinian weaknesses, inter-Arab competition and British pressure on account of London's deep antipathy towards the mufti meant that, as the Mandate came to an end on 15 May, the AHC had little if any effective administration, military force or means of government on the ground in Palestine – in sharp contrast to their Zionist antagonists, who had already gone on the offensive.

Slowly, and in response to the evident supremacy of the Zionist forces in the field and the growing distress and forceful displacement of the Palestinian Arabs, the Arab League began to move towards endorsement of an independent Palestinian government. First, a 'temporary civil administration' was set up in July 1948, despite strong Jordanian reservations, British opposition and Palestinian discontent at what was seen as a half measure. In September, a subsequent decision (led by Cairo and directed mostly against Amman) was taken to set up a twelve-man All Palestine Government (APG), under the premiership of the former AHC Jerusalemite member Ahmad Hilmi Abdelbaqi, to be based in Gaza, then under full Arab (Egyptian) military control. In the first of a series of similar declarations of 'independence' that presaged what was to follow some decades later, the AHC declared that

> the inhabitants of Palestine, by virtue of their natural right to self-determination and in accordance with the resolutions of the Arab League, have decided to declare Palestine in its entirety ... as an independent state under a government known as the All-Palestine Government which is based on democratic principles.[15]

The decision elicited joy and hope among the Palestinians, and in particular the growing refugee population, and the mufti – defying Cairo's will – ended his eleven-year exile by turning up in Gaza to rapturous popular welcome. The AHC/APG set about trying to rebuild some semblance of Palestinian military capability and sought to elicit international recognition from the UN. It issued several thousand 'Palestinian' passports and convened a National Council against ferocious Transjordanian opposition, passed a provisional constitution, designated a national flag and declared Jerusalem as its capital. And it asserted the right of the Palestinian people to a 'free sovereign and democratic state, with its borders defined as Syria and Lebanon in the North, Syria and Transjordan in the East, the Mediterranean in the West and Egypt in the South'.

But the APG was doomed from the start. Confronted with Transjordanian rejection, international indifference, lukewarm Arab support, inter-Arab competition, minimal military muscle and no real political reach into the Palestinian heartland, as well as an overwhelmingly superior Israel-Zionist foe, the entire experiment in independent Palestinian statehood veered rapidly towards a virtual space somewhere between farce and tragedy.

The upshot was that Transjordan effectively imposed itself on the ground on what was to become the West Bank partly by disarming the APG's armed (Jihad Muqadass – Holy War) forces in the areas allocated to the kingdom by dint of the tacit understanding between the newly declared State of Israel and the king. Most critical, however, was a large-scale Israeli offensive in October that drove the Egyptian army out of its positions in most of southern

Palestine. The mufti was recalled to Cairo, the APG fell apart, and in December 1948 the now leaderless, powerless and broken Palestinians responded to a National Congress called by Abdullah, who duly proclaimed the union of what remained of Palestine and Jordan.

The APG represented the highest point of Palestinian political aspirations after 1917, but matched with the least potential for their fulfilment. The notion of an independent and unitary Palestinian state in 1948 was the culmination of a gradual evolution of Palestinian political demands and their most developed and 'modern' manifestation – a self-conscious echo of the similar demands of all the other Arab peoples – indeed, of the Zionist movement itself. But the prospects of independent statehood in the prevailing circumstances were negligible if not non-existent. Whether the Palestinians could have done otherwise is open to debate. That they failed to achieve any of what they sought – or those who purported to speak on their behalf said they wanted – over thirty years of struggle before 1948 is not.

Epilogue

The 1948 *Nakba* left Palestinian society pulverized, its people dispersed, its land occupied, its leadership discredited and broken. With the mufti fading into irrelevance, the APG held on to its seat at the Arab League until 1959. The 23 per cent of Mandatory Palestine that was not occupied by Israel was held in Arab custody – the West Bank integrated into a unitary Jordanian state and the Gaza Strip under Egyptian military rule. The Palestinians went into something akin to national concussion, their cause a moral factor embedded in the Arab consciousness but with no clear voice or direction of their own.

But, by the late 1950s, significant if scattered signs of post-1948 stirrings began to emerge out of the debris of the *Nakba*. Fired by the experience of Israel's six-month occupation of the Gaza Strip in 1956, a new sense of activism and national reassertion gave birth to Fatah – the Palestinian National Liberation Movement. Fatah's original Gaza-based founders, such as Yasser Arafat and Khalil al-Wazir, were inspired by the Algerian model of armed struggle and resistance as a means of reawakening the Palestinian people and keeping the 'cause' alive.

Fatah drew on a number of converging groups and trends, both Islamist (many of its first leaders came from a Muslim Brotherhood background) and nationalist. But, most of all, it set about rekindling a Palestinian sense of pride and self-assertion that was directed as much against the trials and tribulations of the Arab diaspora and the Arab states' iron hold over the Palestine problem as against the injustice that had befallen the Palestinians at the hands of the Zionists. Alongside the call to arms, a much debated issue at the time was that of 'entity-building' (*bina'a al-kayan* and *kayanniyah*) – i.e., reconstructing a collective Palestinian political persona. This was essentially about identity and national empowerment rather than state-building or any programmatic attempt at laying the foundations of statehood along the lines of the Zionist movement.

But this attempt to re-create a Palestinian political persona was also an Arab enterprise. It was aimed both at containing and co-opting any nascent Palestinian activism that could spark a confrontation with Israel and also at preventing other Arab parties from monopolizing or determining the fate of the struggle over Palestine. In 1960, Iraq's new revolutionary leader, Abdulkarim Qassem, then in competition with Egypt's Nasser and Jordan's King Hussein over the Palestine issue, was the first Arab leader to urge the creation of a Palestinian state on the West Bank and Gaza as a concrete manifestation of a Palestinian entity and the first step towards full liberation.

For the emergent Palestinian national movement, however, entity-consciousness was not to be confused with statehood – and certainly not a state in just *part* of Palestine. The dominant theme of the movement as represented by Fatah and other smaller groups was that of full 'liberation' – i.e., of *all* Palestinian lands occupied in 1948. 'Liberation' encompassed a broad notion of 'return', and the two were bound together through the agency of armed struggle. In 1964, Egypt took the lead in giving the 'entity-building' exercise a notional institutional form via the establishment of the Palestine Liberation Organization (PLO), with a seat at the Arab League that replaced the now defunct APG chair.

The 1967 war gave the Palestinian national movement an unexpected but vital boost by providing indisputable evidence of the political bankruptcy of the Arab regimes and by posing the image of the Palestinian revolutionary-guerrilla as a more hopeful political counter-example. By 1968, the PLO began to assert itself as a broad national institution and passed a revised and authoritative version of its original 1964 Charter. Its 'liberationist' language was unequivocal:

> Palestine with the boundaries it had during the British Mandate is an indivisible territorial unit . . . armed struggle is the only way to liberate Palestine . . . The Palestinian Arab people assert their absolute determination and firm resolution to continue their armed struggle and work for an armed popular revolution for the liberation of their country and their return to it.[16]

The Charter goes on to declare that the partition of Palestine in 1947 and the establishment of the State of Israel 'are entirely illegal regardless of the passage of time because they were contrary to the will of the Palestinian people and to their natural right to their homeland.'

By 1969, the Fatah leader, Yasser Arafat, had been elected Chairman of the PLO. In a further and more 'progressive' elaboration of its liberationist line, Fatah adopted the goal of a unitary 'secular democratic state in the whole of Palestine' on the basis of one man, one vote. This echoed some of the previous pre-1948 concepts of statehood and independence, albeit in a sketchy form. But, with no real political drive or traction behind this call (or any positive response from the Israeli side), it quickly faded into political obscurity.

More important was the strategic change in direction after the 1973 Arab–Israeli war. Under the impression that the postwar diplomatic process was about to produce a comprehensive Arab–Israeli settlement, and keen to ensure that the Palestinians would not be bypassed or ignored, the PLO under Arafat quietly began to debate a shift away from the liberationist impulse towards a more pragmatic political programme based on Palestinian statehood in the territories occupied by Israel in 1967 alone, rather than all of Palestine.

In 1974 the PLO's parliament and highest authority, the Palestine National Council (PNC), called for a 'national authority' to be established in any part of Palestine, and in 1977 the PNC openly called for the establishment a Palestinian *state* for the first time since 1948. This process culminated in the PNC's 'declaration of independence' in 1988 and, as part of its political programme, its explicit adoption of the two-state solution and the partition of Palestine between Arabs and Jews based on the 1967 borders, as explicated in UN Resolution 242. The fact that the 1988 decision was a direct and unambiguous violation of the 1968 Charter appears to have been of little consequence either to the PLO's leaders or to the majority of PNC members.

A Palestinian state in the West Bank and Gaza along the June 1967 lines, with East Jerusalem as its capital and the right of return for the 1948 refugees, thus became the PLO's national programme and the point of convergence and lowest common denominator between most nationalist and leftist trends. It has been the consistent demand of the PLO's leadership since, and it remains the core demand of the PLO/PA today as part of its bid for international recognition at the UN.

Statehood in *part* of Palestine, however, can be seen as an anomaly rather than as a historically consistent Palestinian national demand. The post-Oslo experience of the PA may also have soured the prospects and popular faith in any viable form of partial Palestinian statehood, and its appeal may be waning under pressure from scepticism and doubt from the Islamists (including Hamas) and a growing sense among the younger and more active elements of Palestinian society that a two-state solution along the lines of the 1988 PNC program is no longer either feasible or necessarily desirable.

The twin declarations of independence of 1948 and 1988 and the PLO's 2011 attempt to secure recognition of a Palestinian state at the UN provide a convenient set of bookends for the history of the Palestinian national movement and the evolution of its demands. But they mark neither the beginning nor the end of the struggle. Self-rule, national government, independence, entity-building, liberation and the two-state solution can all be seen as part of a continuum whose end remains unfulfilled and whose prospects are uncertain at best. Whether we are heading towards another cycle of Palestinian national farce-cum-tragedy remains to be seen, but the Palestinians' unwavering aspiration for freedom is as undeniable as it is unlikely to dissipate in the near future.

Notes

1 The most reliable statistics suggest that there were some 700,000 Muslims and Christians in Palestine at the time of the First World War, compared to around 65,000 Jews (both local Ottoman and foreign citizens). See the detailed discussion in G. Kramer, *A History of Palestine* (Princeton, NJ, and Oxford: Princeton University Press, 2008), pp. 137–8.

2 'Memorandum from the Muslim–Christian Committee in Jaffa to the [British] Military Governor on the First Anniversary of the British Entry to the City', 16 November 1918, in B. N. al-Hout (ed.), *Documents of the Palestinian National Movement, 1918–1939, From the Papers of Akram Zu'aiter* (Beirut: Institute for Palestine Studies, 1984), p. 7 [in Arabic]. Hereafter, al-Hout, *Documents*. All Arabic translations are by the author unless otherwise indicated.

3 'Memorandum from the Third Palestinian Arab Congress to the [British] High Commissioner', Haifa, 18 December 1920, in Abdelwahab Kayyali (ed.), *Documents of the Palestinian Arab Resistance to British Occupation and Zionism (1918–39)* (Beirut: Institute for Palestine Studies, 1988), p. 1 [in Arabic] [emphasis added].

4 'Memorandum from the First Palestinian Arab Delegation to the British Colonial Secretary regarding the Aspirations of the Arabs of Palestine and their Views of the Mandatory Government and Zionist Immigration', 24 October 1921, ibid., p. 34.

5 Speaking to a Palestine Delegation in London (whom the British refused to grant representative status and met in their 'purely personal' capacity), the Colonial Secretary, Winston Churchill, set the tone for the British response to Arab entreaties: 'The British Government mean to carry out the Balfour Declaration. I have told you again and again. I told you so at Jerusalem. I told you at the House of Commons the other day. I tell you so now. They mean to carry out the Balfour Declaration. They do. What is the use of looking at anything else? The government is not a thing of straw to be blown by the wind this way and that way. It is bound to carry out the Declaration.' 'Report of Conference held at Colonial Office', 22 August 1921. Original English text in B. N. al-Hout, *Political Leaders and Institutions in Palestine 1917–1948* (Beirut: Institute for Palestine Studies) [in Arabic]. Hereafter, al-Hout, *Political Leaders*.

6 'Memorandum from the Arab Delegation to the League of Nations Assembly', 17 February. 1922. Original English text in al-Hout, *Documents*, p. 304.

7 'Founding Document of the Independence Arab Party and its Bylaws', Jerusalem, 1932, ibid., p. 360.

8 'Objectives of the National Defense Party (NDP), 1934', Constitution of the Arab Palestinian Party (APP), 1935', al-Hout, *Political Leaders*, p. 742.

9 'Bylaws of the National Bloc Party (NBP), 1935', and 'Objectives of the Arab Palestinian Reform Party (APRP), 1935', ibid., pp. 743 and 747.

10 'Memorandum Submitted by the Arab Higher Committee to the Permanent Mandates Commission and the Secretary of State for the Colonies', 23 July 1937, ibid., p. 760.

11 *A Survey of Palestine, 1945–46*, Volume 1 (London: HMSO; reprinted Washington, DC, IPS, 1991), p. 94.
12 'AHC response to the British White Paper', al-Hout, *Political Leaders*, p. 766.
13 'Arab Delegation's Proposals to the London Conference, 1946', ibid., p. 820.
14 'AHC Memorandum regarding Modifications to Some of the Clauses of the Arab States' Plan offered to the London Conference, 1946', ibid.
15 Shlaim (1990).
16 See the full text of the Charter, and subsequent amendments made after the 1994 Oslo agreement between Israel and the PLO, on the PA's official website, www.pna.gov.ps/Government/gov/plo.

Further reading

Caplan, N. (2010) *The Isreali–Palestinian Conflict: Contested Histories* (Oxford: Blackwell).
Jankowski, J., and Gershoni, I. (eds) (1997) *Rethinking Nationalism in the Arab Middle East* (New York: Columbia University Press).
Khalidi, R. (1997) *Palestinian Identity: The Construction of Modern Consciousness* (New York: Columbia University Press).
Khalidi, W. (1992) *All That Remains: The Palestinian Villages Occupied and Depopulated by Israel in 1948* (Washington, DC: Institute for Palestine Studies).
Mandel, N. J. (1976) *The Arabs and Zionism before World War I* (Berkeley: University of California Press).
Mattar, P. (1992) *The Mufti of Jerusalem: Al-Haj Amin al-Husayni and the Palestinian National Movement* (New York: Columbia University Press).
Muslih, M. (1988) *The Origins of Palestinian Nationalism* (New York: Columbia University Press).
Muslih, M. (1990) *Toward Coexistence: An Analysis of the Resolutions of the Palestine National Council* (Washington, DC: Institute for Palestine Studies).
Porath, Y. (1974) *The Emergence of the Palestinian National Movement, 1918–1929* (London: Frank Cass).
Porath, Y. (1977) *The Palestinian Arab National Movement, 1929–1939* (London: Frank Cass).
Sayigh, Y. (1997) *Armed Struggle and the Search for State* (Oxford: Oxford University Press).
Shlaim, A. (1990) 'The Rise and Fall of the All-Palestine Government in Gaza', *Journal of Palestine Studies*, 20/1, p. 42.
Swedenburg, T. (2003) *Memories of Revolt: The 1936–1939 Rebellion and the Palestinian National Past* (Fayetteville: University of Arkansas Press).
Swisher, C. (2011) *The Palestine Papers* (Chicago: Hesperus Press).

Part II
Narratives and key moments

3

Competing Israeli and Palestinian narratives

Paul Scham

<table>
<tr><td>

Traditional Israeli narrative
(1882–1949)

</td><td>

Traditional Palestinian narrative
(1882–1949)

</td></tr>
<tr><td>

a) The legitimacy of the Zionist enterprise of returning Jews to Eretz Yisrael is based on Jewish descent from the ancient Israelites. The Jewish people inherited their right to the land religiously, legally, and historically. Jews have always looked and prayed towards Zion (Jerusalem), have never relinquished their relationship to the land, and, despite expulsions, have always maintained a presence since ancient times. Jews were treated as foreigners and persecuted wherever they were during their long Exile.

</td><td>

a) Judaism is a religion of revelation, like Christianity, and has no inherent tie to a particular land. Jews are not a nation but rather a community of believers. In any case, any Israelite presence was a short period in the long history of Palestine. Ultimately, religious myths, without presence and possession, are incapable of creating an ownership right. Palestinians are, in fact, descendants of all previous inhabitants, including Israelites. Those Jews living in Palestine and the Muslim world before 1882 were well treated by Muslim neighbors and rulers.

</td></tr>
<tr><td>

b) Zionism was an authentic response to the persecution of Jews over millennia around the world. Jews did not come as colonizers, but rather as pioneers and redeemers of the land, and did not intend to disrupt the lives of the current inhabitants of the Land of Israel. All land for Jewish settlement was legally bought and paid for, often at inflated prices.

</td><td>

b) Zionism was a European colonialist enterprise like many in the late nineteenth century and continues to be a European ideology superimposed on the Middle East. Moreover, it is an ideology of expansion directed towards robbing Arabs of their ancestral land. Arabs have been systematically expelled by Zionist settlers from the beginning.

</td></tr>
<tr><td>

c) The Arabs of Palestine were not a national group and never had been. They were largely undifferentiated from the inhabitants of much of Syria, Lebanon, and Jordan, with no authentic tie to the Land of Israel. Many came

</td><td>

c) The ancestors of today's Palestinians (Canaanites, Jebusites, and others mentioned in the Bible) were there before the Israelites, as shown by both biblical and archaeological evidence. Palestinians have lived continuously

</td></tr>
</table>

(Continued)

Paul Scham

(Continued)

Traditional Israeli narrative (1882–1949)	Traditional Palestinian narrative (1882–1949)
for economic opportunity only after the Zionist movement began to make the land fruitful and the economy to thrive. In all the years of Arab and Muslim control, from the seventh century, Palestine was never a separate state and Jerusalem was never a capital.	in the land since then. Certainly by the 1920s, and likely much earlier, there was a Palestinian identity and nationality that differed fundamentally from those of other Levantine Arab peoples.
d) Zionist diplomacy legitimately sought a Great Power patron since Herzl, and found one in Great Britain. True, Britain had its own imperial agenda, but this does not detract from the righteousness of the Zionist cause. The Balfour Declaration was ratified by the League of Nations, constituting a statement of international law approving a Jewish homeland in Palestine.	d) The British foisted Zionism on the Palestinians, beginning with the Balfour Declaration, as part of their imperial strategy, with no right whatsoever in international law, and this was illegally ratified by the League of Nations. "He who did not own gave a promise to those who did not deserve." Zionists worked hand in glove with Britain to subjugate the Palestinian people.
e) The riots of 1920, 1929, and 1936 were instigated by unscrupulous Arab leaders for their own nefarious purposes, particularly the mufti of Jerusalem, Haj Amin al-Husseini. The "Palestinian" population had increased rapidly through immigration of Arabs who were attracted by Zionist economic successes, and the Arab population's living standards rose rapidly during this period. The British frequently stood aside when Arabs murdered Jews.	e) All the disturbances were justified and spontaneous revolts by the Palestinian people against the British/Zionist alliance and increasing immigration. The increasing Jewish immigration, facilitated by the British, created the resentment that led to the revolts. The British backed the Zionists, who were responsible for and had provoked the disturbances, and punished Palestinians harshly and illegitimately.
f) The British, who had initially been supportive of the Zionist enterprise through the Balfour Declaration and the early Mandate, began to backtrack early, as reflected in the splitting off of Transjordan in 1922, the issuing of the Passfield White Paper of 1930, and many other incidents. They definitively repudiated the Balfour Declaration with the White Paper of 1939, and were unabashedly pro-Arab after that point.	f) The British were always pro-Zionist, except when occasionally forced to behave otherwise by Arab pressure. They conspired with the Zionists to destroy Palestinian leadership in the 1936–9 revolt, thus making it impossible for Palestinians to prepare for the coming war with the Zionists. The White Paper of 1939 had no effect as it was not enforced. The British deliberately trained Zionist soldiers during the 1936–9 revolt and World War II.
g) The Zionist movement accepted the UN partition resolution of 1947 in good faith. War was forced on the *Yishuv* (Jewish national community) by the Arabs. In self-defense, the Haganah (later the Israeli Army) took over more land than had been allotted in the partition resolution and was justified in holding it, as it would inevitably have become a base for attacks on Israel.	g) The UN partition resolution of 1947 was illegitimate, as the UN had no right to give away the homeland of the Palestinians. The Palestinians cannot be blamed for trying to hold on to what was rightfully theirs. Compromise was out of the question. The Jewish leadership never genuinely accepted the idea of partition; in any case, expulsion (transfer) was always the plan.

(*Continued*)

(Continued)

Traditional Israeli narrative (1882–1949)	Traditional Palestinian narrative (1882–1949)
h) The *Yishuv* was numerically vastly inferior to the combined Arab population; it bordered on a miracle that Israel survived the war ("the few against the many"). The War of Independence was fought primarily against the Arab armies from five states. Jews realized they would be massacred if they lost, and fought with absolute determination to prevent another Holocaust. Arab atrocities proved they had no other choice.	h) The Jews had planned for the war, had organized politically and militarily, had strong support abroad, and were in a much more favorable position when war came. Their armed forces outnumbered all the Arab armies. Palestinians had no infrastructure or military training and were attacked and massacred repeatedly by Jewish gangs. Arab "aid" consisted primarily of attempted land-grabs by other Arab countries of Palestinian land.
i) The Palestinians were not expelled. They fled, in most cases, because they were ordered and cajoled by their leaders and the Arab states, in order to make room for conquering Arab armies. In many cases Jewish officials pleaded with the refugees to stay. The Israeli decision to prevent refugees from returning was justified, as otherwise Israel would be destroyed by a hostile Arab internal majority. Ultimately, the responsibility and blame rests with the Arab leadership for rejecting the partition resolution.	i) Beginning soon after the adoption of the partition resolution in November 1947, the Zionists began to expel Palestinians from their homes, almost certainly according to a plan (Plan Dalet). Deir Yassin was a planned massacre that succeeded in forcing Palestinians to leave. The *Nakba* (Catastrophe) was planned and carried out as ethnic cleansing, reminiscent of the Holocaust. The Zionists recognized that a Jewish state could not exist until most Arabs were expelled, and history proves this was the plan that was carried out.
j) The refugee issue was artificially kept alive by the Arab states, which deliberately used the refugees as pawns against Israel and forced them into refugee (concentration) camps. The real reason for the continuation of the conflict is the refusal of the Arab states to recognize Israel's existence. Israel has repeatedly offered peace, but not at the price of its own destruction, which has been the Arab goal since 1948. The "right of return" is a measure invented in order to destroy Israel as a Jewish state, and will never be accepted.	j) The Palestinian people have never ceased to protest against the illegality and immorality of their expulsion, and Palestinians continue to identify themselves as belonging to their real homes in Palestine. The Arab states have repeatedly betrayed the Palestinians and only grudgingly gave them space in refugee camps. There can never be a settlement without Israel recognizing its guilt and providing appropriate redress, including the right of all Palestinians to return to their homes enshrined in Resolution 194. Palestinians in other Arab countries are still in exile.

Revised and excerpted from Scham *et al.* (2005). This version © 2009 by Paul Scham.

Israeli historical narratives

It is not an overstatement to assert that the Israeli–Palestinian conflict is fueled largely by different understandings of history. Of course, the conflict is ultimately about land. But the rights to the land that are asserted by Israelis and Palestinians respectively rest on how they interpret the events of the past – some ancient, some very modern. Most of the "facts" – i.e., names, dates, the bare bones of events – are not seriously in dispute. But the interpretation and very meaning of those facts have been exacerbated by later events and, especially in the last few decades, by their association with theological perspectives.

To comprehend the nature of historical narratives, it is essential to distinguish between "history" and "narrative," at least as used in this essay. History is *not*, as is often assumed, "what happened in the past." If you reflect for a moment, it is clear that, on any given date, literally trillions of events occur on Earth, most of them trivial even to the individuals involved. The job of the historian is to cull from those that are known and use them selectively to illuminate and create a coherent understanding of some aspect(s) of the past. What we know about the past, therefore, is primarily what historians say it is. Of course, every historian puts their personal and ideological stamp on what they write, and one of the most important stamps is the national interpretation of the historian's own nation. Too strongly stamped, though, and it may be referred to as propaganda. And, to be sure, there is no clear differentiation between history and propaganda in this sense; we rely on professional (and sometimes amateur) historians to help us make this distinction.

However, as a practical matter, individuals or nations do not really consult historians for most of their ideas about their collective past, and especially not for important events of the last few generations. They learn these stories from older relatives, from teachers, from what they see around them (monuments, ruins, etc.), from street names in certain cases, from newspapers, and from politicians, among others. When we generalize about this highly unscientific view held by a nation about its own past, we can refer to it as "narrative."

"History" and "narrative" intersect at certain points, and each influences the other. But, not infrequently, some schools of history at times interpret history in a fundamentally different way than the majority of the population of that nation. The Israeli "new" or "revisionist" historians, discussed below, exemplify that process.

Of course, national narratives tend to glorify the nation's past and emphasize its heroism. If there is a villain in the story, such as a traditional national enemy, that nation (or sometimes a person) is painted in the blackest colors. The further the narrative extends into the past, the more it is likely to shade into myth, or into religion in certain cases, partly because less is known about the distant past even by professional historians.

It is essential to understand that there is no "correct' history against which narrative can be judged. Of course, as noted above, if basic and generally known facts are misrepresented, that is out-and-out falsification. But usually that is not the important issue, as those facts can be and often are pointed out and eventually corrected. Rather, the issue is almost always the interpretation, and, in this, most professional historians of two warring nations disagree as well. However, in many cases, their disagreements are less sharp than those reflected in their respective narratives.

This essay examines the interplay between narrative and history among Israelis and Palestinians and focuses on the crucial role that narrative plays in Israelis' understanding both of themselves and of their adversaries, and how this often tends to exacerbate the conflict. The two basic narratives for the crucial period 1882–1949 are laid out at the beginning of the chapter. For those who grew up with either narrative, one side is comfortably familiar and the other reads like propaganda. Neither one could legitimately be called history.

Origins of the narrative

The Israeli narrative begins with the Jewish narrative as told in the Bible, plus the important addition of the exile of the Jewish people from the Land of Israel/Palestine and their suffering of the last 2,000 years. However, Zionism reframes the story in national terms, explicitly acknowledging the influence of nineteenth-century European political thought and events.

Moreover, since most of the early Zionists were secular, and they understood politics in secular terms, the divine aspects were generally seen in symbolic and historical terms. Jewish return to the land from which their ancestors were expelled was denominated primarily as rectifying a historical injustice. Of course, religious Zionism, which has its own ideology, interprets the return very much in theological terms, but religious Zionism became the primary face of the Zionist movement only well after 1967.

Palestinians see the Jewish return, by contrast, as a naked land-grab dressed up in historical terms but much more akin to colonialism than to justice. They point out that, if every nation laid claim to the land in which its ancestors lived, no country would be secure in its borders – an argument that is hard to refute. Moreover, when Zionism was being formulated and for decades afterwards, there was an almost complete ideological obliviousness to the current inhabitants of the land – i.e., the (Arab) Palestinians. The reason for that is not difficult to find. The Palestinians (a term not then in use) were invisible, for the most part, to Zionists, whether in or outside of the Land of Israel. A popular slogan, indeed, was "A land without *a* people for a people without a land," sometimes misquoted as "A land without people for a people without a land."

The missing particle is crucial to the Jewish/Israeli narrative. The concept of Jews as a distinct people, or nation, was and is crucial to the Zionist worldview. In German, which was the language of many of them, the word is *Volk*; in Hebrew it is *Am*. The German and Hebrew terms convey an almost mystical connection of blood, history, and collective consciousness. Zionists did not, and some still do not, see the Arabic-speaking inhabitants of the land as a "people" and certainly could not imagine that they had the same religious, historical, and existential relationship to Palestine that Jews have to Eretz Israel.

Few Zionists imagined that the Arabs on the land could threaten their enterprise.[1] Theodore Herzl himself, the founder of the Zionist movement, who spent all of three days in the land, fantasized in his book *Altneuland* (Old-New Land) that they would be grateful for the blessings of civilization and wealth the Zionists would bring to them. This wishful attitude also stayed with the Zionist movement for decades, though it was eventually swept away by the violent opposition to Zionism in which Palestinians increasingly engaged over the decades of the British Mandate.

Palestinians have, since the establishment of Israel, and especially in the 1990s, attempted to counter Zionist ideology based on the Jewish historical relationship to the land with their own version of early history. They have claimed descent from various peoples who, according to the Bible, preceded the Children of Israel in the land, such as Philistines (from whom the name "Palestine" derives), Canaanites, and Jebusites. More plausibly, many claim descent from all of the nations and people who have passed through the land since antiquity, including the Jews. Some have even claimed they are really the descendants of the Jewish people, and the current "Jews" have stolen the religion as well as the land.

These attempts have received little attention outside Palestinian circles. It is the Jewish fortune, and the Palestinian misfortune, to have the foundations of the Jewish narrative enshrined in the single most important book in Western civilization. The Jewish claim therefore resonates with much of the Christian world.

Palestinian academic historians have contributed to the Palestinian enterprise by emphasizing the settled nature of Palestinian society, commercial growth, and agricultural development in the last few centuries, in contrast to the Zionist picture of a desolate wasteland populated largely by nomadic Bedouin. Here, the Zionist narrative has been supported by the romantic paintings of David Roberts and travelers' accounts such as Mark Twain's *Innocents Abroad*. A later generation of post-modernists termed this "Orientalism," after the notable book by Edward Said.

Early settlement

The early years of Zionist settlement (1882–1914) are for many Israelis suffused in a romantic glow. Their narrative tells of a small minority of those Jews streaming out of Russia to America having the idealism instead to come to the land of the forefathers, and to suffer extreme hardship and deprivation while "redeeming the land." During this period, they invented the unique institution of the kibbutz (communal settlement), revived Hebrew as a spoken language (the only example in history of a dead language being renewed sufficiently to become the daily language of a country), formed a self-defense force against "Arab depredations," established dozens of settlements (villages), and developed the ideology of rebuilding the Jewish people from its centuries of "parasitism" by engaging in productive agricultural labor. This gave rise to an insistence on "Hebrew labor," the principle that Jewish landowners and employers should hire only Jews, even at higher wages, as a subsidy to the national enterprise.

Arabs regard this period as beginning the process of clearing Palestinians off their land that culminated in the 1948 *Nakba*. In fact, even Palestinian historians acknowledge that comparatively few Palestinians were dispossessed in this period, as many Jewish settlements were built on hitherto unused land. However, most non-academic Palestinians have little use for such distinctions. For them, the whole point of the Zionist enterprise was to rob Palestinians of their land; many will not countenance facts that detract from that narrative.[2]

The Balfour Declaration, the British Mandate, and the Holocaust

Ever since the Zionist movement was founded by Herzl, it had sought a powerful national patron. In 1917 it found one in Great Britain, which believed its postwar aims coincided with Zionist hopes. The Balfour Declaration put the movement on the map and recognized its aspirations.

Palestinians were and remain outraged by the Declaration. They correctly point out that the British were simultaneously promising Sherif Hussein (of the Hashemite family, ancestors of the current Jordanian royal family) an Arab empire and also dividing the postwar spoils with France (the Sykes–Picot agreement). Arab anger was only heightened by the ratification of the Declaration by the League of Nations, as part of awarding the Palestine Mandate to Great Britain. It was only slightly assuaged by the fact that the British immediately divided the Mandate, giving the eastern part to the Hashemites as Transjordan (now the Kingdom of Jordan).

Zionists point out (correctly) that the Declaration was intended primarily to stake a British claim in the region, especially vis-à-vis their erstwhile allies, the French. At the same time, they acknowledge that the romance of the Jewish return struck a biblically inspired chord in many Englishmen, including Prime Minister David Lloyd George. Most of all, however, they see the Declaration and its subsequent ratification as a recognition in modern international law of the Jewish claim to Palestine, thus adding a legal aspect to the existing historical and biblical rights.

Historically, the British remain villains for both Zionists and Palestinians.

Zionists and Arabs agree that British policy shifted in 1929–30 to being more favorable to the Arabs. Zionists regard the Mandate as the stage during which they built their state-in-waiting. The Jewish Agency Executive, headed by David Ben-Gurion, was prepared to take over (as it did in 1948). Immigration, after stagnating in the 1920s, boomed starting in 1933, thanks to German Jews who emigrated, recognizing the danger posed to them by Hitler and Nazi Germany. The true villain of this period for Zionists is Haj Amin al-Husseini, the British-appointed mufti (chief religious officer) of Jerusalem.[3] Zionists argue that he incited Arabs, who would have recognized the economic benefits of the Jewish presence, against the Zionists and the British, leading to the riots of 1929 and 1936–9. Without his intervention, they claim to believe Arabs and Jews would likely have been able to find a modus vivendi.

The "revolt" of 1936–9 was the first sustained period of Palestinian–Zionist violence, and, in retrospect, Palestinian strategy then bore marked similarities to the two *intifadas* of 1987–93 and 2000–04. Palestinians regard them as tragic and heroic enterprises and as inspiration for a struggle that will never be defeated and will inevitably triumph. Israelis view them primarily as murderous rampages, with few goals except for killing Jews. In fact, all three revolts involved significant intra-Palestinian violence and settling of scores, as well as attacks on Jews and, in the first, against the British.

Both sides use this period to foment their resentment against the British. Palestinians accused the British, with justification, of brutal repression, using modern arms against a poorly armed population, and, in the later stages of the revolt, allying with the Zionist militia, the Haganah, to attack Arab villages. Zionists, who shared an interest with the British in suppressing the revolt, felt betrayed immediately after its suppression by the issuance of the White Paper of 1939, a document which repudiated the notion of Palestine as a Jewish homeland and virtually ended Jewish immigration on the eve of the Holocaust.

The Nazi Holocaust is seen as central by both sides, though both narratives are somewhat ambivalent about its real effect. For Jews, it is the final proof that the Zionist diagnosis of the Jewish condition was correct, and that only an independent state can protect the Jewish people. At the same time, there is a reluctance to credit the Holocaust as a necessary element in the creation of the Jewish State. Zionists tend to insist that, even without the Holocaust, Israel would have been created one way or another, as Zionist momentum was unstoppable. The Holocaust is, nevertheless, employed as a justification, while, simultaneously, Jews often resent others who use it as the primary reason for Israel's establishment.[4]

On a deeper level, the Holocaust provides an almost reflexive standard both for Israelis and for the Jewish diaspora by which to measure their enemies. Most of Israel's enemies since 1948 have been referred to by many Jews and Israelis as Hitler. Among these foes have been Hajj Amin al-Husayni, Egyptian Presidents Nasser and Sadat (before the latter made peace with Israel), Yasser Arafat, and Iranian President Mahmoud Ahmadinajad. This identification equates these present-day enemies with ultimate evil, and thus justifies virtually any measure taken against them. And those who make this identification deploy an unanswerable argument: "No one thought Hitler really would try to do what he advocated." Of course, it is inherently impossible to prove conclusively that these or other enemies of Israel are *not* bent on annihilating the Jewish people.

The Arab narrative is not uniform with regard to the Holocaust. There is a strong strain of Holocaust denial, exemplified by Mahmoud Abbas's doctoral dissertation for Moscow University in 1982 – since repudiated – and, more recently, the statements of Iranian President Ahmadinajad. Younger Palestinians tend to eschew Holocaust denial, realizing that it often harms their own cause. Rather, they tend to equate Israeli actions with those of the Nazis and to separate Zionism from the Holocaust justification, thus mirroring the argument of some Zionists. However, all Palestinians agree that they have been unfairly made to pay the price for European anti-Semitism, which had nothing to do with them. "If you want to establish Israel," they say, "do it in Europe."

Perhaps the most important aspect of the Nazi/Holocaust analogy is the frequency with which it is used, often implicitly by Jews and increasingly explicitly by Arabs and other Palestinian supporters. One might have thought that, as the Holocaust recedes from living memory, its use as a political tool would likewise erode. This does not seem to be the case.

The *Nakba*/War of Independence

For Palestinians, the *Nakba*, encompassing all the events surrounding the establishment of Israel in 1948 and the creation of the Palestinian refugees, is the seminal event in their history. To make a very rough analogy, it is comparable in their consciousness to the events in Jewish history and collective memory stretching over 3,000 years, from the Exodus from Egypt to the Holocaust. This is not, it should be clear, in any way equating the magnitude of the Holocaust and the *Nakba* but, rather, the role they play in the historical consciousness of Israelis and other Jews, on the one hand, and of Palestinians and other Arabs and Muslims, on the other.

Palestinians see the *Nakba* as the logical and intended culmination of Zionism. For them, Zionism has always been directed towards the creation of a Jewish state, which necessarily means getting rid of the Palestinians. Palestinians, and some Israeli "new" historians, have collected statements by Zionist leaders from the beginning of the movement which advocate "transfer" (a frequent euphemism for expulsion). They point specifically to Plan Dalet, a strategic plan drawn up by the nascent Israeli military leadership in early 1948, which discusses clearing out Arab villages wherever they might pose a threat to Jewish settlement. This they consider to be a blueprint for what actually occurred.

Palestinians also blame much of the rest of the world for the *Nakba*. Israel's establishment was authorized by the United Nations in its 1947 partition resolution, with the concurrence of most Western nations together with the Soviet bloc. Even the Arab nations, who resisted and voted against partition, are blamed first for their diplomatic ineptitude in failing to stave off the resolution and then for their almost complete lack of success in their war against Israel, beginning on May 15, 1948. Moreover, it is clear that all the Arab states, except for Lebanon, which did virtually nothing in the war, had agendas of their own vis-à-vis Palestine and the Palestinians. While of course Palestinians have cooperated with the Arab countries and the former Soviet bloc over the years, they never forget these initial acts of betrayal. Interestingly, these feelings run parallel, to a significant degree, to those of Jews who blame the West both for not preventing the rise and rearmament of Nazi Germany in the 1930s and for not bombing the extermination camps during World War II.

The Israeli narrative of 1948, its "War of Independence," could not be more different. Israelis are convinced that they did all they possibly could to compromise with the Palestinians, notably accepting the partition resolution which divided the country. For them, the war was purely defensive. When the Palestinians and Arab states refused to accept this international decision, Israel defended itself from annihilation (and Israelis are uniformly convinced that the Jewish population would have been massacred had they lost). They argue that Plan Dalet was primarily a contingency plan, not a blueprint. And they claim that the Arab leaders told the Palestinians to leave their homes to allow the Arab armies to invade, with the plan of returning weeks later after the victory. The last point was the original justification for Israel refusing to allow the approximately 700,000 Palestinian refugees to return to their homes, since they left "voluntarily" and would constitute an immense fifth column if they actually lived in the Jewish state. The Israeli narrative has generally rebutted any claims of massacres or expulsions, though more recent archival work has convinced many Israeli historians (but fewer lay people) that they indeed took place.

It is notable that Palestinians emphasize the first part of the war, until May 15, when Israel was fighting primarily against Palestinian irregulars, and Israelis emphasize the period after May 15, when the armies of five Arab countries entered Palestine.

Post-1948

The period from 1881 until the establishment of the State of Israel in its 1948–67 boundaries and the creation of the Palestinian diaspora constitutes the main battleground for the respective historical narratives. Both sides remain firm in their rectitude, convinced that their behavior was generally consonant with international moral and legal norms. Thus, neither side is able to countenance those who question their narrative, as its elements seem blindingly obvious to each.

With the conclusion of the truces between Israel and the Arab countries that had sent forces into Palestine (except for Iraq), Israelis assumed that, within a generation or two, the Palestinian problem would be solved, since the refugees would be absorbed into the Arab world. Israel therefore defined the remaining problem as the refusal of the Arab states to accept such a solution.

The majority of, though by no means all, Palestinian refugees initially lived in refugee camps in Arab countries. Instead of being absorbed, they carefully nurtured their Palestinian identity, a task made much easier by their living together, generally apart from the natives of the countries in which the camps were located. Israel charges that the camps were set up and maintained so that, instead of permitting the refugees to begin normal lives, Arab countries could use them as a propaganda weapon against Israel. Arabs countered that all Arabs were not the same, and that the refugees preferred to live with their own compatriots. Indeed, in many camps, Palestinians from the same towns or villages lived next to one another, thus perpetuating the memories of their lost homes. Children, even those three or four generations removed from Palestine, would answer with the name of their village when asked where they were from. Many refugee families retained the key to their home in Palestine as a symbol of their intention to return.

For most of the world, the issue of Palestinian refugees seemed closed. Palestinians spent the next twenty years recovering from their experience. Israel assumed its hopes would be fulfilled and continued to deny there was any such thing as a Palestinian. Most notably, Prime Minister Golda Meir scoffed at the notion of the existence of Palestinians, displaying her Mandate-era identification papers describing her as a Palestinian, which was the pre-1948 designation of all inhabitants of the Mandate. (Only after 1948 was the term "Palestinian" reserved solely for Arabs. Jewish inhabitants were henceforth called "Israelis.")

The 1967 war, dubbed the June War by Arabs and the "Six Day War" by Israel and most of the West, thus emphasizing its near-miraculous short time span and its humiliating defeat of Arab armies, has its own separate set of narratives. For Israel, it was again purely defensive. Most Arabs believed it was deliberately and duplicitously instigated by Israel, which fits into their understanding of Zionism as inherently aggressive and expansionist. After this war, Israel and the rest of the world discovered that there was a new generation that considered itself solely Palestinian, and that was ready to fight for its right to return. Israelis defined this as "terrorism," and for several decades, for them, the term "Palestinian" was virtually synonymous with "terrorist."

The latest great Battle of the Narratives concerns the Oslo process of 1993–2000, culminating in the failed second Camp David summit. Both sides tend to regard themselves as well-meaning dupes of the other. For Israelis, the recognition of the PLO and of the Palestinian people was a major concession. The fact that Yasser Arafat and the Palestinians spurned their "generous offer" at Camp David was proof positive to them that the Palestinians would settle for nothing less than Israel's destruction. They regard the outbreak of the Second *Intifada* two months later as carefully planned in order to force Israel into concessions that would endanger its security.

The Palestinian view is almost a mirror image of this. They see the Oslo process as occasioned by their willingness to make a "historic compromise." They would accept the 22 percent of Palestine that lay outside Israel's 1948–67 borders, East Jerusalem as their capital, sovereignty over the Haram al-Sharif (which Jews refer to as the Temple Mount), and, of course, the right of Palestinians to return to their homes. Perhaps some trimming around the edges of this package could be accepted, but this was understood as the basic framework. Israel's refusal of all of these terms without major modifications, and especially its unwillingness even to discuss the right of return, convinced most Palestinians that what Israel wanted was simply to rearrange the nature of the Occupation, with the Palestinian Authority as its enforcer.

Historical "revisionism"

Of course, belief in the narratives has never been uniform; political and religious differences provided some significant differentiation, especially on the Israeli side. However, in the late 1980s, there arose the first substantial movement challenging Israeli historical orthodoxy, known as the "revisionist" or "new" historians. All came from the political left and coupled their historical views with critiques of current Israeli policies towards Palestinians. The best-known figure was and is Professor Benny Morris, a historian specializing in the events of 1948 who, without changing his historical revisionism, around 2002–04 switched his political views and now is a vigorous exponent of a hawkish Israeli policy.

There are as many critiques of the narrative as there are historians, and significant variation between them. However, if there is one theme running through revisionist history, it is that Zionist and, later, Israeli government policy was much more hard-line towards Arabs than the traditional narrative contends, and that there were many possible opportunities for peace that Zionist and Israeli leaders ignored, deliberately or not. Likewise, they frequently find a flexibility on the Arab side that the traditional narrative denies.

In the 1990s, the revisionist arguments coincided with the Oslo peace process, and elements of Israeli society showed a willingness to suspend their traditional views, though by no means accepting most revisionist contentions. However, after the beginning of the Second *Intifada* in 2000, opinion swung back in many instances. Also, following Professor Morris's more recent contentions, many right-wing Israelis now accept there was indeed Israeli brutality in 1948 and afterwards, but insist that Israel had no choice because of its enemies' implacable hatred.

Nevertheless, despite the hardening of attitudes, few if any Israeli historians today believe that Palestinians fled "voluntarily," for example, and they accept that Israeli history is far less pristine than generally portrayed in the traditional narrative. However, among ordinary, non-academic Israelis, the traditional narrative seems almost impervious to the attacks it has received.

Israelis ask why there has been no similar movement on the Palestinian side. While a few Palestinian historians, especially those living abroad, have made some efforts to accept elements of Israeli contentions,[5] the basic outline of the Palestinian narrative remains the same. Perhaps the best explanation is to compare the huge changes in every aspect of Israeli society since it achieved independence in 1948, with the lot of Palestinians, who still lack independence and for whom many aspects of life have deteriorated. Israel has been able to develop in many directions since then; Palestinians are stuck still trying to achieve self-determination, and their historical explanations have also been unable to develop further.

Thus, the changes that have taken place have not really impacted the views of most members of either society.

Conclusion: the use and future of the narratives

Both peoples are introduced to their respective narratives as fundamental parts of their individual and collective identities. Thus, it is impossible for many on both sides to see their adversaries as *not* historically deceptive, and themselves, as Professor Morris (1999) aptly put it, as "righteous victims." Substantial elements in both populations have no frame of reference to understand the grievance of the other side; rather, they see themselves as deserving compensation and the other side as deserving punishment.

On both sides, understandings of history shape and are shaped by ongoing political events. Israeli demands for security are based on a historically shaped set of perceptions that Palestinians have never reconciled themselves to Israel's existence and will seek to destroy it even if they proclaim they accept it. Many Palestinians now despair of the two-state solution because they see Zionism as a movement that has historically been bent on dispossessing them. The distrust that both sides show, and which is perhaps currently the biggest obstacle to peace, is based on each one's perception of its historical experience with the "other."

Can the conflicting narratives be reconciled? Or, can the two peoples live next to each other while still maintaining their narratives?

In this author's view, the latter is more possible and likely than the former. The historical narrative of each side embodies how it understands itself. Without its narrative, neither would be recognizable even to itself. And experience has shown that both narratives are immensely resilient. Thus, what is needed is an "acknowledgement" of the other narrative, not an acceptance of one or an attempt to reconcile contradictions.

However, it is hard to imagine that such a development is imminent.

Notes

1   One of the few who realized this was Yitzhak Epstein, who in 1903 wrote a prescient article entitled "The Hidden Question," warning that, if Zionists did not formulate a policy to deal with the land's inhabitants, their whole enterprise would be endangered. His concerns were not heeded. A. Dowty, "A Question That Outweighs All Others: Yitzhak Epstein and Zionist Recognition of the Arab Issue," *Israel Studies*, 6/1 (2001), pp. 34–55.
2   For an illustration of this dynamic, see Discussion 2 in Scham *et al.* (2006), pp. 84–91.
3   For a balanced treatment of this controversial personality, see Philip Mattar, *The Mufti of Jerusalem: Al-Hajj Amin al-Husayni and the Palestinian National Movement* (rev. ed., New York: Columbia University Press, 1992).
4   See, for example, the reaction to President Obama's speech of June 4, 2009, when he used the Holocaust as a primary justification for Israel's existence, in Martin Peretz, "Narrative Dissonance: What the Cairo Speech Got Wrong," *The New Republic*, July 1, 2009, www.tnr.com/article/narrative-dissonance
5   While their approaches are very different, two of the best-known examples are Philip Mattar and Rashid Khalidi, both of whom have lived in the United States for most of their lives. Dr. Mattar refers to himself half-seriously as "the first Palestinian revisionist historian" (conversation with the author, 2003).

Further reading

Adwan, Sami, and Bar-On, Dan (2003) *Learning Each Other's Narrative: Palestinians and Israelis* (Beit Jala, Prime [Peace Research Institute in the Middle East]).

Bar-On, Mordechai (1998) "Historiography as an Educational Process: The Historians' Debate in Israel and the Middle East Peace Process," in Ilan Peleg (ed.), *The Middle East Peace Process: Interdisciplinary Perspectives* (Albany, State University of New York Press), pp. 21–38.

Ben-Ami, Shlomo (2006) *Scars of War, Wounds of Peace: The Israeli–Arab Tragedy* (New York: Oxford University Press).

Bitterlemons (2006) "Narratives Revisited," September 4, www.bitterlemons.org/previous/bl040906 ed35.html.

Caplan, Neil (2010) *The Israel–Palestine Conflict: Contested Histories* (Malden, MA: Wiley-Blackwell).

Kaufman, Stuart J. (2009) "Narratives and Symbols in Violent Mobilization: The Palestinian–Israeli Case," *Security Studies*, 18/3 (2009), pp. 400–34.

Lazarus, Ned (2008) "Making Peace With the Duel of the Narratives: Dual-Narrative Texts for Teaching the Israeli–Palestinian Conflict," *Israel Studies Forum*, 23/1 (2008), pp. 107–24.

Morris, Benny (1999) *Righteous Victims: A History of the Zionist–Arab Conflict, 1881–1999* (New York: Knopf).

Rotberg, Robert I. (ed.) (2006) *Israeli and Palestinian Narratives of Conflict: History's Double Helix* (Bloomington: Indiana University Press).

Scham, Paul L. (2006) "The Historical Narratives of Israelis and Palestinians and the Peacemaking Process," *Israel Studies Forum*, 20/2 (2006), pp. 58–84.

Scham, Paul, Salem, Walid, and Pogrund, Benjamin (2005) *Shared Histories: A Palestinian–Israeli Dialogue* (Walnut Creek, CA: Left Coast Press).

Tessler, Mark (2010) *History of the Israeli–Palestinian Conflict* (2nd ed., Bloomington: Indiana University Press).

4

The 1948 war

The battle over history

Kirsten E. Schulze

On 29 November 1947 the United Nations General Assembly voted to partition Palestine. The partition plan envisaged the establishment of a Jewish and an Arab state in the territory which had been under British control since the end of the First World War. However, no sooner had the vote been concluded than both Arabs and Jews in Palestine started to arm themselves. In December intercommunal clashes erupted in what became the first phase of the 1948 war. This phase was effectively one of civil war characterized by intense, bitter fighting between the two communities in Palestine. The second phase of the war began with Israel's declaration of independence on 14 May 1948 and the subsequent attack by the neighbouring Arab states of Egypt, Jordan, Lebanon, Syria and Iraq, ostensibly to liberate Palestine. The civil war thus was transformed into an interstate conflict.

On 11 June and again on 19 July a truce was ordered by the UN Security Council in the hope that a new political compromise could be reached. By that time, however, Israel had attained numerical superiority and had managed to import a significant amount of weapons and ammunition despite the UN embargo. The combination of increased manpower and fire-power tipped the balance decidedly in Israel's favour. By December 1948, Israel had broken the Egyptian blockade in the Negev, seized most of the Galilee, and crossed the border into southern Lebanon.

In January 1949, armistice negotiations began between Israel, Egypt, Jordan, Lebanon and Syria. Israel had increased its territory by 21 per cent compared to the partition resolution boundaries. The Arab states, too, had increased their territory. Jordan gained the West Bank and Egypt the Gaza Strip. The Palestinian Arabs, in contrast, had lost any possibility of a state of their own. An estimated 150,000 came under Israeli rule and were granted Israeli citizenship; between 550,000 and 800,000 became refugees scattered across the Arab world. Not surprisingly, the 1948 war went down in Israeli history as the war of independence, while in Palestinian history it became known as *al-Nakba*, the Catastrophe. It is equally unsurprising that Israeli, Arab and Palestinian narratives on the war differ and remain contested to the present day. Moreover, the Palestinian armed struggle for the state they felt they had been denied plunged the region into another four Arab–Israeli wars (in 1956, 1967, 1973 and 1982), as well as two Palestinian uprisings (in 1987 and again in 2000). The unresolved issues of 1948 also haunted the Oslo peace process (1993–2000).

One of the key issues is the origins of the Palestinian refugee situation. Israel's official line since the 1948 war has been that it bears no responsibility for the Palestinian exodus and thus has no obligation to allow any Palestinians who left to return to their former homes. The Palestinian position is that the Arabs of Palestine were expelled and that Israel consequently bears the moral responsibility to set both the past and the present right by accepting a Palestinian right of return. Thus the debate on what exactly happened in the 1948 war and who did what to whom is not just history. It cuts to the heart of the Israeli–Palestinian conflict, past and present, and remains one of the most important factors in achieving a just and lasting peace between Israelis and Palestinians.

Traditionalist Israeli and Palestinian accounts of the 1948 war

Following the 1948 war, an official history of the birth of Israel and the 1948 War of Independence quickly emerged. It was part of the nation-building effort of this new state and was based on the accounts and memoirs of participants in the struggle. The majority of these accounts were highly personal, not written by historians, and portrayed the war as a heroic struggle by a small Zionist community against a vastly larger Arab enemy comprising local Arabs, Arab irregulars and five Arab armies who were all bent on strangling the newborn State of Israel at birth. Moreover, the Arabs were aided both directly and indirectly by the British, who right up to the last days of the Mandate tried to thwart the emergence of a Jewish state and openly supported the Arab side. Yet, against all these odds, Israel survived. The local Arabs left, having been asked by their leaders to make way for the advancing Arab armies, and these armies, in turn, were pushed back and defeated by the Israeli forces by the end of 1948. The infant State of Israel had thus re-created the biblical victory of David over Goliath.

A good example of this traditional narrative can be found in Jon Kimche and David Kimche's book *Both Sides of the Hill: Britain and the Palestine War*, which describes British Foreign Secretary Ernest Bevin as 'bellicosely inclined to support the Arab position' and the British soldiers and administrators in Palestine as being 'pro-Arab' (Kimche and Kimche 1960: 36). In their account it is the Arabs who are clearly to blame for the descent into war following the UN partition resolution, while the Jews were hoping for peaceful co-existence. The book explains: 'With the dawn of November 30th, 1947, there came also the first shots in Jerusalem and the other "mixed" towns, and along the highways. This was the Arab answer to the assumption of the Jewish leaders that all might yet be settled without undue violence' (ibid.: 73). Once violence broke out, the British not only failed to uphold law and order but intervened on the Arab side with 'hostile acts carried out by individual members of the British security services' against Jewish positions, including the planting of explosives (ibid.: 93). However, despite the fact that the Jewish forces and population were on the receiving end of Arab and British violence, they practised restraint, with retaliation 'directed only against "guilty" Arabs' (ibid.: 83). When the State of Israel was declared, the situation became even worse, as five regular Arab armies from the neighbouring states of Egypt, Jordan, Syria, Lebanon and Iraq now swelled the Arab ranks. The Jews were almost hopelessly outnumbered. 'In the Negev (including Beersheva) there were over 100,000 local Arabs, as against 1,000 Jewish settlers' (ibid.: 89), and in the Galilee Arabs 'outnumbered the Jews nearly thirty to one' (ibid.: 104). Yet, miraculously, the Jews not only won but increased the territory of the State of Israel. The exodus of the local Arab population, according to the Kimches, was the result of calls by Arab leaders to vacate the area for the advancing Arab irregulars and armies. This became the official line on the Palestinian refugees. As Israel's first prime minister, David Ben-Gurion, reiterated again and again in his speeches, it was the Arab leaders that were to blame for their departure, not Israel.

Here are more than 600,000 despairing and disappointed people who have lost their all and had nothing in return, deceived by their leaders and 'liberators', and left to fend for themselves in poverty and distress. Yet their wrath and rancour are not turned against the authors of their calamity – the Mufti's men and the rulers of the Arab countries – but against the Jews.

(Ben-Gurion 1997: 101)

Ben-Gurion then continues the official line, saying that, as it was the Arabs who were responsible for the calamity of the Palestinians, it is the Arab countries that should resettle them.

It is exactly this discourse on the Palestinian refugees on which traditional Israeli narratives were almost immediately challenged by Palestinian leaders and later historians. The traditional Palestinian counter-narrative is one that places the blame for the refugee problem firmly on the Israelis and sees the departure of the Palestinians as the result of the Zionist colonization process since the 1880s and a Zionist campaign of expulsion during the 1948 war.

On the sixtieth anniversary of the *Nakba*, the Palestinian Academic Society for the Study of International Affairs (PASSIA) published a special issue of their bulletin. The analysis advanced in this bulletin is exemplary of traditional Palestinian narratives. It starts with what it calls the Zionist colonization of Palestine in the late nineteenth century and proceeds with a discussion of British duplicity during the First World War. This is followed by an account of how various highly aware Palestinian organizations, such as the Muslim–Christian Association, the Arab Executive, the various Arab congresses, and the political parties, tried to counter the threat posed by Zionist funds, institutions and land purchases. However, they were fighting a losing battle, as Zionism's powerful friends in the British establishment – Arthur Balfour, Mark Sykes, David Lloyd George, Herbert Samuel and Winston Churchill – ensured that British Mandate policies were pro-Zionist. They encouraged Zionist proto-state-building, immigration and land purchases, and, when tensions between Arabs and Jews in Palestine turned to violence, 'the British security forces did their utmost to disarm the Palestinians and disrupt the establishment of any Arab paramilitary organization', while 'the Zionists were encouraged to arm and organize and were often given logistical support by the British authorities' (PASSIA 2008: 10).

The narrative proceeds to discuss the Jewish terrorist organizations Lehi and Irgun, which became active in the 1930s and played a prominent role towards the end of the Mandate. It was their violence in addition to international pressure which prompted the British to hand Palestine over to the United Nations. Zionist lobbying of the United Nations Special Commission on Palestine (UNSCOP) then resulted in the latter's recommending the partition of Palestine. Once the partition resolution had been passed in November 1947 in the UN General Assembly, violence erupted between Jews and Arabs in Palestine, and 'the Zionist leadership embarked upon a ruthless program of ethnic cleansing prior to the end of the Mandate.'

Knowing that the Arab armies would not intervene before the British withdrawal, the Zionists could turn their full focus on the Palestinian population with frequent and brutal raids on villages, creating a state of unprecedented fear. Villages near Jewish settlements were forcibly depopulated, and the Jewish forces soon took their manoeuvres further afield to expel as much of the Palestinian population from Mandatory Palestine as possible.

(PASSIA 2008: 12)

By the time the British Mandate ended in May 1948, half the Palestinian population had already been forced from their homes, while the British, 'after tilting the scales firmly in favor of the Zionists during their occupation of Palestine, adopted a policy of non-interference in the conflict, despite their supposed responsibility for law and order in their mandate' (ibid.: 13). With the British gone, the Zionists turned to the USA and found another powerful friend in Harry Truman. Truman's support allowed the Zionists to declare the State of Israel in the full knowledge that they would have unconditional US support in future.

Challenging the conventional narrative: the 'new' Israeli historians

While Arab and Palestinian historians challenged the Israeli narrative on the 1948 war, it was not until four decades after the founding of the State of Israel, in 1988, that a vibrant, controversial, and often acrimonious historiographical debate emerged between 'new' or revisionist and 'old' or traditionalist Israeli historians. This hiatus can be explained by three mutually reinforcing factors: first, it was not until the early 1980s that Israeli documents from the late 1940s were declassified in line with the thirty-year rule. Historians were now able to re-examine Israel's history through Israeli archival sources. Second, there was a generational transition. What became the official Israeli narrative had, more often than not, been written by participants in and witnesses to the birth of Israel. Moreover, views had been heavily influenced by the larger than life figure of David Ben-Gurion, Israel's first prime minister. The younger generation of 'new' historians lacked this first-hand knowledge, approaching the subject with more objectivity, but also within the context of an Israeli state that had not only survived for forty years but had become a regional superpower. That released them from the bonds of writing 'protective' or 'defensive' histories. And last, but certainly not least, was the impact of the ill-fated 1982 Lebanon War, which resulted in widespread soul-searching and moral re-evaluation on the Israeli left and, with it, an environment of criticism of Israeli policy that made it easier to write and publish revisionist histories.

The first book to appear was Simha Flapan's *The Birth of Israel: Myths and Realities* (Flapan 1987). Flapan identified seven myths which he sought to challenge, as he saw them as obstacles to resolving the conflict with the Palestinians: first, the Zionists accepted the UN partition plan and planned for peace; second, the Arabs rejected the partition and launched war; third, the Palestinians fled voluntarily; fourth, all the Arab states united to expel the Jews from Palestine; fifth, the Arab invasion made war inevitable; sixth, defenceless Israel faced destruction by the Arab Goliath; and, seventh, Israel has always sought peace, but no Arab leader has responded.

Flapan's book kick-started a debate among Israeli historians revolving around the military balance, Israeli–Jordanian relations, British policy, Arab war aims, the elusive peace, and the origins of the Palestinian refugee problem. One of the most widely propagated myths within the traditional Israeli narratives on the 1948 war is that Israel won against overwhelming odds – a little Israeli David facing a giant Arab Goliath. The newly born State of Israel was beleaguered and embattled by all its neighbours, who were intent upon pushing the Jews into the sea. Israel's victory is likened to biblical miracles, providing the State of Israel with an almost divine destiny. The revisionist historians were quick to point out that they did not question the heroism of the Jewish fighters or the fact that the *Yishuv* (pre-state Palestine) paid a heavy price in this war. However, they did challenge the numbers and the way they should be viewed. Rather than seeing the 1948 war as one fought by 650,000 Jews against 1.2 million Palestinians and 40 million Arabs, they looked at the numbers of fighters and their military capacity. Very quickly the odds took on a different aspect. During the last months of the Mandate, the *Yishuv* gained the upper hand against the Palestinians because its forces were larger, better trained and more technologically advanced. This did not change significantly when the Arab armies invaded on 15 May 1948. The Arab regular and irregular soldiers numbered between 20,000 and 25,000. The Israel Defence Force (IDF) had 35,000. By mid-July, the IDF had increased to 65,000 and by September to 90,000. At the end of the war the IDF outnumbered the Arab armies nearly two to one (Shlaim 1995: 294).

The discrepancy was even greater when comparing military capacity. Several of the Israeli fighters had been in the British army during the Second World War. Many were well trained, and all of them were highly motivated, as they needed to win this war in order for the state to survive. Firepower was initially a problem. However, during the first ceasefire, in June, a large quantity of arms and ammunition was brought in. The picture on the Arab side differed significantly. Motivation was initially high, as there had been promises of an easy battle followed by the spoils of war. For instance, the Egyptian Adel Sabit, aide to Azzam Pasha and cousin of King Farouk, recalls the belief that this was 'going to be a pushover, that the Jews were going to run away the moment they saw the Arab regular army moving in on them with bayonets and whatever. Therefore, we didn't really make any preparations' (Bregman and El-Tahri 1998: 38). False expectations and lack of preparation were further compounded by the lack of functioning united command, logistical supply lines that were too long, high numbers of deserters, and widely differing fighting capacity across the various armies. The Egyptian army, for example, had little more than parade ground experience, while the Jordanian Arab Legion was highly professional. However, as a result of a secret Zionist/Israeli–Jordanian agreement, the Arab Legion's capacity was never fully employed against the Jewish forces.

Israeli–Jordanian relations and, by definition, Jordanian intentions during the 1948 war became another area for revisionist challenge. Traditionalist accounts portrayed Israel in a struggle against a monolithic Arab enemy intent on the liberation of Palestine. Avi Shlaim's book *Collusion across the Jordan: King Abdullah, the Zionist Movement and the Partition of Palestine* challenged this analysis by looking at secret relations between King Abdullah of Transjordan and the Zionist movement from 1921 to 1951. Shlaim argued that 'in 1947 an explicit agreement was reached between the Hashemites and the Zionists on the carving up of Palestine following the termination of the British Mandate.' He further claimed 'that this agreement laid the foundation for mutual restraint during 1948 and for continuing collaboration in the aftermath of the war' (Shlaim 1988: 1). Thus, the Arab enemy was far from monolithic. Instead Arab rulers were deeply divided on how to deal with the Zionist challenge.

This leads directly to the next two areas contested: British policy and Arab war aims. With respect to British policy, the traditional Israeli narrative during the period between the partition resolution in November 1947 and the end of the British Mandate in May 1948 is that the British were anti-Zionist and pro-Arab and that they were secretly arming the Arabs in order to prevent any Jewish state from coming into being. Foreign Secretary Ernest Bevin, in particular, is charged with deliberately instigating hostilities in Palestine so that the Jewish state could be crushed. Ilan Pappé, in his book *Britain and the Arab–Israeli Conflict, 1948–51* (1988), challenged this notion of British anti-Zionism. He maintained that British, Arab and Israeli documents show that Britain was not anti-Zionist and that it certainly was not pro-Palestinian. While Britain indeed armed and encouraged her Arab allies, this was restricted to the Transjordanian Arab Legion, and the aim of the Arab Legion was to crush not the emerging Jewish state but a possible Palestinian one, which the British associated with their wartime enemy Palestinian national leader Hajj Amin al-Hussayni.

With respect to the Arab states, it was not just the Jordanians who pursued their own nationalist and territorial interests during the 1948 war. The Arabs were far less monolithic than traditional narratives would suggest. While all Arab states with the exception of Jordan rejected the UN partition plan, and while they shared a rhetorical commitment to the liberation of Palestine, a Palestinian state or the fate of the Palestinians was often the last thing on their minds. King Abdullah's aim was ultimately the annexation of the Arab part of Palestine. King

Farouk of Egypt, who was suspicious of Abdullah, intervened against the advice of his experts in order to check Abdullah's ambitions. Similarly, Syria and Lebanon felt threatened by Abdullah's long-standing Greater Syria plans. Moreover, the public demand on the Arab street for a war with the Jews made it virtually impossible for any of the Arab states to remain on the sidelines. So, in the end, they all declared war on Israel. However, selfish national interests ensured that the Jordanian Arab Legion made every effort to avoid full contact with the Jewish forces and that the Lebanese army never even crossed the border. Rather than liberating Palestine, the war disintegrated into what Avi Shlaim called 'a general land grab' (Shlaim 1995: 300).

When the war ended, Israel signed armistice agreements with Egypt, Lebanon, Syria and Jordan. Israeli hopes were high that these agreements were the first step towards full peace treaties with its Arab neighbours. The traditional narrative on why peace proved unattainable is that Israel reached out to Arabs but there was no one to talk to. Arab intransigence was the greatest stumbling block to peace in the Middle East. The revisionist narrative suggests the opposite – namely, that it was Israeli intransigence that was the stumbling block. The 'new' historians further argue that the claim that there was no one to talk to was a complete myth. Indeed, the Israeli Foreign Office files show peace feelers being put out by all of Israel's neighbours, including Syrian president Husni Zaim, Egyptian King Farouk and Jordanian King Abdullah. What the Arab leaders wanted in return for peace was territorial concessions, such as a land corridor to link Jordan with the Mediterranean, and Israel's agreement to accept the return of Palestinian refugees. However, Ben-Gurion was not interested in concluding peace on any basis other than the status quo.

The final area to be challenged by the revisionist historians was the origins of the Palestinian refugee problem. The traditional narrative revolves around three contentions: first, that Arab leaders called on the Palestinians to vacate their villages to clear the way for the advancing troops; second, that the Palestinians left voluntarily; and, third, that Israel neither bears responsibility for their departure nor has any moral obligation to allow them to return. The first comprehensive challenge to this narrative came from Benny Morris, in his book *The Birth of the Palestinian Refugee Problem, 1947–1949*. Morris very clearly challenges the first two contentions. Combing through the archives, he found no evidence that Arab leaders gave blanket orders for the Palestinians to leave their homes. He also found no evidence of a radio or press campaign urging them to flee. Taking on the traditionalist Palestinian narrative maintaining that Israel expelled the Palestinians, he further asserted that there were no blanket Israeli expulsion orders. Morris accepted that there were individual local Jewish and Arab commanders who did give such orders, but in neither case was there evidence of general orders from above or systematic campaigns. He thus concludes that:

> The Palestinian refugee problem was born of war, not by design, Jewish or Arab. It was largely a by-product of Arab and Jewish fears and of the protracted, bitter fighting that characterised the first Israeli–Arab war; in smaller part, it was the deliberate creation of Jewish and Arab military commanders and politicians.
>
> *(Morris 1987: 286)*

Almost two decades later, Ilan Pappé, in his book *The Ethnic Cleansing of Palestine*, went several steps further, arguing that a culture of *Nakba* denial has emerged, led by the Israeli government, that 'totally removes the refugee issue from the peace agenda and side-lines the Palestinian Right of Return as a "non-starter"' (Pappé 2006: 239). Pappé saw this refusal to discuss the right of return as driven by a 'deep-seated fear vis-à-vis any debate over 1948, as Israel's "treatment" of the Palestinians in that year is bound to raise troubling questions about the moral legitimacy of the Zionist project as a whole' (ibid.: 245).

Challenging the challengers: Israeli and Palestinian responses

In 1988, in response to the emergence of the 'new' Israeli historians, the Palestinian historian Walid Khalidi published an article entitled 'Plan Dalet: Master Plan for the Conquest of Palestine'. He acknowledged that the 'new' Israeli historians had moved significantly away from the 'myths' propagated by the official Israeli narrative. At the same time, however, he accused – them of a tendency to write off the Palestinian 'flight' as a tragic situation born out of war and to disregard the imperative for Zionist plans to seize Arab land in order to accommodate the hundreds of thousands of envisioned Jewish immigrants. This, according to Khalidi, not only reduced Plan Dalet (Plan D) to merely a military plan but also 'subliminally placed the moral burden ... not on the invader, but on the invaded, who by resisting or panicking brought permanent exile upon themselves' (Khalidi 1988: 8). Khalidi saw Plan D as crucial to understanding both the origins of the Palestinian refugee problem and the Arab intervention after 15 May 1948. With respect to the Palestinian refugees, Khalidi argued that the offensives of Plan D, which entailed 'the destruction of the Palestinian Arab community and the expulsion and pauperization of the bulk of Palestinian Arabs, were calculated to achieve the military fait accompli upon which the State of Israel was to be based' (ibid.). Plan D did not emerge in a historical vacuum but was the product of Zionist ideology, and thus it cannot be separated from the fundamental notion that the establishment of a Jewish state on already inhabited land would necessitate the 'transfer' of the indigenous population. Khalidi then proceeded to discuss the idea of 'transfer' within Zionist circles and the need to dislodge the Palestinians before the end of the British Mandate and the attack by the neighbouring Arab armies.

This line of argument was taken up in a more comprehensive manner by Nur Masalha in his book *Expulsion of the Palestinians: The Concept of 'Transfer' in Zionist Political Thought, 1882–1948* (1992). Like Khalidi, Masalha argued that Plan D must be seen in the context of Zionist transfer thinking, and it is this evolution of the notion of transfer that he carefully documented and analysed. And, like Khalidi, he further argued that transferring the indigenous population was an ideological imperative. It was not possible for the Palestinians to be allowed to remain *in situ* if large numbers of Jewish immigrants were to be absorbed. Moreover, the removal of the indigenous population would by definition entail expulsion and the destruction of Palestinian society in light of the Arab resistance which the Zionists had encountered since 1882. Returning to Morris's assertion that Plan D was not a blueprint for expulsion as there were no official expulsion orders, Masalha concluded that, in the end, it did not matter whether a policy of expulsion was officially formulated or whether 'it was just *de facto* and clearly understood at every level of military and political decision-making' (Masalha 1999: 218). The outcome was the same.

While the traditionalist Palestinian historians asserted that the Israeli revisionist historians had not gone far enough, the traditionalist Israeli historians charged the 'new' historians with being incompetent researchers who were politically motivated and thus biased to the extent that they were deliberately misrepresenting the facts. Moreover, to complicate matters further, both the Palestinian and the Israeli traditionalist historians used exactly the same documents as the Israeli revisionists to challenger the latter.

The traditionalist Israeli historian Shabtai Teveth, whose writings were the object of much of the revisionist criticism, responded quickly. In his article 'The Palestine Arab Refugee Problem and its Origins' (1990) he dissected Morris's book, asserting that Morris's research was flawed as he did not consult Arab sources or conduct any interviews, and that it was deliberately ahistorical in its periodization in order to obfuscate patterns. Teveth further claimed that Morris 'creatively' filled out the picture and distorted reality by elevating obscure documents to the status of mainstream views, such as presenting a document of the Haganah Arab section as an IDF intelligence report or Yosef Weitz's proposals on transfer as official Zionist policy. He also charged him with a complete misrepresentation of David Ben-Gurion, which Teveth saw as personal bias. Teveth's final verdict on Morris's work was harsh:

> Had Morris agreed to conduct interviews, had he been qualified to do so in Arabic, had he been given access to Arab archives, or, most of all, had he been free of bias, he might have shed more light on the mystery of the first 'two waves'. He might even have drawn the inevitable conclusion from his own story: The leaders of Palestine's Arabs voted with their feet. The very orders for evacuation, whatever the excuse, and the example of the leaders and commanders set before their people amounted to an unmistakable instruction to flee.
>
> *(Teveth 1990: 229)*

One of the most vociferous challenges to the revisionist historians came from Efraim Karsh. In his book *Fabricating Israeli History: The 'New Historians'*, Karsh launched what he himself described as a 'frontal assault on Israel's fashionable "revisionist" school of thought' (Karsh 1997: xv), targeting three key revisionist theses: first, the transfer idea; second, the collusion between the *Yishuv* and Jordan; and, third, British policy. On the first of these, Karsh asserted that Morris failed to put the Zionist discussion of the transfer idea within its true context, namely the 1937 Peel Commission report, and that Morris deliberately omitted to state that transfer had initially been mooted by the British. He then charged Morris with distortion and falsification of evidence through the creative rewriting of original texts (ibid.: 43). Second, Karsh stated that the collusion between the Zionists and King Abdullah of Jordan was no more than a myth propagated by Shlaim based 'on the single episode approach' and misrepresentation of the record; moreover, Shlaim was 'not even "new" in being wrong'" (ibid.: 107), as this myth had been around for decades. An explicit agreement was never reached, Palestine was not divided between the Zionists and Hashemites, and the Jewish Agency had no awareness of such a partition. Karsh points to Meir's verbal report, which he claims Shlaim failed to consult:

> As is clearly shown by Meir's verbal report, the meeting [with Abdullah] left her and the Zionist leadership at large deeply suspicious of Abdullah's expansionist ambitions, the precise nature of which [was] to be gauged in a future meeting shortly after the passing of the UN resolution. In the event, this meeting did not take place until 11 May 1948, and Jewish suspicions of Abdullah's real agenda remained unabated until the Arab attack on the newly-established State of Israel, in which Transjordan's Arab Legion participated.
>
> *(Ibid.: 97)*

Karsh then turned to British policy, reasserting the traditionalist position that Britain was anti-Zionist and was never a party to an attempt to frustrate the UN partition plan and divide up Palestine between Abdullah and the Jews. He asserted that Shlaim's and Pappé's thesis that Bevin resigned himself to the emergence of a Jewish state but was intent on frustrating the emergence of a Palestinian one is 'totally misconceived' and a 'fantastic claim' (ibid.: 112). Karsh concluded his book by stating that he had 'conclusively demonstrated that the self-styled "new historians" are neither new nor true historians but partisans seeking to provide academic respectability to long-standing misconceptions and prejudices relating to the Arab–Israeli conflict' (ibid.: 195).

The *Nakba*: alternative Palestinian narratives

While the bulk of the revisionists have emerged on the Israeli side of the historiographical debate, some Palestinian historians have also challenged the traditional Palestinian narrative on the *Nakba*, as well as engaging with the Israeli revisionist historians. They have moved away from blaming exclusively outsiders for the refugee problem. While they agree with the traditionalist histories that the British were anti-Palestinian, that the Zionist forces were superior and often ruthless, and that the Arab states were interested more in their own expansionist agendas than in liberating Palestine, the revisionist Palestinian historians assert that this version of history 'conveniently' absolves the Palestinians of any responsibility for their own fate. Foremost among these are Issa Khalaf and Rashid Khalidi, who both asked the question why Palestinian society was so weak that it collapsed within weeks of the partition resolution.

Issa Khalaf in his work focused on the socio-economic changes in Palestinian society and their effects on social cohesion. In his article 'The Effect of Socioeconomic Change on Arab Societal Collapse in Mandate Palestine', Khalaf argued that the process by which migrant peasants became agricultural wage labourers in the second half of the Mandate had a destabilizing effect on Palestinian society (Khalaf 1997: 94). He saw the Palestinian peasants being dislocated by three interlinked processes: the administrative reforms of the Ottoman Empire, the competition with the Zionists, and the expansion of the world market into Palestine under the British. His analysis showed how the Ottoman reforms from the 1830s did little for the peasants while reinforcing the patronage system and elites. Palestinian farmers remained at the mercy of landlords and creditors, poor weather conditions, and the Islamic inheritance laws which called for equal shares for all sons. This problem was further compounded by Jewish land purchases. These were mainly from non-Palestinian absentee landlords and resulted in the eviction of Palestinian peasants working that land. These peasants then became wage labourers and urban workers. However, in the absence of progressive labour legislation, the urban drift often became the first step to unemployment. These processes climaxed after the Second World War, leaving Palestinian society at its most vulnerable just as the Mandate was drawing to a close.

> Increasing unemployment, growing political antagonism between Arabs and Jews, heightened Arab working-class political and social consciousness, simmering peasant resentment against land sellers, severe social disruption, and intensified urban overcrowding weakened and frayed the Palestinian Arab social structure at the very moment, in 1948, when it faced its first military challenge from an organised, determined foe.
>
> *(Ibid.: 95)*

Rashid Khalidi too asked the question why more than half of the Palestinian population was driven from or fled their homes and ended up dispossessed and under alien control. Like Khalaf, Khalidi argued that the decisive blows to the cohesion of Palestinian society were struck before 15 May 1948 and that the underlying causes for the collapse of Palestinian society and the Palestinian political failure lay even further in the past. However, while Khalaf focused mainly on socio-economic factors, Khalidi looked at political-institutional ones. Thus Khalidi's central argument was that Palestinian society collapsed so quickly because of the structural weaknesses of its political institutions, factionalism among the notables, and grave shortcomings in leadership (Khalidi 2001). The Palestinian National Movement faced unique challenges because the Palestinians were denied international recognition as a people and, with it, the attributes of 'stateness' and access to state power. Instead it was the Jewish people who were given the right to a national home, and the Zionist movement that received 'international legitimacy and guaranteed access in London and Geneva, which were invaluable, besides providing the framework within which the Israeli para-state could be constructed without hindrance, and with ample British support.' The lack of effective power over the state resulted in the Palestinian notables' inability to develop into a cohesive stratum. This lack of cohesiveness was further exacerbated by the increasing dominance of a religious leadership 'authorised, encouraged, and subsidised by the British' (ibid.: 22). British divide and rule tactics pitted the Hussaynis against the Nashashibis and incited a growing discontent among younger Palestinians and landless peasants towards the elites.

Like Khalaf, Khalidi challenged traditional Palestinian and Arab accounts that the Palestinians were overwhelmed by massively superior Zionist forces which had British, US and Soviet support. While he acknowledged that Jewish forces were superior and did have international recognition, he asserted that the Palestinians had several advantages, including their dominance of the rural areas and along many of the strategic roads, as well as some experienced fighters from the 1936–9 Arab Revolt. Yet they were defeated in all decisive battles in spring 1948. Khalidi concluded that the1936–9 revolt, which he sees as a massive failure as it achieved no lasting gains, played a profound role in the military defeat of the Palestinians in spring 1948.

> Purely in terms of Arab casualties of approximately 5,000 killed and 10,000 wounded, and those detained, who totalled 5,679 in 1939, the suffering was considerable in an Arab population of about a million: over 10 percent of the adult male population was killed, wounded, imprisoned or exiled. A high proportion of the Arab casualties included experienced military cadres and enterprising fighters. The British also confiscated large quantities of arms and ammunition during the revolt, and continued to do so during later years. These heavy military losses were to affect the Palestinians profoundly a few years later when Britain handed the Palestine question over to the United Nations, and it became clear that an open battle for control of the country between Arabs and Jews would take place.
>
> (Khalidi 2001: 27)

The Arab Revolt also contributed to the collapse of Palestinian society, as it crippled the Arab economy and shattered the traditional Palestinian leadership. With the Palestinians militarily, economically, politically and socially weaker than the *Yishuv*, the outcome of the 1948 war was a foregone conclusion.

The battle over history

The 1948 war was concluded with the 1949 armistice agreements. The battle over history, however, is far from over. Each nation's narrative on who did what to whom has retained and arguably increased in importance. The Palestinian and Arab belief that Israel was created at the expense of Palestine, dispossessing the Palestinians, as well as the Israeli belief that it was fighting a battle for survival in which the Palestinians simply fled, fuelled subsequent Arab–Israeli wars. They drove both the Palestinian quest for statehood and justice and Israel's quest for security and recognition. And while Israeli and Palestinian revisionist historians since the 1980s made concerted efforts to challenge their own national narratives, politicians on both sides continued to cling to what they perceived as historical truths. Thus the core issues of 1948 remained at the centre of the Arab–Israeli conflict and attempts at negotiating peace, albeit often obscured by other factors such as the Cold War or competition for hegemony over the Levant.

References and further reading

Ben-Gurion, David (1997) *Like Stars and Dust: Essays from Israel's Government Year Book* (Sede Boqer, Israel: Ben-Gurion Research Center).

Bregman, Ahron, and El-Tahri, Jihan (1998) *The Fifty Years War: Israel and the Arabs* (London: Penguin).

Flapan, Simha (1987) *The Birth of Israel: Myths and Realities* (New York: Pantheon Books).

Karsh, Efraim (1997) *Fabricating Israeli History: The 'New Historians'* (London: Frank Cass).

Khalaf, Issa (1997) 'The Effect of Socioeconomic Change on Arab Societal Collapse in Mandate Palestine', *International Journal of Middle East Studies*, 29/1, pp. 93–112.

Khalidi, Rashid (2001) 'The Palestinians and 1948: The Underlying Causes of Failure', in Eugene L. Rogan and Avi Shlaim (eds), *The War for Palestine: Rewriting the History of 1948* (Cambridge: Cambridge University Press).

Khalidi, Walid (1988) 'Plan Dalet: Master Plan for the Conquest of Palestine', *Journal of Palestine Studies*, 18/1, pp. 3–70.

Kimche, Jon, and Kimche, David (1960) *Both Sides of the Hill: Britain and the Palestine War* (London: Secker & Warburg).

Masalha, Nur (1992) *Expulsion of the Palestinians: The Concept of 'Transfer' in Zionist Political Thought, 1882–1948* (London: I. B. Tauris).

Masalha, Nur (1999) 'A Critique on Benny Morris', in Ilan Pappé (ed.), *The Israel/Palestine Question: Rewriting Histories* (London: Routledge).

Morris, Benny (1987) *The Birth of the Palestinian Refugee Problem, 1947–1949* (Cambridge: Cambridge University Press).

Morris, Benny (2007) *Making Israel* (Ann Arbor: University of Michigan Press).

Pappé, Ilan (1988) *Britain and the Arab–Israeli Conflict, 1948–51* (Basingstoke: Macmillan).

Pappé, Ilan (2006) *The Ethnic Cleansing of Palestine* (Oxford: Oneworld).

PASSIA (2008) Nakba: The Process of Palestinian Dispossession, www.passia.org/publications/bulletins/Nakba%20website/NakbaFull.pdf.

Shlaim, Avi (1988) *Collusion across the Jordan: King Abdullah, the Zionist Movement and the Partition of Palestine* (Oxford: Clarendon Press).

Shlaim, Avi (1995) 'The Debate about 1948', *International Journal of Middle East Studies*, 27/3, pp. 287–304.

Teveth, Shabtai (1990) 'The Palestine Arab Refugee Problem and its Origins', *Middle Eastern Studies*, 26/1, pp. 214–49.

The First and Second Palestinian *Intifadas*

Rami Nasrallah

Introduction

The Arabic term *intifada*, literally a "shaking off," when applied to conflicts usually takes on the meaning of an uprising, popular resistance, or rebellion. In the context of the Palestinian experience, one must further differentiate between the First *Intifada* and the Second (al-Aqsa) *Intifada*. The first is best understood as a popular or people's resistance movement, fundamentally but not totally non-violent, that sought an end to Israeli occupation of the West Bank (including East Jerusalem) and the Gaza Strip and the creation of a sovereign Palestinian state. It relied very heavily upon local, civil society leadership rather than on the guidance of the then exiled PLO. It began in 1987 and ended essentially with the Madrid Conference in 1991, although some date its formal termination as 1993 with the onset of the Oslo Accords.

The Second or al-Aqsa *Intifada* began in 2000, and, while many of its actions and effects are still playing out today, most authorities assign an end date of July, 2005. While the goals of the two *intifadas* were similar – statehood, sovereignty, and an end to the occupation – the strategies and tactics adopted in the al-Aqsa *Intifada* were distinctly more violent. Civil disobedience played a much reduced role. It is also fair to say that this *Intifada* was effectively led or abetted by the formal Palestinian political establishment (the PLO was no longer in exile) rather than the local indigenous civil society, whose powers had diminished in the period between the *intifadas*. The Second *Intifada* was much more a story of cycles of attacks and counter-attacks than a sustained popular resistance campaign.

The First *Intifada*

Context and causes

According to Arafat's advisor Mamdouh Noufal, the causes of the First *Intifada* are fourfold: 1) the poverty the Palestinians had been living under throughout 1948–87; 2) the feelings of humiliation arising from the conditions of living under occupation; 3) the loss of belief in the idea that they would be saved by Palestinian armed resistance from abroad; and 4) the feeling that their cause had been abandoned by the Arab states at the Arab Leaders' Summit in Amman in October 1987, when the leaders focused on threats from Iran and did not address the Palestinian struggle.[1]

Further, the cumulative effect of four decades of defeat, futile asymmetrical resistance, colonial suppression, land expropriations, and occupation had laid the groundwork for an uprising. All that was required was a triggering event. It came on December 9, 1987, in the form of an auto collision in the Gaza Strip, when four Palestinians in a car on their way to work were killed by an Israeli truck. According to journalists Ze'ev Schiff and Ehud Ya'ari, there would not have been anything suspicious about that accident, for traffic deaths were commonplace in Israel and the territories, but what triggered an unprecedented wave of demonstrations – the onset of the First *Intifada* – was a rumor that the crash "had not been an accident at all but a cold-blooded act of vengeance by a relative of [an] Israeli stabbed to death [in Gaza] two days earlier."[2] The rumor spread throughout Gaza and the West Bank, and on the next day *al-Fajr*, an Arabic-language newspaper published in East Jerusalem, denounced the "murder" of the four passengers as "maliciously perpetrated." The opening act of the First *Intifada* began with Palestinian youth throwing stones against the forces of the Israeli occupation, but it quickly became a widespread movement. After a very brief start-up period, these objectives of the "shaking off" morphed into the broader objective of self-determination, and, in short order, nothing less than an end to the occupation and the achievement of statehood would satisfy Palestinian grievances.

By the end of 1988 there was a clear consensus among the local leadership (the UNLU umbrella organization discussed below) that the way forward was to be based on a wide array of civil disobedience or popular resistance activities. The First *Intifada* was special, however, not only for its rather non-violent character but also for the vast active support it received from Palestinian society at large. With the *intifada*, the broad civil society united and, indeed, organized and led the resistance. There are exceptions to these generalizations that the *intifada* was non-violent and based in the civil society, and they will be discussed later. The most common non-violent strategies of resistance, passive and active, by the Palestinians comprised a set of economic actions: the boycotts of Israeli products, commercial strikes, and the withholding of VAT payments, income taxes, and fees to Israel. The Palestinians also challenged the Israeli administrative and military authority through resigning from the Israeli police force and from tax collecting authority; the destruction of Israeli-issued ID cards; the ignoring of government and military instructions – for example, orders against public and commercial curfews, public gatherings, marches, demonstrations, sit-ins, and the display of the Palestinian flag; the creation of an underground radio station; and the widespread use of anti-Israeli graffiti and posters.

Developing self-reliance, independence, and Palestinian alternatives

During the First *Intifada*, the Israelis imposed various forms of closure and extended curfews, withheld public services, and restricted access to the necessities of everyday life. For example, schools were closed for months on end and power and communication utilities were often shut down. The Palestinian response to these actions was to create alternatives, such as developing street markets to counter store closures and curfews; developing alternative public services, including underground schools, health-care facilities, street sanitation, security services, emergency services, and provisions to store and distribute food; increased self-reliance by developing backyard gardens as well as small dairy operations to provide milk for children; self imposed taxes (donations, really) to support the activities of the *Intifada* and to aid its victims; and the creation of popular committees to assure delivery of services.

Beit Sahour, a small Christian town adjacent to Bethlehem, exemplifies many of the Palestinian strategies. It was an especially important center of non-violent resistance during the First

Intifada. Along with boycotting Israeli products, illegally flying the Palestinian flag, ignoring military orders, destroying Israeli ID cards, and educating children in underground schools, the people of Beit Sahour pushed for self-reliance that included backyard gardening and secret dairy farms. More famously, the town is still known today for organizing a tax revolt in 1989. Individuals withheld taxes, and several hundred small businesses refused to pass on the collected VAT to Israel. The Israeli army responded harshly to this non-violent resistance: forty residents were arrested, and their possessions were confiscated to cover the debts of the Beit Sahour citizenry. The value of the money – both cash on hand and from seized bank accounts – and the property taken is estimated to have been between $1.5 and 7.5 million. Neither amount bore any relationship to the amount of taxes owed.[3] Beit Sahour was declared a "closed military zone," and during the 42-day siege of the town no telephone or electricity services or food supplies were provided, nor were journalists allowed to enter.

Israeli strategies

While some of the Palestinian strategies were proactive, designed actively to confront the Israeli regime, others were reactions to the efforts of the Israelis to break the back of the resistance. The most notorious Israeli action was the implementation of Yitzhak Rabin's "bone crushing policy." In mid-January 1988, Rabin, then Israeli defense minister, announced a policy to restore order in the Occupied Territories by "force, might, beatings." More specifically, he reportedly urged Israeli soldiers summarily to beat Palestinian demonstrators. Israeli soldiers implemented this policy, breaking the hands or arms of many demonstrators with methodically directed blows, using sticks and stones. In some cases, Palestinian youngsters were rounded up from their homes, brought to remote areas, and there, while soldiers held them, had their bones smashed.

Israel responded to the uprising by outlawing popular committees, holding tax raids, imposing severe travel restrictions, and arresting and deporting leaders. Some towns were declared a "closed military zone" and placed under siege without telephone or electricity services, and only approved residents could leave such villages for work or school during the day. Finally Israel imposed long curfews on wide areas as a form of collective punishment, making it difficult for the community to purchase food.

Major players in the *Intifada*

The Unified National Leadership of the Uprising (UNLU)

In the West Bank, representatives of the local Palestinian leadership of Fatah, the Popular Front for the Liberation of Palestine (PFLP), the Democratic Popular Front for the Liberation of Palestine (DPFLP), and the communist Palestine Popular Party (PPP) met and decided on their own, without the guidance of their "outside" leadership abroad, to establish a framework of local "inside" leadership that would lead the popular movement and issue manifestos (*bayanat*) on its behalf. At first, disagreements arose concerning the name and functions of the leadership framework, leading each of the factions to act independently and issue its own proclamations under the name and functions of its choice. But within two weeks, and before the end of 1987, the various representatives reconvened and agreed to unite and establish a unified framework called the Unified National Leadership of the Uprising (UNLU; *al Qiyada al Watnia al Muwhhada*). All of their orders, manifestos, and proclamations were issued under the shared slogan "No voice is louder than the voice of the *intifada*." During the First *Intifada* the UNLU played the central role in mobilizing grassroots support.

Membership in the UNLU frequently rotated, making it difficult for the occupation authorities to apprehend the leaders. There was a hierarchy of cells and popular committees that were subordinate to the organization. The main subordinate group was the Shabiba, founded by Fatah in 1982 and outlawed by Israel in 1988. Shabiba took root in universities and high schools before the outbreak of the *intifada* and was active in providing community and social services. Shabiba groups usually numbered around fifty per town or village, with fewer units within the refugee camps. After the eruption of the *intifada*, Shabiba set up small cells or "strike forces."

In addition to Shabiba, which was Fatah led, the other factions of the UNLU organized strike-force cells. They usually consisted of five- to fifteen-members and were supervised by "central security cells," which monitored their activities. Both, however, were subordinate to the General Command, which transmitted all UNLU directives to them. Leadership of each cell was rotated, usually monthly. Manifestos or *bayanat* of the *intifada* were issued solely by the UNLU, usually one every fifteen days.

The rise of Hamas

On January 14, 1988, the Muslim Brotherhood in Gaza issued a *bayan* calling for the Palestinian people to stand up against the occupation (see chapter 20, by Khaled Hroub). This manifesto is considered the founding statement of HAMAS, the Islamic Resistance Movement (in Arabic, an acronym for *Harakat Al-Muqawama Al-Islamia*). It quickly became involved in street confrontations against the occupation. Later a military wing, the Izz ed-Din al-Qassam Brigades, was established. It was involved, *inter alia*, in investigating collaborators and, indeed, claimed responsibility for executing a number of them.

The Hamas leadership refused to become involved with the UNLU national framework. Rather, it proposed merely coordinating their respective work in the field. Hamas soon began issuing *bayanat* independently and conducting its own activities. The "coordination" was far from perfect. Hamas often called strikes on days that were not in sync with those called for by the UNLU.

Hamas considered all of historical Palestine to be an Islamic *waqf* (a land that cannot be given away, sold, or entitled to another entity) belonging to the Palestinians, and thus called for resistance to expel the Israeli occupation and establish an Islamic state. It rejected any type of political settlement with Israel and also rejected the principle of two states. Nevertheless, it did not declare open hostility against the UNLU despite the latter's rejection of its Islamic programs.[4]

Hamas, which was an arm of the Muslim Brotherhood, and the Islamic Jihad (which split off from the Muslim Brotherhood) were the only serious challenges to the UNLU. Both sought the end of Israel and the triumph of an Islamic religious state. Neither took orders from the UNLU; each habitually resorted to violence to press its cause; and both were against a two-state solution and negotiations with Israel. They participated in the uprising by conducting similar or parallel actions but without accepting the leadership of the UNLU or its goals. The Islamic Jihad was a small secretive organization with fewer than 400 members. But the military arm of the Muslim Brotherhood, Hamas, represented real competition to the PLO-backed UNLU. Hamas and the Islamic Jihad were responsible for most of the violent acts of the *intifada* – street violence, murder, stabbings, and kidnappings. Their rejection of the UNLU leadership and the two-state principle, along with their predilection for violence, placed them outside the mainstream of the First *Intifada*.

Effects and consequences of the First *Intifada*

Elevation of the local civil society leadership

It became obvious to most Palestinians that the *intifada* had corrected the status of the Palestinian national movement hierarchy and had restored political heft from abroad back to its natural place, the homeland. The "outside" basis of the decision-making process before the *intifada* would not be retained unchanged, and those on the inside must be involved in the process in an actual rather than a figurative manner.

A new elite

The First *Intifada* had created a new elite: the local leaders and activists who organized the popular resistance and addressed basic community needs in the West Bank and Gaza. Indeed, the UNLU, which played the main leadership role, may be the First *Intifada*'s central achievement. Its multi-party cadres galvanized Palestinian society, overcoming divisions among regions, religious groups, political factions, sexes, and social classes. While Israel chose to ignore this new elite, the local organizations and personalities forged an effective civil society that demonstrated the people's ability to be self-governing and generally non-violent even in the face of an oppressive occupation.

Losses

Both sides incurred losses. They were far greater on the Palestinian side, given the dramatically asymmetrical forces created by the superior Israeli arms and manpower, and the Israelis were not inhibited by non-violent impulses. Fatalities among the Palestinians for the years 1988–93 totaled slightly over 1,200, including 200 under the age of sixteen. In Gaza alone during 1988–92, Amira Hass (2000) reports there were 60,706 injured by shooting (live and rubber bullets), beating, or tear gas. Citing UNRWA reports, Hass reckons that

> between August 1989 and August 1993, 1,085 persons treated in its clinics had been shot in the head: 302 of these were between the ages of 17 and twenty-four, 163 of them (15%) were women, and 545 were under sixteen – of whom 97 were children under the age of six.
>
> *(Hass 2000: 56)*

Indeed, a report by the Palestinian Physicians for Human Rights notes that, "during the first five years of the *intifada*, a child under six was shot in the head once every two weeks." The losses were not confined to the Palestinian territories. A number of Palestinian resisters who infiltrated into Israel were killed in bombings and shootings.

Leadership also suffered losses. Key among them was the bloody assassination of Khalil al-Wazir, in the presence of his wife and children, by Mossad and Israeli commandos in Tunis on April 16, 1988. It was an important symbolic and strategic loss for the Palestinians. Al-Wazir had been a founder of Fatah, and in the 1980s had organized a number of anti-Israeli actions. From his base in Tunis it is said that he organized youth committees in Palestine which eventually became the backbone of the First *Intifada*. The Palestinians considered his assassination an attempt by Israel to end the *intifada* or at least to strike at the morale of the Palestinian people. In fact the period after this assassination was defined by the Palestinians as a new chapter in the

Table 5.1 First *Intifada* fatalities

Year	Israeli deaths		Palestinian deaths
	MFA	B'tselem	
1987	11		22
1988	16	12	310
1989	40	31	305
1990	33	22	145
1991	21	19	104
1992	34	34	138
1993	45	61	180
	200	**179**	**1,204**

Source: Adapted from www.mideasteeb.org/Middle-East-Encylopedia/Intifada.

intifada. Al-Wazir was given a martyr's funeral with a procession led by Arafat, and his demise reverberated in demonstrations throughout the Occupied Territories.

What about losses on the Israeli side? The Ministry of Foreign Affairs (MFA) and the Israeli human rights group B'tselem report 200 and 179 deaths respectively. Injuries are reported as totaling 3,100 (1,700 soldiers; 1,400 civilians). While human loss should not be overlooked, the primary effect of the First *Intifada* on Israel may have been economic: the Palestinian boycott of Israeli goods and the outlay of significant military expenditures. But beyond the loss of life and money, and perhaps more enduringly, the First *Intifada* polarized Israel into two camps: those that sought a political solution to the conflict and those who would rely upon draconian measures – the IDF's might, settlement expansion, population transfer, and expulsion. That division persists today.

The re-emergence of the PLO and the rise of Hamas

One of the most significant consequences of the First *Intifada* was the re-emergence of the PLO and the rise of Hamas – and the conflict between them. Since the 1960s the PLO had been in exile, and in 1982 the PLO established its headquarters in Tunisia, absent from the territories and removed from the everyday struggle of the occupation. Into this vacuum stepped Hamas. Its Islamic orientation and emphasis on confrontation – violent and otherwise – was gaining increasing credibility, and Hamas worked hard to become the PLO's rival. Secular Palestinian activists in the Occupied Territories (notably but not exclusively Fatah) demanded that the PLO adopt a clear political program to guide the struggle for independence. In response, the Palestine National Council (a Palestinian parliament-in-exile), convened in Algeria in November 1988, proclaimed an independent Palestinian state in the West Bank and the Gaza Strip and accepted the two-state concept. Moreover, this marked a moment when the external leadership listened to the troops on the ground, the local Palestinian leadership. Indeed, the First *Intifada* had shifted the gravity of the Palestinian political initiative from Tunis to the Occupied Territories. The 1988 Declaration of Independence also marked a shift in the PLO platform from armed struggle to a peace strategy and historical compromise – the acceptance of a state within the 1967 borders. At this point, the PFLP and the DPFLP both dropped out of the PLO, unwilling to accept the two-state solution to the conflict.

The Israeli response was ambiguous. On the one hand, while it had earlier encouraged the Muslim Brotherhood's development as an alternative to the PLO, by May 1989 its violence against Israelis had become intolerable and its goal (the triumph of Islam and the elimination of the Israeli state) existentially threatening. Israel exiled the Hamas leadership and arrested several hundred of its cadres. During the *intifada*, Hamas urged Palestinians in the West Bank and Gaza Strip to confront Israeli authorities. It coordinated labor strikes against Israel and conducted a campaign to try to make Muslims adhere to a strict Islamic code. In 1989, Hamas members kidnapped and killed two Israeli soldiers in a direct attack on Israel. In response, Israel declared Hamas an illegal organization and arrested its head, Yassin. After several more violent actions, in December 1992 Israel expelled more than 400 Hamas members and supporters to a remote area inside the Lebanese border.

The Palestinian proffer of a two-state solution represented a major turn in the course of the conflict. In the West, it resuscitated and legitimized Arafat as the leader of the Palestinians. In addition, it reawakened the interest of the international community in the conflict and led to efforts by the United States and Europe to find a solution. Those efforts led ultimately in 1991 to the Madrid Conference, which was effectively the beginning of the end of the First *Intifada*. Its final breath expired with the Oslo Accords in 1993. By all but the most strenuous standards the First *Intifada* may be considered a non-violent, civil society success. It must also be acknowledged that the competition that developed between Hamas and the PLO for the hearts and minds of Palestinians would haunt the post-*intifada* years.

Jordanian disengagement

In 1988, shortly after the onset of the First *Intifada*, Jordan declared a total disengagement from the Palestinian West Bank – legally, administratively, and financially. While a number of nationalistic and demographic factors figured in the Jordanian decision (i.e., the perceived threat of a growing Palestinian population within Jordan), the decision was also taken in recognition of the fact that the *intifada* was a struggle for liberation and independence not merely from the Israelis but from foreign Arab regimes as well.

Persisting images

For the world at large, the First *Intifada* produced two broad images, both to the advantage of the Palestinians: first, that of Israel as conveyed through the international media as a bully who confronts children with armed fire; and second, and parallel to that, the sympathetic image of the Palestinians, finally recognized as an oppressed people who faced weaponry with mere stones.

The Second *Intifada*: the al-Aqsa *Intifada*

What caused the outbreak of the al-Aqsa *Intifada*? The conventional wisdom places the blame on one of two central figures, Ariel Sharon or Yasser Arafat. In one version, Sharon, then leader of the Israeli opposition, started the *intifada* by going on an intentionally provocative visit to the Temple Mount al Haram al-Sharif on September 28, 2000. Alternatively, the Israeli view has it that Arafat, President of the Palestinian Authority (PA), decided to unleash Palestinian militants against Israel rather than accept a negotiated resolution of the conflict. Both simple scenarios may contain a measure of truth (although Arafat was certainly not in charge of the uprising at the onset), but they omit critical elements of the historical and political context that had developed in the period between *intifadas*.

Primary causes: the inter-intifada period, post-Oslo

The years between the *intifadas* (1993–2000) could not be called pacific. In 1994, an Israeli massacred twenty-nine Palestinians at prayer in the Ibrahimi Mosque in Hebron. In response, Hamas intensified its military actions and targeted Israeli civilians. The inter-*intifada* period also witnessed the September Riots after the opening of the Hashmonaim Tunnel in Jerusalem in 1996; the riots left eighty-five Palestinians and sixteen Israelis dead and 1,200 Palestinians and eighty-five Israelis wounded. Indeed, throughout this period, hardly a week passed without some fatal conflict between Israelis and Palestinians. In some measure, the clash at al-Aqsa and the Western Wall, which launched the Second *Intifada*, was a dramatic flare-up of an ongoing process of mutual destruction.

Palestinians had expected that the 1993 Oslo agreement would lead to better lives, greater freedoms, the end of Israeli occupation, and, at the end of five years (1999), Palestinian statehood. When such changes failed to materialize, and rapid settlement advanced, entailing the loss of significant Palestinian lands, the situation on the ground worsened. This dynamic – the clash between expectations and a worsening reality – explains much of the popular support for the Second *Intifada*[5] The failure of the Camp David summit in July 2000 only reinforced the belief that diplomacy was at an end and that confrontation was the only alternative.

Culpable leadership

Sharon and Arafat helped shift the status quo from a tense situation to a violent one. Sharon's visit to the al-Aqsa area – accompanied by a security detail 1,000 strong – was *une provocation enorme* and set the Second *Intifada* in motion. Arafat's contribution, on the other hand, was more a sin of omission: he and several other Palestinian leaders decided not to try to rein in the violence once it started. Indeed, in seven of the nine days following the onset of the al-Aqsa *Intifada*, Arafat was out of the country. He incorrectly assumed that the violence could improve the Palestinian negotiating position.

Internal factors

The public's perception of Arafat's leadership, his cabinet, and his party (Fatah) contributed to the energy of the Second *Intifada*. Many Palestinians viewed his leadership as rife with corruption, nepotism, and cronyism. Former civil activists who had been the backbone of the First *Intifada* felt marginalized by the return of Arafat and the PLO to the homeland and joined in the *intifada* out of frustration with Arafat and his cabinet, which they viewed as ineffective and corrupt.

The course and strategies of the Second *Intifada*

While the spark that set off the *intifada* came from a clash at the al-Aqsa Mosque in the Old City in East Jerusalem, the uprising gained much of its original momentum from civil activists in peripheral areas (Rafa, Nablus, and Jenin) who had been marginalized by the PA. But, rather than follow geography or personality, the path of the Second *Intifada* may best be charted by examining the violence it unleashed and the tightening of Israeli controls, coupled with increased expropriation of land and the further development of settlements.

Violence against violence

In contrast to the First *Intifada*, the al-Aqsa *Intifada* was marked by a very high degree of violence. On the Palestinian side, this involved virtually no military or security cadres. The Palestinian weapon of choice appears to have been suicide bombings: fifty-six from September 2000 until December 2005, of which thirty-four were conducted by Hamas, Islamic Jihad, or other jihadist groups, fourteen had some Fatah involvement, and eight were by undetermined parties. (The Palestinian Authority was often faulted by Israel for not stopping suicide bombers; ironically, most of the suicide bombers came from "Area B" localities which were under full Israeli security control.) Additionally, there were twenty-one non-suicide bombings (including fifteen car bombings and two that were remote controlled) and thirty-one attacks involving ambush shootings, gunman attacks, grenades, primitive rockets, and mortar fire. To these must be added an undetermined number of deaths by stabbing and one horrific incident of a Palestinian bus driver turning his vehicle into a crowd, killing eight and injuring twenty-one. The bombing venues were diverse: shopping malls, pedestrian malls, outdoor markets, seaports, soccer fields, nightclubs, markets, outside schools, vacation resorts, hotel lobbies, buses, bus stops, hitchhiking posts for soldiers, restaurants, cafes, pizzerias, discos, pool halls, promenades, outside synagogues, and bar mitzvahs.

Palestinian violence erupted with considerable momentum, and Israel responded with a mix of conventional and modern weaponry – tanks, missiles, F-16 bombers, Apache helicopters, and aerial bombardments. These weapons and Israeli army ground troops were used to invade refugee camps, to destroy Palestinian police stations and commercial and public facilities, and to demolish over 1,000 homes, as well as to uproot tens of thousands of olive and fruit trees. Among other actions were the use of human shields, targeted assassinations, and administrative detentions of Palestinian leadership throughout the territories. In sum, Israel followed the doctrine of "overwhelming force" in what was distinctly an asymmetrical conflict.

Israeli control

In addition to violent events and strategies, Israel employed a concert of actions designed to impose their colonial writ and fragment the territories. Areas from which the Israeli army had previously withdrawn were now reoccupied, and isolated and closed "military zones" were created around towns and villages to which the UN, the press, and outsiders were denied entry and from which residents could not exit without special permits – closure implemented with an intricate system of several hundred road blocks. But perhaps the most significant Israeli imposition of control was the massive separation wall begun in 2001. Ostensibly erected as a security barrier to stop suicide bombers, the 700+ kilometer structure winds it way through Jerusalem and around the West Bank, annexing land within the Green Line and separating Palestinian communities from one another and from their hinterland, resulting in an occupied land of bantustans.

Another of Israel's most powerful tools was its comprehensive control of borders – international borders with Jordan and Egypt as well as borders within Israel itself, including borders between it and occupied East Jerusalem, internal borders between Palestinian cities and towns, and control of the borders that framed the linkage between Gaza and the West Bank. Throughout the Second *Intifada* (and, indeed, up to the present), Israel frequently closed any and all of these borders, thereby disrupting travel, trade, taxation, postal services, banking, and medical and educational activities. Continued Israeli control of Palestinian life has led to a resentment that boils just below the surface today.

Israeli expansion and the further fragmentation of Palestinian territory

Throughout the post-Oslo period and into the al-Aqsa *Intifada*, Israeli settlement-building continued apace, regardless of changes in Israeli administration. Indeed, during the years 1993 to 2000 the population of Israeli settlers in the West Bank increased from 115,000 to 200,000, in addition to the 180,000 in East Jerusalem settlements. The number of settler housing units increased by 17,190 during this period, and three new "official" settlements (Lapid, Kiryat Sefer, and Menora), as well as forty-two "unofficial" settlements, were erected.[6] In the first two years after the signing of the Oslo Declaration of Principles, Israel confiscated 41,000 acres of West Bank land and, in 1999, another 10,000 acres. The development of the Har Homa Israeli settlement (1997–9), built in part on Arab-owned lands, effectively completed a belt of settlements around Palestinian East Jerusalem; this sparked fierce demonstrations throughout the West Bank and Gaza and led to a nineteen-month breakdown in the peace process. Moreover, land transfers taken from the Palestinian Authority also led to the proliferation of Israeli bypass roads in the West Bank. In the period 1994–7, 140 kilometers of new Israeli bypass roads were built, skirting Palestinian cities and villages. The roads cut the West Bank into pieces. This further limited the possibility of finding a political resolution in which the Palestinians could realize a state composed of contiguous territory.

Results and consequences of the Second *Intifada*

In many respects, the effects of the al-Aqsa *Intifada* are still unraveling and playing out today. But, if we take the onset date of September 2000 and the somewhat arbitrary end date of 2005, one can come to an assessment of its impact in terms of human losses, economic decline, and the fall of Arafat.

Human losses

Most NGOs report a 3:1 ratio of Palestinian to Israeli losses. We have eschewed the possibly biased data of both governments and have relied upon B'tselem, an Israeli human rights organization, whose data approximate the 3:1 ratio. In the Occupied Territories 3,135 Palestinians were killed by Israeli forces, including 627 under age eighteen, 181 in extra-judicial executions, and 288 assassinations, plus 54 killed by Israeli security forces in Israel and 34 killed by settlers in the West Bank. On the Israeli side there were 950 fatalities, made up of 431 civilians killed in Israel (78 of whom were under age eighteen), 218 civilians killed (mostly settlers) in the West Bank and Gaza (of whom 34 were under age eighteen), and 301 Israeli security forces (218 in the West Bank and Gaza, and 83 killed inside Israel). Moreover, in what has been styled by the Israelis as "the *intifada* within," seventeen Arab-Israelis were killed in Palestinian solidarity demonstrations that took place throughout Israel in October 2000. To these grim figures must be added Palestinians killed by Palestinians: 130 were put to death under suspicion of collaboration with the enemy.[7]

Economic impact

The World Bank reports that, by 2004, the destruction of enterprises and the disruption of businesses by closures had caused a decline in average incomes by more than 33 percent. Unemployment ranged from 25 percent to 60 percent in the territories, and hundreds of thousands lived below the poverty line. The PA had no realistic response to this crisis. For years, donor money, internal tax receipts, and customs and VAT payments transferred by Israel covered the PA's general operating costs. Significantly, the customs and VAT revenue stream is controlled by Israel, and it made up almost two-thirds of the PA's formal working budget. Shortly after the onset of the Second *Intifada*, Israel refused to transfer these VAT payments; at the same time donor concerns about the integrity of the PA leadership caused them to bypass Arafat's ministries and funnel emergency aid through such international agencies as UNWRA and UNDP. Other crucial sources of revenue were sharply reduced: with the destruction wreaked by the war, profits from state or state-linked business concerns in the private sector plummeted, and revenues from the control of major commodity flows (such as gasoline, cement, and gravel) were non-existent or dismal.

Marginalization of the PA

Perhaps more significant than the budgetary crisis was the unabated criticism of the PA's short-comings as a government. Public sentiment against its ineptness and corruption intensified, as most PA institutions proved poorly equipped to respond to public needs during a national emergency. Thus, civil defense measures from the police and security forces were rare; instead, local municipalities had to carry the burden of dealing with the physical destruction from Israeli military attacks. The PA also was largely absent in other areas. The PLO's Palestine Red Crescent Society, along with NGOs such as the Union of Palestinian Medical Relief Committees, was more active in emergency medical services than the Ministry of Health. By bombing the installations of the PA security forces and assassinating individual Hamas and Fatah activists, former Prime Minister Ehud Barak and, later, Sharon sent a message that reinforced a sense among Palestinians of the Israeli army's almost supernatural powers of surveillance, as well as the PA's impotence. The segmentation of Palestinian territory, including the Gaza Strip, into dozens of blockaded areas made the practice of self-government by the PA virtually impossible. The nominal institutions of collective decision-making, weak in the past, now seem almost defunct.

The demise of Arafat

It is important to remember that Arafat had been looking for a face-saving exit from the *intifada* since March, 2001, and a life-saving exit since June. In March, none of the PA's hoped-for gains from the *intifada* had materialized; the second Arab summit drove home the fact that it could not expect any real political leverage from the Arab regimes. Two "honorable" exits were proffered after that summit: the Jordanian–Egyptian proposal in April and the Mitchell report released in late May. But neither offered more than minimal face-saving gains to the Palestinian leadership and an ambiguous settlement freeze. Sensing that Arafat was cornered, Sharon declared a unilateral but loosely defined ceasefire. It was impossible for Arafat to enter Sharon's "ceasefire," especially given that all Palestinian factions had discounted the significance of the settlement freeze. Then came the turning point of the June 1 suicide attack in Tel Aviv, in which twenty Israeli teenagers were killed.

Arafat, already seen as an obstacle to the peace process in the West and threatened with political excommunication by the US, was forced to reciprocate Sharon's ceasefire and accept Israel's timetable for implementing the Mitchell report. Then the Bush administration went on summer vacation, apparently unready to exert much further effort in a conflict that seemed interminable.

Arafat's charismatic hegemony was proven to be true through the Second *Intifada*. Jammed between the imposed obligations of the Oslo Accords, on the one hand, and the growing popular frustration with his inability to make progress towards a Palestinian state, on the other, Arafat chose effectively not to lead the *intifada*, but also not to suppress it. Instead he allowed it to run its own course. When the Israeli offensive escalated the armed resistance of the Palestinians, Arafat abstained from taking any real leadership role. Since his charismatic authority was the glue that maintained the coherence of the fragmented political system, his abstinence from playing a firm role opened the door for an open conflict between internal rivals. In response to the announcement by Israel and the United States that he had become "*irrelevant*," Arafat gave the green light for more internal degradation and random violence to send out a message with the tenor "*deal with me . . . or otherwise chaos*."[8]

Mutual violence resumed and climaxed in the siege of Arafat's headquarters, the Muqata. In 2003 the Palestinian Basic Law was changed to create the position of a prime minister, which, under American pressure, passed to Mahmoud Abbas (Abu Mazen). Arafat died in 2004 and Abu Mazen, who was against military resistance from the beginning, became president. Abbas was bested in an election by Hamas. After a near civil war in Gaza between Hamas and Fatah, Abbas was able to cling to power as president in the West Bank by sharing power with the new PM, Salam Fayyad, who enjoyed the support of the USA and the West.

In some respect, the al-Aqsa *Intifada* continues today. At this writing, direct negotiations are in hiatus and there is widespread popular resistance: Palestinian demonstrations (often met by violent Israeli responses), boycotts of settlement goods, and the threat of withholding Palestinian labor from the settlements. This may be a nascent return to the strategies of the First *Intifada*.

Third intifada?

Although it received little media coverage at the time, in late July 2007 the Palestinian cabinet released a new policy platform that, for the first time in the Palestinian Authority's history, omitted any reference to "armed resistance" to Israel as a core principle. Dropped from the platform was the Arabic term for resistance – *muqawama* – widely employed by Palestinian militant groups. The new PA platform, which has been endorsed by President Abbas and Prime Minister Fayyad, instead calls on Palestinians to fight for statehood with a different form of resistance – "popular struggle."[9] Fatah had thus made a strategic decision effectively to declare a third *intifada* against Israel, citing the failed peace talks as the essential reason for their resolution. One of Fatah's top officials said that a third *intifada* would have a widespread popular base, adding, however, that, unlike the al-Aqsa *Intifada*, the movement will not endorse an armed struggle or the use of firearms.[10]

Perhaps the two most successful "popular struggle" campaigns have been the protests against the separation wall in the villages of Budrus and Bil'in and the movement to boycott goods produced in Israeli settlements. Prime Minister Fayyad has been among the Fatah advocates of both causes. He has called for weekly anti-separation fence rallies in locations across the West Bank, and has encouraged Palestinians to adopt a strategy of "peaceful resistance" with regard to a boycott of settlement products. In a recent speech he noted, "There has been progress in the boycott of settlement products, which comes from the idea of popular peaceful resistance, and I hope we will rid our markets of all settlement goods by the end of the year."[11]

Notes

1 Noufal (2000), pp. 107–8.
2 Schiff and Ya'ari (1990), p. 18.

3 A. Grace, "The Tax Resistance at Bayt Sahur," *Journal of Palestine Studies*, 19/2 (1990), pp. 99–107.
4 Noufal (2000), pp. 109–10.
5 Pressman (2003).
6 "Facts on the Ground since the Oslo Agreement, September 1993," *Palestine-Israel Journal*, 7/3–4 (2000), www.pij.org/details.php?id=269.
7 B'tselem report, BBC News online, 2 August 2005.
8 Ali Jarbawi and Wendy Pearlman, "Struggle in a Post-Charisma Tradition: Rethinking Palestinian Politics after Arafat," *Journal of Palestine Studies*, 36/4 (2007), pp. 6–21.
9 M. J. Stephen, "Dropping 'muqawama,'" 27 September 2007, www.opendemocracy.net/article/dropping_muqawama.
10 J. Khoury, "Fatah Officials Warn of Third Palestinian *Intifada*," *Haaretz*, 20 November 2009.
11 Carmel Gould, "Salam Fayyad and the Drive towards Palestinian Statehood: A Comparison of British and US Media Coverage," *Just Journalism*, special report, www.justjournalism.com/specialreports/download/Just_Journalism_Report__Salam_Fayyad_in_the_media_-_May_2010.pdf.

Further reading

Baroud, R. (2006) *The Second Palestinian* Intifada*: A Chronicle of a People's Struggle* (London: Pluto Press).
Baylouny, A. M. (2010) "The Palestinian *Intifada*," in N. Young (ed.), *The International Encyclopedia of Peace* (New York and Oxford: Oxford University Press).
Carmon, Y., and Feldner, Y. (2000) *The* Intifada *of Al-Aqsa*, Middle East Research Institute, Inquiry & Analysis Series, Report no. 42, October 11.
Hamami, R. (2001) "Intifada in the Aftermath," *Middle East Report Online*, October 30, www.merip.org/mero/mero103001.
Hamami, R., and Hilal, J. (2001) "An Uprising at a Crossroads," *Middle East Report*, no. 219, www.merip.org/mer/mer219/uprising-crossroads.
Hass, A. (2000) *Drinking the Sea at Gaza* (New York: Henry Holt).
Jarbawi, A., and Pearlman, W., "Struggle in a Post-Charisma Tradition: Rethinking Palestinian Politics after Arafat," *Journal of Palestine Studies*, 36/4 (2007), pp. 6–21.
Noufal, M. (2000) *The Search for a State* (Ramallah: MUWATIN – the Palestinian Institute for the Study of Democracy).
Pressman, J. (2003) "The Second *Intifada*: Background and Causes of the Israeli–Palestinian Conflict," *Journal of Conflict Studies*, 23/2, pp. 114–32.
Schiff, Z., and Ya'ari, E. (2000) Intifada*: The Palestinian Uprising – Israel's Third Front* (New York: Simon & Schuster).

6

The Camp David summit

A tale of two narratives

Joel Peters

On 11 July 2000, Israel and the Palestinians met at the US presidential retreat of Camp David to resolve their outstanding issues and tackle the status of Jerusalem, borders, settlements, refugees, security arrangements, and water. Discussion of those issues comprised the final stage of the negotiation process laid out by 1993 Oslo Accords.

The impetus for holding the Camp David summit came from Israeli Prime Minister Ehud Barak, who believed discussions over interim arrangements had run their course and that the only way that Israel and the Palestinians could resolve their differences was by addressing all outstanding final-status issues at a high-level summit meeting. Palestinian leader Yasser Arafat was from the outset resistant to the idea, maintaining that conditions were not yet ripe and insisting that more time was needed. President Clinton, however, shared Barak's vision that only a summit meeting offered the possibility of a breakthrough. And once he issued invitations to the parties, the Palestinians had little option but to agree.

Israel and the Palestinians entered the summit questioning the intentions and commitment of each other to take the steps necessary to resolve the conflict. The Camp David summit followed nearly six years of daily interaction between Israel and the Palestinians, with the two sides struggling to implement the various interim arrangements and agreements signed during the preceding years – years which had seen missed deadlines, setbacks, and the failure of both sides to translate the hopes and promises of the Oslo Accords into reality.

The choice of Camp David – the site of the dramatic Carter–Begin–Sadat breakthrough – held huge symbolic power. Like the 1978 summit, the July 2000 meeting featured the extended sequestration of the Israeli, Palestinian, and American negotiating teams led by their respective presidents and prime ministers, a virtual media blackout, and the personal mediation of the American president. Unlike its predecessor, the second Camp David summit ended in failure. After being locked in intense negotiations for two weeks, Israel and the Palestinians were unable to arrive at any shared understanding on the issues under discussion.

The Camp David summit has been the subject of numerous and differing accounts, many of which have been authored by the summit's participants (Ben-Ami 2006; Hanieh 2001; Indyk 2009; Miller 2008; Ross 2004; Sher 2006). Contradictory accounts abound as to what occurred at the meeting and who was to blame for its failure. The accounts coalesce around two principal narratives. The first maintains that Israel was ready to make unprecedented and far-reaching concessions at Camp David and that Yasser Arafat, uninterested in making peace with Israel, was unwilling to make the necessary comprises to end the conflict. The second narrative holds that Israel's offer fell far short of Palestinian expectations. This narrative shifts the blame away from Arafat and argues that Israel and the Americans, and to a lesser extent the Palestinians, shared responsibility for the summit's failure. This chapter will not detail the discussions held during the two weeks at Camp David. Instead it will focus on those competing narratives that emerged following the summit and assess how they have impacted on policy choices in the years thereafter. It is the claim of this essay that, twelve years on, those narratives continue to impact on the public's perceptions (especially within Israel) of the peace process.

At the conclusion of the summit, Israeli officials presented an account that quickly became the dominant and unchallenged narrative within Israeli society as well as within the American political establishment. According to this version of events, Ehud Barak made an unprecedented and generous offer to the Palestinians, who rejected it without presenting any counter-proposals. According to reports and various accounts of the summit, the ideas that Barak conveyed to Clinton one week into the talks would have allowed for a Palestinian state on 91 percent of the territory plus the Gaza Strip. Israel would annex 9 percent (from land inside the West Bank) in exchange for a land swap equivalent of 1 percent south of the Gaza Strip (i.e., a 9:1 swap). Israel would lease an additional 10 percent in the Jordan Rift Valley for no more than twelve years. For the first time, Israel was prepared to consider the idea of Palestinian sovereignty over most of Arab East Jerusalem and the Muslim, Christian, and Armenian quarters of the Old City. Its proposals allowed for Palestinian "custodianship" over the Temple Mount/Haram al-Sharif, though sovereignty over the area would rest with Israel (see chapter 8, by Galia Golan).

In a somber parting statement, Barak laid full blame for the setback at Yasser Arafat's door, claiming that he had missed a golden opportunity to achieve a permanent peace for his people. Barak asserted that Israel had been prepared for "every possibility" but, instead, because of Arafat, "the vision of peace had suffered a major blow." Barak continued to negotiate with Arafat after Camp David through to his election defeat in January 2001 and even ran his election campaign on a platform of a continuation of the peace process. Once out of office, he was unrelenting in his attacks on Arafat. In an interview on the anniversary of the Camp David summit, he described Arafat as a cunning rival and claimed that he had come to power to reveal Arafat's true face. Barak boasted that at Camp David he had shown Arafat to be a leader lacking both the character and the will to make peace with Israel.[1]

In a wide-ranging interview two years after the summit, Barak described Arafat's behavior as a sophisticated performance designed to extract from Israel as many concessions as possible without ever seriously intending to sign a peace treaty. For Barak, Arafat did not come to Camp David to negotiate in good faith; rather: "He just kept on saying 'no' to every offer, never making any counter proposals of his own" (Morris 2002).

Barak claimed Arafat saw himself as a reborn Saladdin – the Kurdish Muslim general who defeated the Crusaders in the twelfth century – and Israel as just another ephemeral Crusader state. He charged Arafat with not accepting Israel's legitimacy or the existence of a Jewish nation and went on to accuse Arafat and the Palestinian leadership of secretly planning Israel's demise. For Barak:

> What they [Arafat and his colleagues] want is a Palestinian state in all of Palestine . . .. Israel is too strong at the moment, so they formally recognize it. But their game plan is to establish a Palestinian state while leaving the door open for further legitimate demands down

the road. For now they are willing to agree to a temporary truce a la Hudnat Hudaybiyah. . . . Then they will push for a binational state and then demography and attrition will lead to a state with a Muslim majority and a Jewish minority. This would not necessarily involve kicking out all the Jews. But it would mean the destruction of Israel as a Jewish state. This I believe is their vision.

(Morris 2002)

Shlomo Ben-Ami, Israel's foreign minister at the time of Camp David, also accused Arafat and the Palestinian leadership of not accepting the idea of a two-state solution: "He may be able to make some sort of partial, temporary agreement with us – although I have my doubts about that, too – but at the deep level, he doesn't accept us. Neither he, nor the Palestinian national movement accepts us." For Ben-Ami, no rational Israeli leader could have reached an agreement with Arafat at Camp David. Ben-Ami talked of Arafat as a "mythological leader" who was not looking for practical solutions, but was instead focused on mythological issues such as the right of return, Jerusalem, and the Holy Mount. In his account of the summit, Arafat

would only speak in slogans, catchwords, Islamic metaphors . . . [the]elusive, non-committal, master of double talk turned the negotiations with him into a futile exercise. . . . Arafat's truth is the truth of the Islamic ethos, the ethos of refugees and victimization. This truth does not allow him to end his negotiations with Israel unless Israel breaks its neck. So in this particular aspect, Arafat is not a partner. Worse, Arafat is a strategic threat; he endangers peace in the Middle East and in the world.[2]

The Israeli narrative was further underscored by comments made by President Clinton and other American officials. The Palestinians had sought (and felt they had received) assurances that they would not be blamed should the summit end in failure. However, in his statement marking the end of the summit, Clinton clearly pointed the finger of blame at Arafat and went out of his way to praise Ehud Barak for his "particular courage, vision and an understanding of the historical importance of the moment." In contrast, he damned Arafat with faint praise, merely noting his commitment to the path of peace.

Clinton's comments were born in part out of his frustration with Arafat's passivity and the contradictory positions of the Palestinian delegation at Camp David. They were also designed to bolster Barak's faltering standing among the Israeli public. In an interview on Israeli television at the end of July, Clinton commended Barak for his willingness to cross red lines and break taboos in order to achieve peace with the Palestinians at Camp David. He also warned Arafat not to consider a unilateral declaration of statehood in September and hinted that he was considering moving the American embassy from Tel Aviv to Jerusalem.

In a final effort to bring about an agreement before the conclusion of his presidency, Clinton was forced to temper his criticism of Arafat (see chapter 26, by Steven Spiegel), but on leaving the Oval office he described Arafat as an ageing leader who relished his own sense of victimhood and who was incapable of making peace with Israel. In his memoirs, Clinton bitterly recalls a final conversation with Arafat: he "thanked me for all my efforts and told me what a great man I was." I replied, "I am not a great man. I am a failure and you have made me one."

Dennis Ross, the coordinator for the peace process during the Clinton administration, echoed the Israeli narrative attributing the failure of Camp David, and the collapse of the peace process, to Arafat. For Ross, the negotiations failed because Yasser Arafat was unwilling to confront history and mythology.

> Whilst Clinton and Barak were prepared to do what was necessary to reach an agreement and take the risks inherent in confronting history and mythology, Arafat failed that test . . . At no point during Camp David or in the six months after did the Chairman [Arafat] ever demonstrate any capability to conclude a permanent status deal. I simply do not believe that he is capable of doing a permanent status deal.
>
> *(Ross 2001)*

Not only did Arafat reject all ideas offered at Camp David, but he continued to "repeat old mythologies and invent new ones like, for example, that the Temple was not in Jerusalem but in Nablus." US Secretary of State Madeline Albright added her voice to American criticism of Arafat, lamenting that, instead of trying to forge a new Palestinian consensus, he simply reinforced the old one. Albright was certain that, if Arafat had said yes in 2000, the Palestinians would by now be celebrating their independence and Palestine would have become a member of the United Nations with its capital located in East Jerusalem.

Jerusalem and the question of sovereignty over the Temple Mount/Haram al-Sharif were the major points of contention at Camp David. The refugee issue barely featured at the summit. However, Israeli leaders intimated to the Israeli public that it was Palestinian intransigence over the "right of return," and not differences over Jerusalem, that led to the breakdown of the talks. For Israel, Arafat's refusal to compromise on this issue was seen as indicative of his unwillingness to accept Israel's moral legitimacy. Shlomo Ben-Ami said Arafat conceived of himself as a warrior engaged in a campaign against a state born in sin which had to acknowledge the moral right of Palestinian refugees to return (Ben-Ami 2006: 249). Palestinian advocacy of the "right of return" was portrayed within Israel as a "demographic-political weapon for subverting the Jewish state." Israelis from across the political spectrum were of one mind that, by raising the issue of the "right of return," the Palestinians demonstrated that they were not yet reconciled to the idea of coexistence. On 2 January 2001, thirty-three Israeli intellectuals published a statement addressed to the Palestinian leadership. "We want to clarify," it stated, "that we shall never be able to agree to the return of the refugees within the borders of Israel, for the meaning of such a return would be the elimination of the State of Israel." The signatories included Israeli liberals such as the novelists Amos Oz and David Grossman.

The outbreak of the al-Aqsa *Intifada* in September 2001, combined with protests by Israel's Arab population in its early months, substantially undermined whatever weak support existed for the return of refugees to Israel. The backlash was not just confined to rhetorical statements. On 1 January 2001, the Knesset enacted legislation that stated that any agreement which included the repatriation of refugees to Israel would require the prior approval of the Knesset. The resolution won a majority of ninety votes out of a possible 120, attesting to its overwhelming cross-party support.

On 28 September 2000, Likud leader Ariel Sharon paid a controversial visit to the Temple Mount/Haram al-Sharif. Posturing to his domestic constituency, and accompanied by hundreds of police, Sharon sought to demonstrate his commitment to keeping all of Jerusalem under Israeli sovereignty. The next day, angered by Sharon's visit, Palestinians clashed with Israeli police at the site of the al-Aqsa and Dome of the Rock mosques. Seven Palestinians were killed and over 300 wounded. In the following days violent demonstrations erupted throughout East Jerusalem and the West Bank, spreading to the Galilee in northern Israel. Israeli troops responded with great force using live ammunition, and the Palestinians sustained heavy casualties: by the end of October, 141 Palestinians had been killed and over 500 wounded.

Competing Israeli and Palestinian explanations as to the causes of the Second *Intifada* (see chapter 5, by Rami Nasrallah) were added to narratives on the failure of Camp David. Israelis saw the outbreak of violence as evidence that Arafat had not abandoned the armed struggle to promote Palestinian national goals. Israelis were certain that Arafat had made a strategic decision in the aftermath of Camp David to launch a campaign of terror alongside the diplomatic-political route. Ehud Barak asserted:

> we know from hard evidence that after Camp David Arafat intended to unleash a violent confrontation with Israel and Sharon's visit to the Temple Mount offered him an excellent pretext . . . . The intifada was preplanned, pre-prepared. I don't mean that Arafat knew that on a certain day in September [it would be unleashed] . . . it wasn't accurate, like computer engineering. But it was definitely on the level of planning, of a grand plan.
>
> *(Morris 2002)*

Israeli explanations for the outbreak of the Second *Intifada* were echoed by influential voices in the United States. Dennis Ross maintained that Arafat was at fault and did nothing to prevent the violence even though he was aware that the Americans were about to present a set of ideas similar to the Clinton Parameters issued at the end of the December. The influential *New York Times* columnist Tom Friedman condemned Arafat for doing nothing to rein in the militants and terrorists and dubbed the Second *Intifada* "Arafat's war":

> This explosion of violence would be totally understandable if the Palestinians had no alternative. But this was not the case . . . [the violence] came in the context of a serious Israeli peace overture, which Mr Arafat has chosen to spurn. That's why this is Arafat's war.
>
> *(Quoted in Pressman 2003: 14)*

Not surprisingly, the Palestinians left Camp David with a different interpretation of events. Israel's offer at the summit fell far short of Palestinian expectations and did nothing to end its occupation and control of the West Bank and Gaza. For Akram Hanieh, a member of the Palestinian delegation, the Israelis did not negotiate in good faith. Rather they sought to "consolidate the gains of their war in 1967, and not to make peace that removes the traces of this war. They came to reorganize and legitimize the occupation, instead of searching for a language for dialogue on living and coexisting with partners" (Hanieh 2001). For Ghassan Khatib (2002), Barak

> had two objectives at Camp David – either to reach a final settlement ending the Palestinian–Israeli conflict and achieving Israel's objectives of peace, security, integration and prosperity without compromising on Jerusalem, the refugees or many of the settlements, or to end the entire peace process and place the blame squarely on the other side.

Initially Palestinian arguments were ignored. The Israeli/American narrative on the summit and the failings of Yasser Arafat governed discussions on the peace process. The dominance of this narrative was not surprising given the asymmetrical relationship of power between Israel and the Palestinians, and that it was first articulated by Ehud Barak and reinforced by President Clinton and senior American officials. That narrative was soon challenged for overlooking the dynamics of the negotiating process at Camp David and ignoring the constraints and policy dilemmas facing Arafat and the Palestinians. Moreover, casting Arafat as the villain was viewed not only as misleading but as an excuse advanced by Israeli and American negotiators to absolve them of any responsibility. The counter-narrative on Camp David, and the outbreak of the al-Aqsa *Intifada*, while not exonerating the Palestinians and Arafat, presents them in a more positive light. It shifts the burden of failure onto the approach, negotiating tactics, and specific policies of Ehud Barak, questions the nature and substance of Israel's proposals, and addresses the failings of the Americans in mediating the summit. It also discusses Palestinian disenchantment with the Oslo process and its growing mistrust of Israel's actions and intentions.

Palestinians had welcomed Barak's victory in May 1999. After Binyamin Netanyahu's tenure as prime minister, the return of the Labor Party to power was greeted with expectations of renewed movement on the Palestinian track. However, by the summer of 2000, the Palestinians had become increasingly distrustful of Barak's policies, motives, and strategic priorities. Barak's first move was to impose the Sharm el-Sheikh agreement of September 1999 on the Palestinians, according to which the planned third partial redeployment of Israeli troops from the West Bank as part of the 1995 Oslo II Accord would be further postponed and would become part of a new Framework Agreement which would be concluded by February 2000. Instead of proceeding with negotiations, Barak put the Palestinian track on hold, focusing all his efforts on reaching a peace agreement with Syria. Palestinians were affronted by Barak's decision to pursue the "Syria first" option, viewing it as a calculated move to isolate them and force them to make concessions in the future.

Living conditions for Palestinians in the West Bank and Gaza showed no sign of improvement under Barak. Moreover, Israeli settlement-building continued unabated and even gathered pace. Barak's failure both to implement a number of interim arrangements – including a third partial redeployment of troops from the West Bank, the release of Palestinians imprisoned for acts prior to the signing of the 1993 Oslo Accords, and the transfer to Palestinian control of three villages on the outskirts of Jerusalem – and to develop an intimate working relationship with Arafat only increased Palestinian distrust.

It was only after the collapse of talks with Syria in March 2000, following the failed Geneva summit between Clinton and President Assad, that Barak turned his attention to the Palestinian track. Having ignored the Palestinians, he now set a deadline of only a few months to reach a permanent agreement. Barak had made no secret of his antipathy to the idea of interim steps, which was a central component of the Oslo process, and had abstained in the Knesset vote on the 1995 Oslo II Accord. He viewed territorial withdrawal prior to permanent status negotiations as giving away strategic assets without receiving anything tangible in return.

Although Barak allowed negotiators to meet in Stockholm in May to engage in preliminary negotiations on final status issues, he was skeptical that real progress could be achieved through such a back channel. Instead, he pressed the United States to call for a high-level summit to address all the final-status issues simultaneously. Barak believed that only when confronted with a final and comprehensive Israeli offer would the Palestinians be compelled to reveal their true intentions. Furthermore, he was convinced that only by presenting all concessions and rewards in one package would it be possible to convince the Israeli public to support an Israeli–Palestinian peace treaty.

The Palestinians were resistant to the idea of the summit in July, arguing that more time was needed to prepare the ground for negotiations over final-status issues. Without additional preparatory work the risk of failure was too great. Arafat was persuaded that Barak was setting a trap and that the summit served to address the latter's domestic political concerns and strategic purposes. For the Palestinians, the summit was designed solely to increase the pressure on them to reach a quick agreement and to lower their expectations while heightening the political and symbolic costs if they did not. At a minimum, Arafat requested from the Americans that the third Israeli redeployment take place prior to Camp David as a confidence-building measure. He also sought assurances that he would not be blamed should the summit fail. Ultimately Barak's insistence on convening the summit prevailed. Arafat could not refuse Clinton's invitation, going to Camp David "more intent on surviving than on benefiting from it" (Agha and Malley 2001).

Barak was widely praised for his far-reaching and generous territorial offer. Thomas Friedman, in the *New York Times*, called the move unprecedented and unthinkable. However, a Palestinian state in 91 percent of the West Bank and Gaza fell far short of Palestinian expectations, which viewed implementation of Resolution 242 as the guiding principle for any territorial agreement. In the Israeli narrative, the Palestinians were depicted as uncompromising in their refusal to consider Barak's territorial offer. But, from the Palestinian point of view, Oslo itself was a historical compromise. By agreeing to recognize Israel within its pre-1967 borders, they had already made the most important territorial concession – namely, accepting the principle of achieving a state in only 22 percent of historic Palestine and conceding 78 percent to Israel. The Palestinians had no intention of bargaining over additional territory. For this reason, the Palestinians refused to place a counter-proposal on the table, though they did accept the principle of a land swap that would give the Palestinians state territory from Israel equal to the amount of territory that they would cede to Israel from the West Bank. The notion that Israel was "offering" land, being "generous," or "making concessions" was doubly misleading. "For the Palestinians, land was not given but given back" (Agha and Malley 2001). The territorial proposals put forward at Camp David were never stated in writing but were orally conveyed. Israel never presented any maps, nor did it specify the areas of land it intended to annex. Ultimately, maps were drawn up, but only after the summit and based on differing interpretations of what was proposed there. One of the reasons that Barak refused to meet with Arafat at Camp David was fear that any Israeli concessions would be put on the record. Barak denied that Israel had had any part in the proposals, claiming that they were raised by President Clinton.

According to the Palestinians, Oslo II provided for the annexation of Palestinian territory, legitimized Israeli settlements, and perpetuated Israeli control over East Jerusalem and Palestinian natural resources, airspace, and borders. In short, it would result in the "bantustanization" of the West Bank rather than in the creation of a territorially contiguous Palestinian state. The Palestinians viewed the Camp David proposals as dangerous and inadequate. The territorial land swaps were imbalanced, the question of refugees was largely ignored, and the Temple Mount and most of East Jerusalem remained under Israeli sovereignty. Accepting these proposals in the hope that Barak would then make further concessions risked diluting the Palestinian position. It shifted the terms of debate from the international legitimacy of UN resolutions on Israeli withdrawal and refugee return to imprecise ideas raised by Israel and conveyed by the Americans (Agha and Malley 2001).

The Oslo process, intended to turn a conflictual relationship into a cooperative one, ended in failure. While agreements were signed and promises made, nothing in fact changed. Ghassan Khatib (2002) expressed the views of the majority of Palestinians concerning the outbreak of the Second *Intifada*:

> Barak's decision [weeks later] to encourage the leader of his right-wing opposition, Ariel Sharon, to make his provocative visit to Jerusalem's holiest Muslim shrine . . .. Barak's army and police then activated a military plan to brutally shut down civilian protests against the visit, killing tens of Palestinian demonstrators and decisively transforming relations between the two sides from peaceful negotiations into bloody confrontation.

Surprisingly, Israel's intelligence community arrived at a similar conclusion. Arafat was seen to be exploiting popular discontent, not inciting it. In fact, discontent was directed at him and at corruption within the Palestinian Authority just as much as it was at Israel. In contrast to the messages being conveyed to the public by Israel's political echelon, the intelligence community felt that Arafat and the Palestinian leadership were intent on reaching an agreement with Israel through negotiation and were committed to the two-state solution.

Those assessments came to light only in summer 2004, following a public disagreement between former senior officers in the military intelligence – Amos Malka, Amos Gilad, and Ephraim Lavie. However, by that time, after almost four years of violence, Israelis had lost faith in the peace process. The popular narrative that Arafat (and the Palestinians) had rejected the path of peace and had returned to armed struggle after Camp David had become deeply embedded in Israeli society.

Although the Camp David summit ended in failure, President Clinton emerged with his prestige enhanced for his efforts to broker an agreement. As president, Clinton had invested more time and energy in the Arab–Israeli peace process than any of his predecessors. He had won the admiration of both sides for his mastery of details, commitment, and empathy. The Palestinian leadership saw Clinton as more receptive to its needs than any previous US president.

Questions were soon raised, however, about the role played by the Americans and their (mis)management of the summit. For many, the ability of the US to play the role of honest broker was hamstrung by its acute sensitivity to Israel's domestic concerns. Akram Hanieh accused the Americans of being overly sensitive to the needs of the Israeli government and not questioning Israel's demands. He further charged the Americans of colluding with the Israeli negotiating team, whereby they "coordinated their steps, step-by-step and word-by-word" to the point where "the American and Israeli delegations were melting into one" (Hanieh 2001).

Hanieh's views are echoed by Aaron Miller, who served as deputy coordinator for the peace process under Dennis Ross, and by other prominent Americans. Miller reproaches the US team at Camp David for acting like Israel's attorney:

> With the best of motives and intentions, we listened to and followed Israel's lead without critically examining what that would mean for our own interests, for those on the Arab side and for the overall success of the negotiations. We should have resisted Barak's pressure to go for a make-or-break summit and then blame the Palestinians when it failed. What we ended up doing was advocating Israel's positions before, during and after the summit.

Miller argues forcibly that the United States was also culpable for the failings of the summit:

> The Clinton Administration convened Camp David with the best of intentions, but the president and the rest of us who counseled him bear significant responsibility for what transpired there. Probably no American mediator could have overcome the problems we faced. But at the same time our approach left us poorly positioned to pick up the pieces. . . . We can blame Arafat and praise Barak all day long, but that doesn't address our share of the responsibility once we got to the summit. We didn't run the summit; the summit ran us.
>
> *(Miller 2008: 298)*

Dan Kurtzer and Scott Lasensky (2008) find fault all round, damning the summit as "ill-conceived" and the "most glaring failure" of Clinton's last-ditch diplomatic efforts in the Middle East. They portray a policy-making process that was "too insular and inhibited the development of U.S. positions on the core issues . . . the United States was unprepared, and our negotiators scrambled at the last minute to put together U.S. positions on complex issues such as Jerusalem and borders."

Accounts of the Camp David summit report of mismanagement and bureaucratic infighting in the American team. Gilad Sher (2006) talks of a process that lacked adequate preparation and supervision: "the most serious shortcoming of the American team was that some of its members appeared to be less knowledgeable than the president in the details and implications of the process." His views are shared by Yasser Abd Rabbo: "It was chaos. Every day a different meeting, committee and issue. We didn't know what were our aims, to succeed, to fail, to escape" (quoted in Miller 2008: 301).

Nor is President Clinton let off the hook. In Aaron Miller's assessment, Clinton lacked the toughness to say no to both parties and stay with American bridging proposals. The Americans all too often adapted their ideas to fit the whims and constraints of the parties. Compared with previous US mediators, Clinton lacked the capacity of Jimmy Carter to intimidate, the deviousness of Henry Kissinger, and the toughness of James Baker to push Barak and Arafat to close a deal at Camp David (Miller 2008: 309). American threats and deadlines were ignored, as both Israel and the Palestinians were confident that the Americans were too invested in the process to think seriously of walking away. Shlomo Ben-Ami was damning in his final judgment of the Americans: "the Clinton team did not hold the reins of the summit with authority . . . at Camp David, America looked like a diminished and humbled superpower" (Ben-Ami 2006: 263).

The Camp David summit marks an important chapter in the history of the Israeli–Palestinian conflict. Although it signals the first time that Israeli and Palestinian leaders attempted to reach a comprehensive resolution to their hundred-year-old conflict, the meeting is not especially significant for the ideas it generated. Indeed, many of those ideas were superseded in the six-month of discussions that followed the summit – by the Clinton Parameters of December 2000 and by understandings reached at Taba in January 2001. It is significant instead for the competing narratives that emerged following the failure of the two sides to arrive at any understanding.

The myth that Barak offered the Palestinians a great deal and that Arafat responded with terror became deeply engrained within Israeli discourse. Much of the Israeli public as well as the American political establishment accepted this argument as unchallengeable truth. The narrative that Israel lacked a peace partner emerged as one of the deepest obstacles to the road back to negotiations in the years that followed Camp David. It was a narrative that persisted even after the death of Yasser Arafat at the end of 2004 and still impacts on Israeli thinking vis-à-vis making peace with the Palestinians. The "no partner" thesis was a driving force behind Israel's policies of separation and unilateralism (see chapter 16, by Gerald Steinberg), leading to the construction of the separation barrier and to Israel's unilateral disengagement from Gaza in August 2005. Over a decade on, the story of Camp David, however it is perceived, still casts a shadow over relations between Israel and the Palestinians and on efforts to resolve the conflict.

Notes

1   See Lally Weymouth, "Barak: Die or Separate," *Newsweek*, 23 July 2001.
2   Ari Shavit, "The Day Peace Died: Interview with Shlomo Ben Ami," *Haaretz*, 14 September 2001.

References and further reading

Agha, Hussein, and Malley, Robert (2001) "Camp David: The Tragedy of Errors," *New York Review of Books*, 9 August.

Ben-Ami, Shlomo (2006) *Scars of War, Wounds of Peace: The Israeli–Arab Tragedy* (Oxford: Oxford University Press).

Enderlin, Charles (2003) *Shattered Dreams: The Failure of the Peace Process in the Middle East, 1995–2002* (New York: Other Press).

Hanieh, Akram (2001) "The Camp David Papers," *Journal of Palestine Studies*, 30/2, pp. 75–97.

Indyk, Martin (2009) *Innocent Abroad: An Intimate Account of American Peace Diplomacy in the Middle East* (New York: Simon & Schuster).

Kacowicz, Arie (2005) "Rashomon in the Middle East: Clashing Narratives, Images and Frames in the Israeli–Palestinian Conflict," *Cooperation and Conflict*, 40/3, pp. 343–60.

Khatib, Ghassan (2002) "A Palestinian View: Camp David: An Exit Strategy for Barak," *Bitterlemons*, 15 July. Available at www.bitterlemons.org/previous/bl150702ed26.html (accessed 1 June 2011).

Kurtzer, Daniel C., and Lasensky, Scott (2008) *Negotiating Arab–Israeli Peace: American Leadership in the Middle East* (Washington, DC: United States Institute for Peace Press).

Miller, Aaron D. (2008) *The much too Promised Land: America's Elusive Search for Arab–Israeli Peace* (New York: Bantam Books).

Morris, Benny (2002) "Camp David and After: An Exchange (1. An Interview with Ehud Barak)," *New York Review of Books*, 13 June.

Pressman, Jeremy (2003) "Visions in Collision: What Happened at Camp David and Taba?," *International Security*, 28/2, pp. 114–41.

Pundak, Ron (2001) "From Oslo to Taba: What Went Wrong," *Survival*, 43, pp. 31–46.

Ross, Dennis (2004) *The Missing Peace: The Inside Story of the Fight for Middle East Peace* (New York: Farrar, Straus & Giroux).

Sher, Gilead (2006) *The Israeli–Palestinian Peace Negotiations, 1999–2001* (London: Routledge).

Swisher, Clayton, E. (2004) *The Truth about Camp David* (New York: Nation Books).

Part III
Seeking peace

7

The Israeli–Palestinian peace process, 1967–1993

Laura Zittrain Eisenberg

1967 as a turning point

1967 was a watershed in the evolution of the Arab–Israeli peace process. The Six Day War in June ended in defeat for Egypt, Syria, and Jordan and Israel's seizure of considerable territory. A critical outcome of the war was the passing in November 1967 of UN Security Council Resolution 242, which encapsulated the idea of the exchange of land for peace. However, regional actors, having approved the resolution only reluctantly and conditionally, resisted outside attempts to make it operational. Ultimately, mutual distrust and hostility prevented its comprehensive application, thus shattering hopes of a peaceful solution to the conflict.

Although Resolution 242 remained the cornerstone of all subsequent peace efforts, with promising breakthroughs in 1974–5, 1977–9, and 1991, the peace process between 1967 and 1993 remained largely immobilized by the conflicting perspectives and behaviors which had obstructed Arab–Israeli peacemaking for generations.

Egyptian–Israeli peace in 1977–9 broke the tradition of futile Arab–Israeli negotiations but failed to inspire other Arab–Israeli treaties in its wake. The Madrid Conference in 1991 launched a promising new process, but it was the 1993 agreements between Israel and the Palestine Liberation Organization, in which each side recognized the other and pledged to resolve their differences peacefully, that finally seemed to mark a departure from the post-1967 period in peacemaking.

Recurrent themes and obstacles in Arab–Israeli negotiations

At the outset one must note that, as long as either party perceived the conflict to be existential, believing that the other side intended to destroy it, a genuine peace process was not possible. For many years the Arabs' stated goal was the destruction of Israel and its replacement by a Palestinian Arab state. Israel's response was to negate the Palestinian issue and maximize its own military strength to preempt or counter an Arab attack. The 1967 war marked the beginning of Arab inference that, under specific conditions, the Arab states might agree to coexist with Israel. But even this retreat from a zero-sum game mentality has not been enough to produce a negotiated solution.

Although Arabs and Israelis are not monolithic in their beliefs and perceptions, some generalizations can be drawn. Arabs (especially Palestinians) and Israeli Jews both see themselves as victims. Israelis look to 2,000 years of Jewish persecution which culminated in the Holocaust as necessitating and justifying the establishment of a Jewish state in their ancestral homeland. Arabs claim centuries of habitation also reaching back to the biblical period, and, if they acknowledge the Holocaust, see it as a European crime that deserves European, not Arab, sacrifices or restitution.

Palestinians see Israelis as their historical oppressors and European colonizers rather than as fellow victims of the European powers. Palestinians see themselves as David against an Israeli Goliath; Israel sees itself as a beleaguered David confronting a much larger pan-Arab and pan-Islamic Goliath. The identity of victim is important because it suggests the existence of a perpetrator; if anyone must make concessions, the guilty party is the obvious choice. In claiming the victim role, each side looks to the other to "give up" more.

The two sides also enter negotiations with different purposes: for the most part, Palestinians seek justice while Israelis are looking for conflict resolution. Accordingly, they interpret the purpose of negotiations differently. Arabs argue that recognizing the State of Israel and accepting its right to exist is the penultimate concession, and that the goal of negotiations should be to establish the modalities by which an independent State of Palestine comes into existence. Israel understands negotiations as a give and take in which both sides must make compromises and whose end result is not necessarily predetermined.

Israel has also traditionally preferred direct negotiations between it and one Arab state at a time, with progress on any one front unconnected from progress on the others. It has thus shied away from a comprehensive approach aiming to solve all problems at once. Israel's preference for a "gradualist" step-by-step process reflects its suspicion that an Arab peace offer might be only a ploy to weaken Israel for a later attack. The Arab perception is that Israeli policy is one of divide and conquer, with no trust in Israel's professed intention to withdraw from Arab territory. The Arab preference has been for multilateral policies. Arab parties which dared to go it alone in negotiations with Israel have been severely criticized. Arab–Israeli diplomacy between 1967 and 1993 evinced many of the characteristics that obstructed the peace process in previous decades, such as negotiating at cross-purposes or appearing flexible while not in fact intending to compromise; refusing to scale back demands, thus perpetuating an unbridgeable chasm between each side's minimum requirements; the negotiators being unable to deliver on the promises they made; deep-seated distrust, hostility, and fear among the people and often among the leaders; and the tendency to manipulate peace talks with the goal of pleasing a powerful third party from whom favors or patronage are desired.

For most of the period from 1967 to 1993 the United States assumed the role of powerful outsider, determined to manage the peace process while denying similar influence to the Soviet Union, traditional patron of the Arab parties. President Jimmy Carter was prepared to soften this stance and invited the Soviets to co-host an international conference, which did not actually occur until President George H. W. Bush, convinced of the Soviet Union's relative toothlessness in 1991, allowed it nominally to co-sponsor the Madrid Conference.

Another recurrent obstacle in negotiations was the refusal of the parties to recognize one another's legitimacy. In the early period neither side was interested in talking to the moderates on the other, since they were obviously unrepresentative, but equally uninterested in talking to the radicals, since they were terrorists and occupiers with whom no peace was possible. The Arab states avoided meetings in which their representatives would be seated with Israelis – initially on the grounds that they did not recognize Israel as a legitimate and co-equal state, and later arguing that normalization was a concession they were not ready to make until Israel had withdrawn from Arab land. Israel tried to solve the Palestinian problem in dialogues with Jordan's King Hussein, refusing to talk to the Palestine Liberation Organization (PLO), whose attacks on Israeli civilians led Israel to classify it as a terrorist organization. The PLO and Israel spent several decades denying the legitimacy of the other while encouraging other nations to boycott their respective foe.

In the late 1980s the PLO adopted a stance that suggested a willingness to coexist with Israel if the latter withdrew to its pre-1967 borders. Although Israel agreed to Palestinian representation at the 1991 Madrid Conference, it insisted upon the inclusion of non-PLO Palestinians only. This chapter ends with the 1993 Oslo Accords because, in mutually recognizing each other and pledging themselves to a negotiated coexistence, the PLO and Israel drastically departed from the historical pattern of Arab–Israeli interaction.

Two other prevailing characteristics of the peace process are ambiguity and gradualism. In the name of building mutual confidence or maintaining diplomatic momentum, negotiators often "agree to disagree" or otherwise fudge remaining disagreements on some issues so as not to derail limited or emerging consensus on others. The 1967 hallmark Resolution 242 was a masterful exercise in constructive ambiguity. With its possibly contradictory calls for both the "inadmissibility of the acquisition of territory by war" and the right of all states to live peacefully "within secure and recognized boundaries" – with no mention of the Palestinians or Jerusalem – Resolution 242 passed unanimously in the Security Council and succeeded in winning the reluctant approval of all the combatants, who could read into it what they wanted.

The Arab side was looking for a comprehensive solution that would result in complete Israeli withdrawal to the 1967 lines and immediate Palestinian independence prior to the normalization of Arab–Israeli relations. As the more powerful party and, more importantly, the one in possession of the contested land, however, Israel set the negotiation pace to suit its own preference for cautious gradualism. The proponents of gradualism argue that there must be trust-building opportunities before the deeply suspicious parties are ready to take the huge risks necessary for resolving the most difficult issues between them.

Stalled diplomacy, 1948–1967

Years of haphazard Israeli–Arab negotiations produced little peace but many peace plans. During the British Mandate over Palestine (1920–48), Britain tried and failed to create a shared sense of "Palestinian" nationhood among Jews and Arabs. In November 1947 the United Nations General Assembly passed Resolution 181, recommending the partition of Palestine into an Arab state and a Jewish state. Jews saw partition as the successful culmination of Zionist efforts towards a much-needed Jewish state in the biblical Jewish homeland. Arabs, however, rejected in principle what they saw as the European Jewish colonization of Palestinian Arab land.

In May 1948 Israel declared independence and the surrounding Arab states invaded. This first Arab–Israeli war ended in 1949 with individual armistice agreements between Israel and Egypt, Jordan, Syria, and Lebanon, mediated by US diplomat Ralph Bunche. At Arab insistence, the General Armistice Agreements (GAA) specifically stipulated that the 1949 borders constituted ceasefire lines only and were not in any sense political or territorial boundaries, which might indicate Arab acceptance of Israel's existence. Those lines demarcated by the GAA are known variously as the 1949 lines, the "Green Line," or the lines of 4 June 1967.

By 1949, what might have become Arab Palestine had fallen to the Egyptians, who seized Gaza, and the Jordanians and Israelis, each of whom took parts of the West Bank and Jerusalem. Palestinian Arabs were now reduced to playing a secondary role as refugees, *fedayeen* (guerrillas), or an Israeli Arab minority, while the real responsibility for their fate lay in the hands of the Arab states, who were embroiled in their own rivalries with one another as well as with Israel.

After the first Arab–Israeli war, various attempts, both private and public, and usually mediated by third parties, failed to achieve peace treaties, leaving the armistices, which were meant to be temporary, frozen in place. In 1956, Britain, France, and Israel coordinated an attack on Egypt in what became known as the Suez Crisis. US and international pressure quickly forced the Europeans to withdraw, but Israel, after having captured most of the Egyptian Sinai peninsula and the Gaza Strip, refused to evacuate until March 1957, when the UN created the United Nations Emergency Force (UNEF) to serve in Sinai as a buffer between Egypt and Israel. Like the 1948–9 war before it, the Suez Crisis ended without political resolution of any aspect of the Arab–Israeli conflict.

The 1967 war as an opportunity for peacemaking

The decade following the 1956 Suez war saw few attempts at Arab–Israeli negotiation and much escalation in tension. By this time *fedayeen* groups had emerged from within the Palestinian refugee population and undertook cross-border strikes against Israeli, usually civilian, targets. Israel retaliated harshly against the guerrillas' host countries; that and competition over limited regional water brought Arabs and Israelis to the brink of another interstate war. In the spring of 1967 inter-Arab competition led to especially strident anti-Israel threats. Israel prepared for what it saw as a defensive war; Egypt charged that Israel was looking for a pretext to expand its borders. Nasser himself provided the trigger by ordering the UNEF out of the Sinai and closing the Straits of Tiran to Israeli shipping. The failure of the international community to mediate a resolution to the crisis led to a preemptive Israeli attack against Egyptian airfields on 5 June 1967; the war quickly spread to the Jordanian–Israeli and Syrian–Israeli fronts.

In the ensuing six days Israel defeated the armies of Egypt, Jordan, and Syria and, most importantly, conquered and occupied large swaths of territory from them, namely the Sinai peninsula and Gaza (from Egypt), the Golan Heights (from Syria), and the West Bank and East Jerusalem (from Jordan). Before 1967 the Arab states had been rhetorically championing, and often manipulating, the Arab claim to Palestine on behalf of the Palestinians; after the 1967 war their focus shifted from the reclamation of Palestine to the retrieval of their own lost territories. Diplomats sensed a new quid pro quo in the offing: Israel would return the areas taken in 1967 and in exchange the Arab states would recognize the State of Israel and make peace with it.

Israel's cabinet was thinking along similar lines. On 19 June the Israeli cabinet voted to return the Sinai to Egypt and the Golan to Syria in exchange for full peace treaties. The biblically significant West Bank was trickier, since it appealed to religious Jews and security-minded Israeli officials. In July Labor Minister Yigal Allon proposed his plan for the partial redivision of the West Bank between Jordan and Israel, with Israel establishing a line of security settlements along the immediate West Bank of the Jordan river; Jordan would have sovereignty over the territory and responsibility for the Palestinian population west of the Israeli security belt in the remaining 70 percent of the West Bank. Israel removed the barriers separating it from East Jerusalem and the Old City, which had been held by Jordan since 1948, and annexed the newly reunited city, which it declared its capital. Within those parameters, Israelis thought they had the territorial chips with which to strike an Arab peace bargain. As Israeli Defense Minister Moshe Dayan famously said, Israel was just "waiting for a phone call" from Arab leaders ready to make the deal.

The Arabs were having none of it, however. Humiliated by their crushing defeat, Arab leaders met in Khartoum, Sudan, in September 1967 to decide upon a common response to the postwar circumstances. In the resulting declaration, dubbed the "Three No's," they vowed that there would be "no peace with Israel, no recognition of Israel, no negotiations with Israel." Backed by the Soviet Union, they demanded an unconditional Israeli withdrawal and an immediate return to the lines of 4 June 1967.

The United States agreed with Israel that it should not return land to the Arabs without receiving some political gain in return. President Lyndon B. Johnson was determined not to repeat the 1956 scenario, in which Israel withdrew from the Sinai without a political settlement only to have war break out there again ten years later. In his "Principles for Peace" speech of 19 June 1967, Johnson argued that, post 1967, Middle East peace must entail mutual recognition between Israel and the Arab states, respect for one another's territorial integrity, negotiated boundary modifications, resolution of the refugee and Jerusalem problem, respect for maritime rights, and regional arms control.

The international community weighed in with the passage of UN Security Council Resolution 242 in November 1967 calling for, among other things, "the inadmissibility of the acquisition of territory by war" (which pleased the Arabs) and "the right of every state in the area ... to live in peace within secure and recognized boundaries" (which pleased the Israelis). Resolution 242 became a benchmark for every attempt at Arab–Israeli peacemaking after 1967. But crucial ambiguities in the text – notably, the omission of the definite article "the" from the phrase calling for Israel's "withdrawal from territories occupied in the recent conflict" – led to legalistic wrangling among the parties. The Arabs believed that the resolution obliged Israel to withdraw from *all of the* territories captured in the 1967 war. Recalling that the Arab states had always insisted that the armistice lines of 1949 did *not* constitute recognized political boundaries, Israel argued that the resolution required withdrawal from *some* of those territories, allowing for some border modifications in order to produce 242's "secure and recognized boundaries." The failure of the resolution to refer directly to the Palestinians (who were not a "state") or seriously to address any of their claims provided a source of future complication. In fact, "Palestine" does not appear in 242, and "Palestinians" can be inferred only in the reference to "refugees." Interestingly, 242 also makes no special reference to Jerusalem, which can be inferred as territory acquired by war (the Arab interpretation) or as an area ripe for modification in the name of secure and recognized boundaries (the Israeli interpretation). For the Israeli cabinet, the link between Jerusalem and Judaism was so obvious that no one considered putting the city on the table.

Many Israelis hoped that Resolution 242, backed by their decisive victory on the ground, would convince Arab leaders that the Jewish state was here to stay and that they could retrieve their captured land only by direct negotiations. But the Arab states insisted upon the full return of their lost territories *before* they would consider dealing directly with Israel. The ambiguity of Resolution 242 has always blunted its effectiveness, and these chicken-and-egg positions effectively re-established the deadlock of the preceding twenty years.

Failure was not from a lack of trying. Immediately upon passage of Resolution 242, UN Secretary-General U Thant appointed Swedish Ambassador Gunnar Jarring to confer with the Arabs and Israelis and to forge a consensus among them for making 242 operational. Jarring shuttled intensively among the Arab states and Israel, but his efforts failed over differing interpretations of the resolution. Israel insisted upon direct negotiations with the Arabs over the captured territories, and the Arabs insisted on full withdrawal as a precondition for any talks, preferably indirect. Jarring finally issued a formal peace proposal in February 1971, but the negative responses from Israel and the Arab states revealed serious differences. President Richard

Nixon's secretary of state, William Rogers, engaged in some shuttle diplomacy during 1969 and 1970. But circumstances shifted his objective from comprehensive Arab–Israeli peace to a narrow ceasefire between Egypt and Israel, who were engaged in a costly "war of attrition" along the Suez Canal. Rogers finally achieved a stable ceasefire, but the protagonists side-stepped the political components of his plan that would have required some concrete land-for-peace applications. Thus another Arab–Israeli war ended without political progress.

The Arab refusal to deal directly with Israel while the latter still held Arab land became more entrenched with every passing year. And, the longer the Arabs held out, the more Israel grew attached to the territories that diplomats had hoped to use as bargaining chips. Groups of Jews who believed in their divine right to Judea and Samaria (the biblical West Bank) estab-lished settlements in the West Bank and Gaza. With government approval, they settled at first in locations removed from Palestinian population centers, in security-sensitive areas; later Israeli governments would actively encourage a wholesale campaign of Jewish settlement throughout the Occupied Territories in an effort to expand and maintain Israeli control. Israeli settlers were protected by Israeli law; Palestinians in the Occupied West Bank and Gaza fell under an oppressive Israeli occupation and administration.

On 6 October 1973, Egypt and Syria launched a successful surprise attack on Israeli front lines. The date was the Jewish holy day of Yom Kippur, when Israel was least prepared. Although Israeli forces initially fell back, the IDF subsequently recovered, and when the two sides accepted a ceasefire on 23 October, Israel still held the 1967 territories. The early suc-cesses in the war, particularly the surprise attack and the fact that they held out three times as long as they had in 1967, allowed the Arab states to recover much of their pride and dignity. Israel, despite having rallied, perceived this war as an intelligence and military failure. Sobered by its close call, and recognizing that military might alone could not guarantee its security indefinitely, Israel was now willing to consider diplomatic tactics.

By leveling the military playing field somewhat between the Arab states and Israel, the 1973 war can be seen in retrospect as the opening salvo in the Egyptian–Israeli peace process, usher-ing in some moderately successful US mediation activities and hopes for a wider breakthrough in the Arab–Israeli dispute. On the international level, the UN Security Council passed Reso-lution 338, which essentially reaffirmed Resolution 242 and called upon the parties to enter into negotiations for its implementation.

The political aftermath of the 1973 war brought to the fore Henry Kissinger, Nixon's secre-tary of state. As national security advisor, Kissinger had worked hard to obstruct Rogers's Middle East peace initiatives, finding them too demanding of the administration's friends, too generous to its opponents, and insufficiently attentive to the Soviet threat in the region. Kissinger moved quickly to assert US primacy (and his own) in the post-1973 war diplomatic environment. In a flurry of political maneuvering he orchestrated a conference in Geneva in December 1973, formally under joint US–USSR stewardship, although the Americans were the moving force behind the event. The conference broke up in rancor after the first day's opening speeches, but the very fact that delegations from Egypt, Jordan, and Israel had openly, if fleetingly, gathered together in the same room for the first time in twenty-five years consti-tuted a notable psychological accomplishment. Syria and Lebanon did not attend. By cleverly recasting an essentially American mediation process in an international format, Kissinger cre-ated a blueprint that became one of the preferred options promoted by other would-be Middle East peacemakers during the following decades.

The immediate usefulness of Geneva was its function as a legitimizing umbrella under which Kissinger subsequently embarked upon several marathon rounds of personal jet-setting diplomacy. In undertaking personally to mediate between Arabs and Israelis at the highest levels, Kissinger made the USA an indispensable actor in the drama while undercutting any Soviet role. He helped Israel and Egypt to negotiate two disengagement agreements, Sinai I (1974) and Sinai II (1975). The Syrian–Israeli Disengagement Agreement (1974) saw Kissinger log more than 24,000 miles in thirty-four days, shuttling between Jerusalem and Damascus some fifteen times and visiting six other countries along the way. His achievements won him both praise and criticism. Fans lauded him for forging the first Arab–Israeli agreements since the GAA twenty-five years earlier, while critics worried that he manipulated and even hindered Arab–Israeli negotiations with his goal of keeping the United States central to the process, and argued that he had set a poor precedent by mediating the negotiations himself. Would Arabs and Israelis ever again take seriously any intermediary of lower rank than the secretary of state?

1977: President Sadat electrifies the peace process

Rejecting Kissinger's Cold War perspective, President Jimmy Carter planned to partner with the Soviet Union to launch a multifaceted international initiative aimed at settling all outstanding claims among Israel, the Palestinians, and the Arab states. The joint US–Soviet communiqué of 1 October 1977 called on the Arabs and Israelis to return to Geneva to begin the process. Anxious to avoid a repeat of the 1973 Geneva Conference, where the demands of the most intransigent party prevented the more moderate participants from acting, Egyptian President Anwar Sadat responded with a surprise offer to visit Jerusalem on a mission of peace. Equally eager to sidestep Geneva, Israeli Prime Minister Menachem Begin immediately issued an invitation. Sadat's historic visit to Jerusalem on 20 November 1977 and his speech before the Israeli Knesset, by turns demanding and generous, finally made the prospect of Arab–Israeli peace seem possible.

The indigenous initiative floundered within months, however. The Egyptian and Israeli teams simply could not overcome the personal incompatibility of Sadat and Begin and proved unable to reconcile the former's sweeping vision and risk-taking with the latter's suspicion and cautious parsing of every detail. In September 1978, Carter invited the leaders and their delegations to meet with him and his foreign policy team at Camp David, the presidential retreat in the Maryland woods. Carter's personal involvement went one better than Kissinger, setting the mediation bar at the presidency. Two weeks of intense and cloistered talks produced two documents, a "Framework for Peace in the Middle East" and a "Framework for the Conclusion of a Peace Treaty between Egypt and Israel." Non-participation by the Palestinians and other Arab states sidelined the framework for regional peace, but in March 1979 Sadat and Begin signed an Egyptian–Israeli Peace Treaty. At its heart was Resolution 242: Israel returned the entire Sinai peninsula to Egypt in exchange for normalization and peace between the two countries. The Camp David Accords included a number of side-letters between the United States and each of the two parties. The combination of an indigenous initiative with American mediation and guarantees produced the first peace treaty ever between Israel and an Arab state and a precedent against which all future Arab–Israeli negotiations would be measured. Along with land for peace and American mediation, however, Egypt's ostracism from the Arab fold and Sadat's 1981 assassination by Muslim fundamentalists provided a potentially negative precedent for other would-be peacemakers.

The 1980s: much process, little peace

Camp David ignited hopes for Arab–Israeli peacemaking in the late 1970s, but, despite a variety of diplomatic initiatives, the peace process failed to maintain momentum in the 1980s.

In August 1981, Saudi Arabia's Crown Prince Fahd unveiled a 242-inspired eight-point proposal designed to resolve the Arab–Israeli conflict and create an independent Palestinian state in Gaza and the West Bank, with East Jerusalem as its capital. At its summit in Fez, Morocco, in September 1982, the Arab League adopted a version of the Fahd plan, which became known as the Fez Initiative. The USA was disappointed that the Arab plans conferred Palestinian representation on the PLO, which it considered a terrorist organization, and precluded the American (and Israeli) preferred solution of a land-for-peace deal over the West Bank between Israel and Jordan. Israel also rejected Fahd and Fez because they provided no accommodation for Israel's security and required a 100 percent return of the 1967 lands, including Jerusalem. Both plans represented a possible shift in Arab policy with their implicit recognition of Israel, but coinciding negative and violent events intervened.

Between 1970 and 1982, the zero-sum battle between Israel and the PLO had made the Lebanese–Israeli border a staging ground for attacks and counter-attacks. Israel was unhappy with the situation in southern Lebanon, where the PLO maintained arms depots and guerrilla training camps from which it launched terrorist attacks, and where Syria had installed missile batteries. A Palestinian (albeit non-PLO) attack on the Israeli ambassador in London served as the trigger for a massive Israeli invasion of Lebanon in June 1982. In its mission to root out the PLO and drive the Syrians from Lebanon, Israel was working in concert with indigenous Lebanese Christian forces, who similarly desired a Palestinian and Syrian-free Lebanon, aligned with the West. By September 1982 the United States had mediated between Israel and Lebanon (and indirectly with the PLO) for the exit of thousands of Palestinian fighters from the country.

On 1 September 1982 President Ronald Reagan announced the "Reagan Plan," which saw in Israel's defeat of the PLO and Syria in Lebanon an opportunity to advance a broader Arab–Israeli peace. Citing Resolution 242 and the Camp David Accords, Reagan sketched out a vision of Palestinian self-rule, "in association with Jordan," which explicitly ruled out both Israeli annexation of and Palestinian sovereignty in the West Bank. The Reagan Plan soon disappeared in a maelstrom of disastrous events in Lebanon, however, among them the assassination of Lebanese Christian leader and president-elect Bashir Gemayel by the Syrians, the massacre of Palestinian civilians by Israel's Christian militia allies in the refugee camps of Sabra and Shatilla, the immersion of Israeli and eventually American troops in the Lebanese civil war, the emergence of Hizbollah, and devastating suicide attacks against the American Embassy and the Marines quartered at Beirut airport. Although Secretary of State George Shultz successfully mediated an agreement in May 1983 between the reluctant and weak Lebanese government and Israel, Syria's reassertion of influence in Lebanon led the Lebanese parliament in March 1984 to abrogate the treaty.

In 1987, Jordan's King Hussein and Israeli Foreign Minister Shimon Peres capped many months of secret talks with a meeting in the United Kingdom where they personally drafted the secret "London Document" of 11 April 1987, which envisioned an international conference followed by bilateral Arab–Israeli negotiations. It broke new ground by de-linking the bilateral talks from one another (failure to progress on the Israeli–Syrian track, for example, would not hinder Israelis and Jordanians from moving ahead on their track) and introduced the Palestinians into the peace process via a joint Jordanian–Palestinian (non-PLO) delegation. Peres, when he was prime minister, had opened talks with the king, but an awkward political "rotation" between the Israeli prime minister and foreign minister made the hard-line Yitzhak Shamir prime minister by the time the document was complete. Shamir rejected the document, objecting to the international conference, Palestinian representation, and the nod towards land for peace. American hesitancy to take sides in the Peres–Shamir dispute and reluctance to allow the Soviet Union into the process via the international conference contributed to the London Document's demise.

The outbreak of the First *Intifada* in December 1987 markedly changed the parameters of the peace process. The uprising reflected local Palestinian frustration in Gaza and the West Bank with both the ongoing Israeli occupation and the ineffectual leadership of the PLO, based in far-away Tunisia. The uprising invigorated the Palestinian population in the Occupied Territories and led to a new Palestinian consensus that Palestinians, and not the Arab states, would represent the Palestinian case from then on. The rise of Hamas, an Islamic fundamentalist Palestinian organization whose charter disallows any compromise with Israel and, indeed, makes Israel's destruction a critical goal, constituted a severe blow to the land-for-peace premise.

In March 1988, three months into the *intifada*, George Shultz put forth his own proposal, which invoked resolutions 242 and 338 and featured a ceremonial regional gathering, hosted by the UN, which would lead quickly to bilateral talks between Israel and each of the neighboring Arab states. Palestinian representation would be through a joint Jordanian–non-PLO Palestinian team. As in the London Document, movement on the Israeli–Jordanian/Palestinian track was de-linked from less promising bilateral talks. Interestingly, Shultz was, at the very same time, juggling an overture from the PLO designed to open a direct PLO–US dialogue. When the PLO met the secretary of state's conditions in December 1988, Shultz reluctantly authorized the dialogue; President George H. W. Bush suspended it in May 1990, when PLO leader Yasser Arafat refused to condemn an attempted Palestinian terror attack on a Tel Aviv beach.

Similarly exasperated by his attempts to work with the PLO, in July 1988 King Hussein had abruptly severed Jordan's ties with the West Bank. Perhaps he calculated – wrongly – that the PLO would panic and authorize him to deal with Israel on its behalf. Some observers argued that King Hussein's West Bank exit might actually enhance the peace process by building upon the momentum of the *intifada* and moving the Palestinians closer to self-representation within the Occupied Territories. But mainstream Western and Israeli assessments held that, in washing his hands of the West Bank, King Hussein had ruined the possibility of Jordan and Israel striking a land-for-peace deal, upon which Israeli and American hopes had been predicated. The 1980s were thus a turbulent decade for Arabs and Israelis, fraught with violence and disjointed efforts at conflict management and resolution.

1991: the Madrid Conference recasts and reinvigorates negotiations

Although it was certainly not what he had in mind, Iraqi President Saddam Hussein provided the catalyst for the next boost to the peace process when he sent his army to invade Kuwait in August 1990. At the request of Kuwait and Saudi Arabia, who feared it might be Saddam's next target, the United States assembled a genuinely international coalition of forces, including nominal participation by important Arab states, particularly Egypt and Syria. Between January and February 2001 the US-led multinational coalition succeeded in liberating Kuwait from Iraq.

Because of the unique alliance between the United States and many Arab states forged in the Gulf War, President Bush and Secretary of State James Baker believed that heightened American influence in the immediate postwar environment boded well for a new attempt at a comprehensive solution to the Arab–Israeli conflict. Organized by the USA, the peace conference opened in Madrid on 30 October 2001. Two days of public speeches by Arab and Israeli delegates were followed by one day of closed-door bilateral talks between Israel and Syria,

Lebanon, and a Jordanian/Palestinian delegation. In literally gathering Arabs and Israelis around a common table, including an official (albeit non-PLO) Palestinian delegation, and then moving them onto separate bilateral tracks, Madrid shattered long-standing taboos of mutual non-recognition and set in motion a mechanism for ongoing negotiations into the 1990s.

Madrid's innovation was a structural formula that created separate but parallel bilateral and multilateral tracks. The multilateral talks focused on five region-wide problems: water, refugees, the environment, economic development, and arms control. They involved eleven Arab states (Syria and Lebanon did not participate) and twenty-seven other states and international agencies. The first international forum opened in Moscow in 1992. For the United States, a drawback to the multilateral conference idea had always been the risk of enhancing Soviet influence in the Middle East, but, from its post-Gulf War apogee, juxtaposed with the obvious Soviet decline, the Bush administration decided that it could safely convene such a conference under its own terms.

From Madrid the bilateral talks moved to Washington, DC, where the State Department hosted another dozen rounds of negotiations between December 1991 and July 1993. Progress appeared to be minimal. Ironically, however, it was the futility of the Madrid-sanctioned talks with the non-PLO Palestinians which finally propelled Israel into secret negotiations with the PLO in Norway. The result was the surprise announcement of mutual Israeli–PLO recognition on 9 September 1993 and the signing of the "Declaration of Principles" (the Oslo Accord) on the White House lawn on 13 September 1993. The ceremony's highlight was a handshake between Israeli Prime Minister Yitzhak Rabin and PLO Chairman Yasser Arafat.

With the taboo over negotiations with Israel broken by Arafat himself, Israel and Jordan quietly signed a "Common Agenda" on the very next day. Although the document was a product of the Madrid–Washington talks (and the harbinger of the Israel–Jordan Peace Treaty of 1994), its coming on the heels of the Oslo Accord signaled that Israel and the PLO had ended the 1967–93 era of the Arab–Israeli peace process and inaugurated another. The prognosis seemed uncharacteristically promising, but the negative negotiating habits of the previous years would prove hard to break, and easy to fall back on.

Further reading

Abu-Odeh, Adnan (1999) *Jordanians, Palestinians and the Hashemite Kingdom in the Middle East* (Washington, DC: United States Institute of Peace Press).

Bar-Siman-Tov, Yaacov (1994) *Israel and the Peace Process, 1977–1982: In Search of Legitimacy for Peace* (Albany: State University of New York Press).

Caradon, Lord, Goldberg, Arthur J., El-Zayyat, Mohammed H., and Eban, Abba (1981) *UN Security Council Resolution 242: A Case Study in Diplomatic Ambiguity* (Washington, DC: Institute for the Study of Diplomacy, Edmund A. Walsh School of Foreign Service, Georgetown University).

Eisenberg, Laura Zittrain, and Caplan, Neil (2010) *Negotiating Arab–Israeli Peace: Patterns, Problems, Possibilities* (2nd ed., Bloomington: Indiana University Press) [the content of this chapter draws heavily on this book].

Heikal, Mohamed (1996) *Secret Channels: The Inside Story of Arab–Israeli Peace Negotiations* (London: HarperCollins).

Korn, David A. (1992) *The Making of United Nations Security Council Resolution 242*, Case 450 (Washington, DC: Institute for the Study of Diplomacy, School of Foreign Service, Georgetown University) [www.guisd.org/].

Quandt, William B. (2005) *Peace Process: American Diplomacy and the Arab–Israeli Conflict since 1967* (3rd ed., Washington, DC: Brookings Institution; Berkeley: University of California Press).

Riad, Mahmoud (1981) *The Struggle for Peace in the Middle East* (London and New York: Quartet Books).

Stein, Kenneth W., and Lewis, Samuel W. (with Brown, Sheryl J.) (1991) *Making Peace among Arabs and Israelis: Lessons from Fifty Years of Negotiating Experience* (Washington, DC: United States Institute of Peace).

Touval, Saadia (1982) *The Peace Brokers: Mediators in the Arab–Israeli Conflict, 1948–1979* (Princeton, NJ: Princeton University Press).

8
Peace plans, 1993–2010

Galia Golan

There have been numerous plans to bring about a resolution of the Israeli–Palestinian conflict since the Oslo Declaration of 1993.[1] With one exception, none has constituted a comprehensive blueprint for peace and none, obviously, has in fact brought about peace. The period has, however, witnessed the formulation of a cumulative body of proposals relating to the core issues of the conflict: borders, security, Jerusalem, and refugees.

The Oslo Accords

The Oslo Accords were actually seven agreements, beginning with the 1993 Declaration of Principles (DOP) and the Rabin–Arafat exchange of letters, taking in the 1995 Interim Agreement on the West Bank and Gaza (Oslo II), and ending with the 1998 Wye River Memorandum plus other protocols and memoranda. Together they formed interim understandings between Israel and the PLO designed both to implement what was already agreed and to regulate the period up to the conclusion of negotiations regarding the final status of the West Bank and Gaza Strip. Almost identical in principle to autonomy plans proposed in the past – for example, in the 1978 Camp David talks with the Egyptians or by Yitzhak Rabin in 1989 – the Oslo Accords provided for a transition period divided into phases and tasks (all with fixed durations) during which Israeli forces would be redeployed and a self-governing Palestinian body (including a Legislative Council) would be elected and gradually assume partial or total control of evacuated areas. Talks for the final-status agreement were to begin no later than three years from the start of the implementation of the Accords and to be completed no later than five years from that date.

Since the core issues of the conflict (borders, security, refugees, settlements, Jerusalem) were explicitly left for the final-status negotiations, the Oslo Accords did not directly address them. Yet there were a number of clauses that related to these issues in one form or another. Two key clauses that would have ramifications with regard to both future borders and the issue of settlements were the affirmations that "the outcome of the permanent status negotiations should not be prejudiced or preempted by agreements reached for the interim period . . . Neither side shall initiate or take any step that will change the status of the West Bank and the

Gaza Strip pending the outcome of permanent status negotiations" and "[t]he two sides view the West Bank and the Gaza Strip as a single territorial unit, whose integrity will be preserved during the interim period."[2]

East Jerusalem, which had been annexed (and expanded) by Israel in 1967, and which was reserved for discussion as a final-status issue, was explicitly excluded from the territory under the jurisdiction of the interim Palestinian Authority. Safe passage for persons and goods from the West Bank to Gaza was guaranteed by the Accords. A third clause that would be of major subsequent importance maintained that all disputes arising from the agreements would be resolved through negotiation, conciliation, or arbitration – in other words, not through violence or force.

Although the settlement issue was left for the final-status talks,[3] the Palestinians were later to argue that the first two clauses were violated by the building of settlements and continued Israeli expropriation of land. Settlement-building was indeed one of the major problems in the Oslo period, viewed by the Palestinians as a sign that Israel did not intend to leave the Occupied Territories or, at the very least, intended to determine future borders. Not only was land expropriated for settlement construction, but the security clauses of the Accords granted Israel responsibility for the security of all Israelis and the settlements, as well as the use of all roads. In fact, in order to guarantee settler security, bypass roads were built, involving more land expropriation. In addition, Israel was to be responsible for "external" and "internal" security, which meant not just border areas but ultimately the boundaries of areas from which the IDF withdrew. On the ground this meant increasing numbers of Israeli security checks around towns or villages within the West Bank and Gaza Strip – further impeding Palestinian movement inside. Moreover, Palestinian access to East Jerusalem from the rest of the West Bank was closed; Palestinians who were not residents of East Jerusalem now needed a permit to enter or transit East Jerusalem (and other Israeli regulations prohibited West Bank residents married to Israelis or East Jerusalem Palestinians from living in Israel or East Jerusalem). Oslo II contained a concession to permit East Jerusalem Palestinians to vote in elections for the Palestinian Legislative Council, using post offices as a pretense of "absentee" voting.

Since the borders were a final-status issue, the exact perimeters of IDF redeployments were not specified; rather, the Accords stated that withdrawals would be to "designated military areas." Oslo II, however, divided the territories into three areas: area A, from which Israel would withdraw and hand over full civil and security responsibility to the Palestinian Authority; area B, from which Israel would withdraw but maintain security responsibility; and area C, which would remain totally under Israeli civil and security control. Ultimately, once the final borders were negotiated, areas C and B were to be reduced and become A. Thus, while Israel maintained responsibility for the security of the settlers, the Palestinians were to create a limited police force, with weapons and responsibilities clearly defined, for maintaining order in the areas under their whole or partial control. In addition, there were various stipulations about prisoner releases and Palestinian responsibility for dealing with terrorists. The failure of the Palestinian Authority to clamp down on the wave of Hamas and Islamic Jihad terrorism that increasingly accompanied the Accords led eventually to Israeli accusations of violations of the security aspects of the Accords and the principle of peaceful dispute resolution.

Indeed, it was mutual incriminations over delays and failures of implementation of many of the promised measures (e.g., prisoner release, opening of a safe passage) and, most importantly, over settlement-building and growing terrorism that led to the failure of the Oslo Accords. Yet flaws in the agreements themselves led to this development. For example, the failure to include a monitoring body (the CIA was brought in at a late stage but only for a limited security role) left implementation up to each party's own interpretation and political will. Moreover, their interim nature created a period in which opponents to the Accords could (and did) do everything possible to prevent implementation. Thus the basic logic of the interim nature – namely, to have a "test" period in which trust could be built before proceeding to the final-status talks – was rapidly proven fallacious. The absence of a clear goal, such as a Palestinian state and an end to the conflict, left both Palestinians and Israelis with little incentive for tolerating the violations or meeting their commitments.

While it is conceivable that Yitzhak Rabin, with his security credentials, could have seen Oslo through despite these pitfalls, his assassination led to the eventual election of Binyamin Netanyahu and the near death of the process, despite a number of limited US-imposed agreements. The final blow came under Ehud Barak, who, with his election in 1999, jettisoned the remaining Oslo commitments (seeking first an agreement with Syria) and eventually chose to move directly to negotiations on final-status issues. With the Americans now deeply involved, President Clinton, backed by Ehud Barak, pressed for the conclusion of a Framework of Principles for a peace agreement before the US elections of 2000. The result was the Camp David meeting of 11 to 24 July 2000.

The Camp David summit

The Camp David summit did not produce a plan but rather a number of proposals, most of which remain ambiguous to this day. What can be garnered from the many accounts by participants and observers is that the plan Barak conveyed to Clinton one week into the talks – Barak's "bottom lines" – would have allowed for a Palestinian state on 91 percent of the West Bank plus the Gaza Strip. Israel would annex 9 percent (the West Bank) in exchange for a land swap the equivalent of 1 percent south of the Gaza Strip (i.e., a 9:1 swap). Israel would lease an additional 10 percent in the Jordan Rift Valley for no more than twelve years. For Israel, this would accommodate roughly 80 percent of the settlers in land annexed to Israel. It would also ensure, at least for a period of time, Labor's traditional security interest in the Jordan Rift Valley border area. For the Palestinians, however, it meant losing 18 percent temporarily and ultimately 8 percent of the West Bank land intended for their state, which, in their view, was in addition to the 78 percent of mandated Palestine which they had conceded in the 1988 PLO decision to limit their demands to the area of the West Bank and Gaza alone.

Over the next few days Barak increased the Israeli demand to 13.2 percent and ended with a proposal to keep 10 to 12 percent. The exact percentages depended upon how one counted such areas as the land for safe passage between the West Bank and Gaza. The Palestinians remained firmly committed to the 4 June 1967 lines, with a willingness only for 1:1 land swaps and Israeli use of some roads to reach settlements (which would accommodate only 30 percent of the settlers).

The amount of land involved, and therefore the question of borders, was further complicated by Israeli security demands for a presence in the Jordan Rift Valley, including a small number of early warning stations and control or use of the roads to reach them in the case of emergencies. The latter demand was perceived by the Palestinians not only as a violation of sovereignty but also as a division of the West Bank into what would amount to cantons. In addition there were Israeli demands regarding the use of air space and control over electromagnetic fields; there was apparently expectation of agreement regarding water issues and some form of de-militarization of the Palestinian state. Two significant concessions in the discussions were the Barak proposal for an international presence on the international border (with Jordan) and, most importantly, Israeli and American agreement on the creation of a Palestinian state. While this had been understood in the discussions at least over the preceding months, the explicit goal of statehood, which had been missing from the Oslo Accords, was finally stated at Camp David, although it was not pronounced publicly.

The refugee issue, a key problem in the conflict, was not extensively discussed at Camp David. Barak's proposal contained only the briefest reference to a "satisfactory solution" of the problem, and in the talks he was willing to offer some Israeli role in compensation and entry of a limited number of Palestinians under family reunification (as had already been permitted for many years). The Palestinians maintained that the basis for solution was UN Resolution 194, but it was the impression of both Americans and Israelis at Camp David that Arafat was not making this a central issue. Compensation was important, as was Israeli acknowledgement of its responsibility for the problem, but the Palestinian position was that implementation of 194 could be negotiated in a way that would meet Israel's security and demographic needs. When the Camp David talks finally collapsed, however, the Palestinians asserted the uncompromising demand for the right of return of all the refugees to their homes.

Barak apparently had not intended to discuss the politically sensitive Jerusalem issue, but he did agree to a proposal by Clinton and subsequently offered one himself. The first proposal allotted Palestinian sovereignty over the Muslim and Christian quarters of the Old City and seven of the eight or nine outer neighborhoods of East Jerusalem, plus functional autonomy (zoning, planning, security, law enforcement, etc.) in the inner ring of East Jerusalem. Barak later modified this to include Palestinian sovereignty over some of the areas within the inner circle as well and a "Presidential Compound" in the Old City (as distinct from a capital for the Palestinian state). While both these proposals went further than anything Barak had intended to offer, they fell far short of the Palestinian counter-proposals, which sought a return of all of East Jerusalem (with the exception of the Jewish Quarter). The real sticking point, however, was the issue of the Temple Mount/Haram al-Sharif area. Sacred to Muslims, and therefore of importance to more than the Palestinians alone, this site also had come to symbolize Israel's historic bond to Jerusalem and, indeed, to the Land of Israel itself. The Clinton–Barak proposal called for Palestinian "custodianship" over the site (a situation which in effect already existed) in addition to continuation of Israel's self-proclaimed sovereignty there. Barak eventually added the demand that Jews be permitted to pray on the Temple Mount, but, in any case, the Palestinians were unwilling to accept continued Israeli sovereignty. Although Clinton suggested a number of alternatives, it was this issue that finally led to the collapse of the talks. While agreement had not been reached on all or even any of the other issues, at least some of the ideas – for example, the principle of land swaps – did become starting points for subsequent plans.

For Israeli domestic political reasons, both Barak and Clinton explicitly blamed Arafat for the failure of Camp David. Given the lack of information as to what was or was not in fact proposed in the talks, both Israelis and Palestinians believed that the other side had been totally unreasonable – and concluded that there was "no partner" for peace. Although quiet talks did continue between the two sides, the outbreak of the al-Aqsa *Intifada* at the end of September "confirmed" the Israeli public's belief that Arafat was the problem and behind the outbreak and rapid escalation of violence. Despite the bloody clashes, two more peace plans were forthcoming while Clinton and Barak were still in office.

The Clinton Parameters

In December 2000, Clinton presented Arafat and Barak with what became known as the Clinton Parameters. These were not intended as negotiating principles; rather, they were to be accepted or rejected, within four days, as the basis of a plan that could be refined in subsequent talks. The proposed borders would allot the Palestinian state 94 to 96 percent of the West Bank, with a land swap equal to 1 to 3 percent (Clinton later said his plan meant 97 percent for the Palestinian state, although Barak had previously indicated 93 percent as his bottom line). The criteria for the lines would be territorial contiguity for the Palestinians and accommodation of 80 percent of the settlers in blocs annexed by Israel, but a minimum amount of annexation and Palestinians affected. The security arrangements would involve an "agreed upon" international presence on the border with Jordan replacing Israeli forces over a three-year period. Israel would maintain a limited force in the Jordan Rift Valley for no more than an additional three years, under the authority of the international force. The international force would be removed only with the agreement of both sides. Israeli reentry – presumably meaning use of the roads to this area – would be permitted in an emergency, defined as the occurrence of an imminent threat to Israel's national security. Israel would also be able to maintain three early warning posts there, to be reviewed after ten years and removed only with the agreement of both sides. Air space would be under Palestinian sovereignty, but arrangements would be made for Israeli use (for training or operational needs). The Palestinian state would be "non-militarized" – that is, not necessarily de-militarized but limited with regard to the type and size of security force it could maintain. A major Israeli concession would be final withdrawal from the Jordan Rift Valley and the acceptance of an international force – both more or less conceded in principle at Camp David. Less than what Israel sought for its security but nonetheless limiting somewhat Palestinian sovereignty, these proposals were clearly an effort at bridging the earlier differences.

Clinton offered two types of solution to the refugee problem, both of which accepted Israel's right to determine its immigration policy and preserve the Jewish character of the state. According to one idea, there would be recognition of the Palestinians' right to return "to historic Palestine" or their "right to return to their homeland" – namely, the Palestinian state. The second solution was a more complicated one, discussed informally in the past. Refugees would choose between five options: "return" to the Palestinian state; integration into the countries where they currently resided; "return" to the land transferred to the Palestinians by the swaps; resettlement in a third country; and admission to Israel. The last three options would be subject to the immigration policies of the countries involved, including Israel, with priority given to refugees in Lebanon (whose plight was the worst). According to Clinton, these solutions would constitute implementation of Resolution 194. While there was reason to believe the formula would be acceptable, it would not be easy for Arafat as head of the PLO. This organization represented all Palestinians, and many in the Palestinian diaspora had opposed Oslo because it had dealt only with those under Israeli occupation. Clinton, and possibly Arafat, however, might view this solution as a trade-off for a more favorable resolution of the Jerusalem issue.

With regard to Jerusalem, Clinton ignored the complex ideas presented at Camp David and proposed an ostensibly simpler proposal: Jewish neighborhoods to be under Israeli sovereignty, Arab neighborhoods under Palestinian sovereignty. Thus Jerusalem would in fact be divided: the Palestinians could have their capital in East Jerusalem, and Israel could finally have (West) Jerusalem recognized as its capital. What the proposal failed to note was that over 250,000 Israelis were now living in post-1967 East Jerusalem, most of them in what Israel considered simply "neighborhoods" and the Palestinians considered "settlements." Clinton's solution to the Temple Mount/Haram al-Sharif problem was closer to the failed Camp David proposals. The Haram al-Sharif at the top, namely the mosques, would be under Palestinian sovereignty; the area below, namely the Western Wall and its surroundings, would be Israeli, with either a mutual commitment not to excavate or a joint committee to decide upon matters of excavation underground.

Despite objections to the territorial and security aspects, Barak gave Clinton an affirmative answer within the deadline. Arafat voiced reservations on almost every issue and then let the deadline pass with no final response. An Israeli–Palestinian meeting a few weeks later at Taba (18–27 January 2001) – a last-ditch effort by Barak to achieve something before his own clearly futile attempt at re-election, did, nonetheless, tackle some of the same issues.

The Taba talks

Little could in fact be expected from Taba given the ever escalating violence on the ground and the imminent demise of Barak's government, and, indeed, no agreements were acknowledged. There were detailed discussions, with maps, of the size and location of land swaps, apparently coming close to the 97 percent of the Clinton Parameters, accommodating roughly 70 percent of the settlers. Most of the Clinton security arrangements were accepted (non-militarization, an international presence, early warning stations), but Israeli demands regarding lease or access to the Jordan Rift Valley, control of air space, and others remained unsettled. Generally accepting the Clinton formula for Jerusalem, the future status of a number of "neighborhoods" in East Jerusalem also remained elusive, although quite detailed proposals were tabled. Among these were arrangements for the Temple Mount/Haram al-Sharif area, but the issue of sovereignty remained a problem, despite discussion even of "international sovereignty." The working group on the refugee issue (led by Yossi Beilin and Nabil Sha'ath) was the only one said to have actually achieved agreement at Taba. Though never officially acknowledged, this group agreed to the Clinton refugee proposal, including, according to EU observer Miguel Moratinos, an understanding that Israel would allow 40,000 returnees over a five-year period.

The Road Map

The fact that Israel's most "dovish" politicians had been unable to find solutions at Taba did little to change the "no partner" attitudes among Israelis and Palestinians. The election of Ariel Sharon in February 2001 and the continued *Intifada* shifted subsequent efforts to international proposals for a ceasefire and a resurrection of the peace process. The more formal of these were the Mitchell Committee Report and Recommendations, the Tenet Plan, and the Zinni Proposals – all focusing primarily on ending the violence. Their failure gave rise to work on a more comprehensive proposal from the newly formed Quartet (the USA, Russia, the UN, and the EU) first outlined, in part, as a plan for a "provisional Palestinian state" by President Bush in a speech on 24 June 2002 and finally presented on 30 April 2003 as a "Performance Based Road Map." The significance of the speech, however, was Bush's reiteration of comments made by him and by then Prime Minister Sharon in a White House press conference on 7 February 2002 endorsing the creation of a Palestinian state and the two-state solution – a first for both the USA and Israel.[4]

The two-state solution was presented in the very title of the Road Map as the explicit goal of the new process. The plan itself consisted of three "performance-based" phases culminating in the creation of a Palestinian state, the end of the occupation, and the end of the Arab–Israeli conflict. While progress from one phase to another was to be based upon evidence of "good-faith efforts" and "compliance," as determined by the Quartet, beginning and ending dates were assigned to each phase. At the beginning of the first phase (May to June 2003) each side was to initiate a ceasefire and make the following declarations: the Palestinians were to declare their recognition of Israel's right to exist in peace and security (as already declared in the Oslo Accords), while Israel was to issue an "unequivocal statement affirming its commitment" to the two-state solution, with "an independent, viable sovereign Palestinian State" alongside Israel (as Sharon had said in February 2002). The use of the term "viable" (added earlier by Bush), along with a reference to contiguity, may have been designed to allay Palestinian concerns over possible cantonization. There was far greater emphasis in the Road Map on Palestinian institution-building and democratization, however, reflecting Israeli suspicions regarding Arafat and the recently added Israeli (and American) linkage of peace with democracy.

The first phase required numerous detailed democratization measures on the part of the Palestinians, consolidation of their security services, and the dismantling of the terrorist capability infrastructure. Israel was required in this phase to freeze all settlement activity ("including natural growth of settlements"), dismantle settlement outposts created after March 2001, improve the humanitarian situation, and withdraw the IDF to the (pre-*Intifada*) 28 September 2000 lines. Most of these tasks were to be continued in the second phase (June to December 2003), in which there would be the option of creating a Palestinian state with provisional borders, possibly including UN membership. The state would be launched by an international conference, beginning also a peace process with Syria and with Lebanon and the resumption of the Oslo-era links with Arab states and multilateral talks. The third phase (January 2004 to 2005) would consist of completion and consolidation of all the earlier steps so as to ensure democracy and security in preparation for the final-status agreement. A second international conference would launch negotiations on permanent-status issues – namely, permanent borders, security, refugees, and Jerusalem, along with Israeli–Syrian and Israeli–Lebanese peace talks. This phase would end in 2005 with the creation of the Palestinian state, end of the 1967 occupation, and the end of the conflict.

The only references to the nature of the permanent-status solutions envisaged by the Road Map dealt with Jerusalem and the refugees, but only in the most general of terms. The negotiated solution for Jerusalem was to take into account the "political and religious concerns of both sides" and to protect the religious interests of Jews, Muslims, and Christians "worldwide." For the refugees, there was to be an "agreed, just, fair and realistic solution." The choice of the words "agreed" and "realistic" were presumably included in deference to Israel's interests – namely, that nothing would be forced upon Israel, in particular an unrealistic demand that the country jeopardize its Jewish character by allowing large numbers of refugees to return.

The architects of the Road Map apparently did seek to correct some of the errors or problems of the Oslo Accords, and not only by providing clear incentives in the form of statements at the outset of the final goals (Palestinian statehood, an end to the conflict). Although once again a three-year period of interim measures was called for, with the risk of spoilers impeding the building of trust, steps were to be taken to avoid such pitfalls of a transition period. For example, although it left the settlement issue to the final-status talks, the Road Map called for an immediate building freeze – along with humanitarian measures, including the lifting of road blocks and the suspension of punitive measures such as deportations – in order to provide some improvement for the Palestinian population. Similarly, detailed demands were made to eliminate terrorism and incitement, thereby preventing further deterioration of Israelis' safety. Additionally, the Road Map provided for monitoring of each phase in order to ensure implementation – a key lacuna of the Oslo Accords. The problem, however, was that during the first phase only "informal monitoring" would be conducted by existing organs on the ground, to be turned into a formal monitoring group with "enhanced international" participation only in the second phase. While it was understandable that it might take time to form a monitoring group, it would appear that the greatest need for such a body would be during the first, most critical phase of the process. Presumably it would be the monitoring group that would provide the Quartet with the information necessary to determine (by consensus) whether performance warranted transition to subsequent phases, but the composition, the mandate, and the mechanisms for the work of the monitoring body were not stipulated.

Indeed, the issue of performance became the major problem even before the question of moving to the second phase arose, but it revolved mainly around interpretation of the very beginning of the process. Although Israel accepted the Road Map – with fourteen reservations – it did not begin its part of the first phase because of its interpretation that the measures within each phase were to be sequential – namely, that the Palestinians first had to implement their requirements. The most important of these for Israel was the dismantling of the infrastructure of terrorism. The Palestinians and the Quartet viewed the measures within each phase as parallel, not sequential. As we shall see below, some years later the Palestinians were to argue that they had in fact made great progress in fulfilling the democratization-institutional measures and even the security measures of phase I and demanded that Israel do its part. They were never satisfied about the option in the second phase of a state with just "temporary" borders, but phase II remained purely theoretical. Without a monitoring group ever being formed, and with Israeli insistence upon terrorism prevention prior to action on its part, the dates and processes of the Road Map seemed to disappear. In fact, Prime Minister Sharon chose to proceed on another path altogether, reassuring President Bush, who considered the Road Map his initiative, that one day Israel would return to it.

The Arab Peace Initiative

Other plans preceded Sharon's alternative and the later revival of the Road Map. The first of these actually preceded the Road Map almost unnoticed. In March 2002, an Arab League summit in Beirut unanimously adopted a plan originally proposed by Saudi Arabia. Apparently increasingly concerned over the use of the Palestinian issue as a rallying call for the spread of radicalism in the region – threatening many of their regimes – the Arab states took a major step towards Israel in what became known as the Arab Peace Initiative. This plan posited the usual demands for Israeli withdrawal from lands occupied since 4 June 1967 (including Syria and Lebanon) and the creation of a Palestinian state with its capital in Jerusalem, but the formulations employed and some new features made this a most significant innovation. The specification of *East* Jerusalem as the site for the Palestinian capital was intended to clarify the limit of the demand, but far more important was the new wording of the demand regarding the refugees. Avoiding an explicit call for the "right of return" – which in any case was often absent from Arab statements – the Arab League plan added a new term, "agreed upon," to its call for a "just solution" of the refugee problem, based upon Resolution 194. Resolution 194 was, of course, open to interpretation but, inasmuch as Israel maintained that the resolution did not entail the "right of return," the key word was "agreed," meaning Israeli agreement. That the intention was indeed to allay Israeli fears was indicated by one of the drafters of the initiative, then Jordanian Foreign Minister Marwan Muasher.[5] Such wording might imply what had often been said privately by Palestinian leaders – namely, that agreement could be reached so as to meet Israeli security and demographic interests. To protect Arab – presumably Jordanian and Lebanese – interests, the plan also allowed for Arab states to reject "patriation" that conflicted with the "special circumstances" of Arab host countries.

The most significant innovation of the initiative, however, was what the Arab states were offering in return. Rejecting a "military solution," limiting territorial demands to 1967, and accepting the principle of land for peace, the Arab states pledged to consider the Arab–Israeli conflict ended, enter peace agreements with Israel, normalize relations, and provide security for all the states of the region. Here, too, the hand of Muasher, formerly ambassador to

Israel, could be detected, for the terminology reflected the various demands, especially for normalization, an end to conflict, and security, that most Israelis had traditionally considered essential.

Initially Israel appeared to ignore the initiative. It was almost immediately eclipsed by a particularly serious terrorist attack during the Passover meal in an Israeli town, provoking an Israeli military offensive and reoccupation of parts of the West Bank. A year later, however, reference to the initiative was included in the preamble of the Road Map, and over the years the plan began to elicit American support and greater Israeli attention. It found its way into most international pronouncements on the conflict, along with Resolution 242 and other landmark decisions. The Arab League reaffirmed the initiative a number of times and claimed that it had secured its endorsement by the fifty-seven-member Islamic Conference (which includes Iran). By 2007 Israel agreed to discuss the plan and began suggesting that Arab states implement some of the promised normalization as confidence-building measures. There were signs that this suggestion may have been taken up by the Obama administration, although the official Arab position remained that normalization was promised only as part of the "comprehensive peace" outlined in the initiative.

The Geneva Accord

While neither the Road Map nor the Arab Initiative provided any detail regarding the major issues, a group of Israeli and Palestinian officials and former officials, including former military leaders and negotiators, undertook a two-year-long effort to produced a detailed blueprint for a peace agreement, calling it the "Geneva Accord." Led by former Justice Minister Beilin and the Palestinian Information Minister Yasir Abed Rabbo, the group built on the Clinton Parameters and provided plausible solutions for all the problematic issues. The major contribution was the highly detailed, thoroughly planned and delineated nature of each solution. It was published on 12 October 2003.

Regarding borders, "Geneva" maps accorded the Palestinians the Gaza Strip and 97.3 percent of the West Bank, with 1:1 land swaps for the remainder. These consisted not only of the barren area south of Gaza previously proposed but also better land south of the Hebron hills. Duration and procedures for Israeli withdrawal and removal of settlements were included, along with previously missing stringent, complex, and detailed monitoring mechanisms in addition to provisions for a multinational force for a limited period. America, rather than an international team, was to monitor anti-terrorism measures. Israeli security demands regarding a presence in the Jordan Rift Valley, early-warning stations, and use of air space remained, but they were more limited in time and scale than previously proposed. The "non-militarized" nature of the Palestinian state was spelled out regarding type and number of weapons for the Palestinian security force. One innovation was a reference to the need for a regional security regime to be pursed by Israel and the new state.

The refugee problem was addressed by the Clinton five-option formula, with the stipulation that each receiving country was sovereign regarding the numbers it would accept. An addition was a stipulation that Israel "will consider ... as a basis" the average number accepted by third states. This was assumed but not stated to be roughly 40,000 (as suggested at Taba). There was no mention of the "right of return" – an omission that rendered "Geneva" unacceptable to many Palestinians, while a reference to Resolution 194, nonetheless, was viewed, and opposed, by many Israelis as constituting the right of return. Many clauses dealt in some detail with compensation, rehabilitation, and development, with numerous provisions for international involvement. The proposal for Jerusalem was perhaps the most complicated part of "Geneva," with elaborate provisions for access to the various parts of Jerusalem, the Old City, and the Temple Mount. Maps, but not the texts, indicated the division of sovereignty, so that it was not entirely clear how the controversial neighborhoods/settlements would be handled, although it was stipulated that each state would have its capital in the area under its sovereignty. The Old City, except for the Jewish Quarter and part of the Armenian Quarter, was to be under Palestinian sovereignty, and the arrangement for the Temple Mount followed the Clinton formula. There were to be two municipalities for the city with a joint coordinating committee, but international elements were to be involved in matters concerning the Old City. These international bodies would consist not only of the monitoring group established for the whole accord but also of a consultative body from the Arab states and the Islamic Conference.

Aside from the innovations mentioned above, an important formulation appeared in the agreement for the first time. Going beyond the recognition by the PLO and the Oslo Accords of Israel's right to exist, the "Geneva" Preamble affirmed that the agreement marked "the recognition of the right of the Jewish people to statehood," along with the same right for the Palestinians. To overcome habitual Palestinian opposition to any hint of the Jewish nature of the state, primarily out of concern for the Arab minority in Israel, the Preamble added "without prejudice to the equal rights of the Parties' respective citizens." Nonetheless, the formulation did squarely face the right of the Jews to a state (the basis of political Zionism and historically anathema to the Palestinians), strengthened in the body of the document by a clause recognizing "Palestine [the name given to the new state] and Israel as the homelands [note the plural] of their respective peoples."

The importance of the Geneva Accord lay not only in the support Arafat gave the agreement and its relatively favorable reception among the Israeli and Palestinian publics (at its peak, as much as 64 percent and 54 percent support, respectively, according to a press release from the Palestinian Center for Policy and Survey Research on 18 January 2005), but mainly in the detailed material it provided for possible application of the Clinton Parameters in the future. More immediately, it was one of the factors leading to Sharon's decision to offer a plan for unilateral disengagement.

The Gaza disengagement plan

Presenting the disengagement plan to the Knesset on 15 March 2004, Sharon referred to the need to "repel" various initiatives, including the Arab League plan and "Israeli plans which could lead us into the abyss." There were a number of additional factors that led to the decision to act unilaterally. Of an immediate nature, terrorism had reached intolerable levels, but there was also criticism from the public, the military, and, most notably, former security chiefs regarding the failure of the government to move towards peaceful resolution. At a more strategic level, there was an increasing realization by the political right that continued occupation was rapidly leading to a demographic balance in favor of the Arabs between the Jordan and the sea. Sharon may have had other strategic considerations, but unilaterally withdrawing from the Gaza Strip would rid Israel of the responsibility for 1,300,000 Palestinians and eliminate the (unpopular) security burden on the IDF inside Gaza. Removing settlements there and in four places on the West Bank would constitute what could be construed as a move forward without the requirements of the Road Map and without having to deal with the Palestinians.

Aside from the redeployment of the IDF outside the Gaza Strip and the abandonment of the settlements and four small settlements in the northern part of the West Bank, the plan called for Israel to remove all its personnel and relinquish all governmental authority within the Gaza

Strip. Yet Israel was to maintain control over what was called the "Gaza envelope" – namely, land, sea and air access, in addition to infrastructure (the supply of clean water and electricity) – while reserving the right to "use preventive measures as well as the use of force against threats originating in the Gaza Strip." Initially the plan called for Israel to maintain an IDF presence in the "Philadelphi" corridor bordering Egypt. There were a number of ambiguities, particularly in the initial plan, and particularly with regard to the future status of the Gaza Strip. Israel insisted that the move would end the occupation there, but the international community did not accept this view. The death of Arafat, the election of Abu Mazen, and the latter's imposi-tion of a ceasefire changed the atmosphere and led to a slight softening of the conditions of the plan. Sharon maintained his unilateral approach, but agreed in principle – and later retracted – permission for the opening of a sea port, but he did decide to remove the IDF from the Philadelphi corridor. Astonishingly, perhaps, he agreed both to have Egypt take responsibility for that border and, after some indecision and American intervention, to relinquish control of the Rafah crossing point from Gaza to Egypt. An EU presence was to monitor the Palestinian side, although Israel apparently unofficially maintained a role in decisions to close the crossing if secu-rity warranted. The plan also called for third-party (Egyptian, US, British, EU, Quartet) involve-ment in such matters as economic development, the training of a Palestinian security force, and other security-related issues. No measures were dictated for the areas of the four settlements removed in the West Bank; the IDF remained there in occupation.

Two important precedents were set by the disengagement plan, the first of which was the role provided by third parties. While this did not change Israel's traditional opposition to the sta-tioning of peacekeepers on Israeli soil, it did represent the transfer of important security con-cerns to outsiders. That an Arab state was one of them attested not only to the strength of the Israeli–Egyptian peace but also to a new Israeli openness, with possibilities for future coopera-tion with its Arab neighbors. The removal of 7,500 Jewish settlers from areas considered part of historic Israel, and by the person considered the "father" of the entire settlement project, was not only bold but politically risky for Sharon. Ultimately he successfully handled settler resis-tance to the move, but he alienated his own party, leading him to create a new more centrist political party. Moreover, the results of the disengagement – namely, the economic costs (compensation to the settlers) and settler hostility – would make future withdrawals far more difficult.

Politically, the refusal to disengage through negotiations weakened Abu Mazen and those Palestinians who had favored peaceful means. Unilateralism strengthened the Islamists, for Palestinian public opinion, already negatively affected by the failure of Oslo, tended to credit the violence of Hamas with "expelling" Israel from Gaza. Inasmuch as Israel maintained con-trol of all access to and from the Gaza Strip, the boycott it introduced once Hamas was elected, five months after the disengagement, led to near total disruption of life there. For many Israelis, the resumption of violence from the Gaza Strip once Hamas took over cast serious doubt over the wisdom of any future withdrawals.

Ehud Olmert: from "convergence" to the Annapolis process

In January 2006, shortly before the election of Hamas, Olmert replaced Sharon and introduced the "Convergence Plan," a modified unilateral plan for withdrawal from areas of the West Bank. Never fully amplified, the plan entailed withdrawal roughly to the lines created by the separation barrier (which, according to the planned route at the time, would take up 9 to 10 percent of West Bank territory) and the transfer of settlements to settlement blocs on the west-ern side of the barrier. It was not clear if the IDF would be fully withdrawn, since Israel was apparently to maintain responsibility for security for the whole West Bank, including a presence in the Jordan Rift Valley. Indeed, the future status of the evacuated areas was entirely unclear.

In any case, following the Second Lebanon War, Olmert dropped unilateralism and his Convergence Plan. The war, as well as the violence from Gaza, had demonstrated the grave risks of withdrawing unilaterally, without agreements to provide for security interests and the like. Olmert therefore undertook direct negotiations with Abu Mazen, chair of the PLO and still president of the Palestinian Authority despite the Hamas takeover in Gaza and the collapse of the PA "unity government." The declared purpose of the talks was to reach agreement on the core issues of the permanent settlement leading to the creation of the Palestinian state and peace. At the same time, the Road Map was to be revived, with the explanation that the permanent-status agreement reached would be a shelf agreement until the Road Map commitments were met. It appeared to be phase I and phase III of the Road Map simultaneously. Without agreeing to the shelf agreement concept, the Palestinians actually championed the Road Map at this point on the grounds that they had fulfilled most of their commitments, and they demanded that Israel fulfill its commitments, namely a settlement freeze. Both the top-level talks and the negotiations conducted by the two teams, under Tzipi Livni and Saeb Erekat, disbanded once Israeli elections were announced near the end of 2008. No official disclosure was made as to what had been agreed up to that point, but published interviews with Olmert, Abu Mazen, and Erekat, along with published excerpts of a forthcoming book by Olmert, printed speeches by Abu Mazen, and the documents published by Wikileaks/al Jazeera in 2011, provide some, albeit frequently contradictory, evidence of a planned agreement.[6]

With regard to borders, the two leaders came close to, but did not reach, an agreement. Abu Mazen's position (and map) called for Israel to retain 1.9 percent of the territory of the West Bank (including East Jerusalem) while Olmert's map reportedly called for retention of 6.5 percent (one version says 6.3 percent). Both leaders spoke of land swaps to compensate for the areas to be annexed by Israel, but here too there were differences over just what would be included (area for safe passage, for example, between Gaza and the West Bank, certain areas of "no-man's land," and so forth). Each leader's map was designed with the settlers in mind – Abu Mazen based his offer on the 1 percent of the West Bank actually built upon by settlements; Olmert apparently based his on an effort to leave as many settlers in place as possible. There was no agreement over which settlements would remain, most notably the more populous ones such as Ariel (which juts into the West Bank), Maale Adumim (close to Jerusalem), and Efrat (in the historical Gush Etzion area south of Jerusalem). However, the two leaders were, according to Abu Mazen, scheduled to try to bridge the gap between their positions on 3 January 2008, in a meeting in Washington, but this was canceled by Olmert on account of the war in Gaza. Remaining issues, according to most accounts, were basically resolved. Sovereignty in Jerusalem was to be divided according to the Clinton formula – Jewish neighborhoods to Israel, Arab neighborhoods to Palestine – which meant that Abu Mazen agreed that the "neighborhoods" built by Israel in expanded East Jerusalem (with the exception of Har Homa) would revert to Israel. The "holy basin," which would take in more than just the Old City and the holy places (though it was not decided how much), would be under international control. The USA, Saudi Arabia, Jordan, and Egypt would all join Israel and Palestine in this international body, while the rest of the city would be run by two separate municipalities with, possibly, an overall coordinating body – with no physical division between the two sides. According to Abu Mazen, there were some minor security matters to be decided, but there was agreement as to Israeli access to airspace and the electromagnetic field. On the two key security issues, demilitarization and the eastern border of Palestine, the two leaders agreed to the Clinton term "non-militarized state," meaning that Palestine would have a strong police force, but no army, air force or heavy armor. The border would be manned by an international force (possibly NATO), and no foreign armies would be permitted to enter. Nor would Palestine enter military agreements with any state that did not recognize Israel. While details such as pursuit of terrorists remained open, virtually all relevant security matters were resolved.

Finally, the most difficult issue of all, that of the refugees, was also reportedly resolved – in principle. Neither the right of return nor Israel's responsibility for the refugee problem itself was explicitly acknowledged, though Israel would express its recognition of the suffering of the Palestinian refugees. Olmert suggested adding recognition of the suffering of Jews forced to leave Arab countries as a result of the conflict. The Clinton formula was accepted – namely, that the refugees stay in the countries where they were, go to the new Palestinian state, move to a third county, or settle in Israel. However, discussion of numbers to return to Israel was not resolved; Olmert did not go beyond some thousands (no more than 15,000), which was not acceptable to Abu Mazen. Finally, Israel would participate in an international effort to compensate the refugees, and that would mark the end to all claims, as well as an end to the conflict.

All the above was finalized by the two leaders and conveyed to the Americans, but nothing was formally agreed. The principle of the negotiations had been basically that "nothing is agreed until all is agreed." The question of numbers – territory and refugees – remained to be worked out. The Gaza war and the announced pending resignation (and indictment) of Olmert brought to a halt the steps planned to bridge the gap and hoped-for American involvement. Neither side said a final yes or a final no. By all accounts, the two came closer than anyone previously to a workable plan.

The Netanyahu government

When, in spring 2009, the Netanyahu government came in, it accepted the Road Map as still relevant, but Netanyahu spoke of seeking "economic peace." Under US pressure he accepted the goal of the two-state solution – that is, the creation of a Palestinian state – but he conditioned this primarily upon Palestinian recognition of Israel as the "state of the Jewish people."[7] Netanyahu explained that, while the borders were to be negotiated, they were to be "defensible borders" for Israel, and the Palestinian state would be demilitarized, with "iron-clad" security arrangements, including Israeli control of air space and electromagnetic fields, monitoring of imports, and a ban on military alliances. Jerusalem would be the united capital of Israel, and resolution of the refugee problem would be "outside the borders of Israel."

Only a very brief round of talks actually took place between Netanyahu and Abu Mazen, begun in Washington in September 2010 and abruptly halted with the Israeli decision to resume settlement construction (after a ten-month freeze). The two sides had yet to agree on an agenda, with Israel demanding that the first item be security, and the Palestinians insisting it be borders. In a speech to the Knesset on 23 February 2011, Netanyahu clarified that the crucial issue was security, specifically demilitarization of a Palestinian state and "an Israeli presence in the Jordan Valley over the years."[8] He implied that the demand for recognition of Israel as the state of the Jewish people was not of the same "crucial" nature. Some days later, however, he spoke of his intention to present a plan for an interim agreement along the lines of the creation of a Palestinian state in temporary borders. Such a plan would appear to be a response to international pressure on the Netanyahu government and specifically, perhaps, an effort to counter the growing Palestinian campaign to gain recognition of the Palestinian state within the 1967 borders. However, no plan was presented and no frontier talks took place.

Conclusion

There has been much speculation over the years as to why no peace plan has yet been realized successfully. Some ascribe the failure to the absence of leadership or political weakness of the leaders, even though strong leaders have been involved on both sides. Another factor often cited is simply the lack of political will to take the steps necessary for peace, whether for ideological or religious reasons, security-related fears, psychological barriers (such as a sense of victimhood on both sides, scars of past suffering and injustices), or simple mistrust. Negotiations are said to have failed on account of asymmetrical power relations, cultural differences, and even personality traits, while the cumulative effect of past failures has itself rendered success less likely.

Yet, or perhaps despite all this, the general plan for Israeli–Palestinian peace has taken root. Both sides, including the majority of both Israelis and Palestinians, recognize the other's right to a state. The two-state solution has been accepted with borders roughly equivalent to those that existed for Israel before June 1967. The principle of agreed-upon land swaps – to make up for any deviation from the 1967 line – has been accepted. The precedent of settlement dismantlement and settler relocation has been achieved, just as negotiations over the future of Jerusalem – once a taboo – have occurred, and numerous plans for the governing of the city and even the holy places have emerged. Similarly, the difficult issue of the refugees has been tackled, with the sides coming closer to an understanding of the critical elements for each. Israel has accepted the involvement of international actors – including Arab actors – even in security-related matters. And the entire membership of the Arab League, once rejecting Israel entirely, is now, and still, willing to end the conflict, make peace, and normalize relations with Israel. Whether it will be the Clinton Parameters or the Geneva Accords, or some other refinement of the many plans, the outline of a peace agreement is now relatively clear.

Notes

1 Analysis of the proposals may be found in Golan (2009).
2 www.mfa.gov.il
3 Palestinian efforts to include a settlement freeze in the Accords were rejected by the Israelis, with the explanation that the Labor Party had already frozen settlement construction (Savir 1998).
4 An earlier reference to a US "vision" of a Palestinian state had been made in answer to a question at a press conference on 2 October 2001. Reiteration in the Rose Garden speech in June gave this more formal endorsement.
5 Muasher (2009).
6 See *Newsweek*, 22 June 2009; *Haaretz*, 30 March 2009, 10 April 2009, 26 May 2009; *Agence France Presse*, 28 March 2009; *Jerusalem Post*, 17 June 2009; *Washington Post*, 29 May 2009; *New York Times*, 7 February 2011.
7 *Haaretz*, 14 June 2009.
8 www.mfa.gov.il.

References and further reading

Abbas, Mahmoud (1995) *Through Secret Channels* (Reading: Garnet).
Beilin, Yossi (2004) *The Path to Geneva* (New York: RDV Books).
Clinton, Bill (2004) *My Life* (New York: Vintage Books).
Golan, Galia (2009) *Israel and Palestine: Peace Plans and Proposals from Oslo to Disengagement* (2nd ed., Princeton, NJ: Markus Wiener).
Indyk, Martin (2009) *Innocent Abroad* (New York: Simon & Schuster).
Kurtzer, Daniel, and Lasensky, Scott (2008) *Negotiating Arab–Israeli Peace* (Washington, DC: United States Institute of Peace Press).
Miller, Aaron David (2008) *The much too Promised Land* (New York: Bantam Books).

Muasher, Marwan (2009) *The Arab Center* (New Havem CT: Yale University Press).

Qurie, Ahmed (Abu Ala) (2006) *From Oslo to Jerusalem* (London: I. B. Tauris).

Rabinovich, Itamar (1998) *Brink of Peace* (Princeton, NJ: Princeton University Press).

Ross, Dennis (2005) *The Missing Peace* (New York: Farrar, Strauss & Giroux).

Savir, Uri (1998) *The Process* (New York: Vintage Books).

Shamir, Jacob, and Shamir, Michal (2000) *The Anatomy of Public Opinion* (Ann Arbor: University of Michigan Press).

Sher, Gilead (2006) *Israeli–Palestinian Negotiations* (New York: Routledge).

Part IV
Issues

9

Palestinian refugees

Rex Brynen

There can be little doubt that the Palestinian refugee issue is one of the most central and politi-cally sensitive dimensions of the Israeli–Palestinian conflict. For Palestinians, shared experiences of forced displacement and involuntary exile have helped to shape the very core of their modern identity. Understandably, they have sought recognition and redress of these past wrongs. For Israelis, the refugee issue raises uncomfortable questions about the events that accompanied the establishment of their state. Moreover, Palestinian calls for the refugees' "right of return" are seen by most Israelis as an existential threat to their country's very survival as a Jewish homeland.

The refugee issue was one of the so-called permanent-status issues on which discussion was deferred under the 1993 Declaration of Principles between Israel and the Palestine Liberation Organization (PLO). In the interim, Israel did agree to permit the return to the West Bank and Gaza of those Palestinians who had been displaced from these areas as a consequence of the June 1967 War. Further discussion on the 1967 "displaced persons" stalled, however, and this part of the agreement was never implemented.

When talks on permanent-status issues eventually took place at the Camp David summit in July 2000, the two sides made little headway in narrowing the differences between them on the refugee issue. Compromises were suggested by then US President Clinton as part of the Clinton Parameters in December 2000, and significant – if still insufficient – progress was made on the issue in the Israeli–Palestinian negotiations at Taba in January 2001. After that, how-ever, all permanent-status discussions were suspended until the start of the Annapolis round of talks in 2007–08. When Benjamin Netanyahu was elected as prime minister of Israel in February 2009, meaningful permanent status talks essentially came to an end. (For an overview of refugee negotiations and key negotiating texts, see Brynen 2008.)

This chapter will offer a brief overview of the refugee question. It will then go on to discuss the key aspects of the issue that would need to be addressed by any Israeli–Palestinian peace agreement: return, repatriation, and resettlement; restitution, reparations, and compensation; moral acknowledgement, and refugee development.

Origins and scope of the Palestinian refugee issue

With the establishment of the State of Israel in 1948 came the first Arab–Israeli war. In the course of those hostilities, almost three-quarters of a million Palestinians fled or were driven

Table 9.1 UNRWA-registered refugees, 2012

	Number of registered refugees	Percentage of refugees living in refugee camps
West Bank	727,471	24
Gaza	1,167,572	43
Jordan	1,979,580	18
Syria	486,946	30
Lebanon	436,154	50

Source: United Nations Relief and Works Agency (January 2012).

from their homes within the nascent Jewish state to seek refugee status in the (Jordanian-controlled) West Bank, the (Egyptian-controlled) Gaza Strip, Syria, Lebanon, and further afield. In 1949, the United Nations Relief and Works Agency for Palestine Refugees in the Near East (UNRWA) was established to help address the humanitarian, social, and economic needs of these refugees (Schiff 1995; Bowker 2003). When Israel occupied the West Bank and Gaza in June 1967, a further 300,000 Palestinians (many of them also earlier 1948 refugees) fled these areas for neighboring Arab countries.

Today there are some 4.8 million refugees registered with the UNRWA in its five areas of operation (see Table 9.1). Palestinian sources put the total number of refugees and displaced persons as high as 7 million (PLO 2008). Roughly half of all Palestinians today live in the diaspora, in involuntary exile from historic Palestine.

The questions why Palestinians fled in 1948, and why they have remained refugees since then, have long been subjects of political controversy. Israel has generally maintained that the refugees fled of their own choice, or at the command of Arab leaders, in a war that itself arose from Arab and Palestinian refusal to accept the creation of the Jewish state. In this view, the Palestinians are ultimately responsible for their flight. Moreover, Israeli officials and commentators sometimes also argued that "population exchanges" have been a common characteristic of conflicts, and that Israel's absorption of nearly 600,000 Jews from Arab countries effectively cancels out any Palestinian claims. With this comes the implication that the Palestinians are also to blame by maintaining their sense of being refugees rather than forgetting their homeland and fully integrating into their host countries.

In the Palestinian view, their dispossession in Palestine in 1948 was the consequence of the conscious and deliberate policy of a Zionist movement that was explicitly committed to the establishment of a Jewish state in an area that otherwise would have had a Palestinian (Muslim and Christian) majority. To achieve this, the refugees were forced into exile in a form of "ethnic cleansing." Once the refugees had fled, their lands were seized by the Israeli state, and most were prevented from returning.

As is immediately evident, the historical debate over the origins of the refugee issue is not simply a matter of differing perspectives, but rather a broader struggle over moral and political responsibility. However, while the debate remains highly politicized, recent scholarship on the refugee flows of 1948 has shown that the flight was due to a complex mixture of factors: military conflict, widespread fear among Palestinians, specific Jewish attacks and atrocities, Arab disorganization and demoralization, and occasional incidents of people being driven from their homes by force (Morris 1989). There is little dispute that, once the refugees fled, Israel had little desire to permit the return of substantial numbers of Palestinians to their homes within

Israel, perceiving them as a threat to the security and Jewish character of the state. Virtually all refugee properties, and even those of some internally displaced Palestinian citizens of Israel, were seized by the Israeli government under the 1950 Absentees Property Law.

Palestinian refugee advocates argue that the refugees have an inalienable "right of return," expressed both in UN resolutions and in international human rights law. They point in particular to UN General Assembly Resolution 194(III) of 1949, which declares that:

> refugees wishing to return to their homes and live at peace with their neighbors should be permitted to do so at the earliest practicable date, and that compensation should be paid for the property of those choosing not to return and for loss of or damage to property of those choosing not to return and for loss and damage to property which, under principles of international law, or in equity, should be made good by the governments or authorities responsible.

By contrast, Israel has long regarded this as a non-binding recommendation of the UN General Assembly, rather than an obligation under international law.

The social and political conditions of Palestinian refugees vary significantly from place to place. In the West Bank and Gaza, refugees fell under Israeli occupation after the June 1967 War. Since the establishment of the Palestinian Authority in 1994, refugees and other Palestinians in these areas enjoyed a limited degree of self-rule, but they still lack self-determination in an independent state.

Overall, there is relatively little difference in the living conditions of refugees and non-refugees in the Palestinian territories, although camp residents are somewhat worse off than the general population. Following the takeover of Gaza by the Islamist movement Hamas in 2007, conditions there deteriorated sharply as a consequence of Israeli border restrictions, suspensions of foreign aid, and violence. As a result, the UN has had to operate emergency feeding programs to prevent widespread malnutrition. Conditions further worsened with Israel's punitive attacks in Gaza in December 2008 and January 2009, which inflicted approximately $1.6 billion in damage on local infrastructure. Many UNRWA facilities were damaged, and some 50,000 or so Gazans were rendered homeless.

The vast majority of Palestinian refugees in Jordan have been given Jordanian citizenship, and indeed it is likely that a majority of the population is of Palestinian origin. Palestinians participate fully in the political and economic life of the country. Indicative of this integration is the large majority of refugees residing outside the camps. While there are few differences in average living conditions between Palestinian refugees and non-Palestinian Jordanians, conditions in the camps are below national averages.

Political tensions have arisen in the past between the regime (which ultimately rests on an East Bank powerbase) and segments of the Palestinian population. In 1970–71 these exploded into a full-scale civil war between the Palestinian nationalist movement and the Hashemite monarchy, resulting in the expulsion of the PLO from Jordan. While relations today are far more amiable, East Bank–Palestinian tensions do occasionally resurface, and the regime remains extremely wary of the refugee issue and how its future resolution might affect Jordanian and Hashemite interests. Palestinians in Syria, unlike those in Jordan, do not enjoy citizenship. However, they do enjoy full legal equivalency with local nationals in almost all areas, including both employment and access to government services. There are some restrictions on Palestinian property ownership. Moreover, as with all persons in Syria, there are tight controls on all political activity. Mobility in and out of the country is restricted by dependence on UNRWA refugee documents, which other countries may not accept for the purposes of international travel. Like others in the country, Palestinians in Syria have been deeply affected by the civil war that has raged there since 2011.

In Lebanon, Palestinian refugees have long been marginalized. A few Palestinians (mostly Christians) have managed to obtain Lebanese citizenship. Refugees are forbidden to own real estate and are excluded from employment in many professions. Palestinians are also generally denied access to government services and hence depend heavily on UNRWA. As a result, a large segment still resides in refugee camps, in adverse social conditions. As in Syria, refugees in Lebanon are dependent on refugee documentation, which limits international travel.

Lebanese policy has its roots both in that country's delicate sectarian balance and in its history of civil and regional conflict. In the past, the adverse conditions of Palestinians in Lebanon would appear, at least in part, to be a deliberate strategy intended to discourage them from remaining there. In this regard, it may have enjoyed some success: many researchers suspect that the number of Palestinians actually residing in Lebanon may be roughly half of what UNRWA figures suggest.

Palestinian refugees are also found in a number of other Arab countries, as well as elsewhere around the world. In Kuwait, the once very large Palestinian community dwindled sharply after the1990–91 Gulf War. In Iraq, Palestinians have found themselves particularly vulnerable to the violence in that country since the US intervention in 2003, and many have sought to flee (Brynen and Romano 2006). In Egypt, the Palestinian refugee community has only limited rights, and its members continue to be treated as temporary residents (El-Abed 2009).

Negotiating the refugee issue

As noted earlier, Israelis and Palestinians have sought on several occasions to negotiate a resolution of the refugee issue as part of a larger Israeli–Palestinian peace agreement. While those efforts have been unsuccessful, they have contributed to a greater understanding of the various questions involved. So too have various informal discussions (notably the unofficial Geneva Accord, written by prominent Palestinian and Israeli figures in 2003), dialogues, and academic and policy research initiatives (for an overview, see Brynen 2008). All of these proposed solutions, it should be emphasized, presuppose that the refugee issue is resolved as part of an overall Israeli–Palestinian peace agreement that also leads to the establishment of a Palestinian state in the West Bank and Gaza.

Return, repatriation, and resettlement

The single most important – and controversial – dimension of the refugee issue has been the question of the return, or non-return, of refugees and their descendants to those areas from which they were displaced in 1948 (Aruri 2001). At the Camp David negotiations in July 2000, the PLO demanded that Israel recognize the refugees' right of return. In exchange for acceptance of the *principle*, the Palestinians would be prepared to show flexibility on issues of *implementation*, so that Israel did not receive an excessive number of returnees. Palestinian negotiators expressed the view that many refugees would not wish to live in Israel, but would rather repatriate to a Palestinian state in the West Bank and Gaza or accept permanent resettlement in current host countries or elsewhere. However, it was essential that each refugee be given a free choice from a full range of options.

Israel rejected this. It did not accept that there was a Palestinian right of return to begin with, nor were Israeli negotiators prepared to accept a "right" that had unclear or unknown future implications for the Jewish character of the state. Instead, they argued that the refugees would be limited largely to repatriation to the Palestinian state or resettlement outside it. At most, Israel might be prepared to accept a very limited and largely symbolic number of refugees returning, on humanitarian grounds, under the rubric of "family reunification."

Fundamentally there were two issues at stake here: the question of principle and the issue of numbers. In an attempt to bridge the gap between the two parties, then US President Bill Clinton suggested the following compromise formulation in December 2000:

> The solution will have to be consistent with the two-state approach that both sides have accepted as a way to end the Palestinian-Israeli conflict: the state of Palestine as the homeland of the Palestinian people and the state of Israel as the homeland of the Jewish people.
>
> Under the two-state solution, the guiding principle should be that the Palestinian state would be the focal point for Palestinians who choose to return to the area without ruling out that Israel will accept some of these refugees.
>
> I believe that we need to adopt a formulation on the right of return that will make clear that there is no specific right of return to Israel itself but that does not negate the aspirations of the Palestinian people to return to the area.
>
> In light of the above, I propose two alternatives:
>
> 1 Both sides recognize the right of Palestinian refugees to return to historic Palestine, or,
> 2 Both sides recognize the right of Palestinian refugees to return to their homeland.
>
> The agreement will define the implementation of this general right in a way that is consistent with the two-state solution. It would list the five possible homes for the refugees:
>
> 1 The state of Palestine
> 2 Areas in Israel being transferred to Palestine in the land swap
> 3 Rehabilitation in host country
> 4 Resettlement in third country
> 5 Admission to Israel.
>
> In listing these options, the agreement will make clear that the return to the West Bank, Gaza Strip, and areas acquired in the land swap would be the right of all Palestinian refugees, while rehabilitation in host countries, resettlement in third countries and absorption into Israel will depend upon the policies of those countries.
>
> Israel could indicate in the agreement that it intends to establish a policy so that some of the refugees would be absorbed into Israel consistent with Israel's sovereign decision.
>
> I believe that priority should be given to the refugee population in Lebanon.
>
> The parties would agree that this implements Resolution 194.

The Clinton Parameters essentially proposed the return of only a limited and symbolic number of refugees to Israel, but wrapped this in the rhetorical trappings of the "right of return" and Resolution 194. These proposals became the basis for further talks in Taba in January 2001, where the parties did make some additional progress on the issue. In oral communications, members of the Israeli negotiating team suggested that 25,000 refugees might be accepted over three years or 40,000 over five years, in the context of a fifteen-year program of absorption. This ambiguous formula could be read as representing the return of anything from a low of 25,000 to a high of 125,000 or more refugees. It is unclear how much – if any – support these numbers had from the Israeli prime minister or cabinet, however. As an alternative to this,

Israeli negotiators had also suggested granting the "right of return" to original 1948 refugees only – a relatively small number who were well past reproductive age and therefore posed no demographic threat to the Jewish character of the state. This proposal was deemed unacceptable by the Palestinian side. Palestinian negotiators had been urged to press for refugee return "in the six figures" by their leadership, but with no more explicit political guidance. They also continued to demand more explicit recognition of the principle of the right of return.

With the gradual collapse of the peace process and the upsurge of violence that accompanied the Second *Intifada* (September 2000 to 2005), attitudes eventually hardened. By the time that permanent-status negotiations were renewed at Annapolis in November 2007, Israel was much less willing to accept the return of even a purely symbolic number of refugees. Prime Minister Ehud Olmert, while stressing that "under absolutely no circumstances will there be a right of return" (*Haaretz*, 15 September 2008), was willing to consider the admission of some refugees – perhaps 1,000 per year for a period of five years, according to press reports. On the Palestinian side, amid criticism from his Hamas rivals that he was prepared to abandon the principle, President Mahmud Abbas reiterated the importance of the right of return. In any event, the subsequent Netanyahu government declared its opposition to any refugee return whatsoever.

Sometimes lost in the focus on the emotive issue of return to 1948 areas are the other residential options that would likely also be presented to refugees as part of a peace agreement. The question of *refugee repatriation to a future Palestinian state* is perhaps the least controversial, although it has not always been so. Until 2001, it was not clear that Israel would agree to the free movement of Palestinians from the diaspora to the West Bank and Gaza even with a peace agreement. It is extremely unlikely, however, that Palestinians would accept a state with restrictions on that most crucial element of sovereignty – namely, the ability to confer citizenship and admit citizens. Questions are also sometimes raised regarding the ability of the new state to accept large numbers of repatriates without destabilizing political and economic consequences. In recent years considerable work has been done on this issue by the Palestinian Authority, the World Bank, and others. The general consensus is that, given appropriate policies, refugees are likely to make rational and appropriate decisions about repatriation that match the absorptive capacity of the nascent state, with population flows linked to employment and investment opportunities, wages, prices, and social conditions (for a detailed discussion, see Brynen and El-Rifai 2007).

Permanent settlement in current host countries is a sensitive issue, especially in Lebanon, where there is both a broad national consensus and a constitutional amendment against the naturalization of Palestinian refugees. Perhaps, in the context of an overall agreement, Lebanon might be willing to accept the settlement of some refugees, albeit as Palestinian citizens with permanent Lebanese residency rather than as Lebanese citizens. This might be the case especially for the substantial number of mixed Palestinian-Lebanese families. However the Lebanese would certainly want to see many Palestinians depart. Because of this, Israeli–Palestinian negotiations on the issue in 2000–01 often assigned particular priority to the return or repatriation of refugees from Lebanon to Palestine. Syria, for its part, long supported the refugees' right of return. It is unlikely, however, that any Syrian government would strip them of their residency or push them to leave in the aftermath of a peace agreement. Its precise attitude might depend, however, on the status of Israeli–Syrian relations. Absent the return of the Israeli-occupied Golan Heights to Syria, Damascus may have little incentive to cooperate with implementation of an Israeli–Palestinian peace deal. In Jordan, most refugees are already Jordanian citizens, and – while it might raise concerns among some (non-Palestinian) East Bank Jordanians, there would be little obstacle to their remaining in Jordan if they so chose. The Jordanian authorities would like to see the much smaller number of non-Jordanian Palestinians (for the most part, Gazans or later arrivals from the West Bank) repatriated to the

Palestinian state. However, given the realities of Jordanian domestic politics, they are unlikely to force them to leave abruptly.

Finally, there is the possibility of some refugees being resettled in third countries outside the Middle East, such as in Europe, the USA, Canada, and Australia. While there are some modern precedents for large-scale third-country resettlement – notably the case of Ugandan Asian and Indochinese refugees in the 1970s and 1980s – it appears unlikely that Western countries would offer large numbers of places to Palestinian refugees. This is especially true in a post-9/11 era of heightened security concerns and tightened immigration and refugee laws. Indeed, despite the rumors sometimes found in the Middle Eastern press about plots to resettle the refugees in third countries, there has been no serious discussion by governments about doing so.

Restitution, reparations, and compensation

Officially, the Palestinian position on refugee properties has been that Israel should, where possible, return these to their original owners. Israel has flatly refused to consider any sort of *property restitution*, however. Given the very large number of Israelis today living in homes or on lands that were seized from their former Palestinian owners, such restitution would be extremely unpopular with the Israeli Jewish public.

Instead, negotiations have tended to focus on the question of *reparations* or *compensation* for refugee property. Palestinians tend to favor the former term, since it suggests righting a past moral wrong or criminal act. Israelis prefer the latter term, since it has no implicit admission of guilt. While the question of compensating refugees was controversial for many years – with Israelis reluctant to pay, and Palestinians fearful that accepting compensation would be at the expense of their other rights as refugees – this sensitivity had faded by the time permanent-status negotiations began in 2000. Nevertheless, the issue is a highly complex one, with a number of areas of disagreement (Fischbach 2003).

The most obvious of these is *who should pay*, and *how much*? Estimates of Palestinian losses in 1948 range from $3.4 billion to over $235 billion, depending on what losses are considered (fixed property, moveable property, various immaterial losses), how they are valued, and how 1948 losses are converted to current values (PRRN 1999). The PLO has pressed for an agreement to include an Israeli commitment to finance levels of compensation, following a full evaluation by an international commission of Palestinian refugee losses. Israeli negotiators, by contrast, have been wary about agreeing in advance to pay an amount that is yet to be determined, and have instead proposed that Israel offer a fixed sum to an international compensation fund to which international donors would also contribute. The amount that Israel would be willing to contribute has yet to be clearly specified, but typically it is thought to be around $3 billion. This is well below most estimates of Palestinian property losses, and would be inadequate to compensate some 4.6 million or more refugees. While the USA suggested at Camp David that a total of $20 billion might be available from an international fund for refugees, many Western donors have privately expressed a reluctance to finance compensation. Since Israel still holds refugee properties, they argue, it is appropriate that it – and not Western taxpayers – pay for these. Western aid agencies would much rather finance other aspects of the peace agreement, such as assisting the social and economic development of the Palestinian state or facilitating the return, repatriation, resettlement, and development of refugee communities.

The question of which party funds refugee compensation is not just about the financial burden. It is also about responsibility for the refugee issue. Palestinians argue that it is appropriate that Israel bear primary responsibility for compensation – whatever the amount might turn out to be – since it was Israel that forcibly displaced the refugees, seized their property, and prevented their return. Israel would prefer to be only one of several countries contributing to an international fund for Palestinian refugees, in part because it does not accept that it bears primary responsibility for the refugee issue.

Further complicating all of this is the question of Jews who left from Arab countries to Israel in 1948 or afterwards. Israel has claimed that, because these Jews often faced attacks, discrimination, or a lack of protection from their own Arab governments, they should also be considered refugees and receive compensation (Fischbach 2008). Palestinian negotiators have responded that this ought to be an issue between Israel and the Arab governments concerned and not a matter for an Israeli–Palestinian peace agreement. Israel's failure to demand compensation from those countries with which it already has peace agreements – Egypt and Jordan – is seen as confirmation that the issue is raised largely in an attempt to offset Palestinian claims, rather than on its own merits.

Even were there to be agreement on the amount and source of refugee compensation, there are also complex challenges in deciding *to whom it should be paid, and how*. Should compensation be collective and paid to the Palestinian state and host governments? Or should it be paid to individuals? In the latter case, should it be paid to first-generation refugees or to all? Should it be a flat per capita amount or based on documented property losses? Should it be paid in cash, or should part of it take the form of vouchers and entitlements?

In past negotiations there has been general agreement that compensation should be paid to individuals, both to redress their past suffering and because individual compensation was thought to be much more effective at mobilizing refugee support for a deal. At Camp David, the positions put forward by both sides envisaged compensation being paid for particular, documented property losses. By the time of the Taba negotiations in January 2001, however, the idea of compensation payments to all refugees on a per capita basis was discussed, in addition to claims-based payments to former property-holders and their heirs. This idea was further developed in the unofficial Geneva Accord of 2003.

Per capita payments have several advantages. They assure that compensation is paid to all refugees for the suffering they have experienced, and not just those able to show former ownership of specific properties. By contrast, a wholly claims-based system would tend to reproduce the inequalities of pre-1948 Palestine, where relatively wealthy landowners owned a large share of agriculture land. It would also assure that female refugees would receive an equal share of compensation. A per capita system of payments would be much faster and easier to administer than attempting to determine the ownership and value of properties more than a half century – and several generations of refugees – after their loss. A compensation scheme might be designed, for example, whereby claims below a certain monetary value are treated on a fast-tracked basis with a standardized payment, and only larger claims are subject to later adjudication.

With regard to what form compensation payments might take, some have suggested that refugees should be encouraged to spend their compensation in productive ways by paying part of it as vouchers that could be used for education, vocational training, or other services. There has also been some concern that multi-billion dollar compensation could have inflationary or other dislocating economic effects. In general, however, most analysts have regarded cash payments as the most effective and flexible, with refugee households best placed to determine how they can most effectively utilize additional resources.

Moral acknowledgement

As is evident from the preceding discussion, the refugee issue is not simply about questions of residency and financial resources. It is very much a dispute over moral responsibility too.

Attempts to underplay this element and focus instead on more technical solutions ignore the weight of history, the sense of injustice involved, and the extent to which the refugee issue touches upon an existential nerve for Palestinians and Israelis alike. On the Palestinian side, this is not something that is unique to the refugees alone. Public opinion surveys show that non-refugee Palestinians view the issue as just as important as do refugees. Nor, as is sometimes charged, is the refugee question an aspect of the conflict that has been artificially kept alive by Palestinian leaders, Arab regimes, refugee camps, UNRWA, or academics. Given that Jewish communities mourned their historical expulsion from the Holy Land for millennia, it is hardly surprising that Palestinian refugees – most of whom still reside within 100 kilometers or so of their original homes – would still harbor a deep sense of historical attachment to Palestine and a sense of grievance at their expulsion.

The issue of moral acknowledgement is also not one that can simply be "bought off" with offers of financial compensation. Indeed, recent social science research shows that, while addressing such normative issues directly increases Palestinian willingness to compromise, attempting to circumvent them through offers of financial assistance tends to alienate and anger respondents (Atran and Ginges 2009).

Because of its importance, PLO negotiators have consistently pressed for any refugee agreement to contain some expression of Israeli regret and responsibility for what happened in 1948. Israelis, viewing that period through a different historical lens (and, at times, a certain amount of historical amnesia), tend to reject the idea that they *were* responsible. Israeli negotiators are also wary about the longer-term legal implications of admitting fault. Ironically, there is something of a trade-off between the issue of symbolic responsibility and the material issues of return and compensation. The more regret and responsibility Israel expresses in any future agreement, the less return it may have to accept and the less compensation it may have to pay. Conversely, refusal to address the issue of moral acknowledgement may increase the material "price" that Israel has to pay in any agreement.

Discussions on the question at Camp David were largely a dialogue of the deaf, with the two sides exchanging mutually incompatible views of the events of 1948 and about who was responsible for what. Perhaps because US mediators failed fully to appreciate the importance of these issues, there was little attention to the question of moral acknowledgement in the Clinton Parameters. However, there was a serious and good faith effort by Israeli and Palestinian negotiators to come to grips with the issue at Taba, in the form of a joint "narrative" of their fundamentally entwined pasts. Ultimately this was unsuccessful. The Israeli discussion paper presented at Taba did, however, express "sorrow for the tragedy of the Palestinian refugees." While this was less than the Israeli full acceptance of "moral and legal responsibility for the forced displacement and dispossession of the Palestinian civilian population during the 1948 war and for preventing the refugees from returning to their homes" sought by the PLO, it did go beyond the rather limited statement that Israel had been prepared to offer at Camp David six months earlier ("The parties are cognizant of the suffering caused to individuals and communities on both sides during and following the 1948 War . . . "). Much later, during the Annapolis rounds of negotiations in 2008, then Israeli Prime Minister Ehud Olmert largely reiterated the Taba formulation when he expressed "sorrow for what happened to the Palestinians and also for what happened to the Jews who were expelled from Arab states."

While moral acknowledgement has been a Palestinian priority, Israeli negotiators have sought something else in an agreement: a definitive statement of the end of refugee claims and final resolution of the refugee issue. References to this abound in Israeli negotiating documents. The PLO has been prepared to state this, but only on condition that refugee rights and Israeli obligations are fully addressed.

Development of refugee communities

Cross-cutting many of the issues above is the challenge of the social and economic development of refugee communities in the aftermath of an agreement. This is especially the case for the large number of refugees who would reside in, or repatriate to, a future Palestinian state or who would remain in their present host countries.

The World Bank and the Palestinian Authority undertook significant research and planning on these issues in the years 1999 to 2003, as they contemplated possible future repatriation of refugees to the West Bank and Gaza. Among the key lessons of this work were that repatriation flows should be voluntary and linked to economic realities, rather than distorted by perverse incentives and pressures; that refugee planning ought to be part of a broader policy of planning for demographic change in the Palestinian territories, especially with regard to housing policies; that, while it was possible to improve living conditions in former refugee camps, eliminating or replacing these residential areas entirely was likely to be too costly; that donor resources are likely to be limited; and that compensation payments to refugees will be a key part of the development process (Brynen 2006; Brynen and El-Rifai 2007).

There is also the question of what happens to UNRWA. While few doubt that it would eventually be wound down in the aftermath of a comprehensive peace agreement, Israelis and Palestinians tend to differ as to how fast this should be done. The former would prefer it to be terminated sooner rather than later, as a concrete expression of the end of the refugee issue. Conversely, the latter would prefer that it stay in existence until an agreement is fully implemented. For their part, host countries (and the future Palestinian state) worry about the cost of eventually assuming responsibility for the health and education services that are currently provided to many refugees by UNRWA and financed by donor contributions (PRRN 2000).

Conclusion

In two public opinion surveys conducted in December 2008, a large minority of both Palestinians (40 percent) and Israelis (40 percent) expressed a willingness to accept a resolution of the refugee issue based loosely on the Clinton Parameters, the Taba negotiations, and the Geneva Accord (PCPSR 2008). A slight majority, however – 58 percent of Palestinians and 54 percent of Israelis – opposed such a deal. An earlier 2003 poll of Palestinian refugees in the West Bank and Gaza, Jordan, and Lebanon found relatively few enthusiastic about such a arrangement, but half or more would be prepared to accept it were it to be agreed between the PLO and Israel (PCPSR 2003).

Such responses highlight the significant gulf that exists between the two sides on the issue. Indeed, the refugee component of any future deal will likely be a focal point of efforts by both right-wing Israeli and Palestinian rejectionists as they seek to mobilize political opposition to a peace agreement. It is also important not to underestimate the challenge of implementing a refugee agreement should one ever be reached. As this chapter has noted, the resources required are immense, the technical complexities are myriad, and the political sensitivities involved are enormous. As one simulation of Palestinian refugee negotiations by academic experts and former officials noted, the parties will need to meet the challenges of public communication, building political support, managing expectations, coordinating the international community, consulting refugees and other stakeholders, and making sure that the intricacies of an agreement are workable (Chatham House 2008).

As large as these challenges are, however, they are not insurmountable. Polling data indicate that substantial proportions of *both* populations can agree on the general parameters for resolving the refugee issue, if not the precise details. There also seems to be growing support among Arab states for such a compromise. The Arab peace initiative adopted by the League of Arab States in March 2002 called for "achievement of a just solution to the Palestinian refugee problem to be agreed upon in accordance with UN General Assembly Resolution 194" – a statement noteworthy for not explicitly invoking an unlimited right of return, while at the same time emphasizing the need for Israeli concurrence. (A second clause rejected "all forms of Palestinian settlement which conflict with the special circumstances of the Arab host countries" – a reference to Lebanon's unwillingness to naturalize its Palestinian refugee population.)

In practice, however, the prospects for meaningful resumption of permanent status talks seem rather grim at present. The Palestinian polity remains split, between a Fateh-controlled West Bank and a Hamas-controlled Gaza Strip. Israeli Prime Minister Netanyahu and his right-wing coalition government are unlikely to make the sorts of reasonable compromises that would make an agreement possible. In the meanwhile, illegal Israeli settlement activity continues in occupied Palestinian territory. In this context, resolution of the refugee issue – and, for that matter, achievement of a Palestinian state – is unlikely to occur for some considerable time to come.

References and further reading

Aruri, Naseer (ed.) (2001) *Palestinian Refugees: The Right of Return* (London: Pluto Press).

Atran, Scott, and Ginges, Jeremy (2009) "How Words Could End a War," *New York Times*, 25 January.

Bowker, Robert (2003) *Palestinian Refugees: Mythology, Identity, and the Search for Peace* (Boulder, CO: Lynne Rienner).

Brynen, Rex (2006) "Perspectives on Palestinian Repatriation," in Michael Dumper (ed.), *Palestinian Refugee Repatriation: Global Perspectives* (London: Routledge).

Brynen, Rex (2008) *Past as Prelude? Negotiating the Palestinian Refugee Issue*, Chatham House Briefing Paper MEP/PR BP 08/01 (London: Chatham House); available online at www.chathamhouse.org/sites/default/files/public/Research/Middle%20East/0608palrefugees_brynen.pdf.

Brynen, Rex, and Romano, David (2006) "The Palestinians: Finding No Freedom in Liberation," in Rick Fawn and Raymond Hinnebusch (eds), *The Iraq War: Causes and Consequences* (Boulder, CO: Lynne Rienner).

Brynen, Rex, and El-Rifai, Roula (eds) (2007) *Palestinian Refugees: Challenges of Repatriation and Development* (London: I. B. Tauris).

Chatham House (2008) *The Regional Dimension of the Palestinian Refugee Issue: Simulation Exercise Report* (London: Chatham House); available online at www.chathamhouse.org/sites/default/files/public/Research/Middle%20East/12092_prsimulation0608.pdf.

El-Abed, Oroub (2009) *Unprotected: Palestinians in Egypt Since 1948* (Washington DC: Institute for Palestine Studies and International Development Research Centre).

Fischbach, Michael (2003) *Records of Dispossession: Palestinian Refugee Property and the Arab–Israeli Conflict* (New York: Columbia University Press).

Fischbach, Michael (2008) *Jewish Property Claims against Arab Countries* (New York: Columbia University Press).

Morris, Benny (1989) *The Birth of the Palestinian Refugee Problem* (Cambridge: Cambridge University Press).

PCPSR (Palestinian Center for Policy and Survey Research) (2003) "Results of PSR Refugees' Polls in the West Bank/Gaza Strip, Jordan and Lebanon on Refugees' Preferences and Behavior in a Palestinian–Israeli Permanent Refugee Agreement," January–June, available online at www.pcpsr.org/survey/polls/2003/refugeesjune03.html.

PCPSR (Palestinian Center for Policy and Survey Research) (2008) "Following Obama's Election, Palestinians and Israelis Seek a More Active Role of the US in Moderating the Conflict," Joint Israeli–Palestinian Poll, December, available online at www.pcpsr.org/survey/polls/2008/p30ejoint.html.

PLO (Palestine Liberation Organization) (2008) *Fact Sheet: Palestinian Refugees* (Ramallah: Negotiations Affairs Department).

PRRN (Palestinian Refugee ResearchNet) (1999) Workshop on Compensation as Part of Comprehensive Solution to the Palestinian Refugee Problem, Ottawa, 14–15 July (Ottawa: International Development Research Centre), available online at http://prrn.mcgill.ca/prrn/prcomp.html.

PRRN (Palestinian Refugee ResearchNet) (2000) Workshop on the Future of UNRWA, Minster Lovell, UK, 19–20 February; available online at http://prrn.mcgill.ca/prrn/prunrwa.html.

Schiff, Benjamin (1995) *Refugees unto the Third Generation: UN Aid to Palestinians* (Syracuse, NY: Syracuse University Press).

Sher, Gilead (2006) *The Israeli–Palestinian Peace Negotiations, 1999–2001* (London: Routledge).

Zureik, Elia (1996) *Palestinian Refugees and the Peace Process* (Washington, DC: Institute for Palestine Studies).

10
Jerusalem

Michael Dumper

Overview

Jerusalem is one of the most ancient and famous cities in the world. Its political, cultural and religious significance is unparalleled, making the control of the city hotly contested throughout its history. Nowadays, although a bustling modern city, Jerusalem bears the heavy weight of its past, and the competing historical and religious narratives, claims and counter-claims of ownership and sovereignty have produced ideologically driven policies creating further division and prolonging conflict between Israelis and Palestinians. The analyses found in contemporary literature on the subject of Jerusalem are similarly contested, with every manner of political, religious and historical bias represented. This chapter attempts to steer a course through such difficult waters.

Jerusalem is located approximately 60 kilometres east of the Mediterranean coast and the port city of Tel Aviv–Jaffa. It is set in the barren central highlands of the former territory of Mandate Palestine, and the land surrounding the city has little agricultural value and extremely limited water supplies. This, combined with the historical lack of strategic value either as a centre of trade or as a military asset, appears to have endowed Jerusalem with little scope for economic activity and growth. Its significance in history and in contemporary politics is derived, therefore, not from any economic or strategic concerns, but from its essential character as a city holy to the three monotheistic faiths of the Middle East: Judaism, Islam and Christianity.

The city is the site of the of the Crucifixion and burial of Jesus of Nazareth, the site of the earliest Israelite Temple, and the site where the Prophet Muhammad first turned in prayer when he founded the Islamic faith. The history and politics of Jerusalem have been inexorably linked to the rituals and beliefs of these three faiths, which have held it as the focus of their religious and political aspirations for centuries. The walled Old City in the heart of Jerusalem, an area layered with ancient archaeological remains and important religious sites, exemplifies the religious and cultural importance of the city. It contains the Jewish Western Wall, the Muslim Haram al-Sharif and the Church of the Holy Sepulchre. The economy of the city has historically been based on these and other holy sites and the revenue generated by the pilgrims that visit each year.

Of Jerusalem's current population of approximately 700,000 people, two-thirds are Israeli Jews and the rest are Palestinian Arabs.[1] Because of its centrality to the ongoing conflict between the two national groups, Jerusalem is claimed by both sides, although it remains under Israeli control. Israel declared West Jerusalem as its capital in 1948 and in 1967 unilaterally declared sovereignty over the entire city, proclaiming it as the 'eternal, undivided' capital of Israel. The status of Jerusalem as the Israeli capital is disputed both by Palestinians and by a large corpus of international legal rulings which challenge the legality and legitimacy of Israeli actions. The contestation of these declarations provides the background for the contemporary political significance of the city.

Historical background

Ancient period

Jerusalem has been subject in its history to constantly changing rulers, destruction and rebuilding. The earliest evidence of human settlement can be traced to the Jebusite period, around 1800 BCE, with evidence of a walled settlement, housing foundations, water supply and tombs. Jerusalem was conquered by the Israelite tribes under King David and became the capital of their kingdom, uniting the tribal areas of Judah and Benjamin. King Solomon expanded the city and built the Jewish Temple. The enlarged city became a significant commercial centre on the trade route leading to the Arabian heartland. The Babylonian invasion in 587 BCE ended Israelite control in Jerusalem; its rulers were executed and the population deported to Mesopotamia. Under Persian rule, the Israelites returned to Jerusalem in 539 BCE, but they were prevented from establishing political control over the city, although the Temple was rebuilt. Jerusalem passed into Greek control between 332 and 168 BCE, ushering in a period of tolerance when Jewish law and ritual were renewed. The Hellenic period also saw a number of Jewish uprisings against the ruling Seleucid Greeks after Torah observance was outlawed, and the city was destroyed. In 141 BCE the Maccabee Revolt established a period of Jewish control.

Roman period

The Roman period succeeded Hellenic rule, lasting from 63 BCE until the Muslim invasion in 638 CE. Roman rule over Jerusalem can be divided into two periods. In the first period, the Empire was subject to direct rule from Rome, and the established order of Roman pagan worship allowed some religious autonomy and freedom for the Jews. However, all aspirations to Jewish political independence were ruthlessly crushed. Roman domination of Jerusalem reached its zenith between 69 and 70 CE with the destruction of the Second Temple. Emperor Hadrian exiled most of the population and made the city a Roman colony, which was renamed Aeolia Capitolina. During this period, the first Christian communities in Jerusalem were established. In the second period, the Roman Empire was divided in two. Jerusalem became part of the Eastern Empire, ruled from Byzantium. As Emperor Constantine converted to Christianity, the status of the city within the Christian Empire was greatly raised: churches, such as the Holy Sepulchre, Christian colonies and pilgrimages became a central feature of economic and cultural life in Jerusalem.

First Islamic period and Crusader period

The Islamic conquest of Jerusalem in 638 CE led to nearly 1,300 years of Islamic rule in the city that lasted, with the exception of the Crusader Kingdom of Jerusalem, until the mid-twentieth century. The Prophet Muhammad's successor, 'Umar ibn Khattab, conquered Jerusalem in order to secure the holy sites for Islam. Jerusalem had been the first *qibla*, or direction of prayer in Islam, as well as the site of the Prophet Muhammad's ascension to Heaven, according to the Qur'an. 'Umar and his Umayyad successors fostered good relations with the Christian churches and permitted annual Jewish pilgrimages to the city, as well as raising its profile and prestige in the Islamic world by building the al-Aqsa and Dome of the Rock mosques between 685 and 709 CE. Changes in regional politics forced a decline in Jerusalem's prestige and allowed Christians and Jews to become involved in its administration, leading to increased Christian pilgrimage and a weakening of Muslim rule. In 1099, European Crusader armies entered the city, slaughtered or expelled most of the residents, and embarked on a sustained period of Christian construction and pilgrimage which lasted until the recapture of the city by Salah ed-Din in 1187.

Second Islamic period: Ayyubid, Mamluk and Ottoman period

From this point in the city's history there was a long period of unbroken Islamic rule. The Ayyubid period that followed Salah ed-Din's capture of Jerusalem was characterized by large-scale economic investment in the construction of housing, public baths, markets and facilities for pilgrims. A number of large Muslim religious endowments, or *waqfs*, were established in order to attract investment and income for Jerusalem, particularly for the restoration of the Haram al-Sharif. But the city's lack of strategic value in military and economic terms and lack of resources instigated a decline in its importance and a degree of economic and social stagnation during most of the thirteenth century. This stagnation emphasized Jerusalem's lack of importance as a political or administrative centre, but the subsequent rise to power of the Mamluk dynasty renewed its importance as a Muslim sacred site. The Mamluks offered protected *dhimmi* status to the small insular Jewish community, ensuring a measure of religious freedom. The wealth of the Mamluk princes in Jerusalem attracted funds from large endowments, which were directed into the construction of buildings of exceptional architectural splendour. The reaffirmation of Jerusalem's sacred status and its new-found wealth attracted large numbers of Muslim pilgrims, who revitalized the city's economy, and also led to a large number of creative works by religious poets and scholars praising the city.

In 1517 the Ottoman Turks took over Jerusalem, founding a dynasty that remained unbroken until the early twentieth century. The Ottomans laid the foundation for the development of modern Jerusalem, expanding beyond the old walls of the city. European influence was guaranteed by the 'capitulation' treaties with European countries, giving them powers over many Christian holy sites and establishing a hierarchy for the various Christian denominations which became known as the 'Status Quo' arrangements. These arrangements, with some significant changes, have formed the basis of the administration of the holy sites in Jerusalem to the present day. The declining power of the Ottoman state in the nineteenth century allowed Britain to become more involved in Jerusalem as sponsors of Jewish immigration. In 1917, during the course of the First World War, Britain took control of the city, then the largest in Palestine.

British Mandate

The British Mandate of Palestine, established in 1922, oversaw Jerusalem's transition to a European-style city in terms of demographics, culture and appearance. British administration was centred in the city, improving its economy, and British support for Jewish immigration saw the Jewish population of Jerusalem treble between 1922 and 1946. Jewish immigration,

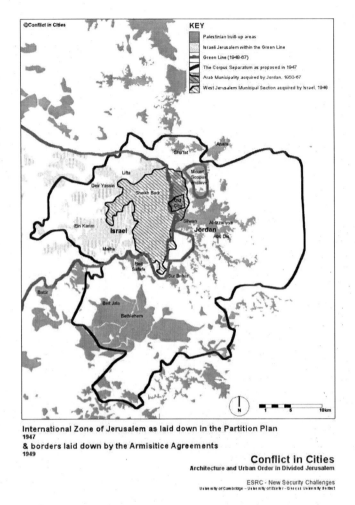

International Zone of Jerusalem as laid down in the Partition Plan
1947
& borders laid down by the Armisitice Agreements
1949

Conflict in Cities
Architecture and Urban Order in Divided Jerusalem

ESRC - New Security Challenges
University of Cambridge - University of Exeter - Queens University Belfast

Figure 10.1 International zone of Jerusalem as laid down in the partition plan, 1947, and borders laid down by the armistice agreements, 1949

the sidelining of Muslim political authority in the city and disputes over access to holy places led to a rise in communal tensions between Jews and Arabs. The United Nations, in Resolution 181, advocated partitioning Palestine and creating an international *corpus separatum* around Jerusalem. Palestinians rejected this proposal, and the war that broke out following British withdrawal in 1948 led to an armistice and the partition of the city into an Israeli-held west and a Jordanian-held east.

The division of Jerusalem in the aftermath of the 1948 war lasted until June 1967, when Israel conquered East Jerusalem. During this period, Israel annexed West Jerusalem and proclaimed it as the capital of the new state of Israel (see Figure 10.1). The Israeli government invested heavily in West Jerusalem, attempting to address the economic disadvantage of being cut off from its natural hinterland to the east and the lucrative holy places in East Jerusalem. The government offices of the new Israeli state were built in West Jerusalem, and water and power supplies to the area were ensured. These activities led to the population doubling to

200,000 Jews, but the lack of economic stimulus caused hardship and dependency on government employment. In the same period, the Hashemite Kingdom of Jordan had annexed East Jerusalem, but the population for that part of the city remained unchanged. Palestinian Arab refugees from the western part of the city balanced the outward migration of people seeking work and a move away from hostile territory. The presence of the holy places in the Old City boosted the economy, but being cut off from the coastal plains and ports offset this advantage. The 1967 war and the Israeli occupation of East Jerusalem and the West Bank brought a number of new dimensions to an already tense conflict. Nowhere was this more obvious than in Jerusalem.

Key issues since 1967

Political annexation

Israel's dominance of Jerusalem culminated in an act of *de facto* political annexation, whereby Israel assumed sovereignty over the entire city shortly after the war. The annexation of Jerusalem, from the viewpoint of Israel, was a legitimate act as well as a political and national imperative. Israel has argued that it was forced to occupy East Jerusalem in self-defence against Jordanian attack, and that it assumed sovereignty and political control in the ensuing vacuum after the war. It is important to note that this *de facto* annexation of East Jerusalem comprised a new expanded municipal boundary which included territory that extended to the outskirts of Ramallah in the north and Bethlehem in the south (see Figure 10.2). In addition, the Jordanian municipal authority in East Jerusalem was dissolved and absorbed by the Israeli municipality. The issue of Israeli sovereignty, and the passing of a Knesset bill in 1980 asserting Israel's unassailable national right to the entire city, denies or ignores Palestinian claims of national or territorial rights in East Jerusalem, although significant ambiguities concerning Israeli sovereignty and legal authority do exist. Tensions between the Palestinian Arab and Israeli Jewish communities have been constant since the unification of the city under Israeli rule. The Palestinian residents view the Israeli occupation and annexation of East Jerusalem as illegal, and most residents have responded to it with boycotts of local elections. The annexation of East Jerusalem brought with it a number of coercive unilateral measures, taken at both municipal and governmental level, which blur perceptions of the reality of Israeli occupation.

Exclusivist ideology

The capture and annexation of Jerusalem was viewed positively in Israel. After the war there was a sense of renewed national pride and religious fervour on account of the re-establishment of Jewish control over the Old City and the holy places. The Israeli conception of Jerusalem as a fundamentally Jewish city led to the expression of an exclusivist ideology that sought to assert the Jewish nature of Jerusalem, physically, demographically and culturally, often at the expense of the Palestinian Arab residents. For example, the Palestinian quarter around the Western Wall was demolished in order to construct a large plaza for Israeli Jewish worshippers. Palestinians in East Jerusalem can obtain residency of the city, but they are not citizens of Israel and they are not permitted to vote in Knesset elections; nor are Israeli laws applied with equal measure in both sections of the city. Although it represents one-third of the population, the Jerusalem municipality proportionately spends significantly less money: only 11 per cent of its budget is spent in Arab areas. As a result the provision of municipal services is much smaller in the Palestinian areas of the city. In addition, the Israeli government has adopted a policy of ensuring a

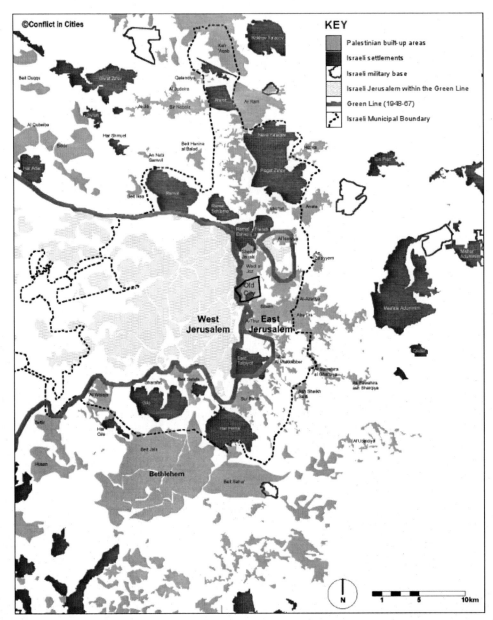

Jerusalem: new Israeli municipal border and settlements
after 1967

Figure 10.2 Jerusalem: new Israeli municipal border and settlements after 1967

minimum two-thirds Jewish majority in the city, encouraging Jewish migration and settlement in the eastern suburbs and making the expansion of Palestinian neighbourhoods all but impossible. The ostensible principle of this Israeli policy is the creation of a united 'open' city where free access to residential and sacred sites is guaranteed to all. However, much of the evidence suggests an ideological focus on Judaizing the city and eroding the Palestinian Arab identity and presence in East Jerusalem.[2]

Land acquisition and the construction of Israeli settlements

The acquisition of Palestinian Arab-owned land in East Jerusalem is perhaps the most politically sensitive of Israeli post-1967 policies in the city. The issues of demography and land ownership have been central to the Israeli–Palestinian conflict since its inception, and have particular relevance in Jerusalem. In keeping with the ideological predisposition of the Judaization of Jerusalem, Israel expanded the municipal boundary and began to acquire as much land in the east of the city as possible. The methods of land appropriation that have been utilized include the manipulation of land zoning and building permit laws. The municipality and central government acted to reserve as much real estate as possible for Jewish residents and severely inhibited construction and expansion in Palestinian Arab neighborhoods. Similarly, by amending its 'Absentee Property' law, Israel simultaneously facilitated the confiscation of 'enemy' properties in the east as well as preventing the reclamation of Palestinian Arab property in West Jerusalem. These policies have been backed by the extensive use of punitive property demolition and land confiscation in order to prevent unauthorized Palestinian construction. The result of this is that approximately 35 per cent of East Jerusalem has come under direct Israeli control, and the use of some 80 per cent is denied to Palestinians through restrictive zoning and planning decisions. Invoking the 'open city' principle has facilitated Israeli appropriation of Arab land in East Jerusalem in order to create pockets of Jewish settlement in the east.[3]

In order to attain and ensure control over East Jerusalem, the Israeli government sought to increase significantly the Jewish population, creating a Jewish Israeli demographic bloc which would prevent the eastern part of the city from ever returning to Palestinian or Jordanian rule. Acting on this imperative to strengthen its position on the ground, the Israeli government encouraged Jewish migration to the east of the city, often settling new immigrants in the area, and has to date settled over 180,000 Jews in East Jerusalem. The policy of Jewish settlement of East Jerusalem has had a dual impact. The settlements offer a consolidation of Israeli physical control over the city, creating rings of Jewish suburbs that surround and isolate Palestinian areas, making them enclaves in a modern Israeli city. The Jewish settlements also serve as buffers between the Palestinian neighbourhoods of East Jerusalem and the West Bank, cutting off the Palestinian areas from their natural economic, political and population hinterland. From the Israeli perspective, East Jerusalem is an integral part of the state, and Jewish residency in any part of the city is an incontrovertible right. From the Palestinian perspective, these Israeli policies are interpreted as attempts to negate Palestinian claims to sovereignty as well as to preclude the possibility of East Jerusalem being included in any final peace agreement.

Holy sites

Israeli policy towards the holy sites in East Jerusalem and the religious communities that administer them is subject to much scrutiny and debate. In this context, one can see how Israeli policies have been geared largely towards the placation and reassurance of the international community that Israel would ensure the protection of the sites and freedom of access to them.

However, a concurrent ideologically led policy was pursued of extending state control over religious sites, which restricted the autonomy of non-Jewish groups and gave significant influence to the Jewish religious hierarchy. The issue of sovereignty over the holy places is extremely controversial, particularly with regard to the Haram al-Sharif. Israeli attempts to assert control over the Haram, which incorporates part of the remains of the Jewish Temple, have been fiercely resisted, leading to rioting in 1996, although the construction of a police station on the site and considerable excavations and tunnelling underneath it have gone ahead. The issue of authority over the Haram remains a contested one. However, the framework of Muslim religious administration has remained relatively unchanged since Jordanian rule. The many Christian communities, which are often in conflict with one another, had enjoyed the protection of the 'status quo' agreement since the Ottoman period, but since 1967 have been unable to secure an Israeli commitment to the continuation of this arrangement. This leaves them exposed to potential state intervention, although their sites remain under the ownership of the controlling Christian denominations.[4]

The separation barrier

The cultural isolation of East Jerusalem from the West Bank has been achieved with the establishment since 1967 of groups of Israeli Jewish settlements that encircle Palestinian suburbs, cutting them off from the large Palestinian population reservoir and economic centres in the Jerusalem hinterland. The separation barrier or wall which marks the physical division of East Jerusalem from the West Bank is an ominous presence that looms over any discussion of East Jerusalem. Consisting of 20 kilometres of concrete between 4 and 9 metres high, and an additional 57 kilometres of fencing, the barrier carves directly through a number of Palestinian villages and suburbs in Jerusalem, potentially separating 100,000 Palestinian Jerusalemites from the city's education, hospital and religious sites, as well as cutting off the Palestinian population of the city from an invaluable reservoir of labour and commercial markets (see Figure 10.3).

The construction of the barrier was a measure taken by Israel as a drastic security response to the devastating series of suicide bomb attacks on Israeli Jews in Jerusalem from Islamic and other militants based in the West Bank. It has damaged Israel's standing in the international community, and the International Court of Justice ruling in 2003 further highlighted the illegal nature of its presence in East Jerusalem. It also led to an increase in the Palestinian population on the western side of the barrier, as Palestinians moved to ensure their access to education and services there. For the Palestinians in the city, the construction of the barrier caused major physical damage to the functioning of East Jerusalem, economic stagnation by denying the West Bank labour force access, and further internal displacement. Finally, the barrier has introduced a serious political impediment to the pursuit of a negotiated settlement between Israelis and Palestinians over the future of the city.

Jerusalem and the peace process

Jerusalem in international law

The position of the international community, through UN fora and the rulings of international law on Jerusalem, has frequently been invoked throughout the long-running Arab–Israeli conflict. UN General Assembly Resolution 181, passed in 1947, recommended the creation of a *corpus separatum* in Jerusalem, highlighting the UN's refusal to acknowledge any party's claim to sovereignty over the city. International opinion on the 1948 Israeli annexation of West

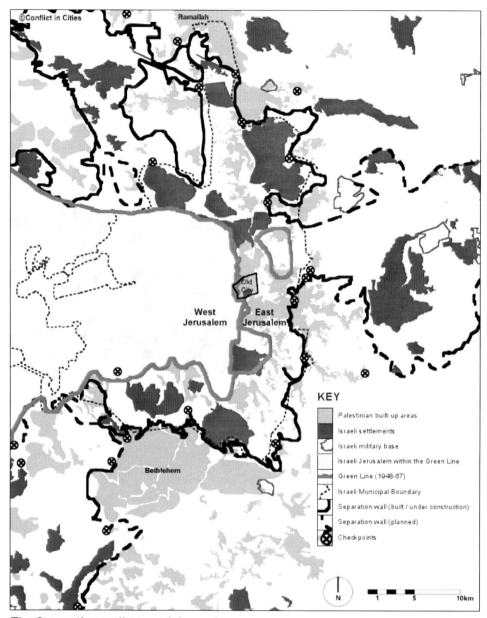

The Separation wall around Jerusalem
March 2007

KEY

- Palestinian built-up areas
- Israeli settlements
- Israeli military base
- Israeli Jerusalem within the Green Line
- Green Line (1948-67)
- Israeli Municipal Boundary
- Separation wall (built / under construction)
- Separation wall (planned)
- Checkpoints

N   1   5   10km

Conflict in Cities
Architecture and Urban Order in Divided Jerusalem

ESRC - New Security Challenges
University of Cambridge – University of Exeter – Queens University Belfast

Figure 10.3 The separation wall around Jerusalem, March 2007

Jerusalem also reflected this position, promoting a consistent refusal to recognize any part of Jerusalem as Israeli territory, let alone as the capital. This position remains the official international consensus and official UN stance to this day, although to some extent Resolution 181 has been subsumed in subsequent decisions.

After Israel's occupation of East Jerusalem in 1967, the UN Security Council passed Resolution 237, condemning the annexation of East Jerusalem. Resolution 242, although not mentioning Jerusalem directly, demanded a withdrawal of Israeli forces to the 1949 armistice lines, thereby relinquishing control of East Jerusalem. The passing of the 1980 Knesset law on Jerusalem was interpreted as an attempt by Israel to prevent the implementation of the legally binding existing UN resolutions and elicited a resolution containing a strongly worded condemnation from the Security Council. The International Court of Justice, the judicial arm of the UN, ruled in an advisory opinion in 2004 that the separation wall was illegal and stressed the illegitimacy of the Israeli occupation of East Jerusalem. Taken together, these resolutions comprise a forceful corpus of binding international law that denies the legitimacy and legality of Israeli actions in all of Jerusalem, and in the east of the city specifically. While the overall direction of international law on Jerusalem is clear, Israel has been able to point out the contradictions between Resolution 181, recommending a *corpus separatum*, and Resolution 242, demanding a withdrawal to the 1949 armistice lines, as an example of the lack of clarity in international law. In addition, the lack of action taken by the UN to enforce its rulings exhibits a deficiency of political will among the key players in the international community. The USA has adopted a policy of vetoing or abstaining from UN resolutions concerning Israeli actions in Jerusalem, and the EU is constrained by the existing American monopoly over Arab–Israeli mediation, as well as by the lack of coordination between member states. This has led Israel to interpret the absence of enforcement as acquiescence on their part and therefore to act without hindrance in Jerusalem.

The Israeli perspective of its acquisition of Jerusalem is that it gained possession of the city through lawful acts of self-defence in times of war, and was entitled to do so as a historical and national right. The 1967 unification of Jerusalem was not held to be an annexation, but rather an act of administrative and municipal integration. Israel constantly and publicly asserts the legitimacy of its sovereignty over the city, and has consistently refused to acknowledge the international legal rulings that delegitimize its rule in East Jerusalem. Jerusalem is officially deemed beyond negotiation. Given the city's symbolic and religious importance to Israel, as well as the Jewish population investment in East Jerusalem, many governments have declared that there is no possibility of its inclusion in a peace agreement. This position has been tempered in recent years with the tacit recognition of the necessity and also the desirability of including at least some Palestinian suburbs of East Jerusalem in the territory of any future Palestinian state. Israel has been aided by the relative ambiguity in international law. As the internationally accepted basis for peace negotiations, Resolution 242, contains no explicit reference to Jerusalem, Israel has maintained that there is no binding resolution on its future.

On the other side, the Palestinian perspective of the Jerusalem issue is firmly rooted in Resolution 242. The call for Israeli withdrawal from territories conquered in 1967 and the assertion of the inadmissibility of territory conquered by force are integral features of Resolution 242. International law gives considerable backing to Palestinian political aspirations and to claims that East Jerusalem is being occupied and settled in violation of legally binding resolutions. For Palestinians, East Jerusalem is the religious, cultural and economic centre of the territory that they claim, and was, until Israeli settlement, a predominantly Arab city that was forcibly taken from their control. Palestinians claim Jerusalem as no less significant in their history and culture then it is for Israelis.

From Oslo to Geneva

Jerusalem has played a pivotal role in the peace process as a 'final-status' issue since the Israelis and Palestinians first negotiated and signed the Oslo Accords in 1993. It is impossible to foresee any stable political agreement between the two sides without an agreement on Jerusalem. The Oslo Accords explicitly refer to the city and are based partly on Resolution 242, implying an Israeli withdrawal from East Jerusalem. In the Accords, Jerusalem was categorized as a 'final-status' issue, to be discussed after other phased aspects, including the establishment of an interim regime (the Palestinian National Authority – PNA), were implemented in the West Bank in the framework of a lasting peace.[5] However, the Oslo Accords began to unravel soon after they were implemented. The Israeli reluctance to cease settlement-building and the inability of the PNA to curb Islamic militancy led to profound mutual suspicions, both of each side's commitment to the Accords and of their true intentions. Any serious discussion of Jerusalem under the Oslo Accords was thus continually deferred and has yet to take place.

The Camp David summit in 2000, between Israeli, Palestinian and US leaders, proved similarly unfruitful in addressing the issue of Jerusalem. Israel proposed allowing the PNA to administer some northern suburbs of the city and the devolution of administrative power in some of central East Jerusalem, but Israel was to retain overall sovereignty and control of the Old City (see Figure 10.4). The Palestinians countered with a demand of adherence to Resolution 242 and the implied withdrawal from East Jerusalem, resulting in a stalemate and a breakdown in trust. In an attempt to rescue the peace process, negotiators met again in the Egyptian resort of Taba in 2001. Here both sides agreed to delineate sovereignty in Jerusalem, accepting Israeli settlements in the east and Palestinian sovereignty up to the 1949 armistice line, with an agreement in place to discuss the holy sites. This was the first time that Israel accepted the possibility of Jerusalem being shared by two states.[6] The informal Geneva Initiative of 2003 continued the Taba proposals and included phased Palestinian sovereignty over the Haram, Israeli sovereignty over the Mount of Olives and the Western Wall, and a special regime for the Old City. The Geneva Initiative also allowed for third-party intervention, creating a role for UNESCO and a monitoring religious body.[7] The combined effect of these talks has been to move opinion away from the maximalist demands of both sides and towards a compromise, but at the time of writing no further convergence in positions has been reached.

Alternative models

There have been proposals for alternative models to the two-state solution and the division of Jerusalem that is implied, although they remain somewhat on the fringe of current discussions on the future governance of the city. In order to avoid the division of Jerusalem, and to ensure the freedom of access to holy sites, the possibility of creating either a bi-national federation, a confederation or a unitary state in Israel/Palestine has been explored by a number of writers since the 1930s. Such models are loosely referred to as 'one-state' solutions, as they advocate some form of political arrangement such as federalism, consociationalism or a single unitary polity, which would effectively create one state, resulting in coordination, joint access and political control of Jerusalem for both parties.[8]

One scenario, for example, would be for the entire territory of Israel and Palestine to be united under a single political authority which would contain two component states, one for each national group, with Jerusalem as the capital of each and for the united polity. This would ensure shared sovereignty between both national groups and access to all areas of the city, including the holy places. The other model that as been explored is the creation of an

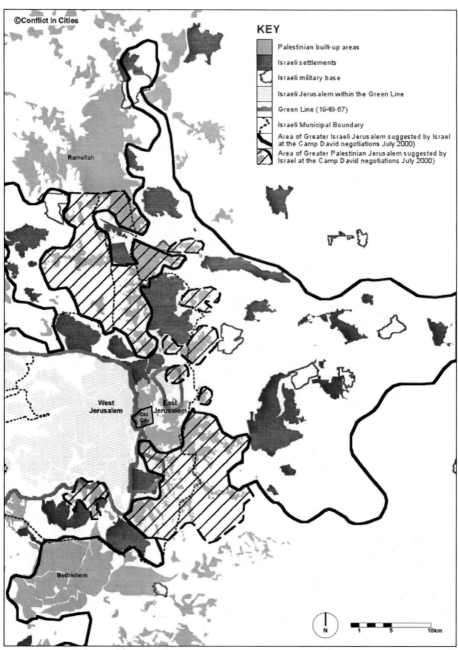

KEY

Palestinian built-up areas

Israeli settlements

Israeli military base

Israeli Jerusalem within the Green Line

Green Line (1948-67)

Israeli Municipal Boundary

Area of Greater Israeli Jerusalem suggested by Israel at the Camp David negotiations July 2000)

Area of Greater Palestinian Jerusalem suggested by Israel at the Camp David negotiations July 2000)

©Conflict in Cities

Ramallah

West Jerusalem

East Jerusalem

Old City

Bethlehem

N

1   5   10km

Jerusalem: Camp David proposals
2000

Conflict in Cities
Architecture and Urban Order in Divided Jerusalem

ESRC - New Security Challenges
University of Cambridge - University of Exeter - Queens University Belfast

Figure 10.4 Jerusalem: Camp David proposals, 2000

extra-territorial entity in Jerusalem, in line with the *corpus separatum* plan from 1947. The Jerusalem area would become an independent entity, the rule of which would be coordinated between the resident national groups. Central to the alternative models is their capacity to offer reconciliation in Jerusalem through shared sovereignty, freedom of access and residency, and shared control of sites crucial to religious and national identity. These options have largely remained on the periphery of any discussion of Jerusalem, labelled as politically unfeasible by external actors, and as unthinkable capitulations to the 'other' by the main protagonists. Nevertheless, they continue to receive attention both for their promotion of political coordination between Jews and Arabs in the governance of Jerusalem and for their role as catalyst in focusing efforts on a two-state solution.[9]

Conclusion

Jerusalem has been a contested city for much of its history and remains one today. It reflects the major issues of the Arab–Israeli conflict in a microcosm, making it a useful unit of analysis. Jerusalem also brings its own issues to the conflict. The sacred nature of the city drives the religious and political aspirations of all parties and feeds the clash between competing national and historical narratives. The attempts to consolidate a Jewish hegemony in East Jerusalem, while successful in demographic terms, have been somewhat undermined by the relatively ambiguous nature of Israeli sovereignty and legal authority in the east of the city. In the same way, Israel's ideological preference for Jewish exclusiveness in Jerusalem weakens its intention to control the entire city. The difficulty inherent in incorporating a hostile population, combined with the exclusionary principles inherent in mainstream Zionism, has led to the construction of multiple overlapping borders in Jerusalem in terms of applying education policies, legal jurisdictions and municipal services. Given the virtual abdication of municipal responsibility for Palestinian areas in Jerusalem, other groups, such as NGOs, religious denominations and political parties, have stepped in to provide services and structure for Palestinian residents separate from the Israeli state, highlighting the fundamental contradiction in Israeli approaches to Jerusalem. At the same time, the growth of Islamic militancy and intolerance over the future of the city has constrained the room for manoeuvre of the PNA, and the possibilities of some shared governance of the city have receded in recent years.

Jerusalem is a city that lacks many basic resources, yet ideological imperatives will continue to influence the growth of the city's population and the separateness of its communities. The emotions associated with the issue of control do not bode well for its future. However, the acknowledgement of the necessity to address realistically the Jerusalem issue in peace negotiations, in terms of a partitioned territory or the implementation of some form of cooperative administration, provides a glimmer of hope for the future of the city. A resolution in the framework of a negotiated settlement between the parties remains the outstanding desire of the international community, as well as of the majority of Israelis and Palestinians.

Notes

1   According to the Jerusalem Institute for Israel Studies, the population of Jerusalem in 2008 stood as follows: total (Palestinian, Israeli and Other) 763,600; Jewish and Other 495,000; Palestinian Arab 268,600. During 2007 the total population grew by 1.9 per cent (14,300 people), the Jewish population by 1.3 per cent (6,100) and the Arab population by 3.2 per cent (8,200). From 1967 to 2007 the population grew by 181 per cent, the Jewish population by 146 per cent and the Palestinian Arab population by 280 per cent. Further details are available at www.jiis.org/.upload/publications/

facts-2008-eng.pdf. Note that these figures refer to the municipal borders established in 1967 and not only those areas inside the separation wall.

2 Dumper and Pullan (2010).

3 Further details can be obtained from a report by the UN Office for the Coordination of Humanitarian Affairs (UN-OCHA), *The Planning Crisis in East Jerusalem: Understanding the Phenomenon of 'Illegal' Construction* (April 2009), available at: http://unispal.un.org/UNISPAL.NSF/0/2F8FB6437DB17 CA5852575A9004D7CB4.

4 Dumper (2001).

5 For the legal aspects of the Oslo Accords, see G. R. Watson, *The Oslo Accords: International Law and the Israeli–Palestinian Peace Agreements* (Oxford: Oxford University Press, 2000).

6 Akiva Eldar, 'The "Moratinos Document": The Peace that Nearly Was at Taba', *Haaretz*, 14 February 2002.

7 Geneva Accord, *The Geneva Accord: A Model Israeli–Palestinian Peace Agreement* (1 December 2003), available online at www.geneva-accord.org, at article 6.3.

8 For a fuller discussion of this issue, see As'ad Ghanem, 'The Bi-National State Solution', *Israel Studies*, 14/2 (2009), pp. 120–33; Leila Farsakh, 'Israel–Palestine: Time for a Bi-national State', *Electronic Intifada*, 20 March 2007, available at: http://electronicintifada.net/v2/article6702.shtml; Virginia Tilley, 'From "Jewish State and Arab State" to "Israel and Palestine"? International Norms, Ethnocracy, and the Two-State Solution', *Arab World Geographer*, 8/3 (2005), pp.140–46.

9 Michael Dumper, *'Two-State Plus': The Binationalism Debate and the Future of Jerusalem*, Working Paper no. 16, 2010; available online at: www.conflictincities.org/workingpapers.html.

References and further reading

Armstrong, K. (1996) *Jerusalem: One City, Three Faiths* (London: HarperCollins).

Asali, K. J. ed.) (2002) *Jerusalem in History: 3000 BC to Present* (London: Kegan Paul).

Benvenisti, M. (1996) *City of Stone: The Hidden History of Jerusalem* (Berkeley: University of California Press).

Blum, Y. Z. (1974) *The Juridical Status of Jerusalem* (Jerusalem: Hebrew University).

Cattan, H. (1981) *Jerusalem* (London: Croom Helm).

Dumper, M. (1997) *The Politics of Jerusalem since 1967* (New York: Columbia University Press).

Dumper, M. (2001) *The Politics of Sacred Space: The Old City of Jerusalem in the Middle East Conflict* (Boulder, CO: Lynne Rienner).

Dumper, M., and Pullan, W. (2010) *Jerusalem: The Cost of Failure*, Briefing Paper MENAP 2010/03 (London: Chatham House).

Friedland, R., and Hecht, R. D. (2000) *To Rule Jerusalem* (Berkeley: University of California Press).

Kark, R. (2001) *Jerusalem and its Environs: Quarter, Neighborhoods, Villages, 1800–1948* (Detroit: Wayne State University Press).

Klein, M. (2001) *Jerusalem the Contested City* (London: Hurst).

Lapidot, R., and Hirsch, M. (1994) *The Jerusalem Question and its Resolution: Selected Documents* (Dordrecht: Kluwer Academic).

Ricca, S. (2007) *Reinventing Jerusalem: Israel's Reconstruction of the Jewish Quarter after 1967* (London: I. B. Tauris).

11

Territory and borders

David Newman

The evolution of Israel's interstate boundaries

Only two of Israel's five potential land borders have the status of internationally recognized boundaries, a fact that is unique to states in the contemporary world. The two borders, between Israel and Egypt and between Israel and Jordan, achieved that status only following the respective peace agreements between the countries, in 1979 and 1994. Before those dates, all of Israel's borders were, at best, agreed armistice lines drawn up in the wake of its War of Independence in 1948–9 or imposed lines of administrative division following the Six Day War of 1967. The ultimate demarcation and location of the recognized boundaries with Egypt and Jordan were based largely on the boundaries that had existed before the wars, and the same is to be expected if, and when, boundaries are eventually demarcated with Lebanon and Syria – although the case of Syria is more problematic given the dispute, because of its strategic importance, over the Golan Heights. For as long as there is no formal agreement between the neighbouring states, boundaries remain officially designated as armistice lines and open to modification in future peace talks.

The history of boundary demarcation in this region is recent, dating from the final break-up of the Ottoman Empire, in the second decade of the twentieth century, and the division of the territory by the League of Nations between the two Mandate powers, France and Great Britain. The northern boundary of the British administered territory (the southern boundary of the French territory) is almost identical to Israel's northern boundary with Lebanon, the line which was determined in the armistice talks in Rhodes in 1948–9, and to which Israel withdrew in 2000 following their eighteen-year-long occupation of southern Lebanon. Israel's southern boundary with Egypt, formally agreed as part of the Israel–Egypt peace accords in 1979, is based on the southern boundary line of the British Mandate area. The ultimate control of the Taba area was disputed between the two countries before the finalization of the Camp David peace agreements but was eventually awarded to Egypt following international arbitration. Israel's eastern border with Jordan (not including the section which borders the West Bank) is the line drawn up by the British Mandate authorities in 1921, following the partition of historical Palestine and the creation of the new State of Transjordan. The line follows the course of the Jordan Rift Valley from the Syrian border in the north until the Gulf of Aqaba in the south. In the northern section, the Jordan River constitutes the boundary, and, on a number of occasions, the border has shifted in accordance with slight shifts in the course of the river. Given the lack of water flow during the past three decades, the course of the river, and hence the boundary, has remained in situ. Israel's border with Lebanon was also drawn up by the Mandate authorities following the division of the area between the British and the French. At the time, the British wanted the boundary to be located further to the north, to include the Litani River, but this was not accepted by the League of Nations. The border to which Israel withdrew in 2000, following almost two decades of its occupation of southern Lebanon, was almost identical to that of the Mandate division, although there remains a dispute over the small region around the Shabah farms. The most contested boundary is that with Syria, given the fact that Israel now controls the entire Golan Heights which, before 1967, had been under Syrian control. Israel is reluctant to withdraw from this area, given the strategic importance of the region and the fact that it overlooks the farms and villages of northern Israel. For its part, Syria refuses to undertake any peace agreement with Israel without the return of the Golan Heights to its control and the evacuation of all Israeli settlements which have been established there in the post-1967 era.

The rest of this chapter deals with the fifth boundary – that between Israel and the West Bank, which will potentially constitute the border between Israel and a sovereign State of Palestine if and when such a state is established as part of a peace agreement. This is more complex than any of the other four boundaries, not least because of its location in the geographical centre of Israel and the fact that it divides populations. The essay will examine the history of this boundary, known as the 'Green Line', and will analyse the various components through which it will be reconstituted and potentially redemarcated as part of a future peace agreement.

The Green Line: the evolution of a boundary in conflict

Israel's most famous border is, in effect, non-existent in international terms. The Green Line, separating Israel from the West Bank, was drawn up as an armistice line immediately following the War of Independence in 1948–9, following the Rhodes armistice talks which took place between Israel and Jordan. The line largely reflected the position of the respective troops at the cessation of hostilities. It was delimited and fortified during the subsequent two years, and remained as the official line of separation between Israel and the West Bank (a territory administered by the State of Jordan) until the Six Day War in 1967, during which Israeli troops conquered the West Bank and extended their control as far as the Jordan River in the east. Since 1967, Israel has constituted the occupying power throughout the West Bank, such that the Green Line was relegated to the status of an internal administrative boundary between sovereign Israel and those territories under occupation and governed according to the civil administration of the military government.

Despite successive Israeli governments pronouncing the demise of the Green Line and even removing it from all official maps and atlases, it continued as the line dividing Israel from the Occupied Territories, if only because no Israeli government attempted to annex the newly acquired territories to the State of Israel (with the notable exception of East Jerusalem). As such, the laws appertaining to the civilian administration of the Palestinian population residing inside the West Bank (and Gaza Strip) were different to those inside Israel. No citizenship rights were granted to the Palestinian residents of this region, who remain – to the present day – stateless for as long as there is no formal international recognition of an independent and sovereign Palestinian state in this region.

Following the outbreak of the First *Intifada*, which took place in 1987 (some twenty years after the Six Day War), the Israeli government began to re-impose a boundary regime on the

West Bank as a means of preventing the unchecked flow of Palestinians from the Occupied Territories into Israel, even as daily commuters to fill the menial labour jobs within the Israeli economy. Continual curfews and closing down of the Occupied Territories took place along the course of, or in close proximity to, the Green Line almost by default, the major exceptions being in those areas where the construction of Jewish settlements had served to blur the clear distinctions between the two sides. Over the next twenty years, the boundary was reinforced, largely because of a series of security concerns, as defined by the Israeli government and military authorities, culminating in the construction of what has become known as the separation barrier from 2004 onwards.

This barrier, in part electrified fence, and in smaller part concrete wall (especially in around the urban areas), has redefined the Green Line according to new physical realities. It is true to the course of the Green Line for approximately 70 per cent of its length, deviating mostly in those areas where the government has desired to keep the Israeli settlements on the Israeli side of the line. Many of these deviations were ruled as illegal by both the International Court of Justice and the Israeli Supreme Court during the 2000s, resulting in their being redrawn in some locations. In no case has the line deviated to the west, inside Israel – meaning that all such deviations have effectively annexed Palestinian land from the West Bank to Israel. It is this reality which has given rise to the idea of land exchanges as part of a permanent territorial solution to the conflict based on the two-state solution, in which the Palestinian state will have no less land than was originally the case following the drawing up of the Green Line in 1949.

The physical construction of the separation barrier has meant that the border discourse inside Israel has been transformed from an abstract notion into one which is concrete and tangible. Many Israelis encounter the border as they drive through Jerusalem or along the trans-Israel highway. The vast majority of Israeli citizens, who never travel into the West Bank, either out of fear for their personal safety or because they are opposed to driving into what they perceive as illegally occupied territory, are now more fully aware of the specific point beyond which they should not cross. Five distinct border crossing points have been constructed along the course of the separation barrier, at which point travellers have to show their documents or be recognized as bona fide travellers to pass from one side to the other. Palestinians require special permits to enter Israel (Israelis do not require any special documents to enter the West Bank), and cars with Palestinian licence plates are not allowed beyond the border.

Palestinian claims to a sovereign territory of their own have focused increasingly around the calls for a return to 'borders of 1967' – namely, the Green Line. For them, this is a minimalist demand given the fact that such a demand is recognition of the fact that they no longer lay claim to the rest of Mandate Palestine (over 70 per cent of the territory), which now constitutes the State of Israel. For Israel, the calls for a return to the Green Line is perceived as being a maximalist demand, as though the Palestinians should be prepared to 'compromise' over some parts of that territory, given the geographical and demographic changes which have taken place in the forty-five years which have passed since the 1967 war, most notably the construction of Israeli settlements beyond the Green Line. It is this counter-claim to boundary demarcation which serves as the basis for understanding the political discourses surrounding the territorial arrangements and negotiations as part of a final resolution of the conflict.

Conflict resolution and the process of border demarcation: territorial and cartographic imaginations

Since the signing of the Oslo Agreements in 1993 and 1995, there have been ongoing discussions and negotiations concerning the future demarcation of a border as part of a proposed two-state solution to the complex problem of Israel–Palestine. This has taken place at a number of levels, largely within the context of the Track II meetings, which provide important professional input for decision-makers and government leaders if, and when, Track I – namely, direct political negotiations between heads of state – takes place, but also in various Israeli 'offers' at the Track I level, such as Camp David, Taba and Prime Minister Olmert's territorial offer.

The default position for border demarcation is the Green Line. From a Palestinian perspective, this is the border which existed before the events of the Six Day War in June 1967 and would transform the armistice line of 1948–9 into an internationally recognized boundary. It would also signify the Palestinian acceptance of the West Bank as constituting the territory of an independent Palestinian state, and their abandoning of claims to other parts of Israel which were also part of the pre-state single Mandate territory of Palestine between the Jordan River and the Mediterranean Sea. From a Palestinian perspective, this is perceived as a significant concession, accepting only 22 per cent of the Mandate Palestine territory as constituting their sovereign state.

From an Israeli perspective, a return to the Green Line is more problematic, owing to the settlement infrastructure which now exists within the West Bank, encompassing a network of small towns and communities consisting (as of 2012) of over 300,000 residents. This figure does not include the neighbourhoods of East Jerusalem, with a further 300,000 residents. Israel insists that East Jerusalem is not part of the area defined as 'occupied' or 'administered', as a result of the Israeli annexation ('extension of civilian law') of the eastern part of the city by a vote in the Israeli parliament (the Knesset) shortly after the Six Day War in 1967. This annexation led to a redrawing of the municipal boundaries, to include the entire city, but it has become physically divided again – albeit along entirely different lines – following the erection of the separation barrier through parts Jerusalem.

The alternative scenario to an automatic return to the Green Line is based around the argument that an Israeli government (even of a left-wing persuasion) is unwilling, or unable, forcefully to remove over a quarter of a million settlers, a large percentage of whom have settled this area for ideological and religious reasons and are therefore unwilling to give up their homes in return for generous financial compensation and resettlement back inside Israel proper. The scenes which accompanied the forced removal of the 7,000 settlers of the Gaza region in the summer of 2005 are seen as being no more than a small prelude of what could be expected if a similar scenario were practised with respect to the entire West Bank settler population, and could potentially lead to levels of violence between settlers and soldiers of an extent which the government is unable to manage, and even bring about fatalities. As such, Israeli governments are wary of their ability to commit to such a scenario and have constantly sought to legitimize part of their occupation policy by seeking alternative border demarcations which would enable a significant part of the settler population to remain in their homes and under Israeli sovereignty.

The initial proposals for the redrawing of boundaries to retain control of much of the settlement infrastructure in situ was assumed, by Israeli policy-makers, to mean that the extent of a Palestinian state would be smaller than that encompassed by the West Bank, a scenario which is of course unacceptable to even the most moderate of Palestinian negotiators. This has been reflected in the erection of the separation barrier, which deviates from the Green line along about 30 per cent of its course, but only in an easterly direction – namely, inside the West Bank, never inside Israel. In all those parts, the deviation takes into account the Israeli desire to retain territorial control of major settlement blocs which are located in close proximity to the Green Line.

This reflects a basic dissonance in the respective territorial discourses of the two sides. While the Israeli territorial perspective is based on a discourse which views the West Bank only as the source of the conflict and therefore a territory which can be further divided, the Palestinian territorial discourse is one which sees the entire pre-state area of Palestine as the territory to be divided and, as such, the entire West Bank is a minimalist territorial demand on their part. Thus the concept of the 'whole' territory is different for Israelis and for Palestinians. For Israel, the Palestinians insist on retaining control of the 'whole' territory and are not prepared to compromise on a single metre, while, for the Palestinians, the 'whole' territory – namely Mandate Palestine – has already been divided and therefore the 'whole' of the West Bank is no more than the remaining quarter part of that territory, to which Israel should have no claims whatsoever.

In the later stages of border discourse there has therefore been acceptance that, even if the territorial shape of the West Bank undergoes change as a result of bilateral conflict resolution, the size of the Palestinian territory must remain the same, without further encroachments. Notions of territorial exchange and land swaps, ideas which would have seemed fictional to the average Israeli as recently as the period of the Oslo Agreements in the mid-1990s, have now become a central part of the discourse. This is based on the idea that, if Israel were to demand the redrawing of the border in such a way as to annex anything up to 10 per cent of the region to the State of Israel, the Palestinian state would have to be compensated by an equal amount of land along and around those parts of the Green Line which are unsettled on the Israeli side of the border.

Imaginative land-swap alternatives have also included such ideas as compensating the Palestinian state with an area of land adjacent to the densely populated Gaza Strip region, which, in current thinking, and despite the political rise to power of the Hamas movement, is still perceived by most as constituting part and parcel of a Palestinian state consisting of two territories, connected by a land link and safe passage through the south of Israel. Professor Ben-Arie, a geographer and past rector of the Hebrew University of Jerusalem, went as far as proposing a regional series of land swaps and territorial exchanges which would include both Israel and Egypt transferring land to the Gaza area in order to expand its land base and allow it some breathing space; Israel, Jordan and Egypt exchanging land in the Red Sea Eilat–Aqaba regions; and the transfer of land in the West Bank to Israel. A territorial solution of this nature would, in the view of Ben-Arie, add an important regional dimension to the nature of conflict resolution.

Regarding land swaps around the Green Line, two areas of potential exchange have been identified, with vastly different political and demographic significance for both Israel and a Palestinian state. The area to the south of the Green Line, south of Qirya Gat and bordering on the Beer Sheba and Hebron Hills region, is largely unsettled inside Israel, although there have been attempts to bolster the Jewish presence in this region during the past two decades. This is also an area where the country's growing Bedouin population (roughly estimated to be around the 200,000 mark at the beginning of 2011) is concentrated. Cross-border links between the Bedouin population of this region and the Palestinian residents of the southern parts of the West Bank exist, although this has become increasingly complicated with the construction of the physical separation barrier and the difficulty of crossing from one side to the other.

The second area of potential land swaps to have been identified is in the northern section of the West Bank. Unlike the relatively unsettled southern area, the northern region consists of a dense population of Arab-Palestinian citizens of the State of Israel, including such major towns as Um el Fahm and Tayibe and numerous smaller townships and villages. Right-wing politicians within Israel, many of whom are still opposed to the principle of a two-state solution to the conflict, have stated their reluctant acceptance of such a solution, but only if the land swaps were to take place in this northern region, resulting in the relocation of some of the Arab villages presently located in Israel to the Palestinian side of the redrawn boundary. This would, in effect, be a 'silent transfer' of population, redefining the citizenship of the residents simply by redrawing the border, as happened in many European countries following the end of the First World War. In this way, the right-wing parties would reduce the percentage of the Arab minority in Israel overnight, from approximately 20 per cent to less than 15 percent.

The land-swap ideas do not deal with a critical issue concerning settlement – namely, the fact that there still remain at least a third of the settlements (approx 100,000) which are on the 'wrong' side of the line and, as such, would have to be evacuated by the Israeli government. Not only is this a large number, but it consists of the most ideologically oriented groups among the settler population – those who came out of a historic or religious belief that the Land of Israel belongs to them, and not for economic incentives such as cheap houses or the interest-free mortgages offered to Israeli residents by right-wing governments as an incentive to get them to relocated beyond the Green Line – most of whom reside in close proximity to the Green Line, not in the interior regions of the West Bank. There is a geographic paradox here, in that many of the settlers who would be prepared voluntarily to evacuate, if and when they were offered adequate economic compensation to purchase a house back inside Israel, would not have to relocate because of border changes which would leave their settlements inside Israel, while those who would refuse to relocate under any circumstances, and would have to be forcefully evacuated by the government, with real fears of physical violence and fatalities, are located mostly in those areas which, under any form of territorial redrawing of the borders, would remain on the Palestinian side of the line. This politico-geographic reality makes the implementation of the two-state solution even more difficult for Israeli governments.

Securitization discourses and border demarcation

The demarcation of borders within the Israel–Arab context have traditionally focused around notions of security and defence in a country which perceives itself as being subject to constant threat from each of its neighbours, even those with which it has a peace agreement. The Israel–Egypt border negotiations were finalized only after agreement was reached concerning much of the Sinai peninsula as a demilitarized zone, controlled by an international peacekeeping force. The peace agreement with Jordan included clauses which forbid Jordan from allowing any form of foreign military intervention or presence of foreign troops in their country, which would be seen by Israel as a legitimate *casus bellum*. The on–off discussions concerning a potential Israeli withdrawal from the Golan Heights as part of a future peace agreement with Syria are concentrated almost entirely around security dimensions and the perceived threat to the Israeli settlements in the Galilee region if the area was to be returned to Syrian control, with memories of the shelling which took place before the 1967 war.

The ongoing discussions concerning an eventual territorial withdrawal from the West Bank also have a strong security component, although this has become of lesser significance in recent years, with the major focus being on the issues discussed in the previous section of this chapter – namely, the presence of Israeli settlements and the possibilities of land swaps and territorial exchanges along the course of the Green Line.

But the securitization discourse has emerged afresh as a result of the construction of the security barrier between Israel and the West Bank, on the one hand, and the firing of rockets from the Gaza Strip (following Israeli withdrawal from this region), on the other. The construction of the separation barrier was, first and foremost, a unilateral Israeli response to the worsening of its national security and the infiltration of suicide bombers from the West Bank and Gaza into Israel's main population centres. Although, in reality, the security barrier has become transformed into an international border, with electrified fences, sophisticated surveillance technology and a limited number of crossing points, its initial rationale was, as far as the vast majority of Israelis were concerned, to prevent the movement of potential security risks (terrorists) from entering Israel. It is for this reason that it enjoyed the support of most Israeli citizens, regardless of their positions along the right–left political spectrum and the fact that it was initially implemented by a right-wing prime minister, Ariel Sharon, who – at that time – was opposed to the idea of creating a political border between Israel and the West Bank. It continues to be opposed by the settler community, who now find themselves on the 'wrong' side of the barrier, which has rapidly become associated in the minds of most Israelis as a future political border between two independent states. It has also transferred incidents of violence and terrorism from inside Israel proper to the settlements, as perpetrators of violence are no longer able to cross into Israel. For most Israelis, the construction of the separation fence has indeed resulted in a significant decrease in the incidents of violence and terror, and it is for this reason that they see a peace agreement as containing a clear commitment to boundary demarcation, and a closed, almost sealed, border between the two countries, at least in the first stages of implementation.

Before the 1990s, the return of the entire West Bank to Palestinian control was portrayed, mostly by right-wing politicians, as constituting a major security threat. It was common for maps of the region to show the missile radius from points along the Green Line border into the major Israeli cities and population centres. It was argued that the return of the area to the Palestinians would put almost the whole of Israel under threat of missile attack. This discourse has developed in the intervening period in two contrasting ways. On the one hand, following the first Gulf War in the early 1990s when, for the first time, long-range ballistic missiles were fired from Iraq into the heart of Israel, it was understood that the border played little significance in preventing such attacks, since the origin of the missiles was hundreds, even thousands, of kilometres distant. As weapons technology developed, so too would the long-range accuracy of such missiles and, as such, the precise location of the border would have little significance for this dimension of the securitization discourse. On the other hand, the return of the Gaza Strip to Palestinian control resulted in the firing from close range of small-scale missiles into the towns of southern Israel, such as Sderot, Ashqelon and even Beer Sheba, causing damage to civilian infrastructure, which had not previously been experienced in Israel's wars. This was repeated with the firing of missiles from southern Lebanon into the towns of northern Israel, reaching the major metropolitan centre of Haifa and its oil refineries. In both cases, Israel undertook major reprisal actions in Lebanon and the Gaza Strip, raising questions in the minds of many Israelis concerning the need to control (occupy) areas just beyond the border so as to prevent them from becoming transformed into missile launching sites, be it of the Iranian-supported Hizbollah in the north or Hamas-supported groups in the south. As such, the significance of the border vis-à-vis this aspect of securitization is an open question, while Israel's long-term strategy is to develop, in cooperation with the United States, a sophisticated 'iron dome' policy by which missiles can be detected and intercepted immediately after launching and before they hit any of their targets.

There has also been a major change in thinking concerning the security discourse of the country's eastern border. Immediately following the June 1967 War, Israeli government policy until 1977 was governed by what became known as the 'Allon Plan'. This, before the mass settlement of the West Bank region, was aimed at returning large parts of the area to Jordanian control through the granting of autonomy to the Palestinian residents of the region, while at the same time maintaining direct Israeli control over the eastern border running along the Jordan Rift Valley. The autonomous area would be linked to Jordan through a territorial corridor running from the West Bank town of Ramallah, north of Jerusalem, in a south-easterly direction, to include the one Palestinian town in the Jordan Valley, Jericho. As such Israel would not have to exercise direct control of the civilian population, while it would, according to its security perceptions of that time, maintain control over what became known as its 'defensive boundaries'. The notion of defensible boundaries was central to Israeli military and strategic thinking until the 1990s, while for some it remains a major component. But this concept has been brought into question during the past two decades, initially following the first Gulf War and the firing of long-range ballistic missiles into the heart of Israel in 1991, and then again following the ease with which both short- and long-range missiles were fired into northern and southern Israel respectively from southern Lebanon (Hizbollah) and the Gaza Strip (Hamas).

It was also increasingly understood by Israeli policy-makers that any attempt to reach a territorial solution to the conflict which would argue for the retention of the entire Jordan Valley by Israel would be automatically rejected by the Palestinians. Such a solution would mean that the Palestinian state would be denied huge areas of land, much of it – despite its difficult climatic conditions – available for development and even the settling of potential returning refugees, as well as turning the new state into a virtual enclave, surrounded on all sides by Israel. Thus, the combination of these reasons – the changing security environment and the realization of political realities, has gradually removed the Jordan Valley defensible border concept from Israeli territorial thinking. Under the present government (under Binyamin Netanyahu, 2012), the issue of the Jordan valley as a defensible border along the eastern margins of the country, never to be relinquished, has been raised afresh within public debate. But this is seen by many commentators as a means of fractioning the peace discourse which had already arrived at a conclusion that it could be implemented only through the establishment of a Palestinian state in a single compact territory, with a clear border with the State of Jordan.

Thinking beyond the box: territorial alternatives to a two-state solution

Much of the border discourse in this chapter could conveniently be described as being 'traditional', focusing on such issues as the drawing of lines, the role of borders in enhancing physical security, and the relationship between borders and territorial sovereignty. It is the type of discourse which many theorists have argued is no longer of relevance, either because almost all of the world's land boundaries have long been demarcated, and there are only a few contemporary examples of territorial and political conflict which arise out of 'positional disputes', or because theories of globalization and postmodernity argue for an era in which territorial fixation and rigid compartmentalization is passé, and that we have moved into a period in which borders are opening up, becoming increasingly porous, and in which we move beyond borders into a world of shared and hybrid political and social spaces.

The Israel–Palestine case study is clearly one where much of the traditional discourse is prominent: a country whose borders have not yet been determined, which claims sovereignty and control over pieces of disputed territory, and for which the security discourse remains a central part of the national psyche. Moreover, given the rapidly changing political realities, there are serious questions concerning the possibility of implementing a traditional solution of territorial separation and the delimitation of physical borders. Not least are the problems relating to the evacuation of settlements – regardless of the morality or legality of their construction in the first instance – as they become strongly implanted as part of a new geographic and territorial reality.

This has resulted in 'thinking beyond the territorial box', in which alternative ethno-territorial and ethno-political solutions have been suggested, at least as part of an interim period of conflict resolution. Such notions as a state in temporary borders, cross-citizenship (settlers remaining in the West Bank but retaining their Israeli citizenship, and Palestinian residents of Israel having the opportunity of choosing between Israeli or Palestinian citizenship), ethnocracy, and even a return to largely discarded notions of federalism and cantons have provided fertile ground for political and territorial imaginations.

As far fetched as some notions may appear at any specific political juncture, the Israel–Palestine case does prove that ideas that were deemed totally unacceptable only a few years previously, if pushed strongly enough within the public discourse, can have a significant impact upon political thinking and ultimately become acceptable. This is as true of the concept of a Palestinian state and a two-state solution (which were not even part of the Oslo Agreement terminology as recently as the mid-1990s) as it is of the idea of territorial exchange and land swaps (which would have been deemed a figment of the imagination less than a decade ago). The Israel–Palestine conflict proves that territorial and political solutions which might earlier have given rise to conflict resolution cannot necessarily be adopted when the political and geographical realities have changed the conditions on the ground. This has been a constant theme, and failure, of the conflict resolution process in the region – namely, the willingness to embrace solutions which could have been implemented had they been endorsed at a previous time, but when eventually adopted have proved to be almost impossible to implement. The constant failure of the so-called windows of opportunity, which reopen every few years but are invariably sealed very quickly, each time with greater frustration and disappointment at the inability to realize the opportunities, is in great part due to the willingness to adopt solutions which are no longer compatible with the contemporary realities. Both Israeli and Palestinian policy-makers are responsible for this situation, even at the times – few and far between – when there has been a real desire on both sides to reach the first stages of conflict resolution, which would include the necessary territorial arrangements. Such arrangements, in turn, require the demarcation of borders and the delineation of clear spaces of sovereignty and control, although the most recent phases in the conflict would indicate that even this necessitates a structural reassessment, as this small piece of real estate, the source of the world's single longest ongoing conflict of this nature, becomes transformed into patchwork of micro territories increasingly difficult to separate one from the other.

Future borders would not just be territorial constructs. A peace agreement would have to deal with the functional dimensions of border control, determining whether such borders would be open, allowing movement across them, or sealed to movement from both sides. There is a real economic interest for Palestinians to be able to cross into Israel, while for some Israelis there would be an interest in crossing into the Palestinian state to visit Jewish holy sites. Part of a State of Palestine would be entirely landlocked, with its only access to major ports being a land corridor with the Gaza Strip and the Mediterranean or a land corridor through Jordan via Aqaba and the Red Sea. But, from a Palestinian perspective, the political imperative of retaining sovereign control over their own territory and desiring to turn their backs on the former 'occupiers', and the desire by Israel to retain strong control over its physical security through the establishment of a closed border regime, would seem, at least in the first stages of the implementation of conflict resolution, to be stronger than the economic and social logic of flexible and open borders.

Further reading

Falah, Ghaza, and Newman, David (1995) 'The Spatial Manifestation of Threat: Israelis and Palestinians Seek a "Good" Border', *Political Geography Quarterly*, 14, pp. 689–706.

David Newman

Harker, Christopher (2010) 'New Geographies of Palestine/Palestinians', *Arab World Geographer*, 13/3–4, pp. 199–216.

Long, Joanna (2011) 'Geographies of Palestine–Israel', *Geography Compass*, 5/5, pp. 262–74.

Newman, David (1989) 'Civilian and Military Presence as Strategies of Territorial Control: The Arab–Israel Conflict', *Political Geography Quarterly*, 8/3, pp. 215–27.

Newman, David (1997) 'Creating the Fences of Territorial Separation: The Discourses of Israeli–Palestinian Conflict Resolution', *Geopolitics* 2, pp. 1–35.

Newman, David (2002) 'The Geopolitics of Peacemaking in Israel–Palestine', *Political Geography*, 21, pp. 629–46.

Newman, David (2010) 'The Renaissance of a Border which Never Died: The Green Line between Israel and the West Bank', in A. Diener and J. Hagen (eds), *Borderlines and Borderlands: Political Oddities at the Edge of the Nation-State* (Lanham, MD: Rowman & Littlefield), pp. 87–106.

12
Water

Julie Trottier

Introduction

Water in the Israeli–Palestinian conflict is usually portrayed as an international competition between two bodies, Israel and the Palestinian Authority, each attempting to secure as large a quantity of water as possible. This is an oversimplification of a complex situation. It is problematic because it prevents us from understanding the multi-scalar interactions that determine water management in this area and from recognizing the myriad of actors involved in deploying a variety of property regimes concerning water. It prevents us from comprehending the manner in which these overlapping modes of management affect water quality within shared aquifers, which in turn generates problems concerning water quantity, since poor quality limits its uses. More crucially, it prevents us from elaborating an effective proposal for a water agreement between Israel and a future State of Palestine. We must therefore understand both the issue of water in the Israeli–Palestinian conflict and the history of its narrative to grasp its impact on the progression of the conflict.

This chapter first sketches the physical resources at stake in the conflict. It then details the manner in which these resources became split among various states and were managed very differently by Israel and by the Palestinians. It ends by examining the issues and prospects that lie ahead.

The Jordan Basin

Both surface and groundwater are objects of competition. An overview of the manner in which water flows through the region is necessary to understand this competition. Much of the territory of Israel and of the Occupied Territories lies outside the Jordan Basin. Yet, locating this basin and the manner in which it came to be split remains essential to appreciating the present conflict over water. Three main tributaries – the Dan, the Banyas and the Hasbani – flow into the Upper Jordan, which feeds into Lake Tiberias/Sea of Galilee/Kinneret). The Jordan River flows south from Lake Tiberias into the Dead Sea. The Yarmuk River feeds into the Jordan River 10 kilometres downstream of Lake Tiberias after having flowed from the east and the north-east. A basin is the territory of a watershed, the space within which water trickles

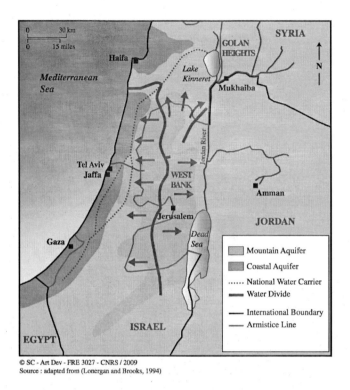

© SC - Art Dev - FRE 3027 - CNRS / 2009
Source : adapted from (Lonergan and Brooks, 1994)

Figure 12.1 The Jordan Basin and the Israeli and Palestinian aquifers

towards the same river or the same sink, such as the Dead Sea. The south-west limit of the Jordan Basin is the mountain ridge that runs from north to south, mostly through what is now the West Bank, roughly linking the cities of Nablus, Ramallah, Jerusalem and Hebron. Water trickles east of this ridge towards the Dead Sea and feeds the eastern aquifer, west of this ridge towards the Mediterranean Sea and feeds the western aquifer, and north-east of this ridge towards the north and feeds the northern aquifer. As illustrated in Figure 12.1, this means that, as far as surface water is concerned, the West Bank is now a downstream riparian and Israel is an upstream riparian. However, as far as the main aquifers are concerned, the West Bank is located upstream and Israel lies downstream.

Dividing the Jordan Basin

The Franco-British Boundary Treaty of 23 December 1920 divided up the territory of the Ottoman Empire, splitting the Jordan Basin between the French Mandate in the north and the British Mandate in the south. Priority in water use was granted to the upstream riparian body, as article 8 specified that the territories lying in the French Mandate would 'receive prior satisfaction'. However, the French government would give its representative 'the most liberal instructions concerning the use of the surplus of these waters for the advantage of Palestine' (Caponera 1993). The territory that now constitutes Israel and the Palestinian Occupied Territories became a downstream riparian Mandate along the Jordan River. According to the Anglo-French agreement, of the three tributaries of the Upper Jordan, only one, the Hasbani, was located inside the French Mandate. However, when the border was demarcated in 1923 by the Paulet–Newcombe team, another of these three tributaries, the Banyas, became located inside the French Mandate over Syria and only the Dan was left inside the British Mandate (Medzini 1997).

When the British Mandate over Palestine was established, water had always been managed at the local level. Spring or well users themselves determined the rules governing water use, access and allocation. Water was very rarely sold. Farmers sharing a spring developed rotations on a time basis whereby they successively directed water to their respective plots via gravity-fed irrigation networks. The Mandate authorities, realizing that water law literally varied from one village to another, and facing the absence of any real definition of water rights and land tenure deeds, were reluctant to invest in hydraulic infrastructure. They deployed much effort between 1929 and 1937 in formulating a water law that would apply uniformly to the territory of the Mandate and would allow for 'efficient' use of water in irrigation according to a narrow engineering understanding of that term. Their efforts failed.

British efforts to develop a water law corresponded to an attempt to depoliticize Jewish immigration to the Mandate over Palestine. Churchill's White Paper of 1922 declared the 'absorptive capacity' of Palestine would determine the number of Jewish immigrants allowed to enter the territory (El-Eini 1996). The Zionist leadership claimed this absorptive capacity could be limitless if the country was modernized. Its water experts developed a discourse of water abundance in the area according to which technology alone was necessary (Alatout 2008). Water was available, they claimed; all that was needed was a means to extract and channel it. Mekorot was created in 1937 within this context, for the purposes of planning, executing and running waterworks for irrigation and consumption throughout the Mandate over Palestine.

After the emergence of Israel, the water discourse changed from one of abundance to one of scarcity. By 1957, they had progressively reviewed their 1950 estimate of renewable resources, 2,800 million cubic meters per year, downwards to 1,850 million cubic meters per year (Alatout 2008). Israeli Law 5715-1955 concerning drilling and 5716-1955 on water metering went through in 1955. Law 5718-1959 on drainage and flood control was passed in 1957. These three laws were consolidated in 1959 into the Israeli Water Law, which withdrew water once and for all from the private and communal spheres – a challenging political decision that was legitimized by the new water scarcity discourse. Within ninety days of the promulgation of the Water Law, control of water in Israel switched from a totally fragmented situation, where every well and every spring had its own law, to a completely centralized process. All users had to apply for a one-year production licence from the water commissioner, who could stipulate any new condition judged necessary in order to conserve water stocks and to improve the efficiency of management and use.

This centralized water management system in Israel was accompanied by the development of large infrastructure. The National Water Carrier was completed in 1964 to bring water from Lake Tiberias through the north of Israel to the south of the country, as the goal of greening the southern desert was a fundamental tenet of Zionism. This reduced the flow of the Lower Jordan, which runs south from Lake Tiberias to the Dead Sea, and amounted to a deviation of the Jordan River away from what was Jordan at that time, which elicited protestations from neighbouring states. As a consequence, Arab states decided at the January 1964 Cairo summit to deviate the Hasbani and Banyas towards the Yarmuk. Work started to that effect in November 1964 but ceased after Israeli bombings in April and August 1965. These events have often been invoked as evidence that the states in the region were willing to go to war over water. However, they could also have been invoked to argue the opposite: Nasser chose not to go to war over these incidents. Clearly, the deviation of water was already serving a greater role as a battle cry than as an actual motivation for a state to go to war.

The gradual drop in the water level of the Dead Sea began with the construction of the National Israeli Water Carrier, and was later accelerated by the construction of King Abdullah Canal by Jordan in the 1960s, which fed on water from the Yarmuk, a tributary of the Lower Jordan. This canal, initially intended to develop irrigation within the Jordan Basin, was later also used to bring water to Amman. Both uses decreased the amount of water that actually flowed to the Lower Jordan to replenish the water the Dead Sea lost every year through evaporation. The drop in the level of the Dead Sea was also accelerated by the activities of Israeli and Jordanian companies that developed evaporation ponds at the southern extremity of the sea in order to mine the salt and minerals in its water.

In 1950, the West Bank was annexed by Transjordan, which changed its name to Jordan. The former situation continued regarding water management, whereby tight social control existed over the use of the resource, but was fragmented among a multitude of local institutions. Wells are much more easily drilled along the coastal plain than in the rocky soil of the West Bank, and until 1950 most water used in the West Bank originated from springs and rain collection. Capital and technology became available in the 1950s and 1960s, enabling villagers to drill wells along the north-western edge of the West Bank. Farmers pooled their savings and created 'well companies' in order to gather the necessary funds. Communal property regimes had long been used to manage spring water, and farmers adapted such regimes to manage the water from these new wells. Usually referred to as 'private' wells, they show many aspects of communal property regimes to this day. Some state development of water management did take place in the West Bank during its Jordanian period, however. The Jerusalem Water Utility was created by the Jordanian government in the mid-1960s, with the aim of providing piped domestic water to urban dwellers in Ramallah, Jerusalem and Bethlehem. Its progression was stopped by the 1967 war, when it had reached only the northern part of East Jerusalem.

In 1967 Israel occupied the West Bank (including East Jerusalem), the Gaza Strip, the Golan Heights and the Sinai. It annexed East Jerusalem in 1967 and extended Israeli law to the Golan Heights in 1981, but it never annexed the Gaza Strip or the West Bank. As a result, the Israeli Water Law was not extended over these territories, which were ruled by military orders. A few weeks after the occupation began, Military Order no. 92 granted complete authority over all issues concerning water in the Occupied Territories to a military officer named by the area commander. Later, Military Order no. 158 submitted the drilling of any well in the Occupied Territories to the previous obtainment of a licence and allowed confiscation of any resource lacking a permit. The Israeli authorities delivered only twenty-three such permits to Palestinians between 1967 and 1990.

In practice, Israel did not extend its powers over water as far as its military orders allowed in theory. Israeli authorities barely interfered with the control of spring water. They limited the drilling of Palestinian wells and the quantity of water the existing irrigation wells could pump by imposing their metering and a yearly quota on each of them. However, they did not attempt to modify the local property regimes that existed in Palestinian villages governing the management of water at the well or spring level. As a result, while academic literature focused increasingly on the overall quantities of water consumed by Israelis, on the one hand, and Palestinians, on the other, little attention was paid to the fact that these bulk numbers reflected smaller overall quantities of resources.

Each drop of water is used several times between the moment it falls as precipitation on the West Bank and the time it reaches the sea, or some other sink, or evaporates or evapotranspirates. It is used within different polities, each with its own structure of power

Table 12.1 Interim period water allocations according to the Oslo Agreements (million cubic metres)

	Israel	*Palestinian Authority*
Eastern aquifer	40	54
		+ 78 to be developed
North-eastern aquifer	103	42
Western aquifer	340	22

determining the rules of management. It may be used a first time within a Palestinian farmer-operated irrigation system based on a communal property regime before it returns to the aquifer, laden with some pesticide. It may then reappear in a well operated by the Palestinian Authority to supply drinking water to an urban network. Then it may return to the aquifer laden with bacterial contaminants and reappear in an Israeli well operated by Mekorot to supply drinking water to either an Israeli or a Palestinian municipality. Every time the set of actors determining what will be done to prevent that drop of water from evaporating or from being contaminated is organized differently. These polities are all related, and all of them need to be considered in the elaboration of a final-status agreement.

The issue of water was left to the final-status negotiations when the Declaration of Principles was signed in 1993, the Gaza–Jericho Agreement in 1994, and Oslo II in 1995. The quantification narrative was already so well established by then that it guided the interim measure that was adopted. The Oslo Agreements detailed quantities of water from each of the West Bank aquifers that would be allocated to Israel and the Palestinian Authority during the interim period until the final-status agreement was reached. These numbers corresponded roughly to the quantities already consumed by Israelis and Palestinians, except for the additional 78 million cubic metres which the Palestinians were supposed to 'develop' from the eastern aquifer. Schedule 10 referred to in paragraph 20 of article 40 of the Protocol Concerning Civil Affairs within the Oslo II Accord stipulates the quantities (see Table 12.1).

The Oslo Agreements did not recognize the existence of the numerous local, usually informal, Palestinian institutions that managed water but conferred the responsibility of managing the water Palestinians were already using to the Palestinian Authority alone. Annex II of the 4 May 1994 agreement (article II, section B, paragraph 31a) specifies: '[a]ll water and sewage (hereinafter referred to as "water") systems and resources in the Gaza Strip and Jericho Area shall be operated, managed and developed (including drilling) by the Palestinian Authority, in a manner that shall prevent any harm to the water resources.' Harm can be understood here to mean the degradation of groundwater quality.

The definition of the conflict over water as one strictly in terms of quantities to be controlled centrally by Israel and the Palestinian Authority suited the international community. Since 1993, the international community has been subsidizing the creation of the Palestinian Authority. Between 1994 and 2005, over $6 billion was thus directed to the Palestinians, the bulk of it after 2000 (Keating, Le More and Lowe 2005). Water infrastructure started being funded in the Palestinian territories by international donors, who believed they were thus supporting the creation of a Palestinian state. The Palestinian Water Authority was created by the Oslo Agreements as the regulatory authority for water. International donors funded international consultants to draft the Palestinian water law, declaring the resource public property as Israeli law had done in Israel in 1959. These consultants did not build on the myriad institutions already existing at the local level that managed the resource according to communal property regimes, and, sometimes, private property regimes, well by well and spring by spring. They drafted a law relying on the typical principles put forward by the Food and Agriculture Organization's development law office. Such principles were deemed to have universal value.

Approaching the issue of water as a quantitative problem to which the solution would be the allocation of a certain amount of water to Israel as well as to the future state of Palestine rallied many different actors. International donors, such as the United Nations Development Programme (UNDP), for example, were under a tight delivery constraint whereby they had to disburse large amounts of money within a calendar year, over a relatively small territory and facing the competition of many other donors. Large, state-controlled water infrastructure is especially expensive, so it catered well to that concern. The Palestinian Authority was composed largely of Palestinian Liberation Organization members who had returned from Tunis after the Oslo Agreements were concluded. Their families were often from areas that now lay inside Israel. Acknowledging the fact that water used by the Palestinians was already managed by informal institutions, usually deploying communal property regimes and controlled by local families, would have been perilous to its quest to construct a central authority controlling water as a public property. While its water law, drafted in English by international consultants, allowed the Palestinian Authority to win the favour of international donors, it sometimes had to manage reality with decrees, written in Arabic only, which recognized the authority of such informal institutions. The recognition of the Ein Sultan Water Association, an association of irrigation farmers based in Jericho, via decree no. 38 in 1998, illustrates this (Trottier 1999).

Israel also benefited from defining the water allocated to the Palestinians as public property. The Oslo Agreements created the Joint Water Committee (JWC), composed half of Israeli representatives and half of Palestinian representatives, the decisions of which had to be made by consensus. The apparently sweeping powers over water granted the Palestinian Water Authority, cited above, were severely limited by the role of the JWC, which had to grant its authorization for any decision made by the Palestinian Water Authority before it could become effective. In effect, this allowed Israel to decide on the infrastructure that the international community was funding in the Occupied Territories. The centralization of power in the hands of the Palestinian Water Authority, through the designation of water as public property, centralized this power in the hands of Israel, through the role of the Joint Water Committee.

The Oslo Agreements gave an enormous impetus to a supply management approach, whereby the demand for water was not questioned. It was to be satisfied by technological means, the bill footed by the international community. This placed even greater pressure on already stretched natural resources. A demand management approach could have been considered, whereby the demand for water would have been examined as the result of social and economic processes which can be acted upon. For example, the quantity of water Israel allocated to its agriculture could have been challenged. But defining water rights in terms of quantities allocated to each party conveniently allowed Israel, the Palestinian Authority and international donors to skirt this issue. Once a quantity was allocated to a party, the decision what to do with it was in its control.

The Israeli 'separation fence'

The construction of the 'separation fence', to isolate Israel from the Palestinians, began the same year the Palestinian Water Law was promulgated. This had declared water public property and had designated the Palestinian Water Authority the regulator. However, it had remained unimplemented because the Palestinian Authority did not have the political or social means to wrest control over water from the multitude of communal, formal and informal institutions that already managed the water allocated to the Palestinians according to the Oslo Agreements. The surprisingly serpentine path of the separation fence has a variety of causes. A detailed look at the Palestinian wells it affected negatively suggests that water was among the concerns determining its meandering path. While Palestinian NGOs such as PENGON protested early on, claiming loss of water quantity, the Palestinian Authority did not protest until a year after the start of construction of the wall. PENGON calculated the quantity of water purported to be lost by adding the quotas allocated to the wells that lay west of the wall. Yet, many wells located east of the barrier were also affected negatively. The irrigation networks they supplied lay west of the wall and were severed, for example, or the reservoirs they supplied were destroyed because they lay in its path. Interestingly, the wells that were affected negatively by the first phase of construction were all operated by formal or informal institutions deploying communal property regimes. The separation fence, however, left unharmed the wells that were operated by the Palestinian Authority (Trottier 2007).

The construction of the fence did not affect the allocation of water as specified in the Oslo Agreements. As less water was drawn from wells harmed by the barrier, the Palestinian Authority could ask to extract more water from the wells it operated in order to claim its entire 1995 allocation. This would represent a net sectoral reallocation from irrigation to domestic use and a net transfer of power over water from informal, often traditional, structures to the Palestinian Authority. Israeli officials had been deploring the 'inefficiency' of the Palestinian Water Authority since its creation. The construction of the separation fence seems to have championed their vision of what water management in the Palestinian Territories should be.

Evolutions since the 1990s

Throughout the 1990s, a fledgling environmental movement in Israel drew attention to the degradation of the aquifers. As the Palestinians are located upstream, aquifer-wise, from Israel, the absence of waste-water treatment plants in the West Bank worried Israel. Feitelson (2002) noted several evolutions in the Israeli discourse concerning water. An environmental strand drew attention to the sustainability of water use and to the degradation of water quality in the aquifers. Another strand portrayed access to water of sufficiently good quality as a human right. Desalination now appears to many to satisfy these concerns.

Desalination

The production of water through desalination corresponds to a supply management approach. It is energy intensive, technology intensive, capital intensive and centralized. Israel embarked on large-scale desalination when it completed a Desalination Master Plan in 1997 and approved and budgeted extensive seawater desalination facilities in 1999. It now expects to have coastal plants providing over 500 million cubic meters of water by 2013 (Garb 2008). Desalination increases the overall amount of water available for consumption. It has transformed Israeli preoccupations with quantities of water available in the aquifers into preoccupations with the quality of the water in those aquifers, while the Palestinian main preoccupation remains accessing a greater quantity of water. In 2008, the Israeli National Building Commission proposed allowing the construction of a desalination plant on land next to Caesaria, inside Israel, to produce domestic water for the Palestinian Authority.

Defining the water conflict as a quantitative one to which desalination offers a solution allows a paradigmatic transformation of a problem of joint natural resource management, first, into a technical issue and, as a consequence, into an issue of international aid. Clearly, in this case, the existence of a technical solution – desalination – to increase overall supply contributed to the definition of the problem. Desalination eliminates Israel's vulnerability to climate change, which models predict will reduce rainfall in the area. But desalination is not without its own environmental cost and is making Israel dependent on water quality in the Mediterranean and vulnerable to energy price variability.

The Red–Dead canal

In 2007, the World Bank launched a call for proposals for a feasibility study of a canal linking the Red Sea and the Dead Sea. A very similar project had already been examined between 1995 and 1997. It had included three components: the conveyance of sea water from the Red Sea to the Dead Sea, a desalination facility by the side of the Dead Sea, and the transmission of desalinated water to Amman and Jerusalem. The initial project was turned down as too expensive a way of generating domestic water. The idea of a 'peace conduit', for which a feasibility study is currently under way, caters only for the first component of the 1995 project – that is, the canal linking the Red Sea and the Dead Sea, which represented more than one-third of the overall project's estimated costs. The present project is now promoted to save the Dead Sea from disappearing. It has met opposition from environmentalists, however, who point out that the Dead Sea has received a supply of fresh water, not marine water, throughout its history. Filling it with Red Sea water, they argue, could hardly restore it to its earlier condition.

The beneficiaries of the Red–Dead project are the governments of Israel, the Palestinian Authority and Jordan. The stakes are different for each and the realization or not of this project will affect them in different ways. If realized, it will completely transform the ecology and the water management situation of the region. If the desalination component is completed, it will pursue the supply management logic that has been at work in the region since the 1950s.

Solving the water conflict?

Devising a final-status agreement with respect to water has been plagued by several historic legacies: the faith in technology that originated in the Mandate days and still promotes supply management; the discourse promoting centralized water management as the only response to scarcity, which originated in Israel shortly after its independence; the unequal overall water allocation for Israelis and Palestinians, resulting from over forty years of occupation; and the creation of a Palestinian Water Authority by the Oslo Agreements, modelled on the Israeli method of centralized management that never had the institutional capacity to gather the power which these agreements theoretically conferred on it. Most of the proposals for a solution to the water conflict have fallen into these traps. Shuval (1996), Marei and Weinthal (2002) and Phillips and his colleagues (2007a, 2007b; Phillips, Jagerskog and Turton 2009) all made propositions heavily modelled on such legacies.

Daring to recognize legal pluralism?

In 2007, the Geneva Initiative, a non-governmental effort at elaborating a peace treaty between Israel and the future State of Palestine, asked an Israeli–Jordanian–Palestinian NGO, Friends of the Earth Middle East (FOEME), to devise a proposal for article 12, the article dealing with water between the two parties. This environmental NGO has contributed to what Feitelson has called 'an environmental strand' to the Israeli discourse on water. In 2002 it produced a proposal (www.informationclearinghouse.info/article5019.htm) that broke with the quantitative approach to water. The Geneva Initiative did not include this text in its final proposal, but FOEME launched a campaign to promote it in November 2010.

This article proposes to recognize the asymmetry between Israeli and Palestinian water management. Legal pluralism in water management has been widely acknowledged around the world (Bruns and Meinzen-Dick 2001). Strengthening existing local institutions that already allocate water and deal with conflicts systematically proves more efficient and effective than imposing new institutions. The FOEME proposal acknowledges the fact that Israel has a centrally managed system while the Palestinians have a decentralized water management system. It suggests integrating the myriad formal and informal institutions on the Palestinian side into an institutional structure of joint management of the resource. It breaks with past proposals that defined water rights in terms of quantities of the resource allocated to one or another party and, instead, recognizes priorities according to the types of use – granting a minimum of domestic use highest priority – and recommends an institutional set-up that would allow ongoing mediation to determine abstractions on the basis of continuous monitoring of the aquifer according to the priorities established for the uses made. Such a system effectively de-securitizes water because it refuses to ascribe a bulk quantity to one party or another. It caters to the Israeli concern with the quality of the aquifers and it caters to the Palestinian concern with accessing more water. It ties both parties in a duty of mutual help which would stir them towards demand management, putting an end to the destructive process of supply management funded by international donors that has been at work since the 1950s and has soared to dangerous heights since 1993.

References and further reading

Alatout, Samer (2008) '"States" of Scarcity: Water, Space, and Identity Politics in Israel, 1948–59', *Environment and Planning D: Society and Space*, 26, pp. 959–82.

Bruns, Bryan Randolph, and Meinzen-Dick, Ruth S. (2001) 'Water Rights and Legal Pluralism: Four Contexts for Negotiation', *Natural Resources Forum*, 25, pp. 1–10.

Caponera, Dante A. (1993) 'Legal Aspects of Transboundary River Basins in the Middle East: The Al Asi (Orontes), the Jordan and the Nile', *Natural Resources Journal*, 33/3, pp. 629–63.

El-Eini, Roza I. M. (1996) 'The Implementation of British Agricultural Policy in Palestine in the 1930s', *Middle Eastern Studies*, 32/4, pp. 211–50.

Feitelson, E. (2002) 'Implications of Shifts in the Israeli Water Discourse for Israeli–Palestinian Water Negotiations', *Political Geography*, 21, pp. 293–318.

Garb, Yaakov (2008) 'Desalination in Israel: Status, Prospects, and Contexts', in A. Tal (ed.), *Water Wisdom* (New Brunswick, NJ: Rutgers University Press).

Keating, Michael, Le More, Anne, and Lowe, Robert (2005) *Aid, Diplomacy and Facts on the Ground: The Case of Palestine* (London: Chatham House).

Marei, Amer, and Weinthal, Erika (2002) 'One Resource, Two Visions: The Prospects for Israeli–Palestinian Water Cooperation', *Water International*, 27/4, pp. 460–67.

Medzini, Arnon (1997) 'The River Jordan: The Struggle for Frontiers and Water: 1920–1967', PhD dissertation, University of London.

Phillips, D., Attili, S., McCaffrey, S., and Murray, J. (2007a) 'The Jordan River Basin, 1: Clarification of the Allocations in the Johnston Plan', *Water International*, 31/5, pp. 16–38.

Phillips, D., Attili, S., McCaffrey, S., and Murray, J. (2007b) 'The Jordan River Basin, 2: Potential Future Allocations to the Co-Riparians', *Water International*, 31/5, pp. 39–62.

Phillips, D., Jagerskog, A., and Turton, A. (2009) 'The Jordan River Basin, 3: Options for Satisfying the Current and Future Water Demand of the Five Riparians', *Water International*, 34/2, pp. 170–88.

Shuval, Hillel (1996) 'A Water-for-Peace Plan', *Palestine–Israel Journal*, 3/3–4, pp. 74–83.

Trottier, Julie (1999) *Hydropolitics in the West Bank and Gaza Strip* (Jerusalem: Palestinian Association for the Academic Study of International Affairs).

Trottier, Julie (2007) 'A Wall, Water and Power: The Israeli "Separation Fence"', *Review of International Studies*, 33, pp. 105–27.

13
Terrorism

Magnus Norell

Introduction

This essay aims to give an overview and introduction to various forms of Jewish and Palestinian terrorism during the Israeli–Palestinian conflict, mapping out the larger trends of the conflict and the role played by terrorism. A comprehensive study of the topic is not within the scope of this study. For that, the reader is encouraged to look at the further reading section at the end of the chapter. Neither will it be a list of attacks; for that there are a number of statistical references available.

The aim of this essay is, rather, to give the reader a more general understanding of terrorism as it has been used and developed by the primary actors – Israelis and Palestinians – during the last half of the twentieth century and into the first decade of the twenty-first, roughly since the creation of Israel in 1947–8 until the Gaza war in December 2008 and January 2009. These dates give a convenient framework by which to assess the history of terrorism in the conflict.

This time frame is also used because terrorism as a tool in the conflict became more pronounced after Israeli independence in 1948. The choice of the Gaza war in 2008–9 is because that conflict marks – for now at least – a rather clear break between two strands of thought on the Palestinian side – namely, between Fatah and the Hamas movement. That is, the more pragmatic (as it developed over time) strategic thinking of Fatah represented by President Mahmoud Abbas and Prime Minister Salaam Fayyad, whereby terrorism as a tool is more or less cast aside in favor of a political, negotiated peace-deal with Israel, is now on a collision course with the Islamist movement Hamas, which is still arguing for armed struggle as a way to solve the conflict with Israel. It should be pointed out that, although Fatah (and by extension the PLO) has yet to renounce "armed struggle" (a well-used euphemism for terrorism) in pursuit of its stated aims, for all intents and purposes Fatah, especially under Abbas, after the death of Yassir Arafat, has chosen political strategy as a means to solve the conflict.

Pre-independence terrorism

Terrorism is here defined as:

> The systematic use of illegitimate violence – specifically aimed at non-combatants and/or civilians – by non-state, sub-state actors to achieve specific objectives. These objectives

could be political, social or religious depending on the group/individual in question. Terrorism becomes international when it is carried out beyond the borders that define a specific group's/individual's country of origin, or when it is targeting foreign nationals within s specific group's/individual's country of origin.

(Norell 2001: 2)

This does not mean that terrorism was not used before independence. On the contrary, both sides used terrorism as a tool during the decades preceding Israeli independence.

In the struggle leading up to independence, the *Yishuv* (Jewish community in British Mandate Palestine) had over the years developed a well-structured political entity. Modeled on democratic structures used in Europe, the community had, on the eve of independence, overwhelmingly chosen to gain strength by building a civil, democratic community among its citizens. When the UN-sponsored partition plan was presented, a majority chose to go along with it, but, at the same time, a minority saw it as treason and vowed to fight partition by all means available. It was among this minority that terrorism by choice – directed both at Palestinian Arabs and at the British – developed.

The struggle in the months preceding the implementation of the UN partition plan, between the vote in the UN General Assembly on November 29, 1947, and the end of the British Mandate on May 14, 1948, was more a civil war than anything else. The Jewish and Palestinian communities both tried to prepare for the showdown that was expected on May 14, when the Mandate was to end. Both sides used indiscriminate attacks against the other. There was, however, a certain asymmetry to it. On the Jewish side, unapologetic attacks were carried out by the radicals in some terrorist organizations, such as the Irgun and the Stern gang. It was a tit-for-tat war, with grenades thrown into vegetable markets, ambushes of buses carrying civilians, and bombs in cinemas.

After the massacre by the Irgun of Palestinian civilians (including women and children) at the village of Deir Yassin in April 1948, David Ben-Gurion, leader of the *Yishuv*, decided once and for all to clear the deck. With help from supporters in the United States and Europe, the Irgun was bringing in weapons in order to act independently of the Haganah (a precursor to the Israeli army). Ben-Gurion and the political leadership of the *Yishuv* first demanded that the Irgun concede the weapons to the Haganah. When it refused, Ben-Gurion took the radical decision to shell the transport ship, even though it meant that desperately needed weaponry would be lost. The ship (the *Altalena*) was sunk with the loss of several Irgun fighters. This marked the end of these groups, whose members were forcefully integrated into the Haganah. The terrorism used by the Jewish radicals was never blessed by the mainstream political and military powers of the *Yishuv*, and the *Altalena* affair (as it came to be known) became an important watershed in the domestic Jewish political struggle.

Terrorism, as used during these months (as well as in the future), never became condoned as a legitimate tool in the conflict with the Palestinians. This was underlined after the murder of the UN-appointed mediator – Swedish Count Folke Bernadotte – in September 1948. The murder (carried out by the Stern gang) was roundly condemned by the Israeli government. That incident led to harsher measures being taken against radical Jewish fringe-movements.

Some notable exceptions to the terrorism carried out by the Jewish terrorists in the Irgun and the Stern gang were the attacks on the Semiramis Hotel in Jerusalem, which killed, among others, the Spanish consul, and the attack on the King David Hotel. Both were launched as 'joint-ventures' between the mainstream Haganah and the Irgun (whose leader was Menachem Begin). While the aim was not to kill non-combatants per se (the King David Hotel was used by the British as both political and military headquarters), the high number of civilians working there at the time was well known. Warnings were sent by telephone before the bombings, but no evacuations took place. The attack had significant political repercussions. For the British it arguably added to pressure to withdraw from Palestine altogether.

For the Palestinian Arabs during the pre-independence period (especially the period November 1947 to May 1948, when the fight against the Jews was taken over by regular Arab armies from Jordan, Egypt, and Syria), terrorism was viewed as a legitimate tool in the struggle against the Jews. On the Palestinian side the war was conducted very much as a guerrilla war, with irregulars rallied for specific operations from nearby villages and with no real structured forces (unlike the Jewish Haganah). Fighting often took the form of ambushes and assaults on small groups of Jews (or even on individuals). Jews, whether armed or not, were all seen as legitimate targets in the fight for Palestine.

As implementation of the UN partition plan drew near, the lack of structure on the Palestinian side (both politically and militarily) began to turn in favor of the *Yishuv*. The Palestinians, lacking the political leadership and organization of the *Yishuv*, never received the promised support from their Arab neighbors. Instead, when partition came in May 1948, they were told to move aside and let the regular Arab armies do the job of crushing the Jews.

Stages in the Israeli–Palestinian conflict

With Israeli independence the conflict entered a new stage. The partition plan was never fully implemented, and what was supposed to become the Arab Palestinian state was either lost in the war or occupied by Jordan (the West Bank, later annexed by Jordan) and Egypt (the Gaza Strip). The conflict has developed through three stages, each defined by the way in which it was seen by the actors themselves.

1948–1973

The first period stretches roughly from Israel's declaration of independence in 1948 to the October War of 1973 (the Yom Kippur War). During this time, opposition to Israel was dressed in the garb of pan-Arabism: the goal was to build coalitions based on Arab unity in order to isolate and destroy Israel militarily by waging war on two or more fronts simultaneously. Pan-Arabism (with Nasser, who died in 1970, as the figurehead) was the ideology around which Arab politics revolved.

Between 1948 and 1967 terrorism in the Israeli–Palestinian conflict was conducted mostly through Palestinian cross-border raids aimed at Israeli settlements and farms. The raids were launched from around Israel, from Gaza, at the time occupied by Egypt, and from Jordan, Lebanon, and Syria. Since these attacks were targeted mostly at civilians and non-combatants, they were defined as terrorist attacks. Arabs, however, viewed them as legitimate resistance aimed at reversing what was seen as Jewish occupation of Arab land. The UN partition plan of November 29, 1947, was accepted neither by the Palestinians nor by the neighboring Arab countries.

These attacks were mainly in the form of small-arms ambushes or raids on settlements. The larger aim was to prevent Israeli society from developing a normal economy and to render life in these outlying farms and settlements so dangerous as to force people to abandon them. Tactically, the aim was to kill (and sometimes to kidnap) civilians. On a strategic level, the attacks were supported by other Arab states, although the actual individuals participating were recruited almost exclusively from among Palestinian refugees forced in 1947–8 to flee their homes when Israel was established. The effort was labeled pan-Arab to redress an injustice done to the Arab people by the international community. The specific conflict between the Israelis and the Palestinians constituted the cutting edge of that larger Arab–Israeli conflict.

The Israeli victory in June 1967 also forced a change in the way the Arabs conducted terror attacks against Israel. No longer able to launch attacks from Gaza or from a weak Jordan, the Arab states, although still verbally (and to some degree economically) committed to an armed solution to the conflict, were forced by the overwhelming Israeli victory to reconsider their options. With Israel within striking distance of their own borders, attacks launched from their territory carried the risk of triggering retaliatory attacks, and the war of October 1973 put an end to the notion that Israel could be defeated militarily. The six years between 1967 and 1973 saw a decrease in cross-border terrorism. Israel was transformed into a fully fledged occupier, and the shock felt by Arabs as a consequence of the Israeli victory in 1967 took some time to overcome.

What also happened at the tail-end of the first period, between 1967 and 1973, was that Palestinians and Israelis confronted one another more often on a day-to-day basis. The war in 1967 saw the birth of the settlement movement in Israel. At the beginning this movement was led by people who saw the Israeli victory as divine intervention on the Jewish side and, as a result, an open invitation to settle "liberated" lands in the West Bank. The settlement movement fostered within it the seeds of a Jewish terrorism that in later years would become much stronger.

The fundamental problem with the pan-Arab strategy that defined the first stage was rooted in the very idea of pan-Arabism. It proved impossible to create unity in strategic goals. This led to Arab defeats in the wars of 1948, 1956, and 1967. Ironically, the partially successful attack on Israel launched in October 1973 led to Egypt's abandoning the entire failed project of collective Arab strategic thinking and to pursue a separate peace with Israel, eventually achieved in 1979. The war spelled the end of the "classic" period of the Arab–Israeli conflict.

1973–1994

In the second period or stage, the Israel–Palestine conflict came to the fore, pushing the broader Arab–Israeli conflict to the sidelines. Combining political initiatives and armed struggle, including terrorism, the PLO (at that point dominated entirely by Arafat's Fatah faction) was able to open several fronts against Israel, as well as against Jewish targets around the world. The armed struggle was presented as part of a worldwide revolutionary struggle against colonialism. That way, the PLO was able to ally itself with a host of left-wing groups, most notably in Europe. This provided political support that reached beyond the most radical and violent groups, such as the German Red Army Faction and the Italian Red Brigades.

Terrorism in this period also changed considerably, from cross-border attacks in the region to attacks on Israeli and Jewish targets in Europe. Hijackings of airplanes also began at this time. It was a relatively cheap way of pushing the Palestinian issue to the forefront. Media coverage was assured, and the audacity and daring with which some of the attacks were carried out ensured a constant stream of new recruits.

Terrorism also became much more international during this period. The Palestinians took their struggle to the global arena, targeting Jews and Israelis in several countries. The fact that the PLO allied itself with the "third-worldism" of left-wing groups in Europe opened up the number of potential targets to include anyone who could be perceived as supporting Israel – US and NATO targets, for example. Under headings such as "anti-colonial" or "anti-imperialist," terrorism widened. What also changed were the tactics. From small arms used in firefights and ambushes, bombs now became the favorite weapon, manufactured by specialists, often trained in Eastern bloc countries. The localized terrorism in the Middle East thus became entangled with power politics in the East–West conflict.

A number of highly publicized terror attacks occurred during this period, with plane hijackings and perhaps the most (in)famous attack of all: that on the Israeli Olympic team in Munich in September 1972 (Burleigh 2009: 157–67). The perpetrators belonged to "Black September," a group created by Arafat, whose name alluded to September in 1970, when King Hussein of Jordan crushed Palestinian armed groups posing a real threat to his regime.

This attack put the Palestinian issue onto the world stage with a vengeance, with millions of people watching events unfold on their TV screens. The Munich massacre also heralded the era of "media war," whereby terrorism became something that the perpetrators projected onto the world stage to highlight whatever cause they were pursuing. And the media happily played along. It also triggered a retaliatory string of attacks by the Israelis, wherein several Palestinians (allegedly those having had something to do with the attack) were killed throughout Europe.

Despite the internationalization of terrorism, this period also saw the emergence of political initiatives to confront the conflict with negotiations instead of violence. This led to terrorism becoming more radicalized, as various Palestinian groups resisted this change. A number of leading Palestinian politicians, most notably Issam Sartawi, who had been arguing for an end to the armed struggle as well as an end to using terrorism, at least against non-combatants, were murdered by radical Palestinians such as Abu Nidal (who, in late 1974, formed "Fatah: The Revolutionary Council" as a way to counter what he, and other radicals, saw as treason to the Palestinian cause). As the 1970s progressed, this trend become more pronounced, and, if the first half of the 1970s saw a kind of undercover war between Israelis and Palestinians, the latter half witnessed a progressively bloody Palestinian civil war, often fought in Europe (Burleigh 2009: 152–88).

This period also witnessed something that, in hindsight, can be termed the high-water mark of Jewish terrorism directed at the Palestinians. During the 1980s various Jewish terrorist groups emerged from the settler movement in the West Bank and Gaza. The tit-for-tat picture that to some degree defined the struggle during the years leading up to Israeli independence came back with a vengeance. Jewish terrorism reached a dramatic level, with conspiracies to blow up the Dome of the Rock and in attacks against Palestinian officials and civilians in the West Bank (Shipler 1986: 98–137). Examples include car bombs directed against the Palestinian mayor Bassam Shakaa of Nablus (who lost both his legs on June 2, 1980) and the Ramallah mayor Karim Khalaf (who lost half a foot), as well as a bomb planted on the garage door of the mayor of el-Bireh, Ibrahim Tawil, which blinded an Israeli soldier who tried to defuse it. These radical movements gave birth to trends that were to plague Israeli society for several years, leading to domestic terrorism attacks as well. The most well-known attack in this regard was perhaps the murder of then Premier Yitzhak Rabin on November 4, 1995, at a political rally in Tel-Aviv.

As it would turn out, the tactics of the PLO under Arafat (who dominated the decision-making to a significant degree) were hampered by the fact that they lacked coherent strategy. During Arafat's rule, a long series of decisions culminated in an equally large number of poli-cies. On the tactical level, there were some successes, with the PLO claiming support from dif-ferent, mostly left-wing, groups in Europe, but, as a large-scale strategy towards a political solution, it amounted to a dead end. Despite peace initiatives such as the Oslo process, Arafat, a quintessential tactician, never fully renounced the "armed option" (including terrorism). This remained an impediment to any strategic change in Palestinian thinking, thus helping to usher in an era where religiously motivated Islamic terrorism would come to define the conflict. Plagued by corruption and internal violence, the PA suffered as a result of Arafat's unwillingness to share power with people who understood better the needs for state-building (Ross and Makovsky 2009: 106–30). During his last years the peace process stalled and sputtered to a halt.

This period saw a transition for the PLO from the political wilderness to the negotiation table. For many years, in the minds of the Israelis, the PLO was no more than a terrorist group bent on the destruction of Israel. This didn't change until 1988, when Arafat (who held the monopoly on decision-making in the PLO) made the necessary changes for the United States officially to open talks with the PLO. It took several more years before the Israelis would contemplate direct negotiations with the PLO.

1994–2009

Long before Arafat's death in 2004, a new form of religiously motivated terrorism had begun to assert itself. It took some time before this form of terrorism was really taken seriously because, as long as he dominated the Palestinian polity, Arafat could hold these trends down. In addition, it took some time to build up alternative political and militant organizations to counter Arafat and Fatah effectively.

As a phenomenon, religiously motivated terrorism had of course been around for some time. The mother of all Islamist movements, the Muslim Brotherhood in Egypt, emerged as early as 1928. And the religious underpinnings for the radicals could be based on readings of the Qur'an and on Islamic thought going back to Ibn Tamiyyah in the thirteenth century.

A similar trend was apparent on the Jewish side. As the settler movement grew over the years, a certain percentage of its adherents came to define themselves as liberators of the ancient Jewish homelands of Judea and Samaria. A number of these went further and saw not only the Palestinian Arabs, but also their Israeli brethren who disagreed with them, as enemies that had to be defeated. An interesting twist in this domestic Israeli conflict was that Israeli governments, regardless of whether they were on the right or the left, came under fire from these radicals for "giving in" to pressure and "selling out" Jewish interests. The murder of Rabin was a watershed in that it highlighted the very real danger of domestic Israeli terrorism, directed at Israeli targets. However, it was not only Yitzhak Rabin (who was murdered by a radical religious terrorist) from the Labor Party who was vilified. Ariel Sharon, himself an architect of the settler movement, was criticized when he decided to leave Gaza and evacuate the settlements there.

One of the worst terrorist atrocities carried out towards Palestinians by Israelis came as a result of a messianic trend, namely the murder of Palestinian worshipers at the Macpela cave in Hebron on February 25, 1994 (twenty-nine people were killed and 200 wounded before the crowd overpowered and killed the perpetrator, a doctor named Baruch Goldstein). The killer, who came from one of the more radical and messianic settler communities in Kiryat Arba, just outside Hebron, was acting alone without any kind of organization behind him, and was roundly condemned across the political spectrum in Israel. Thanks to massive resistance from the population as a whole and skilled intelligence work, terrorism on the scale of the radical Islamists never took root. Nevertheless, vigilante settler violence directed at Palestinians in the West Bank has continued and increased with the stalemate in the peace process and in the wake of pressure on Israel to freeze settlements or remove them altogether.

This third period has witnessed the addition of a strong religious component in what had previously been primarily a nationalist conflict. Its beginnings can be traced to the Islamic Revolution in Iran, in which Ayatollah Khomeini brought forth a whole new vision of the role of Islam in the conflict with Israel. Unimpressed by Israel's military victories, Khomeini rejected the notion that the State of Israel was a fait accompli. He viewed the conflict and the establishment of Israel as an affront to God and the struggle against Israel as a test for Islam. If Muslims stayed true to their faith, Israel would be annihilated.

But, for this to become possible, Islamists could not content themselves with acting merely in a passive, supporting role. In order to defeat Israel, a more activist role was necessary. The war in Lebanon provided such an opportunity. With Israel's invasion in the summer of 1982, an opportunity was presented to Iran to strengthen and expand its role in Lebanon. Iran already had a toehold in the country as a result of its support of the Shi'ite population in Lebanon. The creation of Hizbollah made it possible for Iran to open a front against Israel that was entirely independent of other Arab states or the PLO, which Khomeini saw as incompetent and corrupt.

The strategy used by Hizbollah during the years of Israeli occupation of southern Lebanon was directed against Israeli soldiers and occasionally Lebanese allies of Israel. Attacks were often conducted in the form of suicide bombings. Although Hizbollah has not used this particular form of terrorism since Israel's withdrawal in 2000, armed struggle was perceived to have proven results in the fight against Israel.

During the 1990s, various other Islamist movements gained influence in the region, becoming an ever more important political actor in the Israeli–Palestinian conflict. In addition to the Lebanese Hizbollah, Hamas became increasingly powerful at the expense of the PLO. This process culminated in Hamas's electoral victory over the PLO and the PA in the Palestinian elections in 2006, a victory that was further solidified when Hamas ousted Fatah from Gaza in June 2007.

Religiously motivated terrorism entered center stage in Israel in the 1990s (Pedahzur 2005; Juergensmeyer 2000). While occasional stabbings and kidnappings still occurred, the period came to be defined by suicide bombings. Hamas and Palestinian Islamic Jihad were the two best-known groups in this regard, but even Fatah-affiliated groups (such as Force 17 or the Al Aqsa Martyrs' Brigades) launched such attacks. Very often these coincided with political initiatives to further the peace process. For example, on August 31, 2010, on the eve of direct negotiations in Washington between Israeli Prime Minister Binyamin Netanyahu and his Palestinian counterpart, Mahmoud Abbas, on the subject of settlements, Palestinian gunmen shot and killed four Israelis in their car outside Hebron, in an attempt to derail the peace process once again.

Suicide bombings led to a boycott of Arafat and a mistrust of the PLO (and later the PA), which was seen as ineffective in combating terrorism. After a string of bus bombs in Jerusalem in the late 1990s, there were political demands to disengage from the Palestinians altogether. In April 2002, following the bombing of a Passover meal in a hotel in Netanya, Israel launched operation Defensive Shield and reoccupied the Palestinian towns in the West Bank, finally putting a stop to any meaningful negotiations. A further result of the bombings was Israel's decision to build a separation fence between Israel and the Palestinian territories.

By adding a religious component to a national conflict, the Islamists – who came to dominate the way in which the conflict was defined during these years – managed to narrow the scope for negotiation and compromise. By targeting not only Israelis and Jews (consciously blurring the lines between the two) but also reform-minded Muslims, the conflict became tied to larger issues, such as what Islam should look like and what it entailed to be a Muslim (Kepel 2004).

Conclusion

If terrorism was used as a tool by both Israelis and Palestinians during the pre-partition period, it has since developed into a device used more "exclusively" by perpetrators defining themselves in religious terms. Terrorism as a tool has undergone various transformations which mirror the conflict at large and the wider regional circumstances framing it.

The impact of terrorism and political violence in the Israeli–Palestinian conflict can hardly be underestimated. In addition to mirroring the conflict, terrorism has helped shape the situation. While the political leadership on both sides has constantly condemned the use of terrorism, it has at the same time been unable – or sometimes unwilling – to stop it completely. The use of terrorism by radical Islamists has placed the conflict in a religious context, making it harder to contain or solve. This is a result of larger trends in the region as a whole, but, since the Israeli–Palestinian conflict looms so large in the Middle East, the use of terrorism will continue to have an impact on how the conflict plays out as well as on how it is depicted.

References and further reading

Benvenisti, M. (1995) *Intimate Enemies: Jews and Arabs in a Shared Land* (Berkeley and Los Angeles: University of California Press).

Burke, J. (2003) *Al Qaeda: Casting a Shadow of Terror* (London and New York: I. B. Tauris).

Burleigh, M. (2009) *Blood & Rage: A Cultural History of Terrorism* (New York: HarperCollins).

Collins, L., and Lapierre, D. (1972) *O Jerusalem!* (London: Weidenfeld & Nicolson).

Cook, D. (2005) *Understanding Jihad* (Berkley and Los Angeles: University of California Press).

Horovitz, D. (2004) *Still Life with Bombers: Israel in the Age of Terrorism* (New York: Alfred Knopf).

Husain, E. (2007) *The Islamist* (London: Penguin).

Juergensmeyer, M. (2000) *Terror in the Mind of God: The Global Rise of Religious Violence* (Berkeley and Los Angeles: University of California Press).

Kelsay, J. (2007) *Arguing the Just War in Islam* (Cambridge, MA: Harvard University Press).

Kepel, G. (1997) *Allah in the West: Islamic Movements in America and Europe* (Cambridge: Polity).

Kepel, G. (2004) *Fitna: guerre au coeur de l'islam* (Paris: Gallimard).

Klein-Halevi, Y. (2002) *At the Entrance to the Garden of Eden: A Jew's Search for Hope with Christians and Muslims in the Holy Land* (New York: HarperCollins).

Laqueur, W. (2001) *The New Terrorism: Fanaticism and the Arms of Mass Destruction* (New York: Oxford University Press).

Laqueur, W. (2006) *Dying for Jerusalem: The Past, Present and Future of the Holiest City* (Naperville, IL: Sourcebooks).

Michael, G. (2006) *The Enemy of my Enemy: The Alarming Convergence of Militant Islam and the Extreme Right* (Lawrence: University Press of Kansas).

Norell, M. (2001) *The Role of the Military and Intelligence in Combating Terrorism* (Stockholm: Swedish Defence Research Agency).

Norell, M. (2002) *A Dissenting Democracy: The Israeli Movement 'Peace Now'* (London: Frank Cass).

Pedahzur, A. (2005) *Suicide Terrorism* (Cambridge: Polity).

Reuter, C. (2004) *My Life is a Weapon: A Modern History of Suicide Bombing* (Princeton, NJ: Princeton University Press).

Ross, D., and Makovsky, D. (2009) *Myths, Illusions, & Peace: Finding a New Direction for America in the Middle East* (New York: Viking Books).

Roy, O. (1994) *The Failure of Political Islam* (London: I. B. Tauris).

Shipler, D. K. (1986) *Arab and Jew: Wounded Spirits in a Promised Land* (New York: Penguin).

14
Religion

Yehezkel Landau

Introduction: religion and conflict in Israel/Palestine

The land of Israel/Palestine is not just the homeland of two peoples locked in conflict. It is also considered holy by several monotheistic traditions tracing their origins back to the patriarch Abraham/Ibrahim. This overlay of national identities and religious affiliations creates a potentially explosive mixture, especially when either identity marker becomes ideologized and rendered absolute, inviolable, and essential to one's very existence.

Many commentators have observed that the conflict over Israel/Palestine is not, at its core, a religious conflict comparable to the medieval Crusaders' war against the Muslims. However, religious traditions that sanctify territory and history are invoked to justify nationalistic claims. Religion, with its powerful symbols and loyalties, is fundamental to the identities of both Arabs and Jews, even for those who do not define themselves as traditionally observant. The holy city of Jerusalem, in particular, evokes associations, attachments, and aspirations that are rooted in historical memories and eschatological hopes integral to the self-understandings of Jews, Christians, and Muslims.

Unlike many liberal Western societies, the Jewish and Palestinian cultures in Israel/Palestine are not conducive to total separation of religion and state governance. Throughout the Middle East, religion is a public concern, not just a private pursuit. There are pluses and minuses to this, as there are in the complementary reality that most Americans, for example, take for granted. Even in Israel, whose culture is more westernized than Palestinian society or Arab culture generally, the religious dimension is close to the surface. As a self-defined Jewish state, it is a hybrid of secular democratic political norms – the social fruits of modernity – and an ancient covenantal call at Sinai, reiterated by later prophets, commanding the Children of Israel to be a "kingdom of priests and a holy people" (Exodus 19: 5–6). The homecoming of Jews to the Land, and now the State, of Israel has created a radically new setting in which they can define who they are and, out of that recast self-understanding, relate differently to Christians and Muslims. For their part, the Palestinians are trying to define themselves as a distinct Arab nation under conditions of dispossession, exile, and brokenness. The political turmoil over the last century has created a cycle of violence, retaliation, and ongoing mutual threat. As a result, both national identities have been tragically skewed and defined as mutually exclusive rather than complementary. Spiritual energies that could otherwise be invested in collective healing and renewal are constantly sapped, or misdirected, by the state of war.

The intermingling of religion and power politics corrupts both. Invoking God's name to justify territorial claims that end up harming others perverts what is professed to be sacred. But protracted conflicts have always generated this spiritual contamination, which is exacerbated by politically motivated violence. The exclusivist or triumphalistic tendencies of the different Abrahamic traditions only add fuel to the fire.

Judaism, Zionism, and their impact on the conflict

As Arthur Hertzberg noted in his landmark anthology of Zionist thinkers and activists, the phenomenon known as Zionism cannot be explained by using conventional political categories. Other modern nationalist movements, struggling to overcome home-grown tyranny or colonialist occupation from outside, had an existing land and language as the dual foundation for their political aspirations. The Jewish nation-building project had to reclaim both, mobilizing Jews to return to their ancestral homeland and resurrecting Hebrew as a vernacular language that could unite immigrants from over 100 diaspora communities.[1] From the beginning, the Zionist undertaking forged a creative synthesis of nineteenth-century nationalist ideology and centuries-old messianic hopes to end the Jewish condition of exile by returning to the ancestral and still-promised homeland. Those hopes were based on a profound faith orientation common to Jews everywhere, linking a collective return to the Holy Land with the redemptive transformation of history anticipated at the "End of Days." The Hebrew prophets, reflecting on the ultimate purpose of exile within the covenantal relationship between God and the Jewish people, foresaw an eventual return that would restore the people to the land and to its vocation as a priestly community chosen to bless all of humanity. This messianic vision was enshrined in Jewish prayers recited every day and reaffirmed with special intensity on religious festivals. For close to 2,000 years, these liturgical affirmations animated and consoled a dispersed, politically marginalized, and often persecuted people. It is this unbroken chain of covenantal faithfulness that serves as the spiritual underpinning of the political movement called "Zionism," which takes its name from the prophetic and messianic term "Zion," connoting redemption for both land and people.

It should be noted that, even for Ben-Gurion and other secularized Jewish nationalists, the Hebrew Bible was the spiritual, historical, and cultural touchstone for Jewish identity and the Jewish people's link to the Land of Israel. And, throughout the development of Zionist thought and activism, there were visionaries such as A. D. Gordon (1856–1922) and Ahad Ha'am (the pen name of Asher Ginsberg, 1856–1927) who envisioned a Jewish national homecoming in very practical terms, encompassing politics and economics and, at the same time, viewing that political revolution as a means to redeem spiritually a suffering, landless, and powerless people. Their religious symbolism challenged the *realpolitik* pragmatism of Theodore Herzl and many other Zionist leaders, and their "messianic" visions challenged, quite deliberately, the passive pietism of classical rabbinic Judaism. Nevertheless, their this-worldly notion of redemption, melding ideology and praxis, was inspired by the core values of justice and human dignity championed by the Hebrew prophets.

This combination of traditional values and symbolism with modern political norms stretches conventional categories of "religion" and complicates the task of identifying a Jewish religious dimension to Zionism, the State of Israel, or the Middle East conflict. The term "secular messianism," which Hertzberg and others use to define the spiritual essence of the Zionist enterprise, may sound like an oxymoron, or at least a paradox (which, on some level, it is). It reflects the reality that Jewish piety or spirituality is characterized more by practice than by belief. If one sees in the Hebrew Bible the basis of all Jewish existence, then one cannot avoid or deny a central feature of the biblical worldview – namely, that many of the Torah's injunctions presume a Jewish collective existence in the Land of Israel as the locus for a covenantal mission consecrating space (land) and time (calendar). In ancient times, when agriculture and livestock formed the basis of an economy, specific injunctions in the Torah were meant to create an ecologically holistic framework for communal life – for example, the commandments regulating tithing or consecrating first fruits, as well as the sabbatical rhythm allowing the land to lie fallow every seven years.

In the modern era, translating these ancient practices and their spiritual rationale into idioms that make sense, and that appeal to large numbers of Jews, has been the challenge facing religious Zionists of all ideological hues. In the pre-state period, the preeminent figure in the traditionalist wing of the Zionist movement – a minority outnumbered by the secular, either socialist or nationalist, leaders – was Rabbi Abraham Isaac Kook (1865–1935). His mystical, messianic understanding of the national renewal unfolding around him transcended the duality of religion vs. secularity. Rabbi Kook saw the Zionist homecoming as part of a divine plan for global redemption. He pointedly embraced the socialist, non-observant pioneers who established the kibbutzim, the Zionist labor federations, and other national institutions in pre-state Palestine. His visionary synthesis became a model for many other religious Zionists, including the political activists who transformed the Mizrahi movement into the National Religious Party once the state was established.

The watershed for religious Zionism was the Six-Day War in June of 1967. In less than a week, Israel found itself controlling four times the territory it had had jurisdiction over during the previous nineteen years. Jews everywhere saw the war as having averted a catastrophic defeat by the armed forces of Egypt, Syria, and Jordan. In the postwar euphoria, a new spirit of national idealism and determination emerged. One of the fruits of that spirit was the impulse to establish Jewish settlements or neighborhoods in the newly occupied territories of the West Bank, the Gaza Strip, the Golan Heights, and East Jerusalem. There were security-related reasons for holding onto these areas, to create defensive buffers around Israel's main population centers. But there was a "religious" motivation as well, amply supplied by the Gush Emunim (Bloc of the Faithful) settlement movement and its charismatic rabbinic leaders.

Chief among those leaders was the son of the pre-state Rabbi Kook, Rabbi Zvi Yehudah Kook, who became the spiritual head of Gush Emunim. He saw the outcome of the 1967 war as portending the messianic deliverance of the Jewish people, and so he opposed any territorial compromise that would involve ceding any of the conquered lands to Arab sovereignty. He and his disciples (younger rabbis and lay activists, including Haim Druckman, Eliezer Waldman, and Hanan Porat) gradually took control of the formerly moderate National Religious Party and created a vast infrastructure of economic and political interests undergirding the settlement movement. If one were to pinpoint a key "religious" element on the Jewish/Israeli side helping to perpetuate the Israeli–Palestinian conflict and making a viable peace agreement more difficult to achieve, it would be the messianic determinism of Gush Emunim and its political heirs, along with the forces in government and society that have emerged to implement their partisan ideology. As the religious aspect of the conflict has intensified over the years, with the parallel rise of Islamist movements on the Arab side, a heightened militancy has emerged among the Jewish settler population, especially in the younger generation. This development is exemplified by the "hilltop youth" who have established unauthorized outposts in the West Bank.

The other major Orthodox Jewish viewpoint in Israeli politics is the non-Zionist position represented by the parochial *haredi* parties. Although in earlier decades their leaders expressed more dovish views, in recent years they, too, have tended towards right-wing positions favoring Jewish rule over all, or at least most, of the Holy Land. They share the Gush Emunim belief that God promised the whole land to the Jews, based on certain biblical texts and later rabbinic interpretations. According to this self-referencing and self-preferencing worldview, no Arab territorial claims in Palestine are valid.

Mention should be made of a small counter-movement within the ranks of religious Zionism. This group of religious "doves," called Oz veShalom-Netivot Shalom (Strength and Peace/Paths of Peace), favors political and territorial compromise to save human lives and to end what is perceived as a long-term, dehumanizing, and corrupting occupation of the Palestinian people by Israel. Members of this movement, who take biblical and rabbinic tradition as seriously as do Gush Emunim supporters, either cite alternative religious texts or interpret the same Torah sources differently. The following statement appears on the movement's website:

> As the only religious Zionist peace organization of its kind, we are in a unique position to counter fundamentalist and extremist political arguments that have erroneously placed the value of the Land of Israel ahead of human life, justice, and peace – concepts which have always been central to Jewish law and tradition.[2]

Out of the ranks of Oz veShalom-Netivot Shalom came the leaders of the Meimad religious Zionist party, which allied itself with Labor for a time and offers an ideological alternative to the right-wing National Religious Party. Meimad's leader and former representative in the Israeli Knesset (parliament) is Rabbi Michael Melchior, the former chief rabbi of Norway.

The role of Islamist ideologies and movements

In the pre-1948 period, before the State of Israel was established, the Palestinian leadership under the British Mandate did what it could to thwart the influx of European Jews and what they saw as the gradual takeover of their country by foreigners. Two personalities, legendary figures from a Palestinian perspective, stand out in any historical account of the first half of the twentieth century. The first is Izz al-Din al-Qassam, a Syrian-born sheikh who led a militant revolutionary movement in the 1930s against both the British Mandate and the Zionist movement. A deeply religious man and a fiery preacher, he and his underground fighters (*mujahideen*), motivated by their religious convictions, waged a violent struggle, or *jihad*, to advance Palestinian Arab and Muslim interests. When British troops killed the charismatic sheikh on November 19, 1935, he became a martyr to the Palestinian cause, an idealistic patriot whose fervor and self-sacrifice still inspire Palestinian Muslims today. In fact, the "military wing" of Hamas, the al-Qassam Brigades, bears his name, as do the al-Qassam rockets fired from the Gaza Strip into Israel. The sheikh's radical politics offered an alternative to the less extreme ideology and tactics of the established, or more recognized, Palestinian leadership of that time, personified by the second key figure: the mufti of Jerusalem, Haj Muhammad Amin al-Husseini (1895–1974).

Al-Husseini was, and remains, one of the most controversial Palestinian leaders of the twentieth century. Arab nationalists have idealized him as a patriot waging a war of principled resistance against Zionism, while Israeli Jews have vilified him as a genocidal anti-Semite and fanatic. A sympathetic, but critical, biography of the mufti by Philip Mattar (1988) analyzes his role in Middle East affairs over a long and influential life, during which he managed to antagonize more pragmatic Arab leaders (such as King Abdullah of Jordan in the 1940s), as well as British authorities and the Zionist leadership. After rising to power at age twenty-four as head of the Supreme Arab Council under the British Mandate – appointed by High Commissioner Herbert Samuel, himself a Jew and a Zionist – he used his office, with its resources and its network of mosques in Palestine, to mobilize anti-Jewish violence. He also used his contacts in other Muslim countries to encourage international pressure against the Zionist movement.

The British exiled the mufti to Iraq in 1936, in response to the outbreak of the Arab Revolt. He made his way to Berlin and made common cause with Adolf Hitler and other Nazi leaders. He recruited Muslim soldiers in Bosnia and elsewhere for the Axis cause, yet he wrote in his memoirs (published in Damascus in 1999) that the Palestinians were not in favor of exterminating the Jews. Mattar and others claim that his political alliance with the Nazis was forged mainly because the Germans were fighting his two principal enemies, the British and the Zionists, and because Germany had supported the Ottoman Empire in World War I, when al-Husseini was an officer in the Ottoman army.[3]

Placed in their historical context, the lives of al-Qassam and al-Husseini shed light on more recent events. Islamist movements such as Hamas (the "Islamic Resistance Movement") or the more radical Palestinian Islamic Jihad did not emerge in a vacuum, and it is important to realize that throughout the twentieth century religion played a profound role in Palestinian politics. Those politics were, in turn, influenced by developments elsewhere in the Middle East, especially the growth of the Muslim Brotherhood (*Al-Ikhwan al-Muslimun*). This movement was founded in Egypt in 1928 and has inspired branches in other Arab countries, including Palestine.[4] The Palestinian branch, formally established in the 1940s, was motivated by two major imperatives that converged in its ideology and activism: (1) to resist the growing strength of Zionism and then Israel, and (2) to further the creation of one pan-Islamic nation using political and military means in a sacred struggle (*jihad*) on behalf of God and Islamic principles. Khaled Hroub traces the evolution of the Muslim Brotherhood in Palestine, its ties to the Ikhwan branches in Egypt and Jordan, and its ambivalent relations with the more secular nationalist movement Fatah. For decades, especially during the time of Egyptian President Nasser's popularity (and his suppression of the Egyptian Brotherhood), the

> Palestinian Brotherhood continued to maintain that mobilization for the war of liberation had to have a proper Islamic foundation. A generation of Muslims committed to their faith and prepared for sacrifice had to be raised by shaping the character of individual members of that generation in a true Islamic mold.[5]

While Fatah and other PLO groups engaged in guerrilla warfare against Israel, the Brotherhood opted for a "cultural renaissance designed to instill true Islam in the soul of the individual" before engaging in a collective liberation struggle in concert with the rest of the Islamic *umma* (worldwide community). From the late 1960s through the 1980s, Palestinian Islamists consolidated their influence through the creation of mosques, student societies, and charitable societies, drawing Muslim youth into their circles. The decline of Nasserism following the debacle of June, 1967, helped attract followers, as the appeal of secular nationalism and leftist ideologies waned and as Israel consolidated its occupation of the territories won in the Six-Day War.

The Islamic revolution in Iran, bringing Ayatollah Khomeini to power in 1979, reverberated throughout the Middle East, as Islamists drew inspiration and hope from this watershed development. Fathi al-Shikaki, Abd al-Aziz Awad, and other radical students broke away from the Brotherhood, considered too moderate, to form Palestinian Islamic Jihad (PIJ). Even though these militants were Sunni Muslims, they saw the revolutionary theocratic regime in

Tehran as a model for an Islamic government in all of historic Palestine. In addition, the Shi'ite focus on martyrdom has influenced the ideology and tactics of PIJ, which adopted suicide bombing against Israeli civilian targets as a central element of its jihadist struggle. Its uncompromising ideology has kept PIJ outside of any political negotiations, doctrinally committed to armed struggle against Israel.

The ideas and policies of Hamas, the Islamic Resistance Movement, are more nuanced and variegated than those of PIJ. As discussed in chapter 20 in this volume, Khaled Hroub demonstrates how the movement adjusted its doctrine and tactics in response to events. It was founded in conjunction with the First *Intifada*, which broke out in December, 1987. The earlier Islamic Brotherhood movement, along with Sheikh Ahmed Yassin's existing activist group (founded in 1983), helped to found Hamas, thus initiating a new phase in the Islamist struggle against Israel. An "Introductory Memorandum," issued by Hamas in 1993, offers a succinct rationale for the movement's existence and includes these statements:

> Hamas is a popular struggle movement that seeks to liberate Palestine in its entirety from the Mediterranean Sea to the River Jordan. It bases its ideology and politics on the teachings of Islam and its juridical tradition. It welcomes all those who believe in its ideas and stands and who are ready to bear the consequences of sacred struggle (*jihad*) for the liberation of Palestine and the establishment in it of an independent Islamic state.... Hamas believes that the ongoing conflict between the Arabs and Muslims and the Zionists in Palestine is a fateful civilizational struggle incapable of being brought to an end without eliminating its cause, namely, the Zionist settlement of Palestine.... Believing in the sacredness of Palestine and its Islamic status, Hamas believes it impermissible under any circumstances to concede any part of Palestine or to recognize the legitimacy of the Zionist occupation of it.

Hamas bases its position on traditional Islamic jurisprudence (*fiqh*) and the doctrine of *Dar al-Islam* (or Domain of Islam).[6] According to this view, Jewish national sovereignty over any part of Palestine violates God's will, and a territorial compromise with Israel is therefore prohibited. Hamas (along with other Islamist movements) perceives the Zionist enterprise as part of a general Western campaign against Islam and Muslims, making militant resistance to Zionism a pan-Islamic imperative.

One of the crucial differences between "Islamist" movements and traditional Islamic thought is their attitude towards Jews and Judaism. Muslims are taught by the Qur'an and later sources that Torah Judaism is a revealed religion, since Moses and the other biblical prophets are also Muslim prophets. This basic teaching leads many Muslims to distinguish between Judaism (seen as legitimate) and Zionism (perceived as an illegitimate corruption of the Torah).[7] Ironically, there are some strictly observant (*haredi*) Jews who make a similar distinction and value judgment,[8] and the Palestinian leadership has, on occasion, enlisted these *haredi* Jews to bolster their political claims.

One rarely hears Jews making a distinction between "Islamic" and "Islamist," probably because most Jews do not know enough to distinguish between the two, and media stereotypes tend to paint Muslims in general as inherently anti-Jewish. Part of the challenge in seeking a just and lasting peace in Israel/Palestine is finding ways to rehumanize the demonized "enemy," in a spirit of mutual respect and appreciation.

It remains to be seen whether Hamas leaders, or their followers, are capable of sufficient doctrinal flexibility to enter into fruitful negotiations with Israel, aiming for a two-state compromise. Over time, strategic considerations have allowed Hamas representatives to make a distinction between a "historic solution" (ultimate victory) and an "interim solution" (either a temporary armistice, or *hudna*, or a popular referendum to forge a national consensus). Since the ascendancy of Hamas in Palestinian elections, and then its violent takeover of the Gaza Strip following confrontations with Fatah and the Palestinian Authority, Hamas leaders have had more opportunities to demonstrate flexibility and pragmatism. Political empowerment brings responsibility, and revolutionary rhetoric usually gets tempered by realism. In this respect, Hamas faces the same challenge facing fervently partisan religious Zionists: whether to compromise on divinely revealed principles (considered theoretical "truth," but not realizable in practice) in favor of benefits that can be realistically achieved – including freedom, dignity, sovereign control over territory, material prosperity, and, above all, the saving of human lives sacrificed for an absolutist objective.

Any political resolution to this conflict will require courageous acts by Muslim and Jewish leaders who place life and peace above religiously sanctioned violence. The political compromises they endorse, at the cost of maximum territorial aspirations, will mean renunciation of doctrinal positions that fuel religious extremism. Some of them may risk their lives or their livelihoods in the process, but they will do so to ensure a better future for their children and the generations to come.

The influence of Palestinian Christians

For Christianity, Israel/Palestine is also a holy land. Places associated with the life and ministry of Jesus – including Bethlehem, Nazareth, the Jordan River, and Jerusalem – have been pilgrimage sites for Christian tourists for centuries. Although the vast majority of Palestinians living in the land today (some 97 percent) are Sunni Muslims, the spiritual and political influence of Palestinian Christians, linked by faith and history to their fellow Christians abroad, is far more significant than their numbers would suggest. In recent decades prominent Christian Palestinian writers have had considerable influence presenting their people's experience to a largely Western public. Among them are George Antonius (*The Arab Awakening*, 1938), Edward Said (*The Question of Palestine*, 1979, and other works), and Hanan Ashrawi (*This Side of Peace: A Personal Account*, 1995).

Given their position as a tiny minority living in the midst of two larger religious populations locked in conflict for the last century, the Christians of Israel and Palestine face many challenges. Among them is a basic identity issue: which is paramount, their Christian faith or their Palestinian nationality?[9] For most, both elements are essential for defining themselves, and it could be that whichever is more threatened at any particular moment becomes, at that instant, more salient. Since all Palestinians, including those who hold Israeli citizenship, feel the pressure of Israeli rule beyond the 1967 borders, the mutual solidarity of Christians and Muslims struggling to forge a self-governing society in the midst of violent conflict and economic hardship has usually taken precedence. But there are, at the same time, ongoing tensions between Christians and Muslims within Palestinian society, exacerbated by Islamist aspirations to create an Islamic state in their own image. The Christians of the West Bank – and, even more, the tiny community in Gaza – can feel intimidated either to conform to the Islamists' agenda or to remain silent. Their coreligionists in East Jerusalem are in a special bind of their own, since the seats of the different churches are there, under Israeli rule. Even in Nazareth, within Israel, tensions were evident when Muslims sought to construct a mosque close to the historic Church of the Annunciation.

Palestinian Christians are also caught up in the wider religious battles between various Christian communities abroad. There are two main Christian factions in the West that take opposing stands on the Israeli–Palestinian conflict. In the first group are the evangelical Protestant churches, which tend to be pro-Israel/Zionist, seeing modern-day Israel as the fulfillment of biblical prophecies which also presage (in their interpretation) a Christian eschatological victory in the Second Coming of Christ. For some of these apocalyptic "Christian Zionists," Islam as a religion is inherently evil and functions, in their religious worldview, as the archetypal anti-Christ. In the second faction are the pro-Palestinian "liberationists," who tend to see Palestinian Christians and Muslims as oppressed victims of Zionism and Israel, or at least of Israel's occupation of Palestinian territory after 1967. Some of them are theological supersessionists, denying a continued Jewish covenant with the God of history that links Jews everywhere with the land of Israel. Others reflect a "liberation theology" that views the conflict dualistically, with the Jews as the oppressors and Palestinian Arabs as the oppressed. Yet others hold theological views that emphasize social justice, and they see the indignities suffered by Palestinians as a profound matter of faith and conscience, but without embracing anti-Judaism. Given this range of Christian attitudes outside Israel/Palestine, Palestinian Christians appeal to their coreligionists abroad to take them seriously and to offer them support.

A recent public statement issued by an ecumenical group of sixteen Palestinian Christians has prompted considerable controversy, especially among Jewish groups in the United States. Called *The Kairos Palestine Document*, modeled on a similar statement from churches in South Africa during the apartheid era, it was released in Bethlehem on December 14, 2009.[10] The authors seek to bear witness to an inclusive love that does not discriminate or favor either side in the conflict over the Holy Land. Yet their Palestinian loyalties, deepened by the prolonged anguish of their communities, make that kind of nonpartisan love virtually impossible to share with Jews and Muslims, who are in need of such a faithful Christian witness. "The mission of the Church is prophetic," they assert, "to speak the Word of God courageously, honestly and lovingly in the local context and in the midst of daily events. If she does take sides, it is with the oppressed" – and that means, for them, their fellow Palestinians. But, by taking sides, their courage is minimized, and the honesty and love they profess become self-referencing.

While the document's signatories affirm that "our presence in this land, as Christian and Muslim Palestinians, is not accidental but deeply rooted in the history and geography of this land," they do not affirm any Jewish connection to the land, historically or spiritually, and so they never call for a two-state arrangement that would allow both peoples to exercise the right of return and self-determination. Moreover, they do not offer any acknowledgement that Muslim or Christian Palestinians might share responsibility for holding both peoples hostage to continued violence and suffering. Their calls for repentance are directed to two different Christian constituencies. The first call is to their own Palestinian community for "our silence, indifference, [and] lack of communion," weakening the Christian witness by remaining internally divided or putting institutional interests before solidarity with other Palestinians who have suffered. There is no suggestion that Jews deserve empathy for *their* suffering, and there is no direct criticism of violence perpetrated against innocent Israelis. The second call to repentance is to other (mostly Western) Christians who use the Bible to favor Jewish claims, while ignoring or rejecting the claims of Palestinians. By omitting any reference to the long history of Christian anti-Judaism or to Christian animosity towards Muslims from the time of the Crusades, the authors of the *Kairos Palestine Document* have missed an opportunity to speak effectively to the hearts and consciences of their non-Christian neighbors. This missed opportunity is very unfortunate, given that most Israeli rabbis and Palestinian Muslim clerics are paid by governmental authorities, making the Christian religious leaders freer to speak their minds, hearts, and consciences than their counterparts in the other two Abrahamic communities.

The challenge of interreligious peace-building

At the outset of this essay, it was acknowledged that, even though the Israeli–Palestinian conflict is not essentially a religious war, nonetheless religious traditions that sanctify territory and history are invoked to justify nationalistic claims, and they are fundamental to the identities of both Arabs and Jews. Given this assessment, it follows that the identities and loyalties underlying the conflict might be transformed in the direction of peaceful coexistence by unconventional, or counter-cultural, religious teachings, rituals, and other spiritually resonant actions grounded in one or more of the Abrahamic faiths.

One illustrative example is a campaign by the Bereaved Families Forum, a coalition of Israeli and Palestinian families who have lost loved ones in the course of the conflict. The group organized a display of coffins, hundreds of them, covered with Israeli and Palestinian flags. They represented the number of casualties incurred until then during the Second *Intifada*. Along with the rows of coffins was a banner with the organization's slogan: "Better the pains of peace than the agonies of war." Since Judaism and Islam both teach that saving one human life is tantamount to saving the entire world, this powerful symbolic act – repeated in various places, including the UN Plaza in New York – affected people deeply. Another spiritually resonant act was a peace demonstration held several years ago by a group of Israeli Jewish women. They called on their fellow Israelis to relinquish sovereignty over the West Bank ("Judea and Samaria" to religious Jews) for the sake of peace. Among the holy sites in that territory are the Tomb of the Patriarchs in Hebron/Al-Khalil, Joseph's Tomb in Shechem/Nablus, and Rachel's Tomb near Bethlehem. The women held aloft a huge sign with the message: "Better to cry over the graves of our ancestors from afar than to cry over the graves of our children up close."

In addition to public demonstrations by religious peace activists, there is evidence that Jewish, Christian, and Muslim clergy have been instrumental in lessening the level of violence in Israel/Palestine, or at least preventing an escalation of the fighting.[11] On occasion they have been proactive in forging fruitful contacts between representatives of the two sides. The historic Alexandria summit in January 2002, for example, was an attempt by high-ranking clerics of all three Abrahamic faiths to find common spiritual and ethical ground in the midst of the Second *Intifada*. Courageous personalities such as Rabbi Menahem Froman, from the West Bank settlement of Tekoa, and Sheikh Talal el-Sider, a former Hamas leader, have met to discuss elements of a peace agreement based on Jewish–Muslim reconciliation. In addition, many grassroots interfaith dialogue and social action projects are facilitated by faithful activists in both Israel and Palestine.[12]

The potential for the religious dimension of Israeli–Palestinian peace-building would command greater attention, vying with the religious extremists in newsworthiness, if clergy and grassroots educators were included in the negotiations, if professional training of diplomats included sensitivity to religious factors in intercommunal conflicts, if the media gave religious peacemakers greater coverage and legitimacy, and if philanthropic agencies would support their efforts.

Rabbi Dr. Marc Gopin, a leading theorist and practitioner of religious peacemaking, pointed to Israelis and Palestinians who are living out their convictions by building bridges between their embattled communities:

> Many do have followings in the West who sustain them with modest support, but they plainly would be far more effective if policymaking circles and political leaders had seen them from the beginning as assets to the peace process. In fact, they have sustained vital relations at times when everyone else has given up. Furthermore, their visibility from time to time on the streets of Israel, in the public square, has been among the few signs of hope

that many Jews and Arabs ever see. I have personally witnessed how meaningful that has been for otherwise hopeless citizens on both sides of the conflict.[13]

I share Gopin's assessment that religious peacemakers have a unique potential to break through conditioned reflexes that are reinforced by conventional religious thinking. They can share stories of spiritual transformation stimulated by encounters with neighbors, colleagues, and even strangers of a different faith. Those stories can, in turn, help transform others, creating a chain reaction rooted in the Spirit.[14]

At the level of communal leadership, a different understanding of the sacred has to be taught by clerics and educators. They need to exemplify a "hierarchy of holiness" that places the sanctity of human lives above holy land and holy places. This is especially true in addressing the sensitive issues concerning Jerusalem, above all the area Jews call the Temple Mount and Muslims call the Haram al-Sharif. In a more conducive context of trust and goodwill, it might be possible for Jews, Christians, and Muslims to design a political framework for peaceful coexistence in a shared Jerusalem. With the holy city serving as a dual capital of Israel and Palestine, both nations could agree to offer up to God the sacred plateau at its heart, deeming it extraterritorial space in terms of sovereignty, with the *waqf* Islamic trust continuing to administer the al-Aqsa Mosque and Dome of the Rock. This was proposed by the late King Hussein of Jordan, and others have endorsed his idea. But, in the meantime, voices are heard in both national communities delegitimizing the other's attachments to this sacred site. Such mutual denial adds poison to an already lethal atmosphere.

Jews, Christians, Muslims, Druse, and others in the Holy Land are hungry for an experience of true holiness, rooted in an awareness of the all-loving and inclusively just God. That God has created individuals and nations with such striking differences in order to create a variegated human community that can celebrate diversity instead of feeling threatened by it (cf. Qur'an 49: 13). If both Jews and Palestinians could affirm that the land belongs to God alone, and that by the grace of God both peoples belong to the land (cf. Exodus 19: 5–6), they could build a life-affirming political framework on this spiritual foundation.[15] All the children of Abraham can be partners in the task of collective consecration, rather than rivals competing for divine favor on the basis of a scarcity principle. With regard to truth and holiness, the principle of abundance, of gracious generosity, has to take over. And, for this to happen, religious educators must learn from one another, pray for one another, and work together to support the political agenda of reconciliation. Without a shared commitment to genuine sacrifice – humility and renunciation for the sake of God – all the peace plans advanced by diplomats will fail. God's Holy Land is meant to be a laboratory for practicing justice and compassion towards all. If we rise to that challenge, we will all be blessed by the holiness of *Shalom*, *Salaam*, Peace.

Notes

1 Hertzberg (1997).
2 See: www.netivot-shalom.org.il
3 Mattar sees al-Husseini as a political opportunist whose main objective was "to stop the Jewish emigration to Palestine that he saw as leading to displacement or eviction of his own people."
4 Hroub (2000).
5 Ibid.: 28.
6 The classical doctrine anticipates that lands not under Muslim rule, comprising *Dar al-Harb* (the Domain of War), will eventually be subsumed under *Dar al-Islam*. This kind of historical determinism mirrors, in principle, the Gush Emunim position on the Jewish side – with one significant difference: its eschatological vision encompasses the entire globe.

7 Hamas's "Introductory Memorandum" includes a rare denigration of Judaism in explaining its anti-Zionist position, saying its political stance is based on a "profound understanding of the Zionist enemy, its intellectual background in the Torah and Talmud, the writings of the founders of the Zionist movement, and its attachment to the myths of the promised land, God's chosen people, and Greater Israel" (Hroub 2000: 299). This disparaging connection between traditional Jewish sources and modern Zionism turns the claims of religious Zionists on their heads.

8 The Neturei Karta (Guardians of the City) movement and the Satmar Hasidim oppose political Zionism as a sinful rebellion against God, looking forward to a messianic kingdom in place of the State of Israel.

9 Sennott (2001).

10 See www.voltairenet.org/article163282.html.

11 Landau (2003).

12 For the text of the Alexandria Declaration and reports on grassroots interfaith meetings and activities, see ibid.

13 Quoted ibid.: 8.

14 One initiative demonstrating this transformative power is the Open House Center for Coexistence and Reconciliation in Ramle, Israel. Its unique story of two families – one Israeli and one Palestinian – and their shared home in Ramle, is reverberating around the world through Sandy Tolan's book *The Lemon Tree* (Tolan 2007). See www.friendsofopenhouse.org.

15 For a kabbalistic approach to healing the Israeli–Palestinian conflict, see Landau (2008).

References and further reading

Burrell, D., and Landau, Y. (eds) (1992) *Voices from Jerusalem: Jews and Christians Reflect on the Holy Land* (New York: Paulist Press).

Chacour, E. (with Jensen, M. E.) (1990) *We Belong to the Land* (New York: HarperCollins).

Gopin, M. (2002) *Holy War, Holy Peace: How Religion Can Bring Peace to the Middle East* (New York: Oxford University Press).

Gopin, M. (2009) *To Make the Earth Whole: The Art of Citizen Diplomacy in an Age of Religious Militancy* (Lanham, MD: Rowman & Littlefield).

Hertzberg, A. (ed.) (1997) *The Zionist Idea: A Historical Analysis and Reader* (Philadelphia: Jewish Publication Society).

Hroub, K (2000) *Hamas: Political Thought and Practice* (Washington, DC: Institute for Palestine Studies).

Landau, Y. (1989) "Blessing Both Jew and Palestinian: A Religious Zionist Perspective," *The Christian Century*, 20–27 December.

Landau, Y. (2003) *Healing the Holy Land: Interreligious Peacebuilding in Israel/Palestine* (Washington, DC: United States Institute of Peace Press); available at www.usip.org/files/resources/pwks51.pdf.

Landau, Y. (2008) "The Land of Israel in Jewish–Christian–Muslim Relations," *Studies in Christian–Jewish Relations*, 3/1: 1–12; available at: http://ejournals.bc.edu/ojs/index.php/scjr/article/view/1501/1354.

Little, D. (ed.) (2007) *Peacemakers in Action: Profiles of Religion in Conflict Resolution* (New York: Cambridge University Press).

Lustick, I. S. (1988) *For the Land and the Lord: Jewish Fundamentalism in Israel* (New York: Council on Foreign Relations).

Mattar, P. (1988) *The Mufti of Jerusalem: Al-Hajj al-Husayni and the Palestinian National Movement* (New York: Columbia University Press).

Raheb, M. (1995) *I am a Palestinian Christian* (Minneapolis: Fortress Press).

Ravitzky, A. (1996) *Messianism, Zionism, and Jewish Religious Radicalism* (Chicago: University of Chicago Press).

Sennott, C. M. (2001) *The Body and the Blood: The Holy Land's Christians at the Turn of a New Millennium* (New York: PublicAffairs/Perseus Books).

Tolan, S. (2007) *The Lemon Tree: An Arab, a Jew, and the Heart of the Middle East* (New York: Bloomsbury).

15

Economic aspects

Arie Arnon

Introduction

Economic factors rarely receive mention in a general discussion of the Israeli–Palestinian conflict. The most obvious reason for this omission is that the more directly political dimension of
the conflict overshadows all others. This has not always been the case. During the British Mandate, when Jews and Arabs lived side by side in Palestine, the economic dimension did not
enjoy secondary importance at all. In fact, the disparate economic performances of the Jewish
and Arab populations in Palestine at the time transformed the balance of power between the
two sides and had a major role in shaping the conflict. Economic factors, while frequently
overlooked, continued to characterize the conflict in later periods too.

The second section of this chapter elaborates on the years before 1967, emphasizing the formative experience of the Mandate period as well as the post-1948 experience. The 1948 war
led to the creation of the refugee problem and with its devastating economic impact, shaped
the economic aspect of the conflict for at least nineteen years. In 1967, a new war transformed
the region. The third section addresses the various economic aspects of this new era, emphasizing labor and trade, the public sector, money and banking, and the economic performance of
the Palestinian economy in the West Bank and Gaza under occupation. Economic factors were
of primary importance, although now, as intended by Israel, they supported the status quo and
did not change the fundamental balance of power between the warring sides.

The First *Intifada*, in 1987, and the subsequent political process, resulted in attempts to
reshape the political and the economic dimensions of the conflict. While both attempts have so
far failed, the two sides agreed on a new framework for economic relations in the form of the
1994 Paris Protocol. The fourth section analyzes these new arrangements and assesses their
impact. The final section covers the years after 2000, when a series of events – "closures", the
Second *Intifada*, the election in 2006 – led to the *de facto* collapse of the 1994 arrangements.
The fact that no formal alternative to the 1994 Paris Protocol was agreed upon, or even
proposed, testifies to the damaging lacuna that exists in the economic sphere in 2012.

The economic dimension before 1967

The conflict's most basic attributes are demographic changes and the struggle over land; both have clear economic implications. Together they indicate that the conflict arose out of the desire of two communities – one indigenous and one claiming to have been indigenous – to live on the same land. The demographic changes in Palestine during the British Mandate years are well known. In 1922, when the British conducted the first census, they counted 84,000 Jews and 680,000 Arabs in Palestine. Thus, the Jewish population amounted to less than 12 percent of the Arab population. The fact that Jews immigrated in large numbers in the following years changed this ratio: by 1947 about 600,000 Jews lived in Palestine compared with about 1,300,000 Arabs. Thus, the Jewish population was now close to 45 percent that of the Arab.

Changes in economic indicators were even more striking: the Jewish economy measured by its Gross Domestic Product (GDP) was about 25 percent of the Arab economy in 1922; by 1947 the Jewish GDP outperformed the Arab GDP by almost 20 percent. The standard of living, measured by Gross National Product per capita (GNP-PC), saw a less dramatic change: in 1922 the average standard of living in the Jewish population was around twice that of the Arab; by 1947 it was two and a half times higher than the Arab standard of living. These changes reflect the very different performances of the Arab and Jewish economies during those twenty-five years. Although the two economies existed side by side, with no border and almost no distance between them, actual economic interactions were fewer than one might expect. The two traded in goods and services, and some Arab workers found employment in the Jewish economy. However, interactions were not welcomed; in particular, there was some resistance to trade links on both sides, and on the Jewish side there was a campaign against employing Arab workers, under the slogan "*Avoda Ivrit*" ("Hebrew work").

The proximity of the two economies, the lack of borders, and the fact that both were governed by the same foreign authority did not prevent diverging tendencies between them. The Jewish economy and society managed to bring in more human and non-human capital, was better organized, tended to concentrate less on agriculture and more on services, and enjoyed high levels of growth. The Arab economy tended to have a more traditional structure, with more agriculture, far fewer capital-intensive sectors, and less growth. By the end of the Mandate period, the Jewish economy, while lagging far behind the more developed economies in the world, was more advanced than the Arab economy.

The different growth rates of the two populations are behind the story of the Mandate period. Although the data presented in Table 15.3 show that both economies performed quite well, the Jewish economy overtook its Arab rival. The Jewish population increased eightfold between 1922 and 1947, while the Arab population only doubled; the Jewish and Arab economies measured by their GDP reflected the strength of the former, while the standard of living of the Jewish population rose much faster than that of its Arab counterpart.

New circumstances prevailed for both the Jewish and Arab societies in Palestine following the 1948 war. First, the geographic partition of the land: around 77 percent of the area between the Jordan River and the Mediterranean Sea came under the jurisdiction of the newly created State of Israel, while 23 percent, known as the West Bank (of the Jordan River), came under Jordanian jurisdiction. Thus, after 1948 and up to 1967, an economic border existed between Israel and the West Bank, as well as between Israel and the much smaller Gaza Strip. Second, the war led to a massive population movement: about 700,000 Palestinians became, and remain, refugees.

The refugees constituted about 80 percent of the Palestinian Arabs who before 1948 had been living in the area that became Israel. Only 160,000 Palestinian Arabs stayed in Israel and

Table 15.1 Population data, 1922–1947

Year	Jews	Arabs
1922	84,000	680,000
1931	175,000	860,000
1935	322,000	941,000
1939	432,000	1,040,000
1947	610,000	1,334,000

Source: Metzer and Kaplan (1990); Metzer (1998).

Table 15.2 Jewish economy vs. Arab economy: ratios between the population, GDP, and GNP-PC, 1922 and 1947 (percentages)

	1922	1947
Population	11.9	45.7
GDP	26.1	119.1
GNP-PC	191.1	260.5

Source: Metzer (1998: 16).

Table 15.3 Jewish economy vs. Arab economy: growth rates of population, GDP, and GNP-PC, 1922–1947 (percentages)

	Jewish economy	Arab economy
Population	8.5	2.8
GDP	13.2	6.5
GNP-PC	4.8	3.6

Source: Metzer (1998: 16).

lived under military rule up to 1966. The 700,000 who left, under coercion or by choice, found themselves in the West Bank, in Gaza, and in the surrounding areas. After 1949, the majority of the refugees, about 300,000, resided in the West Bank, which increased its population from 400,000 to 700,000 in just a few months. Gaza, which had had a population of only 75,000, became the place of residence of 150,000 refugees. The remaining 250,000 refugees resided mainly in Jordan (in the East Bank), in Lebanon, and in Syria. Thus, the war saw a massive movement of the Palestinian population, with tremendous economic consequences. After the war, Jewish population movements, mainly from Arab countries but also from Europe, reshaped the population mixture.

The refugees left their property behind. Israel took possession of Palestinian properties via a chain of rules and newly created authorities that in effect confiscated them. The UN created an authority, UNRWA (United Nations Relief and Work Authority), that was responsible for providing basic services to the refugees in the five areas where the majority resided: Gaza, the West Bank, Jordan, Syria, and Lebanon. It also created the UNCCP (Nations Conciliation Commission for Palestine) in an effort to promote a solution to the refugee problem.

From 1949 to 1967, the West Bank was part of the Jordanian economy and less developed than the East Bank. Gaza was a separate region in Egypt, suffering high unemployment and low standards of living. The 1967 war and the occupation of the West Bank and Gaza reshaped the geography and transformed the conflict yet again.

The new reality after 1967: Israeli occupation of the West Bank and Gaza

The 1967 war marks a turning point and demonstrates how unforeseen consequences can transform reality. According to most observers, no thought had been given in advance to the economic implications of the West Bank and Gaza coming under the military occupation of Israel. The new political reality borders would dramatically change the economic dimension of the conflict. For a while, Israel hesitated as to whether to keep open the economic border along the pre-1967 Green Line. After a year or so of internal debate, Israel decided to allow Palestinians into Israel to work.[1] Thus, the pre-1967 closed labor borders were now open to Palestinians seeking employment within the Israeli economy. In addition, Israel imposed its trade protocol along the new external borders of the Palestinian economy, creating a customs union (CU), albeit an unusual one. This Israeli–Palestinian customs union was imposed on the Palestinians. No new trade protocol was negotiated, as is usually the case with CUs, and no "revenue sharing" arrangement, which is a customary feature of CUs, was specified. Thus, since 1967 most revenues from taxes on imports to the Palestinian economy has ended up financing the Israeli public sector. On the other hand, Israel has provided financial support to the public sector within the Palestinian economy. Trade borders along the old Green Line ceased to exist. Palestinian and Israeli producers could, in principle, sell their products on the other side of the border without paying customs duty or facing barriers to trade. In reality, there were some restrictions on Palestinians selling in Israel, in particular agricultural goods. More significantly, Israel implemented some restrictions on what Palestinians could produce.

The next few years saw a transformation in the Palestinian economy in the West Bank and Gaza, with significant changes in employment structure, trade relations, the public sector, money, and banking. The new economy, coupled with higher standards of living, meant job seekers could receive higher wages, and Palestinians increasingly sought work in Israel; at the same time, Israeli employers could now pay lower wages to Palestinian workers than to their Israeli counterparts. This dual attraction based on economic interests threatened traditional employment patterns within the Palestinian and Israeli economies that had until this point been separate. The Israeli government's first reaction in 1967 was to try to maintain the pre-1967 labor borders, declaring that, while trade in goods would be permitted, Palestinians would not be allowed to work in Israel. This initial decision was influenced both by the high unemployment rate in Israel before the war, when the country experienced its worst recession since 1948, and by early reservations concerning the integration of the two societies and economies. However, in less than two years the restrictions on employing Palestinian laborers in Israel had disappeared. The economic boom after 1967 and the outcome of the government debate on economic integration led to a canceling of labor borders between the Palestinian and Israeli economies. The hegemonic idea among Israeli policy-makers was that maintaining high employment levels in the West Bank and Gaza served Israel's interests; supporting normal and even prosperous economic life in the Occupied Territories was in line with the strategic priority of weakening any potential opposition to Israel's continued occupation.

The economic patterns that emerged in such a dual, segmented labor market for Palestinians – where one segment exists in the West Bank and Gaza and another in Israel – confirm basic economic predictions. Palestinian workers and Israeli employers found each other in the market place. A significant number of Palestinians turned to the Israeli economy for employ-ment, where at first wages were much higher than in the Palestinian economy. The decrease in the number of seeking employment close to their homes, and the increase in the number commuting and looking for work away from home, led naturally to a decline in the initial gap in wages paid in the two economies to Palestinian workers. During the first five years of the occupation the number of workers from the West Bank and Gaza employed in Israel reached about 30 percent of the labor force; at the same time the gap in wages paid to Palestinians in Israel and those paid to Palestinians in the West Bank and Gaza declined to only 20 percent. Thus by 1972, and for the next fifteen years, we find a stable pattern in the dual labor market for Palestinians.

The trade regime between the Israeli and Palestinian economies after 1967 as described above was an involuntary, one sided, impure custom union. Exchange between Israeli and Palestinian traders was ostensibly free, and the geographical area comprising Israel and the West Bank and Gaza Strip had no internal trade borders, or trade barriers.[2] Trade with the rest of the world was carried out under the Israeli trade regime and according to Israel's (changing) policies. Thus, Israeli customs and other barriers to trade operated along the external borders of the combined area. Since there was no Palestinian (economic) authority and Palestinians did not participate in policy-making, all decisions were made by the Israeli authorities.

In theory, such a one-sided customs union should have resulted in different economic processes from those that actually evolved. Thus, in spite of the asymmetrical trade regime, the difference in real wages between Israel and the Palestinian economy should have led to more Palestinian goods being sold on the Israeli market and fewer Israeli goods being sold on the Palestinian market. The fact that this did not happen was the result of political causes or inter-ventions in the economic process. The actual trade pattern between the Israeli and Palestinian economies also reflects the uneven relations between the two. Israel exported more to the West Bank and Gaza than would be expected under normal conditions; it also imported more than one might predict, but less than it exported. The result was a very significant trade deficit, covered in part by the massive export of labor to Israel (see Tables 15.4 and 15.5, columns 4, 5, and 6).

One major intervention in the economic process took the form of direct administrative measures related to production capacity in the Palestinian economy. Palestinian entrepreneurs had to apply for licenses from the Israeli authorities for every economic activity they sought to initiate. Israel's policy, at least until the 1990s, was not to encourage local economic devel-opment.[3] This policy, and the measures taken to enforce it, turned important sections of the Palestinian market into a captive market in which Israeli producers had a significant advan-tage; it also put the Israeli market almost out of reach of potential Palestinian entrepreneurs who would otherwise have been able to compete with Israeli and foreign producers. Under the economic circumstances that prevailed between 1968 and 1994, when imposed economic integration was in force, theory would have led us to predict the emergence of tough competi-tion between Israeli and Palestinian producers in both markets. Such competition was prevented in many spheres.

As is clear from the data presented in Tables 15.4 and 15.5, the Palestinian economy was not only much smaller than that of Israel (column 7), it also became dependent on the former in both employment and trade. Although the growth rate of the Palestinian economy was impres-sive, especially during the first five years, its relative size as measured by its GDP remained throughout less than 5 percent that of the Israeli GDP. Dependency on employment in Israel characterizes relations between the two economies: in the West Bank, around 30 percent of

Table 15.4 Basic data on the West Bank, 1968–1993

	(1) GDP growth rates (average annual % change)	*(2)* GNP per capita growth rates (average annual % change)	*(3)* Employed in Israel (% of total employment)	*(4)* Factor income from abroad (% of GDP)	*(5)* Imports (% of GDP)	*(6)* Exports (% of GDP)	*(7)* GDP as % of Israel's GDP
1968–72	15	20	21[a]	20[a]	67	22	2.6
1973–9	6	4	30	32	73	25	3.1
1980–87	5	2	32	28	63	24	3.5
1989–93	8	5	31	30	n/a	n/a	3.7

Source: ICBS (1996).

Note: [a] For the years 1970–72.

Table 15.5 Basic data on the Gaza Strip, 1968–1993

	(1) GDP growth rates (average annual % change)	*(2)* GNP per capita growth rates (average annual % change)	*(3)* Employed in Israel (% of total employment)	*(4)* Factor income from abroad (% of GDP)	*(5)* Imports (% of GDP)	*(6)* Exports (% of GDP)	*(7)* GDP as % of Israel's GDP
1968–72	11	18	17[a]	9[a]	64	21	1.0
1973–9	7	6	37	28	109	36	1.1
1980–87	3	2	45	57	123	43	1.0
1989–93	7	5	34	46	79	14	1.1

Source: ICBS (1996).

Note: [a] For the years 1970–72.

total employment was in Israel; in Gaza, the percentage climbed to 45 percent in the 1980s, before the First *Intifada*. The income of the laborers, known by economists as "factor income from abroad," contributed significantly to domestic activity in both areas.

The trade deficit was high: aggregate trade figures for the West Bank show a stable pattern for exports and a less stable one for imports. After 1968, exports constituted about 20 percent of GDP and imports about 60 to 80 percent of GDP, the latter alternating in keeping with the "olive crops cycle."[4] The West Bank's largest trade partner was Israel. Most exports (60 percent on average) and most imports (90 percent on average) were to and from Israel; the second-largest partner was Jordan (about 39 percent of exports and only 3 percent of imports). Trade with the rest of the world was marginal. The result of this trade pattern was a high and persistent annual average trade deficit of about 45 percent of GDP. Aggregate trade figures for the Gaza Strip show a less stable pattern than the one found in the West Bank. Since 1968, exports have risen steadily, from about 15 percent of GDP to around 50 percent in the mid-1980s. Imports at the beginning of the period were around 50 percent of GDP, rising to over 120 percent of GDP by the 1980s. Most exports (65 percent on average) and most imports (91 percent on average), were to and from Israel; exports to Jordan were less important for the Gaza Strip than for the West Bank economy (18 percent of total exports on average) and consisted almost entirely of agricultural goods, mainly citrus. Trade with the rest of the world was negligible.

The Gaza Strip's trade deficit was higher than that of the West Bank: about 68 percent of GDP, on average, from 1968 to 1987, and about 64 percent between 1988 and 1993, compared with "only" 45 percent of GDP for the West Bank from 1968 to 1987.

Investment in the Palestinian economy tended more to investment in housing than in production, leading to a very low accumulation of capital per worker that further restricted domestic employment opportunities. Several reasons may explain this phenomenon. One is the almost complete lack of mediation in the West Bank and Gaza. After 1967, Israel ordered existing local banks to close; a few Israeli banks started to operate, but their activities were limited. For this and other reasons, the population preferred to use traditional networks – especially family ones – to channel savings into building homes for young couples and the extended family. The result was high formation of housing capital accompanied by low accumulation of equipment and productive assets.

The economic dimension after Oslo: the Paris Protocol

In September 1993, with the signing of the Oslo Accords between the government of Israel and the Palestine Liberation Organization, exclusive Israeli power over economic policy concerning the West Bank and Gaza Strip ended. Paradoxically, just as the new economic regime with the declared objective of encouraging economic development was adopted, a serious economic crisis commenced which, in various ways, pertains to the present day. Negotiations on the economic aspects of the Oslo Accords continued for six months, and in April 1994, after agreeing to implement the Declaration of Principles in Gaza and Jericho, "The Protocol on Economic Relations between the Government of Israel and the PLO Representing the Palestinian People" (the "Paris Protocol") was signed in Paris.[5] After more than a quarter of a century the era of Israeli economic policy imposed on the Occupied Territories ended, at least according to the agreement. The economic regime of the Paris Protocol is very similar to that designed at the end of the 1960s, with just few modifications discussed below.

The protocol assumed that there will be no trade border between the Israeli and Palestinian economies, as was the case since 1967, and thus, with some modifications, it continued the previous trade regime. As discussed in the previous section, the trade regime that existed between Israel and the Occupied Territories from 1967 to 1993 corresponded to the conceptual framework of a customs union, albeit one implemented unilaterally by Israel. An irregular and unusual feature of this customs union was that it did not provide any arrangement for sharing the proceeds from import taxes; the lion's share of revenues was transferred to Israel. The modifications proposed in the Paris Protocol were meant to ease certain conditions for the Palestinians – that is, the right to import certain goods in limited quantities at rates not regulated by Israeli customs (see lists A and B in the agreement).[6] It promised only limited and temporary protection for Israeli agricultural products and, most importantly, included a more reasonable arrangement for dividing import duty revenues. A bitter argument broke out during the Paris negotiations concerning the preferred trade regime. The Palestinians preferred a free trade area (FTA), such as the 1994 NAFTA agreement between the USA, Canada, and Mexico. Members of an FTA do not share a single exterior border; each partner decides its own trade regime with "the rest of the world." There are no trade borders among the partners to the agreement, but goods manufactured within the joint area – in our case Israel and the Palestinian Territories – are not subject to customs or other trade limitations when sold within the free trade area. When the Oslo Agreements and Paris Protocol were signed, Israel opposed any defined border, thus rejecting any system other than a customs union. The "reward" that was offered to the Palestinians for agreeing to a customs union related to the labor links: allowing Palestinians to continue working in Israel. Thus, along with the "carrot" in the form of a customs union appeared the "stick" – a threat to discontinue Palestinian entrance to the Israeli labor market. The Economic Protocol states that movement of workers will be as "normal" as possible and permanent blockage of the movement of workers would not be permitted; there was, however, no clarification concerning implications of frequent limits on movement.

While the Paris Protocol assumed almost complete free movement of labor and goods, in reality more and more obstacles to free movement were introduced. The restrictions started before Oslo during the first Gulf War; but after Oslo a series of violent attacks and counter-measures by Israel created a system of restrictions that culminated in what is known as the "closure" system. This began in the form of restrictions on movement to Israel but later deepened to involve restrictions on movements within the Palestinian economy. The impact of this *de facto* not-so-free movement of goods and services on the economy, including labor flows to Israel, can be seen in Tables 15.6 and 15.7.

The first three years after the signing of the Paris Protocol were particularly bad. The income brought into the economy by workers in Israel declined as a result of restrictions on labor flows. Before the 1994 interim agreements, as stated above, 30 percent of total

Table 15.6 Basic data on the West Bank, 1994–2007

	(1) GDP growth rates (average annual % change)	(2) GNI per capita growth rates (average annual % change)	(3) Employed in Israel (% of total employment)	(4) Factor Income from abroad (% of GDP)	(5) Imports (% of GDP)	(6) Exports (% of GDP)	(7) GNI as % of Israel's GDP	(8) Unemployment (%)
1994–6	6[a]	1[a]	18[a]	12	75	23	2.6	17
1997–2000	8	4	23	15	80	22	2.8	13
2001–5	1	3	14	6	81	16	2.3	23
2006–7	7	5	13	9	63	19	2.4	18

Source: PCBS and World Bank since 1994 and the author's calculations.

Note: [a] For the years 1995–6.

Table 15.7 Basic data on the Gaza Strip, 1994–2007

	(1) GDP growth rates (average annual % change)	(2) GNP per capita growth rates (average annual % change)	(3) Employed in Israel (% of total employment)	(4) Factor income from abroad (% of GDP)	(5) Imports (% of GDP)	(6) Exports (% of GDP)	(7) GNI as % of Israel's GDP	(8) Unemployment (%)
1994–6	2[a]	5[a]	6[a]	10	68	4	1.3	31
1997–2000	3	0	14	15	69	6	1.3	21
2001–5	7	2	2	4	65	6	1.2	3
2006–7	13	14	0	3	65	3	1.0	32

Source: PCBS and World Bank since 1994 and the author's calculations.

Note: [a] For the years 1995–6.

Palestinian employment in the West Bank and more than 40 percent of that in Gaza was in Israel. In 1995–6, the percentage of workers from the West Bank in Israel dropped to 18 percent and those from Gaza to only 6 percent. Thus income created by workers from the Palestinian Territories employed in Israel declined; remittances dropped from more than 30 percent of the GDP in the West Bank to about 12 percent, while in Gaza remittances dropped from some 50 percent of the GDP in the 1980s to about 10 percent.[7] At the same time, the rate of unemployment in the Occupied Territories, which had been relatively low until 1993, rose dramatically: around 17 percent in the West Bank and more than 30 percent in Gaza. GNI per capita decreased accordingly, by 1 percent in the West Bank and by 5 percent in Gaza in the years 1994–6. When a major closure ended in 1996, after the Israeli elections, economic performance improved somewhat from 1997 to 2000; more workers were allowed into Israel (see Tables 15.6 and 15.7) and unemployment rates dropped a little, allowing GNI to recover in the West Bank and to stagnate, rather than continue to decline, in Gaza. However, after the failure of the negotiations in Camp David in July 2000 and the eruption of the Second *Intifada* in the last quarter of 2000, a new negative stage began which has persisted for over a decade.

The characteristic deficit in the balance of payments continued. After 1994, the deficit was covered partly by international aid which, instead of creating conditions for sustainable development and productive growth, served mainly to prevent an even sharper drop in the standard of living. The private sector, slated to drive development in the Palestinian Territories in 1994, failed to do so mainly because successive closures, political instability, and economic uncertainty undermined the confidence of local and foreign investors. The newly formed public sector faced many difficulties, particularly the challenging process of transforming a stateless organization into a political body building national institutions. To some extent, the public sector depended upon Israel's good will: according to the Paris Protocol, Israel was responsible for transferring various funds to the Palestinian Authority, including its revenues from import taxes and other payments. Between 1995 and 2000, more than 60 percent of the revenues of the Palestinian Authority, excluding international aid, came from Israel.

To sum up, dependency on Israel did not decline after 1994 but rather transformed from dependency on Israel's labor and goods markets to financial dependency on the Palestinian public sector. One early manifestation of this trend occurred in the summer of 1997. After a wave of bombings, and contrary to the terms of the agreement, the Israeli government voted not to transfer the revenues it had collected to the Palestinians. It was not the last time that Israel would implement such measures.

2t Camp David in July 2000, another chapter unfolded in the Israeli–Palestinian dispute. From "striving to end the dispute" with a permanent two-state solution wherein Israel and Palestine would live side by side in peace, there evolved a razor-sharp rhetoric according to which, as Israeli Prime Minister Ehud Barak argued, we "unmasked our enemies" who "spoke of peace but were actually trying to destroy us." Barak convinced most Israelis that "there is no partner." When Ariel Sharon, who had always believed this to be true, came to power, he turned his back on negotiations, eliminating the possibility of repairing the failures of previous negotiations.[8]

A decade of economic failure

Those who signed the Paris Protocol anticipated a deepening of economic integration between the two economies, political stability, and a prosperous Palestinian economy; the reality was growing separation, unilaterally imposed by Israel, the creation of economic borders, and serious economic decline. After the agreement was signed in 1994, more restrictions were introduced on the movement of both goods and labor between Israel and the Occupied Territories; moreover, free movement within the Territories was now also restricted.[9] The reasons for the restrictions were cited as pertaining to security but, obviously, there were also other political calculations on the Israeli side. Without elaborating on Israel's intentions, the result was a *de facto* "closure regime" – both internal and external – very far from the openness espoused in the Paris Protocol. Violent hostilities between Israelis and Palestinians and the new economic regime contributed to fading hopes for economic prosperity in the Palestinian economy. The frequent closures and the replacement of Palestinians with foreign workers brought about a dramatic change in the pattern of relations between the Israeli and Palestinian economies.

The failure to reach a permanent agreement at Camp David, along with the outbreak of the Second *Intifada*, ended efforts to implement a permanent agreement. Since 2000, the economy has become an inextricable part of the battlefield where, as in military strategy, both sides try to achieve a decisive victory. Economic policy became an accepted tool for applying pressure as each side did its best to hurt the other. Even for public relations purposes, Israel no longer claimed to be interested in the economic prosperity of the Palestinians. The hostilities dramatically affected the economy. Israel suffered a three-year recession that damaged its GNP, but the Palestinians suffered an economic collapse on a different scale. From 2000 to 2002, living standards dropped by about 30 percent and the unemployment rate rose to levels unknown in modern economies: about 30 percent in the West Bank and nearly 40 percent in Gaza (according to ILO definitions). The poverty rate – with a poverty line fixed at a mere $2.1 per person per day – rose from 13 percent before the collapse to a peak of 40 percent in the West Bank and from 32 percent to about 65 percent in Gaza.

Several new tendencies characterize the years after 2000. On the one hand, fewer Palestinian workers were employed in Israel; this tendency was even stronger in Gaza than in the West Bank. On the other hand, after 2000, aid to the Palestinian economy from the donor community rose to unprecedented levels. Whereas between 1994 and 2000 the West Bank and Gaza received about $3 billion, in the following seven years they received around $8 billion.

Table 15.8 The West Bank and Gaza, 1994–2007: GDP, GNI, GDI, and transfers from abroad (international aid) (current million $; average per year)

	West Bank				Gaza			
	(1) GDP	*(2)* GNI (% of GDP)	*(3)* GDI (% of GDP)	*(4)* Transfers (% of GDP)	*(5)* GDP	*(6)* GNI (% of GDP)	*(7)* GDI (% of GDP)	*(8)* Transfers (% of GDP)
1994–6	2036	2341 (115%)	2608 (128%)	266 (13%)	1102	1221 (111%)	1388 (126%)	167 (15%)
1997–2000	2717	3182 (117%)	3452 (127%)	269 (10%)	1287	1487 (116%)	1658 (129%)	171 (13%)
2001–5	2632	2843 (108%)	3403 (129%)	560 (21%)	1369	1436 (105%)	1800 (131%)	364 (27%)
2006–7	3274	3674 (112%)	4687 (143%)	1013 (31%)	1372	1459 (106%)	2131 (155%)	672 (49%)

Source: PCBS and the author's calculations.

Notes: GNI equals GDP plus "factor income from abroad," mainly wages for work in Israel; GDI equals GNI plus "transfers from outside," which practically equals international aid. See PCBS (2009) *Guidebook of Statistical Definitions and Glossary*, pp. 36–7, 41–2; available at: www.pcbs.gov.ps/DesktopDefault.aspx?tabID=4036&lang=en.

However, rather than helping to build the Palestinian economy, this assistance became an emergency safety net. Table 15.8 opposite summarizes the decline of the importance of work in Israel and the rise in the weight of transfers from the donor community. Looking at the differences between GDP, GNI, and GDI,[10] one can see that GNI became only 12 percent higher than GDP in the West Bank in the years 2006–7; but GDI was 43 percent higher than GDP as a result of impressive transfers from the donors of almost a third of the GDP in those years. In Gaza, the trends are even more acute. The GNI is only 5 to 6 percent above GDP, while the GDI is 55 percent higher than GDP. This is because of transfers of close to half of GDP to the Gazan economy in 2006–7 and the almost complete stoppage of work in Israel. This high level of aid is unprecedented worldwide.

The significant injection of funds from abroad cannot solve the economic crises in the Palestinian economy, and in particular the deep crisis in Gaza. The economy cannot function when there is no way the unemployed can find jobs and when the trade regime is abnormal. The fact that the Paris Protocol is now a dead letter in Gaza and, furthermore, that there are no discussions about a normal trade alternative leaves 1.5 million people in extreme poverty. The economic environment in the West Bank is more promising, though uncertainty concerning its political future hangs in the air and prohibits prosperity. Ten years after the failure to achieve a permanent agreement, the economy in both the West Bank and Gaza is in deep trouble.

While economic factors in the Israeli–Palestinian conflict might seem secondary in the short run, their impact in the long run and their significance in shaping the form the conflict takes cannot be underestimated.

Notes

1 For a detailed description of this crucial decision, see Arnon *et al.* (1997).
2 There were certain exceptions. See below.
3 The study of Israel's economic policy regarding the West Bank and the Gaza Strip suffers from a paucity of reliable sources. However, the written evidence of retired high-ranking officials (Gazit 1995) and from the report of the 1991 Sadan Committee, which recommended changing Israel's policy towards the Gaza Strip economy, support the claims made in the text.
4 Records show a two-year alternating cycle in olive crop yield in the West Bank. There is also, apparently, a six-year cycle.
5 The economic agreement known as the Paris Protocol was signed on April 29, 1994. One week later it was one of the annexes to the Cairo Agreement that dealt with implementing the Oslo Accords first in Gaza and in Jericho.
6 The official exceptions to the customs union were a list of products A1 and A2 and B and were also applied temporarily to agriculture. See Elmusa and El-Jafari (1995) and Arnon *et. al.* (1997).
7 There is some confusion and lack of consistency in the figures published by various organizations relating to that period.
8 An analysis of the failure at Camp David is not within the realm of this essay.
9 See Diwan and Shaban (1999: chapter 4).
10 GDP (Gross Domestic Product) measures the local production; GNI (Gross National Income) measures the GDP plus the income received from abroad for local factors of production employed outside of the local economy; GDI (Gross Disposable Income) measures the GNI plus transfers to the local economy from outside.

References and further reading

Aix Group (2004) "Economic Road Map: An Israeli Palestinian Perspective on Permanent Status," available at: www.aixgroup.org/research.html [in English, Arabic, Hebrew, and French].
Arnon, A. (2007) "Israeli Policy towards the Occupied Palestinian Territories: The Economic Dimension 1967–2007," *Middle East Journal*, 61/4, pp. 573–95.

5

Arie Arnon

Arnon, A., and Gottlieb, D. (1995) "A Macroeconomic Model of the Palestinian Economy: The West Bank and the Gaza Strip 1968–1991," *Bank of Israel Review*, 69, pp. 49–73.

Arnon A., and Weinblatt, J. (2001) "Sovereignty and Economic Development: The Case of Israel and Palestine," *Economic Journal*, 111 pp. F291–F308.

Arnon, A., Luski, I., Spivak, A., and Weinblatt, J. (1997) *The Palestinian Economy: Between Imposed Integration and Voluntary Separation* (Leiden: Brill).

Cobham, D., and Kanafani, N. (eds) (2004) *The Economics of Palestine: Economic Policy and Institutional Reform for a Viable Palestinian State* (London: Routledge).

Diwan, I., and Shaban, R. A. (eds) (1999) *Development under Adversity? The Palestinian Economy in Transition* (Washington, DC: MAS [Palestine Economic Policy Research Institute] and World Bank).

Elmusa, S., and El-Jafari, M. (1995), "Power and Trade: The Israeli–Palestinian Economic Protocol," *Journal of Palestine Studies*, 24, pp. 14–32.

Gazit, S. (1995) *The Carrot and the Stick: Israel's Policy in Judea and Samaria, 1967–1968* (Washington, DC: B'nai B'rith Books).

ICBS (Israel Central Bureau of Statistics) (1996) *National Accounts of Judea, Samaria and the Gaza Area 1968–1993*, Special Report #1012 (Jerusalem: ICBS).

Kleiman, E. (1999) "Fiscal Separation with Economic Integration: Israel and the Palestinian Authority," in A. Razin and E. Sadka (eds), *The Economics of Globalization: Policy Perspectives from Public Economics* (Cambridge: Cambridge University Press), pp. 246–63.

Metzer, J. (1998) *The Divided Economy of Mandatory Palestine* (Cambridge: Cambridge University Press).

Metzer, J., and Kaplan, O. (1990) *The Jewish and Arab Economy in Mandatory Palestine: Product, Employment and Growth* (Jerusalem: Maurice Falk Institute for Economic Research in Israel) [in Hebrew].

PCBS (Palestine Central Bureau of Statistics) (various issues) *National Accounts, Labor Force Data*, available at: www.pcbs.gov.ps/DesktopDefault.aspx?tabID=3341&lang=en.

Protocol on Economic Relations between the Government of the State of Israel and the PLO, representing the Palestinian People (1994) The English version is part of the Cairo Agreement of May 1994: Gaza–Jericho Agreement Annex IV – Economic Protocol.

Shaban, R. A. (1993) "Palestinian Labor Mobility," *International Labour Review*, 132, pp. 655–72.

World Bank (1993) *Developing the Occupied Territories: An Investment in Peace*, 6 vols (Washington, DC: World Bank).

World Bank (2002) *Long Term Policy Options for the Palestinian Economy* (West Bank and Gaza: World Bank).

16

Unilateralism and separation

Gerald M. Steinberg

The decision to withdraw the Israeli presence – military and civilian – unilaterally from Gaza in August 2005 marked the most fundamental change in Israeli policy since the 1967 war and the resulting occupation of the West Bank and Gaza. The disengagement, which extended beyond Gaza, reflected the widely held recognition that neither the status quo (occupation) nor the remnants of the Oslo negotiation framework (1993–2000) served Israel's interests. But the implementation of an alternative policy was traumatic and dramatic for both proponents and opponents.

Prime Minister Ariel Sharon, who, in previous positions, had been the major architect of the settlement program for over thirty years, led the withdrawal. After repeatedly rejecting this approach, he delivered a major policy speech on December 18, 2003, announcing the disengagement plan, and proceeded to implement it. Sharon faced strong opposition within his governing coalition, as well as threats of civil disobedience and more violent resistance. In August 2005, the process began, and thousands of Israeli soldiers battled settlers and their supporters who sought to prevent the withdrawal. A few months later, the Likud Party split, with Sharon leading one group to form Kadima, a new party based on an alliance between center-right and center-left (Labor Party) members of Knesset.

This chapter examines the many complex factors that led to the withdrawal (which also involved four settlements in the West Bank), the reasons for its unilateral nature, and the lessons drawn. While it is often described as a "surprise move" by Prime Minister Sharon, evidence shows that the unilateral withdrawal strategy evolved gradually as a carefully considered response to developments.

As will be demonstrated, some factors stemmed from foreign policy issues, particularly following the failure of the Oslo peace efforts, the mass terror attacks (the Second *Intifada*), the death of Palestinian leader Yasser Arafat, and pressure from the United States and Europe to implement the new "Road Map." Additional factors leading to unilateral separation were related to domestic politics and societal change, including the decline of the settlement lobby and ideological political frameworks, opposition to maintaining the post-1967 status quo, and what became known as "demographic concerns" related to the long-term status of Israel as a Jewish democratic state.

The legacy of Oslo

In the late 1980s and early 1990s, a series of events created a sense of optimism among many Israelis that the long impasse in the conflict with the Palestinians could be ended through negotiations. The Palestinian *intifada* that began in 1987 ended over twenty years of relative stability following the 1967 war, the result of which was Israeli control over the West Bank (Judea and Samaria) and Gaza. By the early 1990s, many Israelis became concerned over the long-term costs of maintaining control over a hostile and growing Palestinian population, and support for a political solution increased.

This period was also marked by a growing recognition that the "Jordanian option" and various proposals based on federation-type frameworks that would not have involved an independent Palestinian state were not realistic. In 1988, King Hussein renounced claims to a major role in the West Bank and in Palestinian affairs. In parallel, the 1991 Gulf War against Iraq marked a major increase in the American presence in the region and triggered the formation of a US-led alliance involving most other Arab states, Egypt and Syria among them. This isolated and weakened the "rejectionist" front (referring to Arab leaders who continued to oppose all peace negotiations with Israel) led by Saddam Hussein. Yasser Arafat, who was aligned with the Iraqi leader, was also isolated and under pressure to make concessions. Many Israelis saw this situation as an opportunity to accelerate change and disengage from Palestinian entanglements through a negotiated peace treaty.

In the 1992 elections, Israelis (by a narrow margin) voted in a Labor-led coalition, headed by Prime Minister Yitzhak Rabin, in part because some voters saw Prime Minister Shamir and the Likud as moving too slowly in promoting the negotiations that began with the 1991 Madrid peace conference. The secret "Oslo negotiations" took place under this government, and, in August 1993, followed by a grand signing ceremony on the White House lawn, the Declaration of Principles (DOP) was announced. The Israeli public was generally supportive and even enthusiastic. The DOP created the framework for the Palestinian Authority, as well as the opportunity (and, for many, the expectation) for the creation of a Palestinian state and the "two-state solution" that had been sought since Arab rejection of the 1947 UN partition plan.

But, within a few years, the continuing and escalating violence led to a change in Israeli public opinion, and in 1996, following a series of Palestinian mass terror attacks, the Likud, headed by Binyamin Netanyahu, was returned to power. Many "swing voters" who had supported Rabin and Labor in 1992 veered to the right and voted for parties in the Netanyahu coalition. This changed again in December 1998, after Netanyahu's allies left the government, forcing new elections, in which Labor was returned to power, with Rabin's protégé, former IDF Chief of Staff Ehud Barak, as prime minister.

This change in Israeli leadership did not result in the successful conclusion of the Oslo negotiations, and by 2000, with the failure of the Camp David summit, remaining support among the Israeli public for this approach was largely gone. The violence and escalation into bus bombings and other forms of mass terror led to a break-up of Barak's coalition government, followed by a no-confidence vote and elections for prime minister, which brought Ariel Sharon to power in 2001. In a span of nine years, Israeli politics had twice gone full circle, from Likud to Labor and back.

While Sharon's primary task was focused on restoring security, this required the development and implementation of an appropriate diplomatic dimension. In the United States, the newly elected administration of George W. Bush had examined the deep American involvement in the Oslo process, which consumed considerable resources without positive results. As a result, President Bush and his administration initially decided against involvement in Palestinian–Israeli negotiation efforts.[1]

As the terror attacks and Israeli responses increased, pressures mounted for an American initiative aimed at a ceasefire and resumption of negotiations. Bush, Secretary of State Colin Powell, and National Security Advisor Condoleezza Rice added their voices to those of UN and European leaders, such as EC External Relations Commissioner Chris Patten, criticizing Israeli military actions. Bush also dispatched a number of high-level special envoys, including CIA director George Tenet and former General Anthony Zinni, in the effort to broker an end to the violence and resume negotiations. Sharon rejected calls for reopening negotiations, in any form, with Arafat. In January 2002, the Israeli navy seized a large shipment of arms and explosives from Iran aboard the *Karine A*, which had been arranged by Arafat. In the wake of this act of war, the option of killing or exiling the Palestinian leader was raised, but reportedly vetoed by the United States.[2] In March, following a series of Palestinian bombing attacks that killed and wounded hundreds of Israelis, the IDF put Arafat under house arrest – which continued, in different forms, until the Palestinian leader's death in November 2004.

After the 9/11 al-Qaeda terror attacks on the United States, the Bush administration was more inclined to accept the Israeli position on Arafat, and in June 2002 the president delivered a speech that called for Arafat's replacement as precondition for peace negotiations. Like Sharon, Bush had come to the conclusion that Arafat was not interested in reaching any realistic peace agreement. At the same time, the Israeli leadership understood that an alternative was necessary, and a group of officials and analysts advocated unilateral approaches to change the status quo. The non-negotiated withdrawal from southern Lebanon in May 2000, which was implemented by Prime Minister Barak, was seen, at the time, as a successful example, both domestically and internationally.

The unilateral approach had the advantage of detouring around the obstacles to negotiated agreements created by recalcitrant leaders and of allowing for policy change in the absence of what negotiation theorists refer to as "ripeness."[3] In Lebanon, the UN demarcated the international border and declared that Israel had withdrawn to this boundary, thereby providing rare international approval for an Israeli policy.

As the architect of Israeli settlement policy, Sharon initially rejected any withdrawal from the West Bank and Gaza, warning that this territory would then be used for terror attacks. He also rebuffed calls for the extension of the small sections of a physical barrier that had been constructed following Palestinian attacks in the mid-1990s (the fence built around Gaza in earlier years had proven successful in ending suicide bombings launched from there). Sharon recognized that a physical division also had important political ramifications, since areas that were outside the "fence" would be seen as having been conceded to the Palestinians, even prior to negotiations. On this basis, in the 2001–2 period, Sharon refused to consider proposals for the construction of a comprehensive security barrier in the West Bank.

Following each major terror attack, however, public demonstrations and newspaper articles demanded immediate construction of a comprehensive security barrier, and by the end of 2002 the prime minister publicly announced acceptance of the concept. In public speeches and a later exchange of letters with President Bush, Sharon declared that the "fence is a security rather than political barrier,"[4] but this position could not be maintained.

Sharon's recognition of the broad public support for a barrier to separate large parts of the West Bank physically from Israel was a prelude to acceptance of the wider unilateral separation strategy. On May 27, 2003, following his second election victory, Sharon went much further than at any previous stage, declaring that the "occupation" was "a terrible thing for Israel and for the Palestinians" and "cannot continue endlessly."[5]

A few months later, in his Herzliya speech of December 18, 2003, Sharon announced that, "if in a few months the Palestinians still continue to disregard their part in implementing the

Road Map – then Israel will initiate the unilateral security step of disengagement from the Palestinians." The stated objectives included reducing terror, granting "maximum security and minimize[ing] friction between Israelis and Palestinians."

The cumulative result of these developments was firmly to end the Oslo negotiation process. In the 2002 Operation Defensive Shield, the Israeli military had restored its security control over the territory that had been under the Palestinian Authority. Gradually, the dispatch of envoys, meetings, and the search for an agreement with Arafat and the Palestinian leadership stopped. In some ways, the peace process and overall relationship had not simply reverted to the status quo before the beginning of the Oslo negotiations, but the differences between Israeli and Palestinian perceptions had increased significantly.

No partner: the end of the Arafat era

In the Middle East, a diplomatic vacuum is understood to be particularly dangerous, and, with the end of the Oslo negotiations, pressures for alternative negotiation frameworks developed immediately. As noted, the Israeli and US governments had decided that negotiations with Yasser Arafat were not useful. With Arafat remaining the primary Palestinian decision-maker regarding negotiations with Israel, the possibility of reaching a stable peace agreement was seen as non-existent. The Israeli leadership, almost across the board, had come to view Arafat as ideologically committed to the destruction of the Jewish state, and this notion came to be shared by many American policy-makers. Similarly, Israeli public opinion polls showed that, while a majority supported peace based on compromise and "painful concessions," including territorial withdrawal, they did not view Arafat as capable or interested in ending the conflict.

To break this impasse, the United States led attempts to push Arafat aside and promote potentially more pragmatic leaders – specifically Mahmoud Abbas (Abu Mazen) and Ahmed Qurei (Abu Ala) – but with little impact. Although Israel had isolated Arafat in his Ramallah compound and prevented him from traveling abroad (other than on a one-way trip into exile), he maintained control over key policies. In contrast, European governments and EU officials continued to hold regular meetings with Arafat, but with no results other than undermining American pressure for an alternative Palestinian leadership.

In this situation, the Israeli government, and Sharon in particular, concluded that there was no negotiation partner on the Palestinian side, and there probably would not be one for the foreseeable future. Thus, in his Herzliya speech of December 18, 2003, announcing the disengagement plan, Sharon declared: "We are interested in conducting direct negotiations, but do not intend to hold Israeli society hostage in the hands of the Palestinians. I have already said – we will not wait for them indefinitely." Instead of more dead-end negotiations, or maintaining the increasingly costly status quo, Israel would pursue unilateral policies to reduce these costs through disengagement.

In November 2004, Arafat died and was replaced by his deputy, Mahmoud Abbas. Israeli policy-makers concluded that Abbas would not have the authority that Arafat commanded and was likely to remain in his mentor's shadow. In parallel, Hamas – the Islamist organization challenging Arafat and the PLO – continued to gain power, later reflected in their victory during the January 2006 elections for the Palestinian legislature. Thus, the chances that a Palestinian leader would emerge who could and would reverse Arafat's legacy in peace negotiations were very low.

In this context, and while support for the unilateral strategy grew, other options were discussed. For example, the informal "Geneva Initiative" was promoted vigorously, but this was anathema to the Sharon government. Geneva involved a group of Israeli opposition figures, many of whom played leading roles in the Oslo process, and their Palestinian counterparts. Dubbed by Israelis as "Oslo II," this initiative was funded by the Swiss and other European governments and was perceived as an attempt to undermine Sharon's policies.[6] Dov Weisglass, Sharon's personal advisor and the lead person in contacts with the US government, frequently cited concerns about potential support for the Geneva Initiative as one reason for moving quickly to implement the unilateral withdrawal.

In parallel, Palestinian strategists increasingly emphasized the "one-state" approach, in which Israel would have been locked into a political framework extending from the Mediterranean to the Jordan River. Over time, the growing Palestinian population would exceed 40 and eventually 50 percent of this combined entity, and so lead to the dismantling of Israel as the nation-state of the Jewish people, as embodied in the Zionist framework.

The "one-state" approach was perceived by many Israelis as another expression of the history of Palestinian rejection of the legitimacy and permanence of Israel and of Jewish national sovereignty. In order to avoid this and similar scenarios, a realistic alternative was necessary, and this contributed to the support for unilateral separation among Israeli decision-makers, eventually including Sharon.

The impact of the Road Map and the Quartet on unilateral separation

In parallel, and to avoid a diplomatic vacuum, the newly formed Middle East Quartet (consisting of representatives from the United States, the European Union, Russia and the United Nations) introduced another initiative, known as the Middle East Road Map to Peace. The details contained in this document, and the dangers perceived by Sharon and the Israeli government, contributed significantly to the decision to implement unilateral withdrawal as an alternative.

The Quartet's Road Map initiative reflected the ongoing international pressure for the resumption of a peace process (a "political horizon") following the demise of the Oslo framework. In June 2002, President Bush spoke in general terms about a road map that would be "a starting point towards achieving the vision of two states ... It is the framework for progress towards lasting peace and security in the Middle East." The development of the parameters took place, largely under European direction and without Israeli input, over a period of months.

Broader regional and global factors also influenced the process – particularly the build-up to the US-led war against Iraq that began in March 2003. As tensions increased, European leaders sought to offset Arab reactions to the Iraqi conflict by demonstrating efforts to resolve the Israeli–Palestinian conflict. On April 30, 2003, a detailed framework document was published under the title "Road Map for Peace in the Middle East: Israeli/Palestinian Reciprocal Action."

The Israeli government viewed the proposed process as unrealistic and, if implemented, likely to end again with violence, as in the Oslo process, particularly given Arafat's continued control, as well as the growing capabilities of Hamas. The Road Map was seen as reflecting European demands, including a lack of realism, a low priority for security concerns, and an overemphasis on Palestinian perspectives. In response to US pressure, Israel did not reject the terms, but formal acceptance was accompanied by fourteen reservations.

The introduction of the Road Map accelerated the Israeli search for alternatives, contributing to Sharon's embrace of unilateral disengagement. Palestinian terror attacks continued, and the pressures on Israel for concessions involving security risks and territorial withdrawals increased. In his December 2003 Herzliya speech, Sharon claimed that the unilateral approach "does not prevent the implementation of the Road Map. Rather, it is a step Israel will take in the absence of any other option, in order to improve its security." In reality, the announcement of the unilateral strategy essentially ended discussion of the Road Map.

On February 13, 2004, the US government announced acceptance of Ariel Sharon's plan for a unilateral withdrawal of most Israeli settlements from the Gaza Strip. This announcement strongly restated the conclusion that "negotiations were impossible because of Palestinian recalcitrance." In addition to much needed diplomatic support, the US statement gave Sharon important backing in the internal Israeli political debate over unilateral withdrawal (see detailed discussion below). He pressed for a more detailed American government statement on future borders and on Palestinian refugee claims which would offset some of this criticism.

On April 14, 2004, following intense negotiations, President Bush gave a letter to Prime Minister Sharon focusing on final status negotiations, which addressed these concerns. The letter stated:

> In light of new realities on the ground, including already existing major Israeli population centers, it is unrealistic that the outcome of final status negotiations will be a full and complete return to the armistice lines of 1949, and all previous efforts to negotiate a two-state solution have reached the same conclusion. It is realistic to expect that any final status agreement will only be achieved on the basis of mutually agreed changes that reflect these realities.

In the press conference held following this meeting, Bush also stated that:

> It seems clear that an agreed, just, fair and realistic framework for a solution to the Palestinian refugee issue as part of any final status agreement will need to be found through the establishment of a Palestinian state and the settling of Palestinian refugees there rather than Israel.

Thus, although the withdrawal was unilateral, and reflected the perception that negotiations towards a peace agreement were not realistic under the existing conditions, this policy was also seen as a step towards confidence-building and resumed negotiations towards peace.

Domestic factors: the post-ideological consensus and the demographic threat

The Israeli domestic context of the August 2005 disengagement and withdrawal from Gaza was as important as the external context. Disengagement, which included four settlements in the West Bank and was unofficially expected to go beyond Gaza and determine Israel's borders, was the result of a long and major transformation of Israeli society and politics. Over the previous two decades, both active and passive support for the post-1967 settlement activity had declined. The *intifada* (1987–90) ended a relatively stable status quo while increasing internal political support for a workable framework to replace Israeli control over and responsibility for the Palestinian population.

The 1993 Oslo process reflected and accelerated this domestic political change, while the failure and accompanying violence led to a search for alternatives. Public opinion polls and election returns from 1992 through 2003 showed that a consensus viewed the post-1967 status quo, including the "occupation" and its growing costs for Israeli society, as unacceptable.

The 2001 elections for prime minister brought Ariel Sharon to power after a decade of frequent shifts between Labor and Likud-led coalitions. The outcome, as well as polling data and other indicators, showed that the ideological divide over war, peace, settlements, and borders had been replaced by a pragmatic and centrist majority that supported a shift away from the post-1967 stalemate. At the same time, there was little expectation that negotiated peace efforts would succeed. In opinion polls conducted by the Tami Steinmetz Center at Tel Aviv University (the Peace Index), over 80 percent of Israelis agreed that the Palestinians were solely (49 percent) or mostly (35 percent) responsible for the continuation of the conflict. Polls from 2002 showed that 70 percent of Israelis perceived Palestinians as not wanting peace and seeking to kill as many Jews as possible, conquering all of Israel – an increase of over 20 percent on previous years. (Palestinian polls reported that 47 percent saw the goal of the violence as Israel's destruction.) According to the Peace Index, even among those Israelis who supported Labor Party leader Ehud Barak in 2001, only 27 percent reported that they continued to support the Oslo process. Since the Israeli left was strongly associated with the Oslo negotiations, its credibility on peace and security had been severely damaged.

This trend continued in the 2003 Knesset election campaign, which showed further weakening on the left, accelerated by the cooptation by the Likud and Sharon of the separation agenda.[7] In the process, Sharon had both led and adapted to the wider changes in the Israeli polity, moving towards the centrist consensus against maintaining the status quo. He even endorsed the principle of Palestinian statehood, which had been anathema for many years, and made numerous references to the need for "painful compromises" necessary for Israeli security. In this context, Sharon also sought to demonstrate that separation was possible without lengthy and problematic negotiations.

At the same time, the Israeli public, like Sharon, saw no positive outcome resulting from the possibility of renewed peace negotiations with Arafat and the PLO. The Peace Index showed that 70 percent of Israelis viewed Arafat as a terrorist rather than as a statesman, a 30 percent increase over the average during the 1990s. A similar proportion expressed agreement with the view that, even if Israel agreed to all the Palestinian demands, Arafat would not be willing to reach an agreement based on a two-state solution to end the conflict. While polls showed that a plurality of Israelis retained their belief that ultimately the conflict could be resolved only by negotiations, in the short-term, the majority gave priority to strengthening Israel's military capability to defeat the terror attacks.

Having ruled out both negotiations with Arafat and the long-term one-state scenario, Israelis, including Sharon, looked for realistic alternatives. In this framework, discussion of unilateral withdrawal expanded. General Uzi Dayan, who headed the Israeli National Security Council, had proposed a detailed model for this process a few years earlier, which Sharon initially rejected. (Dayan was also replaced as head of the NSC.) But, in the context of the search for a political option that would satisfy both international and domestic pressures, Sharon gradually adopted the unilateral withdrawal option.

In presenting separation to the Israeli public, Sharon echoed the words of the late Prime Minister Yitzhak Rabin, from the Labor Party. In 1994, following a suicide bombing near the city of Netanya, Rabin declared support for separation (at the time, through negotiations and the Oslo process).

> This path must lead to a separation, though not according to the borders prior to 1967. We want to reach a separation between us and them. We do not want a majority of the Jewish residents of the state of Israel, 98% of whom live within the borders of sovereign Israel, including a united Jerusalem, to be subject to terrorism.

This dynamic demonstrates the importance of "bottom-up pressure" in the process that led to the unilateral disengagement decision. In a wider analysis of Israeli political evolution, Waxman argues that demands for changes in the post-1967 status quo reflected the "profound cultural changes that had taken place in Israel during the 1990s." Based on constructivist approaches in international relations, and citing the "new historians" who challenged traditional Israeli narratives of the conflict, as well as growing cultural divisions, Waxman asserts that, "in the 1990s, attitudes and opinions that were once shocking and unspeakable began to openly circulate in the public realm, and gradually became more acceptable."[8]

This convergence was reflected in Sharon's speech of December 2003, which adopted many positions that had been previously taboo in any Likud framework:

> In the framework of a future agreement, Israel will not remain in all the places where it is today. The relocation of settlements will be made, first and foremost, in order to draw the most efficient security line possible, thereby creating this disengagement between Israel and the Palestinians.... Settlements which will be relocated are those which will not be included in the territory of the State of Israel in the framework of any possible future permanent agreement. At the same time, in the framework of the "Disengagement Plan," Israel will strengthen its control over those same areas in the Land of Israel which will constitute an inseparable part of the State of Israel in any future agreement.

These fundamental changes, which, as noted, were widely shared by the Israeli public, were also closely linked to the "demographic threat," reflecting concerns resulting from the different growth rates of the Jewish and Palestinian Arab populations. According to some research extrapolations, in a single political entity between the Mediterranean and the Jordan River (in other words, the post-1967 status quo), the number of Palestinian Arabs would equal and then exceed the Jewish population within a few decades. Israel would then since cease to be a democratic national home for the Jewish people, who would become a minority. This was clearly antithetical to the objectives of Zionism.

On December 18, 2003, in his speech at the Herzliya conference announcing the disengagement plan, Sharon declared that this approach "will reduce as much as possible the number of Israelis located in the heart of the Palestinian population." Earlier, Deputy Prime Minister Olmert warned publicly about the "cloud of demographics" which hovers over Israel, and which will "come down on us not in the end of days, but in just another few years."[9] Professor Sergio DellaPergola, from the Hebrew University's Demography and Statistics program, published data in 2003 claiming that, while the current division is 55 percent Jewish and 45 percent Arab, the higher Arab fertility rate would lead to an evenly balanced population in this undivided territory by 2020.

In response, opponents of disengagement, including Finance Minister Binyamin Netanyahu, cited research publications that rejected DellaPergola's analysis, including the claim that "a careful review of the data reveals that the source of much of Israel's demographic anxiety may be traced to inaccurate numbers issued by the Palestinian Authority, and accepted – if not actively promoted – by prominent Israeli academics." The authors concluded that, while "the Jews of Israel face a demographic threat... the threat has been greatly exaggerated.... Israel must realize that it has time, demographically speaking, to evaluate [policy] choices, and to make the right decisions."[10] But this evaluation did not defuse the demographic concerns and the threat posed by the "single-state" option.

The demographic threat and the wider concern regarding the costs of maintaining the post-1967 status quo and stalemate were at the core of the growing Israeli political centrist consensus, as reflected in public opinion polls, election results, and other measures. Sharon and Olmert did not initiate these political changes among Israelis, but rather responded to the changes. In appealing to this consensus, Olmert declared: "We are approaching a point where more and more Palestinians will say: 'There is no place for two states between the Jordan and the sea. All we want is the right to vote.' The day they get it, we will lose everything." He added: "I shudder to think that liberal Jewish organizations that shouldered the burden of the struggle against apartheid in South Africa will lead the struggle against us."[11]

Disengagement and centrism in Israeli politics

Opposition to the overall policy of separation and the specifics of unilateral withdrawal was intense, but, as noted above, ideological claims on both the left and the right had weakened significantly in the 1990s. The traditional Zionist left was led by the Labor Party, challenged by the newer and more ideological Meretz bloc. After the failure of the Oslo process, which was led by Labor, and in particular the perceived ineffectiveness of the government led by Ehud Barak between 1998 and 2001, Labor suffered as unprecedented loss of support. In the process, a number of former Labor leaders involved in the Oslo process joined the Meretz bloc, among them Yossi Beilin, leaving Labor in a position to join the expanding centrist framework.

Within the Likud Party and its political allies and coalition partners further on the right of the political spectrum, opposition to Sharon's unilateral disengagement was fierce. Despite the decline in support among the general population, the settlement movement maintained strong representation and influence within these structures and sought to block the endorsement and implementation of the departure from Gaza and from the four smaller settlements in the West Bank. Over Sharon's objections, the Likud held a non-binding referendum in May 2004, in which half of the registered members participated; over 60 percent opposed disengagement. (A Palestinian attack in Gaza which killed a pregnant Israeli woman and her four daughters may have increased the opposition vote.)

The opposition to disengagement continued and intensified, with Sharon increasingly isolated in his Likud Party and challenged by Netanyahu for the leadership. Sharon was accused of using the disengagement and the growing alliance with the Labor leadership to maintain power and deflect attention from an influence-peddling and corruption investigation which also involved his sons and close colleagues. (Eventually, Omri Sharon, who was elected to the Knesset, was convicted for his role.) Adversaries reminded Sharon of his earlier dismissal of calls to remove the 7,800 Israeli civilians in Gaza settlements, which he had declared were "no different than Tel Aviv," and whose fate "is the fate of Jerusalem."

As the August 2005 disengagement neared, opponents launched legal challenges and media campaigns, held large demonstrations and protest vigils, and engaged in highly disruptive civil disobedience. But the impact of these efforts was minimal and even counter-productive, as sympathizers were alienated by the disruptions and violence. An effort to mobilize maximum support in a mass march towards Gaza was blocked by the government before reaching the border. Another mass protest in Tel Aviv drew up to 300,000 participants. While an impressive number, the total fell far short of demonstrating wide opposition to the disengagement.

To offset the dissension within his Likud Party base, as well as the departure of coalition partners, Sharon moved to create a centrist-based coalition. The Labor Party supported the disengagement legislation in the Knesset, creating a *de facto* alliance, and then Labor entered the coalition, with Shimon Peres as deputy prime minister. Peres, who had served as foreign minister under Rabin, was widely seen as the chief architect of the Oslo process. This coalition, which implemented the disengagement, marked a major change in Israeli politics, demonstrating the strength of the centrist approach and the weakness of the ideological poles, both left and right. In cementing this process, Sharon and his supporters from the Likud joined with the centrist elements in Labor to create the Kadima ("Forward") Party, based on a platform of additional unilateral withdrawals as well as other non-ideological positions on the Israeli political agenda.

In the 2006 election campaign, despite Sharon's incapacitating stroke, Kadima, led by Olmert, received strong support, ending the domination of the two ideological blocs in Israeli politics.

The impacts of disengagement

Although Israel's unilateral withdrawal from Gaza in 2005 was the most significant political change since the 1967 war and ended four decades of status quo, the impact was far from what had been expected. Kadima and its centrist approach, including policies based on further unilateral disengagement, survived Sharon's stroke and the party received broad support in the 2006 elections, enabling Olmert to lead the government coalition. But the escalation of rocket attacks from Gaza targeting Israeli towns, particularly after Hamas took full control in 2007, led to a large-scale Israeli military response in December 2008. To a large extent, the public viewed the unilateral withdrawal as a failure, and this ended consideration of applying the same approach to the West Bank.

Stripped of its primary political platform, and of its founding leader, Kadima began to lose support. Olmert's conduct of the Second Lebanon War following the attack by Hizbollah forces in mid-2006 was widely criticized, and, in 2008, corruption allegations forced him to resign. After the 2009 elections, Netanyahu and the Likud returned to lead the governing coalition.

By this time, the factors that led the majority of Israelis, including Sharon, to adopt the unilateral disengagement strategy, had faded. Five years after Arafat's death, Abbas and the Palestinian Authority agreed to resume peace negotiations with Israel, and the international pressure to do so was very strong. Perhaps, if these efforts also fail, tempered by the lessons from the initial effort, Israelis and their leaders will again turn to a form of unilateralism in parts of the West Bank as the least bad option.

Notes

1 Freedman (2004).
2 Yossi Klein Halevi and Michael Oren, "Israel's Unexpected Victory over Terrorism", *Jewish World Review*, 20 September 2004; available at: www.jewishworldreview.com/0904/halevi_israeli_victory.php3?printer_friendly.
3 Zartman (1989).
4 Letter from Prime Minister Sharon to President George W. Bush, Israel Ministry of Foreign Affairs, April 14, 2004, available at: www.mfa.gov.il/MFA/PeaceProcess/ReferenceDocuments/Exchange oflettersSharon-Bush14-Apr-2004.htm.
5 Kelly Wallace, "Sharon: Occupation 'Terrible' for Israel, Palestinians," *CNN*, May 27, 2003, available at: http://edition.cnn.com/2003/WORLD/meast/05/26/mideast/index.html.
6 Schiff (2010).
7 Rynhold and Steinberg (2004).
8 Waxman (2008).
9 Ori Nir, "Demographics Drive Likud's Shifting Agenda," *Forward*, 26 December 2003, available at: www.forward.com/articles/7386/#ixzz1123bgtpQ.
10 Zimmerman, Seid and Wise (2006).
11 Nir (2003).

References and further reading

DellaPergola, Sergio (2003) "Demographic Trends in Israel and Palestine: Prospects and Policy Implications," *American Jewish Year Book*, 103, pp. 3–68.

DellaPergola, Sergio (2007) "Sergio DellaPergola vs. the authors of 'Voodoo Demographics,'" *Azure*, no. 27, available at: www.azure.org.il/article.php?id29 [response to article by Zimmerman *et al.* cited below].

Freedman, Robert O. (2004) "The Bush Administration and the Arab–Israeli Conflict: The Record of the First Three Years," *Jerusalem Viewpoints*, 516, pp. 14–29.

Rynhold, Jonathan, and Steinberg, Gerald (2004) "The Peace Process and the Israeli Elections," *Israel Affairs*, 10/4, pp. 181–204; available at: http://faculty.biu.ac.il/~steing/election%20PDFs/LOW-RES-FISA-10-4-100409-181-204.pdf.

Schiff, Amira (2010) "Quasi Track-One Diplomacy: An Analysis of the Geneva Process in the Israeli–Palestinian Conflict," *International Studies Perspectives*, 11/2, pp. 93–111.

Waxman, Dov (2008) "From Controversy to Consensus: Cultural Conflict and the Israeli Debate over Territorial Withdrawal," *Israel Studies*, 13/2, pp. 73–96.

Zartman, I. William (1989) *Ripe for Resolution: Conflict and Intervention in Africa* (New York: Oxford University Press).

Zimmerman, Bennett, Seid, Roberta, and Wise, Michael L. (2006) "Voodoo Demographics," *Azure*, no. 25, available at: www.azure.org.il/article.php?id130.

17

Gaza

Joel Peters

At the start of 2004, Israel's prime minister, Ariel Sharon, declared that Israel would evacuate all settlements and unilaterally withdraw its military forces from Gaza. Sharon was true to his word. In August 2005, Israel dismantled the Gazan settlements and military outposts, thus ending its thirty-eight years of military occupation. At the time, many observers regarded Israel's disengagement from Gaza as a defining moment in Israeli–Palestinian relations. Supporters of the disengagement plan heralded it as a move that would reignite the moribund peace process, allowing the Palestinians to build the institutions for self-government and set the foundations for Palestinian statehood. Such optimism proved illusory. The hoped-for momentum in the peace process failed to materialize. Instead, the disengagement has led to a marked decline in the socio-economic and living conditions in Gaza, and to a deterioration in the security environment for both Gaza and Israel.

Since Israel's withdrawal in the summer of 2005, the future of Gaza has emerged as a new issue within the Israeli–Palestinian conflict. Gaza has become a separate entity, effectively cut off from the West Bank and the outside world. Palestinian politics and society has become bifurcated, with Hamas in control of Gaza and the Palestinian Authority governing the West Bank. This separation has been reinforced by the international community, which has directed its diplomatic and financial efforts to bolstering support for Mahmoud Abbas while maintaining a political boycott of Hamas.

Background

Gaza is a narrow piece of land along the Mediterranean coast between Israel and Egypt. It is just 40 kilometers long and 10 kilometers wide and is home to more than 1.5 million Palestinians. Two-thirds of the population are registered refugees, of which half live in the eight refugee camps run by the United Nations Relief and Works Agency (UNRWA). Gaza is one of the most densely populated places on the planet, with an annual population growth of 3.5 percent per year. Over half of the population is under the age of fifteen.

Israel captured the Gaza Strip from Egypt following the Six Day War in June 1967. In 1972, the first Israeli settlements were established in Gaza, initially as paramilitary outposts. Following the 1979 Israeli–Egyptian peace treaty, the number of settlements grew, with many of the new settlers arriving from Yamit, evacuated by Israel following its withdrawal from the Sinai peninsula. Gaza, however, does not possess the same religious and ideological attachment for Israelis as the West Bank. In all, Israel created twenty-three settlements in the Gaza Strip, home to some 8,000 settlers. The settlements, however, together with Israel's military installations, accounted for almost 40 percent of the total area.

Gaza remained under Israel's direct military rule until May 1994, when under the Gaza–Jericho Accord, signed between Israel and the PLO as part of the Oslo peace process, a phased transfer of governmental and civilian authority to the Palestinians took place. Israeli forces withdrew from 60 percent of the territory, primarily the urban areas and refugee camps, leaving the newly established Palestinian Authority to govern and police Gaza. From 1994 through the collapse of the Oslo process at the end of 2000, the Palestinian Authority began to establish the institutional foundations of a Palestinian state in Gaza and the West Bank. In this enterprise they were assisted by the international community through the flow of considerable economic aid and investment. Although the Palestinians were afforded some elements of sovereignty, the Israeli military remained deployed in Gaza, and no Israeli settlements were dismantled. Critically, Israel retained control over the borders and the roads leading to the settlements and constructed a fence surrounding Gaza, thus sealing it from the outside world and allowing Israel to control the flow of goods and people to and from the territory. With the start of the Second *Intifada* in September 2000, Israel tightened its control of Gaza and ended most of the cooperative arrangements with the Palestinian Authority. It restricted the entry of Palestinian workers into Israel, causing severe stress to the Gazan economy. It also set up a series of roadblocks and crossing points, limiting the internal freedom of movement of the Palestinian population and effectively dividing Gaza into three segments.

The Gaza disengagement plan

It was Israel's disengagement plan and its withdrawal from Gaza in August 2005 that fundamentally changed the geopolitics of Gaza. On December 18, 2003, in his address to the annual Herzliya conference on Israel's national security, Israeli Prime Minister Ariel Sharon served notice that, should the Palestinians continue to disregard their obligations under the Road Map – the plan for peace devised by the United States, the European Union, Russia, and the United Nations – then Israel would have no alternative but to

> initiate the unilateral security step of disengagement from the Palestinians. . . . The "Disengagement Plan" will include the redeployment of IDF [Israeli Defense] forces along new security lines and a change in the deployment of settlements, which will reduce as much as possible the number of Israelis located in the heart of the Palestinian population.[1]

Initially, Sharon offered no details of the geographic scope or the extent of his proposed disengagement plan. Two months later, in an interview with the Israeli newspaper *Haaretz*, he became more specific, revealing for the first time his intention of evacuating all Israeli settlements in Gaza and from certain areas in the northern part of the West Bank. "This vacuum, for which the Palestinians are to blame, cannot go on forever," Sharon asserted.

> So as part of the disengagement plan I ordered an evacuation – sorry, a relocation – of 17 settlements with their 7,500 residents, from the Gaza Strip to Israeli territory. . . . Not only settlements in Gaza, but also four problematic settlements in Samaria [the West Bank].[2]

No Israeli prime minister had ever spoken before in such detail about removing Israeli settlements from Gaza and the West Bank.

Sharon's decision to withdraw unilaterally from Gaza and to dismantle settlements without demanding any reciprocal undertakings or guarantees from the Palestinians represented a sea change in Israeli strategic thinking. The territories captured in the Six Day War had always been viewed by Israel as offering it vital strategic depth, or to be used as a bargaining chip and to be returned only in exchange for peace. For Ariel Sharon, it signaled a remarkable change of heart. No Israeli leader was more closely associated with Israel's settlement enterprise, and specifically with Gaza, than Sharon. Over the years, Sharon had been the driving force behind the expansion of settlements in the West Bank and Gaza, seeing their construction as a security imperative rather than as an ideological or religious obligation. And, throughout the Oslo process, he had continued to profess the importance of maintaining a presence in Gaza and of the strategic value of the Gazan settlements for Israel's security.

The disengagement plan had its roots in the growing demand in Israel for a physical separation from the Palestinians and in the ideas presented by Israeli "security doves," who had been advocating a policy of reducing Israel's military commitments in the Occupied Territories (see chapter 16, by Gerald Steinberg). It was generally welcomed by the Israeli public, which had become weary of the cost of protecting the Gazan settlements – requiring an estimated 5,000 soldiers to protect roughly 8,000 settlers. By handing over Gaza, Israel would no longer control the daily lives of Palestinians and would extricate its soldiers from conflictual encounters with them. Yitzhak Rabin expressed the sentiments of most Israelis when in 1992 he said that he wished that Gaza would simply sink into the sea. The isolated Gaza settlements and the considerable manpower and resources required to protect them was widely viewed as a strategic burden for Israel. This backing of the Israeli public enabled Sharon to stare down his critics and secure the necessary political and legislative support required to implement the disengagement plan.[3]

Sharon came under widespread criticism for his intention to withdraw unilaterally from Gaza and dismantle Israeli settlements. In particular, he was vilified by members of his own Likud Party and by the settler movement for what they regarded as his act of betrayal and his willingness to sacrifice the Land of Israel. The disengagement plan was decried as a cynical move, with the sole aim of ensuring his personal political survival by diverting attention from the ongoing criminal investigations by the Israeli attorney-general against him and his sons. By proposing an Israeli withdrawal from Gaza, Sharon's critics argued that he was simply seeking the support of the political left and center in Israel in the hope that they would be less intent on pressing for his removal from office.

Many Israelis also attacked the disengagement plan as strategic folly. Withdrawing from Gaza without demands for reciprocal measures on the part of the Palestinians, it was argued, would only undermine Israeli deterrence and security and be understood by the Palestinians and by the Islamic world as a sign of weakness and as attesting to the success of the wave of terrorist attacks against Israeli citizens. That interpretation was echoed by the Palestinian reaction to Sharon's plan. Many Palestinians celebrated it as an important achievement of the *Intifada* and as justifying the armed struggle. Hamas leaders hailed Israel's retreat as a great victory for the Palestinian resistance movement and the "end of the Zionist dream and a sign of the moral and psychological decline of the Jewish state."

On the other hand, supporters of the disengagement plan heralded it as an important confidence-building measure, one that would allow the Palestinians to establish the institutions for self-government and serve as an important catalyst for reviving the moribund peace process. That optimism was not based on a shrewd analysis of Israel's strategic motives. Although he paid lip service to the Road Map, Sharon spoke little of his hopes of bringing the Palestinians back to the negotiating table and did not foresee any prospect of ending the conflict in the immediate future.

A more pessimist, and hard-headed, interpretation viewed Sharon's decision to leave Gaza as a calculated move designed to derail other political initiatives (including the Road Map), with the ultimate aim of strengthening Israel's long-term hold over the West Bank. This required a political trade-off: the sacrifice of Gaza, and the evacuation of the Gazan settlements, for the long-term imposition of a weak truncated Palestinian state that the Palestinians would eventually be forced to accept. This interpretation became increasingly popular following a wide-ranging and often-quoted interview given by Dov Weisglass, Sharon's chief of staff and a close personal adviser. Weisglass described the disengagement plan as

> the bottle of formaldehyde within which you place the president's [Bush's] formula so that it will be preserved for a very long period of time. The disengagement is actually formaldehyde. It supplies the amount of formaldehyde that's necessary so that there will not be a political process with the Palestinians. . . . The American term is to park conveniently. The disengagement plan makes it possible for Israel to park conveniently in an interim situation that distances us as far as possible from political pressure. It legitimizes our contention that there is no negotiating with the Palestinians. There is a decision here to do the minimum possible in order to maintain our political situation.[4]

For Weisglass, the Israeli settler movement should have celebrated Sharon's plan and "danced around the Prime Minister's Office." Although the disengagement plan required the evacuation of a small number of settlers from their homes, Ariel Sharon was "strengthening the other 200,000, strengthening their hold in the soil." Formally, Sharon distanced himself from Weisglass's remarks and continued to express his support of the Road Map. But, in a letter to members of his Likud Party, he expressed similar sentiments: "We cannot fulfill all our dreams but through the means of disengagement we can achieve most of them. . . . As a result, Ma'aleh Adumin will grow stronger, Ariel, the Etzion bloc, Givat Ze'ev will remain in Israel's hands and will continue to develop. Hebron and Kiryat Arba will be strong."[5]

With the announcement of the disengagement plan, Ariel Sharon not only regained control of the political agenda but also was afforded unprecedented international acclaim. Many in the international community remained distrusting of Sharon and expressed their concerns over the unilateral nature of Israel's thinking and the exclusion of the Palestinian Authority as stakeholders in the process. Those concerns were tempered by the fact that no Israeli prime minister had been bold enough to express publicly as a precondition for peace the need to remove settlements – a step long called for by the Palestinians and the international community – nor have the vision to initiate a plan to such an end. The Middle East Quartet welcomed Sharon's initiative, describing it as "a rare moment of opportunity in the search for peace in the Middle East," though they were less confident that this initiative would lead to progress on the Road Map and the creation of a Palestinian state. The European Union was more qualified in its response, pledging its support so long as the disengagement plan "did not involve a transfer of settlement activity to the West Bank; there was a negotiated handover of responsibility to the Palestinian Authority; and Israel facilitated the rehabilitation and reconstruction of Gaza."[6]

US President George Bush lavished praise on Sharon for his "bold initiative" and the risks he was prepared to make for peace. In April 2004, Sharon traveled to Washington with the aim not only of shoring up American support for the disengagement plan but also of translating his initiative into long-term political gains for Israel. He returned home having extracted a series of commitments from the United States over the contours of final settlement that would have been much harder, if not impossible, to achieve in the context of negotiations with the Palestinians. Specifically, in his letter to Sharon of April 14, 2004, on the disengagement plan, President Bush reassured the prime mininster that any resolution of the Palestinian refugee issue would involve the resettlement of the refugees in a Palestinian state and not Israel. More critically, on the future of Israeli settlements in the West Bank:

> In light of new realities on the ground, including already existing major Israeli population centers, it is unrealistic to expect that the outcome of final status negotiations will be a full and complete return to the armistice lines of 1949.... It is realistic to expect that any final status agreement will only be achieved on the basis of mutually agreed changes that reflect these realities.[7]

In doing so, Bush significantly modified America's position on the future of the settlements and the borders between Israel and a Palestinian state, a step seen at the time as a major gain for Israel.

Throughout 2004, Israel set about planning its withdrawal from Gaza. It took the better part of eighteen months to make the necessary preparations and to pass the legislation in the Knesset for evacuating the settlements. On August 7, 2005, the Israeli cabinet approved the first phase of the disengagement process. Ten days later the Israeli army began to evict settlers from Neve Dekalim, Ganei Tal, Bedolah, Morag, Tel Katifa, and Kerem Atzmona. Within the space of five days, in a skillful and well-prepared operation, the Israeli army completed the evacuation of the remaining eleven Gaza settlements, encountering little resistance from the settlers. On August 22, the last Israeli settlers were removed from their homes in Netzarim. In the lead up to disengagement, the settler movement had vowed to launch a campaign of civil disobedience. Talk abounded in Israel of violent clashes between the settlers and the Israeli army. In some quarters there were even fears of civil war. Yet, to the surprise of all observers, the eviction passed without serious incident. This was largely the result of meticulous planning, discreet coordination with the leadership of the settler movement, and overwhelming public support for disengagement. The evacuation of the settlements created an important precedent, shattering the belief that the removal of settlements was politically unfeasible for Israel.

The disengagement plan initially called for the Israeli army to remain positioned in the Philadelphi corridor, an 8-mile (13-kilometer) military zone along the Gaza–Egypt border. Israel's military leaders were concerned over the future militarization of Gaza and argued that, without a permanent military presence along the border, new weapons systems – including anti-aircraft missiles and improved rocket systems – could be smuggled into Gaza. There was even talk that Israel might need to widen the Philadelphi route. Ultimately, other considerations prevailed. It was clear that the continued Israeli military presence would constitute a major source of Israeli–Palestinian friction. Israel turned to Egypt for support in preventing the smuggling of weapons across the border. On September 1, 2005, following lengthy negotiations, Egypt and Israel signed the Agreed Arrangements Regarding the Deployment of a Designated Force of Border Guards along the Border in the Rafah Area (the Agreed Arrangements). This document amended the 1979 Egypt–Israel peace treaty and called for the deployment of a 750-strong Egyptian patrol along the Egyptian side of the border. In an unprecedented move, Israel transferred responsibility for control of part of the external perimeter of Palestinian territory to an external party. On September 12, with the deployment of the Egyptian force along the border, Israel withdrew its forces from the Philadelphi corridor and dismantled its last military installations in Gaza. Israel's thirty-eight-year civilian and military occupation of Gaza had come to a close.

Gaza – post disengagement

The Gaza withdrawal was heralded as a turning point in Israeli–Palestinian relations. But the progress anticipated by many of the supporters in the peace process failed to materialize. For the disengagement plan to have been successful, it required two outcomes. Palestinians needed to acquire immediate and tangible economic benefits and Israelis needed to feel that their security environment had been enhanced. Neither of these conditions was fulfilled.

Visions of turning Gaza into a prosperous economy proved to be illusory, despite the concerted efforts of the international community. In order to meet the economic challenges posed by the disengagement plan the Quartet appointed James Wolfensohn, the former head of the World Bank, as the special envoy to oversee international efforts to rebuild the Palestinian economy, and in May 2005 the leaders of the G8 summit pledged up to $3 billion a year to support those efforts. A package of so-called Quick-Impact Projects was identified, and $750 million was earmarked by the donor community for disbursement between July and December 2005. Attracting little attention, Israeli and Palestinian technical experts, facilitated by experts from the World Bank and Wolfensohn's team, began to meet to ensure the smooth transfer of settlement assets, specifically the greenhouses, to the Palestinians and to work out new border arrangements that would ease the long-standing Israeli restrictions on the free movement of Palestinian workers and goods.

The efforts to establish a new border regime for Gaza proved to be difficult. Given its overriding security concerns, Israel was unwilling to relinquish control over the external perimeter of Gaza, including seaports, air space, and, most critically, the passage of people and goods. As a consequence, economic development, post-disengagement, remained dependent on Israeli decisions. The number of Palestinian workers entering Israel dropped from an average 6,500 per day before the withdrawal in August to virtually zero by October. Similarly, the number of truckloads of exports from Gaza during the same period declined from about thirty-five per day to a barely a handful. It took a further month of painstaking negotiations, requiring the intervention of the US secretary of state, Condoleezza Rice, for Israel and the Palestinians to reach agreement on a new border regime. On November 15, 2005, the two sides signed the Agreement on Movement and Access. As part of this agreement, Israel and the Palestinian Authority asked the European Union to send an observer force to monitor the performance of the Palestinian border control, security, and customs officials at the Rafah crossing point. The plans for the post-disengagement economic development of Gaza never got off the ground. For Gazans, living conditions following disengagement declined rapidly. At the start of 2006, the United Nations and the World Bank issued warnings of the collapse of the Gazan economy, but the World Bank's work on reviving this was shelved, and the Agreement on Movement and Access went largely unimplemented. The proposed Erez industrial estate was first looted by Palestinians, and then many of the buildings were destroyed by an Israeli military incursion in response to the firing of Qassam missiles into Israel in June 2006.

The most consequential aspect of disengagement unilateralism was its impact on the Palestinian leadership of Mahmoud Abbas, who had succeeded Yasser Arafat as chairman of the Palestine Liberation Organization. Proponents of the disengagement plan had hailed Sharon's move as an important confidence-building measure for Israeli–Palestinian relations. But the Palestinians were not stakeholders in either the process or its outcome. They were suspicious of Sharon's motives, seeing that his true intention was to ensure Israel's hold on the West Bank. The Palestinian leadership was effectively neutralized, as Israel planned its withdrawal from Gaza and at the same time accelerated the construction of the "separation fence" in the West Bank and Jerusalem. Their concerns and fears over disengagement were largely ignored and were interpreted as further Palestinian intransigence.

Sharon had refused to deal with Arafat, who died in November 2004. The election of Abbas in January 2005 led to renewed prospects for dialogue. The two leaders declared a mutual ceasefire at a summit hosted by Egypt on February 8, formally signaling an end to the four-year Palestinian *Intifada*. But there were no sustained diplomatic efforts to build on this rapprochement. Israel was not interested in developing a political strategy that might allow Abbas to take political credit for Israel's withdrawal from Gaza. Thus, Israel left without any formal handover or ceremony. The Palestinians celebrated Israel's departure, but it was Hamas, not the Palestinian Authority, that was able to capitalize on the moment. Hamas claimed Israel's withdrawal as its victory and a vindication of its armed struggle. Nor could Abbas point to any immediate benefits for the Palestinians following disengagement. The Rafah crossing point was closed for three months, and commercial trade though Israel ground to a halt. In short, the Palestinian Authority inherited a rump state with Israel still controlling its borders. Five months after disengagement, Hamas won the popular vote in the parliamentary elections to the Palestinian Legislative Council and formed a new Palestinian government led by Ismail Haniyeh.

In response to Hamas's electoral victory, Israel imposed a set of sanctions on the new Hamas-led Palestinian Authority, including the withholding of tax revenues it collected on imports and by introducing additional restrictions of the movement of goods to and from Gaza. The international community also withdrew its financial assistance from the Palestinian Authority, insisting that any future support was conditional on the acceptance by Hamas of the three principles laid out by the Middle East Quartet: 1) recognition of the State of Israel, 2) recognition of previous agreements, and 3) renunciation of violence. Although defeated in the elections, Fatah refused to cede control of Palestinian Authority institutions, in particular the security institutions, to Hamas. Armed clashes between the two political factions erupted throughout 2006 in the West Bank and Gaza. Eventually, following intensive mediation efforts by Saudi Arabia, the two sides signed an agreement in Mecca in February 2007 that led to the formation of a coalition government. Within a few months that agreement collapsed as forces loyal to Hamas and Fatah once again clashed. By June 14, Hamas forces and armed groups had taken control of all security installations and government buildings in Gaza. In response Mahmoud Abbas dismissed the Hamas-led government and declared an emergency government based in the West Bank.

From this point on, Palestinian politics and society has remained divided into two separate geographical and political entities – Gaza and the West Bank. In September 2007, Israel declared Gaza to be a "hostile territory" and imposed further reductions on the transfer of goods and supplies of fuel and electricity. Since then Israel has only sporadically allowed goods into Gaza and has at times closed all the crossings. Gaza has been effectively blockaded and sealed from any contact with the outside world. The international community has reinforced this geographic division of Palestinian society by channeling all its diplomatic efforts and financial assistance to the Palestinian Authority in the West Bank, while at the same time maintaining a complete political and economic boycott of Hamas and the governing institutions in Gaza.

As discussed earlier in this chapter, many critics of disengagement plan in Israel saw Israel's planned withdrawal from Gaza as strategic folly, maintaining that it would be interpreted by Palestinians as a sign of weakness. Leaving Gaza without any security guarantees, it was argued, would result only in a decline in Israel's deterrence capacity and an increase in the number of terrorist and rocket attacks from Gaza on its cities in the south. Those fears were immediately realized. In the first four months after its pullback, 283 rocket attacks were launched from Gaza into Israel. Israel responded by launching more than 100 air strikes on Gaza. With the electoral victory of Hamas the rocket attacks only intensified, bring in response an increase in the number of airstrikes and the firing of heavy artillery into Gaza by Israel. The escalating violence culminated at the end of June 2006 with an Israeli military incursion into Gaza. Israel's stated goals in Operation Summer Rains were to suppress the firing of Qassam rockets from Gaza and to secure the release of Corporal Gilad Shalit, who had been captured by Hamas militants on June 25 following a cross-border raid. Operation Summer Rains was followed by a similar military operation, code-named Autumn Clouds, at the beginning of November.

Following extensive mediation by Egypt, Israel and Hamas agreed to a six-month ceasefire (*Tahdiyah*) in June 2008. The ceasefire was not set out in any formal written document but comprised an agreement by Hamas to stop and prevent attacks by armed groups operating in Gaza against Israel and a commitment by Israel to cease its airstrikes and military operations in Gaza. Israel also reportedly agreed to ease its blockade of Gaza and gradually lift its ban on the import of a large number of commodities. The ceasefire held for the duration, with only a few minor violations. However, following its expiration on December 19, 2008, tensions quickly mounted on the Israeli–Gaza border, with a sharp in sharp increase in the number and frequency of rocket attacks into Israel. In response to the escalating tension Israel launched on December 27 Operation Cast Lead, consisting initially of airstrikes against Hamas security installations, personnel, and other facilities in the Gaza Strip. This was followed on January 3 by a full-scale Israeli military ground operation in Gaza. Intense shelling and fighting between Israeli forces and Hamas fighters lasted for three weeks until a ceasefire was drawn up, with Israel withdrawing its troops from Gaza on January 21, 2009.

While Israel could claim that Operation Cast Lead was successful militarily, and that it had weakened Hamas's military capabilities, its international reputation was significantly harmed by the intensity of its armed assault on Gaza. Initial understandings over the need to defend its citizens from rocket attacks quickly turned to widespread international criticism. Human rights organizations estimated the number of dead at close to 1,400 Palestinians, including more than 1,000 civilians, and the wounded at more than 5,000. Much of Gaza's infrastructure and many of its buildings were also destroyed or badly damaged. Israel's military operation led to calls for the setting up of an international commission of inquiry. In response the UN Human Rights Council (HRC) established the United Nations Fact Finding Mission on the Gaza Conflict to investigate Israeli violations of international human rights and humanitarian law in the context of military operations in Gaza, whether before, during, or after Operation Cast Lead. On September 29, 2009, Justice Richard Goldstone, who headed the mission, presented the report (commonly known as the Goldstone report) to the HRC in Geneva. The mission had investigated thirty-six incidents of alleged violations by the IDF in Gaza, as well as alleged violations by Palestinians. This reflected an effort by Goldstone to broaden the scope of his report beyond the original mandate, which was limited only to violations by Israel. Among its many conclusions, the report claimed that members of the IDF were responsible for the deliberate targeting of civilians, for the destruction of critical infrastructure in Gaza, and for using weapons such as white phosphorous in highly populated areas, all of which it deemed to be violations of international humanitarian law.[8] The Goldstone report was widely criticized by supporters of Israel (and Goldstone vilified) for its legal and factual errors, as well as for devoting insufficient attention to the asymmetrical nature of the conflict and the fact that Hamas and other Palestinian militants were deliberately operating in heavily populated urban areas of Gaza. The government of Israel also rejected the charge that it had a policy of deliberately targeting civilians.[9]

Israel's economic blockade of Gaza and the living conditions of the Gazan population came under the international spotlight the following year with the Gaza Flotilla/*Mavi Marmara* incident. In May 2010, six ships carrying humanitarian aid and construction materials set sail from

Turkey with the intention of breaking the Israeli naval blockade of Gaza. The "Gaza Flotilla," organized by the Free Gaza Movement and Turkish Foundation for Human Rights and Freedoms and Humanitarian Relief, was manned by over 1,000 human rights activists. On May 31, the Israeli navy intercepted and manned the flotilla. On the Turkish ship *Mavi Marmara* the Israeli naval commandos encountered fierce resistance. During the struggle, nine activists were killed and many others were wounded, among them ten Israeli commandos. The five other ships in the flotilla were boarded without major incident. The ships were towed to Israel, where all passengers were detained and later deported. The boarding of the *Mavi Marmara* and the deaths of the nine activists led to widespread international condemnation and to a further deterioration in Israeli–Turkish relations. Paradoxically, Israel's actions succeeded only in drawing attention to its blockade and the living conditions in Gaza, one of aims of the organizers of the flotilla.

In response to this mounting international criticism, Israel announced in June that it would ease the restriction of goods and, in particular, allow the entry of construction materials into Gaza. The loosening of the economic blockade resulted in a limited reactivation of the Gazan economy, arising from the increased availability of consumer goods and some raw materials. The opening of the Rafah crossing point between Egypt and Gaza in May 2011 allowed for some limited access and travel for Gazans (men aged between eighteen and forty require a permit). Trade, however, remained prohibited, and Gaza remains isolated politically and economically, effectively cut off from the West Bank and the rest of the world.

Conclusion

Hamas's takeover of Gaza has led to a policy vacuum over the future of Gaza as far as the international community is concerned. The demand that Hamas accept the Quartet principles, and its resultant diplomatic isolation, has failed to shift its position over recognition of Israel and the peace process. This failure has led to a growing questioning of the utility of the Quartet principles, but the policy of isolating Hamas politically has, so far, remained firm. Israel's attempt to loosen Hamas's control of Gaza has also met with little success. Operation Cast Lead weakened its military capabilities and its willingness to launch rocket attacks on Israeli cities in the south, but only to a certain degree. The security environment along the Israel–Gaza border consists of a fragile unofficial ceasefire punctuated by periodic cycles of mounting tension marked by the launching of rocket attacks on Israeli cities in the south and retaliatory strikes by Israel on Gaza. In May 2010, Fatah and Hamas signed a reconciliation agreement in Cairo which called for the setting up of a transitional government to pave the way for new legislative and presidential elections within a year and for the entry of Hamas into the PLO. This agreement offered the prospect of reintegrating Palestinian society and politics, and of bringing an end to the division of Palestine between Gaza and the West Bank. However, its implementation quickly ran into trouble. Instead, the impoverishment and isolation of Gaza and the prevailing unstable security environment continues, with little hope of significant change in sight.

Notes

1 For the full text of Sharon's speech, see www.mfa.gov.il/MFA/Government/Speeches+by+Israeli+leaders/2003/Address+by+PM+Ariel+Sharon+at+the+Fourth+Herzliya.htm.
2 Yoel Marcus, "PM's Pullout Plan: 20 Settlements to Go within a Year or Two," *Haaretz*, 3 February 2004.
3 Rynhold and Waxman (2008).
4 Quoted in Ari Shavit, "The Big Freeze," *Haaretz*, 8 October 2004.

5   Quoted in Nathan Guttman and Aluf Benn, "Bush Says Disengagement Plan Must Be Part of Road Map," *Haaretz*, 13 April 2004. These are all references to Israeli settlements in the West Bank.

6   Brussels European Council, Presidency Conclusions, 25–6 March 2004. Document available in Sharon Pardo and Joel Peters, *Israel and the European Union: A Documentary History* (Lanham, MD: Lexington Books, 2012), pp. 329–31.

7   See www.mfa.gov.il/MFA/Peace+Process/Reference+Documents/Exchange+of+letters+Sharon-Bush+14-Apr-2004.htm. Bush's letter of assurance to Sharon is a reversal of the letter of assurance given to the Palestinians by his father, President George H. W. Bush, before the Madrid peace conference of October 1991, which stated that the "United States has opposed and will continue to oppose settlement activity in the territories occupied in 1967 which remain an obstacle to peace."

8   The Goldstone report can be found at www2.ohchr.org/english/bodies/hrcouncil/specialsession/9/factfindingmission.htm.

9   Richard Goldstone retracted some of the findings of the report in an opinion piece published in the *Washington Post* in April 2011. See Richard Goldstone, "Reconsidering the Goldstone Report on Israel and War Crimes," *Washington Post*, 2 April 2011; available at: www.washingtonpost.com/opinions/reconsidering-the-goldstone-report-on-israel-and-war-crimes/2011/04/01/AFg111JC_story.html.

References and further reading

Chomsky, Noam, and Pappe, Ilan (2010) *Gaza in Crisis: Reflections on Israel's War against the Palestinians* (Chicago: Haymarket).

Hass, Amira (2000) *Drinking the Sea at Gaza* (New York: Picador).

Peters, Joel (2012) "Gaza," in Richard Caplan (ed.), *Exit Strategies and Peace Building* (Oxford: Oxford University Press).

Rynhold, Jonathan, and Waxman, Dov (2008) "Ideological Change and Israel's Disengagement from Gaza," *Political Science Quarterly*, 123/1, pp. 11–37.

Part V
Domestic actors

18

The Palestine Liberation Organization

Nigel Parsons

The evolving role of the PLO

The Palestine Liberation Organization (PLO) has evolved as it has endured, shifting over five decades from anti-colonial radicalism to enervating diplomatic pursuit of the nationalist agenda. That the organization has persisted for so long is a measure of both its durability and of frustration.

The PLO was established in 1964 in Jerusalem on the initiative of the League of Arab States, prompted by Egyptian president Gamal Abdul Nasser. It was intended as a mechanism for the aggregation and articulation of a Palestinian political voice, subject to Arab tutelage. But by the late 1960s, with a new leadership typified by the charismatic guerrilla leader Yasser Arafat, the PLO had assumed the role with which it is more commonly associated: an independent means of determining the direction of a Palestinian national project. The organization's record judged by its mandate is something of a curate's egg. On the one hand, the PLO can claim credit for reconstructing modern Palestinian national identity and securing recognition of the right to self-determination in international law. On the other hand, it is responsible for the Declaration of Principles, concluded with Israel in 1993, whereupon the bulk of personnel and resources were transferred to the troubled semi-autonomy of the Palestinian Authority (PA).

The twenty-first century found the remnant PLO far from its peak, operating adjacent to the PA but still performing important functions within the polity. In lieu of the conversion of semi-autonomy into sovereignty, the organization retained authority over negotiations and pursued wider Palestinian diplomacy. It continued to provide representation for the Palestinian people as a nation, bridging the Occupied Territories and the diaspora; and it maintained a substantial network of diplomatic missions, increasingly afforded embassy status, around the world.

PLO institutions

The Charter and Basic Law

The original PLO Charter adopted in 1964 was subject to major amendment in 1968, following the entry of independent guerrilla groups into the organization. Besides lending the PLO a more independent and national character, from this point forth, of thirty-three articles, seven made some reference to 'arms', 'armed struggle', 'armed Palestinian revolution' or 'armed popular revolution'. Guerrillas were logically central to the project. For example, article XXX asserted that 'Fighters and carriers of arms in the war of liberation are the nucleus of the popular army which will be the protective force for the gains of the Palestinian Arab people' (Hartley 2006: 383–7). However, by 1993, compliance with the Israel–PLO letters of mutual recognition framing the Oslo process necessitated textual emendation, and the PLO's senior decision-making body, the Palestine National Council (PNC), met twice to that effect. In 1996, the twenty-first PNC convened in Gaza and comfortably reached the two-thirds majority required to amend the contested articles. However, provisions for the drafting of a new charter were not utilized. Under Israeli and international diplomatic pressure, the twenty-second PNC convened, again in Gaza, during December 1998, this time in the presence of US President Bill Clinton. The PNC affirmed that a specific list of contentious articles had indeed been abrogated (Parsons 2005: 52, 186). Further to the PLO Charter, a rather less controversial Basic Law determines internal procedure, including means of election to PLO bodies and the frequency with which those bodies are to convene and reconstitute (Musallam 1990).

Constituent factions

Following the entry of guerrilla groups into the PLO in 1968, the organization became an umbrella for multiple factions with contrasting views and patrons. Eight are represented on the organization's Executive Committee (EC). The Fatah movement, officially unveiled in 1965 but on the move from the late 1950s, constitutes the nationalist mainstream, currently led by Mahmoud Abbas. Providing leftist opposition and helping frame national debate are the Popular Front for the Liberation of Palestine (PFLP) and a related faction to which it gave rise in 1969 (as the Popular Democratic Front for the Liberation of Palestine until 1974), the Democratic Front for the Liberation of Palestine (DFLP). The DFLP itself gave rise to a splinter group during 1990–91, the Palestine Democratic Union (known by its reverse Arabic acronym FIDA), ostensibly in a dispute over participation in the post-Gulf War Madrid conference. FIDA is closely allied to Fatah and the PA. The former Palestinian Communist Party joined the PLO in 1987; the end of the Cold War saw it rename itself as the Palestinian People's Party (PPP) from 1991. The PPP was unique among PLO factions in that it emerged in the Occupied Territories rather than the diaspora. The Arab Liberation Front (ALF) was established in 1969 and represented the interests of the Iraqi Ba'ath Party. During the al-Aqsa *Intifada*, the ALF gained a measure of grassroots appreciation for distributing funds from Baghdad to families of Palestinian martyrs. ALF chief Rakad Salim was arrested by Israel for his efforts in 2002. The Palestine Liberation Front (PLF) is another offshoot of the PFLP (via an offshoot of that, the PFLP-General Command); the PLF was established in 1977, also under Iraqi auspices, and is perhaps best known for the public relations fiasco of the *Achille Lauro* operation in 1985 and an assault on a Tel Aviv beach that brought the US–PLO dialogue to a halt in 1990. PLF history is informed by schism and uneven participation in the PLO EC. Finally, the Palestinian Popular Struggle Front (PPSF) emerged in 1967, also from PFLP orbit (Sayigh 1997: xlii); it has a negligible following in the West Bank and Gaza.

Outside of the EC, but with the minimum two seats reserved on the intermediary Central Council (CC), are four additional factions. The Palestinian Arab Liberation Front and Islamic Jihad retain two seats each, allocated to named individuals. Two further factions have seats reserved but do not assume them. The first is the PFLP-GC, which broke away from the PFLP in 1968 and has been very closely allied with Damascus. The second is the Vanguards of

Popular Liberation War Organization, better known as al-Sa'iqa (Thunderbolt); backed by Syria, it was at one point a major military presence in the PLO. However, bitter fallout following the Israeli invasion of Lebanon left Sa'iqa confronting the mainstream PLO, and terminal decline set in. Both the PFLP-GC and Sa'iqa are diaspora-era relics with little relevance to the Occupied Territories.

Besides the Islamist opposition, two factions outside the PLO framework are of historic note. In 1974, encouraged by Iraqi intelligence, Fatah dissident Sabri al-Banna, better known as Abu Nidal, established his own radical faction (akin to a cult), the Fatah Revolutionary Council. He was expelled from the PLO and sentenced to death in absentia for plotting the assassination of his former Fatah colleague Mahmoud Abbas (Seale 1992: 98). The other non-PLO, non-Islamist faction of historical import was Fatah al-Intifada, established in 1983 with Syrian support by the rebel commander Sa'id Musa Maragha.

Chairman and secretary general

The founding PLO EC chairman was the lawyer and diplomat Ahmad Shuqayri. Incumbent from 1964 to late 1967, Shuqayri was removed in the aftermath of the calamitous Six Day War. He was replaced on a caretaker basis by a figure sympathetic to the guerrilla cause, Yahya Hammuda, who held the reins through 1968. Then, on 3 February 1969, Arafat became the third chairman, and by far the most famous. Upon his death in November 2004, Arafat was succeeded by the then PLO secretary general, Mahmoud Abbas. The current secretary general is Yasser Abed Rabbo, formerly of the FIDA faction until 2002, and closely associated with Fatah. In the PA elections of 2006, Abed Rabbo lined up alongside Prime Minister Fayyad on the Third Way list.

The Palestine National Council

The Palestine National Council (PNC) constitutes the supreme PLO decision-making body; the rough equivalent of a national parliament for a dispersed refugee people, it remains the ultimate source of authority on decisions of national import within the Palestinian polity. The inaugural session convened in Jerusalem in 1964 with 422 members (Sayigh 1997: 97). Reflecting the PLO's peripatetic trajectory, the PNC has congregated in four different Arab capitals – Cairo, Damascus, Algiers and Amman – in addition to Gaza in 1966, and three decades later in 1996 and again in 1998 (Parsons 2005: 323). The Hamas takeover of 2007 rendered the coastal strip a problematic venue and so a subsequent PNC special session convened in August 2009 took place in Ramallah. The meeting of some 300 PNC members followed swiftly on the heels of the sixth Fatah General Conference in Bethlehem, part of a concerted effort to boost the legitimacy of nationalist institutions. Hamas dismissed the meeting as 'a desperate attempt to return [the] soul to a dead body' (Xinhua 2009). Nevertheless, negotiations on national unity have routinely addressed the incorporation of Hamas into the PNC, although the terms on which this might happen remain in dispute. Negotiations in Tunis in late 1992 reportedly saw Fatah offer Hamas 'eighteen guaranteed seats in the PNC (compared to Fatah's 33 and the PFLP's fifteen)' (Mishal and Sela 2000: 98). During follow-up talks in Khartoum in 1993, Hamas allegedly claimed 40 per cent of PNC seats, a concession firmly rejected, along with other demands, by Arafat (ibid.: 99). More recently, article 2 of the 2006 National Reconciliation Document (commonly known as the Prisoners' Document), negotiated by representatives of Fatah, Hamas, Islamic Jihad, the PFLP and the DFLP, called for a new PNC constituted 'in a manner that secures the representation of all Palestinian national and Islamic forces, factions and parties and all sectors of our people'. Reflective of ongoing negotiation, the 2007 Mecca Agreement that brokered the PA's short-lived national unity government called for moving ahead with 'measures to activate and reform the Palestine Liberation Organisation and accelerate the work of the preparatory committee based on the Cairo and Damascus Understandings'.

Besides political factions, the formula determining PNC composition reflects a corporatist vision, with representatives drawn from various functional, as well as geographic, units of the Palestinian polity. The components include military forces (historically, the Palestine Liberation Army, reorganized from 1983 as the Palestine National Liberation Army), mass organizations (unions), and representatives of communities worldwide, with a specific allowance for refugee camp and Bedouin representatives (Musallam 1990: 12–13, 30–32). PNC members are to be elected or nominated by committee, subject to circumstance. Following election in 1996 of the PA's parliament, the Palestinian Legislative Council (PLC), the eighty-eight PLC members plus 100 of the nearest runners up were to be added to the roll (Parsons 2005: 186). In the pre-Oslo era, the historic guerrilla leader could usually rely on the heft of the PNLA within the PNC to support his position (ibid.: 130). The post-election incorporation of PA PLC members, consistent with bylaws of the PNC, performed a similar function when it came to amending the Charter.

The Central Council

The Central Council (CC) was not an original component of the PLO but was added by the eleventh PNC in 1973. Diplomatic success and the unwieldy nature of the PNC were felt to necessitate an intermediary body (Musallam 1990: 18–21). CC members are drawn from the PNC and include all members of the EC, plus members of the PNC secretariat, the military committee, mass organizations, standing committees, political factions and a number of independents, as well as a batch of legislators from the PLC. Historically, the CC ratified conclusion of the Declaration of Principles plus the establishment, in October 1993, of the PA via the 'Phased Plan' from the twelfth PNC (Parsons 2005: 125).

The Executive Committee

The EC constitutes a sort of coalition cabinet with members typically afforded a portfolio akin to a government ministry. It is deemed to be 'in permanent session and its members work on a full-time basis'. In principle, the EC 'and its members are responsible to the PNC individually and collectively for the execution and implementation of the policies, plans and programs drawn up and adopted by the PNC' (Musallam 1990: 22). The EC has expanded over time to reach eighteen members, drawn, in accord with the Basic Law, from the PNC. There are several constituent factions of varying import. The revamped PNC of 2009 saw Fatah maintain its allocation of three official seats, with senior Fatah members holding another two seats as independents (certain other independents remained reliable Fatah allies); each of the other factions held a single seat, the smaller among them as observers. One seat is reserved for the head of the Palestine National Fund (PNF), with the remainder held by other independents. The EC is responsible for selecting the chairman from among its number; in practice, this is the head of Fatah. The PNC special session convened in August 2009 broke new ground: nominated replacements for four (now deceased) factional representatives were approved by the PNC in the usual way, but two independents were elected by free vote. Hanan Ashrawi narrowly secured one of the seats and, in so doing, became the first woman elevated to the EC.

Table 18.1 The PLO Executive Committee following the special session of 2009

Name	Affiliation	Portfolio
Mahmoud Abbas	Fatah	Chairman
		Supervisor of the Political Dept
Yasser Abed Rabbo	Independent	Secretary General
Faruq al-Qaddumi	Fatah	Member only
Sa'eb Erekat[a]	Fatah	Negotiations Affairs Dept
Abd al-Rahim Malluh	PFLP	Arab Relations Dept
Taysir Khalid	DFLP	Ex-patriot Affairs
Hanna Amira[a]	PPP	Social Affairs Dept
Salih Ra'fat[a]	FIDA	Military and Security Dept
Ahmad Majdalani[a]	PPSF	Planning Centre
Mahmoud Isma'il	ALF	Popular Organizations Dept
Ali Ishaq	Ex-PLF/Independent	Youth and Sports Dept
Muhammad Zuhdi al-Nashashibi	Independent	Palestine National Fund
Ghassan al-Shak'a	Independent	Dept. of International Relations
Zakariyya al-Agha	Independent (Fatah)	Refugees' Affairs
Riyad al-Khudari	Independent	Education and Higher Education Dept.
As'ad Abd al-Rahman	Independent	Research Dept.
Ahmad Qurei[a]	Independent (Fatah, elected)	Jerusalem Affairs Dept.
Hanan Ashrawi[a]	Independent (elected)	Dept. of Culture and Media
Jamil Shihada[a]	Palestinian Arab Front	Observer
Wasil Abu Yusuf[a]	PLF	Observer
Salam Fayyad[a]	Independent	Economics Dept. (acting head), observer

Source: Based on a report in *Al Ayyam*, 28 August 2009, conversation with staff at the Palestine Media Center, and an interview with EC member Dr Wasil Abu Yusuf, Ramallah, July 2011.

Note: [a] Indicates new members.

Participation in the EC is prone to fluctuation. For instance, controversy accompanying the PLO's initial and implicit recognition of Israel in 1974 famously led to the formation of the Rejection Front, composed of the PFLP, the PFLP-GC, the ALF and the PPSF. Members suspended participation in the EC. Fallout from the invasion of Lebanon precipitated further dramatic internal fissures and finally left Sa'iqa utterly marginalized by the mid-1980s (Gresh 1988: 184–7, 238–44). Oslo amplified the trend in the 1990s: disoriented by a diplomatic process in which they had not participated and for which they were not prepared, the PFLP, the DFLP, the ALF, the PPP, and on occasion the Fatah dissident Faruq al-Qaddumi, could all boycott the EC. So might leading independents. The passage of time took a further toll on an aging membership, to the point that a somewhat diminished EC typically offered little resistance to the dictates of its long-serving and charismatic chairman. However, the Abbas era marked a modest revival in EC fortunes: the troubles besetting the PA as a national project, and the concomitant ascent of Hamas over Gaza, saw Abbas invest in the PLO leadership as a source of additional legitimacy. The 2009 PNC meeting can be understood in this light.

The Palestine National Fund

The PNF is akin to the treasury of the PLO; based in Jordan, it also has an office in Ramallah. The PNF is responsible for funding PLO departments, including diplomatic missions, although sympathetic host governments routinely contribute to the upkeep of Palestinian posts overseas. PNF coffers historically drew upon a 'liberation tax' extracted from Palestinians in the diaspora. The era of the PA found tax returns much diminished but still collected, especially in Egypt and the Gulf. PLO employees contribute around 3 per cent of their salaries. The PLO once held a celebrated investment portfolio; the Palestine Martyrs' Society Workshops (SAMID) generated substantial employment and income (Sayigh 1997: 460), although the Oslo process saw it reduced to a modest archive in Abu Dis. The PLO may technically be in charge of the PA, but the influx of donor funding to the Occupied Territories found the PA at least partially responsible for funding its parent organization.

The PLO's historic contribution

Reconstructing national identity

The PLO may not have realized Palestinian statehood, but it has done much to build the conceptual foundations upon which statehood might stand. Not least has been the reconstitution of modern Palestinian national identity. The 1948 catastrophe, commemorated as *al-Nakba*, left Palestine's largely peasant society dislocated, fragmented and deeply vulnerable. The PLO's achievement would be to rally this critical human resource around the concept of armed struggle; the transformation from refugees to a guerrilla-led nation with self-respect and a clear sense of purpose was not a foregone conclusion (Sayigh 1979; 1997: vii). Moreover, this psychological, cultural and social transformation continues to underpin the remarkable capacity of Palestinian society to resist Israeli occupation.

The PLO at its inception has been described in Patrick Seale's irresistible phrase as 'a sort of corral in which Palestinians could charge about harmlessly letting off steam' (Seale 1988: 121). The organization established a conventional military in the Palestine Liberation Army, but for the most part it remained a state-sponsored forum for venting frustration; Palestinians were enjoined to wait for Arab states to liberate and reintegrate Palestine into the Arab fold. But, independent of the PLO, two main activist currents were coalescing. From southern Palestine to Gaza, via Cairo to the Gulf, Arafat and his colleagues were forging the nationalist Fatah movement. From northern Palestine to Lebanon, and specifically at the American University of Beirut, Christian Palestinians George Habash and Wadi Haddad, with Arab and Muslim colleagues, were building the Arab Nationalists Movement, the group that would develop and bifurcate to form the principal left-wing opposition to Fatah within the PLO. Both currents were committed to armed struggle, but, whereas Fatah held to an essentially non-doctrinaire nationalism, the leftist factions adopted Marxist–Leninist platforms and an avowed hostility to the Arab status quo. Fatah commenced a modest armed struggle under the title *al-Asifa* (the Storm); it was no great success, but 1 January 1965 would soon be commemorated as the birth of the Palestinian revolution.

Trounced by Israel in June 1967, discredited Arab regimes were ill-placed to support the incumbent PLO leadership around Ahmad Shuqayri. Momentum behind the independent guerrillas then increased tremendously in March 1968. Responding to Palestinian raids on the newly occupied West Bank, a large column of the Israel Defense Forces (IDF) crossed the Jordan, intent on destroying a base at Karama. The IDF met uncommonly stiff resistance and suffered major casualties, mostly at the hands of the Jordanian army. A courageous guerrilla contribution was militarily marginal, and yet it proved politically seismic. The myth of guerrilla triumph spread rapidly, 'because it met critical human needs amongst the Palestinians' (Terrill 2001: 91). Karama restored self-respect; guerrillas offered hope amid gloom and were duly propelled to the forefront of popular consciousness. Recruits presented in numbers; oil-rich patrons from the Gulf offered financial support in return for legitimacy. Momentum was such that confident guerrillas entered the PLO at the fourth PNC in July 1968. By the close of the fifth PNC, Fatah alone had secured thirty-three of the 105 seats, rendering it the major bloc. The PLO's guerrilla leadership now commanded an array of assets: a bureaucracy, a military in the Palestine Liberation Army, guerrilla units in the Popular Liberation Forces, diplomatic representation and financial resources (Sharabi 1970: 32–3).

Psychological and institutional progress was substantial, but the course of armed struggle ran far from smoothly. Post-occupation rebellion in the Occupied Territories was quickly suppressed by Israel. Then, discomfited and finally affronted by guerrilla activity on the East Bank, the Hashemite regime launched a bloody purge from September 1970 to July 1971; the events would be recalled by Palestinians as Black September. The PLO then decamped to Lebanon, drawing on a combination of weak domestic state apparatus and receptive refugee constituency. The 1969 Cairo Accords guaranteed PLO autonomy over the camps and operational freedom to confront Israel. Headquartered in the Fakhani quarter of Beirut, secure in the 'Fatahland' of southern Lebanon, the PLO would, in conventional terms, reach its military apogee through the mid-1970s and early 1980s.

Securing recognition and the right to self-determination

The practical impossibility of defeating Zionism through military means necessitated a diplomatic strategy that would translate socio-psychological and institutional progress into regional and international legal success. This unfolded unevenly, with landmarks in 1974, 1988 and 1993.

The goal of Arab nationalist liberation gave way to a discrete 'democratic state' of Palestine between 1969 and the eighth PNC in 1971 (Gresh 1988: 9, 17–57). But this aspiration too would erode under pressure of events on several levels. In the Palestinian polity, the gravitational pull of the Occupied Territories – where the post-1967 priority lay with ending the occupation – counselled further compromise; the Palestine National Front, based in the territories, declared allegiance to the PLO in 1973 and gained admittance to the EC. In the region, calamity in Jordan urged caution in future relations with neighbouring regimes. The strictly national goals of Egypt and Syria in the 1973 war with Israel checked ambition again. In the international arena, the USA proved an elusive interlocutor: US Secretary of State Henry Kissinger precluded the possibility of negotiation with the PLO from 1975 onwards, until it accepted UN Security Council resolutions 242 and 338 and Israel's right to exist. The 1979 Camp David accords then conceived of no role for the PLO. But this was a bipolar world, and pragmatic advice from the USSR maintained the lure of diplomatic initiative. The conceptual bridge to diplomacy emerged in the radical idea of an interim 'national authority', put forward in 1972 by the PDFLP with Fatah's encouragement. The twelfth PNC in June 1974 then produced the ten-point 'Phased Political Program', point 2 of which called for a 'people's national, independent and fighting authority on every part of Palestinian land that is liberated' (Gresh 1988: 168). The USSR then invited the organization to establish an official mission in Moscow. The following month the Arab summit in Rabat accorded the PLO the status of 'sole legitimate representative' of the Palestinian people (ibid.: 179). In November, Arafat was invited to address the UN General Assembly, whose Resolution 3236 defined Palestinian rights as including '(a) The right to self-determination without external interference; (b) The right to national independence and sovereignty'. Resolution 3237 invited the PLO 'to participate in the sessions and work of the General Assembly in the capacity of observer'. The majority in the Occupied Territories approved and in 1976 would vote in municipal elections for pro-PLO candidates (ibid.: 186). Tentative contacts were even forged eventually with the United States: a ten-month cross-factional ceasefire on Israel's northern border from July 1981 constituted an operational achievement for Fatah and accrued appreciation in Washington (Cobban 1984: 112). The situation was deemed intolerable by Israel's right-wing Likud government; an assassination attempt against Israel's ambassador to London by the non-PLO Abu Nidal group served to trigger the invasion of Lebanon in July 1982. The demolition of the PLO was intended to expedite an Israeli diktat in the Occupied Territories (Sayigh 1997: 507–8).

The PLO relocated to Tunis and cast about for ways to remain relevant. Redemption came with the First *Intifada* in late 1987, driven by a confident local leadership, often from refugee backgrounds and educated through PLO scholarships. Local leaders organized the secular-nationalist Unified National Leadership of the Uprising (UNLU), composed of representatives from Fatah, the PFLP, the DFLP and the communists (Robinson 1997: 19–37, 97). The manifest nationalism of the First *Intifada* prompted Jordan finally to concede its claim on the West Bank in 1988. The PLO looked to fill the gap with the resolutions of the nineteenth PNC in November. The Declaration of Independence of the State of Palestine drew upon UN General Assembly Resolution 181, the original partition resolution from 1947 that endorsed the idea of an Arab state alongside Israel. Denied a visa for the United States, Arafat then addressed a special meeting of the General Assembly in Geneva. He eventually foreswore recourse to terrorism and accepted, subject to PLO interpretation, UN resolutions 242 and 338. The PLO Charter was disavowed, and Israel was finally explicitly acknowledged under US pressure at a post-meeting press conference (Sayigh 1997: 624).

However, converting diplomatic momentum into institutional form would take six more years. The PLO's regional standing reached a low ebb following an ambivalent if misrepresented stance on the Iraqi invasion of Kuwait. It played well with domestic constituents but alienated patrons in the Gulf. The post-liberation destruction of the Palestinian community in Kuwait, a key source of tax revenue for the PNF, added to the turmoil in Palestinian finances. The crisis was such that salaries could not be paid to portions of the PNLA (Parsons 2005: 128–9). Alienation from Arab sponsors and the USA then helped keep the organization out of postwar negotiations in Madrid and Washington. For Tunis, already wary of UNLU autonomy and fearful of an ascendant Hamas, the spectre of alternative leadership loomed. Thus it was that Israel chose a propitious moment to engage with the PLO. For the organization, the Declaration of Principles secured Israeli recognition as the legitimate representative of the Palestinian people, conditional on an end to armed resistance.

The PLO adjacent to the Palestinian Authority

Co-option

The Oslo process allowed the State of Israel to incorporate the bulk of PLO personnel, resources and energy into restructured governance arrangements for the indigenous population of the Occupied Territories. The PA presented a new array of institutional opportunities for employment and the extension of patronage. Funding poured in from previously unlikely sources, including the European Union, the United States, the International Monetary Fund and the World Bank. PLO cadres merged with local staff from the IDF's bureaucratic wing in the territories (the Civil Administration) and technocrats from NGOs and the private sector. Duly embedded in governing structures and variously well resourced, the mainstream PLO leadership might deem the PA an essential, if disappointing, national project. Their disposition speaks to Lyons's observation that, given the right sort of incentive, 'actors may become trapped in a politics of moderation' wherein the benefits of perpetuating the status quo outweigh the costs of renewed confrontation (Lyons 2009: 101). Put another way, the PLO leadership through Oslo have 'invested too much for too long, and their power depends too heavily on the process to accommodate a swift and radical shift' (ICG 2010: i). However, Oslo-era and post-Oslo negotiations such as the Annapolis process have steadfastly failed to produce an agreement that meets the basic terms of the PLO's mandate or the reasonable expectations of ordinary constituents. This means most obviously the right to self-determination and, in consequence, key items on the nationalist agenda, among them sovereignty, borders, settlements, water, Jerusalem and refugees. Herein is found scope for the continuing role of the PLO.

Negotiations and diplomacy

The PLO's right to negotiate derives from its status as the 'sole legitimate representative' of the Palestinian people accorded by the Arab League since 1974, with representative status affirmed by the UN the same year. Israel eventually recognized the PLO in 1993 in the letters of mutual recognition exchanged between Arafat, Israeli Prime Minister Yitzhak Rabin and Norwegian Foreign Minister Holst. Rabin's letter to Arafat declared:

> In response to your letter of September 9, 1993, I wish to confirm to you that in light of the PLO commitments included in your letter, the Government of Israel has decided to recognize the PLO as the representative of the Palestinian people and commence negotiations with the PLO within the Middle East peace process.
>
> *(Parsons 2005: 90)*

The Islamist position was clarified somewhat in the National Reconciliation Document of 2006, which affirmed that Hamas and Islamic Jihad acknowledged the PLO's role. Article 7 read:

> Administration of the negotiations falls within the jurisdiction of the PLO and the President of the PNA, which will be on the basis of adhering to Palestinian national goals as mentioned in this document on condition that any agreement must be presented to the new PNC for ratification or a general referendum to be held in the homeland and the Diaspora.

The massive leak of confidential PLO documents, made public by *Al Jazeera* and *The Guardian* during January 2011, led Hamas publicly to revoke the PLO's authorization to negotiate, although the impact remained unclear.

The PLO pursued bilateral negotiations with Israel throughout the Oslo process, the post-Oslo revival mechanism of the Road Map (managed by the Quartet of the USA, the EU, the UN and Russia) and the Annapolis process. The last of these ground to a halt amid the carnage of Operation Cast Lead launched in late 2008. But lack of progress, in conjunction with relentless settlement-building by Israel in the West Bank, stimulated a search for alternative strategies that might be pursued in parallel with the PA's state-building programme under Salam Fayyad. The shift in nationalist thinking was captured in the platform that emerged from Fatah's sixth General Conference; this required a halt to settlement construction as a precondition to further negotiation, in addition to clear terms of reference and a resumption of talks at the point they had previously concluded. The impact on the PLO's position quickly became evident. It affected the approach to negotiation and wider diplomacy. The altered approach to negotiations constituted a paradigm shift, effectively a reversal of the early 1990s turn from Washington to

Oslo. Whereas the delegation to Washington had stuck resolutely to principle, Oslo largely suspended principle in favour of progress on select, practical detail. It expedited the PA but offered no resolution to key items from the nationalist agenda. The organization now looked 'to turn the paradigm [back] on its head... seeking to enshrine principles first, and from there, work backwards to fill in the details' (ICG 2010: 15). Israel balked, and bilateral negotiations stalled. In conjunction, a prospective shift in diplomatic strategy sought the international community rather than Israel as key interlocutor. The UN in particular held promise, and certainly offered a more favourable playing field than anything cultivated by the United States.

The strategy reached a landmark of sorts on 23 September 2011, when PLO Chairman Mahmoud Abbas requested that Palestine be granted full membership of the UN. The application was received in person by Secretary General Ban Ki-moon before proceeding to a committee of the Security Council. The USA worked tirelessly to subvert the initiative and threatened ultimate use of the veto. The Palestinians retained the option of an appeal to the General Assembly, which had the authority to upgrade the Permanent Observer Mission of Palestine to the status of non-member state. The upgrade held practical implications for Palestinian diplomacy, including membership rights in UN agencies such as UNICEF, UNESCO and the WHO, as well as the prospect of access to the International Criminal Court and the International Court of Justice. Platforms such as these could lend Palestine a degree of leverage with Israel that had previously been lacking.

Palestinian foreign policy

The formation of what might be termed Palestinian foreign policy is not a simple business; notwithstanding the importance of Fatah, it is in effect arrived at through a four-way competition between the PA President's Office, the PLO's Negotiation Affairs Department and its related Negotiations Office, the PA Prime Minister's Office and the PA Ministry of Foreign Affairs. Bilateral relations with major states such as the USA, and any state party to negotiations, fall under the purview of the President's Office. Negotiations per se are the business of the Negotiation Affairs Department. The Prime Minister's Office can also contribute, to the extent that its policies are compatible with those of the presidency. The role of the Ministry of Foreign Affairs is primarily to market the policies thus formulated. Indeed, foreign ministers visiting Ramallah may opt to call directly on the president.

Before Oslo, Palestinian foreign policy was the business of the PLO's Political Department under its long-standing head Faruq al-Qaddumi. But after the Declaration of Principles the office waned for two reasons: location outside the Occupied Territories made it difficult to coordinate with foreign envoys coming to the PA; and Qaddumi himself remained a stalwart opponent of Oslo. The decline of the Political Department allowed influence to accrue to the PA's Ministry of Planning and International Cooperation, transformed during 2003 into the Ministry of Foreign Affairs. The role of the Political Department then effectively ended in 2005 as the PA passed the Palestinian Diplomatic Law and the PLO CC mandated the minister to manage embassies and consulates. The achievement owed something to the forceful personality of then minister, Nasser al-Qudwa.

The Negotiations Support Unit

The PLO established the Negotiation Affairs Department in Gaza in 1994 to help expedite the Israel–PLO Interim Agreement. The Negotiation Affairs Department was led by Abbas until his appointment as prime minister of the PA in 2003, whereupon Sa'eb Erekat took charge.

The need to prepare for complex final-status negotiations led the department to the UK government in search of support in 1998. The upshot was formation of the Negotiations Support Unit in Ramallah, under the guidance of Adam Smith International. Besides the UK, funding was received from Scandinavia and the Netherlands. Adam Smith International's role ended in 2010. The unit was mandated to provide legal, policy and communications advice to the Palestinian side in negotiations. Up until 2011, it was best known for maintaining a high quality website. But that changed when it emerged as the key source of the controversial leak to *Al Jazeera*. Not part of the classic PLO structure, the Negotiations Support Unit had already provoked controversy for its influence, its reliance on Palestinian-American and other Western-trained diaspora Palestinian lawyers and the substantial salaries paid to its most senior managers. Scandal hastened the demise of the contested unit; when it was dissolved in March 2011, staff were laid off, particularly Palestinians with Israeli citizenship. The affair did not reflect well on the Negotiation Affairs Department chief, Erekat, but he was maintained in office by Abbas.

Diplomatic representation

Besides the headline work of negotiation and strategic diplomacy, the PLO shares with the PA in a substantial network of diplomatic offices attending to the routine business of the Palestinian nation worldwide. The Arab League and Non-Aligned Movement accord PLO offices the status of embassies of Palestine, as do former Eastern bloc states. Proactive PLO diplomacy looked to upgrade that status where possible, with a flurry of activity taking place in Europe and the Americas. Brazil afforded the PLO an embassy in late 2010, to be followed by several neighbours during early 2011. On a symbolic level, the PLO General Delegation to Washington, DC, was first allowed to fly the Palestinian flag at around the same time. In Europe, Ireland followed three EU states plus Norway to accord the PLO office the title of Mission of Palestine, under an ambassador. Further upgrades were anticipated as renewed PLO diplomacy gathered pace.

Major embassies are located in Arab League states, determined by politics and the size of Palestinian community on the ground. Embassies in Egypt and Jordan employ perhaps forty diplomats and administrators. Concentrations of refugees in Lebanon and Syria necessitate a major presence, as do Palestinian communities in Saudi Arabia and the Gulf. Despite severe cutbacks, the PLO continues to take some responsibility for non-UNRWA education in the diaspora, and, in the field of health care, the Palestinian Red Crescent Society (PRCS) operates as best it can. However, the steep decline in PLO services in the diaspora left a vacuum that, in Lebanon at least, could be partially filled by radical Islamist offshoots (Robinson 2010). Fatah al-Islam at the Nahr al-Barid camp was a case in point.

Outside the Arab world, important posts are maintained in Indonesia, as the world's most populous Muslim state; in South Africa, where the ANC government identifies with the struggle; and in Vietnam and China, fellow anti-colonial allies, with the Beijing embassy dating from the earliest days of the PLO. Russia has of course constituted an important post of long standing. Typical Western European missions are not so big and serve primarily as centres for media and communication; they may have just three to five staff. The largest post in Latin America is in Chile, thought to be home to perhaps 100,000 citizens of Palestinian descent. In North America, the PLO maintains the General Delegation in Washington, DC, plus the Permanent Observer Mission of Palestine to the UN in New York (designated 'Palestine' rather than 'PLO' since 1988); it was led at the time of writing by Riyad Mansour of the DFLP. Both posts have around half a dozen staff. There is a similar mission in Geneva.

The Palestinian diplomatic service is estimated to employ between 350 and 400 personnel, with PLO and PA staff and tasks tightly interwoven. During the tenure of the national unity government, PLO staff hosted senior Hamas figures such as Mahmud al-Zahhar. Diplomatic staff coordinate with host governments on mundane but critical capacity-building tasks such as the supply and receipt of aid. Diplomatic posts also receive batches of Palestinian students for professional development, particularly in fields appropriate to state-building such as engineering and education, although since Israel's clampdown on Gaza these opportunities have been increasingly restricted to Palestinians from the West Bank. Diplomatic personnel also work to raise awareness of Palestinian issues, both within the host government and foreign embassies and within local universities and civil society.

Conclusion

The early twenty-first century found the PLO far from the pomp of its heyday. The bulk of Palestinian nationalist energy now infused the constrained semi-autonomy of the PA in the West Bank and the encircled Hamas administration in Gaza. The PLO, a once vital forum for interfactional debate and dissent, could increasingly seem a dated, even marginal, anti-colonial relic. And yet the power against which the PLO defined itself had still to yield on the demand for self-determination. Credit for securing that right and reconstructing the national identity upon which it is based rests in large part with the venerable organization. It is in these circumstances, and adjacent to the PA, that the PLO might still be said to perform multiple key roles within the Palestinian polity. It continues to contribute to the formation and implementation of Palestinian policy. It provides a recognized address for interlocutors and (controversy notwithstanding) an enduring institutional capacity to negotiate. Diplomatic posts provide national representation and a point of contact for Palestinians abroad, including the refugee heart of the nation. As the PA endeavours to build the state on the ground, the PLO carries the case, with some efficacy, to the international community. If a final-status agreement with Israel is ever concluded, it is likely to be through the PLO, with the PNC convened for ratification.

References and further reading

Sections of this chapter draw on an earlier publication: Parsons, N. (2009) 'The Palestine Liberation Organization and the Oslo Process: Incorporation without Accommodation', in B. W. Dayton and L. Kriesberg (eds), *Conflict Transformation and Peacebuilding: Moving from Violence to Sustainable Peace* (London and New York: Routledge). The author would like to thank Yezid Sayigh for reading an earlier version of this text.

Cobban, H. (1984) *The Palestinian Liberation Organisation: People, Power, and Politics* (Cambridge: Cambridge University Press).
Gresh, A. (1988) *The PLO: The Struggle Within* (London: Zed Press).
Hartley, C. (ed.) (2006) *A Survey of Arab–Israeli Relations* (3rd ed., London: Routledge).
ICG (International Crisis Group) (2010) Tipping Point? Palestinians and the Search for a New Strategy, *Middle East Report*, 26 April; available at: www.crisisgroup.org/en/regions/middle-east-north-africa/israel-palestine/095-tipping-point-palestinians-and-the-search-for-a-new-strategy.aspx.
Lyons, T. (2009) 'Peacebuilding, Democratization, and Transforming the Institutions of War', in B. W. Dayton and L. Kriesberg (eds), *Conflict Transformation and Peacebuilding: Moving from Violence to Sustainable Peace* (London and New York: Routledge).
Mishal, S., and Sela, A. (2000) *The Palestinian Hamas: Vision, Violence, and Coexistence* (New York: Columbia University Press).
Musallam, S. (1990) *The Palestine Liberation Organization: Its Function and Structure* (Brattleboro, VT: Amana).

Parsons, N. (2005) *The Politics of the Palestinian Authority: From Oslo to al-Aqsa* (London and New York: Routledge).

Quigley, J. (2010) *The Statehood of Palestine: International Law in the Middle East Conflict* (Cambridge and New York: Cambridge University Press).

Robinson, G. (1997) *Building a Palestinian state: The Incomplete Revolution* (Bloomington: Indiana University Press).

Robinson, G. (2010) 'Palestine Liberation Organization', in *The Oxford Encyclopedia of the Islamic World*, Oxford Islamic Studies Online, www.oxfordislamicstudies.com/article/opr/t236/e0618.

Sayigh, R. (1979) *Palestinians: From Peasants to Revolutionaries* (London: Zed Press).

Sayigh, Y. (1997) *Armed Struggle and the Search for State: The Palestinian National Movement, 1949–1993* (Oxford: Oxford University Press).

Seale, P. (1988) *Asad of Syria: The Struggle for the Middle East* (London: I. B. Tauris).

Seale, P. (1992) *Abu Nidal: The World's Most Notorious Terrorist* (London: Arrow).

Sharabi, H. (1970) *Palestine Guerrillas: Their Credibility and Effectiveness* (Beirut: Institute for Palestine Studies).

Terrill, W. A. (2001) 'The Political Mythology of the Battle of Karameh', *Middle East Journal*, 55/1, pp. 91–11.

19

The Palestinian Authority[1]

Nigel Parsons

The Palestinian Authority in concept

The concept of the Palestinian Authority (PA) took shape in negotiations leading to the 1993 Israel–Palestine Liberation Organization (PLO) Declaration of Principles on Interim Self-Governing Arrangements, through which the PLO was mandated to form a semi-autonomous Palestinian Interim Self-Governing Authority (PISGA) responsible for limited administration of the indigenous population in the West Bank and Gaza Strip. Article VII noted that

> Upon the entry into force of this Declaration of Principles and the withdrawal from the Gaza Strip and the Jericho area, a transfer of authority from the Israeli military government and its Civil Administration to the authorized Palestinians for this task, as detailed herein, will commence.

The interlude between conclusion of the Declaration and PLO redeployment the following year saw the PISGA morph into the Palestinian Authority; the PLO inserted the word 'national' into the Arabic title, but Israel insisted on its absence from the authoritative English version. The revised title granted the new body a measure of historical resonance by drawing upon the ten-point 'phased political programme' adopted in 1974 by the twelfth session of the PLO's quasi-legislature in exile, the Palestine National Council. Couched in the language of the time, but understood to indicate movement towards a two-state solution, point 2 of the plan called for the establishment of a 'people's national, independent and fighting authority on every part of Palestinian land that is liberated' (Gresh 1988: 168). The decision to adopt the title was ratified by the PLO Central Council on 10 October 1993 (Parsons 2005: 125).

In line with the 1978 Camp David Accords concluded between Egypt and Israel, but which at Sadat's insistence touched on the Palestinian issue, the Declaration of Principles stipulated that the PA would function for 'a transitional period not exceeding five years', with final-status negotiations to open 'not later than the third year after the beginning of the transitional period'. The end point to be reached in that time, however, remained ambiguous. Project advocates in the PLO and beyond assumed that the PA would serve as an interim step towards the fulfilment of the Palestinian right to national self-determination, with an independent state the logical outcome of the process. Critics, including some on the PLO's secular left as well as Islamists outside of the organization, were less certain. Textual ambiguities lent support to this concern. Neither the Declaration, nor the letters of mutual recognition that directly preceded it, specified an outcome. Consistent with precedents set at the Madrid conference in 1991, and further back at the 1978 Israeli–Egyptian Camp David summit, United Nations Security Council resolutions 242 and 338 provided the benchmark: they did stipulate Israeli withdrawal from territories conquered in 1967, but did not specify a Palestinian right to self-determination. In contrast, the PLO's 1988 Declaration of Independence of the State of Palestine had drawn upon UN General Assembly Resolution 181, the original partition resolution from 1947, which did endorse the idea of an Arab state alongside Israel. Technical ambiguity was resolved somewhat in 2002 with US sponsorship of UN Security Council Resolution 1397, a landmark that explicitly referred to 'a vision of a region where two states, Israel and Palestine, live side by side within secure and recognized borders'. The launch of the Road Map in 2003 drew qualified Israeli consent to the same goal. The Annapolis conference of 2007 convened on the same basis. The Obama administration extracted grudging consent, again heavily qualified, from right-wing Israeli Prime Minister Binyamin Netanyahu in 2009. This being so, at an official level at least, key parties to the conflict aligned on the apparent destiny of the PA: the PLO and Israel, all four members of the Quartet overseeing the Road Map (the USA, Russia, the European Union and the UN), plus the League of Arab States, supported the establishment of an independent Palestinian state. The territorial and institutional infrastructure upon which this might be built inhered in the PA.

The Palestinian Authority in practice

Notwithstanding a somewhat inglorious reputation, the PA did expedite a series of modest practical advances in Palestinian governance that survived the al-Aqsa *Intifada*; the Road Map reaffirmed the PA (albeit in a single sentence), and, on a technical level, aspects of administrative performance were enhanced in the post-Oslo era. The enduring features of the PA included the demarcation of a measure of accepted territory for Palestinian semi-autonomy, as well as the development of an array of quasi-state institutions that extended through an executive, a legislature and a judiciary to an extensive bureaucracy and police, intelligence and quasi-military apparatus. The advent of Hamas rule over Gaza from June 2007 complicated arrangements, but the PA headquartered in Ramallah endured.

Territorial foundations of the Palestinian Authority

The Declaration of Principles demarcated an initial territorial basis for PA rule; subsequent agreements, among them the 1994 Agreement on the Gaza Strip and Jericho Area, then provided for the redeployment on the ground of the Israel Defense Forces (IDF). Mindful of textual ambiguities, and concerned that Gaza and Jericho might constitute the limits rather than the beginning of Palestinian self-rule, early sceptics contended that a new Palestinian flag was in order: a chilli for Gaza and a banana for Jericho to capture the new territorial reality (Parsons 2005: 44). In late 1995, the Interim Agreement opened the way for further IDF redeployment, this time facilitating the extension of PA authority over most West Bank urban centres. But it did so only within a scheme that subdivided Palestinian space. Area A contained 'populated areas', including Jenin, Tulkarm, Nablus, Qalqiliya, Ramallah, Jericho and Bethlehem; here, the PA was endowed with full civil and security responsibility. Area B encompassed 'populated areas' outside of urban centres, with a list of 'built-up areas and hamlets' specified by an appendix; the PA would run civil affairs and hold limited control over policing. Area C extended to IDF military installations, settlements, and much in between; Israel retained full civil authority over territory (including the critical authority to plan) plus responsibility for security. The Interim Agreement provided for further subdivision, with Hebron separated into areas H-1 (PA administration) and H-2 (Israeli control); the 1997 arrangements agreed separately for the city reiterated the division. Providing for the extension of PA territorial reach, the Interim Agreement scheduled three additional IDF redeployments to occur at six-monthly intervals pending inauguration of the PA's legislature, the elected Palestinian Legislative Council (PLC). But the process quickly stalled. Specific territorial values were reallocated in the 1998 Wye River Memorandum, mostly providing for the transfer of parts of Area C to Area B and some expansion of Area A. In total, Israel agreed to transfer '13 percent from Area C (1 percent to Area A and 12 percent to Area B) and 14.2 from Area B to Area A'. Renegotiation through the 1999 Sharm el Sheikh Memorandum saw PA semi-autonomy extend to its fullest reach: following the last Oslo-era IDF redeployment in March 2000, Area A had grown to constitute some 18.2 per cent of the West Bank; Area B extended to 21.8 per cent. The IDF thus retained official control of some 60 per cent of the West Bank, in addition to around 40 per cent of the Gaza Strip.

The onset of the al-Aqsa *Intifada* later in 2000 put the IDF redeployment process into reverse. By the spring and summer of 2002, more or less full-scale reoccupation was under way in the West Bank, first through Operation Defensive Shield and later through Operation Determined Path. Emblematic of the clampdown, Palestinian areas were further subdivided by an extensive and dynamic network of military checkpoints. Looking to restore political momentum, the Road Map called for Israel to withdraw 'progressively from areas occupied since September 28, 2000', adding provision for subsequent arrangements to 'enhance maximum territorial contiguity'. The re-extension of the PA in practice proved to be a stop–start affair, but by late 2007 Palestinian policing had been reintroduced to Nablus, with Jenin and Hebron following the next year. By the time the Fatah movement's sixth General Conference convened in Bethlehem during 2009, PA police were back on the streets for the event. In the meantime, the parameters of Palestinian space had been shaped by two unilateral Israeli initiatives – construction of the separation barrier in the West Bank and decolonization of the Gaza Strip. The path of the barrier, originally formulated by Labor but adopted by Ariel Sharon in 2002, departed widely from the Green Line to encompass Israeli settlements in East Jerusalem and the bulk of them in the West Bank, most prominently Ariel. The 2004 ruling by the International Court of Justice against the barrier added to the battery of Palestinian legal claims, but the edifice remained. Israeli disengagement from Gaza was realized in September 2005; all Jewish settlements in the strip were abandoned, along with four isolated communities in the northern West Bank.

Movement between or out of PA territory proved fraught. The subdivision of the West Bank into enclaves was ratcheted up during the al-Aqsa *Intifada* as the IDF augmented physical force with bureaucratic measures mediating Palestinian movement. PA-issued passports and ID cards in lieu of supporting Israeli documentation were of little value at IDF or Border Guard checkpoints: indeed, the PA's own ID cards carried a number that could be issued only by Israeli authorities. Israeli-issued internal travel permits were introduced to govern movement within the West Bank during the al-Aqsa *Intifada*. Permits for travel across the Green Line or into East Jerusalem became much harder to obtain. Internal travel restrictions did ease slightly as PA policing reappeared in the West Bank – part of an integrated policy of distinguishing conditions there from the calamities of Gaza. Unilateral withdrawal removed the IDF settlement-checkpoint network from within the coastal strip, but Israel retained full control over land, sea and air around the territory. Concluding in early 2009, the controversial Operation Cast Lead caused extensive Palestinian casualties; combining heavy bombing with ground operations, it demonstrated Israeli readiness to reinvade Gaza, albeit briefly and without taking the casualties necessary for a serious effort to uproot the Hamas-controlled government. In better times, the Interim Agreement provided for safe passage between the West Bank and Gaza, some reassurance for the PLO that the West Bank and Gaza were understood as 'a single territorial unit'. Northern and southern routes were foreseen, with the latter actually functioning for just under a year from October 1999. For movement from Palestine to the outside world, Gaza airport at Rafah opened in November 1998; it too operated briefly until closed by Israel on account of the second uprising. The IDF then shredded the runway. Unable to move across or above the earth, Gazans increasingly went underneath it; a booming tunnel network developed from southern Rafah into Egypt.

Institutional basis of the Palestinian Authority

The Declaration of Principles and additional components of the Oslo process facilitated construction of the institutions of semi-autonomy. PLO personnel returning from the diaspora were at the heart of the process; cadres from the dominant Fatah faction under Arafat, and in particular Fatah's senior echelons, the Central Committee (CC) and the Revolutionary Council (RC), were central. The PLO chairman himself arrived in Gaza on 1 July 1994. In lieu of a constitution to accompany statehood, the PA organized itself according to an interim Basic Law; this was first passed by the PLC in 1997, but promulgated by Arafat only in 2002 and published in the Palestinian Official Gazette the following March. Multiple amendments were made in 2003 to permit the creation of the post of prime minister; rather fewer changes were made in 2005 to accommodate a modified electoral system, with the latter amended again by presidential decree in 2007.

Executive

For the first eighteen months or so of operation, the PA executive constituted an appointed Council of Ministers chaired by Arafat. Thereafter, elections to the presidency and PLC saw members enlisted into an executive authority, with the Interim Agreement granting the president (*ra'is*) the right to appoint up to 20 per cent non-PLC members. The 2003 Basic Law permitted a cabinet membership of twenty-four to what it termed the Council of Ministers.

President

To begin with, ministerial independence was tempered somewhat by the heft of Arafat's personality and the political culture around him. The distribution of portfolios among Fatah CC and RC members reinforced the trend – a pattern that persisted until interrupted by the process of reform and then Hamas (Parsons 2005: 142–207; Parsons 2009: 245–6). The president's penchant for convening PLO Executive Committee meetings alongside the less-familiar cabinet also helped neutralize potential opposition (Shu'aybi 2000: 90). Initial readiness to keep a lid on Palestinian resistance encouraged international acquiescence in the president-centric arrangements. But the al-Aqsa *Intifada* altered the reckoning; with Arafat once again equated with 'terrorism', foreign actors, especially Israel and the USA, sought to unravel the presidential powers in his grip. The 2003 amendments to the Basic Law allowed for the introduction of the post of prime minister to that end, with article 45 granting the president the right of appointment and dismissal.

Elections for the presidency were held in January 1996 and 2005. Neither poll was contested by Hamas. In the first election, Arafat triumphed, with just over 87 per cent of the vote; the remainder went to Samiha al-Khalil, a women's welfare campaigner affiliated to the Democratic Front for the Liberation of Palestine. The PLO chairman remained PA president until his death in November 2004, whereupon he was buried in a mausoleum built within the presidential compound (*muqata*) in Ramallah. The PLC speaker and legislator from Rafah, Rawhi Fattuh, served as interim president until the second poll could be arranged, whereupon Fatah's Mahmoud Abbas was elevated to the presidency. As on the previous occasion, the election result was never in serious doubt, and Abbas secured a decisive 62 per cent of the vote. Of his six competitors, Mustafa al-Barghuthi proved his closest rival, gaining almost 20 per cent; another independent leftist, Barghuthi was an ex-member of the formerly communist Palestinian People's Party. Abbas endured a very difficult tenure, and doubts arose as to his willingness to seek a second term. Lacking Arafat's charisma and iconic status, Abbas invested heavily in an express disavowal of armed struggle in the hope that US support would deliver critical traction on Israel. Lack of progress in negotiations undermined his position. So too did a series of political missteps and related internal schisms, including the 2006 electoral loss of the PLC to Hamas and the 2007 rout of Fatah forces from Gaza. The dispute with Hamas would take constitutional form. The 2005 amendments to the Basic Law set a four-year limit on the president's term. However, articles 2 and 11 of the election law passed shortly afterwards provided for simultaneous elections to the presidency and the PLC; crucially, the PLC timetable was given precedence for the first presidential poll under the new law. Thus Abbas could claim that, according to the election law, his term ran until 2010. This limit too was exceeded.[2] Opponents aired the view that, following precedent, PLC speaker Aziz Dwik should inherit the role from 9 January 2009. The speaker himself showed no interest in pursuing the claim.

Prime minister

Following the amended Basic Law of 2003, the president appoints the prime minister, with the latter then responsible for forming a government. There is no stipulation that the prime minister be drawn from the PLC. However, the legislative body is required to approve the cabinet by absolute majority in a vote of confidence. The initial prime minister back in 2003, Abbas was the first person granted the title since Ahmad Hilmi Abd al-Baqi headed the All Palestine Government in 1948 (Parsons 2005: 211). Set firmly against armed resistance and looking to unpick presidential powers, Abbas struggled to organize a unilateral Palestinian ceasefire just as he struggled to manage a recalcitrant Arafat. Furious internal politicking centred on control of the Interior Ministry and, through that, branches of the security apparatus. In Gaza, Abbas relied upon Hamas's tormentor-in-chief Mohammed Dahlan; the strongman from Khan Yunis refugee camp was well placed to contain the opposition but was deeply resented as a result. Resisted by Arafat and those dependent upon him, Abbas resigned later in the year. He was replaced by his fellow Fatah CC member Ahmad Qurei, based in the Jerusalem suburb of Abu Dis. Qurei proved somewhat more adept at managing Arafat and, as a member of the PLC, could claim at least some sort of constituency. He also kept a public distance from Israel and the United States. Qurei faced similar issues to Abbas, threatening to resign and actually doing so, but found himself maintained in office by Arafat. Qurei relinquished the post briefly at the end of 2006 to run for the PLC, during which time Fatah CC member Nabil Shaath held the reins. Qurei ultimately withdrew from the race for the PLC and remained in office until after the election. Real trouble arose when the poll generated a Hamas majority. Qurei was succeeded by Hamas's Isma'il Haniyya, a resident of al-Shati refugee camp in Gaza. Haniyya was sworn in during March 2006, whereupon his Hamas-led government struggled on for just under a year in the face of Israeli and international sanctions. Hope of sorts appeared with a Saudi-brokered national unity government. But the arrangements quickly collapsed: Fatah provocations, at least partly engineered by Mohammed Dahlan, prompted Hamas to launch a pre-emptive coup in Gaza during June 2007, from which the Islamist movement emerged triumphant. From Ramallah, Abbas dismissed Haniyya by presidential fiat, with the latter continuing in office but restricted to Gaza. In the West Bank, Haniyya was replaced by Salam Fayyad, an economist with experience of the World Bank and IMF. Fayyad served as finance minister under Arafat from 2002 and continued under Abbas. Respected by Western donors, he was a pivotal figure in the history of PA reform; drawing on this reputation, he ran in the 2006 PLC elections as a member of the independent Third Way, winning a seat along with Hanan Ashrawi. The legality of Fayyad's position was disputed by Hamas on the grounds that the PLC had not been afforded a vote on his appointment. Had it done so, the Hamas majority seemed likely to preclude a successful outcome. Fayyad resigned during 2009, seemingly to pave the way towards Fatah–Hamas reconciliation. But a renewal of national unity proved elusive, and Fayyad too continued in office.

Legislature

The Palestinian Legislative Council

The preamble to the Interim Agreement stipulated that an elected Palestinian council be realized for 'a transitional period not exceeding five years', with the timetable set in motion by the signing of the Gaza–Jericho Agreement on 4 May 1994. The PLC established two physical headquarters: one in the relatively comfortable Rimal neighbourhood of Gaza (destroyed during Operation Cast Lead) and another in Ramallah, across town from the *muqata*. The PLC held its inaugural session in Gaza during March 1996, which technically gave it a term of just over three years. In the event, new elections would take almost a decade, during which time the legislative body endeavoured to assert its authority but found itself deeply constrained for structural and internal political reasons. On a structural level, article XVII of the Interim Agreement excluded PLC jurisdiction from 'issues that will be negotiated in the permanent status negotiations: Jerusalem, settlements, specified military locations, Palestinian refugees, borders, foreign relations and Israelis'. This removed most of the headline issues on the Palestinian nationalist agenda from the PLC's remit. Moreover, while article XI granted the body jurisdiction over land in Areas A and B, including powers of 'planning and zoning', in Area C Israel agreed to transfer only 'civil powers and responsibilities not relating to territory'. The PLC thus found itself powerless to do much more than protest as Israel accelerated the pace of Jewish settlement around the PA's delineated enclaves. In addition, article XVIII noted that any PLC 'legislation which amends or abrogates existing laws or military orders . . . shall be void ab initio'. Such PLC legislation as was passed was then to be 'communicated to the Israeli side' of a joint Legal Committee for review. In practice, oversight may have been less intrusive than anticipated (Frisch 2008: 125); this likely reflected the limited consequences of many PLC decisions. Restrictions on movement also undermined PLC members' ability to work. On the internal political front, the first PLC faced a highly assertive president in Arafat, although it could, on occasion, defy him. Legislators refused to take their oath of office alone before the president. The Basic Law first proposed by Arafat was rejected. Cabinet nominees could be declined, and presidential amendments to legislation defining the role of the prime minister did not obtain the necessary majority (Parsons 2005: 209–11). The PLC also ran a series of competent parliamentary committees that examined, among other things, the malfunctioning of the security services. The second PLC faced a Fatah president with a Hamas majority, but the opportunity to practise cohabitation proved very limited amid a state of almost permanent crisis. Following the kidnap and detention in Gaza of an IDF soldier, Gilad Shalit, in June 2006, Israel arrested many Hamas PLC members and denied them a quorum (ICG 2007: 17, n. 143). The loss of Gaza a year later then prompted the Fatah-run PA to take an even closer interest in Hamas in the West Bank.

Legislative elections

The Interim Agreement first specified the system and rules governing election to the PLC, with separate ballots for presidency and legislature to be conducted simultaneously. Further elaboration was undertaken by a Central Elections Commission, following which the 1996 poll was held on a multi-member majority basis: sixteen electoral districts (eleven in the West Bank and five in Gaza) held up to twelve or as little as one seat each. Of the eighty-eight seats in total (fifty-one in the West Bank and thirty-seven in Gaza), six were reserved for Christians and one for the Samaritan community in Nablus. The campaign reflected the dislocation and boycott of much of the secular and Islamist opposition, as well as the transient optimism that followed IDF redeployment. The results were an easy success for Fatah: the movement's official candidates secured fifty seats (57 per cent), but with unofficial allies the total was much higher (Parsons 2005: 186–203). The 2006 poll took place within a different system. The new electoral law of 2005 created a mixed majority-proportional system: sixteen electoral districts remained, but would now account for only half of the expanded 132-seat body. This meant that sixty-six PLC members would be elected in the same manner as before. Six seats were again reserved for Christians. But the remainder would be chosen on the basis of proportional representation, with the West Bank and Gaza Strip treated as a single sixty-six-seat constituency contested by parties or coalitions on closed lists. Women were guaranteed third place on each list and places at intervals thereafter. More than the system had changed in the decade since the first PLC poll. Settlement construction and the consequent al-Aqsa *Intifada* had hardened attitudes. The iconic Arafat was in his grave. The credibility of Fatah had eroded along with the failings of the PA as a national project. Poor governance and a failure to manage internal renewal reinforced disillusion and finally prompted a split in the movement; the dissident leader Marwan al-Barghuthi was persuaded to rejoin, but Fatah's vote dissipated amid the fracas. Following success in a series of local elections, Hamas sensed an opportunity. But the results still came as a shock; campaigning as the Change and Reform list, Hamas won. The Islamist movement scored particularly well in the electoral districts; the proportional list competition was close, Hamas edging Fatah by twenty-nine to twenty-eight, but overall the Change and Reform list secured seventy-four PLC seats to Fatah's forty-five.[2] Following the Fatah–Hamas split, sceptical Palestinians noted that Prime Minister Fayyad represented a party with around 2.5 per cent of the popular vote. Abbas then annulled the election law of 2005 by presidential decree in favour of an entirely proportional system.

Judiciary

The PA judiciary is addressed between articles 97 and 109 of the Basic Law as amended in 2003. The principle of judicial independence is established and followed by a call for a series of courts to be determined by law; the Judicial Authority Law was published in the official gazette in 2002. The Basic Law stipulates a High Judicial Council to consider draft laws regarding judicial authority, including public prosecution, and to recommend candidates for the post of attorney general to the president; the High Judicial Council was established in law in 2000. The courts essentially fall into three streams: religious, special and regular. The Basic Law allows for Sharia and religious courts responsible for personal status, with military courts (deemed to be special courts) restricted to martial affairs and administrative courts as needed. On the ground, the nuts and bolts of the regular judiciary worked upwards from magistrates court to district court/court of first instance to appellate court, with a Court of Cassation and High Court of Justice to follow. The Basic Law stipulates a High Constitutional Court to interpret the PA's foundational document as well as PLC legislation and to resolve judicial and administrative disputes between branches of government, with the High Court empowered to act in lieu; the Constitutional Court Law was passed in 2006. A controversial High Court of State Security was introduced to shore up the writ of the PA in 1995; it attracted much criticism and was abolished amid the process of reform. The law upon which the PA judiciary draws hails from multiple sources that reflect Palestine's tumultuous history; legal legacies have been left by Ottoman, British mandatory, Jordanian, Egyptian and Israeli civil and military authorities. The Interim Agreement stipulated that pre-Oslo arrangements ought not to be unpicked by PA legislation, and indeed the PA's first published order in 1994 reaffirmed the existing legal framework; thereafter, local officials endeavoured to align the West Bank and Gazan legal systems while simultaneously putting as much distance as possible between the PA and Israel (Brown 2003: 18–58). Judicial efficacy suffered from Israeli colonial rule and Palestinian internal politics; short of investment, judges, staff and kudos, the al-Aqsa *Intifada* prompted further degradation through military assault, restriction of movement and the erosion of institutional authority. Post-Oslo, the externally supported impetus for reform provided welcome encouragement and donor support for the PA judiciary, at least in the West Bank.

Bureaucracy

Created by the PLO in advance of the PA, the Palestinian Economic Council for Development and Reconstruction was an early institutional initiative responsible for coordinating with donors, receiving funds and planning for investments. It has been described as 'the runway on which the PA landed from Tunis' (Parsons 2005: 142). Then, between 1994 and 1995, the Oslo process steadily granted the nascent PA authority over a range of indigenous civil affairs: the Gaza–Jericho Agreement operationalized provisions for Palestinian administration set out in the Declaration of Principles, article VI (2), as 'education and culture, health, social welfare, direct taxation, tourism, and other authorities agreed upon'. Appended to the Gaza–Jericho Agreement, the Protocol on Civil Affairs provided an extended list of thirty-two spheres of responsibility for the joint enclaves, ranging from newspaper licensing and censorship, through fisheries and surveying, to postal services and archaeology. Israel retained a role in several areas, including nature reserves and environmental protection, and the PA remained bound to Israeli contracts for electricity and water. Palestinian jurisdiction expanded beyond Gaza and Jericho with the Agreement on the Preparatory Transfer of Powers and Responsibilities, which reiterated the core spheres from the Declaration of Principles and added indirect taxation. The subsequent Protocol on Further Transfer of Powers and Responsibilities, negotiated along with the Interim Agreement, extended PA jurisdiction across the West Bank in eight spheres, listed as 'Labor, Commerce and Industry, Gas and Petroleum, Insurance, Postal Services, Local Government and Agriculture'. Staffing the nascent PA bureaucracy were former employees of the

IDF Civil Administration, redeployed cadres of the PLO, and local technocrats, often drawn from the NGO network. They were joined by graduates of the burgeoning Palestinian tertiary education sector and many recently released prisoners. The politics of the PA put Fatah cadres at the heart of the process; alongside the senior CC and RC figures in the executive, mid-rank cadres released from jail were typically appointed at director-general level (Parsons 2005: 141–5). The occupation, ongoing colonization and restrictions on movement limited the opportunities for private-sector economic growth, rendering the public sector a critical new source of income, prestige and leverage. The disruption of the al-Aqsa *Intifada* accentuated the phenomenon, with the PA effectively serving as an extended social safety net. It has been calculated that it 'employed almost nine times more people than the eighteen thousand Palestinians who worked for the Civil Administration before the transfer of authority in 1993 (Gordon 2008: 186). Following the Hamas takeover of Gaza, PA employees there were instructed not to work, in return for which they would continue to receive salaries from Ramallah.

Police, intelligence and military

The construction of a Palestinian security apparatus was *the* defining feature of the PA in concept and practice. For the PLO leadership, the initiative provided a Western-financed mechanism for the transformation of the diaspora-based armed forces into the quasi-military branches of the new national project; in the process, the PA could absorb the bulk of independent-minded Fatah cadres (such as the Black Panthers in the West Bank and the Fatah Hawks in Gaza) propelled upwards by the First *Intifada*, and then coerce the secular nationalist or Islamist opposition from a position of strength. For Israel, weary of policing a civilian population across the Green Line, the PA offered a proxy mechanism for containing Palestinian resistance to occupation and colonization. The Declaration of Principles set the tone, article III calling for Palestinian police 'to ensure public order' during elections, and article VIII elaborating:

> In order to guarantee public order and internal security for Palestinians of the West Bank and Gaza Strip, the Council [PLC] will establish a strong police force, while Israel will continue to carry the responsibility for defending against external threats, as well as the responsibility for the overall security of Israelis for the purpose of safeguarding their internal security and public order.

Annex II to the Declaration stipulated 'a joint Palestinian–Israeli Coordination and Cooperation Committee for mutual security purposes'. The Cairo Agreement then provided for joint PA–IDF patrols in Jericho, with Israel remaining in control of border crossings with Jordan and Egypt. The Gaza–Jericho Agreement permitted the first contingent of PLO forces to deploy in the territories, with article XVIII on 'The Prevention of Hostile Acts' specifying the remit:

> Both sides shall take all measures necessary in order to prevent acts of terrorism, crime and hostilities directed against each other . . . In addition, the Palestinian side shall take all measures necessary to prevent such hostile acts directed against the Settlements, the infrastructure serving them and the Military Installation Area.

A subsequent annex provided for a Joint Security Committee and a series of District Coordination Offices to expedite cooperation between the PA and the IDF on the ground. The Interim Agreement allowed for the extension of PA security across West Bank indigenous population centres and reiterated the remit; under the heading 'Security Policy for the Prevention of

Terrorism and Violence', annex I stipulated that 'The Palestinian Police will act systematically against all expressions of violence and terror . . . arrest and prosecute individuals suspected of perpetrating acts of violence and terror . . . and cooperate in the exchange of information and coordinate policies and activities.' The 1998 Wye River Memorandum introduced a supporting role for the CIA, developed under director George Tenet to some effect; CIA operatives continued to advise the PA in the West Bank as a means of containing Hamas. The 1999 Sharm el Sheikh Memorandum obliged the PA to collect unauthorized weapons, further apprehend suspects, and submit a list of PA officers to Israel for vetting. Remit in hand, the number of staff in the PA security services grew. The exact proportions were somewhat elusive on account of organizational change as well as inconsistencies in methods of counting (e.g., whether to include contractors, municipal employees and pensioners), but one authoritative estimate put '86,000 active and retired personnel on the PASF [Palestinian Authority Security Forces] payroll in early 2007'. The same report noted that reformed security forces counted just 23,000 in the West Bank three years later (US GAO 2010). The politics of institutional expansion were reflected in a corresponding boom in bureaucracy; the combined civil and security PA payroll was thought to have reached around 165,000 personnel (United Nations 2007: 3).

The upheaval of the al-Aqsa *Intifada* left officers torn between their role as security personnel and a background in resistance. Many were injured and killed in the rebellion. When the dust began to settle, a major effort was undertaken to reorganize the multiplicity of forces and retrain personnel. International support came from several sources. For the USA, Lieutenant General Keith Dayton was alleged to have supported Dahlan against Hamas. The EU ran the EUPOL-COPPS initiative (formerly EUCOPPS), linked with judicial reform. Regional partners Jordan and Egypt offered support. Domestically, training took place at the police academy in Jericho. The PA's coercive forces were rearranged into three clusters. First, the Civil Police included branches for criminal investigation and a drugs squad and also provided the traffic police; the police were aligned with the Preventive Security Force and Civil Defence. These forces answered to the Ministry of the Interior and by extension to the prime minister. Second, General Intelligence stood alone, but was rumoured to be likely to absorb the Preventive Security Force. Third, National Security Force provided an army of sorts, aligned with Military Intelligence and the Special Presidential Guard. The intelligence and military services answered to the president, as did the governors of the sixteen governorates into which the PA was organized. The advent of Hamas government led to a bitter struggle over the Civil Police and associated forces; recalcitrant Fatah, egged on by Israel and foreign donors, helped make the case for units loyal to the Hamas government that would eventually prevail in the struggle for Gaza.

Conclusion

From the perspective of the PLO leadership and the texts that frame the Oslo process, the PA was conceived as an expressly 'transitional' or 'interim' arrangement, destined to be replaced in a permanent settlement realized within five years of the first IDF redeployment. The clock started ticking in 1994, and the PA has endured for at least three times as long as foreseen by Palestinians leading the project. This can be read in different ways. From the perspective of the original time frame, the fact that the PA still exists is an indication of failure: semi-autonomy continues only in the absence of an independent Palestinian state, while Sisyphean negotiations between the PLO and Israel (when under way at all) seldom promise to bring the moment of self-determination any closer. From the perspective of a contemporary optimist, for all of its manifest shortcomings, the PA does constitute the territorial, institutional and human foundations upon which a Palestinian state seems most likely to be built; all key actors officially subscribe to that outcome. The PA has been shaken, most obviously by the al-Aqsa *Intifada* and the Fatah–Hamas split, and yet – in the West Bank at least – it continues to stand and even to strengthen. Ramallah continues to generate considerable support from the international community. Hamas has not dismantled the PA entirely in Gaza, and Israel does not look keen to resume the occupation. The less sanguine observer might argue that the ossification of the PA into a semi-permanent status quo is not a historical accident, with semi-autonomy the beginning, and likely end point, of the PLO's national project.

Notes

1 The author would like to thank Yezid Sayigh for comments on an earlier version of this chapter.
2 Central Elections Commission – Palestine (2005) *Full text of Elections Law No. 9 of 2005*; available at: http://aceproject.org/ero-en/regions/mideast/PS/palestine-elections-law-no.9-2005/view.

References and further reading

Brown, N. J. (2003) *Palestinian Politics after the Oslo Accords: Resuming Arab Palestine* (Berkeley: University of California Press).
Frisch, H. (2008) *The Palestinian Military: Between Militias and Armies* (London and New York: Routledge).
Gordon, N. (2008) *Israel's Occupation* (Berkeley: University of California Press).
Gresh, A. (1988) *The PLO: The Struggle Within* (London: Zed Press).
ICG (International Crisis Group) (2007) 'After Gaza', *Middle East Report*, 68, Amman/Jerusalem/Gaza/Brussels, 2 August; available at: www.crisisgroup.org/en/regions/middle-east-north-africa/israel-palestine/068-after-gaza.aspx.
Khan, M., Giacaman, G., and Amundsen, I. (2004) *State Formation in Palestine: Viability and Governance during a Social Transformation* (London and New York: Routledge).
Le More, A. (2008) *International Assistance to the Palestinians after Oslo: Political Guilt, Wasted Money* (London and New York: Routledge).
Lia, B. (2006) *A Police Force without a State: A History of the Palestinian Security Forces in the West Bank and Gaza* (Reading, UK: Ithaca).
Parsons, N. (2005) *The Politics of the Palestinian Authority: From Oslo to al-Aqsa* (London and New York: Routledge).
Parsons, N. (2009) 'The Palestine Liberation Organization and the Oslo Process: Incorporation without Accommodation', in B. W. Dayton and L. Kriesberg (eds), *Conflict Transformation and Peacebuilding: Moving from Violence to Sustainable Peace* (London and New York: Routledge).
Roy, S. M. (2007) *Failing Peace: Gaza and the Palestinian–Israeli Conflict* (Ann Arbor, MI: Pluto Press).
Rubenberg, C. A. (2003) *The Palestinians: In Search of a Just Peace* (Boulder, CO: Lynne Rienner).
Sayigh, Y. (2007) 'Inducing a Failed State in Palestine', *Survival*, 49/3, pp. 7–40.
Shu'aybi, A. (2000) 'A Window on the Workings of the PA: An Inside View', IPS Forum, *Journal of Palestine Studies*, 30/1, pp. 88–97.
United Nations (2002) *Security Council Resolution 1397*, available at: http://daccess-dds-ny.un.org/doc/UNDOC/GEN/N02/283/59/PDF/N0228359.pdf?OpenElement.
United Nations (2007) *Report of the Commissioner-General of the United Nations Relief and Works Agency for Palestine Refugees in the Near East, 1 January–31 December 2006*. General Assembly, Official Records, Sixty-second session, Supplement No. 13 (A/62/13); available at: www.unrwa.org/userfiles/20100118134924.pdf.
US GAO (United States Government Accountability Office) (2010) *Palestinian Authority: U.S. Assistance Is Training and Equipping Security Forces, but the Program Needs to Measure Progress and Faces Logistical Constraints*, Report to the Committee on Foreign Affairs and its Subcommittee on the Middle East and South Asia, House of Representatives; available at: www.gao.gov/new.items/d10505.pdf.

20

Hamas

Khaled Hroub

I'm a physicist. And I believe in the equations of physics and mathematics. Therefore I respect the laws of math and physics because they're direct. Very simply, there is occupation and it calls for resistance. When does resistance stop? When the occupation is finished.

Khaled Meshaal, Hamas leader[1]

This chapter attempts to describe milestones in Hamas's historical chronology and intellectual development and the political challenges it faces in a region beset by turmoil. The analysis pays particular attention to the tension between utopian and ideological ideals driven by religious aspirations within the movement, on the one hand, and the political realities which have compelled Hamas to adopt pragmatic positions with a visible relaxing of its ideology, on the other.

The mother organization: the Palestinian Muslim Brotherhood in the 1940s

Hamas's official inception is normally dated to late 1987, but its origins go back as far as the mid-1940s, when the formation of the Palestinian Muslim Brotherhood in Jerusalem was announced. The 'Palestinian Brothers' was in fact a branch of the original Egyptian Muslim Brotherhood organization, which was established in Egypt in 1928. That organization's initial aim was to reinstate the Islamic Caliphate, which had been effectively ended by Ataturk and his Young Turk comrades in 1923. The collapse of the Ottoman Caliphate was viewed as the ultimate manifestation of Muslim weakness and defeat in the face of Western powers resulting from the Muslims' abandonment of true Islam. Thus, to bring back power, unity and advancement of the Muslim *Ummah* (an all-encompassing pan-Islamic nation), efforts needed to focus on the re-Islamization of Muslim societies. This Islamization, as actively advocated by the Muslim Brotherhood, would encompass a bottom up process, starting with the smallest unit, the individual and family, then moving into various aspects of society and ending up guiding government and politics.

The Palestinian chapter of the Muslim Brotherhood was marginal to other Palestinian parties and movements, which were concerned more by the rising military power of Zionism within the country and with the fate of Palestine after the end of the British Mandate. In the 1948 Palestine war the Egyptian Brothers took part in the military effort, in coordination with the weak Egyptian army, boosting the image of the Brothers for many years as a group sincere in their concern about the fate of Palestine.[2] In the three decades that followed the war, the Palestinian Brotherhood stood on the margins of the political scene due primarily to three interrelated factors. First, the weakening of the Muslim Brotherhood in Egypt, which had suffered crackdowns after Gamal Abdul Nasser took power in 1953. Second, the Palestinian political scene was dominated by nationalist and leftist movements mostly supportive of Nasser. Third, the Muslim Brotherhood insisted on the Islamization of Muslim society at a time when the national priority was the 'liberation of Palestine'.

From the mid-1950s, in the face of voices within the Brotherhood itself calling upon their movement to engage militarily against Israel along with other nationalist organizations, the Palestinian Brothers' Islamization efforts needed to be redefined in Palestinian terms. These efforts would have to be moulded into a long-term strategy aimed ultimately at the liberation of Palestine. However, this redefinition implied that any fight against a powerful Israel would require a long 'preparation of generations', where Palestinians and other Muslims behind them would have to become stronger and ready for the battle. The only way to achieve such a strength and readiness would be through a long-term process of education and the training of individuals and societies to become true Muslims – that is, Islamization.

There were, however, those who thought the Islamization approach was too open ended and that Palestine would be lost forever before achieving the ultimate goal of 'preparing the generations'. Also, national and leftist movements had been attracting more young Palestinians who were ready to take up arms and fight Israel. At the end of 1950s and in the early 1960s the internal debate within the Gaza branch of the Palestinian Brothers intensified between those groups more willing to adopt an active confrontational strategy against Israel and the mainstream movement that adhered to the Islamization strategy. The dispute ended up with some prominent members splitting and joining forces with other active Palestinian cells and eventually forming the Palestine National Liberation Movement (Fatah), led by Yasser Arafat. Some roots of the deep hostility between the Brothers (which morphed into Hamas after 1987) and Fatah can be traced back to those days.

Despite the fact that the Brothers were reluctant to engage in any meaningful confrontation against the Israeli occupation of the West Bank and Gaza Strip following the June 1967 war, the Islamization process continued apace during the 1970s. There was a noticeable increase in the number of mosques, Islamic charities and social networks across Palestinian cities, villages and refugee camps. At universities and higher education institutions the 'Islamist bloc' started to make visible inroads despite the dominance of nationalist and leftist forces. The 'Islamist solution' in the region as a whole was regaining confidence lost after the 1967 Arab defeat, with the Islamists linking that defeat to the reliance on the ideologies of pan-Arab nationalism, Nasserism and Marxism. The Palestinian Islamists also used the same argument on university campuses and elsewhere. The waxing and waning of nationalism and Islamism in the 1970s reached its peak with the stunning victory of the Islamic revolution in Iran and the overthrow of the Shah in 1979. The impact of the Iranian revolution on Palestinian Islamism, and Arab Islamism at large, was tremendous. Intellectually, and for the mainstream Brothers, it proved their point that Islam could bring about radical change and that long-term and incremental steps at the grassroots level would eventually pay off. Practically, and for more revolutionary members, the Iranian model inspired ideas for action and confrontation with the Israeli occupation. Almost replicating the episode when members of the Brotherhood had defected to form Fatah, members who were greatly influenced by the Iranian experience defected and regrouped in a new formation in the early 1980s under the name 'The Islamic Jihad Movement in Palestine'. According to the Islamic Jihad, Fatah was engaging in the struggle using 'a rifle without Islam' and the Brothers were using 'Islam without a rifle'. The way to achieve the liberation of Palestine was by uniting these two: Islam and the rifle, a practice and strategy that, from that point onwards, the Islamic Jihad would adopt and offer.[3]

The splitting off of the Islamic Jihad Movement played a crucial role in accelerating the debate within the Brothers over their long-term and open-ended Islamization in the form of their 'preparing for generations'. Around the mid-1980s the Israeli army arrested a number of Brothers, led by Sheikh Ahmad Yassin (who would become the founder and spiritual leader of Hamas), after discovering the formation of secret military cells within the Brothers themselves. Internal pressures to adopt a confrontational strategy against the Israeli occupation prevailed side by side with the external intensification of pressure and humiliation imposed on the Palestinians by the occupation itself. The widespread base of Islamist networks that had been built over the years also gave the Brothers further encouragement to change their strategy. The question soon became not whether they should change strategies, but when.

Active resistance: the emergence of Hamas, 1987

In December 1987, the Palestinian *Intifada* erupted and gathered momentum at an accelerating pace, first in the Gaza Strip then in the West Bank – surprising both Israel and the PLO leadership (see chapter 5, by Rami Nasrallah, in this volume). While the main momentum of the *Intifada* manifested popular resistance by the occupied against the occupying power, its internal dynamics featured fierce rivalry between emerging and declining legitimacies among the Palestinians – the Hamas movement on the one hand and the PLO factions on the other.

A few days after the outbreak of the *intifada* the Palestinian Muslim Brotherhood morphed into a new movement, Hamas, which threw itself fully into the wider national confrontation against the Israeli occupation. Fatah and other PLO factions found in the *Intifada* an opportunity to rebuild their ruptured legitimacies after the devastating defeat in Lebanon in 1982, which left their leaderships abroad shattered and disillusioned. Expelled from southern Lebanon from what had come to be known as 'Fatah Land', and now stationed in Tunis far away from the land it set out to liberate, the PLO suffered lack of confidence and a sense of defeat now that the 'resistance project' faced a harsh *de facto* paralysis. The *Intifada* came at the right time, unleashing another form of fully fledged resistance, this time inside Palestine itself, extending a badly needed lifeline to the PLO, who jumped immediately, through its factions in the West Bank and Gaza, to assume leadership of the uprising.

For the Muslim Brotherhood, the *Intifada* was the ultimate test: either join the national effort or watch their movement and its members splintering and joining other factions. On the evening of 9 December 1987 a historic meeting of the political bureau of the Palestinian Muslim Brotherhood was held leading to the formation of the Islamic Resistance Movement, soon to be known as Hamas. Those who attended that meeting were to be considered as the founders of Hamas, among them Sheikh Ahmad Yassin, Abed Al-Aziz Al-Rantisi, Salah Shehadeh, Muhammad Sham'ah, Isa Al-Nashshar, Abed Al-Fattah Dukhan and Ibrahim Al-Yazuri. All of these individuals had been veteran Muslim Brothers and had led the movement in the Gaza Strip for many years.[4]

Some months after its foundation, in August 1988 Hamas issued its 'Charter'. The Charter is one of the first basic documents that was published with the aim of introducing the new movement first to its immediate and then to its broader constituencies. It was meant to be the founding treatise – the embodiment of Hamas's objectives, vision and beliefs and the guideline for its strategy and worldview. The main emphasis of the Charter was to assert that Palestine is an Arab and Muslim land that should be liberated from Zionist domination, and that Israel was a 'usurper' and an alien entity which was 'transplanted' in Palestine only with the support of Western superpowers. Ironically, the Charter failed to articulate clearly the central positions in Hamas's political thinking; a few years after its publication it was shunted into the margins with little reference to its content. It was deemed by many Hamas leaders, both inside and outside of Palestine, to be simplistic and overloaded with claims and arguments that would reflect a naïve, rather than a sophisticated, image of the movement.[5]

The Charter is a long document which in English runs to twenty-four pages[6] and consists of five chapters with thirty-six articles that tackle a wide array of issues and positions. Its general language is distinctively polemical, characteristically religious, and contains anti-Semitic overtones unlike the more politically nuanced language that Hamas adopted in the following years. All the chapters are infused with Koranic verses, *hadiths*, quotations from prominent religious people, ancient and contemporary, and sometimes classical Arabic poetry. A considerable measure of obscurity in the Charter somehow produced a de-Palestinized discourse which made it hard to understand the specifics or relevance of certain statements or discussions in the text.

With its rhetoric, heavy religion-riddled language and limitless generalizations, the Charter inflicted much damage upon Hamas. The movement's literature since 1990 has become far more sophisticated, and its current discourse is politically driven. Actually to change or to replace the Charter would be very difficult and demand considerable courage, and Hamas leaders fear that such a step would be construed by many as giving up on the basic principles of the movement. Yet, by simply downplaying its existence, the cost remains high, since the Charter is still formally taken to be representative of Hamas.[7]

The politics of resistance and the Oslo Agreements, 1993–4

The *Intifada* allowed the Palestinian Muslim Brothers to evolve from a non-violent religious organization, concentrating on proselytizing and the Islamization of society, into a popular and militant movement whose major focus has become resisting the Israeli occupation. Yet the resistance and liberation dimension did not replace the Islamization and religious aspect. In fact it could be said that, since the early days of its inception, two drives within Hamas, one religious and another nationalist, have shaped and influenced the politics and positions of the movement. If in the pre-Hamas days the Islamists focused harmoniously on religious functions and social work, the introduction of a resistance/nationalist programme with room for further national legitimacy, outreach and recruitment has indeed created new challenges and tensions.

Engaged in the daily activities of the *Intifada* between 1987 and 1993, Hamas grew strong and succeeded in creating its own name and stamp. Two concerns, however, posed a particular challenge to its 'resistance project': how the *Intifada*, with its modest military impact on Israel, could ever 'liberate Palestine', and the how to compete with the PLO over the leadership and representation of the Palestinians. The answer to the first concern was to perceive the *intifada* just as a part of the long-term *jihad* and struggle aimed eventually at the liberation of Palestine. The *Intifada* on its own represented only a link in the long chain of *jihad*. As to the second concern, Hamas strove to maintain a position and strategy distinctive to that of the PLO, which, since 1989, was seeking to achieve Palestinian rights through peace talks and not exclusively through armed struggle. The PLO saw resistance and *Intifadas* as mere tactics of coercion to achieve a more favourable negotiating position, in the hope of reaching a peace deal that would conclude with the establishment of a Palestinian state alongside Israel. For Hamas, by contrast, the *Intifada* represented a unilateral and long-term resistance project that was no mere limited tool for achieving 'small' political gains. During the First (and the Second) *Intifada* Hamas criticized the PLO and Fatah for 'exploiting' these uprisings in order to attain political ends that would lead to the recognition of Israel. Yet Hamas realized that the grand goal of the liberation of Palestine would obviously require more sophisticated military strategies and capabilities than a popular uprising was going to provide. The movement thus attempted to reconcile its long-term perspective of liberation with the immediate activities of *Intifada*, which in fact seemed to be heading towards a deadlock. Hamas formulated its *Intifada* and resistance discourse and action around the concept of 'driving the Israeli occupation out the West Bank and the Gaza Strip'. This strategy implied making the cost of the occupation unbearable to Israel; its mantra became 'wherever the occupation exists, resistance should exist'.

The convening of the Madrid conference in November 1991 initiated a set of bilateral and multilateral peace negotiations between Israel and the Arab countries. This would eventually lead to the secret Israeli–Palestinian talks in Oslo resulting in the signing of the Declaration of Principles between the PLO and Israel in September 1993. These agreements (discussed by Galia Golan in chapter 8 of this volume) were strongly opposed by Hamas, which saw them as a sell-out. However, the implementation of the Oslo Agreements, starting in 1994 with the establishment of the Palestinian Authority, first in Gaza and the West Bank city of Jericho, then in other parts of the West Bank, restructured the Palestinian political landscape with respect to leadership rivalry and legitimacy and also shifted the nature of the relationship with Israel radically; Israel and the PA had now become 'peace partners', whereas Hamas was sidelined as an 'enemy of peace'.

The post-Oslo political developments slowed down, even temporarily halted, Hamas's rise and expansion. Exhausted because of the long years of the *Intifada*, many Palestinians pinned high hopes on the Oslo process and looked away from Hamas. At the heart of the new security arrangements stipulated by the Oslo Agreements and to which the PA was committed was the necessary ending of all forms of Palestinian violence. 'Fighting terrorism' became the label applied to all cracking down on Hamas's activities and other resistance factions that did not sign up to the Oslo Agreements. The new security regime, which heavily involved the PA, drastically affected Hamas's military activism, posing hard questions as to the rationale and effectiveness of its resistance strategy as a whole. Externally, the regional and international atmosphere was also unfavourable to Hamas as optimism prevailed that Oslo would lead to an end to the conflict. The summation of internal and external circumstances seemed, in a nutshell, to have exposed Hamas's open-ended 'resistance project' as being out of touch with reality.

In response, Hamas toned down its military activities but kept up its verbal criticism of Oslo. Its strategy of dealing with Oslo was thus 'minimum action, maximum rhetoric'. Hamas's opinion was that the agreement would fail as a result of its own shortcomings and that there was no need to become engaged and exhausted in a battle whose outcome was preordained. The years following the signing of Oslo seemed to prove Hamas's view correct, as hopes in Oslo gradually evaporated, allowing for the reigniting of Hamas's 'resistance project'. In particular, two sets of factors played into the hands of the movement and bestowed considerable legitimacy on its opposition discourse. The first was the continuation of major aspects of the Israeli occupation, in particular the expansion of settlements, keeping thousands of Palestinians in Israeli prisons, and the security crackdowns on Palestinian factions. This continuation of Israeli occupation ran against the premise and promise of Oslo that after an 'interim period' of five years an independent Palestinian state should be in the making. The second set of factors surrounded the provocations by Israeli settlers in the West Bank and Gaza against Palestinians. A landmark incident took place in February 1994, when a settler killed twenty-nine Palestinian worshippers in the Abraham Mosque in Hebron. In response to this bloody and shocking attack, Hamas launched a series of suicide operations in Israeli cities, marking the beginning of a tactic that would stay with Hamas until 2005.

After the Hebron massacre a vicious circle of violence erupted where Israeli security and military strikes against Hamas and other Palestinian groups would intensify, ironically in parallel with the 'peace process' track which remained active with the PLO and the PA. Therefore, and despite initial caution in the aftermath of the establishment of the PA in the Palestinian Territories, Hamas kept the 'resistance' strategy active, exploiting the successive failure of rounds of the peace talks. All this led inevitably at the level of Palestinian national struggle to a clear divide between two polarized strategies: a peace-talks strategy championed by the PLO/PA and a resistance strategy championed by Hamas, both underpinned by fierce rivalry over representation and leadership. The two contending strategies have in fact worked against each other more than against the common enemy, Israel. And, because they were employed by two fiercely competing players, they could never complement each other. Instead, the incremental achievements realized by one strategy would be whittled away by the actions and policies of the other.

The Second *Intifada* and Hamas's road to power

In September 2000, Ariel Sharon visited the Haram al-Sharif in Jerusalem. Hundreds of Palestinians gathered to prevent him from entering the Muslim holy area, and clashes erupted which ended in the Israeli security forces killing thirteen Palestinians and injuring more – and opening the first page of the Second *Intifada*.

In many ways the Second *Intifada*, or al-Aqsa *Intifada* as it was called by Hamas, which effectively would end in the election of Mahmoud Abbas as president in 2005 following the death of Yasser Arafat, paved the way for Hamas's ascendance to power. In the first place the rival PLO/PA strategy of a peace process with Israel collapsed dramatically, giving credence and legitimacy to Hamas's alternative 'resistance'. The widespread activities of the Second *Intifada* – ironically staged by Yasser Arafat himself and his movement, Fatah – had soon gone out of control. All Palestinian groups took part in the *Intifada*, and Hamas joined in with jubilance. Not only had its approach now been endorsed by developments on the ground, but it was also being adopted by those who for the previous decade had championed peace talks.

But Hamas's own reading of the Second *Intifada* was exaggerated. Arafat and Fatah's involvement in the *Intifada* was not a strategic shift away from the peace talks towards resistance, but rather a tactical policy aimed at strengthening the Palestinian negotiating position at those talks.[8] Nevertheless, Hamas exploited this Second *Intifada* to the maximum. Practically and effectively it rebuilt its military wing, the Izz ad-Din al-Qassam Brigades. It also enhanced its wounded social membership networks in both Gaza and the West Bank. The Palestinian security forces that reduced Hamas's activities in the past and almost crippled them had become a prime target of Israeli incursions and air bombardment. Arafat, declared by Israel and the USA (now under George W. Bush) to be an incompetent peace partner, had gambled in playing the 'resistance' card himself. A new Arafat policy of turning a blind eye to Hamas's social rebuilding helped the latter's efforts greatly as well as the movement's escalation of attacks against Israeli targets. Thus, the al-Aqsa *Intifada* was in fact a gift to Hamas. If the First *Intifada* of 1987 moulded the Palestinian Muslim Brothers into Hamas and opened the door to resistance and confrontation with Israel, the Second *Intifada* pushed the gate open wide for contesting the political legitimacy and leadership of the Palestinians.

In the aftermath of Yasser Arafat's death in November 2004, President Mahmoud Abbas vowed not only to re-embrace the peace talk strategy but also to fight terrorism. Hamas anticipated trouble for its military wing, which was by then no longer condoned by the Palestinian official leadership as it had been under Arafat. Hamas adapted to the new situation rather quickly, taking dramatic decisions with significant strategic implications. In October 2005, three major decisions were taken: unilaterally to halt suicide attacks, to join the PLO, and to take part in the coming elections for the Palestinian Legislative Council. That year Hamas took part in municipal elections in the Gaza Strip and the West Bank, winning the majority of the councils for which it competed. Preparation for the January 2006 legislative elections was under way. However, Hamas needed to justify running for a body that was, in effect, a by-product and integral part of the Oslo Agreements, to which the movement objected vehemently.

Sami Khatir, a member of Hamas's Political Bureau, offered a number of reasons for the movement's participation in the elections. The first was the effective death of the Oslo Agreements, which nullified any comparison between Hamas's refraining from participation in similar elections in 1996 and its participation in the 2006 elections. The second was that the Palestinian Authority was seen as corrupt and had evolved in a way that impacted negatively on the project of resistance. The third reason was the expansion of Hamas itself, which brought pressure on the movement to respond to popular demands, especially in curbing the corruption of the PA.[9] However, the main driving force behind its participation in the elections, as expressed by many of its leaders, inside and outside of Palestine, was to protect its military wing, which had been under the worried and vigilant eyes of Israel and the USA. In order to guarantee it such protection, the movement's goal was to place itself at the heart of the Palestinian legislative institution and polity.

The wider context helped Hamas implement the new strategy. The regional implication of the American 'war on terror' after 9/11 could only exacerbate Israeli efforts that lumped Hamas under the target 'terrorist group'. Hamas leadership anticipated that the translation of the war on terror in the West Bank and the Gaza Strip would mean a concerted Israeli and PA effort to stem its military power. Yet, in tandem with the war on terror, Washington declared another policy of promoting democratization across the Middle East and pressing Arab regimes to open up politically. By participating in the Palestinian elections, Hamas was using one part of the American strategy – democratization – to shield itself from the brunt of the other part – the war on terror. In effect, Hamas was conducting a preventive strike by taking part in the elections.

On 25 January 2006, Hamas, which was still officially branded a terrorist organization by the USA and the EU, won seventy-four of the 132 seats of the Legislative Council elections, making it the ruling party. Surprised by the victory, it was ill-prepared to create a Palestinian government. Hamas candidates to the Legislative Council knew how to function as an opposition party but not as a ruling party. Beyond internal lack of readiness, the movement was aware that Israel and the Western powers would never deal with a Hamas-led government and called upon other Palestinian factions to form a coalition government. Leaders of the movement spent almost two months trying to convince other parties to join them. Fatah refused, hoping that Hamas's inexperience would bring them (Fatah) back to power. Leftist Palestinian factions and other independent personalities opposed Hamas's 'government political programme'. Their position was strengthened by Hamas's refusal to declare the PLO the sole and legitimate representative of the Palestinian people. In the end, on 29 March, Hamas formed an exclusive government of its own members and close supporters.

The Quartet (the USA, the EU, Russia and the UN) imposed three conditions before they would establish normal relations with (and provide aid to) the Hamas government: recognition of Israel, acknowledgement of all previous agreements between the PA and Israel, and a complete cessation of terrorism. The three conditions were rejected by Hamas, leading to its isolation internationally. Osama Hamdan, a member of Hamas's Political Bureau, pointed out that

> the negative position of the EU toward the Palestinian elections sent a depressing message to the Palestinian people, which included not only the complete lack of respect for the free choice of the Palestinian people, but also the collective punishment of the Palestinian people for having made their free choice.

Western and non-Western diplomatic relations with the Hamas government were either immediately severed or not established. Hamas ministers were unwelcome almost everywhere. Many Arab and Muslim countries carefully synchronized their moves towards the Hamas government with Western policies. The immediate and disastrous outcome of the embargo placed on the government was felt most catastrophically at the level of ordinary Palestinians. European and other international funding to the PA, one of the two main sources of income for Palestinian public functioning, was stopped. The second main source of income, the monthly Palestinian tax revenues controlled and collected by Israel in accordance with the Oslo Agreements, were also frozen.[10] Caught between the hammer of rising internal dissatisfaction and the anvil of external embargo, Hamas's policies started to fray at the edges. Yet the movement and its government demonstrated a great level of steadfastness.

Boycotted by the international community and with the leader of Fatah as president, the Palestinian political system ended up being two-headed. Mahmoud Abbas had been elected Palestinian president following the death of Yasser Arafat in 2005. The office's four-year term meant that Hamas would have to contend with Fatah at least until January 2009. All security and key financial positions, as well as the presidency itself, remained in the hands of Fatah, stripping the Hamas government of any effective power. For example, Hamas's interior and finance ministers could exert no power on senior staff in their ministries, who would listen only to their Fatah superiors. The smooth transfer of power at the very top and the handing over of ministerial posts was not matched with any acknowledgement of the new power structure by the Fatah high- and middle-ranking functionaries who occupied the vast majority of key positions in the security and civil services.

In addition to the above, the Hamas-led government had to endure Israeli military pressure and incursions into the West Bank and the Gaza Strip. At the risk of eroding their own legitimacy, Hamas leaders pressured their military wing to exercise restraint and to maintain the shaky truce (hudna) that had been in place since months before the elections. But at the same time they allowed other factions, such as Islamic Jihad, to resume rocket launches and other military activity in response to Israeli raids on Gaza.

On the ground the security situation and Hamas–Fatah friction, particularly in Gaza, intensified because of the two-headed security authorities. By January 2007, marking exactly one full year since Hamas's victory, the spectre of civil war had become very real. Egyptian, Syrian, Qatari and Jordanian attempts to mediate between the two fighting factions failed one after the other. In early February Saudi King Abdullah took an initiative and called the leaders of both Hamas and Fatah to convene in Mecca.

The Saudi initiative was successful, and between 6 and 8 February 2007 Fatah and Hamas concluded what would be known as the Mecca Agreement. Putting an immediate end to Palestinian in-fighting in the Gaza Strip, the agreement paved the way for the formation of a Palestinian National Unity Government, which took place in March 2007. The political programme of the would-be government confirmed the pragmatic compromise line from Hamas, in which it agreed to respect previous agreements signed between the PLO and Israel. The programme also stipulated the establishment of a Palestinian state using the 1967 borders as the national aim of the government, yet without conceding recognition of Israel. The Mecca Agreement was a breakthrough, offering a potential Palestinian consensus, however shaky, on a unified political programme.

However, the National Unity Government did not change the Quartet and Israel's policy of isolating and boycotting Hamas. In particular the new government did not succeed on two critical fronts: breaking the international boycott and unifying the internal security forces under the Interior Ministry. The skirmishes between the Fatah-affiliated groups and security forces, on the one hand, and Hamas's forces, which were a combination of the Executive Force set up by the Interior Ministry under Hamas's old government and its al-Qassam Brigades, on the other, intensified greatly. A new round of violent internal fighting by May–June culminated in mid-June in Hamas taking control of the security forces in the Gaza Strip. Dozens of Palestinians on both sides were killed, and hundreds were wounded. Gaza fell entirely under Hamas control. Immediately, Palestinian President Mahmoud Abbas nominated a non-Hamas government in the West Bank, headed by the Western-welcomed Palestinian technocrat Salam Fayyad, whose government was quickly recognized and supported by the Quartet and Israel. At that point the Palestinian polity, society, demography and geography of the West Bank and the Gaza Strip was split, with the former coming under the control of Fatah and the latter under Hamas, each claiming to rule in the name of the Palestinian people. The international community sided with the government in the West Bank, while at the same time tightening the blockade against Hamas and the Gaza Strip and its almost 1.5 million Palestinians.

Hamas's experience in power shifted from the formation of an exclusive government in March 2006, to a short-lived National Unity Government in March 2007, to a military-controlled Gaza in June 2007, and to an Israeli war on Gaza in December 2008–January 2009. The movement's reactions and adaptations to such developments are mixed at best. Many Palestinians have absolved Hamas and its government of much of the responsibility for failing to live up to their original promises. This failure was blamed on Western and Israeli policies, which were meant to punish Palestinians for their democratic choice of Hamas.[11] But, within Hamas as a political movement, the experience was, and is still, painfully diverse. A sentiment heard often by Hamas's leaders about their reign in power reflects the views of Ahmad Yousef, the former political advisor of the Hamas-appointed prime minister Ismail Haniyya: 'It was a tough year but a great one as well, like an intensive course on politics where we had to learn in one year what would otherwise have required us ten or fifteen years to learn.'[12]

Two conclusions can be drawn from the above. The first is that Hamas's eventual shift from 'opposition' to 'power' in the Palestinian political system, occasioned by the election victory of 2006, has structurally changed the rules of the game in the Palestinian–Israeli conflict. The same shift has also caused structural changes within Hamas itself at the levels of discourse, practice and regional and international relations. Hamas, acknowledged as a major party on the Palestinian political scene, has become an integral part of the Palestinian leadership. Without its participation, or tacit approval at the very least, and as long as it remains unified and not fragmented, any lasting peace agreement between the two sides is inconceivable.

The second conclusion relates to Hamas's orientation along military, political and religious lines and its vacillation between 'moderation' and 'radicalization'. The trajectory and the historical experience of the movement have shown that external political gains, achieved or perceived, produce more moderate discourse and practice. Such gains would offset any internal discomfort which may equate moderation with concessions. Engaging politically usually produces this kind of trade-off between external benefits and internal pressures. By contrast, with lack of any external gains, the movement looks more inward. If politics and conditions are coercive and isolating to Hamas, undermining its political choices (as opposed to its resistance choices), its responses tend to shift into more radical mode in an effort to satisfy internal criticism and maintain the coherence and unity of the movement.

Notes

1 'Hamas Sticks to the Hard Line', *Newsweek*, 14 October 2010; available at: www.newsweek.com/2010/10/14/hamas-sticks-to-the-hard-line.html#.
2 El-Awaisi (1998).
3 Author interview with Dr Fathi Shikaki, founder of the Islamic Jihad Movement in Palestine, Beirut, 17 April 1994. Shikaki was assassinated by the Israeli Mossad in Malta in November 1995.
4 Hroub (2000: 36–41).
5 In several interviews over the years this author has been told by a number of Hamas leaders that the Charter was written by one leading personality in the Gaza Strip and distributed hastily without prior consultation, and that it no longer reflects Hamas's sophisticated visions.
6 For the full text of the English version, see Hroub (2000: 267–91).
7 Hroub (2010: 15–33).
8 Sayigh (2001).
9 Khatir (2007).
10 In 2005, according to World Bank statistics, the PA expenditure was $1.92 billion, of which international aid provided $349 million and tax and customs transfers controlled by Israel accounted for $814 million. See World Bank, *Coping with Crisis: Palestinian Authority Institutional Performance* (Jerusalem: World Bank, 2006).
11 Ben Bot, the Dutch foreign minister, was quoted on the record as saying: 'The Palestinian people have opted for this government, so they will have to bear the consequences.' *Associated Press*, 10 April 2007.
12 Interview, Gaza, 7 March 2007.

References and further reading

Cohen, A. (1982) *Political Parties in the West Bank under the Jordanian Regime, 1949–1967* (Ithaca, NY: Cornell University Press).
El-Awaisi, Abd al-Fattah M. (1998) *Muslim Brothers and the Palestine Question, 1928–47* (London: I. B. Tauris).
Gunning, J. (2008) *Hamas in Politics: Democracy, Religion, Violence* (London: Hurst).
Hroub, K. (2000) *Hamas: Political Thought and Practice* (Washington, DC: Institute of Palestine Studies).
Hroub, K. (2010) *Hamas: A Beginner's Guide* (2nd ed., London: Pluto Press)
International Crisis Group (2003) 'Islamic Social Welfare Activism in the Occupied Palestinian Territories: A Legitimate Target?' *Middle East Report*, no. 13, 2 April; available online at: www.crisisgroup.org/en/regions/middle-east-north-africa/israel-palestine/013-islamic-social-welfare-activism-in-the-occupied-palestinian-territories-a-legitimate-target.aspx.
International Crisis Group (2004) 'Dealing with Hamas', *Middle East Report*, no. 21, 26 January; available online at: www.crisisgroup.org/en/regions/middle-east-north-africa/israel-palestine/021-dealing-with-hamas.aspx.
International Crisis Group (2006) 'Enter Hamas: The Challenges of Political Integration', *Middle East Report*, no. 49, 18 January; available online at: www.crisisgroup.org/en/regions/middle-east-north-africa/israel-palestine/049-enter-hamas-the-challenges-of-political-integration.aspx.
International Crisis Group (2007) 'After Mecca: Engaging Hamas', *Middle East Report*, no. 62, 26 February; available at: www.crisisgroup.org/en/regions/middle-east-north-africa/israel-palestine/062-after-mecca-engaging-hamas.aspx.
Khatir, Sami (2007) 'Assessing Hamas's political experience in 2006–2007', in M. M. Saleh (ed.), *Critical Assessments of Experience of Hamas & its Government* (Beirut: Al-Zaytona Centre), pp. 17–23 [in Arabic].
Klein, M. (2007) 'Hamas in Power', *Middle East Journal*, 61/3, pp. 442–59.
Milton-Edwards, B., and Farrell, S. (2010) *Hamas* (Cambridge: Polity).

Mishal, S., and Sela, A. (2000) *The Palestinian Hamas: Vision, Violence, and Coexistence* (New York: Columbia University Press).

Sayigh, Yezid (1999) *Armed Struggle and the Search for State: The Palestinian National Movement 1949–2003* (Oxford: Oxford University Press).

Sayigh, Yezid (2001) 'Arafat and the Anatomy of a Revolt', *Survival*, 43/3, pp. 47–60.

Tamimi, A. (2007) *Hamas: A History from Within* (Northampton, MA: Olive Branch Press).

21

Palestinian civil society

Michael Schulz

Introduction

This chapter demonstrates the important role that Palestinian civil society has played in the West Bank and Gaza Strip. The concept 'civil society' covers 'those areas of social life – the domestic world, the economic sphere, cultural activities and political interaction – which are organized by private or voluntary arrangements between individuals and groups outside the *direct* control of the state' (Held 1993: 6). Civil society is often seen as a benign societal force which pushes for the improvement of the public good, in areas such as human rights, democracy, development, education, and so on. By challenging the state, it constitutes a balancing force to the state. However, there is nothing inherently benign about civil society, since it is made up of various interest groups that primarily serve themselves and do not necessarily work towards the broader social good. Hence, the important empirical question to address is the extent to which civil society actually serves the interests of society in general, if it *is* benign, and how it functions.

This essay looks at how Palestinian civil society (in Arabic *mujtama madanî*) in the West Bank and Gaza Strip changed in scope, activity and outreach before, during and after the Oslo process (1993–2000). Civil society functioned as a mobilizer in the pre-Oslo period and during the First *Intifada*. Since then, it has served as a safe haven for many Palestinians, in parallel to the extended family structures (*hamula*) that fulfil the same purpose.

The Oslo process led to the creation of the Palestinian Authority (PA), which took on the responsibility of providing for the socio-economic welfare of the Palestinian population. The majority of Palestinians quickly lost faith in the PA, seeing it increasingly as corrupt or power-less. Civil society was viewed as an alternative to the pre-state system that took care of health, education, child care, human rights, and so on. However, most civil society organizations are also linked to political parties and factions within and outside of the Palestine Liberation Organization (PLO). They are thus seen as tools of different factions and not as independent players. The donor community and political commentators tend not to consider Islamic charity organizations as part of civil society, but rather as connected to Islamic political movements. At the same time, Islamic as well as secular civil society organizations have played an important role in promoting debate about democratization of the PA, the peace process and the social service sector.

While Palestinian civil society cannot be seen as a completely autonomous player, it has – despite political party links – played a semi-independent role vis-à-vis the PA, not least in relation to the formation of the latter's political system within areas of self-rule. In Palestinian society, the intersection of political parties and civil society organizations/movements constitutes something of a grey zone. The roles played by different voluntary organizations, social movements and other civil society agencies, in terms of serving the Palestinian public and also contributing to peace-building and democratization, are elaborated below.

Understanding Palestinian civil society

In order to grasp the role of Palestinian civil society it is important to outline its relative size and to describe its activities and the societal sectors in which it operates. Using data from the University of Gothenburg–Birzeit University[1] questionnaires, we find that around 11 to 12 per cent of the Palestinian public is active in civil society or in a charitable organization. Generally speaking, Palestinians are not part of associational life. In comparison with Sweden, where the figure is around 85 per cent of the population, we can draw the conclusion that formal civil society is relatively small in the Palestinian self-rule areas. This explains its relative lack of influence in comparison with the historical and contemporary situation in European societies.

Table 21.1 Number of NGOs in the West Bank and the Gaza Strip

Date	Number of NGOs
1990	2,000
1994	1,400
1996	1,850
1997	1,200
1999	1,200
2001	982
2006	*c.*1,000

Source: Challand (2009: 68).

Table 21.2 Percentage of NGOs according to their period of establishment

Date of creation	Source: MAS (2001)[a]	Source: MADAR (2000)[b]
Post Oslo (1994–)	37.6	46
Before Oslo		54
1988–93	18.8	
1980–87	13.3	
1968–79	15.4	
1949–67	11.5	
Before 1948	3.4	

Source: Challand (2009: 69).

Notes: [a] MAS (2001) *Mapping of Palestinian Non-Governmental Organizations in the West Bank and the Gaza Strip* (Ramallah: MAS, Economic Policy Research Institute) [in Arabic].
[b] MADAR (2000) *The Palestinian NGOs: Facts and Figures* (Ramallah: MADAR Centre for the Development and Study of the Palestinian Society).

Table 21.3 Number and percentage of NGOs according to the main types of activity

Type	Number	Percentage
Charitable organizations	374	40.4
Youth and sport	282	30.4
Culture	94	10.2
Relief	44	4.8
Development	45	4.9
Research	32	3.5
Training and rehabilitation	25	2.7
Human rights	24	2.6
Others	5	0.5
Total	**926**	**100**

Source: Challand (2009:70).

Research into Palestinian civil society can be divided into several areas. Much has been written about civil society and its role as a forerunner of democratization. Many researchers have emphasized that the Oslo process was the result of civil society action to put pressure on the elite from below. Policy-makers and donors also placed hope in the role of civil society in peace-building and flooded the NGO sector with funds. Civil society and development studies (Brynen 2000) are another important area of academic study. One of the most debated issues in this field concerns the relationship between social capital and development. Putnam's seminal work (Putnam 1993) shows that civil society can build collective trust which in turn impacts positively on development and democracy. In the 1990s several policy-makers, not least the World Bank and other global institutions and donors, placed their trust in civil society to bring about much-needed changes.

Challand, in his seminal work, talks about a potential field that sees civil society as a 'source of autonomy', indicating its relative autonomy vis-à-vis the state (Challand 2009: 34–6). In the Middle East, democratization literature has been linked to hopes that civil society will bring about the looked-for change from authoritarian rule in the region. However, as Challand and others warn (Schulz 2006), civil society does not inherently work for the public good, but should be viewed as interest or advocacy groups which are capable of creating conflict and political tension. Hence, we need to ascertain in what way civil society acts, in whose name (the public's or the organization's) and its impact on society writ large.

Palestinian civil society before the Oslo process

Palestinian civil society has its roots in the 1920s under the rule of the British Mandate. In these early days it consisted mostly of welfare organizations and was grassroots oriented (Sullivan 1996).

Later civil society organizations were influenced by the authorities that controlled the West Bank (Jordan from 1949 to 1967) and the Gaza Strip (Egypt from 1948 to 1967). Until 1988, when Jordan ceased to have any administrative responsibilities, many charity organizations in the West Bank actually received funding from the Jordanians. Jordan thus paved the way for the PLO to claim and establish its presence in the area. Interestingly, civil society organizations were registered under British Mandate law until the PA Law on Civil and Charitable Associations came into being in April 2000. When Jordan stopped engaging in the West Bank at the time of the First *Intifada*, in December 1987, donors (in particular, Europeans) came to the support of Palestinian non-governmental organizations (Challand 2009; Brynen 2000; Bouillon 2004).

Most Palestinian NGOs were established in the Bethlehem–Jerusalem–Ramallah areas. Any new NGO had to follow Israeli military Order 686, which stated that only NGOs with a non-Palestinian nationalist orientation were allowed to be registered and conduct activity. As a result of this order, the PLO came to disguise its activities under the umbrella of NGO activities. After the 1967 war the PLO had increasingly taken over its political role from pro-Jordanian family elites in the West Bank, but in the Gaza Strip Egyptian influence also declined. Israeli repercussions against the PLO and other factions followed.[2] When the Palestinian uprising against Israeli occupation erupted in 1987, many PLO activists were deported and the formation of new popular committees intensified. These committees, made up of members of the different political factions, became active in the fields of education, women's issues, trade unions, professional organizations, health, and so on. They came to serve the Palestinian public, and thus the PLO indirectly began to administer civil affairs.

Public support for these committees created competition in which each faction wanted to establish its own committee, and hence a process of duplication occurred wherein different NGOs doing similar things were established. With the outbreak of the uprising, dependency on European donors increased. The need to cooperate during the *Intifada* gave donors the opportunity to put forward different suggestions as to how to work in a more democratic spirit. This external link had a great impact on Palestinian society in terms of how democratization took shape (Challand 2009).

In the pre-Oslo period, after the 1967 war, researchers drew attention to the strong presence of Palestinian civil society and its impact on democratic performance (Giacamen and Lønning 1998; Abu Amr 1996). It has been claimed that it was civil society which created those institutions that enabled Palestinians to cope with the Israeli occupation in the West Bank and the Gaza Strip. When the Oslo process began in 1993, great hope was invested in the role civil society would play in Palestinian democratization. Despite the categorization of the PLO as at best a semi-democratic organization, these internal associational forms were seen as the forerunners of future democratization. Furthermore, the vibrant character of the various associations and voluntary organizations constituted a social security system during the Israeli occupation.

Despite their relatively small size in comparison with their European counterparts, these numerous voluntary associations, political workshops, women's organizations, trade unions, human rights groups, cooperatives and social work organizations in the West Bank and Gaza constituted a vibrant civil society, especially when compared with those in other Arab states (Robinson 1997). Although many of these initiatives have been crippled by the involvement of factional(ist) as well as extended family politics, the number and scope of the activities have informed the intensity of political discussion and serve (partly) as a counter-voice to the state in the making. Roy (1995) argues that, in contrast to the relatively pluralist civil society in the West Bank, there is no such thing in Gaza, largely because of the greater degree of repression which characterized Israeli politics in the Gaza Strip before Israel's withdrawal in 2005.

In the pre-Oslo period, before 13 September 1993, civil society constituted virtually the only acceptable Palestinian player as far as the Israeli occupation administration was concerned. It was responsible for civil administration within the Occupied Territories and built up a much-needed infrastructure in addition to the Israeli civil administration (i.e., the military authority). However, it was often linked with the various factions within the PLO, and a duplication of, for instance, health clinics, was linked to the fact that each political group wanted to establish its own social institution. Hence, student councils, social movements, women's organizations, and so on, that dealt with the Israeli–Palestinian conflict risked being taken as mobilization arenas for Palestinian factions, thereby incurring potential Israeli repercussions.

The Palestinian Authority and Palestinian civil society

When the Oslo process began, the Palestinian NGOs realized that the forthcoming PA would take over their responsibilities. Thus in 1994 they organized themselves into a network. It was unclear under which ministry the NGO sector would fall. Civil society institutions were initially placed under the Ministry of Social Welfare but later fell under the Ministry of Non-Governmental Organizations Affairs, established in 1999. Currently, the Ministry of Interior in the West Bank deals with all such issues. A similar structure exists in the Hamas-controlled PA in the Gaza Strip.

In 1994 the newly created Palestinian Authority, led by PLO chairman Yasser Arafat, saw its role as serving the Palestinian public in the area of civil affairs. To this end it took over the responsibilities of the civil society organizations which had more or less been running these activities since the Israeli occupation began in 1967. The general intelligence service, *al-mukhabaraat al 'aama*, requested that each NGO answer two surveys about their members' family background, which party they belong(ed) to, and if they, or their relatives, had ever been charged with spying.

A power struggle arose over roles and resources. In addition, external influences had a serious impact on how Palestinian civil society would act and orient its activities. As Challand (2009) and others have shown, many of the non-Islamist organizations became increasingly donor-driven. Palestinian NGOs repeatedly claimed that their activities were conducted in the name of grassroots needs, but assessment was rarely, if ever, undertaken. As the donors influenced the agendas and priorities of the civil society organizations, real need was often overlooked. In addition, the donors' focus on establishing a vital and democratic PA drained the resources of many previously functional organizations.

The form of social infrastructure and networking established by Islamist organizations might themselves serve as a catalyst for more participatory politics. Islamic institution-building and networking in the form of schools, mosques, health clinics, kindergartens, charities, sports clubs, choirs and computer centres are a form of mobilization from below. With these kinds of network, a sort of parallel institution-building has taken place. Furthermore, the Islamic charity and social welfare organizations serve as a competition to the secular ones (see Michal and Sela 2006; Hroub 2000).

Palestinian civil society and the Israeli–Palestinian peace process

In the years before the Oslo process many civil society organizations were involved in activities that were linked to the Palestinian uprising. Some, however, worked to build bridges with their Israeli counterparts,[3] thus contributing to forging ideas and solutions to core issues of the Israeli–Palestinian conflict. Further, although part of the nationalist struggle to establish a Palestinian state, they differed from other civil society organizations, as well as from major Palestinian factions, in how to achieve their objectives. They explored possibilities for compromise and proposed a two-state solution to the conflict rather than insisting on one state. However, they were much more restricted than their Israeli counterparts, as they ran the risk of being labelled collaborators by the Palestinians. Many contacts with the Israeli side therefore took place in secret. Palestinian individuals who had the courage to meet Israelis risked their lives by doing so. As a result of these meetings, an important new discourse about the 'Other' was established. Hassassian argues that Palestinians:

> began to be able to make a distinction between Israelis as people and Israelis as oppressors dressed in army uniforms. Likewise, the inverse is probably true as Israelis came to see the Palestinians as a people who are fighting for their national rights, and not just a people who are predisposed to 'killing Jews' or 'the destruction of the state of Israel'.
>
> *(Hassassian 2006: 79)*

Organizations, as well as individuals, began to consider ways in which Israelis and Palestinians could meet and engage in dialogue. Civil society-inspired citizen diplomacy meetings increased in number. Also, there emerged a distinction between so-called hard and soft Track II approaches, in which the hard track is more politically oriented and the soft track more concerned with increasing understanding of the other side's position. Many Palestinian NGOs, however, avoided any framework that included Israelis. The more the Oslo process soured, the greater the risk of being labelled as working for 'normalization' with the occupier.

One of the few exceptional organizations with a joint set-up was the Israel Palestine Center for Research and Information (www.ipcri.org). IPCRI saw itself as an NGO that brought together those associated with the leaderships of both societies in unofficial meetings and round-table discussions during the first uprising and, later, in semi-official meetings when the Oslo process began. The signing of the Declaration of Principles envisaged a new role for civil society. The Oslo peace process was seen by the donor community as a post-conflict phase where social reconstruction of Palestinian society could take place and Israeli–Palestinian relations could be healed. The international community was keen to participate in the peace process and turned to the local NGO sector.

Among other initiatives, people-to-people programmes were seen as an important tool to strengthen cooperation between Israeli and Palestinian organizations. The EU was keen to support these activities; within the framework of the Barcelona process (1995–2000), it funded hundreds of such programmes at a cost, according to Hassassian, of $US26 million (Hassassian 2006:95). Among activities promoted were cultural exchanges, educational undertakings with participants from all sides, and grassroots and religious dialogue. What these activities often lacked was a more long-term objective in which the key issues of the conflict were raised. Atieh *et al.* (2005) have proposed five reasons for the failure of the people-to-people programmes:

1 they focused on the individual and did not impact on the perceptions that participants held of the others' nation;
2 they failed to reach important sections of society;
3 they ignored the socio-economic disparities between Israelis and Palestinians;
4 they placed too much emphasis on joint activities rather than on intercommunal dialogue;
5 they were bound to the present with little reflection on the future or the past.

With the outbreak of the al-Aqsa *Intifada* in 2000, these programmes collapsed altogether (Hassassian 2006; Schulz 2008).

Various civil society think tanks, dealing with major issues such as Jerusalem, Palestinian refugees, final status and Israeli settlements, produced similar output. In fact, donors developed a 'politics of spending', while the NGOs focused on a 'politics of receiving'. Little attention was paid to coordination between donors and NGOs. Identifying real need and evaluating and monitoring projects were seen as less important priorities. In sum, many NGO activities came to an abrupt end with the outbreak of the second Palestinian uprising, the al-Aqsa *Intifada*, in

September 2000. The collapse of the peace process halted NGO funding and activity. Paradoxically, the need for citizen diplomacy and NGO initiatives was even greater at this stage than before.

While certain NGO activities focus on non-violent resistance to the Israeli occupation, others, such as boycotting and burning settler products, involve factions such as Fatah and Hamas. Israel thus identifies these activities with the elite and not with the grassroots. Further, these NGOs link up with international NGOs; the 2010 'Gaza Flotilla' incident, in which nine people were killed, attracted considerable media attention and was made up of various international and national NGOs.

Islamic civil society

Most Islamists involved in the Hamas and Islamic Jihad movements would contest that they constitute part of Palestinian civil society. They avoid using the concept 'civil society' and prefer *al-aml al-ahli*, which denotes 'civic work'. The connotations of spiritual and physical *jihad* (struggle) and social mobilization are connected for Islamists to a deeper understanding of civic work. The secular NGO and civil society sector is often seen by Islamists as a modern Western phenomenon, inherently alien to Islamic and Palestinian society. Furthermore, the activities of secular civil society are, according to the Islamists, tainted by the goals and intentions of the donors and thus have no legitimate basis among the broader Palestinian public.

The political goals of a state in the making are different from those of secular civil society. Rather than acting as an independent, autonomous sphere side by side with the state, Islamist institution-building seeks to challenge the state. Despite this challenge Islamists also work side by side with the state, and the kind of social work and grassroots mobilization provided by their kind of organization should therefore be included in the perceptions of civil society.

Challand (2009) emphasizes that the Islamist sectors are primarily an urban phenomenon in which huge social discrepancies occur as a result of the merging of refugee camps and city centres, such as in Gaza City, Bethlehem and Nablus. Increased tension and frustration among the youngsters leads them to support the Islamists. The fact that the majority of Palestinians are young explains to some extent why Hamas was successful in the elections of 2006. At the same time, these youngsters tend to hold less democratic values than the average Palestinian, which in turn influences how Islamic civil society views the democratization process.

In contrast to secular civil society, the Islamists worked closely with the grassroots, viewing their activities as voluntary work for the neediest. Theirs was a 'civil struggle', as distinct from the military struggle against the Israeli occupation. During the 1990s and in the al-Aqsa *Intifada* period that started in September 2000, they gained much public support and respect for their activities. External funding came primarily from non-Western countries, such as Iran and Saudi Arabia. The most important income base, however, which afforded the Islamists a degree of freedom from external funding, came from *zakaat*, a charity within the framework of the mosque system to which Muslims donate a portion of their income to benefit the poor. While Western donors were wary of supporting the Islamists, the Islamists themselves wanted to avoid being influenced and directly supported by donors. The PA, which received considerable donor support, was seen as corrupt and guilty of neglecting basic Islamic values and misusing donations. The Islamists became, in the eyes of the Palestinian public, the alternative and more reliable provider of social services for the people most in need.

Many NGOs that were labelled ideologically leftist lacked grassroots support and were sometimes driven into politics. Several former NGO members became ministers in the Fatah PA,[4] which was seen as non-democratic and alienated from the needs and services the public

Table 21.4 Degree of public trust in Palestinian institutions and organizations (percentages)

	1997	2001	2006	2009 West Bank	2009 Gaza
Palestinian courts	48.0	39.7	39.9	45.6	28.1
Palestinian police	54.9	42.0	36.1	48.3	26.4
Palestinian security forces	55.5	45.3	37.5	44.8	24.7
President's Office	62.5	51.2	48.2	50.8	
Government ministers	33.4	33.9	52.6	37.0	23.1
Prime minister[a]	Not asked	Not asked	Not asked	44.9	31.1
Legislative Council	52.0	41.9	59.6	28.4	
Palestinian political parties[b]	37.7	48.4	42.0	19.1	
Palestinian universities	84.6	82.1	70.7	61.4	
Palestinian press	71.8	75.0	65.1	50.9	
Labor and professional unions	62.6	55.4	51.7	35.8	
Student union/councils	Not asked	69.9	55.5	39.1	
Women's organizations	Not asked	52.7	49.5	32.9	

Source: The University of Gothenburg–Birzeit University surveys.

Notes: The categories are: Do not trust; Trust to a certain extent; Trust; Trust a lot. The results for Trust and Trust a lot are merged.In the 2009 survey we questioned various branches of the West Bank (Fatah-controlled) and the Gaza (Hamas-controlled) PAs.
[a] Prime minister in the West Bank: Salam Fayyad; prime minister in the Gaza Strip: Ismail Haniyyeh.
[b] Political parties could be seen as a sphere between civil society and the PA structures.

needed. This disaffection with the PA enabled Islamist social movements and charity organiza-tions to win the hearts and minds of the ordinary people.

With its electoral victory in 2006, and in particular with its takeover of control of the Gaza Strip in 2007, Hamas had a chance to deliver and implement a more solid strategy for building social welfare. However, its increased isolation by Fatah, Egypt, Jordan, Israel, the USA and the EU made it extremely difficult for Hamas to implement its social programme. Following the Gaza War (December 2008–January 2009) between Israel and Hamas, the situation has become even more complicated for successful Hamas governance.

Table 21.4 reveals that people have less trust in Hamas now than they did in 2006, but the same is true in relation to the Fatah PA in the West Bank. The disappointment with Hamas will have an impact on the trust invested in and the credibility of the Islamic civil charity and social organizations as well

Civil society as driver of democratization

The debate in the Middle East concerning democratization began in the 1990s and was linked directly to the role of civil society in this process. Most studies had previously focused on the importance of elites for political change (see Owen 2004). When the potential for democrati-zation in the Arab world was first perceived, it was linked to the role of civil society (Norton, 1995: 5). Others emphasized the developmental capacity of civil society, not least the 'Islamic' sector of it, claiming that it provided help for those most in need.

Recent research, however, has been critical of civil society, claiming it is still marginal in the Middle East. Islamic civil society has been seen rather as a breeding ground for Islamic radical-ism and jihadists. In the Palestinian case, most observers identified it as vivid and relatively strong. Also, with the establishment of the Arafat-led PA, many saw Palestinian civil society as a potential counterbalance, and were strongly supported by the international community.

In a process of dealing with state-building and democratization simultaneously, two dilemmas are created with regard to aid: 'What should come first – political centralization of power or economic development?' The second relates to:

> the degree of autonomy the state should possess relative to society; the proper ratio between investment in non-governmental developmental tasks on the one hand, and building and maintaining state bureaucratic capacity on the other; the degree of selectivity the state should undertake in promoting economic tasks; and the importance of cultivating civil society and democratic governance as a means of restraining the state.
>
> *(Frisch and Hofnung 1997, quoted in Brynen 2000: 30)*

Palestinian civil society was often in competition with the PA for international donor money. Hence, it became a counterforce to the PA, which was increasingly viewed with distrust by the public and implicitly challenged the potential of the establishment of a future Palestinian state. In the pre-Oslo period, Palestinians were already questioning any central authority. They challenged the occupation by not paying taxes, by avoiding Israeli products and by generally resisting anything that could be linked to the Israeli military authorities.

With the establishment of the PA, initial hopes were soon replaced by a political culture of scepticism and distrust of centralized policies and institutions. Existing non-democratic structures within the PLO and the newly established PA regime further strengthened this mistrust. The public judged the PA in relation to its performance in the peace process with Israel. Political returnees from the PLO who arrived with the establishment of the PA in 1994 were labelled 'the Tunisians'. Between 1986 and 1994 the PLO had its headquarters in Tunis. Returnees were so labelled because they were seen to hold the same values and exhibit the same behaviour as people in countries where corruption and nepotism were rife. There was low public expectation that the PLO/PA would be the forerunner of democracy. Meanwhile, the Palestinian public placed its trust in civil society organizations.

During the entire Oslo process, PA institutions were accused of being more corrupt than civil society organizations. Hence, Palestinian support for a continuation of the resistance culture vis-à-vis the PA continued. When simultaneously the donor community decided to support civil society institutions, NGOs became qualified critics of PA policies. Many of the traditional assumptions behind modernization theory build upon the perception that the strengthening of Palestinian civil society creates the potential for much needed democratization.

Secular civil society became increasingly split and was often donor driven, pursuing activities that frequently had little relevance to the people most in need. In contrast, Islamic civil society was less dependent on donors and became more active in the grassroots sector, establishing kindergartens, schools and health clinics for the poorest Palestinians. These activities had a positive impact on the support base for the Hamas movement in particular. At the same time, trust in the Fatah-dominated PA deteriorated further, with the public becoming increasingly aware of its impotence to deliver services to the people.

Civil society was involved in the question as to how the PA should develop, taking part in debates around gender equality, in issues linked to human rights, and concerning how the democratic system under the PA could best be developed. Some of the better-known human rights organizations[5] challenged the undemocratic behaviour of the PA. Several representatives of the most outspoken of these were arrested and interrogated by the PA. The most successful contribution was to the debate surrounding the formulation of the constitution of the PA, as well as about laws regulating relations between the PA and civil society. The PA first proposed a draft inspired by the Egyptian constitution. However, civil society organizations, with support from the international community, pressed for a reformulation and further draft constitutions were drawn up. In the end the law afforded fewer possibilities for the PA to control civil society activities than the former had originally proposed.

Conclusion

Palestinian civil society, despite its relatively small size, acted as a lobby against undemocratic behaviour within the PA. While it could not entirely prevent the repressive actions of the Arafat regime, by bringing issues into the public arena it contributed to shifting public support away from Fatah.

The grassroots work done by the Islamist social movements and organizations contributed to the surprising Hamas election victory in 2006. Initially, potential for a parliamentary system was created when Hamas formed its first government. However, power struggles between Hamas and Fatah soon caused setbacks. From summer 2007 a *de facto* split within the PA occurred whereby Hamas ruled the Gaza Strip and Fatah the West Bank. The future direction Palestinian civil society will take and how it will work vis-à-vis each authority remains to be seen. There is a risk that it will be marginalized as a result of increased repression by each authority; alternatively, it will continue as in the past – namely, as the only impartial societal force that can criticize the tendency of each authority to monopolize power.

Three possible scenarios for the development of civil society in the West Bank and the Gaza Strip can be envisioned. First, the continuation of the split between Fatah and Hamas will have a number of negative ramifications for both the secular and Islamic sectors of civil society. In the current situation, many Islamic charity organizations in the West Bank have been closed down or harassed by the Fatah-dominated PA. This could cripple the capacities of the Islamists to provide social services such as food, education and free health care for people in need and lead to public criticism of the West Bank Authority. Fatah-linked NGOs in particular risk being harassed in the Hamas-controlled Gaza Strip. Human rights organizations are currently experiencing a reduction in their capacity to report critically on human rights abuses by the Hamas government. However, this too could backfire in the form of public criticism and support of the Hamas government. Hence, both Hamas and Fatah risk mobilizing forces against themselves and creating problems for democratization.

Second, a (re)uniting of the West Bank and Gaza Strip following a Fatah–Hamas reconciliation would probably benefit civil society and pave the way for it to offer a critical voice vis-à-vis the PA. Different interest groups within civil society could form advocacy platforms and create a more vivid democratic debate, and increased competition between Islamist and secular civil society might well challenge the role of donors in relation to civil society groups and the PA. Finally, there could be an attempt by Israel to defeat Hamas militarily – a risky proposition with no clear outcome. If military victory is not achieved, Hamas could end up stronger. If Hamas is defeated, Islamist civil society would be severely hampered, as in the first scenario. Most likely, the West Bank PA would be tempted to exert greater control over secular civil society in order to prevent new grassroots mobilization from below, as Hamas did successfully in the past. This would hinder the creation of a vivid and democratic civil society able openly to challenge and to criticize the PA when it does not follow a democratic process or provide the social welfare people want. In conclusion, no matter which scenario takes effect, Palestinian civil society faces a number of serious challenges. And it will need to work towards the greater involvement of the grassroots that it claims to represent to meet those challenges.

Michael Schulz

Notes

1   The survey data arise from joint research projects between the School of Global Studies, University of Gothenburg (Sweden), and the Department of Sociology at Birzeit University (West Bank). Four surveys were conducted: in November 1997, July 2001, April/May 2006 and, most recently, September 2009. A random sample of 1,308 Palestinians was selected for the 1997 survey, 1,492 for the 2001 survey, 1,500 for the 2006 survey, and 1,504 for the 2009 survey. The surveys contained approximately 150 to 200 questions. The target population was individuals aged eighteen or above, residents of the West Bank and the Gaza Strip, or East Jerusalem (under Israeli control). The samples were made with the help of the Palestinian Central Bureau of Statistics. Although some questions were changed, removed or added between the surveys, several key aspects were measured on all four occasions.
2   The main political factions within the PLO are Fatah, the Popular Front for the Liberation of Palestine, the Democratic Front for the Liberation of Palestine, the Popular Front for the Liberation of Palestine-General Command, Al-Saiqa and the Palestinian Communist Party (later renamed the Palestinian People's Party). Fatah is the largest party within the PLO.
3   Two such NGOs were Women in Black (www.womeninblack.org) and Coalition of Women for Peace (www.coalitionofwomen.org/?lang=en), who work against the Israeli occupation.
4   For example, Palestinian People's Party member and head of Jerusalem Media and Communication Centre Ghassan Khatib became Minister of Labor in a previous Fatah-dominated PA government. Panorama Director Riad Malki became Minister of Foreign Affairs. Mustafa Barghouti, head of the Union of Palestinian Medical Relief Committees, became the Minister of Health in the current PA government in the West Bank.
5   The Palestinian Centre for Human Rights (www.pchrgaza.org) is one of the best-known organizations in the Gaza Strip.

References and further reading

Abu Amr, Ziad (1996) 'Pluralism and the Palestinians', *Journal of Democracy*, 7/3, pp. 83–93.
Atieh, Adel, Ben-Nun, Gilad, El Shahed, Gasser, Taha, Rana, and Tulliu, Steve (2005) *Peace in the Middle East: P2P and the Israeli–Palestinian Conflict*, UNIDIR/2004/33 (Geneva: United Nations).
Bouillon, Markus E. (2004) *The Peace Business: Money and Power in the Palestine–Israel Conflict* (London and New York: I. B. Tauris).
Brynen, Rex (2000) *A Very Political Economy: Peace Building and Foreign Aid in the West Bank and Gaza* (Washington, DC: United States Institute of Peace Press).
Challand, Benoit (2009) *Palestinian Civil Society: Foreign Donors and the Power to Promote and Exclude* (London and New York: Routledge).
Giacamen, George, and Lønning, Dag Jørund (eds) (1998) *After Oslo: New Realities, Old Problems* (London: Pluto Press).
Hassassian, Manuel (2006) 'Civil Society and NGOs Building Peace in Palestine', in Edy Kaufman, Walid Salem and Juliette Verhoeven (eds) *Bridging the Divide: Peacebuilding in the Israeli–Palestinian Conflict* (Boulder, CO: Lynne Rienner).
Held, David (1993) *Political Theory and the Modern State* (Cambridge: Polity).
Hroub, Khaled (2000) *Hamas: Political Thought and Practice* (Washington, DC: Institute for Palestine Studies).
Michal, Shaul, and Sela, Avraham (2006) *The Palestinian Hamas: Vision, Violence, and Coexistence* (New York: Columbia University Press).
Norton, Augustus Richard (ed.) (1995) *Civil Society in the Middle East*, 2 vols. (Leiden: E. J. Brill).
Owen, Roger (2004) *State, Power and Politics in the Making of the Modern Middle East* (London and New York: Routledge).
Putnam, R. D. (1993) *Making Democracy Work: Civic Traditions in Modern Italy* (Princeton, NJ: Princeton University Press).
Robinson, Glenn E. (1997) *Building a Palestinian State: The Incomplete Revolution* (Bloomington: Indiana University Press).
Roy, Sara (1995) *The Gaza Strip: The Political Economy of De-development* (Washington, DC: Institute for Palestine Studies).

Schulz, Michael (ed.) (2006) *Democratization and Civil Society in the Middle East: Case Studies of Palestinian Self-Rule Areas and Iraqi Kurdistan* (Stockholm: Sida and Centre for Middle East Studies, Göteborg University) [first published in 2003].

Schulz, Michael (2008) 'Reconciliation through Education: Experiences from the Israeli–Palestinian Conflict', *Journal of Peace Education*, 5, 1, pp. 33–48.

Sullivan, Denis J. (1996) 'NGOs in Palestine: Agents of Development and Foundation of Civil Society', *Journal of Palestine Studies*, 25, 3, pp. 93–100.

Gush Emunim and the settler movement

David Newman

Introduction

The impact of Gush Emunim and the settler movement on Israeli society and the Israeli–Palestinian conflict can not be underestimated, even though Gush Emunim ceased to exist as a formal organization the 1980s. The movement gave birth to a large number of settlements and political and ideological organizations which continue to implement the basic ideology laid out by its founders, focusing, above all else, on the Greater Land of Israel ideology and spearheaded through its West Bank and Gaza settlement policy. The impact of this policy has been clearly evident in the efforts to draw the boundaries of a two-state solution to the Israel–Palestinian conflict, while the political influence of its supporters as part of the governmental and institutional framework has been a major factor underlying Israeli governmental coalitions during the past thirty years.

And yet, somewhat paradoxically, the widespread public support for the evacuation of settlements in Gaza in August 2005, and the growing consensus within Israeli society that a two-state solution to the conflict will eventually – sooner or later – become a reality, might suggest that the Gush Emunim ideology has failed to take root in the hearts of the Israeli public. The fact that the Gaza disengagement (and the evacuation of four settlements in the northern part of the West Bank) was conceived and implemented by Ariel Sharon, who had been the settlers' major political ally and was instrumental in creating much of the settlement network and infrastructure, posed a great dilemma for the settler movement. The fact that politicians from across the Israeli political spectrum, including the majority of the members of Likud, now freely use the semantics of Palestinian statehood, and talk of 'painful compromises' to be made for the sake of peace, would suggest equally that the impact of Gush Emunim has been less successful than is normally supposed.

This chapter offers a brief history of Gush Emunim and the settler movement, outlining its ideological tenets. It then analyses the ways the settler movement has operated, detailing four specific modes of operation: as a protest movement, as a political movement, as a settlement movement and, finally, as a movement of ideological socialization. The essay concludes by discussing the impact of the settlements on the Israeli–Palestinian peace process and the challenges the settler movement now faces as a result of the Gaza withdrawal of 2005, especially in light of the growing support for separation from the Palestinians and the acceptance by the Israeli public and body politic of the need for a Palestinian state and a two-state solution to the conflict.

History of the Gush Emunim and its ideological tenets

Gush Emunim was formally founded in early 1974, some months after the end of the Yom Kippur War, as a movement of religious Zionists favouring the long-term retention of the West Bank, the Gaza Strip, and the Golan Heights by Israel and their ultimate inclusion within the sovereign territory of the state. Their territorial irredentism was based on a religious ideology which viewed the whole of the Land of Israel, as described in the biblical texts, as having been promised to the Jewish people by God and, once conquered (or, in their terms, 'liberated') in the 'miraculous' events of the Six Day War of June 1967, not to be relinquished voluntarily to any form of non-Jewish (Arab) rule, even through the democratic decisions of an elected government. Fearful that the Israeli government was demonstrating weakness following the near disastrous events of the Yom Kippur War, Gush Emunim set as its objective the creation of a political movement which would ensure that none of the land now controlled by Israel would be relinquished. To that end, it proposed the establishment of Jewish settlements throughout the West Bank and Gaza Strip as a practical means through which land would come under long-term Israeli civilian control. Arguing that all settlement-colonization activity in pre-state Palestine had been influential in determining the ultimate borders of the State of Israel, it was necessary to undertake similar activities within the West Bank and Gaza Strip.

Gush Emunim set out to thwart any government policies which might entail future territorial compromise. It established illegal outposts at Sebastia and Ofra, against the wishes of the Rabin government of the time, though aided initially by the then defence minister, Shimon Peres, who afforded the first squatter outposts the protection of army camps in the area. Following the election of Israel's first right-wing government in 1977, one of Prime Minister Begin's first actions was to visit the Camp Kaddum outpost and to declare that there would be many more Elon Moreh during the lifetime of his government. The Likud government went about assisting in the construction of an eleven further Gush Emunim settlements during its first year in office and helping create the administrative and organizational structure for the future establishment of additional settlements.

Gush Emunim never became a formal movement with membership and official leadership roles. Movement activists, who identified with the basic Land of Israel ideology, became involved in a wide range of private, public and quasi-governmental institutions aimed at furthering the cause of West Bank and Gaza settlement. Over time, Gush Emunim adopted a dual mode of political behaviour as a means of achieving its objectives. On the one hand, it maintained an extra-parliamentary mode of protest whenever it felt that its ultimate objectives were threatened. At the same time, the movement's leaders and daughter institutions underwent a process of governmental co-optation and institutionalization, working from within government to advance their political aims. The latter has taken place through a diverse network of political parties, splinter factions, settlement movements, planning agencies, and local governmental and municipal positions, from which it has been possible to advance the political objectives of settlement with the use of public-sector resources.

A number of basic ideological tenets have underscored the activities of Gush Emunim and the settler movement. Although different messages have been disseminated to different audiences in an attempt to attract wider support and sympathy for its political positions, a number of key themes can, however, be identified: the 'failure' of the Zionist project, religious law as binding, peace and securitization, and democracy and legitimacy.

In general, Gush Emunim and the settler movement have regarded the act of establishing settlements as constituting the 'positive' and 'Zionist' way of protesting any governmental decision which would weaken Israel's overall territorial control of the territories captured in the Six Day War, steps which they see as negating the essence of the Zionist project. From its earliest days, the settler movement portrayed itself as the contemporary manifestation of pioneering Zionism. Arguing that the left wing had forsaken its original idealism (which had brought about the establishment of the state) its activists saw themselves as the carriers of the mantle, as evidenced in the establishment of settlements in difficult and peripheral locations. Any decision by an Israeli government to withdraw from territories and voluntarily to evacuate settlements is perceived by the settler population as the ultimate manifestation of the failure of Zionism to preserve its ideals, even when faced with a hostile world and a perceived loss of 'values' from within. The notion that political Zionism is a pragmatic rather than an irredentist movement is rejected. The necessity of territorial compromise in the past, in the eyes of the settlers, was grounded in different political and demographic realities, which changed as a result of the Six Day War. The settlers use the semantics of the earliest Zionist leaders (such as Herzl) by arguing that the State of Israel would never have been created had the early Zionist leaders paid attention only to the political realities of the period, rather than believing in an objective which appeared unattainable at the time. Territorial withdrawal and settlement evacuation is therefore portrayed as constituting a betrayal of Zionism.

For Gush Emunim, the basic notion of 'Greater Israel' as constituting the 'promised land' is essentially a religious one. For the national religious community, territorial withdrawal and settlement evacuation is in direct contradiction to the law of the Torah, which takes precedence over any form of human decision-making process, however democratic that process may be. As such, the West Bank Rabbis' Forum (Yesha Rabbis) has become the most important ideological forum, to which the political leadership has become increasingly subservient. The Yesha Rabbis have issued public statements that governmental decisions negating the Greater Land of Israel ideology are in contradiction to Torah law and are therefore 'immoral' and not to be observed. As the national religious population has become increasingly fundamentalist in matters of religious observance and ritual in the past two decades, so too the Yesha Rabbis have come to exert greater influence over the political activities and decisions of the settlers themselves.

The focus on the religious dimension of the political struggle has created problems vis-à-vis the secular right wing inside Israel. Those with views on this part of the political spectrum use a combination of historical (biblical) and securitization discourses to justify their demand to retain control of the Occupied Territories, but they do not see the retention of the land as constituting a divine imperative which is above the law of the state and democratic procedures.

For Gush Emunim, secular support for their cause was attributed to both pragmatic and mystical factors. At the pragmatic level, it was seen as being part of a hard-line securitization discourse which emphasized the need to retain territories in the face of enemies as a means of ensuring a strong border and a defensive strategy for the state. At the mystical level, Gush Emunim attributed the support of the secular elements in terms of Rabbi Kook's ideology, inasmuch as he had argued that all of the secular Zionist pioneers had demonstrated an inner (often unconscious) spark of holiness by virtue of the fact that they were building up the Land of Israel, which would eventually bring about redemption. It was for this reason that the Gush Emunim leaders had no qualms about portraying themselves as the contemporary continuers of the pioneering Zionists of the early twentieth century, whose actions they perceived as inherently religious and as speeding the process of ultimate redemption.

The settler movement appeals to the broader Israeli public by arguing that the notion of 'land for peace' is based on false notions of peace. The post-Oslo experience, in which the granting of autonomy to large parts of the West Bank and Gaza and the return of Yasser Arafat to the region was accompanied by increased terror, suicide bombings and violence, is, they argue, an indication that the Palestinians do not really want peace. Territorial compromise and withdrawal will, they maintain, only bring further demands on the part of the Palestinians and will make the life of most Israelis less, rather than more, secure. Given the realities of the Second *Intifada* period, coupled with the impact of the securitization discourse among the Israeli public, this is a powerful argument which appeals to the basic survival instincts of much of the non-settler population and explains the opposition among many to territorial withdrawal and disengagement.

Unlike the religious narratives which lay at the heart of the Gush Emunim *raison d'être* but which appeal to only a relatively small percentage of the Israeli population, it is the securitization and defense discourses which interest much larger groups among society at large, and which have invariably determined the outcome of elections in Israel. Settler leaders have invariably invoked the securitization discourse, especially during times of terror incidents, to attract this support. The argument that giving up land to foreign rule is a religious prohibition, regardless of greater or lesser security, is largely internalized, since it is not a saleable product.

One of the major factors underlying the Gush Emunim settler movement activities has been the issue of democracy vis-à-vis the religious beliefs of the settlers themselves. Inhabiting the Land of Israel has always been seen as constituting an inherent religious belief for the Gush Emunim settler groups. When, as has often happened during the past forty years, this conflicts with the decisions of the democratically elected government of the State of Israel, those decisions are often portrayed as being contrary to the settlers' religious beliefs and as being immoral and undemocratic decisions. When pressed, many will argue that the laws of the Torah (as construed by them in terms of nationalist ideology) occupy greater prominence than the laws of democracy and, as such, are to be preferred in taking decisions. This has always been problematic for the mainstream settler movement, who desire, on the one hand, to be seen as an integral part of modern Israeli society (as contrasted with the ultra-orthodox groups, who do not serve in the army and who do not take part in many of the normal activities of the state) yet, at one and the same time, are not prepared to forego their religious beliefs in favour of governmental decisions, and thus are seen by the wider population as being no more than a fundamentalist group disguised in the education and clothes of modernity.

Modes of operation

Four modes of behaviour can be identified over the past forty years which, taken together, explain the impact of the movement and its ideology on the Israeli body politic: Gush Emunim as a protest movement, as a political movement, as a settlement movement and as a movement of ideological socialization.

Gush Emunim as a protest movement

Gush Emunim and its ideological inheritors have always been at the forefront of all opposition to peace processes which have entailed any form of territorial withdrawal resulting in non-Jewish control/sovereignty over parts of the Land of Israel. The settlers and their supporters have always been the most effective demonstrators against the various peace initiatives, organizing large rallies in the major cities, posting their slogans and billboards throughout the country at the most visible intersections and public places, and generally creating a lobby among right-wing politicians aimed at preventing the implementation of the proposed peace accords. Compared to all other modes of protest in Israel during the past forty years, the settler movement has always been the most vociferous and active, with the ability to mobilize tens of thousands of supporters in acts of public protest whenever necessary. At the same time, the inherent belief in their ultimate objectives has spilled over into acts of violence and extremism which have become associated with right-wing protest in Israel, questioning the extent to which they accept the game rules of protest within a parliamentary democracy.

While Gush Emunim has supported right-wing governments, it has protested equally against both right- and left-wing governments whenever its interests have been threatened. It is precisely in periods of right-wing administrations where it has been most successful at using its institutional legitimacy (in some cases being part of the government itself), together with street protests as dual means of opposing government policies aimed at any form of territorial compromise, settlement freeze or related activities. Thus, the settler movement demonstrated equally against both Begin's evacuation of Yamit (northern Sinai), Netanyahu's signing of the Wye Accords and the Sharon disengagement plan in Gaza and against the Rabin government and the Oslo Accords and the Barak government in its attempt to reach a territorial solution to the conflict at Camp David in 2000.

The activism and enthusiasm of those in the settler movement and their national religious supporters is unequalled among all other political movements in Israel, on both the left and the right of the political spectrum. In the first place, they are spurred on by an essentially religious ideology which they perceive as constituting the one and only truth as ordained by God. Second, the settlers are those most affected by any peace proposal which would necessitate territorial withdrawal and settlement evacuation. For them, it is not an abstract piece of territory but the region within which they reside and have constructed their homes.

But much of the right-wing protest associated with Gush Emunim and the settler movement has moved beyond what is normally conceived of as constituting legitimate protest. What began as extra-parliamentary protest has, for many of the younger and more radical groups, given way to illegalism and acts of violence, increasingly so in the post-Oslo period, not least in the use of Holocaust imagery, the labelling of government officials and supporters of the peace process as 'traitors', the call for 'transfer' of Arab-Palestinian inhabitants out of Israel, and the implicit acceptance by many that the political assassination of a prime minister is an act which could, under certain circumstances, repeat itself. The national religious community has always been quick to argue that the use of violence is limited to a small radical minority, most of whom were to be found in the right-wing Kach movement or, more recently, as part of the 'Hilltop youth', who have adopted even more radical stances than the Gush Emunim founder generation.

A number of grassroots protest movements, organizations and NGOs have been set up to support different aspects of the settler cause. Most notable among these have been the Women in Green, Zo Artzenu, Batzedek movements, the Gamla movement and Professors for a Strong Israel. As in the case of the many pro-peace left-wing NGOs, many of these receive external assistance and funding from supporters in North America and Western Europe. They have all come out strongly against any form of territorial compromise and were at the forefront of the campaign against the Gaza disengagement. Many have adopted the more extreme semantics and slogans of protest, distancing themselves from the mainstream leadership of the settler movement who continually try to adopt a mode of operation which will be acceptable to the population at large.

Gush Emunim as a political movement

While Gush Emunim never became a formal movement with a membership and organizational structure as such, its leaders and ideologues spawned an impressive network of formal institutions within the public sector. This ranged from settlement organizations and political parties to ad hoc membership of right-wing political and educational institutions. In particular, settlers and other Gush Emunim supporters have become active in two main areas of public-sector activity – as members of the Knesset in a variety of like-minded political parties and as elected and paid officials in the local government and municipal administrations created to manage the settlement network. The main political party associated with the Gush Emunim ideology has been the National Religious (Mafdal) party (the NRP). Before 1967, Mafdal was seen as the party of compromise between secular and orthodox Israelis and took part in almost all government coalitions. After 1967, however, the party underwent a clear turn to the right in terms of national politics, becoming self-transformed into the party which supported and promoted the retention of the Occupied Territories and the establishment of settlements throughout this region. All the earliest leaders of Gush Emunim identified with the NRP and, because of the exuberance of their commitment to the 'Land of Israel' cause, were successful in partially taking over the party hierarchy from the 'old guard' leadership, who were perceived as lacking in 'ideological commitment' to the challenges of the day. The earliest governmental supporters of Gush Emunim were the NRP 'young guard', headed by Zevulun Hammer and Yehuda BenMeir. They promoted the cause of the fledgling settler movement within the Labor governments of the mid-1970s, and later, by opting to form a coalition government with Menachem Begin following his victory at the 1977 elections, led the way for the establishment of Israel's first right-wing Likud government.

Other leading settler activists have been members of the Knesset or right-wing parties, ranging from the Likud itself to parties such as Techiyah in the 1980s, Tzomet in the 1990s and the National Union (post-2000). These parties adopted an extremist right-wing position in support of widespread settlement throughout the West Bank and Gaza Strip, were opposed to any form of peace agreement which would necessitate territorial compromise or withdrawal and, unlike the NRP, were composed of a combination of religious and secular politicians. For many, the religious–secular combination was itself an important ideological statement, in the sense that the public should not perceive West Bank settlement as being limited solely to the religious camp. Moreover, because these parties, unlike the NRP, were created around a single policy issue – the territories and the Israel–Palestine conflict – they drew supporters from a variety of social and economic backgrounds.

Given the fact that the settler population has never numbered more than 0.5 per cent of the total Israeli population, its representation in the Knesset, through different political parties, far exceeded its proportionality. In the Sharon administration (2002–6) ten members of the Knesset resided in West Bank and Gaza settlements, providing the settler movement with a foothold in the formal corridors of government which no other protest movement in Israel's history had previously succeeded in attaining. Another form of political institutionalization has been the local government framework which has been created to administer to the interests of the West Bank and Gaza settlements. All told, there are twenty-four Jewish municipalities in the West Bank, of which three are fully fledged cities (Maaleh Adumim, Betar Illit and Ariel), fourteen are independent standing local councils, and seven are regional councils. Local government authorities are responsible for a diverse range of public-sector and service-provision activities. Their budgets are a combination of local taxes (*arnona*) and central government transfers. The local government authorities are responsible for the organization of education and welfare services within their jurisdictional areas, an activity which provides many public-sector resources and employment opportunities. Many of the settler activists find employment within local government at this very practical level of daily life, while the elected mayors are also from among the resident population. This constitutes an enabling influence for the settlers, who are legally permitted to use public-sector resources to consolidate and further promote expansion of the settlement network in line with their political and ideological ambitions.

Various settler leaders have also been appointed on an ad hoc basis to senior civil-service posts by government ministers who share their political views. This has enabled them actively to promote public-sector activities within their areas of responsibility which necessitate the allocation of scarce resources (in such areas as the construction of classrooms and kindergarten facilities by the Education Ministry, local road paving and infrastructural development by the Ministry of Construction and Housing and the Ministry of Infrastructure) or additional positions in a wide range of utility and service provision from within the Interior Ministry. The fact that the publication of the national budget figures by the Central Bureau of Statistics focuses only on particular activities, nationwide, but does not provide any regional breakdown of the budget, has made it difficult to assess exactly how much of the various ministry budgets have been poured into the settlement network, although it is assumed that this runs into many billions of dollars.

A number of additional quasi-public bodies, set up with specific political objectives, provide further indications of the sophisticated organizational system which has formed around the settler movement. The Yesha Council and the Yesha Rabbis are two ad hoc bodies which fall somewhere between the extra-parliamentary protest movements and the formal political institutions of the state. The Yesha Council is an umbrella organization representing all of the municipalities and local government authorities in the West Bank (and Gaza until 2005). Its objective is to promote the settlements and to lobby on their behalf inside government, the political parties and the government ministries. The council is composed of all of the local government mayors in the West Bank and it also employs its own administrative staff, some of whom are seconded from the local government authorities themselves. The Yesha Rabbis council is composed of some of the leading community rabbis and has, over time, become the supreme authority for many of the settlers in determining what form of opposition and political activity is legitimate in the face of government decisions aimed at territorial withdrawal and settlement evacuation.

On the one hand, both the Yesha Council and the Yesha Rabbis' Forum are informal, non-governmental, institutions. At one and the same time, they are composed of activists and functionaries who occupy public-sector positions (local council mayors, state-funded rabbis) and, as such, are making use of their public-sector time to promote political objectives and causes. They have direct access to leading political figures – up to the level of prime minister and state president – and they command a political authority which determines the actions and protest activities of the settlers themselves. As such, they promote the protest activities of the settler movement while using the time and resources available to them as public-sector civil servants and functionaries.

Gush Emunim as a settlement movement

Gush Emunim always focused on the practical and tangible dimensions of achieving its political objectives. Despite its religious worldview, which focuses on the Land of Israel, the State of

Israel, and even the army of Israel, as constituting 'holiness' and part of the process of eventual messianic redemption of the Jewish people, the Gush Emunim ideology argues that redemption can only be brought about through practical actions. That action, which has been undertaken since the inception of the movement and has become the masthead of all Greater Israel ideologists, has been the establishment of settlements throughout the disputed territories as a means of ensuring that the 'miraculously liberated' territories of the Six Day War will never again be relinquished to non-Jewish rule. Settling the territories is, in their view, part of the process through which redemption will be advanced, while surrendering them constitutes a setback in the redemption process.

From their earliest publications, those involved in Gush Emunim presented themselves as the 'true' continuers and interpreters of the Zionist enterprise which began in the late nineteenth century, and which brought land under control of the Jewish collective and eventual sovereignty of the state, by incremental land purchase and land settlement. Their continued attempts to establish new settlement outposts, even against the wishes of the Israeli government of the time, were portrayed as being equivalent to the heroic and pioneering activities of the Zionist movement to create settlements in the face of the anti-settlement and anti-immigration policies of the British Mandate during the pre-state period. They perceived themselves in the same romantic terms of the early Zionist pioneers, arguing that they were now taking on the mantle of pioneering and state-building as part of a continuous ideological process.

The removal or evacuation of settlements is portrayed as essentially an 'anti-Zionist' action which runs against the state-building process as a whole. Settlement is also portrayed by many of the settlers as constituting an essential element in the security and defence policy of the state, arguing that the existence of the settlements in relatively peripheral locations removes the immediate threat of terrorism and katyusha missiles from the metropolitan centre of the country. The use of both the 'pioneering' and 'defence' images is designed to create a discourse which is acceptable to the wider Israeli public, especially those (the vast majority) who are not won over by the recourse to religious justifications for settlement expansion. Many centrist and right-wing Israelis can identify with the notion of settlement pioneers and/or settlements contributing to defence policy, while being equally turned off by a political position based on notions of religion, redemption and divine promises. But there is a strong counter-argument to the pioneering and defence discourses which have made them less relevant during the past decade, especially during a period when the notion of territorial compromise has become more prominent and acceptable and in which settlements are increasingly seen by a growing proportion of the Israeli public as constituting an obstacle to peace. The conditions in the suburban, Western-style communities that constitute much of the settlement enterprise today are not seen as pioneering in comparison with the difficult conditions experienced by the pre-state settlers in peripheral regions. Western-style villas, state-funded mortgages, and commuting to white-collar employment in Tel Aviv and Jerusalem are viewed by many as a means through which the state has been exploited, and middle-class lifestyles subsidized, at the expense of many other social and welfare needs and the peripheral regions in the Negev and the Galilee. Equally, West Bank (and previously Gaza) settlements that have to be defended by extra troops and reservists are seen as constituting a security burden, rather than contributing in any way to the defensive posture or safety of the country's inhabitants.

But settlements have played a role in the ongoing discourse concerning the eventual demarcation of borders and lines of physical separation between Israel and a future Palestinian state. The attempt to annex parts of the West Bank in those places where the major settlement blocs are located, especially in areas in close proximity to the Green Line boundary with Israel, has indicated the powerful impact of settlements in creating new geographical and political realities which then have become difficult to reverse at a later stage, and under changed political conditions. This has been translated into a partial reality following the physical construction of the separation fence, which has effectively annexed parts of the West Bank to Israel under the guise of security considerations.

Gush Emunim as a movement of ideological socialization

Gush Emunim succeeded in creating a new generation of ideologically motivated activists, many of whom have taken on leadership positions in the settler movement. Part of this success is due to the mechanisms of message dissemination and ideological socialization which the national religious community has at its disposal, and over which it maintains rigid control, limiting access only to those who would preach the 'correct' message. The fact that the national religious community maintains its own separate educational framework enables it to maintain a powerful role of social gate-keeping in terms of what messages are disseminated and who has the authority to disseminate them. Schools, *yeshivot* and synagogues are all subject to these gate-keeping constraints, with access limited to rabbis or educators whose interpretation of political events corresponds with the ideology of the settler movement. The religious high school system affiliated with the Bnei Akiva national religious youth movement is the major source for social reproduction and recruitment of the future generations of right-wing activists and settlers. Many of the students at these high schools are themselves residents of the settlements, while most others are from families who are closely affiliated with the settler movement and its irredentist ideology. Many of these schools will bus their students to right-wing demonstrations and justify this on the grounds that it is part of the process through which their students participate in legitimate democratic activities, on the one hand, while strengthening their attachment to the Land of Israel, on the other. With the possible exception of some ultra-orthodox groups, no other political sector in Israel has such direct access to future generations of committed youth, who will fill the role of activists and, eventually, a new generation of leaders.

Socialization also takes place through the special army units, known as *hesder*, which were set up in the 1970s to accommodate the demand of religious Zionist youth to serve and study together as consolidated units. These soldiers were seen by the army hierarchy as constituting highly motivated units, spurred on by the religious nationalist beliefs that they were taught in their schools and *yeshivot*. Unlike the ultra-orthodox community, they consider army service as constituting no less than a religious obligation and were prepared to take part in some of the toughest combat units. From the 1990s on, many of these *hesder* soldiers began to reach high-level command positions for the first time in Israel's history.

The religious nationalist message is also disseminated through many of the country's synagogues. The weekly Friday evening sermon is often devoted to a religious analysis of contemporary political events as interpreted through the texts of the weekly Torah portion. Increasingly, this has become a means of emphasizing the exclusive divine promise of the land to the Jewish people, the supremacy of Torah law over the rule of the majority, and supreme sanctity of the land above all else. Orthodox rabbis, perceived as constituting the authentic interpreters of the Jewish law, preach a right-wing political message through their analysis of the Torah texts.

The use of the public media is another important means of message dissemination. The settler movement has established its own radio channel (*Arutz 7*) and set up its own newspaper, *Mekor Rishon*. While the ideological media of the left wing, such as the Peace radio station of Abie Nathan or newspapers such as *Al Hamishmar* and *Davar*, had all closed down due to a lack of interest and support, the right-wing *Hatzofe* newspaper continued to preach to its national religious audience, while both *Mekor Rishon* and *Arutz 7* found a ready audience for its specific political message. Internally, the settler movement continues to produce its own political and ideological magazine, *Nekudah*, which has been published monthly since the late 1970s and which reflects the major ideological trends within the settler community.

The challenge of the Gaza withdrawal

The decision by the Israeli government unilaterally to disengage from the Gaza Strip in the summer of 2005 and to evacuate all the Jewish settlements constituted a major crisis for the settler movement at both the ideological and the practical level. Ideologically, the Gaza withdrawal, together with the evacuation of four settlements in the north of the West Bank, symbolized the opposite of everything that Gush Emunim had set out to achieve – namely, the extension of Jewish control throughout the entire 'Land of Israel' through the agency of practical actions such as settlement. The withdrawal of Israeli troops and the forced evacuation of the settlements was, for them, the antithesis of what they had come to perceive as constituting the 'true' [*sic*] path of contemporary Zionism, spurred on by a deep religious belief that they were carrying out the authentic will of divine command in the Holy Land. Practically, those in the settler movement and their supporters used every means at their disposal to thwart the implementation of the Gaza withdrawal. This ranged from attempts to overturn the decision within the government, through civil protests in the form of demonstrations and the wearing of orange clothes and ribbons to signify their opposition to the plan, to violent actions such as the blocking of major roadways in the centre of the country, the establishment of illegal outposts, and the positioning of fake terrorist devices at key locations such as bus stations.

The implementation of disengagement raised major ideological questions concerning the success of Gush Emunim ideology in the long term. Having set out to ensure future control and sovereignty over the entire 'Land of Israel' which had been miraculously 'liberated' in the 1967 war, the settlers were forced to give up control over large parts of these areas. The collapse of the 'Greater Land of Israel' dream did not start with Gaza Disengagement – it commenced with the implementation of the Oslo Agreements and the transfer of local control and autonomy in many areas to the Palestinian Authority. But the Gaza Disengagement (and the evacuation of some settlements in the northern sections of the West Bank) was the only the second time that settlers were forced to leave their homes (Yamit in the early 1980s being the first time). The forced evacuation of the Gaza Strip and Northern West Bank settlements represented the most serious ideological and political challenge faced by the settler movement since its inception in the early 1970s. Some of its leaders bitterly noted that the failure to command the support of the vast majority of the country's Jewish population was due to the fact that, while they had 'succeeded in settling the heart of the Land, they had failed to settle in the hearts of the people'.

Conclusion

The settler movement has come a long way since the inception of the Gush Emunim in 1974. At the time, attempts to settle at Sebastia and Ofra were seen as being nothing more than a protest on the part of a relatively small group of national religious youth led by Hanan Porat and Moshe Levinger. Within certain political constraints, the government and the political elite were prepared to suffer these protests, given the fact that they operated within the discourse of Zionism and pioneering, and because they were not initially seen as constituting a threat to the political hegemonies of the elites who had governed the country during the previous thirty years, and to which these religious protest groups had no real access. But the structural changes experienced by the Israeli body politic since the Six Day War in 1967, and even more since the rise to power of the first Likud government in 1977 and the greater distribution of power among a more diverse set of groups, has transformed the settler movement into a powerful political player wielding considerable influence over the policies and decisions of successive Israeli governments.

The question of the future of Israel's settlements in the West Bank lies at the very heart of the Israeli–Palestinian peace process. The international community has long denounced Israel's settlement-building, seeing it not only as illegal under international law but also as a major impediment to the peace process between Israel and the Palestinians. The continual growth of ettlements in the West Bank makes the prospects of a geographically contiguous and viable Palestinian state increasingly remote. The political influence exerted by the settler movement and Israel's refusal engage in any serious and meaningful settlement freeze is viewed by the Palestinians, and by the majority of the international community, as evidence of its ill faith and its unwillingness to relinquish control of the West Bank.

The settler movement has impacted significantly on the territorial discourse within Israel and on the Israeli–Palestinian peace process as a whole. The complexity and the political challenges presented by any large-scale settlement evacuation, especially of the blocs around Ma'ale Adumin, Gush Etzion, Givat Ze'ev and Ariel, has impacted on the discussions over the territorial and border configurations of a future Palestinian state. A withdrawal by Israel to the pre-June 1967 boundaries is no longer seen as viable. Instead discussions have concentrated on a territorial exchange based on the 1967 Green Line, taking into account the geopolitical realities created by the settler movement. In similar fashion, this is reflected in the unilateral construction of the separation fence/wall by Israel since 2003, deviating in some areas from the Green Line so that a large number of settlements would be included within Israeli territory, thereby creating an interim political border/boundary and *de facto* annexation of parts of the West Bank.

Paradoxically, the efforts of the right wing and the settler movement to ensure Israel's retention of the 'Land of Israel' and long-term control of the West Bank has created a new political challenge – namely, the continuation of Israel as a Jewish democratic state. The demographic reality of near parity between Arab and Jewish populations – and the eventual emergence of an Arab majority – has created the conditions of binationalism and power-sharing rather than two states and respective Israeli and Palestinian sovereignty. This demographic time-bomb has given an added urgency to the calls within Israel for separation and withdrawal from the West Bank, and has now led to many earlier advocates of the Greater Land of Israel, including prominent political leaders such as Ehud Olmert and Tzipi Livni, to embrace the logic of the two-state solution.

Further reading

Feige, Michael (2009) *Settling in the Hearts: Jewish Fundamentalism in the Occupied Territories* (Detroit: Wayne State University Press).
Gorenberg, Gershom (2006) *The Accidental Empire: Israel and the Birth of the Settlements, 1967–1977* (New York: Times Books).
Lustick, Ian (1988) *For the Land and the Lord: Jewish Fundamentalism in Israel* (New York: Council on Foreign Relations).
Newman, David (1985) *The Impact of Gush Emunim: Politics and Settlement in the West Bank* (London: Palgrave Macmillan).
Zertal, Idith, and Eldar, Akiva (2007) *Lords of the Land: The War over Israel's Settlements in the Occupied Territories, 1967–2007* (New York: Nation Books).

23

Israeli peace movements

Naomi Chazan

Peace movements have been an integral part of the Israeli political landscape since the inception of the Palestinian–Israeli conflict. From as far back as the beginning of the twentieth century, Jews and Arabs have sought constructive ways to share the land. These efforts, which continued on a small scale after the creation of the State of Israel in 1948, gathered steam after the 1967 war and flourished in the wake of the First *Intifada*. Non-governmental and grassroots initiatives designed to promote a lasting Israeli–Palestinian peace have persisted into the twenty-first century, and many of the positions they promoted have become part of the political mainstream in the country. In recent years, however, their number and range have decreased and their effectiveness has been seriously curtailed (Chazan 2005).

This chapter sets out to examine extra-governmental peace action in Israel since 1967: to map its constituent groups, discuss its dynamics, and assess its impact over time. The "peace camp" in Israel covers a broad array of organizations, groups, and networks which share a basic commitment to the non-violent resolution of the Arab–Israel conflict and engage in a multiplicity of activities to promote this objective. Although never united, its boundaries are the subject of some debate. One school of thought prefers a narrow definition and includes only those groups that are dedicated to actively advancing a political settlement between Israel and its Arab neighbors in general and the Palestinians in particular (Kaminer 1996). Another, dominant, school prefers a much looser construction of peace movements, incorporating into its analysis not only avowedly political organizations on the national level, but also dialogue groups, human rights associations, academic endeavors, professional exchanges, and diverse local initiatives whose aim is to improve the relations between Israelis and Palestinians as part of broader accommodation efforts (Hermann 2002: 96–7). This broad definition of Israeli peace movements, however unwieldy, provides an opportunity to delve into their diversity, explore their commonalities, and comprehend their dynamics.

Peace movements in Israel have developed in four distinct phases, dovetailing clear stages in the progression of the conflict since 1967: an initial period of organization and political definition (1967–87); a stage of consolidation around the demand for direct Israeli–Palestinian negotiations (1987–93); an era of diverse attempts at peace-making during the seven years of the Oslo process (1993–2000); and the present phase of contraction and marginalization (2000–).

The range and emphases of peace movements have varied in each of these stages, as have their objectives, their internal structures, their activities, their influence on decision-makers, and their impact on the resolution of the conflict.

This essay demonstrates the cyclical quality of extra-parliamentary peace action in Israel to date. The first grassroots stirrings emerged at the left fringes of the Israeli political spectrum. These gradually gathered momentum and succeeded in penetrating the uppermost echelons of the political establishment. By the first decade of the present century, the main message of the peace camp – the demand for a two-state solution – had been adopted by a solid majority of Israelis. At the same time, belief in its feasibility waned, leading to the shrinking and subsequently to the renewed marginalization of the vestiges of peace advocacy. The shifting resilience of Israeli peace movements is a function of the interaction between their changing objectives and internal characteristics, on the one hand, and shifts in the social and political environments in which they operate, on the other. They are therefore as much a product of their socio-political context as a key trigger for its transformation.

Phase I: the formative years (1967–87)

Extra-parliamentary peace action developed slowly in the years immediately after the 1967 war and the Israeli occupation of the West Bank, the Gaza Strip, the Golan Heights, and the Sinai peninsula. Nevertheless, during the following two decades the foundations of the peace camp were laid down, its broad characteristics were shaped, and initial mobilization took place.

The cornerstones of Israel's peace movements were laid in the course of the 1970s by academics, journalists, writers, and intellectuals on what was then considered the far-left edge of Israeli politics. A series of initiatives spearheaded by Ha'olam Hazeh (the Israeli journal cum political movement established by veteran activist Uri Avnery) and by members of the Israel Communist Party led not only to initial, sporadic political meetings between Israelis and Palestinians but also to the creation of the Israeli Council for Israeli–Palestinian Peace and the Committee for Solidarity with Birzeit University (Avnery 1986). These later coalesced into the militant pole of the peace camp under the umbrella of Gush Shalom (the Peace Bloc). The objective of these groups, from the outset, was to realize a full Israeli withdrawal from all the territories captured by Israel in 1967 and to create a Palestinian state alongside Israel on the 4 June 1967 borders.

The activities of these small, at times clandestine, efforts during the bulk of the 1970s and 1980s, while concerned with sensitizing Israeli public opinion to the injustice inherent in the institutionalization of an occupation regime and to the dangers of Jewish settlement across the Green Line, focused primarily on establishing initial links with the Palestine Liberation Organization (PLO). Many of these first encounters were brokered by European and American peace networks (the American Friends Service Committee for one) and hosted by academic institutions and think tanks outside the Middle East (Mendelsohn 1982; Kelman 1995), especially after an official ban was placed on such meetings in 1986.

The creation by young reserve soldiers of Peace Now in 1978, on the eve of Menachem Begin's journey to the first Camp David summit with Anwar Sadat, marked the emergence of the moderate pole of Israeli peace activism. The objective of Peace Now was originally to encourage, in broad strokes, the peaceful resolution of the Arab–Israel conflict. It concentrated, at first, on the Egyptian–Israeli peace treaty and subsequently, albeit somewhat belatedly, on the opposition to the First Lebanon War of 1982. Despite some initial publications protesting the expansion of settlement activity, Peace Now turned its full attention to the Palestinian question only in the latter part of the 1980s, when it became the focal point for the mobilization of a large number of more mainstream political activists concerned with the promotion of accommodation with the Palestinians (Hall-Cathala 1990).

In these formative years, the nascent peace camp was not only bifurcated ideologically and narrowly constructed socially; it also lacked political traction at the formal level. The militant pole was represented in the Knesset in the late 1970s and the early 1980s by a series of small factions (Ha'olam Hazeh, HaMoked, Sheli, and, after 1981, Ratz). The moderates also found a home first in Ratz and then among a very small group of up-and-coming Labor Party doves, including Avraham Burg, Yossi Beilin, and, at the time, Haim Ramon. The main political parties (Likud and Labor), however, were preoccupied with socio-economic matters and the Lebanon quagmire. The two national unity governments they formed were incapable of moving on the Palestinian front, and the vast majority of the Israeli public evinced little interest in these matters. During this period, the groundwork for Israeli peace activism was established but not actualized.

Phase II: promoting a negotiated settlement (1987–93)

The outbreak of the First *Intifada* in December 1987 proved a turning point for the Israeli peace camp. Its grassroots quality punctured the prevailing complacency in Israeli society and galvanized civil action pointedly around resolving the Palestinian–Israeli conflict. During these critical years additional organizations decrying the status quo were formed, protest activities expanded substantially, and the political impact of peace-oriented initiatives increased accordingly.

The overarching goal of the peace camp at this stage was to set in motion direct negotiations between Israel and the Palestinians based on the notion, however ambiguously defined, of Palestinian self-determination. Although the vast differences between the various groups regarding the identity of the interlocutors, the details of a permanent settlement, and its ultimate shape persisted (the militant camp arguing for a Palestinian state in the entire territory occupied in 1967; Peace Now and its associates advocating "Territories for Peace" and "No to Violence, Yes to Peace"), the shared focus on launching a process of negotiations temporarily blurred these substantive differences and enabled the coalescence of activities under a common banner.

To promote this end, a series of new, more specialized, organizations was established around the existing peace poles. These included, among others, women's organizations such as Women in Black and Reshet: The Israeli Women's Peace Net, which later evolved into Bat Shalom (Chazan 1991; Sharoni 1995); human rights groups concerned with Israeli activities in the Occupied Territories (B'tselem, Physicians for Human Rights, the Israeli Committee Against Torture, and HaMoked: The Hotline for Victims of Violence); and a spate of networks representing specific constituencies and local communities (East for Peace, Oz v'Shalom/Netivot Shalom, Neve Shalom, Professors Against the Occupation, Osim Shalom – Social Workers for Peace). Opinion-makers became more active with the establishment of the think tank-like Alternative Information Center, the International Center for Peace in the Middle East, the Economic Cooperation Foundation (ECF), and, later, IPCRI – the Israel Palestine Center for Research and Information. For the first time, academic research institutes such as the Harry S. Truman Research Institute for the Advancement of Peace at the Hebrew University and the Tami Steinmetz Center for Peace Research at Tel Aviv University turned their attention to policy-oriented research, frequently conducted with Palestinian counterparts.

Participants in these various undertakings came mostly from well-educated, urban middle-class segments of Israeli society. But by the beginning of the last decade of the twentieth century their numbers had swelled, reaching out to religious as well as to secular activists, *Mizrahim* (Jews from the Middle East and North Africa) alongside *Ashkenazim* (Jews from Europe), and to representatives of development towns and poorer neighborhoods as well. The social roots of Israel's peace movements became somewhat more varied at this time (Bar-On 1996).

The range and types of activities also diversified. In general, the pace of protest action increased, educational initiatives were launched, petitions were circulated on a regular basis, and public advocacy campaigns proliferated. At this time Israeli and Palestinian activists on both sides of the Green Line explored new ways of working together to promote common objectives. Literally hundreds of encounters at the local as well as the leadership level took place, in most instances contributing markedly to dispelling mutual stereotypes and sometimes to serious discussions on the ingredients of a lasting Israeli–Palestinian accord (Saunders 1999). By the time formal negotiations began in the early 1990s, many of the key actors were already acquainted with one another, and some had developed significant working relationships.

The growing salience of peace activities came together, at this time, with enhanced political access as well. The establishment of the peace-oriented parliamentary bloc of Ratz, Mapam, and Shinui (later, after the 1992 elections, merged into Meretz) gave these efforts a clear voice in the Knesset throughout the First *Intifada*. These were echoed by dovish Labor Party members who, following the collapse of the second national unity government in 1990, stepped up their criticism of Likud Prime Minister Yitzhak Shamir. These forces, although in the opposition at the time, were clearly instrumental in amplifying the American demand to participate in the November 1991 Madrid conference which effectively launched the Palestinian–Israeli diplomatic process.

The hope planted in Madrid created a public climate conducive to change. The Labor–Meretz government ushered into office in the wake of the 1992 elections was backed not only by a widespread popular demand for Israeli–Palestinian accommodation but also by a strong belief that the implementation of such a vision was possible. It is hardly surprising that Prime Minister Yitzhak Rabin chose to pursue possibilities both formally and informally, through a variety of civil society initiatives – most notably the ECF–PLO talks, which ultimately matured in the summer of 1993 into what came to be known as the Oslo Accords. Thus, some peace activities at the civil society level during this period were translated first into greater political representation at the formal level and then into the institutionalization of track II negotiations which were subsequently co-opted to promote official policies.

The impact of Israeli peace movements on the Oslo process is nevertheless a matter of not inconsiderable disagreement. While non-governmental efforts unquestionably contributed to reordering the public agenda at this time and to altering the prevalent discourse, external factors, such as the collapse of the Soviet Union and the emergence of a local Palestinian leadership capable of rallying the population around negotiations as a tool for liberation, played a direct role (Nasser and Heacock 1991; Peres 1993).

Equally significantly, the burgeoning of heterogeneous groups concerned with promoting non-violent solutions to the conflict was an integral part of a broader sociological phenomenon – the growth of civil society in Israel. Previously, organizational life in the country had been extremely contained. Rapid processes of economic growth coupled with the loosening of centralized controls over socio-economic life enabled, precisely at this juncture, the flourishing of a wide range of civil society groups – however loosely organized – of which peace movements were just one example.

Nobody, therefore, can seriously suggest that these organizations were inconsequential in molding the setting for the diplomatic breakthrough of the early 1990s (although the contribution of grassroots movements was frequently belittled by policy-makers). Indeed, the joint efforts of various peace groups at this juncture took on enhanced meaning when combined with shifts in the global environment, greater public receptivity to the peace message, and the emergence of a political leadership willing to explore the possibilities it offered.

Phase III: negotiating an agreement (1993–2000)

The seven years between the signing of the Oslo Accords and the collapse of the permanent settlement negotiations at Camp David in the summer of 2000 witnessed the rise, fragmentation, and gradual enfeeblement of vigorous civil society peace activity in Israel. This dynamic echoed the rhythm of excitement which accompanied the signing on the White House lawn of the Declaration of Principles, the confusion attendant upon the assassination of Yitzhak Rabin in November 1995, and the gradual disillusionment which accompanied the renewal of violent resistance and the failure to reach a binding agreement.

The peace camp expanded enormously at the outset of the Oslo process. Not only were additional organizations added to the long list of peace-oriented initiatives, including those aggregating like-minded professionals (Imut – Mental Health Workers for Peace, Rabbis for Human Rights, the security personnel-initiated Council for Peace and Security), but new women's groups were established (Bat Shalom – The Jerusalem Link), youth initiatives were launched (Seeds for Peace, for one), and organizations in the heart of the Jewish establishment began to engage in joint ventures with the Palestinians (Hadassah, the Joint Distribution Committee, Na'amat, a variety of academic institutions). These efforts were followed by the creation of dozens of small dialogue groups at the local level, especially along the Green Line and in the Jerusalem area (Kaufman and Salem 2008). Many of these undertakings were initiated jointly with Palestinian partners.

This organizational proliferation was not always accompanied by ideological consolidation within the peace camp. From the outset of the Oslo phase, divisions over substance were evident: the moderate and militant wings differed on the significance of the agreement themselves, on the contents of a permanent settlement solution, on the final-status issues (from Jerusalem and the refugees to borders and settlements), and, ultimately, on the feasibility if not the desirability of the two-state solution.

Differences of opinion also grew on the tactics of extra-parliamentary action: some moderate groups toned down criticism of the Labor–Meretz government in order to prop up the formal process; others continued to protest governmental ambiguity, to underscore Israeli violations of human rights, and to demand palpable amelioration on the ground. Many of these internal arguments focused on the stepped-up settlement construction which accompanied the Oslo talks (Peace Now Settlement Watch: http://groups.yahoo.com/groups/Settlement-Watch). Ongoing debates on the nature of activities with Palestinians continued: were these designed to bolster human trust, as so many Israelis wanted, or were they meant to promote a political solution to the conflict, as most Palestinians and veteran peace activists urged? Convergence on the need to expedite the peace talks and to combat the growing opposition to the overall trajectory set by the government could hardly mask the renewed splits within the peace camp.

Israeli peace and reconciliation groups nevertheless came together to deflect increasingly well-organized efforts by Oslo opponents to derail the process in its entirety. These were spearheaded by the settler movement and backed by the Likud and parties to its right, which formed a disciplined front united in its outright rejection of the Rabin government's policies. This nationalist bloc succeeded, in the name of patriotism and societal cohesion, to rally many religious, *Mizrahi*, and new immigrants' groups which were concerned primarily with socio-economic matters and felt that the overwhelming preoccupation with peace was the luxury of veteran elites detached from the realities of everyday life.

These tensions came to a head on the eve of the signing of the interim agreement between Israel and the PLO (commonly dubbed "Oslo II") in September 1995. A series of rallies, demonstrations, and strikes organized by the opposition evoked widespread incitement against the government and its proponents. In an effort to counter this campaign, the various components of the peace camp, with government approval, decided to hold a major public show of strength on November 4, 1995, which ended in the fatal shooting of the prime minister.

In retrospect, the assassination of Rabin proved to be a turning point not only in the history of Israeli–Palestinian relations but in the story of the peace camp as well. Immobilized first by the event itself and then by a broad national campaign for domestic reconciliation, civil society peace groups were ill-prepared to deal either with the spate of bus bombings which occurred just before the May 1996 elections or with the subsequent razor-thin victory of Binyamin Netanyahu, which ushered a right-wing government into office.

These changing political circumstances inevitably affected both the vibrancy of Israeli peace movements and the thrust of their activities. The number and frequency of joint Israeli–Palestinian encounters dropped while attention turned to sustaining the peace constituency inside Israel. In the process, many small joint ventures – faced with growing logistical problems emanating from restrictions on Palestinian movement and inadequate resources – dissipated, while the cohesion of the camp in its entirety began to unravel. Divisions between the moderate and radical poles were further compounded by a widening gap between the increasingly institutionalized (and relatively well-funded) groups – among them Peace Now, the ECF and the major human rights organizations – and the smaller, more spontaneous, grassroots initiatives.

With limited access to decision-makers during the first Netanyahu administration and a virtual stalemate in negotiations, Israeli peace movements were increasingly stymied in the latter part of the 1990s. The victory of Ehud Barak in the 1999 elections took place in a markedly different political and social climate than the one that had brought Rabin back to power scarcely seven years earlier – one in which skepticism replaced the enthusiasm of yesteryear and doubts about the possibility of ending the conflict overrode the hope of achieving this result.

The brief Barak incumbency magnified the disarray in the peace camp. Differential access to the government compounded the ideological breach between the two poles of the peace camp, with moderate elements sustaining the government in the hope of resuming negotiations and the more militant groups breaking entirely with its direction. People-to-people activities came to a virtual standstill as many Palestinians shunned contacts which did not address the goal of terminating the occupation. And the policies of the Barak government – especially on the settlement issue – further undermined one of the key tools of mobilization for peace action.

In retrospect, the contraction of peace-oriented movements at this time was a harbinger of the collapse of the Oslo process. With only a few exceptions, mostly clustered around the more radical pole, the peace camp was unusually dormant when the Camp David summit broke down in the summer of 2000 and Ehud Barak announced that Israel no longer had a partner for negotiations (Barak 2001; Malley and Agha 2001; Pressman 2003). It was also virtually silent when, immediately afterwards, the Second (al-Aqsa) *Intifada* erupted at the end of September. By then, the impact of civil society peace groups on public outlooks – or, for that matter, on events – was minuscule.

The reasons for the failure of Israeli movements at this juncture relate, first, to their inability to make the transition from promoting a peace process to dealing with the intricacies of peacemaking. Strategic confusion reigned as key players (including ECF, Peace Now, and, towards the end of this period, the Peres Peace Center) viewed their primary role as providing support and direction for official efforts, whereas others continued to see themselves as movements bent on advocating a just resolution of the conflict regardless of who was in power. This role redefinition inevitably hampered agreement on goals, highlighted problems of leadership, adversely affected the cohesion among the multiplicity of organizations that inhabited the already loosely knit peace camp, and, ultimately, encouraged a variety of uncoordinated activities with diminishing effect.

The disunity in peace circles was related, second, to substantial changes in attitudes towards the peace process and its promoters within Israeli society at large. By the end of the 1990s, popular belief in the possibility of a negotiated accord with the Palestinians (regardless of positions on its desirability) had waned, to be replaced by a disenchantment fueled by its ideologically united and organizationally disciplined opponents (Hermann and Yuchtman-Yaar 2002). The outer support circles of the peace camp, lacking the commitment of the core activists, gradually abandoned its ranks, leaving the survivors with a vastly diminished constituency.

These factors adversely affected official political willingness to pursue a negotiated settlement, which in turn further marginalized the voices of peace advocates. The growing violence associated with the fortification of religious extremism inevitably exacerbated this circular dynamic. The failure of last-ditch efforts by President Clinton to bridge Israeli and Palestinian positions and the premature termination of the Taba talks paved the way for Ariel Sharon's victory in the February 2001 elections. The demise of the Oslo process signaled the breakdown of the broad alliance that had upheld the pre-Oslo call for negotiations and had led the efforts to nurture mutual understanding during the 1990s, pushing the remaining doves increasingly to the sidelines of Israeli politics (Hermann 2009).

Phase IV: seeking a resolution to the conflict (2000–2012)

The first decade of the present millennium has been marked by several rounds of violence involving non-state actors, interspersed by unsuccessful attempts to renew Israeli–Palestinian negotiations which have only cemented the existing diplomatic stalemate. In these deteriorating circumstances – punctuated by the Second *Intifada*, the death of Yasser Arafat, the Israeli disengagement from Gaza in the summer of 2005, the Hamas electoral victory in early 2006, the Second Lebanon War later that year, the subsequent rocket bombardments on the south of Israel, and the Israeli attack on Gaza in December 2008–January 2009 – civil society peace efforts in Israel underwent a substantial reconfiguration. They not only significantly altered their strategic objectives, their tactics, and the thrust of their activities, but also were bifurcated in the process. By the end of this period, extra-parliamentary activities focused no longer on a nebulous notion of a peaceful bilateral settlement, but rather on the pursuit of a variety of alternative approaches to realizing an end to the occupation and the implementation of a durable solution to the conflict.

During the Sharon years (2001–6) the size and shape of the organizations committed to the peaceful resolution of the conflict changed dramatically – a shift that endured throughout the decade. Most small dialogue networks ceased operations, many professionally based groups folded, and almost all youth initiatives disbanded. All the veteran groups – including Peace Now and Gush Shalom – lost much of their popular support base. At the same time, the divisions between these surviving groups became more pronounced as the remnants of the peace camp – which continued to meet under the auspices of the Peres Peace Center – split into two distinct segments.

The first consists of human rights and veteran movements on the left (Gush Shalom, B'tselem, Rabbis for Human Rights, Physicians for Human Rights, the Israeli Committee against House Demolitions, HaMoked) along with newly formed groups such as Ta'ayush (the Jewish–Arab Movement for Peace), the Coalition of Women for a Just Peace, Mahsom Watch, Breaking the Silence, and Ir Amim (this last concentrating specifically on Jerusalem). These were joined by short-lived initiatives of conscientious objectors and by a spate of new militant groups (Anarchists against the Wall, for one). What distinguishes this set of organizations is their preoccupation with Israeli violations in the Occupied Territories and their avowedly activist character. They focus on humanitarian issues and on the amelioration of conditions in the Occupied Territories, often receiving reinforcement from external civil society networks such as the International Solidarity Movement.

The second segment of the reconfigured organizational map comprises moderate groups which have concentrated primarily on bringing about a political settlement, both by altering Israeli public opinion and by suggesting creative approaches to the resolution of the conflict. These include not only the drastically diminished Peace Now, but also such organizations as the Council for Peace and Security, the ECF, and the Geneva Initiative, formed after the publication of the blueprint for a fully fledged Palestinian–Israeli accord (see www.geneva-accord .org/). This bloc engages mostly in advocacy and track II undertakings concerned with developing workable strategies to move the peace process forward.

Very few joint Palestinian–Israeli efforts survived into the beginning of the twenty-first century, among them the Jerusalem Link, the *Palestine–Israel Journal*, IPCRI, and the Alternative Information Center. Several attempts to build new cooperative ventures proved to be short-lived (the Palestinian–Israeli Peace Coalition formed in 2001, the People's Voice initiative of Sari Nusseibeh and Ami Ayalon, the Danish government-sponsored International Alliance for Arab–Israeli Peace). Three important additions, besides the Geneva group, did gain some traction during this period: the internet-based Israeli–Palestinian exchange Bitterlemons, the Palestinian–Israeli Bereaved Families' Circle, and the International Women's Commission for a Just and Sustainable Palestinian–Israeli Peace (IWC), founded in the summer of 2005. However, none of these ventures, which were severely hampered by logistical as well as political obstacles, succeeded in maintaining the kind of continuous personal ties that flourished during the Oslo years. Nor did most (including the IWC and Bitterlemons) make it beyond the second decade of this century.

The successors of the original peace camp have therefore operated in separate, rarely overlapping, coalitions. Indeed, they have often differed on objectives, strategies, tactics, and activities. Although they share the broad goal of ending the occupation and bringing about a just resolution of the conflict, they do no agree on the amount of attention that should be given to immediate concerns (with the solidarity network devoting the bulk of its energies to preventing further Israeli infringements on Palestinian rights and daily life) versus the fulfillment of long-term aspirations (the bailiwick of the political alliance). Behind these disagreements lies a growing ideological rift on the substance of the preferred solution to the conflict. While the majority of activists, including the veteran Gush Shalom, still adhere to the two-state solution, some elements in the solidarity camp have rallied around the one-state option, which envisages a binational, secular, and democratic state in the entire area.

Given these divergent visions of the future, it is hardly surprising that there has been growing discord on the strategic agenda of these non-governmental movements. The grassroots associations came out forcefully against the construction of the separation wall, decried by only a handful of the moderate groupings. These, in turn, initially rallied around the full text of the Road Map, promulgated on April 30, 2003, which was largely dismissed by the human rights organizations. The former were directly involved later that year in drafting the Geneva Initiative, whose provisions became the subject of heated debate in more militant circles. The two broad coalitions then differed on the advisability of the unilateral withdrawal from Gaza, announced by Ariel Sharon as a response to the assertion by the Geneva proponents that a negotiated settlement was still attainable. Differences of opinion on the motives and the manner of the Gaza pullout in August 2005 fractured even the moderate sector, as most of this group applauded the move, while some key personalities questioned its advisability.

Ideological disagreements reached a head with the outbreak of the Second Lebanon War in the summer of 2006. The militant groups immediately denounced the Israeli attack; most of their more moderate counterparts supported the move during its initial phases, calling for a ceasefire only when the ground war was launched. This internal polarization was magnified during the three weeks of the Israeli war on Gaza, which commenced at the very end of December 2008. Members of the politically oriented movements justified the military action (although not always its scope) as a necessary response to the rain of rocket attacks, whereas the human rights and solidarity organizations, along with key Arab civil society groups within Israel, found themselves in virtual isolation in opposition to the assault on heavily populated areas.

Strategically, nevertheless, one significant point of convergence did emerge: the appeal for international involvement in the Israeli–Palestinian arena. The abandonment of a uniquely bilateral track reflects the widespread despondency and frustration prevalent in dovish circles. It also explains the generally favorable attitude of these civil society groups both to the Arab Peace Initiative (particularly after its reaffirmation in Riyadh in March 2008) and to President Barack Obama's attempts to expedite a binding settlement.

The external reorientation of peace organizations has, however, assumed very different practical manifestations. Political activists have intensified their work outside the region, traveling to various capitals in an attempt to rally direct international intervention on the diplomatic front. They have also been involved in intensive efforts to develop formulae for the renewal of a political process and, in a more innovative vein, in exploring other ways to bring about a Palestinian state, either through internationally sanctioned unilateral Palestinian action or through external imposition. Their human rights counterparts, in stark contrast, have not only invited outside participation on the ground (the weekly demonstrations against the separation wall in Bil'in and Na'alin are but one example) but in some instances have joined the call for BDS (boycott, divestment, and sanctions) to force Israel to relinquish its stranglehold on the Palestinian Territories. The entire array of organizations has, significantly, come together to protest settlement expansion throughout the West Bank and in East Jerusalem.

By the end of the decade, these tactical differences split the depleted forces on the left. The response to the report of UN Human Rights Council Goldstone Commission on the Gaza war highlighted this polarization, as the solidarity sector embraced its main findings, while the more political groups sought to attenuate its impact in an attempt to keep diplomatic options alive.

These internal fissures compounded the already obvious organizational weakness of peace movements. The impasse in Israeli–Palestinian relations, coupled with the persistence of Hamas-led violence, had already alienated many supporters. Some, who had nevertheless clung to the peace vision, became disenchanted by the in-fighting and the lack of any palpable progress. In the absence of serious prospects for a settlement, still others opted for disengagement from politics in general. The social foundations of peace activism were seriously undermined as a result.

Intra-group tensions have worsened precisely as the social and political credentials of those engaged in peace and human rights activities have been increasingly questioned in broad sections of Israeli society. The rapid escalation of violence and its extraordinarily cruel progression rendered most Israelis psychologically drained, unspeakably afraid, and unwilling to entertain the possibility of accommodation even if they understood the need for a political separation from the Palestinians. This mood has become the breeding ground for expressions of intolerance and even outright racism. In these circumstances, ironically, public opinion has tended to lump the various factions of the Israeli peace camp together, vilifying their past work and indiscriminately assailing their present operations. This broad-based condemnation of the purveyors of non-violent approaches to conflict resolution is indicative of their social marginalization – bordering on complete isolation – in the post-Oslo environment.

This popular straitjacket has assumed political dimensions as well. The three general elections conducted in the first ten years of the twenty-first century witnessed the progressive diminution of peace-oriented parties. Ariel Sharon's overwhelming victory in the 2003 elections adversely affected the access of even the most moderate non-governmental groups. The rise of Ehud Olmert at the head of the Kadima Party in 2006 severed the last tenuous links to the political establishment, especially after the Labor Party joined the coalition and, proclamations aside, forfeited its claim to represent the peace camp. By the February 2009 elections which ushered Binyamin Netanyahu back to the prime minister's office, the political representation of the original peace constituency in Israel had collapsed almost entirely (Labor, Meretz, and Hadash together accounted for only 16.6 percent of the seats in the Knesset) and that of progressive peace voices had declined to a paltry 5.6 percent.

By 2010, the main message of Israeli peace movements – the two-state solution – had been internalized by the political mainstream. But no real progress had been recorded towards achieving this goal. Extra-parliamentary activities made hardly a dent on prevailing mindsets during this period, nor did they help shape the flow of events. The lack of consensus, cohesion, and coordination, coupled with diminishing human and financial resources, impeded the range and effect of many of these movements. When coupled with an emotionally charged sociopolitical climate distinctly antagonistic to accommodation, it is not too difficult to explain their decidedly negligible impact.

This does not mean that these organizations do not play a significant role in voicing dissent, in safeguarding Israel's democratic values, in continuing the struggle for security based on dignity and justice, and, consequently, in presenting Israel's human face to the outside world. Their message resonates globally, galvanizing Jewish communities and general public opinion abroad. In this respect, despite their political marginalization and the curtailment of their activities, the various movements still active on the peace front hold forth hope even now for a better future for Palestinians and Israelis alike.

Civil society and conflict resolution

The story of Israeli peace movements has come full circle. From a series of small groups subsisting on the outer fringes of Israel's society and polity, they gained support and influence on the eve of the opening of Israeli–Palestinian negotiations, only to lose ground with the breakdown of the Oslo process and to be further marginalized in its aftermath.

Veteran peace activists are not unfamiliar with their renewed protest role. But the challenges they and their second- and third-generation successors face are particularly daunting: they have to overcome past failures and operate in a highly skeptical social and political context very different from the optimism that prevailed scarcely two decades ago.

The content and direction of peace action has thus become a key indicator of unfolding political trends – starting with the appeal for bilateral negotiations in the early 1990s, moving on to the attempt to achieve a permanent settlement in the Oslo era, and, now, to various efforts to seek a solution by these and other non-violent means. Civil society is likely to continue to explore possibilities as long as the Israeli–Palestinian conflict persists.

The results of these efforts, as in the past, will rely not only on the creativity of peace activists and their mobilization capacities but also on their ability to penetrate decision-making circles and to induce them to achieve results. It is also true that, while peace movements cannot bring about a lasting resolution of the conflict on their own, successive Israeli governments – however hard they try – cannot silence their voices.

References and further reading

Avnery, U. (1986) *My Friend the Enemy* (London: Zed Press).

Barak, E. (2001) "Israel Needs a True Partner for Peace," *New York Times*, 30 July, p. 17.

Bar-On, M. (1996) *In Pursuit of Peace: A History of the Israeli Peace Movement* (Washington, DC: United States Institute of Peace Press).

Chazan, N. (1991) "Israeli Women and Peace Activism: A View from the *Intifada*," in B. Swirski and M. B. Safir (eds), *Calling the Equality Bluff* (New York: Pergamon Press).

Chazan, N. (2005) "Peace Action and Conflict Resolution: An Israeli–Palestinian Exploration," in E. Podeh and A. Kaufman (eds), *Arab–Jewish Relations: From Conflict to Resolution?* (Eastbourne: Sussex Academic Press).

Hall-Cathala, D. (1990) *The Peace Movement in Israel, 1967–1987* (London: Macmillan).

Hermann, T. (2002) "The Sour Taste of Success: The Israeli Peace Movement, 1967–1998," in B. Gidron, S. N. Katz and Y. Hasenfeld (eds), *Mobilizing for Peace: Conflict Resolution in Northern Ireland, Israel/Palestine and South Africa* (Oxford: Oxford University Press).

Hermann, T. (2009) *The Israeli Peace Movement: A Shattered Dream* (New York: Cambridge University Press).

Hermann, T., and Yuchtman-Yaar, E. (eds) (2002) *Can the Israeli–Palestinian Conflict be Resolved?* (Tel Aviv: Tel Aviv University Press) [in Hebrew].

Kaminer, R. (1996) *The Politics of Protest* (Eastbourne: Sussex Academic Press).

Kaufman, E., and Salem, W. (eds) (2008) *Searching for Peace* (Utrecht: Center for Conflict Prevention).

Kelman, H. (1995) "Contributions of an Unofficial Conflict Resolution Effort to the Israeli–Palestinian Breakthrough," *Negotiations Journal*, 11, pp. 185–209.

Malley, R., and Agha, H. (2001) "Camp David: The Tragedy of Errors," *New York Review of Books*, 9 August.

Mendelsohn, E. (1982) *A Compassionate Peace: A Future for the Middle East* (New York: Hill & Wang).

Nasser, J., and Heacock, R. (eds) (1991) Intifada: *Palestine at the Crossroads* (New York: Birzeit University and Praeger).

Peres, S. (1993) *The New Middle East* (Shaftesbury: Element).

Pressman, J. (2003) "Visions in Collision: What Happened at Camp David and Taba," *International Security*, 28/2, pp. 5–43.

Saunders, H. (1999) *A Public Peace Process: Sustained Dialogue to Transform Racial and Ethnic Conflicts* (New York: St Martin's Press).

Sharoni, S. (1995) *Gender and the Israeli–Palestinian Conflict* (Syracuse, NY: Syracuse University Press).

24

Palestinian citizens of Israel

Amal Jamal

Introduction

The sociological and political developments within the Arab-Palestinian community in Israel and the ongoing estrangement policies of the state vis-à-vis this community have led to growing tensions and increased confrontation between the two sides. The leadership of the Arab-Palestinian community and the leadership of the state, especially the right-wing government that won power in early 2009, understand that state–minority relations can be viewed in internal Israeli terms but also as a central component of the broader Israeli–Palestinian conflict. Neither leadership has decided clearly which understanding is preferable. As a result, one can speak of a spectrum of relationships between the state and the Arab-Palestinian community within it that keep shifting, mostly in the direction of confrontation rather than conciliation. This shift brings to the fore the need for new models of analysis that go beyond a vertical understanding of Israeli–Palestinian relations. Horizontal conceptions, where the entire Israeli control system is viewed as one entity in which the normalization of Jewish life leads to the fragmentation and ghettoization of Palestinian life, are more accurate to an understanding of Israeli policies and Palestinian reactions in the last decade.

This chapter demonstrates that the gap in the expectations of both sides is the major cause of their bad relationship. Before continuing, it is important to note that, for the sake of clarity, this essay regards the relationship between the state and the Arab-Palestinian community as one between two "homogeneous" players. State and minority are seen as two active agents, operating in circumstances that condition their mutual behavior.

The state is not a unified political agent. It is a complex institutional structure that can have contradictory policies. The Arab-Palestinian minority is also a complex social entity, wherein different groups can have contradictory interests. Notwithstanding this argument, it is claimed that the mechanisms of delegitimizing the Arab-Palestinian minority facilitated by state institutions, especially the Knesset, and the resulting areas of contention exploited by the Arab-Palestinian minority have been on the rise in the last decade. In the triangular relationship between contention, accommodation, and control we witness a clear retreat from the mutual accommodation of both parties and a growing tendency towards contention on the part of the Arab-Palestinian minority and towards new forms of control by the Israeli state.

Recent developments in state–minority relations raise questions as to the future status of the Arab-Palestinian minority in Israel and future trends in this relationship, especially in light of two major external processes. The first is the stalemate in the peace process between Israel and the Palestinian Authority and the continuation of Israel's repressive policies in the Occupied Territories. The second is the policies adopted by a growing number of states, especially in Europe and North America, to accommodate the individual and collective rights of various types of minority (McGarry et al. 2008). These two processes reflect contradictory trends in conflict resolution and management and have negative repercussions on state–minority relations in Israel.

The horizons of expectations of both parties form a central factor in determining the role of past experience and present relationship; it is therefore necessary to look at both sides in order to explain the rising tensions and to predict possible developments. In general, state expectations of the Palestinian minority were based on citizenship as accommodation and submission. The state adopted policies of control and neglect in order to meet these expectations. On the other hand, the Palestinian minority expected the state to recognize its substantial citizenship, respect its indigenous status, accommodate its individual and collective rights, and integrate its members as equals in all realms of public life.

In the early years of the state, the minority accepted the framework of majority–minority relations as determining its status. It submitted itself to policies of integration. But, as a result of state control and neglect, a new discourse of contention arose, involving the basic demand that, as the indigenous people of Palestine colonized by an immigrant-settler movement that uprooted them from their homeland, their collective rights be accommodated. The disappointment of the Palestinians occasioned by state policies led to a major shift in their expectations and a refusal to accept the majority–minority citizenship framework as determining the relationship between the two sides. The state policy of constructing "hollow citizenship," devoid of meaning and the continuation of the occupation encouraged calls by the Arab-Palestinian community for closer bonds with Palestinian communities in the Occupied Territories and for the right of return of the Palestinian refugees. The Arab-Palestinian demand for the normalization of relations between their community and the rest of the Palestinian people was viewed by the state as "radicalization" and as a betrayal of their loyalty.

Turning points in state–minority relations

The Palestinian citizens of Israel are the remaining indigenous inhabitants of Palestine that managed to hold on to their places of habitation in the 1948 war. They turned from a majority people into a small minority in the Israeli state, which became the home of a majority of Jews who had mostly immigrated to Palestine in the fifty years before the UN recognition of the Israeli state in 1948. The Palestinian minority remained in three major areas inside Israel – the Galilee, the Triangle area, and the Negev – with a small number in what has been coined the "mixed" cities of Akka, Haifa, Jaffa, Ramleh, and Lod.

The entire Palestinian population was subject to military government based on the emergency regulations set forth by the British Mandate government in 1945. These regulations bypassed the regular legal and judicial system in order to combat the rising activism of anti-British forces – Jewish and Palestinian – that sought to remove the Mandate government. Despite the condemnation of these regulations by both Jewish and Palestinian political groups, the government of Israel maintained them as part of the legal system of the state and applied them in Palestinian areas, enabling the state to bypass the official legal system and set the entire Palestinian population in a state of exception, where they were ruled by military officers

(Kretzmer 1990). This military rule, which lasted until 1966, was eased gradually after 1960, but only after achieving its declared and undeclared goals.

Although the military administration was justified by the Israeli government as addressing security needs, it is clear that it served other purposes that had strategic importance for the state and which had nothing to do with the immediate security threat. The first of its three main undeclared goals throughout its eighteen-year duration was the institutionalization of the economic dependence of the Palestinian minority on the Jewish economy. This was achieved by two interrelated policies: first, the transfer of lands from Palestinian ownership to the state by means that made martial law necessary and, second, establishing a regime of transport permits that limited the freedom of movement of Palestinian workers and blocked their ability to compete freely with Jewish workers in the job market. The second goal was the intimidation of the national political leaders that remained inside Israel after the Palestinian exodus and ensuring through disciplinary measures that the rest of the population accepted its submissive role inside the new political structure. The third goal of the military government had to do with blocking the return of Palestinian refugees from outside what has become recognized as the borders of the Israeli state, the destruction of the Palestinian villages that were depopulated and where no Jewish settlement was established, and the institutionalization of the demographic reality of the Palestinian population, especially turning the "temporary" residency of the internal refugees in neighboring villages into a permanent situation.

The military government achieved most of its economic and demographic goals. It facilitated the transfer of most Arab lands into the hands of the state, it made the agricultural Palestinian society dependent on the Jewish economy, and it managed to freeze the demographic reality that was established during the 1948 war, segregating the Palestinians from the Jewish population and fragmenting them from within (Lustick; 1980; Jiryis 1976; Zureik 1979).

The first turning point in the history of the relationship between the state and the Palestinian minority unfolded when, six months after the military government was lifted in December 1966, Israel occupied the Palestinian areas of the West Bank and Gaza Strip, as well as the Syrian Golan Heights and the Egyptian Sinai peninsula. The Six Day War in June 1967 made it necessary for the state to change its technologies of control and surveillance tactics and to shift most of its military and policing energies into the newly Occupied Territories. The Palestinians inside Israel were exposed to the Palestinian population of the West Bank and Gaza Strip in which relatives and family members lived as refugees. Furthermore, the Palestinian citizens of Israel were exposed to the political and cultural forces in the Occupied Territories, which instigated trends whose implications were understood more than a decade later.

The 1967 war set the stage for major political and economic changes in Palestinian society in Israel that were translated into the Israeli reality in the decades that followed. One of the events it triggered was the first Land Day, on 30 March 1976, which marked the proactive strategy of struggle by the Palestinian community against policies of discrimination, especially in the field of land confiscation, but also in the allocation of resources and in the job market. The first Land Day, during which the police gunned down and killed six demonstrators, was the first nationwide and centrally orchestrated strike of the Palestinian population in Israel. It became a central memorial day among the Palestinians in Israel and was later marked by all Palestinians no matter where they live.

Another important turning point in the history of the Palestinian population in Israel is the signing of the Oslo Accords between Israel and the Palestinian Liberation Organization (PLO) and the ensuing establishment of the Palestinian National Authority (PA). This was significant since it entailed the separation of the solution of the Palestinian national problem from the future political and legal status of Palestinians in Israel. It resulted in a serious realignment in the

Arab party structure, where two new lists – one Islamic and one national – entered the political game in competition with the Hadash list, which had dominated the Arab scene until then. The 1996 elections to the Israeli Knesset marked a differentiation process by which a clear division was seen between those who sought to influence the future of the Palestinian community from within the Israeli formal political system and those who did not trust this strategy and claimed that the price paid by legitimizing the system was too high relative to the possible gains. While Hadash, which represented the communist-secular voter, Balad, which represented the national-secular voter, and the United Arab List, which represented the Islamist-religious-conservative voter, took over 80 percent of the Arab vote in the Knesset elections, part of the Abna'a Al-Balad movement and part of the Islamic movement chose not to participate in the elections. The latter represented national and Islamic potential voters that were not convinced that representation in the Knesset was the way to gain Palestinian rights, especially since the Knesset had enacted the laws that had led to the suppression and disenfranchisement of the Palestinian community in the first place. Since 1996 these splits between the two camps and within each of them have remained more or less the same, weakening the political effectiveness of the entire community vis-à-vis the Israeli state.

Another crucial turning point in the history of the Palestinian minority in the Israeli state was marked by the events of October 2000, in which thousands of Arab citizens marched the streets to express their protest against Israel's repressive policies in the Occupied Territories and against the regression in the equalization and liberalization policies initiated by the second Rabin government and retracted by the first Netanyahu government and then the Barak government. The fierce reaction of the Israeli police, leading to the killing of thirteen Palestinian citizens, deepened the rift between the Palestinian minority and the state. The years 2006–7 witnessed the publication of several vision documents by Palestinian NGOs, signaling the growing engagement of the latter in determining the social and political agenda of society. The documents echoed the political orientation of most of the Arab-Palestinian community in Israel, despite the fact that the public was not sufficiently consulted. This step led to the intensification of surveillance and control policies by the state, initiated after the October 2000 events. The state policies towards the Palestinian minority revitalized the perceptions of the early years of the state, where the Arab-Palestinian minority was conceived mainly in security terms (Lustick 1980; Reiter 2009).

The rise of an educated elite and new political leadership

The Palestinian community in Israel underwent major changes in regard to its demographic composition and weight. One that had a significant impact on Arab politics was the increase in Arab academics, intellectuals, and professionals. The available data on Arab students and academics show a clear growth in their numbers (Al-Haj 2003). The 1948 war led to the expulsion of most Arab elites, including intellectuals, and so the number of higher degree holders remaining in Israel after the war was very small. In 1956–7 there were forty-six Arab students (0.6 percent of all students in Israeli universities that year). In the school year 1979–80 the number was 1,634 (3 percent). The percentage of Arab students completing their BA studies rose in the decade 1988–98 from 6.7 percent to 8.7 percent. In 1998–9 the number of Arab students rose to 7,903 (or 7.1 percent). According to the Israeli Central Bureau of Statistics, the number of university graduates reached 7,200 in 2000–1 and 9,967 in 2004–5. The figure for students in colleges was 2,000 in 1999–2000 and 4,553 in 2004–5.[1] According to Rikaz, the databank for Palestinians in Israel, the total number of Arabs completing sixteen years of education and above in 2002 was 52,032.[2] This number had reached 94,486 by 2004, showing a very clear trend in the Arab community, where the academic and professional elite is growing rapidly (Manna 2008).

A brief look at the elected Arab leaders, especially in the Knesset, shows that major changes are taking place among this elite group, where there is a rising number of academics – something that is slowly but surely changing its political orientation and influencing its modes and patterns of mobilization towards the state. Among educated Arab citizens, only a small number have managed to gain access to Israeli academic institutions. Nevertheless, those that have done so have become well connected to developments in academic discourse in regard to issues related to the status of the Arab community in Israel, especially as far as political and human rights are concerned. Arab academics have contributed to placing Arab citizens' rights on the academic and political stage in Israel as well as in international tribunes. There is also a large group of Arab professionals, especially lawyers and human rights activists, in organizations in Israel and abroad. These professionals are connected to international human rights organizations and are fully aware of changes in world politics in regard to human – individual and group – rights. The Arab academics and professionals that form the vanguard of the Arab community seek ways to promote the community's civic, political, economic, and cultural rights. They increasingly provide the moral, legal, and political legitimizing foundations for the full incorporation of Arab citizenry into the Israeli decision-making mechanism, especially the right to be effectively represented in institutions that determine the future private and public life of Arabs in Israel (Jamal 2006). Since the Arab elite has very marginal power in state institutions, it has had little influence on public policies towards its constituency (Ghanem and Mustafa 2009; Jamal 2006), and this lack of power is particularly frustrating when it comes to shaping the self-understanding of the Arab community and in determining its relationship to others (Jamal 2006). The demand for collective rights therefore opens new structural opportunities for leadership roles that are lacking at the state level, roles that may unlock new avenues of representation, internally and externally, that empower the leadership and, as a result, the community. Tremendous changes have been taking place among leaders and in leadership in the Palestinian community. Although reasons of space do not allow for expansion on the characteristics of these changes, suffice it to say that the Arab leadership in Israel during the first decades of the new state's existence was a product of the *Nakba*. The 1948 war wiped out almost all the political, economic, and cultural elite from the area that became Israel; in particular, those that were involved in any type of resistance to the Zionist movement and to establishing a Jewish state were expelled (Sa'di and Abu Lughod 2007). The Israeli armed forces had information about all influential persons and targeted them (Cohen 2010; Pappe 2006). Those who had a leading position and remained inside Israel had to submit to new rules set by the state. The imposition of military rule on Arab society at the end of the war severely limited the community's freedom of expression, movement, and organization, as well as any possibilities for real political mobilization. Meanwhile, in their quest to control Arab society, the authorities made a practice of cultivating ambitious young members of large clans remaining in Israel (often from what had been the periphery of Palestinian society) who were willing to cooperate with the state in exchange for seats in the Knesset or other positions of power (Lustick 1980). It was such individuals who dominated the Arab lists affiliated with the dominant Mapai (later Labor) Party in Knesset elections up to the late 1970s (Zureik 1979; Ghanem 2001). Thus, most of the post-1948 leadership was pragmatic, traditional, based on family and religious affiliation, instrumental in its outlook, and subservient to the dictates of the state. Most of the leaders of the Arab lists had hardly any formal basic education (Jamal 2006), and many had attended only elementary school. They belonged to a large family in their area, managed to win the support of a large family that provided them with the social backing needed in order to compete with contenders, or were blindly loyal to the dictates of the state and provided services that no other leaders were willing to or could provide, such as roads, electricity services, and running water.

The exceptions to the rule of Israeli-sponsored Arab leaders during the early years of the state came from the al-Ard movement (which espoused a nationalist platform and called for a Palestinian state on the basis of the 1947 UN partition plan) and the binational Arab–Jewish Communist Party.[3] Leaders in these two frameworks were, like their counterparts on the Mapai lists, relatively young when they rose to prominence, but better educated and "self-made." The al-Ard leaders were mostly descendants of internally displaced Palestinian families who had lost their main sources of income and social power as a result of the Israeli land expropriation policies. Some of them came from lower-middle-class families with a clear national consciousness that viewed the Israeli reality in pure colonial terms, which clashed directly with their own aspirations and the basic interests of the Palestinian people. These leaders, such as Anis Kardosh, Habib Kahwaje, Jabur Jabur, Zaki al-Karmi, Naim Makhul, Sabri Jiryis, Mohamad Miari, Nadim Al-Kassem, Abdel Aziz Abu Isba'a, Tawfik Odeh, Mohamad Sruji, and Sami Nasser, were more educated than the average leaders of the Arab community. They are better seen as a direct continuation of the pre-1948 national leadership but with a more realistic worldview and a greater understanding of the power of the Zionist movement and its clash with the basic aspirations of the Palestinian people and the Arab nation (Farah 1985: 266).

The Arab leaders of the Israeli Communist Party (ICP) were also young and more educated than the leaders of the Mapai Arab lists. Most of them were in their twenties, were active in the Palestinian Communist Party before 1948, and, because of their support of the UN partition plan, were allowed to remain in Israel despite their critique of governmental policies. High-ranking leaders of the party originated mostly from the Greek Orthodox Christian community, such as Emile Habibi, Tawfik Toubi, Emile Touma, Saliba Khamis, and Nimer Murkus. Loyal to their Marxist–Leninist ideology, they viewed Jewish–Palestinian relations mostly in class terms and criticized state policies of discrimination based on class exploitation. Communist Arab leaders supported the establishment of a Palestinian state, demanded the return of Palestinian refugees to their original homes, and appealed against the land expropriation policies of the state. Simultaneously, they spoke of the right of the State of Israel to exist, of the legitimacy of Jewish immigration to Israel, and of Jewish–Arab brotherhood in fighting state discriminatory policies (Farah 1985: 254). They were persecuted for defending Arab interests and for raising issues of high sensitivity, such as the status of refugees, the military government, and land expropriation policies. But since Arab communists were a minority in a Jewish–Arab party, they were not in a position to stop or limit the constructive cooperation between some of the Jewish leaders and leaders of the state (Kaufman 1997). (This situation changed in 1965, when an Arab-dominated faction more sympathetic to Arab nationalist demands split from the ICP to form Rakah, which won three seats – two Arab – in the Knesset elections that year.)

One concrete indicator of change can be seen in the educational level of Knesset members (MKs). Until 1981, most Arab MKs, especially those associated with the Labor Party, were uneducated. Only seven out of all seventy MKs between 1949 and 1984 had a BA degree, and nineteen had not even attended school regularly. In comparison, from 1984 until the eighteenth Knesset (elected in 2009), seventy of the seventy-nine MKs had at least a BA degree, while in the last few years there has been a growing number with MAs or PhDs.

Outside the realm of formal politics, young Arabs with leadership abilities seeking avenues of mobilization autonomous from state control gravitated towards Arab NGOs, which began to be established in the mid-1970s to advocate community interests and provide services to the Arab community in areas neglected by the state. Based on a survey of ninety-seven civil activists in twenty active NGOs, the average age of individuals is thirty-four, 75 percent have an academic degree, and 16 percent have completed some other form of higher education. Of 159 board members of another twenty Arab-Palestinian NGOs, 2 percent hold a professorship, while 12 percent have a PhD, 19 percent a Masters degree, 49 percent a Bachelors degree, and 10 percent a higher education diploma. These data reflect the same trend viewed in Knesset members, who are far more educated and to a large extent also considerably younger than traditional leaders.

Unlike the older leadership, which was nurtured and in some cases "created" by the Israeli establishment, the new generation had to struggle to obtain their positions within formal democratic frameworks. Traditional political mobility, based mainly on familial or clan ties, began to give way to new patterns of mobility shaped by democratic procedures and competition. One result was that individuals from smaller families or lower socio-economic backgrounds could reach positions of power, whether as MKs, party leaders, or heads of municipalities, thanks to their education or professional skills, their ability to operate within the democratic process, and/or their familiarity with Israeli political culture. Many of the main leaders who emerged in the 1990s, such as Muhamad Barakeh, Saleh Salim, Muhamad Kana'an, Hanna Swed, Issam Makhul, Afew Egbarieh, Haneen Zouabi, Masud Ghanayeem, Abdel Wahab Darawsheh, Azmi Bishara, Wasel Taha, Jamal Zahalka, Ahmad Tibi, Said Nafa'a, and Abdel Malek Dahamsheh, exemplify this change, as do many leaders at the local level, for example, the former and current heads of the Follow-up Committee – the highest representative body of the Arab-Palestinian community in Israel – namely, Shawki Khatib and Muhamad Zeidan, and also the mayor of Nazareth Ramez Jaraysi. At the same time, the mechanical and somewhat artificial attention to religious affiliation that went into the composition of the Mapai lists gave way, especially with the rise of Rakah–Hadash, to a religious diversity more representative of the party constituency. A similar pattern exists in the other Arab parties, where religious affiliation is either marginal or relatively representative. This does not mean that religious affiliation is not important. All Arab parties, especially the secular ones, seek to reserve seats for a Christian representative, since Muslims form the vast majority of the Arab community. In Hadash, as well as in Balad, one of the three leading seats of the candidates' list for the Knesset is usually allocated to a Christian candidate, although there is no official quota declared. This issue is not usually acknowledged by party officials, although informally the sectarian composition of the party lists plays a major role before every election.[4] Balad was the first to allocate a quota to women, in the eighteenth Knesset elections in 2009. The party decided that women had to be represented in the first three seats, which led to the election of Haneen Zouabi, the first Arab woman on an Arab list to be elected to the Knesset.

State expectations concerning minority behavior

The Israeli state, established as a Jewish state, expected the remaining Palestinian minority to accept the political realities resulting from the 1948 war. This was manifested in official documentations of the state, especially the Declaration of Independence, in proclamations by Israeli leaders, and in policy statements. Palestinians were required gradually to disconnect from the rest of the Palestinian people, accept their official definition as "Israeli Arabs," and respect the boundaries set by their selective Israeli citizenship. The state began constructing political, educational, and disciplining policies that aimed to create a new minority collective imagination. "Israeli Arabs" were to conceive themselves as Israeli citizens, as if their history as a social group started with the establishment of the Israeli state. The politics of fear and policies of discipline were the main mechanisms for facilitating the resocialization process taking place in the official educational system, which was fully under the control of Jewish educators (Al-Haj 1995; Abu-Asbah 2007). Citizenship was introduced by the state as a "control mechanism," its major characteristics being loyalty and patriotism. An attempt was even made in mid-1950 to draft Arab citizens into the army, though ultimately this was not implemented (Cohen 2010; Jiryis 1976). This theory of citizenship did not succeed in protecting Arab citizens from the interference and penetration of state agencies (Yiftachel 2006). Thus, sentiments pertaining to the Palestinian past or sympathy with the Palestinian cause, especially concerning historical injustice and the miserable refugee situation, were interpreted as a serious security threat by the state authorities and as a betrayal of the commitments entailed in citizenship. Thus a situation was created whereby legal affiliation to the Israeli state should determine the worldview of the Arab minority.

Another expectation of the state entailed making the Palestinian minority accept and respect its secondary status in a Jewish national state. This meant accepting both the formal definition of the state as a "state of the Jewish people" and the material superiority of the Jewish majority, as well as accommodating the Jewish symbolic order of the state. The Arab-Palestinian minority was required to adapt to the priorities set by the state concerning the absorption of a growing number of Jewish immigrants and the allocation of resources in the areas of housing, settlement, development, and education. The state viewed these priorities as both natural and necessary in order to realize its character as the nation-state of the Jewish people. The Arab-Palestinian minority, which conceived of itself as the indigenous inhabitants of the land, was expected to accept the official line and act accordingly. A sophisticated system of control was implemented, establishing what has been termed "good Arabs," "positive Arabs," and "quiet Arabs" – a system that continues in various forms to this very day (Jamal 2010; Cohen 2010; Lustick 1980).

Another embedded expectation of the state has to do with the total submission of the Arab-Palestinian minority to the limited ethnic majoritarian political game. The Israeli regime was and still is officially defined as democratic, despite the fact that the Palestinians had to live under a military government until 1966 and continue to be excluded from real participation in the political process. Yet the Arab-Palestinian minority was expected to play according to the rules of the democratic process and accept polices based on majority rule. The fact that the majority was ethnically based and preserved itself through demographic engineering was left out of the political agenda. The democratic procedures of majority decisions have been translated, as in most deeply divided societies, into ethnic majoritarian despotism, leading to the minority's loss of tangible influence on policy-making, especially in matters related to its own well-being and interests (Jamal 2009b). This pattern has been intensified in the last decade, contrary to claims of liberalization and democratization, leading to a lack of any substantial meaning in Arab-Palestinian citizenship (Jamal 2007a). The ethos of defensive democracy has been utilized in order to justify such politics, despite the fact that the Jewish majority in Israel has absolute power over state mechanisms and an automatic majority that is able to pass any decision it wishes.

Another major expectation of the state of its Arab-Palestinian citizens is that they accept their citizenship as the major determinant of their response to the Israeli–Palestinian conflict. In other words, the state expected them to free themselves of the national aspirations of the Palestinian people and accept their civil status in the Israeli Jewish state as the peak of their political ambitions. That is what Israeli leaders mean when they say that the national rights of the Palestinians, including those in Israel, will be met in a Palestinian state in the West Bank and Gaza Strip. Arab-Palestinian citizens are expected to ignore their national, social, and cultural bonds with their brethren at the same time as the Israeli state seeks to deepen the relationship between the Jewish majority in Israel and the entire Jewish people around the world.

Major efforts and material resources are invested in hosting Jewish Americans and Europeans in Israel, aiming to connect them to Zionist ideology and goals.

State policies of control and neglect

The system developed by the state was translated into policies designed to translate the expectations into reality. The policies were developed in various fields and were coordinated either by the Prime Minister's Office through the advisor on Arab affairs or by the minister in charge of Arab affairs in the Israeli government. Many of the studies of state–minority relations in Israel have focused attention on the politics of control of the minority. Their contribution has been enormous to understanding the micro-politics of control and the mechanisms used to penetrate this society and its social formations. However, one cannot ignore the other side of the control coin – namely, neglect – which has been manifested over the years through the politics of de-development and underdevelopment.

The first policy has been to establish by legal means the economic dependence of the Arab-Palestinian minority on state institutions and the Jewish market, intensifying the proletarianization of Arab society, while constructing a Jewish national material and symbolic space that excludes the Arabs (Haidar 1995; Kretzmer 1990). Another policy has been de-development and underdevelopment of Arab towns and villages by minimizing investment in Arab society and allocating resources to nurture loyalty and patronage among local political forces (Hasson and Karayani 2006). In addition to the elimination of agricultural infrastructure and the land expropriation policy, which has reduced areas under Arab control, sophisticated planning and zoning policies and intensive construction of Jewish settlements has led to the ghettoization of Arab towns and cities (Jamal 2008b). The state established a tradition of discriminatory policy regarding the allocation of resources to Arab municipalities and educational and welfare institutions, which was admitted and condemned in the report of the Or Commission (2003). Israel also sought

- to suppress attempts to establish an effective nationwide Arab leadership, while not recognizing the representative bodies of the Palestinian community, such as the Follow-Up Committee (Jamal 2006; Lustick 1980);
- to restrict the maneuvering space of Arab political parties, while utilizing ethnic majoritarian rule to deny Arab leaders any political influence; and
- to delegitimize popular social movements and public mobilization by calling on the loyalty of the Hebrew media and by a widespread body of informers within Arab society itself.

Minority expectations from the state

The Arab Palestinians who remained within the areas controlled by the Israeli army after the 1948 war did not expect the newly established state to divert from its policy and allow them to stay in their villages and houses. The fear resulting from the rumors concerning the actions of the Israeli army in neighboring areas, together with the population census conducted in November 1948, convinced many Palestinians that the state was preparing for a massive expulsion. The sense of fear heralded by their surprise defeat in the war and by the imposition of a military government in Arab areas influenced the expectations and the reactions of the Arab-Palestinian minority.

The first and most dominant hope of the minority was to be recognized as citizens and to purchase Israeli citizenship. Israeli citizenship became suddenly the insurance policy against expulsion and for the protection of private property. The poverty in Arab-Palestinian society resulting from the 1948 war, the policies of neglect by the state, and the lack of strong Arab leadership resulting from the deportation and fleeing of the social, economic, and political elite during the war led to a deep sense of existential threat and limited expectations of survival. The need to remain in their homeland pushed Arab Palestinians to ask merely to be accepted as citizens of the State of Israel. This did not contain any substantial political or cultural content. The fear of deportation was strong, and therefore Arab Palestinians sought to fulfill the expectations of state representatives in Arab villages and towns. The need to demonstrate loyalty and quiescence determined their minimal expectations. This population hoped merely to be allowed to meet its basic needs for shelter and work to ensure a basic income.

The struggle for citizenship changed over time. After having guaranteed their right to remain in their homeland, Arab-Palestinian citizens began expanding the meaning of citizenship, seeking to win equal status. To that end, most of them were willing to accept their integration in the state on the conditions determined by the Jewish majority. However, according to the democratic principle of non-discrimination, they demanded to be treated equally by state institutions and to be recognized as legitimate citizens on an equal footing in the jobs market.

An important expectation of the Arab homeland minority is that Palestinian national rights should be translated into statehood in the territories devoted to that purpose in the UN partition plan from 1947, and later to the territories occupied by Israel in the 1967 war. This was manifested by intensive participation in the Israeli electoral system in order to strengthen those parties that supported peaceful resolution of the Israeli–Palestinian conflict and Israel's surrender of the territories occupied in 1967, while recognizing the PLO as the sole representative of the Palestinian cause. This expectation was translated into the "two states for two peoples" formula promoted by the Communist Party, which for more than two decades was the major party in the Arab community.

As a result of their negative experience with state institutions, and fully aware of the discriminatory policies adopted by the state towards them, the Arab-Palestinian minority began developing new discourses to guarantee them equal status as full citizens. A major demand was to be recognized and respected as an indigenous and national minority – a new formulation of the older demand for integration. Whereas in the past Arab political parties and civic institutions, especially those affiliated with the Communist Party, had emphasized the integrative rights of individual Arab-Palestinian citizens, this new discourse spoke the language of collective rights based on national and cultural grounds. New political parties established in the mid-1980s and in the 1990s brought to the fore Palestinian national affiliation and the ethnic identity of the state as the major factors behind the secondary status of the Arab-Palestinian minority (Ghanem 2001). The discourse of recognition was added to that of allocation and the demand that Israel be transformed from an exclusive ethnic state into a state for all its citizens. Arab-Palestinian leaders raised the expectation that Israel should guarantee the indigenous minority cultural autonomy as a necessary step towards accommodating their basic human and national rights and as a precondition for historical reconciliation.

Minority behavior: from accommodation to contention

The behavior of the minority cannot be fully discussed in this context. This section summarizes the important patterns which have major implications for state–minority relations.

Since the granting of citizenship to non-Jews immediately after the 1948 war was not automatic, and was based not on the principle of the right of return but rather on location, birth, and naturalization, and since many Arab-Palestinian inhabitants did not dare register their names in the population census of November 1948, many were denied citizenship. Therefore, one of the major efforts pursued by members of the minority was to confirm their citizenship, thereby guaranteeing their stay in their homes or nearby as internal refugees. The political response of the majority of the Arab-Palestinian minority in the initial years of the Israeli state could be depicted as accommodative, although one cannot speak of complete quiescence (Lustick 1980). This accommodative behavior by the majority of the Palestinian population was aimed at ensuring the provision of minimal living conditions to the Arab villages and towns that lacked the most basic economic infrastructure (Rekhess 1993).

The majority of the Arab leadership showed toleration of the Jewish character of the state, as long as it was not invoked in exclusive and discriminatory terms. This led to a clear distinction between the political future of the Palestinians in Israel and the rest of the Palestinian people which was reflected in the slogans of the political parties that dominated the Arab political scene (Smooha 2005). This meant differentiating between the legitimacy of state institutions and the illegitimate policies adopted by them and not challenging the Jewish character of the state. That changed in the mid-1980s when the idea of the exclusive Jewish character of Israel started to be promoted by the state.

Concluding remarks

The recapturing of power by the national right-wing parties in Israel has brought to the fore the centrality of the exclusive ethno-national ideology in Israeli society and the unwillingness of most Israeli Jews to compromise for the sake of peace with the Palestinians living under occupation and to promote equal citizenship to all. The reemergence of the ideological right and the declining influence of the left in Israeli society have been matched by the rise in influence of Islamic and national discourses in Arab-Palestinian society. The Islamic movement began mobilizing social forces to support its ideological and political agenda, and secular political voices have also adopted a stronger national discourse (Ghanem and Mustafa 2009). Both Islamic and secular national forces began targeting the ethno-national character of the Israeli state and simultaneously closing the gaps between the demands of the Arab-Palestinian minority in Israel and the entire Palestinian people, including the refugees. Although these changes in the political discourse were not accepted by all parties in Arab society, especially the Communist Party, they became the dominating slogans and the motivating force behind the political conduct of the Arab-Palestinian minority.

These changes have widened the gaps between the expectations of both sides – the Israeli state and the Arab-Palestinian minority. The future-vision documents and the official reaction to them form an important indication as to this growing gap (Jamal 2007a). They were published when it became clear that the Israeli state did not intend to implement the recommendations of the Or Commission report, but rather to render it void of any substance by introducing a counter-policy of penetration, disciplining, surveillance, and control (Jamal 2008a). Furthermore, they were published when it was clear that the Israeli state did not intend to withdraw from the Occupied Territories, but instead to continue its settlement policies, thus closing the door on the two-state solution.

The future-vision documents were formulated by Arab secular civil institutions, led by a new generation of intellectuals. They reflected popular ideas that were not fully expressed by the political parties for reasons that have to do with the legal limitation imposed on political participation through the amendment of the election laws in 2002. The documents, despite the differences between them, define the common ground accepted in Arab-Palestinian society in

Israel, which demands the full democratization of the Israeli state, its de-ethnicization, the accommodation of the collective rights of the Arab-Palestinian minority, and the just resolution of the Palestinian question, including the internal and external refugee problem. These demands are formulated in political and legal terms and framed within international and humanitarian law.

The future-vision documents share several premises. First, they establish the claim that the Arab-Palestinian minority in Israel is an indigenous people, a national minority, and a homeland minority that deserves a special collective regime of rights (Jamal 2008a). Second, all documents take the existence of the State of Israel for granted, albeit not in its current form. All documents view the exclusive ethnic identity of the state as a source of disturbance in majority–minority relations and demand structural transformations of and in the state. Third, all documents demand a special combination of individual and collective rights if the basic rights of the Arab minority are to be genuinely met. Fourth, all documents take into account the tension between the civic and national identity of the Arab community resulting from defining the state in ethnic terms. Aware that neither national community – Jew or Arab – is willing to give up its national identity, the documents seek to strike a balance between civic identity and national affiliation. In this respect, the documents are optimistic regarding a possible combination between national affiliation and liberal-civic culture. They reiterate what has been called liberal nationalism within a civic political entity that enables the various communities within the two nations to enjoy their rights and protect their identities in an atmosphere of tolerance and reconciliation. The examples of Britain, Canada and Spain, where various ethno-cultural and national groups have established political systems and regimes of rights that accommodate their rights and common life within one state, form a source of inspiration.

The horizon of expectations opened by the future-vision documents does not correspond to the policies adopted by Israeli governments in the last decade, especially the radical right-wing government established in Israel in 2009, which has not halted racist legislation aimed at delegitimizing and controlling the Arab-Palestinian minority. The idea of a fusion of horizons and the preliminary demand of mutual recognition does not seem to be on the agenda in Israel today. Therefore, the current situation of cautious quiescence can be viewed only as a temporary condition.

The trend in state–minority relations explicated so far makes it necessary to shift our analysis if we are fully to understand Israeli–Palestinian dynamics. The classical models that accept the separation between the Israeli state and the Occupied Territories and view state–minority relations as an internal Israeli affair must be replaced by models that look at the entire Israeli control system. The developments of the last decade demonstrate that Israeli policy is aimed at normalizing Jewish life, wherever Jews live, including in the settlements in the Occupied Territories. In order to achieve this goal, Israel has been pursuing a policy of fragmentation and ghettoization towards Palestinians, whether citizens or not. Although there are still inconsistencies between the application of this policy in the Occupied Territories and inside the Green Line, the logic of Judaization and, as a result, of de-Palestinization is the same. Israeli policies are leading to two spheres of existence within the areas of the Israeli control system – one Jewish, which is normalized, and one Palestinian, which is an ongoing state of exception.

Notes

1 Central Bureau of Statistics, "The Arab Population in Israel," *Statisti-lite*, no. 27 (2001), p. 9.
2 See www.rikaz.org.

3 The party, which was Arab–Jewish from its initial years in the 1920s, was split into an Arab party and a Jewish party in 1943 as a result of the intensifying conflict between the Zionist movement and the Palestinian national movement.
4 Personal interview with Mtanis Shihadeh, a potential candidate for Balad, 21 February 2010.

References and further reading

Abu-Asbah, K. (2007) *Arab Education in Israel: Dilemmas of a National Minority* (Jerusalem: Floersheimer Institute for Policy Studies).
Al-Haj, M. (1995) *Education, Empowerment and Control: The Case of Arabs in Israel* (Albany: State University of New York Press).
Al-Haj, M. (2003) "Higher Education among the Arabs in Israel: Formal Policy between Empowerment and Control," *Higher Education Policy*, 16, pp. 351–368.
Cohen, H. (2010) *Good Arabs: The Israeli Security Agencies and the Israeli Arabs, 1948–1967* (Berkeley: University of California Press).
Farah, B. (1985) *From Ottomanism to the Jewish State* (Haifa: Al-Carmel).
Ghanem, A. (2001) *The Palestinian-Arab Minority in Israel, 1948–2000: A Political Study* (Albany: State University of New York Press).
Ghanem, A., and Mustafa, M. (2009) *The Palestinians in Israel: The Politics of the Indigenous Minority in the Ethnic State* (Ramallah: Madar).
Ghanem, H. (2009) *Reinventing the Nation: Palestinian Intellectuals in Israel* (Jerusalem: Hebrew University, Magnes Press).
Haidar, A. (1995) *On the Margins: The Arab Population in the Israeli Economy* (London: Hurst).
Hasson, S., and Karayani, M. (eds) (2006) *Barriers to Equality: The Arabs in Israel* (Jerusalem: Floersheimer Institute for Policy Studies).
Jamal, A. (2006) "The Arab Leadership in Israel: Ascendance and Fragmentation," *Journal of Palestine Studies*, 35/2, pp. 6–22.
Jamal, A. (2007a) "Strategies of Minority Struggle for Equality in Ethnic States: Arab Politics in Israel," *Citizenship Studies*, 11/3, pp. 263–82.
Jamal, A. (2007b) "Nationalizing States and the Constitution of 'Hollow Citizenship': Israel and its Palestinian Citizens," *Ethnopolitics*, 6/4, pp. 471–93.
Jamal, A. (2008a) "Future Visions and Current Dilemmas: On the Political Ethos of Palestinian Citizens of Israel," *Israel Studies Forum*, 23/2, pp. 3–28.
Jamal, A. (2008b) "On the Burdens of Racialized Time," in Y. Shenhav and Y. Yonna (eds), *Racism in Israel* (Jerusalem: Hakibbutz Hameuchad and Van Leer), pp. 348–80.
Jamal, A. (2009a) *EU–Israeli Relations and the Status of the Arab Minority* (Tel Aviv: Israeli European Policy Network).
Jamal, A. (2009b) 'The Contradictions of State–Minority Relations in Israel: The Search for Clarifications', *Constellations*, 16/3: 493–508.
Jamal, A. (2010) *Manufacturing Quiet Arabs: The Role of Mizrahi Jews in Israeli Governmental Arabic Newspapers and the Origins of Palestinian Opposition to Them* (Nazareth: I'lam Center).
Jiryis, S. (1976) *The Arabs in Israel* (New York: Monthly Review Press).
Kaufman, I. (1997) *Arab National Communism in the Jewish State* (Gainesville: University Press of Florida).
Kretzmer, D. (1990) *The Legal Status of Arabs in Israel* (Boulder, CO: Westview Press).
Lustick, I. (1980) *Arabs in the Jewish State: Israel's Control of a National Minority* (Austin: University of Texas Press).
McGarry, J., O'Leary, B., and Simeon, R. (2008) "Integration or Accommodation? The Enduring Debate in Conflict Regulation," in S. Choudhry (ed.), *Constitutional Design for Divided Societies: Integration or Accommodation* (Oxford: Oxford University Press), pp 41–88.
Manna, A (ed.) (2008) *Arab Society in Israel, 2: Population, Society, Economy* (Jerusalem: Van Leer Institute and Hakibbutz Hameuchad).
Or Commission (2003) *Report* (Jerusalem: Ministry of Justice).
Pappe, I. (2006) *The Ethnic Cleansing of Palestine* (Oxford: Oneworld).
Reiter, Y. (2009) *National Minority, Regional Majority: Palestinian Arabs versus Jews in Israel* (Syracuse, NY: Syracuse University Press).
Rekhess, E. (1993) *The Arab Minority in Israel: Between Communism and Arab Nationalism* (Tel Aviv: Hakibbutz Hameuchad).

Sa'di, A., and Abu-Lughod, L. (2007) *Palestine, 1948, and the Claims of Memory* (New York: Columbia University Press).

Smooha, S. (2005) *Index of Arab–Jewish Relations in Israel 2004* (Haifa: Jewish–Arab Center, University of Haifa; Jerusalem: Citizens' Accord Forum between Jews and Arabs in Israel; Tel Aviv: Friedrich Ebert Stiftung).

Yiftachel, O. (2006) *Ethnocracy: Land and Identity in Israel/Palestine* (Philadelphia: University of Pennsylvania Press).

Zureik, E. (1979) *The Palestinians in Israel: A Study in Internal Colonialism* (London: Routledge & Kegan Paul).

Part VI
International engagement

25

The United States, 1948–1993[1]

Steven L. Spiegel

The origins of the relationship of the United States to the Israeli–Palestinian conflict emerge in the immediate aftermath of World War II. At the end of the war, Americans were publicly focused on the Holocaust and Jews in the European displaced persons' camps and on the waning British role in Palestine. There was a fundamental dichotomy in American attitudes towards the emerging conflict in the region. The public and Congress were generally more sympathetic towards the Zionist movement. The government, especially the national security bureaucracy (National Security Council, Defense and State departments, and the intelligence community), on the whole saw the nascent dispute in the context of American policy towards the Arabs and even the Muslim world.

For the national security officials, the problem was a matter of resolving the internal dispute between Arabs and Jews in Palestine so that the United States would not be blamed or held responsible for any resolution the Arabs did not approve. This process came into clear focus in the summer of 1946. A group composed of British and American agents from the Morrison–Grady committee proposed a cantonization of Palestine into semi-autonomous Arab and Jewish regions which was opposed by both Jews and Arabs (Foreign Relations 1946: 667–8, 676). American Arabists saw it as a good way to avoid trouble, and President Truman, at first, appeared to sympathize with it. The plan, which would have meant extending British control, was considered acceptable to the security establishment.

None of the maneuvering was designed with a particular sentiment in favor of the Palestinian Arabs, but with a view towards assuaging negative Arab perspectives in the region. In order to prevent the cantonization idea from being accepted, the Zionists proposed for the first time the partition of Palestine between the two peoples inhabiting the territory. In a speech in October, Truman seemed to acquiesce when he acknowledged that the American public would accept partition.

In early 1947 Britain announced its intention to withdraw from the Mandate. The security bureaucracy was skeptical of the ensuing UN Special Committee on Palestine (UNSCOP) proposal that emerged in September 1947, after three months of deliberation, in which all eleven UNSCOP members agreed on the termination of the Mandate. Seven members endorsed the partition of Palestine into two states – one Jewish and one Arab (Jerusalem was to become an international city). Three members endorsed an independent federal state, and one member country abstained. Despite Arab efforts to torpedo the plan, the United States under Truman voted in its favor.

The security establishment immediately set about making the implementation of the UNSCOP proposal for an Arab and Jewish state, with the internationalization of Jerusalem, impossible. It convinced the president to impose an arms embargo on the area, arguing that the United States should not contribute to violence, knowing full well that the Arab side had access to European, especially British, arms. It also set about convincing him to accept a delay in creating the two new states out of the former Mandate on the grounds that, given Arab opposition, the partition plan could not be implemented in the short term.

The result was an announcement in late March 1948 that the United States supported delaying partition in favor of an international trusteeship of the Palestinian Mandate, which would in effect have meant the continuation of British rule. Both Jews and Arabs opposed the idea; their inability to agree on an American-sponsored UN call for a truce further reduced the likelihood of the partition's success.

Trusteeship was widely viewed as a retreat from the General Assembly's endorsement of partition and as further evidence of American oscillation. Most important, it was generally assumed that trusteeship would have to be enforced by a UN peace force, for which there was little enthusiasm (Foreign Relations 1948: 832). The British were opposed and American military readiness for this task was virtually non-existent. Thus, the notion of trusteeship languished. When the British withdrew on May 15 and Israel declared its independence, the United States was the first country to offer recognition.

None of these decisions was made out of a consideration for Palestinian concerns, interests, or even rights. Those sympathetic to partition, including at times the president, believed passionately both in the Zionist cause and in efforts to create a Jewish democratic state, especially in the wake of the Holocaust. Those who argued that American national security would be harmed by the creation of a Jewish state, given the likelihood of severe Arab opposition, were also not concerned about the Palestinian cause per se, but about bringing stability to the region and advancing American interests with the Arab states. Few, indeed, argued the case that the Palestinians either deserved a state of their own or deserved to control the entire area the British were vacating.

The Arab states attacked Israel immediately. Once the war began and the refugee crisis emerged, the president and most of the national security bureaucracy expressed sympathy for the Palestinians. Hence, the United States supported UN General Assembly Resolution 194 on the refugees, which recommended that "the refugees wishing to return to their homes and live at peace with their neighbors should be permitted to do so at the earliest practicable date, and compensation should be paid for the property of those choosing not to return and for loss of or damage to property." In one note to an American diplomat, the president stated bluntly, "I am rather disgusted with the manner in which the Jews are approaching the refugee problem" (Foreign Relations 1947: 1072–4).

The United States supported the Bernadotte Plan developed by the UN mediator before his assassination by Jewish extremists during the Arab–Israeli war. It fundamentally proposed that Israel relinquish the Negev to the Arabs in return for territories gained during the war (Foreign Relations 1948: 1152–4). Instead, the armistice lines at the end of the war became Israel's borders (although these boundaries were not recognized by its neighbors) and included a larger area of Palestine than had been allotted to the Jewish state under the UNSCOP plan, plus half of Jerusalem. The bulk of the originally proposed Palestinian Arab state was captured by neighboring Arab countries. Egypt occupied the Gaza Strip, and Jordan annexed the West Bank and the eastern half of Jerusalem. (Jordan's acquisitions were also unrecognized by her neighbors and represented a larger slice of the envisioned Palestinian state than Israel gained.) With these precarious arrangements, the Middle East settled into a new, uncertain status quo.

Yet, the American national security bureaucracy was unsatisfied. As a consequence of UN maneuvering over the Bernadotte Plan, a Palestine Conciliation Commission was established consisting of the United States, France, and Turkey. This commission held a conference in Lausanne, Switzerland, in the spring of 1949, attended by key Arab states and Israel, in an attempt to reach a peace settlement. The United States pressured Israel to compromise on territory and/or refugees to facilitate negotiations. For the State Department, and even the president, the original boundaries of the partition plan, not the additional territories Israel now occupied, were the basis for negotiations (Foreign Relations 1949: 1073). Controversy over the Bernadotte Plan had by no means abated. Discussions continued with the Israelis, and the Lausanne talks dragged on for most of 1949. In the end, Israel did agree under American pressure to accept 100,000 Arab refugees, but most American diplomats believed that it should have offered to accept at least 250,000, which was still less than one-third the total number (ibid.: 1062). In the end, the talks disbanded in failure. It was to be the last Arab–Israeli peace conference until a one-day meeting in Geneva in December 1973.

The Truman administration, which pushed the British to accept a greater number of Jewish refugees in the aftermath of World War II, approved the UN partition plan, and was immediately forthcoming in recognizing Israel, is often credited with virtually creating the Jewish state. In fact, its support was quite limited. The US government did not aid the fledgling Jewish state militarily, did not always back Israel at the UN, and provided only minimal economic aid. It did, however, offer moral support and did not interfere with the establishment of programs such as Israel bonds in 1952. But the Truman administration remained ambivalent and uncertain about the Arab–Israeli problem as it struggled to adjust to the Cold War, from Berlin to Korea.

American policy was now set until the 1967 war. It focused on the substantial return of Palestinian refugees and the notion that the basis for discussion was the UN partition plan itself. This policy did not go as far as the Arabs demanded, since they did not recognize the right of Israel to exist, and the issue rarely received much attention from American policy-makers. To make matters more complicated, reducing Israeli territory established by the armistice of 1949, which included its gains from the 1948 war, became a more difficult policy to pursue as time went on.

The Eisenhower administration entered office preoccupied with the possibility that the Soviet Union would make inroads into the Arab world, begin to threaten American interests vis-à-vis oil, and gain influence in the region. In this vision, Israel was a burden, and its very existence interfered with attempts to advance American interests. The Arabs at first continued to support America over the Soviets in the Cold War, but came no closer to achieving a Palestinian state.

During August 1955, in an unusual display of interest in the Palestinian refugees, Secretary of State John Foster Dulles delivered a speech to the Council on Foreign Relations in New York, in which he revealed the conclusion of hitherto secret discussions with the British on a peace plan. He identified three major issues in the dispute: Arab refugees (later known as the Palestinian refugee issue), the "pall of fear" on both sides (later known as the peace issue), and the absence of permanent boundaries between Israel and her neighbors (later known as the territorial issue). Dulles advocated refugee resettlement and repatriation, water development, permanent frontiers, and security guarantees. But, in an indication of how little attention was paid to the Palestinian problem per se, he talked about Arab, rather than Palestinian, refugees. All these lofty efforts were sublimated by the Suez crisis and Sinai campaign in 1956.

The peace efforts that the administration pursued were directed towards enhancing American relations with the Arab world and dislodging the Negev from Israel so that the Egyptians and Saudis could travel between their countries without trespassing on Israeli soil. The administration also believed that the British and French, both post-colonial powers, were a hindrance. The Eisenhower administration pressed Britain to sign, as quickly as possible, an agreement with the Egyptians to withdraw its troops from the Suez Canal. This withdrawal was realized in the spring of 1956. By then, the Egyptians had concluded an arms deal with the Czechs (acting on behalf of the USSR), creating the Russian breakthrough with the Arab world that Eisenhower had feared. All efforts to dissuade Nasser from continuing with the deal, including the offer of aid to build the Aswan Dam, failed.

In keeping with the limited American support for Israel under Eisenhower, the administration suspended aid when it considered Israel had overreacted to Arab attacks – for example, after the Qibya raid in 1953. Eisenhower refused to provide military assistance and, in the aftermath of the Suez crisis, threatened to suspend economic aid to Israel. Although he did not object when Paris and Jerusalem established a close alliance, when the Israelis and French colluded with the British in an effort to overthrow Nasser during the Suez crisis, the president voted against them at the UN and put pressure on them to end military action.

In early 1957, Eisenhower went so far as to threaten to suspend all private aid to Israel (public aid was already suspended during the 1956 war) if it would not withdraw from the Sinai and Gaza – territories that it had captured during the fighting. Israel could not withstand these threats and was compelled to comply, settling for a temporary civility on the Egyptian frontier that would last a decade. Only in Eisenhower's second term would economic aid increase by a marginal degree under the program known as the Eisenhower Doctrine to which Israel was allowed to adhere. This program was designed to stop the ideologies of both the communists and radical nationalists such as Nasser from spreading in the region. There was still no American program for dealing with the Palestinian question, then still known as the refugee issue.

It was John F. Kennedy who broke new ground by pursuing a more direct policy in trying to begin the process of solving the refugee problem. As early as February 1957, a full four years before he assumed the presidency, Kennedy addressed a meeting of the National Conference of Christians and Jews and said, "Let those refugees be repatriated to Israel at the earliest practical date who are sincerely willing to live at peace with their neighbors, to accept the Israeli government with an attitude of *civiatus filia*... The refugee camps should be closed" (Spiegel 1985: 111).

While running for president in the summer of 1960, Kennedy spoke to an Israeli newspaper and stressed the importance of the refugee issue. After entering the White House, he appointed Joseph Johnson, president of the Carnegie Endowment, to produce resolutions on the refugee issue that might be considered at the United Nations. Johnson embarked on a fact-finding mission and on several discussions, but met with a lack of interest on both sides. The Arab states totally opposed, and the Israelis were skeptical of, a "pilot project" he envisioned involving what he called a "relatively small number of refugees" (Spiegel 1985: 57).

Kennedy's more important long-term impact was his offer to sell Hawk anti-aircraft missiles to Israel. The sale arose in response to the continuing Soviet military aid to the Egyptians, which the administration believed could tip the arms balance in Cairo's favor. In terms of the American–Israeli relationship, however, this assistance was a critical step in forging a new policy that broke with the earlier taboo about providing military assistance to Israel.

The Johnson administration made this change in American–Israeli relations clear when in 1966 it agreed to sell Skyhawk jets to the Jewish state. In 1968, towards the end of his presidency, Johnson agreed to sell the more sophisticated Phantom jets to Israel – a major step in the gradual intensification of American military assistance to the Jewish state. But the major event of the Johnson presidency affecting American policy towards both Arabs and Israelis was the Six Day War, won with French, not American, arms. It was only in the aftermath of this event that the United States for the first time confronted the Palestinian question. The Johnson administration, preoccupied with Vietnam, found itself engaged in an unanticipated international crisis when Nasser ordered the international force in the Sinai to withdraw precipitously in May 1967, and Arab armies began to encircle Israel.

Despite Johnson's affinity for the Jewish state, his administration, increasingly bogged down in Vietnam, reacted tepidly to Israel's plight. In response to the Egyptian embargo of the Straits of Tiran, Johnson lamely proposed a "Red Sea Regatta" that would involve an international flotilla sailing through the straits, which would hopefully prevent any unilateral Israeli action. This diplomatic intervention seemed unlikely to succeed. The Johnson administration's efforts began to appear half-baked, an impression encouraged by private Israeli talks with the Defense Department. The West as a whole seemed helpless to prevent impending hostilities, as every diplomatic effort thus far had failed (Spiegel 1985: 137).

The result was an Israeli preemption on June 5, 1967, in which Israel captured the Sinai from the Egyptians, East Jerusalem and the West Bank from the Jordanians, and the Golan Heights from Syria. The impact on the Palestinian question was profound. The Palestinian Liberation Organization (PLO) had been organized at the Arab summit of 1964. It was at first a tool of Egyptian policy to thwart its Arab enemies and to challenge Israel. After 1967 the charismatic Yasser Arafat assumed control of the PLO. In contrast to his predecessor, Ahmed Shoukary, who was both ineffective and a tool of the Arab states, Arafat was independent and a challenge to the Israelis.

The new dynamic could be seen as early as March 1968, when a Palestinian force defeated the Israelis at Karameh in Jordan. There followed a round of Palestinian violence worldwide, with airplane hijackings and attacks on civilians, especially Israelis. These steps raised the profile of the PLO under Arafat, but in ways that often led to greater American opposition to Palestinian objectives. The PLO had become a challenge to American interests, making it more difficult to pursue a policy in which a Palestinian state – probably as part of Jordan – was at least contemplated. Indeed, American opposition to terrorism of any kind made US understanding of Palestinian methods almost impossible, an attitude exacerbated by Arafat's close relations with Moscow.

These early steps came to a head in the Nixon administration in September 1970, when the Palestinians under Arafat challenged the rule of King Hussein in Jordan and sought to take over the country, which already had a majority Palestinian population. The Palestinians were defeated despite a fruitless Syrian invasion, as King Hussein's forces thwarted the Palestinian attacks with the not-so-quiet support of the United States and Israel.

Yasser Arafat and the PLO moved to a new base in Lebanon. In the civil war which began there in 1975, they played an exacerbating role. From the American point of view, the PLO was a dangerous terrorist organization, its power and influence seeming to grow despite its defeat in Jordan. To the Nixon administration, with its concentration on the global balance of power, the significance of the Arab–Israeli dispute was the problems it might cause in Washington's relationship with Moscow. Egypt's war of attrition along the Suez Canal in 1969 and 1970 threatened a direct Soviet–American confrontation. In response, the administration was divided. On the one hand, Secretary of State William Rogers believed that diplomacy should take precedence in the American approach to the conflict, leading to tensions with the government of Golda Meir over his emphasis on concessions by Israel and the slower pace of arms sales advocated by his department. On the other hand, Nixon's national security advisor Henry

Kissinger argued that US backing of Israel should intensify until the Arabs understood that they could gain their territories back only by working closely with the United States.

As the years passed, the focus of the Nixon administration was to prevent another deadly war like that of June 1967, which its leaders believed would inevitably occur as a consequence of Israeli preemption. The focus was on maintaining stability through assuring both Israel's strength and restraint. In this regard, the USA focused on the potential threat that Egypt and Syria might pose given their close relationship with the Soviet Union and their repeated threats to go to war with Israel to regain the territories they lost in 1967 (Nixon 1970: 558). The Palestinians were considered a nuisance, the Egyptians and Syrians central to US concerns.

By contrast, the Israelis were preoccupied with the Palestinian threat and withdrew intelligence assets from Egypt and Syria in order to concentrate on Palestinian terrorism. To some extent, the Americans had a better sense of the actual threat Israel faced, since they were intent upon maintaining the regional balance of power. The administration, however, was incorrect in thinking that Israel might strike first if it perceived an Arab threat looming. Instead, uncharacteristically, the Israelis failed to see the developing peril. The result was the Yom Kippur War of October 1973 initiated by Egypt and Syria under their leaders, Anwar Sadat of Egypt and Hafez Assad of Syria. Though initially demonstrating a surprisingly strong front, the Arab states were defeated by Israeli military gains at the end of the war. Israel's comeback was facilitated by a huge airlift worth $2.2 billion, providing a dramatic intensification in American aid to Israel. But it would soon be clear that the USA expected a trade-off from Jerusalem in the shape of new diplomatic concessions.

In the aftermath of the conflict, new stress was placed on making progress in the Arab–Israeli peace process. American diplomacy was deeply affected by the Arab oil embargo and Israel's initially poor showing. In this regard, the Palestinians were considered neither important nor central, despite the PLO's frequent terrorist attacks. In the wake of the October 1973 war, the new secretary of state, Henry Kissinger, pursued an activist shuttle diplomacy, mediating limited disengagement agreements between Israel and Egypt (January 1974) and Israel and Syria (May 1974).

A key question emerged. As early as late 1969, the Rogers Plan (named after Nixon's first secretary of state, William Rogers) assumed a Jordanian return to the territories Israel had captured in 1967 on the West Bank. The Jordanians had chosen not to attack Israel. The two countries that had initiated the attack, Egypt and Syria, had been awarded limited territorial gains in the territories captured in 1967 as a consequence of their early military successes at the outset of the war, even if these advances were later reversed. It made sense that Jordan would receive a similar slice of territory in the West Bank. Yet, the new Israeli prime minister, Yitzhak Rabin, led a weak government, and concessions to the Jordanians on the West Bank were controversial. He preferred, like Anwar Sadat of Egypt, to move towards further efforts in the Sinai. The result was the loss of an opportunity to establish the precedent of Jordan's return to the West Bank – an opportunity that would not return (Quandt 1977: 255). Without realizing it, the United States and Israel had made a fateful decision they neither recognized nor sought.

Instead, in an Arab summit meeting in October 1974 in Rabat, Morocco, the PLO was anointed "the sole legitimate representative of the Palestinian people." An independent Palestinian state was to be established, according to the summit meeting, "on any Palestinian soil that is liberated" from Israeli occupation (Spiegel 1985: 228). The tide had turned, and, to the astonishment and consternation of both the United States and Israel, even Arab moderates had supported the PLO.

After months of wrangling and conflict, Israel and Egypt finally reached a second disengagement accord in August of 1975. This breakthrough was achieved only after the Ford administration conducted an extensive "reassessment" of American policy towards the Middle East. The exercise was intended to signal to Israel that American support was not inevitable and emerged as a result of Ford's frustration with the Rabin government's stance in negotiations over the prospective disengagement accord with Egypt. In the end, Cairo and Jerusalem both signaled that they sought disengagement, but the episode highlighted the tension in the US–Israeli relationship.

Most important in terms of future American policy towards the Palestinians, in a signed Memorandum of Understanding between Israel and the United States accompanying the disengagement deal mediated by Secretary of State Henry Kissinger, the US pledged not to "recognize or negotiate" with the PLO as long as the organization "does not recognize Israel's right to exist and does not accept Security Council resolutions 242 and 338" (Spiegel 1985: 302). This stipulation effectively assured that the PLO would not participate in negotiations. UN Security Council Resolution 242, after the 1967 war, referred to the Palestinians only as refugees. There was no mention of Palestine, let alone a Palestinian state.

With the victory of Jimmy Carter in the 1976 elections, a new approach was initiated beyond Kissinger's shuttle diplomacy which had sought interim agreements between Israel and the Arab states. The Carter team instead wanted a comprehensive settlement of the Arab–Israeli dispute, including the Palestinian question, which it saw as essential in its own right and important for alleviating the oil crisis that had developed after the 1973 war. The administration's view was that settling the dispute would cause opposition towards the United States to abate and thus end the threat to the flow of oil from the region. This attitude was to some extent a throwback to the late 1940s, when it was assumed that American diplomacy favorable to the Arabs would be amply rewarded. But the Carter administration became the first in which key figures actually seemed genuinely to care about the Palestinians.

For the new president, in particular, but also for some of his aides, support for Palestinian rights became a means of moving beyond old contentions such as Vietnam and the civil rights movement, and instead identifying with Third World aspirations. Carter had not only supported the Vietnam War but had been slow to join the civil rights movement. By resolving the Palestinian dilemma once and for all, the new Democratic administration would show the world that America had truly been born again, a seminal experience for the president himself.

Throughout his term, Carter saw no contradiction between his commitment to Palestinian rights and his oft-expressed support for Israel, but partisan supporters of Israel, and Israel itself, did not always see it that way. Early in his presidency, Carter made a number of statements that suggested that the United States was now sympathetic to the establishment of a Palestinian state – for example, "There has to be a homeland provided for the Palestinian refugees." He muddied the waters in attempting to explain his position by subsequently saying: "I think some provision has got to be made for the Palestinians, in the framework of the nation of Jordan or by some other means" (Carter 1977: 387). Other than affirming a new US interest in the Palestinian question, his public statements left the issue even cloudier. Was Carter advocating a Palestinian state, a province within a Jordanian federation, or something else entirely? When he shook hands with the PLO representative to the UN a couple of months into his administration and argued subsequently that there could not be "any reasonable hope for settlement of the Middle East question without a homeland for the Palestinians," the Israelis and their supporters were left astounded, and the administration spent months trying to undo the political damage at home (ibid.: 842, 845).

But Carter was indeed determined. He understood that the PLO might have a problem accepting Resolution 242, so he and Secretary of State Cyrus Vance made statements suggesting that the American position would be more flexible than it had been under Kissinger

(Carter 1977: 1460; Vance 1983: 188–9). For example, in one such statement, Carter declared that his administration "would immediately commence plans" to talk with the PLO if it accepted *either* Israel's right to exist *or* UN Security Council resolutions 242 and 338 as the basis for negotiations. The administration even made it clear that a provisional acceptance of 242, with the understanding that the Palestinians did not accept the resolution's limitation to just refugees, would be acceptable as well. In addition, there were secret approaches to try to encourage the PLO to accept a more positive approach.

Even Carter's acceptance of their interpretation of the 1948 war proved insufficient for the Palestinians. The PLO rejected the president's overtures. At one point, Arafat sent a secret message to Washington through a prominent American educator whom the administration was using as an intermediary. The PLO chief said that his organization would accept the American initiative only in return for guaranteed American backing of a Palestinian state. Even the Carter administration could not go that far. Wracked by internal dissension, and under pressure from President Assad of Syria, who feared that a major PLO concession would diminish his own influence, Arafat and the PLO finally reiterated their refusal to accept UN Resolution 242. By now, the new prime minister of Israel, Menachem Begin, had made it clear that he intended to expand settlements in the West Bank, which was a frontal challenge to the entire Carter approach.

On October 1, 1977, the administration accepted a Russian initiative for a joint statement. In this document, the United States accepted for the first time the phrase "*legitimate rights of the Palestinian people*," once viewed as Arab code for displacing Israel with a Palestinian state (Vance 1983: 199). Obviously, the administration did not take that point of view, but the document was welcomed by the PLO, denounced by Israel, and vilified by many in Congress, and ultimately the administration recanted.

By this time, Egyptian leader Anwar Sadat, who was ultimately prepared to accept a separate agreement with Israel, had had enough, beginning to think that Carter's maneuvering and condescension to Syria would never bear results in the peace process. Thus, Sadat traveled unexpectedly to Israel on November 19, 1977, and delivered a dramatic address to the Israeli Knesset before a worldwide audience of hundreds of millions. Sadat had single-handedly changed the agenda from a comprehensive agreement with emphasis on the Syrians and Palestinians to once again a concentration on the Egyptians. Over the next year and a half, it was the Egyptians who took center stage.

When talks were unproductive between Israel and Egypt, despite Sadat's visit to Jerusalem, Carter invited both Begin and Sadat to Camp David in September 1978. After thirteen tense days, an agreement on a framework for a peace treaty between the two countries was reached. Begin acceded to Sadat's demand that something be done on the Palestinian question, and yet the resulting autonomy accord provided many loopholes in the Israelis' favor. On the one hand, this document provided a fig leaf to the Egyptians to sign what basically amounted to a separate peace treaty with Israel. On the other hand, it also detailed a framework that would later become deeply influential on the Oslo Accords fifteen years later, in 1993. Envisioned at Camp David was the solution that Egypt, Israel, Jordan, and the representatives of the Palestinian people would participate "in negotiations on the resolution of the Palestinian problem in all its aspects." There were to be three stages. In the first, Egypt and Israel would agree on full autonomy. In the second phase, Egypt, Israel, and Jordan would agree "on the modalities for establishing the elected self-governing authority in the West Bank and Gaza." In the third stage, a self-governing authority or administrative council would be established and inaugurated, and a five-year transitional period would begin.

The parties never reached even the first stage of the autonomy agreement because the Palestinians and Jordanians rejected the Camp David Accords, leaving Egypt in the uncomfortable position of negotiating alone. By this time, the Begin government feared that it had been trapped at Camp David into a process that would ultimately create a Palestinian state. The Carter administration was left in the last busy two years of its term to try to contemplate amending UN Resolution 242 so that it would refer to Palestinians as more than refugees and to try to make progress on the issue of settlements and Jerusalem that had deeply disrupted Camp David. In the end, Begin was able to withstand pressures on settlements at Camp David and its aftermath, and autonomy talks withered on the vine. The PLO had once again lost a major opportunity in American eyes, because it did not accept the autonomy framework as a basis for talks leading to a Palestinian state of some kind, even if it might be at least initially constituted within Jordan.

It is often forgotten that it was the Carter administration that is responsible for Israel and Egypt receiving more aid annually than any other two countries in the world. As part of the tense negotiations for an Egyptian–Israeli peace treaty, finally signed in March 1979, both countries received large amounts of aid (Carter received congressional approval for $5 billion in supplemental economic and military assistance to the two countries) to cover the expenses of signing the treaty (Spiegel 1985: 372). Israel was forced to move three large airbases from the Sinai to the Negev in order to comply with the treaty, and Egypt was recompensed for aid lost when other Arab countries that opposed the agreement cut her off. In the years that followed, the two countries would receive a similarly substantial amount of the US foreign aid budget annually as a means of keeping the peace between Cairo and Jerusalem – an expensive but highly successful enterprise wherein Israel has always received 60 percent or more of the funds.

The next administration, under Ronald Reagan, had little sympathy for the Palestinians' cause and was concerned much more with the terrorist issue, harming Palestinians in the process. However, when Israel attacked Lebanon in June 1982 in an attempt to stop the Palestinians based there from continuing their attacks against Israelis, the Reagan administration reacted angrily to an Israeli intervention it saw as dangerous, destabilizing, and an overreaction, especially when Israeli forces headed for Beirut. Once again, the Arab question loomed larger than the Palestinian issue.

By September 1, the administration was concerned about an impending Arab summit on September 6 and the denouement of the war, which had seen the Palestinian leadership forced to withdraw to Tunis. With the PLO at a maximum point of weakness, the Israeli invasion had, to some extent, backfired. The administration, under new Secretary of State George Shultz, was determined that the United States address the Palestinian question as a way of satisfying the Arab states. As a result, President Reagan delivered a surprise speech on the Middle East known as the Reagan Plan, in which he presented American ideas on the final shape of a Palestinian settlement. Barely mentioning Lebanon, the president rejected both an independent Palestinian state and Israeli sovereignty over the West Bank and Gaza. Instead, he argued, "self-government by the Palestinians of the West Bank and Gaza in association with Jordan offers the best chance for a durable, just, and lasting peace." The president also called upon Israel to freeze all settlement activity in the West Bank. At the last minute, he personally added a paragraph suggesting that Israel could not be expected to return to the narrow, indefensible frontiers it had endured during the nineteen years before 1967 (Reagan 2004: 452).

The plan was undiplomatically rejected by Prime Minister Begin and his cabinet because it would have prevented Israeli sovereignty over the West Bank and Gaza and differed from their interpretation of the Camp David Accords. The Israelis probably need not have bothered. The plan itself required cooperation between Arafat and King Hussein, who had the poorest of relations since their mini-war in September 1970. In April 1983, Hussein announced his failure to reach agreement with Arafat on a joint approach to the Palestinian question. Despite secret

American commitments, he was not prepared to enter negotiations without an accord with the PLO chief.

The program envisioned by the Reagan Plan had collapsed and, for most of the rest of the administration, a new series of steps brought the USA and Israel closer than ever before. A novel strategic cooperation initiative was established between them leading to closer cooperation between the two countries to promote Israel as a "strategic asset" against the Soviet Union and its allies in the region. The USA also came to the aid of Israel when it suffered from rampant inflation in the mid-1980s. And Washington under Reagan added another stipulation for dialogue with the PLO, in addition to those agreed in 1975 between the Israelis and the Ford administration. The US now declared that it would deal with the organization only if it renounced terrorism (Miller 2008: 55).

Meanwhile, the PLO leadership settled in Tunisia, Arafat lost influence in the West Bank and Gaza, and the Israelis grew confident that some kind of self-government could emerge there within the contours of Israeli sovereignty. Arafat's failure to reach agreement with King Hussein led the Reagan administration to lose interest in his people's plight, in part out of anger at what they saw as his continuing negative behavior.

By 1987, any notion of a peace settlement was very limited. One of the ideas that did emerge was for a more constricted international conference than had usually been envisioned favoring the role of Jordan and Israel and negotiated between King Hussein and Israeli Foreign Minister Shimon Peres. Prime Minister Yitzhak Shamir vetoed it in April 1987, without much attention from the Reagan administration. This was to be the last opportunity for a Jordanian–Israeli deal over the West Bank. Instead, on December 9, 1987, an auto accident in Gaza ignited the first *Intifada*, a widespread uprising in both Gaza and the West Bank. It woke the Reagan administration from its slumber and led to increased American diplomatic activity on the Palestinian question.

As a consequence, in early 1988 Shultz presented a convoluted set of concepts that came to be known as the Shultz Plan, where he combined elements of the autonomy proposal in the Camp David Accords, the Reagan Plan, and several other ideas that had emerged in previous months, such as an international conference. Shultz now proposed to begin negotiations hosted by the five permanent members of the UN Security Council, with all parties attending accepting UN resolutions 242 and 338 and renouncing violence. The Palestinians were to be represented by a joint Jordanian–Palestinian delegation, which would negotiate the terms of a three-year transitional period for the territories. As Shamir had vetoed Peres's vehement support for an international conference the year before, there was no diplomatic alternative when the Palestinian *Intifada* broke out several months later. The Israeli right had outsmarted itself.

Although the Shultz Plan itself was stillborn, a movement began to promote direct PLO–American discussions. Talks were initiated within the PLO itself, where particular elements were becoming increasingly interested in American involvement as a way of pressuring Israel. In this belief, the Palestinians were entirely overly optimistic.

In the transition between the Reagan and Bush administrations, Arafat made a number of statements intended to satisfy the United States and finally did so in December 1988, when, at a press conference in Geneva, the Palestinian leader stated, "Our desire for peace is a strategy and not an interim tactic." His key comment was that the 1964 Charter of the PLO was *caduc*, a French word meaning "null and void," which suggested that the offending statement in the Charter would no longer be seen as rejecting the right of Israel to exist.[2] This was not sufficient for the Israelis, but it did satisfy George Shultz, who made matters easier for the incoming administration of George H. W. Bush by accepting that Arafat had renounced violence and that the United States would begin discussions with the PLO (Miller 2008: 85).

The approach of the Bush administration was in some ways a throwback to that of Carter in its profound opposition to Israeli settlement-building and its enthusiasm for moving the Israeli–Palestinian peace process forward. The president and Secretary of State Baker began a quiet dialogue with the Palestinians which was aborted in 1990 when Arafat refused to denounce a terrorist attack by a fringe organization within the PLO. The United States was back to square one.

A newly formed Israeli government in June 1990 was even more negative towards the peace process than its predecessor, but on August 2, 1990, before it could take any action or begin discussions with the Bush administration, Saddam Hussein invaded Kuwait, deflecting American attention for several months thereafter. As part of its diplomacy leading up to the Gulf War, the United States promised that, following Saddam Hussein's ousting from Kuwait, it would pursue a more active peace process. This action encouraged several Arab states to join the American coalition.

True to its word, the administration set out in mid-1991 to accomplish a long-contemplated international conference to begin a new peace initiative. As part of its preparations to sponsor an international conference, the Bush administration insisted on Israeli forbearance on settlements in the West Bank. The USA had provided aid to Israel on the eve of the Gulf War in the form of anti-missile systems to encourage Israel not to enter into the war and thereby to prevent Arab participation on America's side from collapsing. As a result, Israel did not retaliate, even after Iraqi missiles hit its territory.

With an influx of Soviet Jews arriving in Israel, the administration was worried that many of these immigrants would settle in the West Bank and that the Arab parties would not attend the conference. It therefore refused to provide the $10 billion in housing loan guarantees that the Israeli government had requested until settlement expansion was stopped. The Shamir government, however, refused to stop settlement expansion. American–Israeli relations deteriorated sharply, but the international conference went ahead.

The Madrid conference in October 1991, co-chaired by the US and Soviet leaders, Bush and Mikhail Gorbachev, is generally regarded as a major success. It included the major parties to the Arab–Israeli conflict in the region with the Palestinian representatives "linked" to the Jordanian delegation. One of the results was to create a series of meetings with Israelis by Lebanese, Syrian, Jordanian, and non-PLO Palestinian delegations in Washington over the ensuing years. These talks continued, especially between the Israelis and Palestinians, until they were displaced by the Oslo Accords of September 1993. Meanwhile, multilateral talks that emerged from Madrid established as one of its five committees a group that dealt with the Palestinian refugee issue. The Israelis under Shamir boycotted these meetings, but when Yitzhak Rabin was elected in 1992 he joined the talks and made advances in establishing a basis for Palestinian compensation before the multilaterals petered out in the middle of the decade.

Other multilateral committees dealt with arms control and regional security, economic development, water, and the environment. It was the conflict between Egypt and Israel in the arms control group over the handling of Israel's purported nuclear force that led to the weakening and ultimately the demise of most projects within the multilateral framework. Once again, a regional issue clouded potential developments on American policy toward the Israelis and Palestinians.

By the end of the first Bush administration, US policy was a far cry from the confused American policy at the emergence of the State of Israel. The United States was finally center stage in moves towards an Israeli–Palestinian settlement. Instead of Israel being treated as an unwelcome new arrival, the Israeli government was viewed as a partner, a critical regional participant, and at times a nuisance. But even in difficult circumstances, Israel was seen as a powerful regional player – a dramatic change in just over forty years.

As far as the Palestinians were concerned, the United States was no longer just the largest contributor to UNRWA (the UN Relief and Works Agency), responsible for providing the refugees with minimal sustenance. Instead, it was focusing more directly on the Palestinians as part of the solution to the conflict, not merely as the problem. The *intifada* at the end of the 1980s had had a major impact. Israel's constant settlement-building had convinced many pol-icy-makers that it could not be trusted to reach an accommodation with the Palestinians alone, at least until the Labor Party under Yitzhak Rabin returned to power in 1992.

The stage was set for a genuine peace process, but even Madrid and the bilateral committees it had established had not delineated a path for moving forward. In American eyes, the Israelis and Palestinians had advanced immeasurably since 1948, but there had still been no break-through in the conflict.

A potentially promising situation on the Arab–Israeli front seemed to exist a year after Madrid. The Cold War was over and the United States had just won a major victory in the Per-sian Gulf War. The Madrid conference was the first major international conference attended in one way or another by all primary parties in the dispute. Promising multilateral talks had been established to address key issues. Although bilateral talks in Washington were not making prog-ress, the Arab world was beginning to adjust to the implications of Saddam Hussein's defeat. Who would take the next step was the challenge the Bush administration bequeathed when it departed the White House in January 1993.

Notes

1 The author wishes to thank his UCLA student research team, headed by Neda Afsharian, for its valuable assistance in the preparation of this and the following essay.
2 R. Tempest, "PLO's Charter is out of Date, Arafat Declares," *Los Angeles Times*, 3 May 1989; avai-lable at: http://articles.latimes.com/1989-05-03/news/mn-2470_1_plo-leader-yasser-arafat-palestine-liberation-organization.

References and further reading

Bickerton, I. J., and Klausner, C. L. (2007) *A History of the Arab–Israeli Conflict* (Upper Saddle River, NJ: Prentice Hall).

Carter, J. (1977) *Public Papers of the President* (Washington, DC: US Government Printing Office).

Eisenberg, L. Z., and Caplan, C. (2010) *Negotiating Arab–Israeli Peace: Patterns, Problems, Possibilities* (2nd ed., Bloomington: Indiana University Press).

Foreign Relations of the United States (1946) *Diplomatic Papers* (Washington, DC: US Government Printing Office).

Foreign Relations of the United States (1947) *Diplomatic Papers* (Washington, DC: US Government Printing Office).

Foreign Relations of the United States (1948) *Diplomatic Papers* Washington, DC: US Government Printing Office.

Foreign Relations of the United States (1949) *Diplomatic Papers* (Washington, DC: US Government Printing Office).

Miller, A. D. (2008) *The Much Too Promised Land: America's Elusive Search for Arab–Israeli Peace* (New York: Bantam Books).

Nixon, R. M. (1970) *Public Papers of the President* (Washington, DC: US Government Printing Office).

Offner, A. (2002) *Another Such Victory: President Truman and the Cold War, 1945–1953* (Stanford, CA: Stanford University Press).

Quandt, W. B. (1977) *Decade of Decisions* (Los Angeles: University of California Press).

Quandt, W. B. (2001) *Peace Process: American Diplomacy and the Arab–Israeli Conflict since 1967* (3rd ed., Washington, DC: Brookings Institution).

Reagan, R. (2004) *Reagan: A Life in Letters*, ed. K. K. Skinner, M. Anderson and A. Anderson (New York: Free Press).

Ross, D. (2004) *The Missing Peace: The Inside Story of the Fight for Middle East Peace* (New York: Farrar, Straus, & Giroux).

Rubin, B., and Rubin, J. C. (2003) *Yasir Arafat: A Political Biography* (New York: Oxford University Press).

Sheehan, E. (1976) *The Arabs, Israelis, and Kissinger* (New York: Reader's Digest Press).

Spiegel, S. (1985) *The Other Arab–Israeli Conflict* (Chicago: University of Chicago Press).

Tschirgi, D. (1989) *The American Search for Mideast Peace* (New York: Praeger).

Vance, C. (1983) *Hard Choices* (New York: Simon & Schuster).

26

The United States, 1993–2010

Steven L. Spiegel

If in 1993 the Palestinians and Israel seemed on the verge of a major breakthrough, the following nineteen years witnessed the striking failure of the peace process. How could such a promising beginning have gone so wrong for the United States? How could well-intentioned US diplomacy have turned so sour?

At the start of his term, Bill Clinton was poised to build upon his predecessor's success in mending Israeli–Palestinian relations and reinforcing the US connection to both sides. Peace between the two would have huge implications for America's strategic, diplomatic, and economic position in the Middle East.

There was a dramatic breakthrough when secret talks between Israel and the PLO resulted in the 1993 Oslo Accords, signaling mutual recognition, the renunciation of violence, Palestinian acceptance of UN resolutions 242 and 338, and a timetable for confidence-building measures over the next five years leading to full peace between the Palestinians and Israelis. The Accords allowed for the creation of a Palestinian Authority to run Palestinian affairs during the interim period, for Palestinian elections, and for Israel to maintain control over security during this period. Permanent-status negotiations were to begin no later than three years hence on the key questions of borders, Jerusalem, refugees, settlements, and security.

Although not a part of these talks, the US administration quickly came forward in support of the process. The agreement and handshake on the White House lawn that followed subsequently between Arafat and Rabin, with Clinton in the middle, would color administration policy throughout Clinton's years in the White House.

The Accords and the immediate positive American response permanently altered the relationship between the United States and the Palestinians. The USA had in the previous twenty years wrestled with the dilemma of what to do with the PLO. In the American political context, even to suggest rapprochement or dialogue was anathema – implying an anti-Israel position and support of terrorism. When the first Bush administration had tried to establishtentative contacts with the PLO, for example, it failed miserably because of internal Palestinian politics and continuing American reluctance. In the diplomatic arena, talking to the PLO had come to mean an abrogation of American commitment to Israel and a compromise of US credibility on the terrorism question.

Unexpectedly, Israel itself had made talking to the PLO legitimate. Rabin had gone further than any American leader had dreamed possible. For the Clinton administration, talking to the PLO was now not only acceptable, but mandatory in terms of creating a valid American role in the ongoing Palestinian–Israeli talks. Arafat suddenly became a frequent visitor at the White House; he and his aides were involved in complex interchanges, even negotiations, with American representatives from many US agencies, including eventually the CIA.

Yet, the Oslo Accords themselves had fundamental weaknesses. On the one hand, they enumerated a lengthy period of time during which both sides would build confidence in each other. But the piecemeal nature of the process provided plenty of opportunity for the process to go in the opposite direction, with both parties losing trust in their partners and the entire enterprise. Many Palestinian groups, including Hamas, Islamic Jihad, and several factions within Arafat's own entourage, simply did not accept the idea of recognizing Israel and negotiating with it. They engaged throughout Clinton's term in frequent acts of terrorism against the Jewish state in a strategy designed to undermine the peace process and undercut Arafat's Palestinian Authority and his rule atop the Palestinian pyramid.[3] As for the Israelis, many within their polity refused to accept the apparent commitment to withdraw from the West Bank and Gaza or to deal directly with the PLO and its hated leader, Yasser Arafat. Construction within the settlements continued, despite protests from the US, the Palestinians and Arab leaders, and the international community. This construction undermined and undercut those on all sides who supported the peace process because they seemed to contradict the spirit – if admittedly not the letter – of the Oslo Accords.

The Oslo Accords nevertheless created a host of new possibilities in the region, and played to the continuing American preoccupation with the Middle East. Thus, in October 1994, on the border between the two countries, Clinton presided over the signing of the Israeli–Jordanian peace treaty.

This achievement, only a little over a year after the Oslo signing, created a false sense of optimism that more breakthroughs would soon ensue. The Clinton administration also sought to arrange a Syrian–Israeli agreement, an effort which reached a peak in early 2000. At the beginning of the year, unprecedented talks were held at Shepherdstown, West Virginia, between the foreign minister of Syria, Farouk al-Shaara, and the Israeli prime minister, Ehud Barak, with Clinton's sporadic engagement. But the talks broke down, and after a meeting in Geneva on March 26 between Clinton and the ailing Syrian leader, Hafez Assad, it was clear there would be no deal. In May 2000, therefore, Barak ordered a unilateral and somewhat haphazard Israeli withdrawal from its southern Lebanon security zone, where Israeli forces had attempted to prevent Hizbollah from attacking Israel.

All of these developments occurred simultaneously with efforts to promote an Israeli–Palestinian deal. After the Jordan peace treaty, the failures and frustrations elsewhere had the impact of worsening the diplomatic atmosphere in which the United States operated vis-à-vis the Israelis and Palestinians. And they seemed to lessen the time available to the president and his team for addressing the Palestinian question.

Because of these conflicting pressures, because the administration was preoccupied with the US economy, and because the president genuinely believed the two sides should reach a peace agreement themselves, the Clinton administration at first tried to keep up the appearance of direct Israeli–Palestinian contacts without close American engagement. But the façade did not and could not last. The Oslo Accords themselves were signed on September 13, 1993, on the White House lawn, with President Clinton gently, but firmly, almost forcing Arafat and Rabin to shake hands in what became the most famous photo of the Clinton years. From then on, every major turning point of the period was accompanied by American involvement.

In May 1994, the first post-Oslo agreement was signed in Cairo between the Israelis and Palestinians, allowing for the return of Arafat to Gaza and the establishment of a Palestinian Authority under his leadership to rule over both the West Bank and Gaza. It included an Israeli military withdrawal from 60 percent of Gaza and from the town of Jericho on the West Bank (Ross 2004: 167–8). US Secretary of State Warren Christopher presided over the proceedings even as the host, Hosni Mubarak, pressured Arafat against trying to gain more concessions at the last minute.

Over a year later, on September 28, 1995, the Israelis and Palestinians signed the next major document, often called Oslo II, which was the result of American and Egyptian mediation (Quandt 2005: 335). The agreement was signed in Washington in the presence of President Clinton and representatives of other states. Oslo II was a major achievement on the then presumed road to a Palestinian state. As a result of the agreement, the West Bank was divided into three parts: Area A encompassed the major Palestinian towns, where the latter would be in control over both civil authority and security. In Area B, other areas of Palestinian population, the Palestinians would have control over civil authority, but security would be under Israel's control. And, in Area C, the Israelis would retain full control. Over 90 percent of the Palestinian population lived in Area A (2.7 percent of the territory) and Area B (25.1 percent), but Area C constituted about 72.2 percent of the territory of the West Bank (Israel Ministry of Foreign Affairs 1995; Gvirtzman n.d.).

The agreement was barely signed when Prime Minister Rabin was assassinated by a Jewish extremist as he left a peace rally in Tel Aviv on November 4, 1995. A crestfallen President Clinton, who had developed an exceptionally close relationship with the Israeli leader, appeared on international television and uttered a phrase that would inadvertently identify a turning point in the peace process: "Shalom Chaver," or "Goodbye friend." He personally attended Rabin's funeral, along with leaders of many other countries throughout the world.

In retrospect, the assassination was a major blow to the Clinton peace process policy, which would never be the same afterward. It forced the administration to become engaged as it had not previously. After the death of Rabin, the United States gradually became the leader of the peace process, not just its cheerleader and mediator. Instead of helping where possible, it became central to the very continuation of the effort. This change was not Washington's choice, but was forced upon it by events. The new leader of Israel, Shimon Peres, moved forward to implement the Oslo II agreements by withdrawing from all the major towns of the West Bank but Hebron. Yet he paid more attention to a possible Syrian deal.

By early 1996, with elections required in October, Peres made the unfortunate decision to gain a mandate so he could proceed on both the Palestinian and Syrian fronts. His announcement was greeted by intensified suicide bombings sponsored by Hamas and Islamic Jihad, which became a factor, along with attacks from Hizbollah in Lebanon, in evaporating Peres's early lead. Despite obvious American support, in May he nevertheless lost by a razor-thin margin to the young leader of the opposition Likud Party, Binyamin Netanyahu.

The new Israeli prime minister had made no secret of his strong opposition to the policies of Rabin and Peres, and the Clinton administration was left to pick up the pieces of a shattered peace process. It was ironically confronting a situation in which Yasser Arafat, the head of the Palestinian Authority, had been overwhelmingly elected in January 1996 and was clearly ready and able to pursue new deals with Israel towards a Palestinian state (Telhami 1999: 383). But Arafat himself presented problems, given his mercurial and inconsistent policy: sometimes cracking down on Hamas and Islamic Jihad, sometimes willing to wink at their terrorism and that of some members of his own affiliated factions. At the time the Clinton administration was fighting terrorism and pursuing the peace process simultaneously, a policy that the new Israeli government was less willing to endorse than its predecessors.

The result was a dramatic slowdown in the peace process and a growing frustration with Netanyahu that placed the Clinton administration in the politically uncomfortable position of being closer to the Palestinians on major questions relating to pushing diplomacy forward. Progress was further inhibited because the Israeli prime minister had the annoying tendency of riding his own roller coaster when it came to the peace process. Every time he acceded to American preferences, such as to meet with Arafat or to agree to withdraw from the last and most difficult Palestinian town, Hebron (in January 1997, mediated by the US), he would balance his new moderation with announcements of new settlements or take actions such as opening archeological sites that the Americans and the Palestinians opposed (Abraham 2006: 116–18; Ross 2004: 450–52). Arafat's inconsistencies further exacerbated prospects for reaching a deal. Previous administration policy had been based on steady Israeli support for the peace process, but now both sides were mercurial and inconsistent, severely complicating any effective US approach.

With frustration and distrust mounting on all sides, the Clinton team was able to arrange a summit in October 1998 at the Wye Plantation in Maryland. The gathering was attended by Netanyahu, Arafat, and Clinton. At the last minute, the dying King Hussein was persuaded to join in a last-ditch attempt to save the meeting. After eight days, the parties agreed on the so-called Wye River Memorandum. The Israelis acquiesced to their withdrawal from an additional 13 percent of the West Bank, and Arafat accepted the obligation to crack down on terrorism and incitement against Israel among the Palestinians.

Seemingly, this was a major achievement for the Clinton team, demonstrating the new role of the US as mediator between the two sides. But after initial steps by both parties to implement parts of the Accord, it quickly collapsed. Netanyahu confronted mounting opposition in his coalition government to the concessions he had made, and most of the withdrawals were never implemented. Arafat remained as complex as ever, still sometimes cracking down on terrorists, at other times looking the other way. Many of his Wye promises were never kept either. However, the 1990s did witness a decline in terrorism. The decade began with an average of forty Israeli deaths from terrorist attacks annually, but closed with only eight such deaths per year.

At Wye, the Palestinians had agreed to have a meeting of their National Council in the presence of Bill Clinton to reaffirm the redrafting of the PLO Covenant to erase any clauses that called for Israel's destruction. In a dramatic trip on December 14, 1998, Clinton witnessed the Palestinian vote in Gaza demanded by the Netanyahu government, even arriving at the Palestinians' Gaza Airport. The administration had anticipated that this high drama might change the atmosphere and prospects for progress, but it was quickly disappointed. On the other hand, the collapse of the Netanyahu government led to an election in May 1999 in which Ehud Barak defeated the Likud leader. Labor was back in power, and the Clinton administration was filled with new hopes.

To their surprise, Barak had ideas of his own. At a meeting in Sharm el Sheikh in October, he informed the Americans and Palestinians that he did not believe that continuing with incrementalism was a useful strategy. Instead, to the puzzlement of the Palestinians, he made it clear that he wanted to spend the next several months reaching a final agreement. The effect was to delay implementation of the Wye Agreement in favor of reaching a total settlement (Quandt 2005: 357–8). To the Clinton administration, with only a little more than a year left in office, the Barak approach seemed to hold ample opportunity to end the administration with a major diplomatic success. The president was sympathetic and was soon dealing directly with the Israeli prime minister, whom he regarded as a healthy change from Netanyahu and a leader ready to make wholesale concessions. The problem was that the president was also bypassing normal procedures and setting the stage for policy chaos later.

Barak continued to operate according to his own agenda. He promised to appoint an envoy who would lead negotiations with the Palestinians, but tarried, and then selected a leading diplomat but gave him little backing (Miller 2008: 283). He then disappointed the Palestinians by telling the Clinton team he wanted to begin serious negotiations with the Syrians before turning to Arafat (Clinton 2004: 885). By the end of March 2000, those talks collapsed; Barak then became preoccupied with withdrawing unilaterally from southern Lebanon, thereby fulfilling a campaign promise, which he did in May. It was only then that he turned his full attention to the Palestinians (Miller 2008: 287–91).

This dizzying round of detours and new directions left the two other members of the triangle confused, to say the least. The Palestinians reacted with skepticism and suspicion, while the Americans, led by Clinton himself, saw in Barak a courageous figure who was willing to make concessions and deserving of backing in that effort (Indyk 2009: 291–3, 310; Miller 2008: 280–82). In May a leak occurred from Palestinian sources which revealed that the Israelis and Palestinians were making progress in back-channel negotiations in Stockholm, but the leak itself served to torpedo those talks. Meanwhile, the Palestinians weighed the possibility of declaring a Palestinian state unilaterally if there was no fundamental progress. The five-year deadline for a deal inherent in Oslo had now come and gone. The Palestinians began to discuss taking matters into their own hands.

It was at this point that Barak produced a new scheme, a "go-for-broke" summit meeting with Clinton and Arafat at Camp David, analogous to the September 1978 gathering at Camp David between Carter, Sadat, and Begin that had produced the basic accord leading to the Egyptian–Israeli peace treaty. Clinton acquiesced in Barak's proposal; it would clearly be his last chance for a Mideast peace success. Arafat initially refused, arguing that he, his team, and his country were still too divided and unprepared for such a final-status negotiation. But he was finally pressured into proceeding by Clinton, who promised that neither the Israelis nor the Palestinians would be blamed if the talks broke down.

And so the stage was set for the "Hail Mary" of negotiations, a giant gamble on the table of Mideast maneuvers, and it failed miserably. It is unclear in retrospect why the Americans and Israelis believed that all issues could satisfactorily be settled in two weeks in the second half of July. After all, most of the discussions since Oslo had been about territory and terrorism. Why should anyone have anticipated that an issue as deep as Jerusalem, with its huge religious implications for both sides, and the problem of refugees, which involved a threat to the national identity of both, could be so quickly resolved. None of the parties had even begun to wrestle with the concessions that would have to be made.

Nevertheless, it is largely overlooked that some important proposals were put forward at Camp David. The Israelis and Palestinians seemed to concede that they would swap some territory in a final settlement: the Israelis would maintain the large settlement blocs along the 1967 frontier with the West Bank, and in return would relinquish some territory of pre-1967 Israel. But there the agreement ended. The Israelis would not agree to the principle of an equivalent swap, Barak offering 91 percent of the West Bank to the Palestinians, who would take nothing less than a 1:1 exchange (Clinton 2004: 914–15). On that point, the negotiations on territory stalled. There was not even incipient agreement on which territories might be swapped.

The most dramatic step of Camp David occurred on the question of Jerusalem, with Barak becoming the first Israeli prime minister to agree on a division of the city between East and West, allowing both parties to declare their capital there. It was a major step that astonished most observers and contributed to Arafat being blamed when the talks broke down. But wrangling over the future of Jerusalem soon became bogged down over the holy sites sacred to both sides. Arafat refused to make any concessions whatsoever, rejecting innovative American proposals. Sheikh Tayseer Rajab Tamimi, chief Islamic judge of the Palestinian Authority, went so far as to claim that Jews had no history in the city, and Saeb Erekat, Arafat's chief negotiator, remarked, "I don't believe there was a temple on top of the Haram, I really don't."

Yet if some progress was made on the questions of territory and Jerusalem, no common ground could be found at all on the issue of refugees. Within the international community, elaborate international plans had been discussed for years in terms of compensation and movement of the Palestinian refugees out of the camps in which their families had resided since 1948. At Camp David, the Palestinian delegation pursued its traditional and decades-old position that it would accept nothing less than the right of the Palestinians to return to the homes the generation of 1948 had lost in Israel proper (Indyk 2009: 333–4). The Israelis claimed that such a huge influx of Palestinians (now much larger than the original 600,000 to 700,000, given the high birthrate of Palestinians) would destroy the Jewish state if there were no limits on the numbers who could "return" to land now held by Israel in its pre-1967 context. And the Israelis had in mind severe limits indeed.

Because Barak made explicit concessions and Arafat simply said no without countering with proposals of his own, he became the person blamed for the breakdown by American and Israeli leaders. Barak was by now in deep political trouble in Israel, and Bill Clinton – despite his commitment to Arafat not to blame anyone – was so furious that Arafat would not engage with Barak's new positions that he faulted him alone for the unfortunate results. There is no question that, in denouncing Arafat, Clinton was also trying to help Barak politically at home. Over the years that followed, an argument concerning who was actually responsible for the failure of Camp David would become widespread, bitter, and deep, with many analysts blaming Barak and Clinton for their errors as well.

During the summit, anxious American diplomats consulted Arab leaders from Camp David only to have the latter complain that they would not pressure Arafat to make concessions because they had not been properly briefed or consulted beforehand. In retrospect, even in failure US policy had come full circle. The Palestinians were now central to American concerns for the first time, and the Arab states were not pleased.

But certainly for the Clinton administration the only challenge left in the Middle East was possibly to reverse the results of Camp David. Thus, the Clinton team carried on in its last months. Perhaps the aftermath of the meeting did more to solidify an atmosphere of failure than Camp David itself. To its credit, the Clinton team did not give up, but continued with intense negotiations intended to break the Camp David logjams. Yet it was now confronting a situation in which the vehemence of the president's denunciation of Arafat led Clinton to appear partisan.

In the weeks that followed, negotiations resumed under the leadership of Dennis Ross, the Mideast envoy of the administration. They led to the final denouement when, in December, after extensive negotiations, Clinton offered parameters or principles for a final settlement. Barak offered reservations, but Arafat, perhaps anticipating a friendlier attitude from the son of the first President Bush, rejected them. When the two sides were unable to reach agreement, in large measure because Arafat would not accept the package the president was offering, Clinton responded on January 7, 2001, by publicly releasing his "parameters" for a solution.

The Clinton Parameters provided ideas on all the major issues. The president suggested Palestinian sovereignty over 94 to 96 percent of the West Bank and all of Gaza in a geographically viable and contiguous state. Israelis would retain their large settlement blocs on the pre-1967 border with the West Bank; the Palestinians would receive in return some territory from pre-1967 Israel amounting to 1 to 3 percent of the West Bank. Clinton envisioned Jerusalem as the capital of both states, open and undivided (Swisher 2004: 396). Jewish areas would be incorporated into Israel; Arab neighborhoods would become part of the Palestinian state. In addition, regarding the controversial religious areas, the Palestinians would be guaranteed sovereignty over the Haram al-Sharif/Temple Mount and Israel would receive sovereignty over the Western Wall, with a commitment from both sides to refrain from excavation in areas under their control without the approval of the other. For refugees, he suggested compensation for all, with rehabilitation in their places of current residence or resettlement either in the new Palestinian state in the West Bank and Gaza Strip or in other countries (including Israel), subject to the sovereign decisions of those states.

But Clinton also made it clear that he was basing his conclusions on his experiences in the negotiations. The ideas would leave office with him and would not be binding on his successor. It was unfortunate that he took this step, because it inadvertently facilitated a formal break with the past in America's approach to the region.

Despite intense interest on the part of the president and an excellent team, why did Clinton fail to reach agreement? There are several reasons that combined to create a cauldron of confusion, frustration, and disappointment. First, the president himself, whatever his skills and acumen, was both inexperienced and preoccupied during most of his administration with other issues – the economy in his first term and the impeachment during part of his second. The Arab–Israeli dispute assumed center stage only in the last year of the administration.

Second, Oslo itself was flawed. The USA was not involved in its conceptual formulation but found itself trapped in ensuing years by its content. Settlements were not required to be frozen, and they were not. Construction and expansion continued. The PA was given widespread responsibility for which it was not prepared and which permitted it to ignore commitments on such issues as terrorism and incitement. No provisions for building basic institutions to provide for security, welfare, and justice were outlined. Many assumed that a Palestinian state was the objective of the process, but there was no stipulation even for this goal in the Oslo Accords. Worst of all, no agreement could possibly be achieved without concentration on borders, refugees, and Jerusalem. But, until Camp David, there was precious little discussion of any of the three issues except borders.

Third, the success of Kissinger, Carter, and Bush/Baker made it appear easier than the process actually was. For all of these former American leaders, their achievements were a consequence of intensive preparation, outstanding teams, and an enormous amount of time devoted to the issue that ultimately took away from other responsibilities, foreign and domestic. And ultimately each had to redirect his attention to pressures and difficulties elsewhere. It is worth noting that no administration that concentrated on the Arab–Israeli dispute won the following election (Nixon/Ford, Carter, Bush Senior, and Clinton/Gore).

Fourth, Clinton was not prepared to devote the same kind of time and effort as his predecessors, but he also had no one at the top of his administration to do the legwork for him, certainly neither of his secretaries of state. The United States had never succeeded in the Arab–Israeli dispute without the intense involvement of the president or the secretary of state. Neither Warren Christopher nor Madeleine Albright, despite their previous successes, seemed able to offer the skill and guidance that would have served as a critical intermediary between the Dennis Ross-led "peace team" and the president. Instead, the divisions and jealousies within the peace team, and between them and the rest of the administration, were not addressed, exacerbating tensions that might never have emerged otherwise and weakening US effectiveness.

Fifth, the Clinton administration was confronted with a leadership vacuum in the region that ultimately prevented it from achieving its objectives. Any mediator requires the cooperation and effectiveness of both sides. The best combination for a potential breakthrough was the

Rabin–Arafat duo that existed from 1993 to 1995. Both leaders developed an understanding and appreciation of each other. In this light, the assassination of Yitzhak Rabin stands as the single most devastating development in the move towards Israeli–Palestinian peace during the Clinton era. If Rabin had lived, it is certainly possible that much greater progress would have been made. Similarly, had Shimon Peres called for an election immediately after Rabin's death, when Labor was particularly popular, Netanyahu would likely not have won the next election – a victory which posed particular problems to advancing the peace process

There can be no question that Netanyahu was a devastating impediment to progress. He was a prime minister torn between his own ideological origins and his party obligations, on the one hand, and the pressures of a US administration attempting to move forward, on the other. Despite the Hebron and Wye agreements during this period, the controversial Netanyahu policies in effect led to a lost three years, from which the Israeli–Palestinian peace process never recovered.

Even when Barak as head of the Labor Party was elected in May 1999, he proved to be a tantalizingly disappointing participant in the process. His tortured efforts to achieve a final deal when combined with his inability to maintain strong support at home certainly created a high-stakes gamble that was easily susceptible to failure and out of keeping with the more measured and responsible policies of Rabin and Peres. Barak's risk-taking could easily lead him to fall off the tightrope and take everyone else with him, which is exactly what happened. His insistence on dealing with the president himself upset the balance within the administration's key personnel working on the issue.

Of course Arafat was an extremely difficult interlocutor with whom to deal. Totally uncreative, he never took the initiative but simply waited for proposals from the Americans or Israelis. He could restrain violent groups at one turn and then look the other way at the other. It was no wonder that Clinton became so furious at the end of his administration. He had spent almost eight years coddling, and working with the Palestinian leader, only to have it all end in Arafat acquiescing in renewed violence in the form of a Second *Intifada* while turning down all diplomatic initiatives without any counterproposals of his own.

It is worth remembering that both Kissinger and Carter made their names for success in the Middle East working with Sadat. Even the much applauded policy of George H. W. Bush yielded only a peace conference whose follow-up diplomacy failed on the bilateral level and was not sustained on the multilateral plane. In part, the Clinton team was simply unlucky in the way that the Russian roulette of Israeli and Palestinian leadership evolved.

Finally, domestic politics within Palestine and Israel clearly contributed to the headaches the Clinton administration suffered and to making it far more difficult to achieve agreement on the complex issues with which it was dealing. But domestic politics played a major role in the United States as well with the Republican takeover of the House of Representatives in 1994, when the party turned decidedly in favor of support not only of Israel but of the Likud perspective. These attitudes were reinforced by the progressive Christian fundamentalist influence on the party, the full impact of which would be clearer in the next decade.

As a consequence, the Clinton administration found itself far more susceptible to criticism from Congress for its diplomatic achievements than might have been the case if the new Republican attitude towards Israel had not emerged. Thus, the failure of the Clinton administration to achieve a peace deal between the Israelis and the Palestinians was a matter not only of technical deficiencies within the administration, but of the complex factors facing the administration after Oslo as well.

Thus, it is not surprising that the next president and his team entered office with a totally different approach. The combination of factors described above would have made any new administration after Clinton hesitate. George W. Bush was confronting an atmosphere of disappointment, violence, and tension. The Israelis were about to hold an election between Barak and Sharon. In a last-ditch effort to reach a deal or at least make progress on the eve of the election, Israeli and Palestinian teams held partially successful talks in the Egyptian resort of Taba during the new president's first week in office. But the *Intifada* continued to escalate, and Sharon won the election easily. The Taba talks, to which the United States had sent a low-level delegation, did not resume after the Israeli election.

The new Bush administration viewed this entire series of depressing developments with utter disdain. From day one, Arafat was regarded with suspicion and even contempt. Clinton told Bush and Dick Cheney on the way to the inauguration that he regarded the gamble on Arafat as a serious mistake; the new team had no interest in repeating the error (Miller 2008: 322). They would not intervene to help the Palestinians until the violence, which had erupted after Camp David, ended. Arafat was seen as at least acquiescing in, if not promoting, the escalating attacks on Israeli civilians.

By early September 2001, the policy of passively waiting for the parties to take independent action was questionable. Could the USA simply wait and watch while the situation continued to deteriorate? Washington was rife with rumors that the administration would soon embark on a new policy. But, before any policy innovations could be announced, the September 11 attacks altered America's view of the Middle East.

The administration was at first in no mood to become too closely aligned with Israel in a conflict with Islamic fundamentalism and terrorism, especially when the Palestinian leader reaffirmed his willingness to assist the United States and the Saudis vehemently expressed their displeasure with American policy on the Arab–Israeli dispute. In response, Bush became the first president in history to announce explicitly that the US favored a Palestinian state. It would have seemed a major milestone, but, given the growing violence against Israelis and the escalating crisis, even the Palestinians did not celebrate.

With the United States preoccupied with the post 9/11 effort to oust the Taliban from Afghanistan, its policy remained minimalist. In December the administration announced that it would send the retired general and former chief of the US Central Command, Anthony Zinni, to try to negotiate a ceasefire between the Israelis and Palestinians. The mission over the next several weeks was to prove a watershed. Behind the scenes, Zinni came tantalizingly close to making a deal, but Arafat rejected his proposals, and instead the Palestinians escalated their suicide bombings and attacks against Israel. Meanwhile, in January, the Israelis discovered a ship in the Red Sea, the *Karine A*, with a shipment of lethal Iranian arms for the Palestinians aboard.

Arafat had already sabotaged any opportunity to ally himself with the United States. He failed to realize that, to the Americans, suicide bombings resembled miniature versions of 9/11. In a letter to President Bush he denied any involvement in the *Karine A* affair; however, Israeli intelligence had already provided incontrovertible proof of just such complicity. The president was incensed.

But now, in a reversal of the historical pattern, Palestinian violence overshadowed Arab government actions. In early April Israel responded massively to an egregious attack on a religious ceremony, a Passover meal, launching Operation Defensive Shield and beginning a process of reoccupation of the West Bank. At this point no one, including the Bush administration, was thinking about the new Arab peace initiative agreed upon in Beirut at the same time or about any other diplomatic approach. The administration had even accepted a UN Security Council Resolution (1397) in mid-March, in which, for the first time since the Truman administration, the US officially accepted the idea of two states, Israel and Palestine, living "side by side within secure and recognized borders." The resolution quickly became another insignificant historical footnote.

Bush had his own theories as to why Clinton failed: a peace deal alone was insufficient. Democratic institutions and reform were prerequisites to successful negotiations. As the conflict continued to escalate throughout the spring of 2002, Bush delivered a seminal speech on June 24, in which he outlined the new American policy towards the dispute. In some ways the ideas were revolutionary. No longer would the United States be content with mediation. Bush bluntly demanded that the Palestinians produce new leadership, engage in true democratic reform and institutionalization, and hold free and fair elections. Without saying so explicitly, he wanted Arafat ousted, or at least removed to a ceremonial position. Only then would the US reengage and demand major concessions of Israel, including a settlement freeze, withdrawal from areas reoccupied during the *Intifada*, and major territorial concessions resulting in the establishment of a Palestinian state. No Arab state had ever been the recipient of such detailed confrontational demands on its internal governance. The Palestinians were gaining more global attention but still had no state, a prospect diminished by the violence against Israel in which they were engaged.

The question next was how to implement the president's ideas. The first strategy, advocated by Secretary of State Colin Powell, was to involve the international community through formation of a "Quartet," consisting of the USA, the EU, the UN, and Russia. During the next several months this group met to produce a "Road Map" for implementing the Bush vision. While a final draft was ready by December, the US held off releasing the document pending the end of an Israeli election campaign. By now, the administration was preoccupied with preparations for an invasion of Iraq. The Israelis and Palestinians would again have to wait.

Once the war began, Bush came under increased pressure, especially from British Prime Minister Tony Blair, to release the Road Map. When Arafat too came under withering pressure from Arab and European countries to appoint a prime minister, he finally relented and invited Mahmoud Abbas (Abu Mazen) – a long-time associate – to take the job. Abu Mazen was sworn in on April 29, 2003; the next day, Bush released the Road Map.

The new document proposed an innovative way of proceeding on the Israeli–Palestinian issue in three phases. In the first, there would be simultaneous, reciprocal, and mutual confidence-building measures. The heart of the second phase would be the establishment of a provisional Palestinian state without permanent borders, and, in a third phase, the two sides would reach a final settlement on all outstanding issues.

One of the unique features of the Road Map was its performance-based criteria. This mechanism was designed to overcome one of the genuine weaknesses of the 1990s, when non-compliance undermined bilateral agreements. The Road Map contained strict target dates designed to reach the conclusion of Phase 3 by the end of 2005. By the time it was published, the first phase was supposed to be almost completed. In the spring of 2004 it was acknowledged that the 2005 deadline for a Palestinian state was unrealistic.

Bush followed the Road Map announcement in June 2003 with a trip to the region, where he met first with several key Arab leaders in Egypt and then with Abu Mazen and Sharon in Jordan. A three-month *hudna*, or ceasefire, was arranged between the various Palestinian groups, including Hamas and Islamic Jihad. Despite its fragility, the stage seemed set by the end of June for serious movement, a process reinforced by separate meetings the president held at the end of July with Abu Mazen and Sharon at the White House.

But, once again, the process quickly degenerated. The Israelis were reluctant to make concessions, such as substantial prisoner releases or dramatic withdrawals, until the Palestinians took serious steps to dismantle the terrorist infrastructure. Abu Mazen and his team claimed they were too weak to take such action, and sought broader and deeper moves from the Israelis. Both sides looked to the United States, but the president and several key figures were on vacation. Within weeks, the entire process had unraveled and Abbas had resigned as prime minister.

Instead, an initially vague promise from Sharon to take "unilateral action" gradually evolved over the next several months into the Gaza disengagement plan. Sharon proposed to dismantle all settlements in Gaza and four more in the West Bank. The Palestinian reaction was mixed, but mostly negative.[1] Meanwhile, the Bush administration offered little meaningful response, and by early 2004 the United States had largely retreated from Arab–Israeli peacemaking, preoccupied with Iraq and the US election season.

Yet, as it became clear that Sharon was determined to move forward, the administration began to negotiate seriously with his government, resulting in a US endorsement of the disengagement plan in mid-April 2004.[2] Bush was making public agreements with the Israelis while essentially removing the Palestinians from the process. The president also went one step further. To Palestinian and Arab consternation, he officially endorsed Israeli positions on two sensitive issues that had previously been left to negotiations: that Israel would retain some of the settlements in the West Bank, and that Palestinian refugees must return to the future Palestinian state, not to Israel.

With the Bush administration having supported Gaza disengagement, it then took over a year for the actual Israeli withdrawal to occur as a result of domestic opposition from the right in Israel. Meanwhile, President Bush was reelected in November, and a few days later Yasser Arafat died suddenly. Intensifying the diplomatic potential inherent in Arafat's death, the new Palestinian leader, Mahmoud Abbas, was a person highly respected by both Americans and Israelis as a moderate. But, at the same time, he was seen as weak, and proved to be reluctant to make concessions in negotiations. In any case, Sharon refused to negotiate with the Palestinians concerning the details of the withdrawal from Gaza, which finally took place in late August 2005.[3]

Despite the months of internal political wrangling in Israel, the actual withdrawal proved smooth and effective, but because no specific arrangements had been made with the Palestinians the consequences were disappointing. Hamas gained a good deal of credit among Palestinians for Israel's withdrawal. The potentially positive impact of the withdrawal was destroyed when, in January 2006, Hamas participated in and won the elections in the West Bank and Gaza for a new parliament. These were the first parliamentary elections in ten years, and the first national elections in which Hamas participated.

The United States had supported the idea of elections as central to its policy of domestic reform. Most Fatah operatives were opposed, but Abbas acquiesced in Hamas's participation as a means of assuring his own Fatah's legitimacy. The Bush administration also supported the elections because its intelligence reports assured American leaders that Hamas would not win.[4] In the confused aftermath of the election, the Quartet demanded that, for Hamas to be recognized as the leader of the Palestinians, it would have to accept previous Palestinian agreements with Israel, renounce violence, and recognize Israel's right to exist.[5] Hamas refused to take these steps, and the coalition government between Hamas and Fatah collapsed. Finally, after several attempts at Fatah–Hamas unity failed, the issue of internal Palestinian conflict was temporarily settled in June 2007 by a Hamas coup in which it took over leadership of Gaza, and Abu Mazen's Fatah was left with control over the West Bank.

Meanwhile, Sharon suffered a debilitating stroke in early 2006 and Ehud Olmert became prime minister. Olmert was strongly committed to developing Sharon's new Kadima Party and to unilateral Israeli withdrawal from most of the West Bank. He won the March 2006 elections, but was not able to pursue his objectives towards the Palestinians because of his government's diversion into confrontations with both Hamas (over its June capture of soldier Gilad Shalit in a raid into Israel) and Hizbollah's capturing soldiers inside Israel operating on the country's northern border with Lebanon in July. The vehement Israeli reaction to the Hizbollah incursion resulted in the Lebanon War of 2006, in which Israel pummeled Lebanese territory, and Hizbollah responded with Katyusha rockets over the northern sector of Israel in a five-week war. The hostilities ended inconclusively despite the destruction suffered by both sides, especially by the Lebanese from Israeli bombing.

The Bush administration was left to try to attain some serious progress in relations between Israel and the Palestinian Authority, when Secretary of State Condoleezza Rice shepherded an agreement for safe passage between Gaza and the West Bank in November 2005. This effort was an indication that the Bush administration, whose policy on Palestinian–Israeli matters in the second term was led in large measure by Secretary of State Rice, had decided to move energetically on the Arab–Israeli peace process for the first time, in the hopes that it could take advantage of the two comparatively moderate leaders, Ehud Olmert and Abu Mazen. Both were under severe domestic pressure, Abu Mazen because of the conflict with Hamas, and Olmert because of the threat of indictment from several financial transactions before he became prime minister. Nevertheless, in November 2007 the administration held a conference in Annapolis, Maryland, in which sixteen Arab countries and many other states were represented.

There was much talk of additional conferences and considerable activity, but, instead, the Israelis and Palestinians settled into a two-level process of their own. On the first track, Olmert and Abu Mazen conducted a series of private talks to try to reach a settlement. On the second, led by the prominent Palestinian diplomat Abu Alla and the Israeli foreign minister, Tzipi Livni, a series of joint committees were established to deal with a variety of critical issues in the peace talks. The advantage of this approach was that the two sides were dealing directly and energetically with matters involving a possible peace between them. The disadvantages involved the absence of Gaza in this process and the insistence of the parties on leaving the Americans out of the details of the issues being discussed, especially at the Olmert–Abu Mazen level. The United States was then reduced to receiving reports on what was happening and playing the role of interested outsider, a kind of cheerleader position in which the Bush administration had often found itself. As the months proceeded, the Livni–Abu Alla process achieved some progress in a very deliberate, detailed, thorough, but slow pursuit of a resolution on key issues. The "Palestine Papers" released by al Jazeera in early 2011 revealed the seriousness of the Palestinian negotiations and their willingness to make concessions. Although comparable Israeli positions are not included, it is clear that the Palestinians, in their considerations, are responding to potential Israeli concessions.[6]

The Olmert–Abu Mazen process was by its nature isolated, and those working in the larger process (especially on the Israeli side) often resented the private discussions being held by the two leaders. Their talks came to a moment of truth in the fall of 2008 when Olmert tabled the most generous proposal ever made by an Israeli prime minister.

Though it was not published at the time, Olmert himself related in several interviews and in his own memoirs the general details of the proposal. Further details were provided in separate interviews with both Olmert and Abbas published in the *New York Times* in February 2011. The two agreed that a Palestinian state would have no military, but would have a strong police force. It was also agreed that an American-led NATO force, not Israeli soldiers, would be stationed on the Palestinian state's border with Jordan. On the issue of borders generally, Olmert related that all but about 6.3 percent (and hinted he would go down to 5.9 percent) of the West Bank would be given to the Palestinians, and the area that Israel kept would be swapped for an identical piece of land inside pre-1967 Israel and a tunnel "fully controlled by the Palestinians" connecting the West Bank and Gaza. Abbas countered with 1.9 percent.[7]

On Jerusalem, "Jewish neighbourhoods would be under Jewish sovereignty, Arab neighbourhoods would be under Palestinian sovereignty, so it could be the capital of a Palestinian state." Olmert proposed that the "holy basin", incorporating areas holy to Jews, Muslims, and Christians, should be an area of what he called "no sovereignty," and it would be "jointly administered" by Saudi Arabia, Jordan, the Palestinian state, Israel, and the United States. An argument remained between Olmert and Abbas on the precise territory of the Old City and holy basin.

On the refugees, Olmert proposed they would become citizens of the new Palestinian state, and that a token 1,000 a year for five years would be allowed into Israel on a humanitarian basis. Basically, there would be no return to Israel proper, but an international fund for compensation would be created in the light of "Palestinian suffering." Olmert pointed out he was the first Israeli prime minister to speak of "Palestinian suffering." Abbas accepted the principle of Olmert's approach, but not the number he was offering.

The Palestinian leader never responded to this offer, in part because Olmert was by now seen as a lame duck on account of his legal problems and in part because Abbas sought American "bridging proposals" and urged the United States to be a strong broker. But Secretary Rice was unable to salvage a process in which she had been kept largely on the margins, and the new Obama and Netanyahu administrations moved in another direction.

Of course, the inability of the Bush administration to insert itself into this process or to persuade Abbas to agree at least to shelve the agreement officially diminished the possibilities of its success. In the end, the innate caution of Bush and Abu Mazen overcame the almost desperate search by Olmert for a dramatic agreement at the end of his prime ministership.

The last step during the Bush era, in terms of American policy towards the Palestinians, was to watch, with some sympathy, as Israel finally retaliated against Gaza for the years of missile attacks on neighboring towns and villages in the controversial Operation Cast Lead. Over 1,300 Palestinians were killed, many civilian, and Hamas retained power, but in a weakened state. For Israel, the results were mixed. On the one hand, it had increased its deterrence and ended the regular missile attacks against it, but it received widespread condemnation from the international community. Thus, the new American president, Barack Obama, entered office with the tantalizing potential of diplomatic progress, as had been suggested in the hapless process over the previous year, and an urgency created by both Operation Cast Lead and the election three weeks into his term of a new right-wing coalition led by Binyamin Netanyahu.

The new president's approach was distinguished by urgency towards resolving the Arab–Israeli conflict, and, on his first full day in office, he appointed former Senate majority leader George Mitchell as his Middle East envoy. In a throwback to the era of Bush Senior, the Obama administration saw settlements as a major obstacle to peace. It was impatient with the Israelis on this issue in a policy that had been prominent since the Nixon and Ford period, however reduced it had become in the previous two administrations. Thus, the administration moved quickly and controversially to insist on a total freeze by Israel of settlement construction, leading to immediate tangles with the new Israeli government. Prime Minister Netanyahu declared in a speech in June 2009 that he accepted a two-state solution, and he later did accept a temporary ten-month moratorium on further West Bank settlement construction in a move widely considered to be the strongest of any prime minister in Israel's history.

Yet controversies between the Israeli and American leaders were almost constant. For example, in a heralded speech in Cairo in June 2009, Obama reached out to Muslims after the damage to America's reputation during the Bush administration, but the Israelis were offended that his rationale for the creation of Israel in the speech centered on the Holocaust, and not on the Jews' historic attachment to biblical lands or the Zionists' long battle for a state. In another confidence-diminishing incident, to the great dismay of the Americans, an announcement of additional construction in Jerusalem (not affected by the moratorium) occurred when Vice President Joe Biden visited Israel in March 2010. Although it provided diplomatic support to Israel, the administration was clearly unhappy when at the end of May 2010 Israel stopped a Turkish-sponsored flotilla headed towards Gaza to break the blockade imposed after the 2007 victory of Hamas in the Palestinian elections. Eight Turks and one American-Turkish citizen were killed in the process of Israeli sailors' boarding one of the ships. Israel claimed the Turks aboard the ship in question used violence in attacking Israeli troops first. In a reflection of his real attitude, the president called the blockade "unsustainable".

Despite these controversies, both Obama and Netanyahu were hard-pressed to put a positive light on their relationship with each other, both for domestic political reasons and for their ability to move forward in their common interests vis-à-vis Iran, terrorism, and other issues of mutual concern. Thus, the two leaders held a successful "love fest" meeting in July 2010 to attempt to convince the press and public in both countries of their good and solid relations.

By the end of the summer, the Obama administration finally succeeded in convincing Abu Mazen to join direct talks with the Israelis, but by now only one month remained on Netanyahu's settlement freeze. The Palestinians had never before refused to engage in talks with Israel while settlement construction continued. But, because the administration had taken a tough line on settlements, especially in its early months, the Palestinians took the position that they could not be weaker on Israel than Washington. For the first time, they made a moratorium on construction of settlements in the West Bank and East Jerusalem a condition for talks.

The Netanyahu government resumed construction upon the end of its moratorium in late September 2010, and the Palestinians withdrew from the inconclusive negotiations after only a month. Even after the Obama team dangled a somewhat amorphous bundle of diplomatic and security assistance if they would reinstate the freeze even for ninety days, the Israeli coalition would not budge, especially after the Palestinians also demanded for the first time the addition of a moratorium on Israeli construction in East Jerusalem as a condition for talks. For the foreseeable future, the direct talks were over.

Though poorly understood, the Obama administration's policies were different to those of its predecessors. On the one hand, in a throwback to the pre-Clinton era, the Obama team was ready to confront Israel directly when it believed Jerusalem had made mistakes diplomatically or had acted in ways Washington considered unacceptable.[8] In early 2010, the president, the vice president, and General David Petraeus went so far as to express the controversial and oft-questioned opinion that the lack of progress in the peace process was a threat to American lives in Afghanistan and Iraq.[9]

On the other hand, unlike the pre-Clinton presidents, when unhappy with Israel, the administration did not diminish the security relationship with the Jewish state. Instead, it expanded and deepened security ties, in a move perhaps related to the issue of attempting to prevent Israel from attacking Iran to delay its development of nuclear weapons, to give Israel confidence to enable it to make concessions in the peace process, and/or because it genuinely believed that a close security relationship with Israel was important for American interests and worthwhile on its own.

In a pattern that previous presidents had faced, tensions with Israel did not always result in benefits vis-à-vis the Palestinians. They were disappointed by the aftermath of the president's Cairo speech, which had seemed to Arab ears to promise a new dawn in American diplomacy. But, as the months passed, they saw no substantive change. At the same time, the Palestinians limited the possibility of the president's success in their cautious attitude towards negotiations with Netanyahu's admittedly tough government. At the mid-point of his first term, Obama was having no greater success than his predecessors in bringing about Israeli–Palestinian peace.

Conclusion

Why have successive administrations had such a difficult time bringing about Palestinian–Israeli peace? The United States has aided Israel, and since Oslo has provided ample assistance to the Palestinians and engaged other countries to do so. The PA would not otherwise have survived. All administrations have been focused on the Israeli–Palestinian problem in one way or another for at least a period of their tenure. So what went wrong?

First, each administration made critical mistakes. After Oslo, Clinton was too slow to realize the critical importance of American involvement and relied on a devoted peace team and the role of the president without the effective functioning of a secretary of state, despite the latter's periodic involvement in both terms. The Bush administration produced an important innovation in the emphasis on institutionalization and democratic reform, but was utterly ineffective when it came to concentrating on a strategy for precipitating diplomatic progress and implementing plans that it was convinced had no chance of success. Of course, it did not try until its last two years.

As for the Obama administration, it understood that, to have any chance of accomplishing its goals, it had to start early and be engaged. But, by beginning immediately, it also stumbled badly when it insisted on a total freeze on settlement construction – setting the bar so high it caused immediate problems with an Israeli government that would not conform and with Palestinians who now demanded US diplomatic achievement.

Second, the stars must be aligned. If the US, Israeli, and Palestinian leaders do not make a compatible team, they will not succeed. They require at least minimum confidence and trust in one another and sufficient standing at home to make the requisite concessions. Unfortunately, that alignment has almost never happened, and hence only the rare snippet of success in one handshake celebrating the Oslo agreements in 1993, the Oslo II Accords in 1995, or the Wye Agreement of 1998.

Third, domestic politics in each of the three countries frequently wreck plans even when the leaders generally agree. All three countries are seriously divided: in Israel between advocates and opponents of the peace process; in Palestine between those who advocate violence and those who are more moderate; and in America between supporters of Israel who believe that peace is possible and supporters of Israel who do not. These domestic complexities mean that a successful peace process can occur only when the leaders can produce a major breakthrough that becomes a fait accompli, enabling top leaders to withstand spoilers and opposition. Overcoming his own domestic politics and those of the other two parties has been almost "Mission Impossible" for American presidents so far.

Fourth, a deal will only be made when Arab states provide confidence-building measures to the Israelis and bolster the Palestinian leadership. But Arab leaders, often insecure, are reluctant to "stick their necks out," and this factor continues to harm the Israeli–Palestinian peace process. American presidents constantly must figure out how to overcome Arab politics, and none has done so successfully since Oslo, a process made more difficult since the Arab Spring.

Fifth, the problems themselves are exceedingly difficult. In the twenty-first century, few countries must debate the dispensation of territory between them, and fewer still argue on religious grounds. Even the idea of swapping land is likely to lead to major crises if negotiations should ever go that far. Jerusalem is the most hallowed and yet controversial city in the world.

Given the biblical history of the Jews and al Quds being the third most important city in the world for Muslims, every inch will be debated. On the one hand, it makes no sense to divide a Jerusalem that has functioned well under Israeli rule. On the other hand, without doing so in some manner, shape or form, no deal will be reached.

The refugee question is as close to a zero-sum game as it gets. The Palestinians continue to insist officially upon the right of any Palestinian who wishes to return to do so, but that policy would destroy Israel as a Jewish state. For the Israelis, the position has gradually hardened given the continued violent threats from Palestinians, and it is fair to say they are less prepared to accept even a token return of Palestinians to pre-1967 Israel than they were at the time of Camp David in 2000.

Thus, even if the leaders are positive and are somehow in a position to control domestic politics, and the negotiators make all the right moves, a breakthrough is by no means assured. Every American administration must struggle with these inherent difficulties, and none has yet overcome them.

Finally, the best outcome, as seen in the Oslo Accords themselves, is when the parties make the deals alone. It is worth remembering that the breakthrough in Egyptian–Israeli and Jordanian–Israeli relations came secretly and between the parties themselves. Yet no deal has ever been consummated without the engagement of the United States. So far, it has not proved possible to combine a private Israeli–Palestinian initiative with American engagement in a way that has resulted in diplomatic victory. A successful peace process requires a formula of the correct procedures and skilled negotiators. The task of reaching Israeli–Palestinian agreement has continued to elude everyone who has sought to defy the odds and produce an effective method for a breakthrough.

The parties will continue to debate the best approach, whether this be a series of steps known as incrementalism, unilateral efforts by one side or the other, some kind of intervention by the international community, or the traditional effort to negotiate the major issues in dispute. Meanwhile, the United States will undoubtedly continue to be at the center of the effort to achieve an Israeli–Palestinian final settlement. However much both parties may complain about the American role at one time or another, they themselves seem committed to an American engagement, or at least they seem unable to find a way around it. One prediction we can safely make in conclusion is that any major movement on the Israeli–Palestinian peace process will be accompanied by some kind of American sponsorship or contribution.

Notes

1   E. MacAskill, C. Urquhart, and J. Borger, "Sharon: Act Now or We Go it Alone," *The Guardian*, 19 December 2003; available at: www.guardian.co.uk/world/2003/dec/19/israel2.

2   E. Bumiller, "In Major Shift, Bush Endorses Sharon Plan and Backs Keeping Some Israeli Settlements," *New York Times*, 15 April 2004.

3   C. Migdalovitz, *CRS Issue Brief for Congress: The Middle East Peace Talks* (Washington DC: Congressional Research Service, 15 November 2005), pp. 6–9.

4   "Israel's Disengagement from Gaza and Several West Bank Settlements," *Staff Trip Reports to the Committee on Foreign Relations, United States Senate, One Hundred Nineth [sic] Congress, First Session*, October 2005, pp.109–36.

5   C. Migdalovitz, *Israel: Background and Relations with the United States* (Fort Belvoir, VA: Defense Technical Information Center, 2007, 2010).

6   E. Bronner, "Documents Open a Door on Mideast Peace Talks," *New York Times*, 24 January 2011; available at: www.nytimes.com/2011/01/25/world/middleeast/25mideast.html.

7   Sheridan (2009); Avishai (2011).

8   H. Cooper, "Obama Talks of Being 'Honest' with Israel," *New York Times*, 1 June 2009.
9   Perry (2010).

References and further reading

Abraham, S. D. (2006) *Peace is Possible: Conversations with Arab and Israeli Leaders from 1988–Present* (New York: Newmarket Press).

Avishai, B. (2011) "A Plan for Peace that Still Could Be," *New York Times Magazine*, 7 February; available at: www.nytimes.com/2011/02/13/magazine/13Israel-t.html?pagewanted=all.

Clinton, B. (2004) *My Life* (New York: Alfred Knopf).

Gvirtzman, H. (n.d.) "Maps of Israeli Interests in Judea and Samaria Determining the Extent of the Additional Withdrawals," Begin–Sadat Center for Strategic Studies, available at: www.biu.ac.il/Besa/books/maps.htm.

Indyk, M. (2009) *Innocent Abroad: An Intimate Account of American Peace Diplomacy in the Middle East* (New York: Simon & Schuster).

Israeli Ministry of Foreign Affairs (1995) "The Israeli–Palestinian Interim Agreement," available at: www.mfa.gov.il/MFA/PeaceProcess/GuidetothePeaceProcess/THEISRAELI-PALESTINIANINTERIMAGREEMENT.htm.

Kurtzer, D. C., and Lasensky, S. B. (2008) *Negotiating Arab–Israeli Peace: American Leadership in the Middle East* (Washington, DC: United States Institute of Peace Press).

Miller, A. D. (2008) *The much too Promised Land: America's Elusive Search for Arab–Israeli Peace* (New York: Bantam Books).

Quandt, W. B. (1977) *Decade of Decisions* (Los Angeles: University of California Press).

Quandt, W. B. (2005) *Peace Process: American Diplomacy and the Arab–Israeli Conflict since 1967* (3rd ed., Washington, DC: Brookings Institution).

Perry, M. (2010) "The Petraeus Briefing: Biden's Embarrassment is not the Whole Story," *Foreign Policy Magazine*, 13 March; available at: http://mideast.foreignpolicy.com/posts/2010/03/14/the_petraeus_briefing_biden_s_embarrassment_is_not_the_whole_story.

Ross, D. (2004) *The Missing Peace: The Inside Story of the Fight for Middle East Peace* (New York: Farrar, Straus, & Giroux).

Ross, D., and Makovsky, D. (2009) *Myths, Illusions, and Peace* (New York: Penguin).

Sheridan, G. (2009) "Ehud Olmert Still Dreams of Peace," *The Australian*, 28 November; available at: www.theaustralian.com.au/news/opinion/ehud-olmert-still-dreams-of-peace/story-e6frg76f-1225804745744.

Swisher, C. (2004) *The Truth about Camp David: The Untold Story about the Collapse of the Middle East Peace Process* (New York: Nation Books).

Telhami, S. (1999) "Camp David to Wye: Changing Assumptions in Arab–Israeli Negotiations," *Middle East Journal*, 53/3, pp. 379–92.

27

Russia

Robert O. Freedman

Any examination of the triangular relationship between the Soviet Union, the Palestinians, and Israel reveals that, depending on its larger diplomatic interests in the Middle East and in the world as a whole, Moscow has shifted back and forth between the two Middle Eastern peoples. During most of the post-World War II period, until the emergence of Mikhail Gorbachev in 1985, Moscow, despite its initial recognition of and support for Israel in the 1947–9 period, tended to back the Arabs in their conflict with Israel. By the late 1960s, this backing took in the Palestine Liberation Organization (PLO) as well. Under Gorbachev, Moscow pursued an "even-handed" policy between the Palestinians and Israel, and in the first decade after the collapse of the Soviet Union in 1991 Moscow's ties were, for the most part, far stronger with Israel than with the Palestinians. Under Vladimir Putin, however, who became Russia's president in 2000, Moscow's relations with Israel cooled as Putin, while seeking to maintain good bilateral relations with Israel, chose to adopt an anti-Israeli Middle Eastern regional policy which involved not only the selling of arms to Syria and Iran – both enemies of Israel – but also the diplomatic legitimization of Hamas, an Islamic political organization whose avowed goal is the destruction of Israel.

The Soviet era

Initially, during the rise of the Communist Party to power in czarist Russia, the communist leadership under Lenin was strongly anti-Zionist because the Zionist movement, which called for the establishment of a Jewish state in Palestine, was, in Lenin's view, trying to divert the attention of Jewish workers from communist efforts to undertake world revolution. In addition, after the establishment of the Soviet Union, the fact that Britain, a major enemy of the USSR during the interwar period, was instrumental, through the Balfour Declaration and the British Mandate over Palestine, in fostering the growth of the Zionist community in Palestine only reinforced Moscow's antipathy towards Zionism. There was, therefore, a great deal of surprise when the Soviet Union, then led by Joseph Stalin, not only supported the 1947 United Nations plan for the partition of Palestine into a Jewish and an Arab state, but also gave Israel both diplomatic support and military aid (via Czechoslovakia) when the Arab states invaded Israel on May 15, 1948, and condemned the Arabs for the invasion. The primary reason for Soviet support for Israel was that Moscow perceived it as fighting against a pro-British bloc of Arab states which would, along with Britain, be weakened if Israel won the war.

In the latter part of the Stalin era, however, Soviet–Israeli relations deteriorated, in part because of increased anti-Semitism in the USSR, and in part because Israel backed the United States' position when North Korea invaded South Korea in 1950. The USSR severed relations with Israel in 1952. Moscow's deteriorating relations with Israel, however, did not lead to an improvement of relations with the Arab states or with the Palestinians (then under Egyptian and Jordanian occupation) until after Stalin's death in 1953. While relations were restored with Israel by Stalin's successor, Georgi Malenkov, in 1953 as part of the post-Stalin "thaw" in Soviet foreign policy, under Nikita Khrushchev, who rose to power in 1955, there was a distinct tilt towards the Arabs, if not yet towards the Palestinians. Moscow strongly condemned Israel, along with Britain and France, for their tripartite invasion of Egypt in 1956. Following the ousting of Khrushchev in 1964, there was an even stronger leaning towards the Arab position on the Arab–Israeli conflict by his successor, Leonid Brezhnev, leading to a severing of the Soviet Union's diplomatic relations with Israel during the 1967 Six Day War, during which Israel took over the West Bank and Gaza Strip. Moscow was criticized in the Arab world for not providing military aid to the Arabs during that conflict.

Following the 1967 war, and the sharp rise in the PLO's importance in Arab politics, the Soviets paid greater attention to the organization, inviting Yasser Arafat, who had become its leader, to Moscow as part of an Egyptian delegation in 1968. But the real change in relations with the PLO was to come after the 1973 Yom Kippur War, during which Moscow, in addition to sending arms to both Syria and Egypt, threatened militarily to intervene on the side of Egypt when the fighting turned against it. This changed position was the result of two developments. First, in 1974 the Arabs themselves recognized the PLO as the "sole legitimate representative" of the Palestinian people, thus giving the Palestinian organization increased legitimacy. Second, Egypt, which had been Moscow's primary ally in the Arab world, and a country on which it had lavished billions of rubles of economic and military assistance, had switched its allegiance to the United States. Therefore, in addition to cultivating Syria, Iraq, and Libya, the USSR began to develop ties with the PLO. Thus in the summer of 1974 the PLO was allowed to open an office in Moscow, and, following the successful completion of the Israeli–Egyptian negotiations at Camp David in September 1978, Brezhnev announced that the USSR supported the right of the Palestinians to create their own independent state.

The Soviet–Palestinian relationship during the Brezhnev era (1964–82) was somewhat problematic. From the Soviet side there was criticism of the terrorist actions of the PLO, and from the Palestinian side there was deep disappointment that Moscow did not provide them with significant support during their war against Syria in Lebanon in 1976 or during the Israeli invasion of Lebanon in 1982. Moscow was also criticized by the PLO and the Arab world for allowing tens of thousands of Soviet Jews to emigrate to Israel in the 1970s and early 1980s. Still, on balance, the Brezhnev era can be seen as a positive one for Soviet–Palestinian relations and a negative one for Soviet–Israeli relations. This situation was to change when Mikhail Gorbachev became the Soviet leader in 1985. Indeed, the Gorbachev era, which lasted until the collapse of the Soviet Union in 1991, was perhaps the most revolutionary in Soviet foreign policy since the communist revolution of 1917.

Gorbachev radically changed Soviet foreign policy, both in the Arab–Israeli conflict and in relation to the United States. His plan was to revitalize the moribund Soviet economy. After the Chernobyl nuclear disaster of 1986 and the sharp drop in oil prices the same year, he understood that an end to the US–Soviet Cold War was necessary for the Soviet Union's economy to develop. This required, among other things, the pull-out of Soviet troops from Afghanistan, a sharp cut in Soviet military forces in Eastern Europe, and changes in Soviet behavior in the Third World. Among these changes was the reestablishment of diplomatic relations with Israel, first at the consular level and then, after the failed coup against Gorbachev in September 1991, with the establishment of full diplomatic relations. Gorbachev also permitted hundreds of thousands of Soviet Jews to emigrate to Israel in the 1988–91 period, an action that not only helped Israel in its demographic competition with the Palestinians but also greatly augmented Israel's scientific and military power, since many of the emigrating Soviet Jews had worked in the USSR's military-industrial complex. Perhaps of equal importance was Gorbachev's admonition both to Syrian leader Hafiz al-Assad and to PLO leader Yasser Arafat that their conflicts with Israel had to be settled politically and not by war – a signal to both Arab leaders that the time had come to negotiate with Israel, and a not so subtle indication that they could not expect Soviet aid if they embarked on a war against Israel.

Post-Soviet policy

The Yeltsin era, 1991–1999

In the first five years after the collapse of the Soviet Union, there was a honeymoon period in the Russian–Israeli bilateral relationship. Cultural relations boomed as Russian artists appeared in Israel and Israelis performed in Moscow and elsewhere in Russia. Economic relations also developed rapidly, reaching the half-billion dollar level by 1995. Russian Jews continued to emigrate to Israel, and Russian tourists, both Jews and non-Jews, began to visit Israel in large numbers, finding a hospitable welcome in a country where there was Russian-language TV and newspapers. Russia and Israel also agreed to cooperate on jointly producing military equipment for sale to third countries; the most important product of that agreement was the sale of an AWACS aircraft to India, with Russia providing the air frame and Israel providing the avionics. The high point in the Russian–Israeli relationship under Yeltsin came in 1995, when Israeli Prime Minister Yitzhak Rabin delivered a lecture to the Russian General Staff in Moscow.

As far as the Arab–Israeli conflict was concerned, there was also an initial tilt towards Israel, although Moscow kept an even-handed position under its foreign minister, Andrei Kozyrev. Yeltsin warmly endorsed the Oslo I (1993) and Oslo II (1995) peace agreements, but in the immediate post-Soviet period Russia was so embroiled in its own domestic economic problems (Yeltsin was trying to privatize the Russian economy) that it had little time for the Middle East. At the time Moscow was concentrating on relations with the countries of the former Soviet Union, which it called the "Near Abroad," on an ugly rebellion in Chechnya, and on its relations with the United States, from which it hoped to get economic aid.

By 1996, the Russian–Israeli honeymoon had ended, as Yeltsin, under increasing pressure from right-wing forces in the Russian Duma (legislature), and following US intervention in Bosnia, took a tougher position in world affairs. Kozyrev was replaced by Soviet-era hardliner Yevgeny Primakov, who displayed an increasingly critical attitude towards Israel and a sympathetic position towards the Arabs states and the Palestinians. Thus, during the fighting in Lebanon in spring 1996 between Israel and Hizbollah, Primakov and Israeli Prime Minister Shimon Peres (who had succeeded the assassinated Yitzhak Rabin) clashed openly. However, underlining the diplomatic impotence of Russia, it was American Secretary of State Warren Christopher, and not Primakov, who succeeded in bringing the fighting to an end. Peres's successor, Binyamin Netanyahu, sought to improve relations with Russia, even giving Moscow a $50 million agricultural loan during a visit in March 1997 and stating that Israel would consider buying Russian natural gas. In addition, bilateral relations continued to develop as the Israeli food manufacturer Tnuva filmed a "milk in space" commercial aboard the Russian space station *Mir*. However, Moscow was critical of Netanyahu's policies, especially his expansion of Jewish settlements on the West Bank. For his part, Netanyahu was critical of Russian military and economic aid to Iran, which included building a nuclear reactor at Bushehr, because Iran was an avowed enemy of Israel. Indeed, Netanyahu later cancelled discussions of the natural gas deal with Moscow because of Russia's supply of missile technology to Iran. Ariel Sharon, one of Netanyahu's ministers, did, however, gain favor in Moscow by backing the Russian position on Serbia during the US–Russian clash over Kosovo in the late 1990s.

By the late summer of 1998 Russia had become enmeshed in a near disastrous economic crisis which effectively limited its freedom of action in the world, including the Middle East. This situation continued until a sick, and frequently intoxicated, Yeltsin suddenly resigned as Russia's president and was succeeded in January 2000 by Vladimir Putin.

The Putin era, 2000–2004

When Vladimir Putin became Russia's prime minister in the fall of 1999 and acting president in January 2000 (he was formally elected president in March 2000), he had three major objectives. The first was to restore Russia's international prestige to prevent the United States from unilaterally dominating the world. The second was to rebuild the economy so that Russia could again become a great power. The third objective was to curb Muslim and especially Middle Eastern aid to the Chechen rebellion, which had erupted again in 1999, so that Moscow could more easily suppress it. To accomplish these tasks, Putin had to consolidate his power and end the near anarchy that had pervaded much of the Yeltsin era. He ended the freelancing foreign policy activities of such oil companies as Lukoil and brought Russian arms sales under the control of one agency, Rosoboronoexport. He also brought the once powerful Russian oligarchs under control, forcing Boris Berezhovsky and Vladimir Gusinsky into exile (Gusinsky fled to Israel) and arresting Yukos head Mikhail Khodorkovsky. To ensure that he would not be criticized by the media, he gained control of all the major Russian TV networks as well as the major newspapers. In addition he created a ruling political party, United Russia, to control the Duma, so that, unlike the situation during the Yeltsin years when the Duma posed constant challenges to the then Russian president, he would have full support for his domestic and foreign policies. After the popular revolutions in Georgia and Ukraine in 2003–4, he created a youth group called "Nashi" (Ours) – a combination of the Komsomol, the old Soviet youth organization, and the Hitler Youth – to disperse anti-government demonstrations.

While Putin was consolidating power from 2000 to 2004, his foreign policy, like that of Yeltsin, was basically defensive. Initially, with oil still below $20 per barrel, and capital flight still plaguing Russia, Putin's policy was cautiously to cooperate with the United States. The one exception was in regard to Iran, where Putin, in 2000, unilaterally abrogated the 1995 agreement between US Vice President Al Gore and then Russian Prime Minister Victor Chernomyrdin under which Russia had promised to end all arms exports to Iran when existing contracts ran out in 1999. In addition, in March 2001, Putin invited Mohamed Khatami, the president of Iran, for a state visit to Russia. Needless to say, the warming of relations between Russia and Iran was not received well in Israel. However, following 9/11, Putin actively cooperated with the United States – after all, the Taliban and al-Qaeda, as well as their ally the Islamic Movement of Uzbekistan – were threats to Russia too, and Moscow not only provided useful intelligence to the United States but also initially raised no objections to the establishment of US bases in Central Asia to fight the Taliban and al-Qaeda.

In the 2002–3 period, US–Russian relations began to chill, in part because of Putin's crack-down on the Russian media, and in part because US President George Bush both abrogated the US–Soviet ABM (anti-ballistic missile) treaty and sought to move NATO closer to Russia's borders by admitting the Baltic States. The biggest problem, however, was Iraq, where the USA was angry at Russian efforts to weaken the UN sanctions regime against Saddam Hussein, and Russia opposed US plans to invade Iraq. During this period, however, Putin was preoccu-pied with the rebellion in Chechnya, and the Chechen seizure of a Moscow theater in 2002 which caused numerous casualties reinforced this concern. Indeed, when an al-Qaeda group attacked Saudi Arabia in May 2003, Putin was quick to compare that attack to Chechen rebel assaults against Russia, and several months later he invited the Saudi crown prince to Moscow and got him to support his hand-picked Chechen leader, Akhmed Kadyrov. Kadyrov, how-ever, was assassinated by the Chechens the following year as a demonstration of the strength of the ongoing rebellion. Putin's policy of comparing the Chechen and al-Qaeda attacks was similar to the Russian leader's early policy on Hamas, when a visiting Israeli delegation to Moscow, after the start of the al-Aqsa *Intifada* in the fall of 2000 was told by Sergei Lavrov, then head of Russia's Security Council, that the terrorism the Israelis were facing in Gaza and the West Bank was exactly what Moscow faced in Chechnya.

Following the Anglo-American invasion of Iraq in 2003, US–Russian relations deteriorated sharply. However, Putin made common cause with France and Germany, which also opposed the invasion, hoping perhaps to drive a wedge between the NATO allies. Nonetheless, follow-ing the rapid US seizure of Baghdad, and perhaps fearing that the United States would then move on Moscow's ally Iran, Putin was willing to press the latter to reveal information about the secret nuclear installations that had come to light in December 2002. Consequently, Putin backed the European Union negotiations with Iran which offered the Islamic republic major economic benefits if it refrained from continuing its nuclear enrichment program. As a possible signal of cooperation with the European Union, Russia also postponed the date for completion of the Bushehr nuclear reactor and delayed signing an agreement to send nuclear fuel to Iran. Moscow also joined the diplomatic Quartet (Russia, the USA, the UN and the EU), whose mission was to facilitate an Israeli–Palestinian peace agreement.

As US–Russian relations chilled, so did Moscow's relations with Israel. At the same time, there was a clear improvement in Russian–Palestinian relations. Moscow's move towards the Palestinians became evident after the Israeli re-entry into the cities of the West Bank following a series of Palestinian terrorist attacks in 2002. A secondary goal of Moscow's pro-Palestinian tilt was to curb Arab support for the Chechen rebellion. Still, even while moving towards the Palestinians, Putin periodically uttered soothing remarks about how much he valued the bilat-eral Russian–Israeli relationship and the role of Russian émigrés living in Israel. However, on issues of substance, such as Russian aid to Iran and Israel's construction of a security fence to protect itself from terrorist attacks, the two countries held opposing positions.

Putin did, however, have a point about the continuing strength of the bilateral Russian–Israeli relationship. By early 2000 trade had risen to more than $1 billion per year, cultural rela-tions continued to develop, 50,000 Russian tourists were visiting Israel annually, and Russia and Israel signed an agreement under which Russian rockets would put Israeli satellites into orbit. Nonetheless, these areas of bilateral cooperation were increasingly overshadowed by diplomatic conflicts.

By the time of Israeli Prime Minister Ariel Sharon's visit to Moscow in September 2003, the growing diplomatic differences between Russia and Israel had become increasingly evident. While Sharon was in Moscow, Putin promised to take Israeli concerns into account when introducing a UN Security Council resolution codifying the diplomatic Quartet's "Road

Map" for peace. However, following the visit, when Moscow introduced the resolution, it was without the Israeli reservations. As far as Yasser Arafat was concerned, by 2002 Israel had refused to talk to the Palestinian leader, blaming him for the wave of terrorist attacks occurring during the al-Aqsa *Intifada*. By contrast, Putin continued to assert that Arafat was still politically relevant. On the issue of Israel's security fence, Russia joined the majority of EU states in voting to support a UN General Assembly resolution (non-binding) both condemning Israel for building the fence and calling on it to comply with the majority decision of the International Court of Justice to tear it down. The United States and six other countries opposed the resolution.

By September 2004, however, after a series of Chechen terrorist attacks culminated in the seizure of a Russian school in Beslan that led to the deaths of 332 people, many of them children, Russia may have wished that it had constructed its own security fence separating the rest of the Russian Federation from Chechnya. This may have prompted Russian Foreign Minister Sergei Lavrov, on a visit to Israel as part of a post-Beslan Middle East tour during which Russia sought world support against Chechen terrorism, to accept an Israeli offer to cooperate in the area of counter-terrorism. The Israeli offer included the sharing of information on safeguarding critical installations, the training of counterterrorism specialists, and the exchange of intelligence data. Still, any hope that Israel may have had that Moscow would adopt a more pro-Israeli stand in Israel's conflict with Palestinian terrorists as a result of the security agreement quickly faded. In October 2004, just one month after the Russian–Israeli agreement, Moscow supported a United Nations Security Council resolution (vetoed by the United States) condemning Israel for its military incursion into Gaza aimed at rooting out as many Hamas terrorists as possible before the Israeli Knesset vote on Ariel Sharon's Gaza disengagement plan.

Following the UN vote, Putin received a major shock when his hand-picked candidate for president of Ukraine, Viktor Yanukovich, lost to the pro-Western Viktor Yushchenko in an election in which Putin had invested his personal prestige. This development, together with the aftermath of the events in Beslan, prompted Putin to take a far more activist policy in the Middle East.

The Putin era, 2005–2009

Putin's activist policy in the Middle East, which was to impact Israel negatively, began in December 2004, as he saw the region open to a greater Russian role. There were two reasons for this. First, the United States, the dominant power in the region since the 1991 Gulf War, was preoccupied with Iraq and, increasingly, Afghanistan. Second, the sharp increase in oil prices had strengthened the Russian economy and given Moscow the ability to waive the debts incurred with the Soviet Union by a number of Arab countries. Taking advantage of US–Turkish friction over the Iraq War, on a journey to Ankara in December 2004, and during Turkish Prime Minister Recep Erdogan's return visit to Moscow in January 2005, Putin raised the possibility of increasing trade from the 2004 level of $10 billion to $25 billion, signed a number of military agreements with Turkey, and promised to help solve the Azeri-Armenian conflict. In January, Moscow also moved to improve ties with Syria, a major enemy of Israel. Isolated because of its heavy-handed policy in Lebanon, Syria was very much in need of Russian economic, diplomatic, and military support. Putin agreed to waive 90 percent of Syria's debt to the former USSR and sold it short-range surface-to-air missiles and anti-tank missiles, some of which were transferred to Hizbollah and later used against Israel in the summer 2006 Israel–Hizbollah war. Moscow sought to prevent sanctions being imposed on Syria after the latter was accused of involvement in the assassination of former Lebanese Prime Minister Rafik

Hariri in February 2005, in the process coming into conflict with both the United States and France, which wanted to penalize Syria for its actions in Lebanon.

In February 2005 Putin also moved to cement relations with Iran by approving the long-delayed agreement to supply nuclear fuel for the nuclear reactor at Bushehr, which Russia was constructing for Iran. Continuing to show the Russian flag, Putin then visited Egypt, Israel, and the Palestinian territories in April, urging the convening of an international peace conference in Moscow – something he hoped would lead to the growth of Russian influence in the region. He also promised to supply fifty armored personnel carriers to the Palestinian Authority – which Israel immediately vetoed in case the troop carriers be used against it – while telling Israel that he would do nothing to hurt their country, pointing to his decision to refuse to sell mid-range Iskander ground-to-ground missiles to Syria as evidence of his commitment.

Most Israelis doubted Putin, however, given his sale of surface-to-air missiles to Syria as well as Russia's sale of weapons to and construction of a nuclear reactor in Iran. Israel's concerns with Moscow's policies were reinforced when, following the election of the outspoken Iranian President Mahmoud Ahmadinejad in July 2005, Russia did its best to delay discussion of sanctions against Iran in the United Nations Security Council after Iran broke off negotiations with the European Union and announced it had begun to enrich uranium, while also refusing to provide information required by the International Atomic Energy Agency. Making matters worse, Ahmadinejad in the fall of 2005 called for wiping Israel off the map and denied the Holocaust. Despite such statements, in November 2005 Moscow signed an agreement with Tehran to provide it with sophisticated short-range surface-to-air missiles that could be used to protect Iranian nuclear installations against a possible US or Israeli attack.

As Putin was moving to bolster the Russian position in the Middle East by cultivating the Arab states and Iran, he also was trying to prevent the Arab and Muslim worlds from aiding the rebellion in Chechnya, which by 2004 had become thoroughly Islamized. Thus he both sought, and obtained, observer status for Russia in the Islamic Conference in 2005 and exploited the Danish cartoon controversy by denouncing the cartoons, which many Muslims considered insulting to Islam, thereby putting Russia on the same side as the Islamic world over the issue. For the same reason he continued to pursue an improved relationship with Saudi Arabia, an effort that bore fruit as the Saudi government distanced itself from the Chechen rebels and promised to help in the reconstruction of Chechnya.

Putin called the Hamas victory in the Palestinian Legislative Council elections in January 2006 "a very serious blow" to American diplomacy in the Middle East. The event signaled a return to the "zero-sum" influence competition that characterized Soviet–American relations until the advent of Gorbachev. Soon after the election Putin invited a Hamas delegation to Moscow, asserting that Hamas was not on Russia's terrorist list and hence was not considered a terrorist organization – a clear change from its policy in 2000, when a visiting Israeli delegation after the start of the al-Aqsa *Intifada* was told that the terrorism Israel was facing in Gaza and the West Bank was exactly what Russia was battling in Chechnya. By inviting Hamas to Moscow, Putin undermined the consensus of the Quartet, which was not to have anything to do with Hamas until it recognized Israel, renounced terrorism, and accepted all previous Israeli–Palestinian agreements.

Putin had a number of objectives in inviting the Hamas delegation to Moscow. First, he associated Russia with the then Arab consensus, which was to give Hamas time to change its policies and in the meantime to work with a Hamas government and not to sanction it. Russia was widely praised in the Arab world for its invitation, which bestowed a modicum of legitimacy on Hamas – much to the anger of Israel, which saw it as a terrorist foe seeking the destruction of the Jewish state. Another goal for Putin was to get Hamas, an Islamist organization, to downplay the Chechen issue. The delegation complied, with its leader Khalid Mashal stating after a meeting with Russian Foreign Minister Sergei Lavrov that the Chechen separatists were "an internal problem of Russia." This comment drew a bitter reaction from the Chechen rebels, who called Hamas's decision to visit Putin's Russia, which had killed so many Chechen Muslims, not only regrettable but also "un-Islamic."

Another blow to Russian–Israeli relations occurred six months later, when war broke out between Israel and Hizbollah following the kidnapping of two Israeli soldiers. Not only did Moscow look the other way when Syria transferred some of its Russian weapons to Hizbollah, at a meeting of the G8 it also opposed sanctions against Syria, then Hizbollah's main sponsor, and criticized Israel for its overreaction to the kidnapping. In the aftermath of the war, Russia sent a group of engineers to rebuild some of the bridges destroyed in the conflict but did not offer troops for the expanded UNIFIL contingent in southern Lebanon, whose mission, at least in theory, was to prevent the rearming of Hizbollah.

In the face of Israel's deteriorating relationship with Russia, Israeli Prime Minister Ehud Olmert journeyed to Moscow in October 2006, perhaps hoping to secure a reversal of some of Russia's anti-Israeli regional policies. Olmert had three issues to raise with Putin: Iran, Syria's transfer of arms to Hizbollah, and Russia's diplomatic support for Hamas. A secondary list of priorities focused on Russian–Israeli bilateral relations, including trade, especially the potential purchase of Russian natural gas, and Russian–Israeli cooperation in arms sales to third countries. For his part, Putin had a more limited list of goals for Olmert's visit. First was his desire to have Russia recognized as a major player in Middle East diplomacy, which Olmert's visit helped confirm. Second came Putin's efforts to rebuild the Russian economy, which was an element in his efforts to regain great power status, and trade with a high-tech country such as Israel would help him achieve that goal. Given the results of the meeting, it appears that Putin fared far better than did Olmert. Thus, on Iran, Russia made no concessions, with Lavrov, after Olmert's visit, saying that it was still opposed to sanctions. Moscow also played down the issue of weapons transfers, and, as far as Hamas was concerned, Lavrov stated, following the departure of Olmert, "Demanding now that Hamas fully accept the Quartet's conditions such as the recognition of Israel, the denunciation of violence against Israel, and acceptance of all existing agreements is unrealistic at this time."

If Olmert got very little satisfaction from his Russian hosts on issues of major importance to Israel, he proved willing to accede to Putin's goals, perhaps hoping that, if bilateral relations improved further, Russia might change its anti-Israeli regional policies. Thus Olmert agreed to raise trade from the current $2 billion annual level to $5 billion and to discuss the possibility of Israel's purchasing natural gas from Russia by way of a pipeline from Turkey, thereby reversing the stand on natural gas purchases adopted by Netanyahu in 1997. That seemed to be a mutually advantageous deal for Russia and Israel, because Turkey in 2006 had failed to use the amount of gas it had contracted with Russia to purchase. Israel, in addition to the natural gas it purchased from Egypt, had planned to buy natural gas from Gaza but considered this unfeasible after the rise of Hamas. The one concrete agreement to come out of the Moscow talks was the setting up of a working group to coordinate arms sales to third countries. While Russia and Israel have cooperated in the production of weapons systems such as the AWACS, the two countries competed for contracts to refurbish old Soviet equipment such as the MIG-23 and MIG-25 aircraft.

Meanwhile, however, Russia's backing for Iran and its allies conflicted with Putin's goal of improving ties with the Sunni states of the Arab world, especially Saudi Arabia and the other Gulf states, Jordan and Egypt, which, particularly after the Israeli–Hizbollah war, had become increasingly suspicious of Iran and its allies – Syria, Hizbollah, and Hamas. Consequently, as a sop to the Sunni Arabs prior to visiting Saudi Arabia, Qatar, and Jordan in February 2007, in December 2006 Russia finally agreed to limited UN Security Council sanctions against Iran. In March 2007, following the trip, Putin agreed to additional very limited sanctions. During his visit to the Gulf Arabs, Putin sought major investments in Russia's banking and space industries, weapons sales, and joint investment projects in oil and natural gas (he was to have similar goals during a visit to Libya in 2008). The energy deals were especially important to Moscow because its own production of oil and natural gas had peaked. During spring and summer 2007, as part of Putin's efforts to court the Sunni Arabs, Russia also delayed sending Iran promised nuclear fuel, making the dubious claim that the rich Persian Gulf country had not made the necessary payments.

Following the ill-conceived US national intelligence estimate on Iran of December 2007, which erroneously argued that the country had given up its nuclear weapons program and hence was not an immediate threat, Moscow, perceiving diminished pressure from the Gulf Arabs and the United States, went ahead with the sale of the nuclear fuel, completing the shipments by February 2008. Ironically, even as Moscow was helping Iran develop its nuclear capability, Putin, seeking business for Russia's nuclear industry, offered to build reactors for the Gulf Arabs, Egypt, and Jordan as well, as the Arab states sought to keep up with their rival Iran.

The major problem Moscow encountered in the Arab world in 2007 concerned the Palestinians. In June of that year Hamas seized power in Gaza, killing a number of Fatah officials working there. With Fatah and Hamas now at loggerheads (Abbas fired the Hamas prime minister and replaced him with one of his own appointees, Salam Fayyad, who had a reputation for fiscal honesty and was close to the West), Moscow faced a problem of choice. Making matters worse for Russia was that Hamas looked increasingly to Iran for support, thereby alienating key Sunni states and making Moscow's legitimization of the organization problematic. In reaction to this situation, the Russians stepped up their efforts, first announced during Putin's visit to the Middle East in 2005, to convene an international peace conference in Moscow. In addition, they increased their backing for the Arab peace plan, which had been introduced in 2002 and reintroduced in 2007. Most important of all, Russia called for reconciliation between Hamas and Fatah as a necessary precondition for the peace conference to take place.

This was to be the thrust of Russian policy towards the Palestinians for the rest of the decade. On the one hand, it sought to reconcile Fatah and Hamas – albeit without success. It also asserted that its continued meetings with Hamas leaders were aimed at changing the Islamist organization's policy towards Israel and towards Fatah, although by the fall of 2009 it had failed in this endeavor as well. By the summer of 2009 the Russian leadership seemed to have shifted to the Fatah side and distanced itself somewhat from Hamas. It failed to give strong backing to Hamas during Operation Cast Lead and praised the long delayed August 2009 sixth Fatah Congress, with Russian Foreign Ministry spokesman Andrei Nesterenko asserting, "The restoration of Palestinian unity on the PLO platform and on the basis of the Arab Peace Initiative is an integral part of lasting peace."

Putin, at that time prime minister, although considered by most analysts to be Russia's most powerful leader, was even more explicit in his praise for Fatah. In greetings to the congress he stated, "Fatah, the core of the Palestinian Liberation Organization, steadily defends the interests of Palestinians, primarily their right to form a sovereign and viable state." The Russian support was in clear contrast to Hamas, which denounced the Fatah Congress.

Russia's policy towards Israel in the 2008–9 period also fell into an already familiar pattern, as Moscow cultivated its bilateral ties with Jerusalem while at the same time pursuing regional policies that endangered the security of Israel. These included protecting Iran from serious sanctions (another round of minor sanctions were approved by the UN Security Council in

March 2009) and indicating it was willing to sell both sophisticated weapons systems to Iran (the SAM-300 long-range surface-to-air missile system, which, if installed, would seriously complicate an Israeli – or American – attack on Iran's nuclear installations) and the MIG-31E military aircraft to Syria. Indeed, Israeli officials, in numerous meetings with their Russian counterparts during this period, sought to prevent these arms sales from being implemented. It appeared that Israel was even willing to trade its participation in the Moscow Middle East peace conference Putin wanted so much (albeit without Hamas attending as an independent participant) for Russia's agreeing not to provide these weapons systems to Iran and Syria. Israeli Foreign Minister Yevgeny Lieberman went so far as to state, during his visit to Moscow in May 2009, that Israel accepted Russia's role as one of the key players in the resolution of the Arab–Israeli conflict.

As far as bilateral Israeli–Russian relations were concerned, they continued to improve, although Russia, as tensions rose in its relations with Georgia in the months leading up to their August 2008 war, openly complained about Israeli arms sales to that nation, especially reconnaissance drones. Israel, mindful of the need to prevent the Russian arms sales to Iran and Syria, complied with the Russian request to terminate the sales, and Russian Foreign Minister Lavrov publicly praised Israel for complying.

Other areas of the relationship blossomed. Trade neared $3 billion a year, with Russia especially benefiting from Israeli expertise in nanotechnology. A Russian cultural center was opened in Tel Aviv, party-to-party relations were established in 2008 between the Russian ruling party, United Russia, and the Israeli party Kadima, which at the time was leading the Israeli governing coalition, and a visa waiver agreement was signed to facilitate tourism.

In addition, Israel agreed to return to Russia the Sergei Courtyard, a property in Jerusalem once owned by the czars. And, perhaps ironically,, because Moscow had fallen behind in drone technology, Israel agreed to sell to Russia the kind of reconnaissance drones that had been so useful to Georgia in the Georgian–Russian war.

Conclusion

There are two major conclusions that can be drawn from Moscow's relations with Israel and the Palestinians. The first is that, while its regional policy under Putin had major anti-Israeli components, such as its diplomatic and military support for Israel's enemies Iran and Syria and the diplomatic legitimization of Hamas, unlike the situation through most of the Soviet period, Russian–Israeli relations on a bilateral basis are now quite warm. It appears that Putin's Russia has three major goals vis-à-vis Israel. First, since Israel is the homeland of more than a million Russian-speaking citizens of the former Soviet Union, and Putin sees Russian speakers abroad as an element in his quest for world influence, cultural ties have been promoted by Moscow in which Israelis of Russian origin play the dominant role. Second, Putin is determined to develop the non-energy sectors of the Russian economy, and high-tech trade with Israel is part of his plan. Third, the Arab–Israeli conflict is a major issue in world politics, and Putin, ever seeking a major role for Russia in the world, would very much like to play a part in its diplomacy, if not in finding a solution to the conflict. For this reason he has called for an international peace conference on the Middle East to be held in Moscow, and Israel has now agreed to attend.

By contrast, looking at Russia's policy towards the Palestinians, there are many similarities to that in the pre-Gorbachev Soviet period, as since the mid-1990s this has been a component of its overall strategy in the Arab world. Since the Palestinians, at least at the current time, have little to offer Moscow on a bilateral basis, except, in the case of Fatah, a willingness to participate in Putin's hoped-for international conference, Russia has championed the Palestinian quest for statehood, as well as the Arab peace plan, as part of its strategy to gain influence in the Arab world. However, unlike the situation in the Soviet era, when the Palestinians had one acknowledged leader, Yasser Arafat, by 2007 a major split had occurred between Hamas and Fatah that posed difficult problems of choice for Russia. Exacerbating the problem for the Russian leadership was the fact that, as Hamas increasingly gravitated to Iran after 2007, the Sunni Arab states, and especially Saudi Arabia, which Moscow had been cultivating, were angered. Under the circumstances, Russia's only option was to seek reconciliation between the two Palestinian groups. However, unsuccessful in this effort by September 2009, it began tilting towards Fatah in the Hamas–Fatah conflict.

Further reading

Freedman, Robert O. (1991) *Moscow and the Middle East: Soviet Policy since the Invasion of Afghanistan* (New York: Cambridge University Press).

Freedman, Robert O. (2006) *Russia, Iran and the Nuclear Question: The Putin Record* (Carlisle, PA: Strategic Studies Institute, US Army War College).

Freedman, Robert O. (2007) "The Russian Resurgence in the Middle East," *China and Eurasia Forum Quarterly*, 5/3, pp. 19–23.

Freedman, Robert O. (2008) "The Russian Invasion of Georgia: Its Impact on Israel and the Middle East," *Caucasian Review of International Affairs*, 2/4, pp. 179–86.

Golan, Galia (1980) *The Soviet Union and the Palestinian Liberation Organization: An Uneasy Alliance* (New York: Praeger).

Ro'i, Yaacov (1974) *From Encroachment to Involvement: A Documentary Study of Russian Policy in the Middle East, 1945–1973* (New York: John Wiley).

28

Europe

Rosemary Hollis

European involvement in the Israeli–Palestinian conflict has taken various forms over the last hundred years. Certainly the origins of the conflict cannot be understood without reference to racism, nationalism and war in Europe. The political contours of the whole Middle East region were determined by British and French imperial machinations between the 1920s and the 1950s. During the Cold War the superpowers became more instrumental, but when they took opposite sides in the 1967 Arab–Israeli war the Europeans adopted a range of positions somewhere in between.

Latterly the European Union (EU) has emerged as a new player in the quest for conflict resolution and, while its role has been secondary to that of the United States, it was quicker to articulate the goal of independent statehood for the Palestinians in the West Bank and Gaza. Yet even though the EU, the USA, the United Nations and Russia joined forces after 2002 in the so-called Quartet and endorsed a 'two-state solution' to the conflict, the EU has deferred to US leadership on how to get there.

This chapter depicts the story of European involvement in the Israeli–Palestinian conflict in five successive phases. The first covers the period of the British Mandate in Palestine, Nazi ascendancy in Europe and the Holocaust, and concludes with the establishment of the State of Israel in 1948 and the genesis of the Palestinian refugee problem. The second phase sees the demise of European imperialism, the Suez debacle, superpower rivalry, the 1967 and 1973 wars, wherein Israel captured and occupied the West Bank and Gaza Strip, the oil shock, and the US-brokered Egypt–Israel peace treaty of 1979. In 1980 the European Community (EC) issued the Venice Declaration, signalling for the first time a collective European position on the conflict that included recognition of the right of Palestinians to self-determination. This marked the beginning of the third phase, during which the EC was transformed into the European Union. It then adopted a central economic role in what became the Middle East peace process.

The outbreak of the Second Palestinian *Intifada* in 2000 marked the beginning of the fourth phase, during which the advent of 'the war on terror' and the Iraq crisis transformed the international and regional context of the conflict. In the face of Israel's military crackdown on Palestinian resistance and terrorism, the EU poured its resources into keeping the Palestinian Authority (PA) afloat. Simultaneously, it forged closer ties with Israel under the European Neighbourhood Policy. The fifth and final phase in the story began in 2006, when the Islamist movement Hamas won the Palestinian legislative elections that were financed and monitored by Europe. The EU, along with the rest of the Quartet, then refused to deal with Hamas, pending satisfaction on Quartet requirements. After Hamas took sole control of the Gaza Strip in 2007, the EU focused on Palestinian institution-building in the West Bank, while Gaza languished under an Israeli blockade endorsed by Washington. Since Europe is now too embedded in bilateral economic relations with Israel and the PA to walk away, EU policy consists of repeated calls on both to agree a solution.

Europe and the origins of the conflict

In the late nineteenth century, Europe was the context for the development of the Zionist movement. Simply put, were it not for the persecution of Jews in Europe, particularly in Eastern Europe and Russia in the nineteenth century, the impetus for the creation of a national homeland for the Jews might have gained less traction. While this essay does not go into the origins of Zionism, it is important to mention how the British featured in the realization of Zionist aspirations.

Members of the British establishment were divided in their reactions to the Zionist cause, though some saw it as potentially serving British interests in the context of the First World War and Britain's imperial ambitions in the Middle East. In November 1917 the British foreign secretary, Lord Balfour, wrote a letter to Lord Rothschild saying that the British government:

> views with favour the establishment in Palestine of a national home for the Jewish people, and will use their best endeavours to facilitate the achievement of this object, it being clearly understood that nothing shall be done which may prejudice the civil and religious rights of existing non-Jewish communities in Palestine.[1]

In the aftermath of war and the collapse of the Ottoman Empire, Britain and France took the lead in dividing up the Middle East into separate states and spheres of influence. Britain acquired the League of Nations Mandate for Palestine in 1922 and Balfour's letter, which became known as the Balfour Declaration, was incorporated in the terms of the Mandate.[2] At British insistence, a further provision was added by which Transjordan was excluded from implementation of the Balfour Declaration.

The flow of Jewish migrants to Palestine was to swell significantly during the 1930s and 1940s as a consequence of the rise of Nazism in Europe. In the face of this and resulting Arab hostility, the British authorities took steps to control the numbers of Jewish immigrants, only to incur Zionist hostility and international opprobrium (especially in the United States) when they tried to turn away Jewish refugees seeking entry to Palestine.

This friction notwithstanding, some of the measures the British authorities took to counter violent Arab opposition to their rule and to Jewish immigration bolstered the position of the Zionists vis-à-vis the Palestinians. The British also deployed emergency powers to suppress unrest that were later adopted by Israel after the establishment of the Jewish state. From a Palestinian perspective, therefore, the British were deemed responsible both for enabling the Zionist enterprise to take off and for undermining the relative strength of the Palestinians in the ensuing contest.

Victorious but exhausted and overstretched at the end of the Second World War, the British were obliged to regroup. Britain's gradual withdrawal from its imperial domains began with Indian independence in 1947. The same year, the British referred the question of Palestine to the United Nations. However, when the UN voted in favour of partition, between a Jewish state and an Arab state, the Zionists acquiesced but the Arabs declared their opposition, and the British, lacking the capacity and the will to enforce partition, packed up and left, leaving the parties to their fate in the war of 1948. As a result Jordan, with British support, won control of the West Bank, including East Jerusalem, along with many of the 700,000 or so Palestinian refugees displaced in the fighting. Other refugees fled north to Syria and Lebanon. Many also ended up in the Gaza Strip, which came under Egyptian administration from 1948 until 1967.

Europe and the Israeli–Palestinian conflict during the Cold War

Israel's victory was the Palestinians' *nakba*, or catastrophe, and antipathy to the Jewish state became a central feature of the Arab nationalist cause, along with anti-European imperialism in the 1950s and 1960s. The British and French progressively retreated in the face of independence movements across the globe, including in the Middle East.

Following the overthrow of the British-backed monarchy in Egypt, Gamal Abdul Nasser emerged as the president of the republic and champion of Arab nationalism. Opposed to Nasser's regional influence and fearing a curtailment of their access to the Suez Canal – a vital artery for European shipping between the Mediterranean and the Indian Ocean – in 1956 the British and French secretly colluded with the Israelis to seize the canal and topple Nasser.[3]

Their mission was thwarted by the Americans, who forced a withdrawal of the British, French and Israeli armed forces and in the process won favour across the Arab world for countering the Israelis and the old imperialists. The Suez War marked the nadir of British imperial fortunes in the Middle East, after which the monarchy they had installed in Iraq was ousted in 1958 and their influence in Jordan was curtailed. By 1967 they were forced out of Yemen by rebels supported by Nasser. The French retreated also and gave up their campaign to hold onto Algeria in 1962.

By 1967 both France and Britain had ceased to exercise decisive influence in the region. Until that date, France had served as the principal supplier of arms to Israel, but as of the 1967 war the French changed policy and opted for closer relations with the Arabs. Britain left its last outposts of empire in the Gulf in 1971 and during the first oil boom became a competitor with the French, the Americans and others for lucrative commercial contracts in the Arab oil-producing states and Iran. Most European countries, with the notable exception of the Netherlands, accommodated to Arab pressure during the oil embargo that accompanied the 1973 war.

Meanwhile, Cold War rivalry between the United States and the Soviet Union became the overriding determinant of external engagement in the Middle East. In the 1967 war the superpowers were ranged on opposite sides. In the aftermath, however, the British and French, both permanent members of the UN Security Council, were instrumental in the drafting and adoption of UN Security Council Resolution 242.

This milestone bears mention here because Resolution 242 subsequently became the benchmark for official European pronouncements on the Arab–Israeli conflict. In essence, Resolution 242 and the successor Resolution 338, adopted during the October 1973 Arab–Israeli War, called for the exchange of land for peace. The Europeans have repeatedly referred back to this formula as the key to resolving the conflict. They contend that the most sustainable road to peace between Israel and the Arabs depends upon Israel giving up the land it captured in 1967, including the West Bank and Gaza Strip, in return for recognition and acceptance by its neighbours.

By contrast, the Americans have tended to assume that, if the parties to the conflict can arrive at an agreement, so be it, irrespective of whether that agreement is fully in accordance with UN pronouncements. Judging by recent EU statements, however (see below), the Europeans have come to the view that, provided both sides agree, there can be adjustments to the 1967 borders.

From the Venice Declaration to the demise of the Oslo process (1980–2000)

The EC's Venice Declaration of 1980 constituted the first major joint statement of the Europeans on the Arab–Israeli conflict and the beginning of Europe's emergence as a new player in the region. It broke new ground by recognizing the right of Palestinians to self-determination and calling for the inclusion of the Palestine Liberation Organization (PLO) in peace negotiations. However, Israel rejected the declaration out of hand and the Americans pursued their own initiatives. As of the Israeli invasion of Lebanon in 1982 that country became the main focus of such efforts. The emergence of Hizbollah, with Iranian support, hostage-taking and the attacks on US and French marines in Beirut widened the conflict and engendered animosities that still endure.

Escorted out of Lebanon under US and French mediation, the PLO leadership decamped to Tunis. Notwithstanding some unofficial European contacts with the organization, it continued to be barred as a terrorist group by the Israelis. Even the PLO was then taken by surprise when the First Palestinian *Intifada* broke out spontaneously in Gaza in December 1987 and spread rapidly to the West Bank. Television coverage of armoured Israeli forces confronting stone-throwing youths and civilian demonstrators on the streets of Palestinian towns drew international sympathy for the Palestinians and triggered a shift in European thinking about the conflict. Israel came in for much criticism, but the emergence of a strong peace camp in Israel also opened up possibilities for new 'people-to-people' initiatives involving both sides, many of which the Europeans helped to fund and facilitate.

Iraq's invasion of Kuwait in 1990 diverted attention to the Gulf. In the ensuing crisis the Arabs divided, with the PLO taking the Iraqi side. The Europeans contributed troops, armour and funds to the US-led coalition force that defeated the Iraqis in early 1991. Yet, when the United States (and Russia) convened the ground-breaking Middle East peace conference at Madrid in November 1991, the EC was granted only observer status. Europe was not yet considered a serious player. The European case for involvement was not helped by internal disagreement over who should represent European member states on such occasions, and to this day the EU suffers from the difficulties of establishing a unified position on foreign policy issues.

However, in the multilateral talks initiated by the Madrid conference, the EU was made 'gavel-holder' of the Regional Economic and Development Working Group (REDWG).[4] The Europeans also participated in parallel talks on regional security, refugees and environment, but they used REDWG to carve out a role for the EU in the Middle East peace process that became increasingly instrumental in the fortunes of the Palestinians. The purpose of the multilateral talks was to bolster the prospects of the bilateral negotiations between Israel and the Arabs, hosted by Washington. However, it was a Norwegian initiative that produced what became the Oslo Accords between Israel and the PLO, soon to be adopted and managed by the United States. The Europeans embraced the initiative as a means for resolving the Israeli–Palestinian conflict and expected that it would likely lead to Palestinian statehood, alongside Israel, in the West Bank and Gaza.

Meanwhile, in 1995 the EU initiated the Euro-Mediterranean Partnership programme (EMP), the central goal of which was to turn the Mediterranean basin into a free-trade area encompassing Israel as well as the Arab littoral states and Jordan. Security cooperation was also envisaged, as were cultural exchanges and environmental protection. Crucially, through promoting human rights and political reform in the Arab partner countries, the EU hoped to use the programme to transform these states and thereby address its own security concerns about migration and terrorist violence perpetrated by Islamist groups linking militants in Europe and North Africa.

A central assumption of the EMP was that the Middle East peace process would deliver. All the protagonists, including Syria and Lebanon, as well as the Palestinians and Jordan, attended partnership meetings alongside the Israelis, notwithstanding setbacks and reversals in bilateral peace negotiations during the 1990s. This experience encouraged the EU to believe that the EMP could make progress in parallel with, but not dependent upon, the fortunes of the Middle East peace process. However, the vision of the programme could not ultimately be realized without resolution of the conflict. Meanwhile, the institutional frameworks through which the EU pursued its objectives in both arenas overlapped and became fused.[5]

Once the PA was established, the EU and its member states began channelling funds previously dispersed to Palestinian NGOs directly to the PA, along with development aid, though European support for people-to-people initiatives also continued. In addition, European governments identified various infrastructure projects, such as a port facility in the Gaza Strip and an airport, for state and EU funding.

On the diplomatic front, the Americans took the lead and expected the Europeans to be supportive but in the background. For the most part the Europeans went along, but when progress on implementation of the Oslo Accords faltered, particularly during the tenure of the Likud government in Israel from 1996 to 1999, they were frustrated and critical, and they showed it by delaying ratification of successive trade and cooperation agreements with Israel. However, under the EMP, the EU did eventually sign and ratify partnership agreements with both Israel and the PA.

The results were mixed. The agreement with the PA took it for granted that economic protocols between Israel and the Palestinians, which assumed complex interdependence and a customs union between the two, would proceed to plan. In reality, the Palestinian economy was subordinate and constrained by the effects of Israeli security measures. The EU partnership agreement with Israel, meanwhile, drew a distinction between goods made in Israel and those made in settlements in the Occupied Territories, such that only the former could enter the EU without paying customs dues. However, in practice, observance of this distinction was cumbersome and fudged, and it became a source of contention between Israel and Europe.

With respect to US handling of the peace negotiations, European pronouncements indicated a level of scepticism about Washington's capacity to understand Palestinian concerns as readily as those of Israel. Yet they recognized the limits of their own leverage with the Israelis in comparison to that of the United States and therefore looked to Washington to deliver Israel. On occasion the French suggested a new peace conference might be required to trigger progress, but they could not force the issue without US concurrence. British Prime Minister Tony Blair made a number of efforts actually to assist US diplomacy.[6] Yet the Israelis and even the Palestinians remained more attentive to Washington than to any European mediation.

Eventually, following the unsuccessful US summit at Camp David in July 2000, the Oslo process collapsed. The Second Palestinian *Intifada* unleashed a series of suicide attacks on Israeli civilians that destroyed the Israeli peace camp and led to the election of Ariel Sharon. He initiated a crackdown on the Palestinians intended to crush resistance and 'lower their expectations'.

Vain quest to restart the Middle East peace process (2001–2005)

In 2001 George W. Bush became the new US president and initially showed little interest in resolving the Israeli–Palestinian conflict. In the absence of US engagement, the Europeans could do little more than provide the funds to keep the PA from total collapse while the conflict raged. The EU contended that preservation of the PA was essential to counter the Israeli claim that there was no Palestinian partner with which to negotiate. Even so, the suicide attacks on Israeli civilians eroded public sympathy in Europe for the Palestinians. Accusations of corruption in the PA prompted the EU to demand stringent reforms in its accounting practices. Meanwhile, the EU was itself evolving and preoccupied with the absorption of new members and the quest for a European constitution.

Against this backdrop the attacks on the United States of 11 September 2001 (9/11) transformed the context of the Israeli–Palestinian conflict and the hopes for peace. The Bush administration declared a 'war on terror', and the Israelis defined their confrontation with the Palestinians in this context. Arafat, who had been a frequent guest at the Clinton White House, was no longer welcome in Washington and remained holed up in his headquarters in Ramallah. After the Americans cut funding to the PA, it fell to the EU to pay the salaries of PA employees in order to avert a humanitarian crisis in the Occupied Territories. EC officials contemplated cutting support to oblige the Israelis to shoulder responsibility in accordance with the Geneva Conventions – but they baulked for fear that the strategy would backfire.

Meanwhile, attention in Europe and the Middle East became riveted on US plans for Iraq. The Iraq crisis and invasion of 2003 caused a major split in the Atlantic alliance and within the EU. The British stood beside the Americans, but largely failed to use their access in Washington to convince them of the importance of reviving the Middle East peace process. The new Eastern European members of the EU were also supportive of Washington, but Germany opposed the invasion, as did the French, who joined various Arab leaders in predicting mayhem across the Middle East as a result of it.

Against this backdrop, EU engagement on the Israeli–Palestinian issue followed two parallel tracks. Funding of the PA was continued, while diplomacy was focused on Washington – where EU leverage was compromised by the Iraq crisis. Following Bush's pronouncement in 2002 that a Palestinian state alongside Israel was his vision for peace, the EU worked within the Quartet to devise a Road Map for reaching that goal. The plan was finally launched in the wake of the Iraq invasion, but languished thereafter, in part because of US and Israeli manoeuvres to keep Arafat out of the frame. After the latter's death in November 2004 the Israelis began a series of unilateral moves that changed the shape of the conflict. In summer 2005 they withdrew all Jewish settlers from the Gaza Strip but continued to control the borders and curtail the movement of Palestinians and trade. Work began on the security barrier around and within the West Bank, separating major settlement blocs from Palestinian population centres.

The EU expressed concerns about the route taken by the barrier, which was pronounced contrary to international law by the International Court in The Hague. EU statements and approaches to the Israelis included frequent complaints about the effects of Israeli security measures on Palestinian economic life and welfare in both the West Bank and Gaza. When Palestinian elections were called for January 2006, the EU hoped to make this a turning point for the Middle East peace process. It was, but not as anticipated. The victory of Hamas triggered a crisis from which EU diplomacy has not recovered.

The EU decision to put Hamas on its list of terrorist organizations, thereby barring it from receipt of EU funds, was taken in 2004, at the height of the 'war on terror'. Having divided over the issue of Iraq, the Europeans were at pains to demonstrate solidarity with Washington on the terrorism issue at least. In addition, Europe was itself the target of terrorist plots, many of which appeared to be 'home-grown', and European governments began to fear a new phenomenon within, which has been dubbed 'radicalization'. A counter-phenomenon, labelled Islamophobia, also worried the authorities, as well as incidences of anti-Semitic attacks on Jews and Jewish sites. Among government responses were measures to control immigration and taking a tougher line on asylum-seekers.

In theory, the EU remained committed to its political reform agenda in the Middle East, enshrined in the Euro-Mediterranean Partnership programme. When the Bush administration announced its democratization strategy for Iraq and the 'wider Middle East', the EU countered with its neighbourhood policy. In the Mediterranean, this was supposed to supplement the broad brush approach of the partnership programme with a differentiated approach to partner countries, tailored to suit the different economic conditions in each. Action plans were agreed with Europe's southern neighbours that were supposed to bring them into closer harmony with EU internal market standards. In the process Israel, with the most advanced economy among the partner countries, attained a new level of integration with the EU. An opportunity to condition closer EU–Israeli relations on progress in conflict resolution was sidestepped.

With Europe's Arab neighbours, meanwhile, closer security cooperation took precedence over democratization and human rights promotion. Only the Palestinians were held to strict standards of financial accountability and transparency. However, once Hamas won the elections in 2006, the EU, which had called for, financed and monitored the elections, faced a dilemma. Financing a Hamas-run PA would be illegal under EU law, but, according to the Americans and Israelis, pressure on Hamas would eventually force the movement to change fundamentally or relinquish power. The EU opted to join the rest of the Quartet in devising three principles that Hamas was enjoined to embrace in order to gain acceptance: recognition of Israel's right to exist; renunciation of violence; and acceptance of all previous agreements reached between Israel and the PLO and PA.

The EU opts for risk avoidance

Devising a unified position across the EU and agreement within the Quartet have become the objectives of EU policy on the Arab–Israeli conflict, to the neglect of action to resolve it. Whereas in the past individual governments and leaders in Europe saw fit to speak out or propose new initiatives, latterly they appear to have calculated that risk avoidance is the best policy. Seemingly they have little hope that the EU can make a difference, even if it could agree on a more interventionist policy.

Yet, by going along with the status quo while issuing dire warnings about the situation being unsustainable, the EU has become more deeply embedded in the structure of the conflict. By avoiding dealing with Hamas and grumbling compliance with the Israeli blockade of Gaza, it has intervened directly in Palestinian factional politics. When in 2007 Hamas ousted its Fatah rivals and took control of Gaza, the EU quickly embraced the emergency administration formed in the West Bank under President Mahmoud Abbas and steered by Salam Fayyad as prime minister. Since then EU and US funds have been channelled into Fayyad's state-building project and Fatah supporters in Gaza have been paid to stay at home rather than work for Hamas-run organizations. Only the UN Relief and Works Agency (UNRWA) has been able to continue an international presence in Gaza, but under the blockade even UNRWA cannot import the materials it needs to run its operations.

In a calculated response to Hamas intransigence and rocket attacks into Israel from the Gaza Strip, in December 2008 the Israelis launched an offensive that resulted in the deaths of some

1,300 Palestinians, including many children, and thirteen Israelis. Public opinion polls in Europe revealed a surge of sympathy for the Palestinians, and the EU, under the Czech presidency, postponed plans for upgrading existing agreements with Israel. The realization that anger at the Israelis over the plight of the Palestinians could contribute to the radicalization of Muslim opinion and thence threaten European internal security was acknowledged in official circles.

However, the EU looked to the new Obama administration to give the lead on what to do next. When President Barack Obama obliged with an urgent call for action to resolve the conflict once and for all on the basis of a two-state solution, the relief in Europe was palpable, and optimism returned for the first time in years. Obama appointed George Mitchell to head up his new initiative, called on the Israelis to halt all 'settlement activity' in the West Bank, favoured Abbas and his administration with renewed support, shunned Hamas, and appealed to the Arab states to help persuade the Israelis to resume negotiations with the Palestinians.

However, Binyamin Netanyahu, who became Israeli prime minister in 2009, declined to institute a total freeze on settlement-building. Abbas consequently refused to enter into negotiations with him and the Arab states sat on the fence – apart from urging the Palestinian factions to overcome their differences. The EU had been told by Washington to expect a breakthrough in the Middle East peace process by September 2009. It did not materialize, and the Obama administration conceded that they had underestimated the difficulties and constraints on both sides.

By the end of 2009 the EU was set to introduce the new leadership structure outlined in the Lisbon Treaty, inclusive of an EU president and foreign minister. Pending this development, however, Sweden, which was the last to hold the rotating EU presidency before the change, managed to broker a new European policy statement on the Israeli–Palestinian conflict which broke new ground. It became the basis of the policy stance of the new EU foreign minister, Cathy Ashton.

The 'Council Conclusions on the Middle East Peace Process', released on 8 December 2009,[7] was the clearest statement yet of EU thinking on the requirements for a comprehensive peace deal. The core element was a renewed call for 'a two-state solution' to the Israeli–Palestinian conflict, with 'the State of Israel and an independent, democratic, contiguous and viable State of Palestine, living side by side in peace and security'. The Council further stated that the EU 'will not recognise any changes to the pre-1967 borders including with regard to Jerusalem, other than those agreed by the parties' and that, in the interests of 'genuine peace, a way must be found through negotiations to resolve the status of Jerusalem as the future capital of two states'. More broadly, the Council noted that 'A comprehensive peace must include a settlement between Israel and Syria and Lebanon.'

The Council document represented the culmination of successive European statements over several decades, commencing with the 1980 Venice Declaration. Seventeen years on, in March 2010, a joint statement by the Quartet incorporated much of the essence of the EU Council's December 2009 Conclusions.[8] Thus the Europeans have effectively blazed a trail for all the major international stakeholders in the Middle East peace process. Yet, while leading on declaratory policy, the EU has consistently deferred to the United States when it comes to policy implementation.

No exit strategy

Since the mid-1990s, European engagement in pursuit of a negotiated solution to the conflict has grown to an extent that the EU could not now walk away without significant detriment to the fate of the Palestinians and European relations with Israel. European involvement combines a strong EU declaratory position; membership of the Quartet; leading donor support to the PA; co-financing UNRWA; training and equipping the Palestinian Police in the West Bank (EUPOL COPPS); and providing a monitoring mission for the Gaza–Egypt border crossing (inactive).

EU partnership agreements with Israel, the PA, Jordan and Egypt have endured in the case of Egypt even through the fall of Mubarak in the so-called Arab Spring of 2011. Yet Syria's decent into civil war in 2012 and the threat of war between Israel and Iran have subsequently put the quest for resolution of the Arab-Israeli conflict on hold.

European investment in containing the conflict and funding the basic needs of the Palestinians is vital to the continuance of the status quo. If Europe withdrew its personnel and economic support there would be a humanitarian crisis, increased instability, lawlessness, disillusionment and generalized conflict. Yet, without agreement between the opposing sides, there can be no resolution. The Europeans are no more capable of imposing a two-state solution now than were the British of enforcing partition in Mandate Palestine.

Notes

1 John Norton Moore (ed.), *The Arab–Israeli Conflict: Readings and Documents* (Princeton, NJ: Princeton University Press, 1977), p. 879.
2 For an analysis of the genesis of the Balfour Declaration, see D. K. Fieldhouse, *Western Imperialism in the Middle East, 1914–1958* (Oxford: Oxford University Press, 2006).
3 See, for example, Keith Kyle, *Suez* (London: Weidenfeld & Nicolson, 1991), and Mohamed H. Heikel, *Cutting the Lion's Tail: Suez through Egyptian Eyes* (London: André Deutsch, 1986).
4 Joel Peters, *Pathways to Peace: The Multilateral Arab–Israeli Peace Talks* (London: Royal Institute of International Affairs, 1996).
5 Rouba Al-Fattal, *European Union Foreign Policy in the Occupied Palestinian Territory* (Jerusalem: PASSIA, 2010).
6 Rosemary Hollis, *Britain and the Middle East in the 9/11 Era* (London: Wiley Blackwell and Chatham House, 2010), chapter 4.
7 See www.consilium.europa.eu/uedocs/cms_Data/docs/pressdata/EN/foraff/111829.pdf.
8 See www.consilium.europa.eu/uedocs/cmsUpload/113436.pdf.

Further reading

Al-Fattal, Rouba (2010) *European Union Foreign Policy in the Occupied Palestinian Territory* (Jerusalem: PASSIA).
Asseburg, Muriel (2009) 'The ESDP Missions in the Palestinian Territories (EUPOL COPPS, EU BAM Rafah) Peace through Security?', in Muriel Asseburg (ed.), *The EU as a Strategic Actor in the Realm of Security and Defence?* (Berlin: SWP).
Bulut Aymat, Esra (ed.) (2010) *European Involvement in the Arab–Israeli Conflict*, Chaillot Paper 124 (Paris: EUISS).
Gordon, Philip H. (1998) *The Transatlantic Allies and the Changing Middle East*, Adelphi Paper 322 (London: International Institute for Strategic Studies).
Hollis, R. (1997) 'Europe and the Middle East: Power by Stealth?', *International Affairs*, 73/1, pp. 15–29.
Hollis, R. (2011) 'The UfM and the Middle East "Peace Process": An Unhappy Symbiosis', *Mediterranean Politics*, 16/1, pp. 99–116.
Keating, M., Le More, A., and Lowe, R. (eds) (2005) *Aid, Diplomacy and Facts on the Ground: The Case of Palestine* (London: Royal Institute of International Affairs).
Musu, Costanza (2007) 'The EU and the Arab–Israeli Peace Process', in Costanza Musu and Nicola Casarini (eds), *European Foreign Policy in an Evolving International System* (London: Palgrave Macmillan).

Pace, M. (2009) *Liberal or Social Democracy? Aspects of the EU's Democracy Promotion Agenda in the Middle East* (Stockholm: International Institute for Democracy and Electoral Assistance).

Peters, J. (1996) *Pathways to Peace: The Multilateral Arab–Israeli Peace Talks* (London: Royal Institute of International Affairs).

Tocci, Nathalie (2005) *The Widening Gap Between Rhetoric and Reality in EU Policy towards the Israeli–Palestinian Conflict*, CEPS Working Document 217 (Brussels: Centre for European Policy Studies).

29

The Arab world

P. R. Kumaraswamy

By politely but firmly rejecting President Barack Obama's suggestion in July 2009 that he make positive overtures towards Israel, King Abdullah of Saudi Arabia reiterated the traditional Arab position vis-à-vis the Arab–Israeli conflict: no normalization with Israel before a just and comprehensive settlement for the Palestinians. Even though countries closer to the USA, such as Qatar and Bahrain, have been somewhat accommodating, the Arab mainstream has not abandoned its insistence on the centrality of the Palestinian issue for peace in the Middle East. Indeed, since the early twentieth century, even countries and societies which have had no direct conflict with Jewish political aspirations have anchored their foreign policy in the Palestinian cause. The fact that only two Arab countries, Egypt and Jordan, maintain normal diplomatic relations with the Jewish state emphasizes the significance of the Palestinian issue and its resonance in the wider Arab world.

The Palestinians have benefited greatly from the support they receive from Arab states and societies. Indeed, wider international recognition of their political rights is primarily a result of Arab interest, involvement, and support. Over the years, the Palestinians sought and received political, economic, diplomatic, and, at times, military support from their Arab friends. At the same time, the Arab role has not always been positive. Arab rulers occasionally used the Palestinian issue to bestow legitimacy upon themselves or to delegitimize their rivals.

Promoting the Palestinian cause

From the very beginning, the Arab–Israeli conflict has revolved primarily, and even exclusively, around the Palestinians. The Zionist political aspirations as endorsed by the Balfour Declaration of 1917 were confined to Palestine, though the partition of 1922 and the formation of Transjordan limited the territorial scope of Jewish hopes. While the Palestinians were also Arab, the problem was much narrower than commonly recognized. By embracing the Palestinian problem, the wider Arab world (and later the Islamic world too) expanded the scope of the struggle against Zionism. The failure of Zionism to define its territorial limits gave rise to a sense of alarm in the Arab mind.

The Arab factor came into prominence only in 1967 when Israel captured the sovereign territories of Egypt and Syria and the West Bank from Jordan. The Arab states were acting on behalf of a people whom they felt were wronged and with whom they shared a common ethno-religious bond. The nascent nature of Palestinian identity, nationalism, and leadership resulted in the wider Arab world taking over the mantle of the Palestinian cause.

For its part, the Palestinian leadership also encouraged the involvement of its Arab neighbors. Arab support was critical for the internationalization of the Palestinian problem. The Grand Mufti of Jerusalem, Haj Amin al-Husseini, was one of the first to recognize its importance and work towards expanding the support base for the Palestinians. The twin problem of Jewish immigration and British Mandate rule appeared insurmountable. While the former was rapidly transforming the socio-demographic profile of Palestine, the latter remained an unknown quantity. Despite being appointed by British High Commissioner Herbert Samuel in March 1921, the mufti had misgivings about the Mandate powers and their intentions. For the mufti the Balfour Declaration and its incorporation in the League of Nations Mandate made the British a willing partner and collaborator in Zionist political aspirations in Palestine. Moreover, he had to contend with the powerful Nashashibi family, which also coveted favors from the British. Using the dilapidated al-Aqsa mosque as the focus of his cause, the mufti sent teams to various Arab countries and Islamic societies (in India, for example) to raise funds for its renovation.

This strategy proved effective. The Palestine question resonated in a number of Arab countries and Islamic societies. A host of representatives from outside Palestine testified before an international commission following the Western Wall riots of 1929. They articulated Islamic claims and ownership and the need to retain the religious and political status quo. In December 1931, the mufti hosted the World Islamic Conference, which was attended by representatives from twenty-two countries.

The pan-Arab connection became concrete towards the end of World War II when the Alexandria Protocol of October 1944, which formed the basis of the Arab League, adopted a special resolution on Palestine. In its view, "Palestine constitutes an important part of the Arab world and the rights of the Arabs of Palestine cannot be touched without prejudice to peace and stability in the Arab world." Calling for an end to Jewish immigration, it declared that "preservation of Arab lands and the achievement of independence for Palestine are permanent Arab rights." Committing its support for the Palestinians, the Protocol pledged to "work for the achievement of their legitimate aims and the safeguarding of their just rights." In parallel to the Jewish National Fund, it promised an "Arab National Fund" towards safeguarding "the lands of Arab Palestine."[1]

This support was more pronounced in the Pact of the League of Arab States adopted on 22 March 1945. Recognizing the special circumstances, it declared that, while "Palestine was not able to control her own destiny," its independence was not in question. "Even though the outward signs of this independence have remained veiled as a result of a force majeure," it was not to impede "the participation of Palestine in the work of the League." Therefore it was decided that "the Council of the League should designate an Arab delegate from Palestine" who would participate in its work until "this country enjoys actual independence."[2]

These commitments were tested in early 1947 when Great Britain handed over the Palestine question to the newly formed United Nations. The five Arab countries which were then members of the organization tried unsuccessfully to scuttle the formation of the United Nations Special Committee on Palestine (UNSCOP). In their view, the problem was simple and the solution straightforward: an immediate end to Mandate rule and independence for Palestine. This was unacceptable to the majority members of the First Special Session of the UN General Assembly. Because the mufti-led Arab Higher Committee boycotted the UN Committee when it visited Palestine, the responsibility to represent the Palestinian case once again fell to the Arab states. The following July representatives from Arab states (except Jordan) went to Beirut and presented the Arab case before UNSCOP. As support for the partition plan was gathering momentum, the Arab states led the final battle in the UN. Aided by Pakistan, they proposed the transformation of Palestine into one unitary state, an idea that did not find favor with others. Eventually, on 29 November 1947, the UN General Assembly voted on the partition resolution. Out of the thirteen countries that voted against this plan, six belonged to the Arab world.

The period between the adoption of the partition resolution and 15 May 1948, the date announced by Britain for its departure, marked a shift in the Arab role. Having failed to prevent the partition resolution, the Arab countries now sought to scuttle its implementation. At the same time, their ability to act forcefully was impeded by the British presence in Palestine. Most of the Arab states neighboring Palestine depended upon Britain for political support, economic assistance, and military supplies. The Arab Legion of the Hashemites was funded, trained, armed, and, above all, commanded by British officers. Egypt had a large British military presence along the Suez Canal. Iraq was under the imperial sphere of influence, and so were the many future sheikhdoms in the Persian Gulf. Hence, despite their aspirations, the Arab countries had to wait for the departure of the last British soldier before they could intervene directly in Palestine.

This did not mean Arab inaction in the interim. Arab states took a number of concrete measures signaling direct military intervention following the British withdrawal. In terms of planning, Jordan and Iraq were given the responsibility for the eastern sector of Palestine, while Egypt was to command the western sector. Lebanon and Syria were to focus on the northern front. The Arab League also called on its citizens to enlist in a volunteer force commanded by Fawzi al-Qawugji. At its height, the Arab Liberation Army had the strength of 10,000 volunteers from the neighboring Arab states. Not encumbered by the restrictions and political compulsions faced by the Arab states, the volunteer army capitalized on the porous borders and infiltrated Palestine. During the 1948 war, they contributed to a major portion of Arab resistance against the Jewish forces, and some of the bloodiest battles during the war were fought by the Arab volunteers.

While the final outcome of the 1948 war was disappointing, the Arab army played a vital role in preventing some of the Arab-dominated territories of Palestine from falling into the control of Jewish/Israeli forces. In the absence of unity of purpose, the non-Palestinian Arab forces could not prevent the formation of the Jewish state. But they did stop the Gaza Strip, the West Bank and East Jerusalem from falling into Israel's hands.

The loss of territories in the war was accompanied by a far more serious problem: a loss of identity. The Palestinians, who constituted more than 95 percent of the population of Palestine at the time of the Balfour Declaration, were overnight reduced to a minority. Whether they were expelled or forced to leave owing to the circumstances of the conflict, a vast majority of Palestinians fled to neighboring Arab countries. According to estimates by the United Nations Relief and Works Agency (UNRWA), over 700,000 people became refugees following the 1948 war, most of them in Jordan. The June 1967 war witnessed another round of refugee exodus, primarily from the West Bank into Jordan. By 2002, the total number of refugees was over 4 million; by 2005 there were at least 1.8 million Palestinians in Jordan, 404,000 in Lebanon, and 432,000 in Syria.

The Arab states provided refuge to these stateless Palestinians at considerable economic and political cost. Even though UNRWA maintains the camps and provides for the health, education, and welfare of the refugees, their ultimate responsibility rests with the host states. Indeed, most of the countries hosting the Palestinians were (and are) not wealthy or resourceful, and the presence of refugees has been a considerable economic burden for them. While other Arab states sought to limit Palestinian activities on their soil, Jordan granted full citizenship to and completely integrated the residents of the West Bank.

The political motives behind Jordan's action were subsequently challenged. However, in the initial years, it provided a national identity and purpose for a vast majority of Palestinians, especially to residents of the West Bank. The status of refugees in Jordan was far better than that of their counterparts in Lebanon, where they were denied any political or economic rights. Indeed, until recently, most Palestinian refugees were prevented from pursuing even menial jobs in Lebanon.

The failure of the Arab states' efforts to prevent the emergence of Israel did not dampen their support for the Palestinians. Despite internal schism over the fate of the West Bank, now under Jordanian control and sovereignty, the Arab League sought to "liberate" Palestine from Israeli control. Indeed, since 1948 the League has been more united over Palestine than on any other issue that affects the member states. While the efficacy and effectiveness of this stand remain debatable, Arab support for the Palestinian cause has been palpable.

Until over a decade after the 1948 war, the Arab states argued over the leadership to represent the Palestinians. Jordanian annexation of the West Bank made things worse: the Arab states could not clamor for international support when individual states sought to usurp the leadership of the Palestinian people. Partly to mitigate such criticism, in 1964 President Gamal Abdul Nasser backed the formation of the Palestine Liberation Organization (PLO). Though it was supposed to be under the tutelage of Egypt and Nasser, the PLO gradually outgrew Arab control. The war of June 1967 and the loss of vast swathes of Arab territory, especially the West Bank, weakened the Arab states and contributed to the emergence of the PLO as a major player. Despite its opposition, Jordanian acquiescence paved the way for the Rabat Arab summit recognizing the PLO as "sole and legitimate representative of the Palestinian people." This helped attract further support from members of the international community, especially Third World countries.

The Arab states also used regional political platforms to highlight the injustice done to the Palestinians and their plight as refugees. The mufti and other Palestinian figures were included in the official delegation that presented the Palestinian problem to the wider world. At a more tangible level, the Arab countries used the Palestinian issue to institute political and economic boycotts of the nascent Jewish state. Israel's exclusion from the Afro-Asian conference in Bandung in April 1955 was a clear example of this trend, as it institutionalized subsequent Israeli exclusion from the more powerful Non-Aligned Movement.

Coupled with this, the Arab countries instituted a prolonged and effective economic boycott against Israel. By the late 1990s the economic cost of this measure was estimated at over $45 billion. The economic clout of the oil-rich Arab countries was clearly demonstrated during the oil crisis of 1973, when the stoppage of supplies forced a number of US allies to alter fundamentally their approach towards the Arab–Israeli conflict. Their energy dependency upon the Gulf forced both Western Europe and Japan to adopt a pro-Palestinian position.

The Arab willingness to rally behind the Palestinians also affected the behavior of important countries such as China and India and shaped their policy towards Israel. From the early 1950s both countries needed the support of the Arab countries in the United Nations. If China was preoccupied with its drive for UN membership, India was concerned over potential Arab support to Pakistan over the Kashmir dispute. Hence, both settled for influencing the Arab countries by refusing to maintain any diplomatic ties with Israel and adopting a pronouncedly pro-Palestinian foreign policy. In contrast, the national liberation struggle of the Kurds received no support from China and India because the Arab states were opposed to the idea. The absence of any bilateral dispute with Israel did not prevent either country from being at the forefront of many Arab-initiated anti-Israeli measures during the Cold War. It was only after the willingness of the PLO to seek a negotiated political settlement with Israel within the framework of the Madrid conference that both China and India normalized relations with Israel in January 1992.

By pursuing an effective politico-economic strategy against Israel, the Arab states pushed the Palestinian issue on the global scene and made it a sine qua non for peace in the Middle East. These efforts bore fruit in November 1974 when the PLO was given observer status at the UN, and gradually the world body recognized the Palestinian people's political rights to independence and statehood. It would be fair to conclude that, but for Arab support, the Palestinian cause would not have acquired the international recognition and legitimacy it did or would have taken a considerably longer time and a higher cost to do so.

Problems of dependency

For a considerable period of its history, the Palestinian struggle against Zionism – and later on against Israel – was headed by non-Palestinian Arab leaders, societies, and ideologies. Unlike various other liberation movements, the Palestinians relied more heavily upon others than themselves. This reliance often bordered on dependency, thereby undermining progress in the accomplishing of their objectives. This was manifest as early as the Mandate period. The nascent Palestinian identity and nationalism could not offer a strong leadership that was capable of facing the two challenges posed by Zionism and Mandate rule. Reliance on the obvious merits of the Palestinian cause and overconfidence in the power of Arab states to defeat the partition plan proved costly. Even the more moderate federal plan advocated by pro-Arab India was insufficient and unattractive. Both during the First Special Session of the UN General Assembly in April–May 1947 and during the visit of UNSCOP to the region, the mufti-led Arab Higher Committee refused to testify. The arrival of the UN committee in Palestine was greeted by a public strike organized by the mufti. It was therefore left to independent Arab states to convey, articulate, and argue the Palestinian case before the world body. To make matters worse, during the run up to the partition vote, the responsibility for making a strong case on behalf of the Palestinians rested on the shoulders of Islamic, but non-Arab, Pakistan.

As discussed earlier, much of the military campaign during the 1948 war rested on the Arabs, especially the Arab Legion of Jordan. For its part, the Palestinian leadership was conspicuous by its absence from Palestine. Indeed the leaders fled long before the masses did. This was largely because of the British presence in Mandate Palestine and its policies and actions against prominent leaders. Wanted by the Mandate authorities since mid-1930, the mufti escaped in October 1937 and was based in Egypt at the time of the British withdrawal. Thus, prominent members of the Palestinian leadership were in Amman, Cairo, Beirut, and Damascus but not in Palestine.

The performance of the Palestinian leaders contrasted with the activities of the *Yishuv* (Jewish residents in Palestine). With the sole exception of Chaim Weizmann, its entire leadership was present when the Zionist Council met in Tel Aviv on the Sabbath eve of 14 May 1948 and signed the Declaration of Independence. The absence of recognized Arab leaders in Palestine at this critical juncture proved catastrophic in the days and weeks after the British pullout.

In the post-1948 years, the Palestinian leadership remained largely marginalized. The Egypt-controlled Gaza Strip and Jordan-annexed West Bank were used mostly to serve the interests of these two countries. If the All Palestine Government proclaimed in October 1948 collapsed within weeks, the West Bank soon became an integral part of Jordan. For his part, the mufti shuttled between various Arab capitals to drum up support. It was only after the formation of Fatah in 1959 that one could really talk of an independent Palestinian leadership. So long as Fatah and Yasser Arafat remained outside the organization, even the PLO was primarily an Arab appendage.

This trend was reflected in the manner in which the Palestinian problem played out internationally. While the 1948 war was rooted in the Palestinian struggle for independence, in subsequent years their plight was reduced to refugee rights. The Palestinian issue became subservient to the larger Arab–Israeli conflict even though, until 1967, Arab states did not have any direct conflict with the Jewish state. As a result, until the early 1970s the Arab–Israeli conflict was defined primarily as an interstate conflict between Israel and its Arab neighbors. The Palestinian issue was marginal to the Suez War of 1956 and the October war of 1973. Even the Six Day War of 1967, which was fought over the remaining areas of Mandate Palestine, was primarily an interstate conflict and should be viewed within the context of political tensions and rivalry between Egypt and Jordan.

The wording of UN Security Council Resolution 242 clearly highlighted this situation. Although it called for "a just settlement of the refugee problem," this was the only reference, direct or indirect, to the Palestinians, and their marginalization resulted in both the PLO and Syria vehemently rejecting the unanimous resolution. Only after the Arab recognition of the PLO in the Rabat summit in October 1974 did the PLO emerge as an independent player in the Arab–Israeli conflict. The observer status bestowed upon by the UN in November 1974 enabled the organization to participate in international debates pertaining to the Palestinians. Until then this function was carried out by the Arab states and by friendly countries of the Third World.

Second, the first round of Arab–Israeli conflict in 1947–8 exposed not only the internal divisions and schism among various Arab leaders but also the political gulf between the Palestinian leaders and their Arab brethren. The territorial agenda of Emir Abdullah resulted in the Arab Legion capturing those areas of eastern Palestine that were allotted to the Arab state under the partition plan. In tune with his understanding with the *Yishuv* leaders, the Jordanian leader never coveted any areas allotted to the Jewish state. East Jerusalem, which was supposed to be part of the corpus separatum under the UN plan, was the notable exception. The Jordanian army not only captured the Old City, including the Haram al-Sharif, but also annexed the West Bank under the pretext of the Jericho conference in December 1948.

The territorial ambitions of Jordan not only ran counter to the Palestinian aspirations but also went against the prevailing Arab consensus as manifested by their quick recognition of the mufti-headed All Palestine Government proclaimed in October 1948. With the bulk of the Palestinian territory remaining under either Israeli or Jordanian control, efforts to establish an independent Palestinian political entity collapsed. The Arab League, which disapproved of the Hashemite annexation, could not act against Jordan and settled for a justification: the Hashemites would hold the West Bank "in trust" until the complete liberation of Palestine. Even the original Charter of the PLO adopted in May 1964 reflected this Arab consensus. This façade, which was not acceptable to Jordan, continued until 1967, when the West Bank came under Israeli control.

Third, Palestinian dependency resulted in Arab states using, misusing, and even abusing the Palestinian problem in furtherance of their respective national interests. As and when needed they rode on or ignored the plight of the Palestinians. Support for the Palestinian cause at times became a political instrument to belittle or undermine political rivals both within their own country and in the wider Arab world. Partly to position himself as the unquestionable leader of the Palestinian struggle, in 1964 President Nasser presided over the formation of the PLO.

Since the entry of Fatah into its fold, the organization has emerged into something other than Nasser originally planned.

Jordan is the best example of this Palestinization. In the final days of the British Mandate, the Hashemites saw themselves not only as the champions of the Palestinians but also as their representatives. This was acceptable so long as the West Bank remained under their control. The loss of the West Bank and the emergence of the PLO as a major player did not, however, diminish the Hashemite appetite. It was only after the outbreak of the *intifada* in December 1987 and the fear of its possible repercussions for Jordan that King Hussein relinquished administrative claims over the West Bank. As many Palestinians discovered following the conclusion of the Israel–Jordan peace treaty in October 1994, even this disengagement was not complete and could be reversed.[3]

Moreover, if President Nasser sought to consolidate his regional influence by highlighting his support for the Palestinians, the Hashemites blamed him for relying on the UN peacekeeping forces for Egyptian security. The argument was that, if he needed international help to protect his own country, how could he fight for the Palestinians? This war of words ended disastrously in the war of June 1967, which brought the West Bank and Gaza Strip, among others, under Israeli control. Israeli leaders, especially from the Labor Party, had long toyed with the idea of the "Jordanian option," whereby the Palestinian problem would be settled by Israel returning a substantial portion of the West Bank to Jordan. King Hussein was a willing partner in this endeavor, and most political negotiations between him and Israeli leaders revolved around this issue. The secret Peres–Hussein London Agreement of April 1987 was the culmination of prolonged behind-the-scenes discussions between the two countries.

Jordan, however, was not alone in subordinating the Palestinian issue to particular national interests. President Anwar Sadat did precisely that in 1977 when he embarked upon his "Egypt first" policy. Initially he conditioned peace with Israel on progress on the Palestinian front. But his resilience floundered, and he could not persuade Israeli Prime Minister Menachem Begin to offer sufficient incentives to the Palestinians to join the peace efforts. Begin's much touted autonomy plan offered limited self-rule to Palestinians but none to the Occupied Territories; it offered limited civil rights to Palestinian residents without giving them any national rights. While agreeing to allow them to vote in the Israeli or Jordanian elections, Begin did not contemplate any political rights for the Palestinians. In the final analysis, Sadat could not even persuade Begin to use "West Bank" to denote the territories that Israel had captured in June 1967.[4]

By pursuing an independent policy towards Israel, Sadat institutionalized the regional fracture and caused deep divisions within the Arab ranks. At one level, Sadat became the forerunner for a peaceful resolution of the Arab–Israeli conflict. However, for the rejectionist camp led by Iraq and Syria, his policy was a reversal of the Arab position since 1948. By seeking a separate peace with Israel in furtherance of Egyptian national interests, he broke the prevailing Arab consensus enshrined in the three "NOs" (No Recognition, No Negotiations and No Peace with Israel) adopted at Khartoum. In the process, he also contributed to Arab division, disunity, and decline. The peace with Israel prolonged Egypt's regional isolation and expulsion from the Arab League and the Organization of the Islamic Conference.

Saddam Hussein was the third prominent ruler cynically to manipulate the Palestinian issue to wriggle out of a crisis that he had created for Iraq. Faced with Arab as well as international criticism over his invasion of Kuwait in August 1990, he linked his occupation of Kuwait to prolonged Israeli occupation of the Palestinian territories. Positioning himself as an upholder of international norms, he argued that Iraq was prepared to pull out of Kuwait if Israel pulled out of the Occupied Territories. While such a link was unacceptable to the wider international community, it had positive resonance among the Palestinians, especially its leadership. The

Palestinians paid a heavy political and economic price after the liberation of Kuwait for their pro-Saddam stand. The incident once again highlighted the manipulative nature of Arab rulers towards the Palestinian problem.

Fourth, struggling for a state, the Palestinians have been easy prey to various internal and intra-regional power struggles in the Arab world. The proliferation of Palestinian groups is largely the result of rivalries among various Arab regimes and competing ideologies. If Jordan sought to represent the Palestinian people rather openly, others were more subtle but brutal. Some of the assassination attempts on Arafat, for example, were attributed to Palestinian groups controlled by rival regimes. The emergence of Hamas offered a new avenue for the conservative Arab regimes in the Gulf. After the Gulf War in 1991, countries such as Kuwait openly backed the militant Islamic group as a way of settling scores with the Fatah-dominated PLO. Following the liberation of Kuwait over 400,000 Palestinians were expelled from the Gulf region, mostly to impoverished Jordan, for the pro-Saddam stand taken by the PLO leadership. The Madrid conference and the PLO's willingness to seek a negotiated political settlement with Israel resulted in the formation of a rejectionist front. Various secular and Islamic Palestinian groups based in Damascus have indulged in a number of political as well as militant activities aimed at scuttling a peace settlement. Partly to undermine Arafat, in September 1998 King Hussein secured the release of Hamas's founder, Sheikh Ahmad Yassin, from an Israeli prison following a failed assassination attempt against Khalid Mashaal.

Fifth, support for the Palestinians has not always brought benefit to the Arab countries, but in fact unforeseen misery. It had taken the official Palestinian leadership nearly five decades to return to Palestinian lands when Arafat entered the Gaza Strip in July 1994. During this period, it was not just the population but also the leadership that was hosted by the Arab countries neighboring Israel. Until the June war, Palestinian individuals and groups operated from the West Bank and Gaza Strip, controlled by Jordan and Egypt respectively. Following Black September in 1970 the *fedayeen* (anti-Israel militants) moved to Lebanon, from where they carried out operations against Israel. In the wake of the Israeli invasion of Lebanon in 1982, the leadership and militants were parceled off to a number of Arab countries, with the PLO moving to Tunis. While the *fedayeen* campaign against Israel resulted in scores of costly retaliations and reprisals, the Arab states hosted them and provided a territorial basis for their militant campaign against Israel.

The prolonged presence of Palestinians has at times resulted in domestic turmoil and violence in the host countries. In 1970, the Palestinian rebellion against the Hashemites led to a near civil war situation in Jordan, and King Hussein almost lost his throne. Likewise the "state within a state" arrangement in Lebanon worked out by President Nasser later that year eventually contributed to prolonged civil war in the country. The Palestinian population which for decades had benefited from benign Kuwaiti rulers found it prudent to collaborate with the invading Iraqi forces during the Kuwait crisis. Partly because of these bitter Arab examples, both during the Israeli siege following the electoral victory of Hamas in 2006 and during the Gaza war of 2008–9, Egypt was adamant about not letting the beleaguered Gaza residents pour into the Sinai peninsula.

Sixth, the Arab factor also became an impediment when the Palestinian leadership sought political reconciliation with Zionism and Israel. For Jordan, the Oslo Accords and the Palestinian recognition of Israel proved to be opportune, as it enabled the Hashemites to come out of the closet and formalize their prolonged but tacit understanding with Israel. It holds true for countries such as Morocco, Oman, and Qatar, which were prepared to establish low-level diplomatic ties with Israel. At the same time, countries such as Syria have used the internal differences among the Palestinians to further their interests. It was no accident that Palestinian groups opposed to the Oslo Accords operated out of Damascus. The failure of the Camp David summit in July 2000 was attributed partly to differences over the refugee question. Fears over their possible abandonment and demand for absorption by host countries angered Palestinian refugees in Lebanon and Syria. These countries used this concern to undermine Arafat's ability to forge an agreement with Prime Minister Barak. The same trends were apparent when Syrian President Bashar Assad forced Saudi Crown Prince Abdullah to abandon "concession" on the refugee front.

The Arab world and the peace process

Since the early 1990s, the Arab countries, especially Egypt, have been more actively involved in the Middle East peace process on behalf of the Palestinians. Cairo has been using its political and diplomatic capital to narrow down or iron out differences between the two sides. The world watched on television how President Hosni Mubarak cajoled Arafat before the latter signed the Oslo II agreement. Of late, the inter-Palestinian tension and conflict have enabled some states to mediate between the PLO and Hamas. In the immediate aftermath of the Oslo Accords, Sudan and its Islamist leader, Hassan Turabi, sought to reconcile the two. Following the outbreak of the al-Aqsa *Intifada* in September 2000 this responsibility was largely shouldered by Mubarak, who recognized the need to calm the situation down in order to push forward the Israeli–Palestinian peace talks. The Mecca Agreement of February 2007 was the result of the Saudi desire to bring about reconciliation between the PLO and Hamas, which controlled the West Bank and Gaza Strip respectively. Since the mid-1990s, Syria has been hosting the "outsider" elements of Hamas on its territory and wields considerable influence, especially when it comes to negotiating with Israel. The end result, however, has not always been fruitful. The Mecca Agreement collapsed within days and was followed by the militant takeover of the Gaza Strip by Hamas in June that year. These efforts do, however, underscore the role and influence of Arab countries in inter-Palestinian affairs.

The Beirut Arab League Summit in 2002 unanimously adopted the Arab Peace Initiative – a peace plan that offered a formula for ending not only the Palestinian–Israeli conflict but also the wider, lingering Arab–Israeli conflict. The initiative was first proposed in Beirut by Crown Prince Abdullah of Saudi Arabia, and was re-endorsed by the Riyadh summit in 2007.

The plan, as adopted, called for Israeli withdrawal from all territories occupied since 1967 and the return of the Palestinian refugees to Israel in return for recognition of Israel and the normalization of relations between Israel and the Arab world. The Arab Peace Initiative was met with mixed reactions and received little attention when it was first introduced. Israel was particularly wary of this initiative, rejecting the idea that any settlement of the refugee issue should be based on UN Resolution 194 (see chapter 9, by Rex Brynen, in this volume) and offer the Palestinians the right of return. Recently, positive interest in the Arab Peace Initiative has grown, both inside and outside Israel.

Mixed verdict

The role played by Arab countries on behalf of the Palestinians has not always been beneficial to the latter. At one level, it has increased political support for the Palestinians and their struggle against Zionism and the State of Israel. Expanding the political scope of the problem to the wider region was one of the most important accomplishments of the Palestinians confronting Jewish immigration to Palestine and the Mandate authorities, which were sympathetic towards a Jewish national home. As witnessed in the dissent of Emir Abdullah, the Arab countries were not united behind the Palestinians. Gradually this dissent widened, with individual countries pursuing policies that at times came into conflict with Palestinian interests. What began as external support gradually transformed into a dependent relationship whereby the Arab leaders and regimes could use and misuse the plight of the Palestinians to further their national interests. The Arab defeats and dispersal of a large segment of the Palestinian population merely compounded this dependency. The Palestinian relationship with principal countries in the region, especially those bordering Israel, became complicated, uneven, and, at times, violent. Preoccupied with dispossession, statelessness, and their primary conflict with Israel, the Palestinians are not in a position to reflect upon the true implication of the Arab role in their conflict with Israel.

Notes

1 The Alexandria Protocol, 7 October 1944, http://avalon.law.yale.edu/20th_century/alex.asp.
2 Pact of the League of Arab States, 22 March 1945, http://avalon.law.yale.edu/20th_century/arableag.asp.
3 According to Article 9(2) of the treaty, "Israel respects the present special role of the Hashemite Kingdom of Jordan in Muslim Holy shrines in Jerusalem. When negotiations on the permanent status take place, Israel will give high priority to the Jordanian historic role in these shrines" (Treaty of Peace between the State of Israel and the Hashemite Kingdom of Jordan, 26 October 1994, http://avalon.law.yale.edu/20th_century/jordan_treaty.asp). This runs counter to the Oslo Accords, whereby Israel is committed to discussing the Jerusalem question with the Palestinians during the final-status negotiations.
4 According to the exchange of letters between Prime Minister Begin and President Jimmy Carter, the expression West Bank "would be understood by the Government of Israel as Judea and Samaria." For the text of the letter which forms part of the Camp David Accords, see http://israelipalestinian.procon.org/view.background-resource.php?resourceID1541. It was only in the Declaration of Principles with the PLO, signed on 13 September 1993, that Israel for the first time used "West Bank" to denote this area.

Further reading

Abu-Ghazalah, Adnan (1972) "Arab Cultural Nationalism in Palestine during the British Mandate", *Journal of Palestine Studies*, 1/3, pp. 37–63.
Arzt, Donna E. (1997) *Refugees into Citizens: Palestinians and the End of the Arab–Israeli Conflict* (New York: Council on Foreign Relations).
Brown, Nathan J. (2003) *Palestinian Politics after the Oslo Accords: Resuming Arab Palestine* (Berkeley: University of California Press).
Doran, Michael (2002) *Pan-Arabism before Nasser: Egyptian Power Politics and the Palestine Question* (New York: Oxford University Press).
Finkelstein, Norman G. (2003) *Image and Reality of the Israel–Palestine Conflict* (2nd ed., New York: Verso).
Gelvin, James L. (2005) *The Israel–Palestine Conflict: One Hundred Years of War* (Cambridge and New York: Cambridge University Press).
Kazziha, Walid (1979) *Palestine in the Arab Dilemma* (London: Croom Helm).
Khalidi, Rashid (1997) *Palestinian Identity: The Construction of Modern National Consciousness* (New York: Columbia University Press).
Lesch, Ann Mosely (1979) *Arab Politics in Palestine, 1917–1939: The Frustration of a Nationalist Movement* (Ithaca, NY: Cornell University Press).
Lesch, David W. (2008) *The Arab–Israeli Conflict: A History* (New York: Oxford University Press).
Lockman, Zachary (1996) *Comrades and Enemies: Arab and Jewish Workers in Palestine, 1906–1948* (Berkeley: University of California Press).

Matthews, Weldon (2006), *Confronting an Empire, Constructing a Nation: Arab Nationalists and Popular Politics in Mandate Palestine* (London: I. B. Tauris).

Rubin, Barry M. (1981) *The Arab States and the Palestine Conflict* (Syracuse, NY: Syracuse University Press).

Shemesh, Moshe (2008) *Arab Politics, Palestinian Nationalism and the Six Day War: The Crystallization of Arab Strategy and Nasir's Descent to War, 1957–1967* (Brighton: Sussex Academic Press).

Zahlan, Rosemarie Said (2009) *Palestine and the Gulf States: The Presence at the Table* (New York: Routledge).

30

The Jewish diaspora and the pro-Israel lobby

Dov Waxman

Introduction

In recent years, scholars, experts, and policy-makers have increasingly recognized the role, both positive and negative, that diaspora groups can play in violent ethno-national conflict. Although attention is often focused on the way in which members of diasporas can help to fuel and prolong such conflicts by providing money, arms, and political support to hard-line nationalists in their homelands (as has been the case, for example, with the Tamil and Kurdish diasporas in Sri Lanka and Turkey respectively), diaspora groups can also help promote peace processes and peace-building efforts (as occurred with the US-based Irish diaspora and the Northern Ireland peace process). In the case of the Israeli–Palestinian conflict, both the Jewish and Palestinian diasporas have always been actively involved in the conflict. To understand fully the dynamics of the Israeli–Palestinian conflict, therefore, it is essential to take this extra-territorial dimension into account. For many Jews and Palestinians living outside Israel, the West Bank, the Gaza Strip, and East Jerusalem, though the conflict may be far away, it is at the center of their political attention and activity.

The Jewish diaspora is the paradigmatic example of a diaspora group being involved in a "homeland" conflict. Indeed, other diaspora groups have looked at it as an example to be emu-lated. Since its origins roughly two millennia ago during the Greek and Roman empires, the Jewish diaspora has always maintained a strong connection with the Land of Israel (*Eretz Yisrael*), but for most of its history this connection was largely religious and emotional. It was not until the late nineteenth century, with the rise of the Zionist movement in Europe, that Jews really began transforming this religious and emotional bond into practical action. The consequence was wave after wave of Jewish immigration to Palestine (initially from Eastern Europe and later from Central Europe). This mass immigration and the accompanying acquisition and settlement of land were the initial catalysts for the conflict between Jews and Palestinian Arabs that developed during the years of the British Mandate. In this respect, the Israeli–Palestinian conflict itself is a consequence of the actions of diaspora Jews. After all, Zionism emerged in the Jewish diaspora, and was a response to the problems facing Jewry at the time: anti-Semitism and assimilation.

From the very beginning of the Israeli–Palestinian conflict, therefore, Jews in the diaspora have been actively involved. Although the vast majority of Jews were not Zionists before the establishment of Israel and only a tiny minority actually moved to Palestine, those in the diaspora played a crucial role in the creation of the state. Their charitable donations provided the Zionist movement with funds to buy land, build agricultural settlements and towns, and purchase arms, and their political lobbying and advocacy activities helped the Zionist movement gain international support and diplomatic backing. It is no exaggeration to say that the establishment of the State of Israel in 1948 would not have been possible without the economic and political support from diaspora Jews, especially American Jews.

Since 1948, Jews in the diaspora have continued to provide Israel with vital economic and political support. In fact, this support has increased tremendously over time as they have overwhelmingly come to embrace Zionism (albeit a highly watered-down version) in the wake of the Holocaust and Israel's creation. The ideological shift from anti-Zionism (dominant before World War II) to Zionism (especially after Israel's victory in the 1967 Six Day War) has had profound and far-reaching consequences and has made support for Israel the single most important and common expression of Jewish identity around the world. In an age when the religious and cultural ties that once united them have steadily diminished, Israel has become a rallying point for Jews worldwide. Visiting Israel, donating to Israel, lobbying for Israel have all become ways in which many diaspora Jews express not only their solidarity with the country but also their own Jewish identity. Supporting Israel, in short, has become a way of *being* Jewish, especially for secular Jews in the diaspora.

For Israel, the financial, political, and moral support it receives from the Jewish diaspora is an incalculable benefit. Ironically, the success of Zionism – an ideology that harshly condemned Jewish life in the diaspora and scorned diaspora Jews – has partly been due to that diaspora. Even Israeli leaders now recognize this fact, and they have gradually come to view the Jewish diaspora as one of Israel's most important strategic assets. Rather than "negating the diaspora" – expecting and hoping for its eventual demise – Israeli policy-makers now want to sustain it and thus stress the importance of strengthening its Jewish identity.

While they have come to appreciate and acknowledge their vital contribution, Israeli leaders continue to insist, however, that Jews in the diaspora are not entitled to any formal role in Israeli politics (since this is restricted to Israeli citizens). Even informally, diaspora Jews generally exercise very little influence over Israeli policies. Although a few very wealthy individuals, in particular, have become much more involved in domestic Israeli politics in recent years, the input of diaspora Jews into Israeli policy-making remains minimal. This is not only because Israeli policy-makers and the Israeli public at large do not see such an input as entirely legitimate, but also because many diaspora Jews themselves are ambivalent about trying to influence Israeli policies (except on matters that concern them directly – i.e., on the issue of "who is a Jew?" and which Jewish conversions are officially recognized in Israel). On the one hand, they may care deeply about what policies Israel pursues but, on the other, they may not feel entitled to try actively to promote the kinds of policies they favor. Thus, despite all their political and financial support, diaspora Jews have only a minor voice in Israeli politics and policy-making.

Diaspora Jewry has therefore had little to no influence upon the policies Israel has pursued or the actions it has taken, which have been determined by domestic groups and forces within Israel (although these groups do sometimes receive financial support from the Jewish diaspora, most notably the settler movement). The main way in which Jews in the diaspora have been involved in the Israeli–Palestinian conflict is through the influence they have tried to exert upon the foreign policies of the countries in which they live – that is, through their political advocacy in support of Israel in their host countries. A large part of global Jewish political activism is aimed at bolstering international support for Israel. This involves lobbying policy-makers and trying to influence public opinion. To do this, diaspora Jews have established a multitude of "pro-Israel" organizations in different countries around the world whose purpose is to shape their government's policy towards Israel and the Israeli–Palestinian conflict in a way that is believed to be in Israel's interests.

The most important and influential diaspora Jewish pro-Israel organizations are those based in the United States. There are three main reasons for this. First, the American-Jewish community has traditionally been, and for the time being continues to be, the largest Jewish community in the world (numbering between 5 and 6 million; roughly 40 percent of world Jewry lives in the United States). Second, the United States' position as the global superpower increases the power and status of the American Jewish community within the Jewish diaspora. Third, the United States offers a domestic political opportunity structure that allows diaspora groups to become active players in foreign policy (the importance of such a structure is clear when one considers the fact that the Soviet Union once contained the third largest Jewish community in the world, but until the late 1980s Jews there were forbidden from maintaining any kind of relationship with Israel).

The critique of the pro-Israel lobby in the United States

The "pro-Israel lobby" in the United States, as it is generally called,[1] has attracted growing critical attention and controversy in recent years. Its many critics see it as a major obstacle in the way of a just and peaceful resolution of the Israeli–Palestinian conflict. In fact, some blame it not only for preventing the resolution of the conflict, but also for instigating violent conflict elsewhere, most notoriously in Iraq (expressed in the claim that America's 2003 invasion of Iraq was a "war for Israel").[2] There is now a cottage industry on the Internet devoted to uncovering and reporting on the many machinations and misdeeds of the pro-Israel lobby. Denunciations of its nefarious influence, however, are by no means a new thing. It has long been blamed by supporters of the Palestinians in the United States and elsewhere for what they perceive as America's pro-Israel "bias" and for the latter's consequent failure both to hold Israel to account for its aggressive military actions and human rights violations and to pressure it to make the necessary concessions to the Palestinians for the sake of peace.

For many years, this critique of the pro-Israel lobby's influence on American foreign policy-making remained on the margins of political debate about the Israeli–Palestinian conflict. To express it was to become identified as "anti-Israel" and to be positioned on the far left or far right of the political spectrum. Today, that is no longer the case, as this view has migrated into mainstream opinion. Indeed, it has almost become the conventional wisdom in liberal society in the United States, and certainly in Western Europe. It gained new force with the collapse of the Oslo peace process and the resurgence of Israeli–Palestinian violence in 2000, and it gained greater respectability as it found some very prominent advocates, most notably former President Jimmy Carter and Professors John Mearsheimer and Stephen Walt. President Carter's book *Palestine: Peace Not Apartheid* (2006) and Mearsheimer and Walt's book *The Israel Lobby and US Foreign Policy* (2007) both quickly became best-sellers and sparked heated controversies. They were hailed by some as courageous voices willing to challenge the vaunted power of the pro-Israel lobby, while others dismissed them as simplistic and misguided at best, bigoted at worst.

Is this critique of the pro-Israel lobby fair? How powerful is this grouping in the United States? And what impact has it had upon American policy towards the Israeli–Palestinian conflict? Is it really an obstacle to peace in the Middle East? The rest of this chapter will try to answer these controversial questions.

Dov Waxman

The power of the pro-Israel lobby

There are many lobbies in Washington, DC, representing almost every conceivable interest (among the most prominent are the farm lobby, the gun lobby, the tobacco lobby, the pharmaceutical lobby, and the oil lobby). The pro-Israel lobby is widely regarded, by friend and foe alike, as one of the most effective of all. Nothing demonstrates this better than the huge aid package that Israel receives each year from the United States. Over the course of its history, Israel has received more direct aid from the United States than any other country, and it remains the single largest recipient (it now receives about $3 billion per year in military aid, plus additional money for the joint development of missile defense systems). The amount and inviolability of this aid (especially for a country whose per capita GDP is now around $28,000 – almost on par with that of Italy) is in no small part a result of the work of the pro-Israel lobby in Congress. Though it is not the only factor at work,[3] direct campaigning and contributions by pro-Israel groups have undoubtedly helped convince many politicians in Congress always to vote in favor of American aid to Israel, as well as other kinds of largesse.

While the pro-Israel lobby exercises a great deal of influence in maintaining and even increasing American aid to Israel, it has much less sway over US policy towards Israel in general, let alone towards the Middle East region as a whole. The argument made by Mearsheimer and Walt, as well as many other critics, that American foreign policy vis-à-vis the Middle East is shaped to a large extent by the pro-Israel lobby completely overlooks all the other forces – strategic, economic, political, and cultural. The same is true of American policy towards Israel. The United States' long-standing informal alliance with Israel is due to a variety of factors, among them the belief that Israel can help serve US strategic interests in the Middle East and beyond; the perception of Israel as the only democratic state in the region; the identification of Israel and the United States as similar nations; Christian religious devotion to the Jewish state and homeland; and a widespread public sympathy for Jewish suffering in the Holocaust and, more recently, Israeli suffering as a result of Palestinian terrorist attacks. All of these factors (rightly or wrongly) lie behind American support for Israel, and thus to single out the pro-Israel lobby is to underestimate the depth and breadth of this support.

The critique of the pro-Israel lobby, therefore, exaggerates its power and importance (conversely, its defenders have a tendency to minimize its power and importance). It is not omnipotent: it does not control US foreign policy, but it does have an influence, and it can make some difference at the margins. An even more serious problem with the critique of the pro-Israel lobby, however, is its depiction as a highly organized, cohesive political actor. Such a view is grossly inaccurate. It is neither monolithic nor a unitary actor. It is fragmented, internally divided by disagreements over what is in Israel's best interests and what is the proper role that American Jews should play in supporting Israel. The diversity of opinion concerning these basic questions contradicts the widespread perception of the pro-Israel lobby as a right-wing monolith. In pressing the US government for what it believes is in Israel's interests, it rarely, if ever, speaks with a single voice.

The composition of the pro-Israel lobby

Pro-Israel groups seldom agree among themselves, let alone act in unison. While they try to promote Israel's interests, they differ greatly in their views on what those interests actually are (just as Israelis themselves do). Some groups oppose Israel's continued occupation of territories gained in the 1967 war; others staunchly support its control over these territories for security, historical, or religious reasons (or a combination of these). Some support the establishment of a

360

Palestinian state in the West Bank and Gaza Strip; others are adamantly opposed to this. Some fiercely resist any American pressure on Israel; others oppose unconditional American support for Israeli policies and favor a more "even-handed" US role in Arab–Israeli peacemaking. The designation "pro-Israel," therefore, tells us very little about the specific policies for which different organizations actually campaign.

What unites all these groups is not their stance on specific policies but their attitude towards the State of Israel itself. An unwavering commitment to the survival of Israel as a Jewish state is, fundamentally, what distinguishes pro-Israel groups from other organizations involved in lobbying the US government on Middle East issues. Every such group is motivated by a bedrock concern for securing Israel's existence as a Jewish state (the fact that they want Israel to exist as a Jewish state is what differentiates pro-Israel groups from non-Zionist or even anti-Zionist groups that are outside the pro-Israel tent).

There is a core consensus among pro-Israel groups, therefore, over the importance of the country's security. Where they part ways is in their understanding of how best to ensure this, reflecting the broader disagreement among American Jews that has developed since the First Lebanon War (1982), and especially since the First Palestinian *Intifada* (1987–91), over how to safeguard Israel's security. At the center of this disagreement has been the issue of the Palestinian territories controlled by Israel since the 1967 war, which has created deep divisions within the pro-Israel community in the United States. As Dan Fleshler, a long-time pro-Israel activist, has written: "There is more than one lobby within the organized, self-styled, pro-Israel American Jewish community because there are substantial differences of opinion about what Israel needs from the United States."[4]

The pro-Israel community is really made up of three different lobbies: a centrist lobby, a left-wing lobby, and a right-wing lobby. The centrist lobby is composed of many of the most established and well-known Jewish organizations – most notably, the American Israel Public Affairs Committee (AIPAC),[5] the American Jewish Committee, the Anti-Defamation League, and the Conference of Presidents of Major American Jewish Organizations.[6] Although these groups have somewhat different missions and agendas, when it comes to pro-Israel advocacy they all try to represent "mainstream" American Jewish opinion. The centrist lobby is fundamentally oriented towards what may be termed "consensus politics." Consensus politics is based on the conviction that the best way to be influential is to present a united front before Congress and the White House. Hence, it seeks to represent the consensus of the American Jewish community (more precisely, the organized American Jewish community),[7] when such a consensus exists. When there are differences of opinion, it attempts to resolve these differences internally, behind closed doors, then in public to support a common position. As a result, the centrist lobby tries to avoid taking clear, strong stances on controversial and polarizing issues.

Hence, although groups in the centrist lobby support the principle of territorial compromise and favor a two-state solution to the Israeli–Palestinian conflict, they do not loudly and energetically promote the establishment of a Palestinian state, nor do they actively and openly oppose Israel's occupation of the West Bank. In fact, they tend to defend the expansion of Israeli settlements there. In the past, the centrist lobby supported the Oslo peace process and Israel's 2005 disengagement from Gaza, but in both cases its support was widely regarded as unenthusiastic, if not wary. It is concerned more with addressing the threats to Israel's security than in promoting peace processes that will necessarily involve Israeli concessions. Writing about centrist groups, Dan Fleshler notes that

> their organizational cultures are most comfortable when they can take forceful stances against Israel's "enemies" – e.g., Iran, Hamas, Hezbollah, and far-left critics of Israel. They

tend to be less comfortable about enthusiastically supporting peace initiatives that require a certain amount of trust in Arab intentions or bold territorial compromises.[8]

For the centrist lobby, being pro-Israel generally means supporting the Israeli government of the day, whatever the political make-up of that government. But the nature of this support may vary from half-hearted to full-throated. While the centrists will never publicly criticize or challenge the policy positions of the Israeli government, they will not necessarily lend their full support. What matters more than anything else is ensuring American support for Israel. The informal alliance between the United States and Israel is considered to be the cornerstone of Israeli security. Hence, maintaining this alliance is the central mission of the centrist lobby, which means that it opposes any kind of American pressure on Israel. Moreover, it is generally hostile to public criticism of Israel in the United States or elsewhere. In recent years, the centrist lobby has become increasingly concerned with combating what it perceives to be a global campaign spearheaded by Arab and anti-Zionist groups on the left to delegitimize Israel.

The centrist groups have always dominated pro-Israel advocacy in the United States. This dominance reflected the overwhelming desire of American Jewry for unity and solidarity, as well as a widespread unease among American Jews over publicly questioning the decisions of Israeli governments and the choices of Israeli voters. One scholar of American Jewry observed:

> On matters defined as security-related, Americans Jews, who do not bear the direct conse-
> quences of such life and death decisions, are reluctant to second-guess democratically
> elected Israeli governments. In addition, many Jews expressed concern that Israel's detrac-
> tors might use criticism of specific policies to bolster their anti-Israel efforts.[9]

Moreover, while the vast majority of American Jews have always supported Israel, especially after the 1967 war, this support was and is largely an expression of their Jewish identity rather than being ideologically driven. As such, most American Jews naturally gravitate to non-ideological centrist pro-Israel organizations.

The single biggest difference between the centrist lobby and the left-wing and right-wing lobbies is that the latter two are much more willing to challenge and oppose the policies of Israeli governments. Both have strong views that they forcefully advocate, even if they may be at odds with Israeli government policy or the consensus of the organized American Jewish community. It is more important to them to express their beliefs and opinions than echo the views of others. Fundamentally, they believe they are entitled to "save Israel from itself," and they are not willing to muzzle themselves for the sake of Jewish unity.

The left-wing lobby is currently made up of groups such as Americans for Peace Now, J Street, and Ameinu. These groups are "dovish" and favor diplomacy, engagement, negotiation, and concessions over the use of diplomatic isolation and/or military force. The left-wing lobby opposes Israel's occupation of the West Bank, favors a division of Jerusalem, and strongly supports the establishment of a Palestinian state. It wants the United States to take a lead role in bringing this about, even if this means pressuring Israel. Strong US–Israeli relations are, there-fore, of secondary importance. Peace between Israel and the Palestinians, and Israeli–Arab peace more generally, is the chief concern.

The right-wing lobby (which includes American Friends of Likud, the Jewish Institute for National Security Affairs, and the Zionist Organization of America), in stark contrast, is very hawkish, skeptical of the value of diplomacy and negotiations, suspicious of engagement, and opposed to Israeli concessions to its enemies. It embraces the use of military force, and believes that this should be applied ruthlessly and devastatingly when necessary. Above all, it supports

Israel's control of the West Bank (i.e., "Greater Israel") and opposes a division of Jerusalem and the establishment of a Palestinian state. The right-wing lobby tends to regard the Palestinians not as potential partners for peace but as implacable foes of Israel, and considers that Israeli–Palestinian peace is simply not possible for the foreseeable future. For right-wing groups, the greatest challenge Israel faces is from the forces of radical Islamism, represented by Hamas, Hizbollah, and, above all, Iran (whose regime the right-wing lobby often depicts as bent on Israel's destruction).

It should be clear by now that the pro-Israel community in the United States is highly fractious and that advocacy groups frequently oppose one another. While there are times when those in the left-wing and right-wing lobbies can find enough common ground with centrist groups to enable them to work together, those on the left and the right, given their radically different political orientations and views, do not cooperate with each other. Hence, more often than not, American policy-makers hear from many different voices, each of which claims to be "pro-Israel" and to represent the views of American Jews. In the words of former US Secretary of State George Shultz: "Anyone who thinks that Jewish groups constitute a homogeneous 'lobby' ought to spend some time dealing with them." Contrary, then, to the critique of the pro-Israel lobby which implies that it speaks (or shouts) with one loud voice to politicians who ignore it at their political peril, the reality is that there is a cacophony of voices, though some generally command more attention from politicians than others.

AIPAC's influence

The different pro-Israel groups are by no means equal. They vary greatly in size (membership and staff), finances, and political influence. Some are merely "one-man shows" led by a single individual; many others are just "shoestring" low-budget operations run out of a single office and reliant upon volunteers. Only a few are well staffed, with fancy offices and large sums of money at their disposal. The American Israel Public Affairs Committee is the biggest, wealthiest, and most powerful. It is undoubtedly the behemoth among pro-Israel groups, and it exerts a lot of influence in Congress – the bills supporting Israel that it drafts and/or promotes often receive almost unanimous support in both the House of Representatives and the Senate. Although AIPAC has much less influence within the White House, it can still effectively limit the room for maneuver of any US administration on issues related to Israel and the Israeli–Palestinian conflict because American presidents are generally reluctant to carry out a particular policy or launch a foreign policy initiative without congressional backing. They are particularly wary of trying to exert strong pressure on Israeli governments in the face of congressional opposition. This helps explain why successive administrations have not applied much leverage to stop Israeli settlement construction in the Occupied Territories, despite the fact that it goes against American wishes and policy goals.

AIPAC has, therefore, helped forestall pressure, threats, or even sanctions that American administrations, frustrated in particular by the continued expansion of Israeli settlements in the West Bank, might otherwise have applied on Israeli governments. But, while it may sometimes be able to prevent or stall US actions against Israel, it cannot always get its way. For instance, it was unable to prevent President Reagan from officially recognizing the Palestine Liberation Organization, to prevent President George H. W. Bush from threatening to block billions in loan guarantees to Israel, or to prevent President Clinton from offering the Palestinians sovereignty over the Temple Mount in Jerusalem (the holiest of Jewish sites). It also failed to prevent several major US arms sales to Arab states (most famously, the Reagan administration's sale of AWACS aircraft to Saudi Arabia in 1981), and to get the US Embassy in Israel moved from Tel

Aviv to Jerusalem. In short, for all its fearsome reputation, AIPAC is no match for a determined administration.

Pro-Israel groups and the peace process

It would be wrong, then, to blame AIPAC or any other pro-Israel group in the United States or elsewhere for the perpetuation of the Israeli–Palestinian conflict. At most, they may inhibit the willingness of American policy-makers to push forcefully for peace and to cajole Israel into making concessions, but they are not an insurmountable obstacle in the way of Israeli–Palestinian peace. This is clear from the historical record. Right-wing pro-Israel groups were staunchly opposed to the Oslo peace process, and in the early and mid-1990s they actively lobbied against the peace process and tried to torpedo it (for instance, they successfully lobbied Congress to pass a bill requiring the United States to move its embassy from Tel Aviv to Jerusalem and to pass an amendment which linked US aid to the Palestinian Authority to State Department certification that it was complying with the Oslo Accords). Their efforts created complications for American and Israeli leaders,[10] but they did not succeed in derailing the peace process. Similarly, left-wing pro-Israel groups that have lobbied for sustained US pressure to be applied on right-wing Israeli governments reluctant to move forward on the peace process (such as the Netanyahu government in the late 1990s and today) have achieved only limited and short-term success at best (as demonstrated by the Obama administration backing down over its demand for a complete Israeli settlement freeze). Thus, whether they are for or against the peace process, pro-Israel groups have been of marginal significance in influencing US policy towards it. This policy, like every aspect of American foreign policy, is ultimately determined by US national interests. It is when these interests appear to require active American engagement in Israeli–Palestinian peacemaking that US administrations become actively engaged, whether pro-Israel groups like it or not. After all, even the George W. Bush administration, hailed by much of the pro-Israel lobby in the United States as Israel's best-ever friend in the White House, eventually, albeit belatedly, pushed for an Israeli–Palestinian peace agreement including a division of Jerusalem, thereby provoking the ire of right-wing groups.

Conclusion

In sum, the pro-Israel lobby in the United States is not as powerful, or as politically homogeneous, as the popular critique of it suggests. It is by no means irrelevant, and on some issues (most notably, US aid to Israel) it is critically important, but it cannot be blamed for the continuation of the Israeli–Palestinian conflict or for America's failure to resolve it. If this is true for the pro-Israel lobby in the United States – the home of the largest, most affluent and successful Jewish community in the diaspora – it is even truer for pro-Israel lobbies in other countries. Indeed, nowhere else does the power of the pro-Israel lobby come even close to that in the United States. Thus, we should not overstate the significance of pro-Israel advocacy by diaspora Jews, whether in the United States or elsewhere. To be sure, this does not mean that diaspora Jewry as a whole plays no role in the Israeli–Palestinian conflict. Pro-Israel groups within the Jewish diaspora have mobilized for and against peacemaking efforts between Israel, the Palestinians, and the Arab world. Those in the United States, in particular, have played roles both in hindering and in promoting efforts to resolve the conflict. Their impact on the conflict has been both positive and negative, but it is not as significant as many now seem to believe.

Notes

1 It is also sometimes called the "Jewish lobby," but this term is misleading because it includes non-Jews, particularly evangelical Christian Zionists. The pro-Israel lobby is defined by its political agenda, not by religion or ethnicity. This chapter, however, focuses solely on Jewish pro-Israel advocacy. On Christian pro-Israel advocacy in the United States, see P. Merkley, "American Christian Support for Israel," in E. Gilboa and E. Inbar (eds), *US–Israeli Relations in a New Era* (New York: Routledge, 2009), pp.108–22.
2 For a rebuttal of this claim, see Dov Waxman, "From Jerusalem to Baghdad? Israel and the War in Iraq," *International Studies Perspectives*, 10/1 (2009), pp. 1–17.
3 American strategic considerations have also played an important role in motivating US aid to Israel, as A. F. K. Organski has persuasively argued in his book *The $36 Billion Bargain: Strategy and Politics in US Assistance to Israel* (New York: Columbia University Press, 1990).
4 Fleshler (2009: 9).
5 AIPAC is often depicted in the media as a hawkish right-wing organization. This popular image, however, is largely erroneous (it is true that some of the group's leadership and major donors have been supporters of Israel's Likud Party). Although it has frequently supported the policies of Likud governments in Israel, it does so less out of strong ideological convictions than because of its policy of backing all Israeli governments (albeit some more energetically and enthusiastically than others). Moreover, AIPAC has on occasion supported Israeli government initiatives that were deeply unpopular with right-wing hawks, most notably the disengagement from Gaza in 2005. By and large, its activists are politically centrist American Jews (mostly Democrats) who are concerned primarily for Israel's security and survival.
6 An umbrella organization comprising fifty-one national Jewish organizations.
7 Many American Jews are not involved in the organized Jewish community. According to the National Jewish Population Survey of 2001, 44 percent of American Jews are "unaffiliated" – they don't belong to a synagogue, a Jewish Community Center, or any other Jewish organization. United Jewish Communities, *The National Jewish Population Survey 2000–01* (New York: United Jewish Communities, 2003).
8 Fleshler (2009: 64).
9 Raffel (2002: 122).
10 Israel's Labor-led government under Prime Minister Yitzhak Rabin opposed both of these bills at the time, and privately complained that right-wing pro-Israel organizations in the United States were acting against its policies and attempting to undermine the Oslo peace process.

References and further reading

Beilin, Yossi (2000) *His Brother's Keeper: Israel and Diaspora Jewry in the Twenty-First Century* (New York: Schocken Books).
Ben-Moshe, Danny, and Segev, Zohar (eds) (2007) *Israel, the Diaspora and Jewish Identity* (Brighton: Sussex Academic Press).
Carter, Jimmy (1996) *Palestine: Peace Not Apartheid* (New York: Simon & Schuster).
Fleshler, Dan (2009) *Transforming America's Israel Lobby* (Herndon, VA: Potomac Books).
Goldberg, J. J. (1996) *Jewish Power: Inside the Jewish Establishment* (Reading, MA: Addison Wesley).
Liebman, Charles (1977) *Pressure without Sanctions: The Influence of World Jewry on Israeli Policy* (Cranbury, NJ: Associated University Presses).
Mearsheimer, John J., and Walt, Stephen M. (2007) *The Israel Lobby and US Foreign Policy* (New York: Farrar, Straus, & Giroux).
Raffel, M. J. (2002) "History of Israel Advocacy," in A. Mittleman, J. Sarna and R. Licht (eds), *Jewish Polity and American Civil Society* (Lanham, MD: Rowman & Littlefield).
Rosenthal, Steven T. (2001) *Irreconcilable Differences? The Waning of the American Jewish Love Affair with Israel* (Hanover, NH: Brandeis University Press).
Seliktar, Ofira (2002) *Divided we Stand: American Jews, Israel, and the Peace Process* (New York: Praeger).

Chronology

Steve Lutes

---

14 February 1896: Publication of Theodor Herzl's *Der Judenstaat* (*The Jewish State*). Herzl argued that, because of anti-Semitism, it was not possible for Jews to assimilate into other cultures and, therefore, it was necessary to pursue the establishment of a Jewish state. His work helped propel the formation of the Zionist Organization and founding of the First Zionist Congress in 1897 which elected him as its first president.

1882–1903: The First *Aliyah* was the first modern widespread wave of Jewish migration to Palestine. Those arriving in this wave were mostly from Eastern Europe but also from Yemen.

1904–1913: The Second *Aliyah* of Jewish immigrants was a defining event in the development of the *Yishuv*, the Jewish settlement in Palestine. As with the 1882–1903 wave of settlers, most of the Jews in this period were escaping persecution in Russia and Eastern Europe. However, a critical new trait of the Second *Aliyah* was ideological, with many of its immigrants, particularly the youth, influenced by the principles of socialism. The creation of the *kibbutz*, an agricultural community of workers, living on and farming communal land, was a product of this *Aliyah*, and this lifestyle instilled in the Jewish pioneers qualities such as self-sufficiency, safety, and sacrifice which were important to the *Yishuv* in the years before to independence. Another important cultural dimension to the Second *Aliyah* was the revival of the Hebrew language, which became a unifying element of the Jewish community.

24 October 1915: The McMahon letters. Over the course of 1915–16, Sir Henry McMahon, representing the British government, exchanged a series of letters with Hussein bin Ali, the Sharif of Mecca, urging an Arab revolt against the Ottomans in exchange for British support of an independent Arab state within proposed territories. The Arabs accepted the British offer but, while their revolt had little military significance, McMahon's ambiguous language left the specific territorial intentions open to interpretation and became a great source of controversy that would have implications for decades to come. While the British argued that Palestine was exempted from the pledge, Arabs insisted that it was included in the agreement. This disagreement was inflamed when it was learned the British had separately promised the contested land to the French and the Zionist movement.

16 May 1916: The Sykes–Picot agreement was a plan reached in secret by the British and French, with the consent of the Russians, to divide large swaths of territory in the Ottoman Empire into regions of control and influence. The British were allotted areas consisting approximately of what is today Jordan and southern Iraq, while most of Palestine, including Jerusalem, was designated as being under international control. This document contradicted British pledges made to the Arabs, specifically Hussein bin Ali in his correspondence with McMahon. When the agreement, which did not expressly call for the creation of an independent Arab state, was publicly disclosed, many Arabs felt misled. It sowed great distrust and became a focal aspect in the future of Arab relations with the West.

2 November 1917: The Balfour Declaration. In a brief letter to Lord Rothschild, an active Zionist, British Foreign Secretary Arthur Balfour expressed "sympathy with Jewish Zionist aspirations" and British support to facilitate the establishment of a Jewish "national home" in Palestine. The letter, which carried the weight of the British government, marked the first time a powerful state officially signaled support for the Zionist cause. While not specifically endorsing a Jewish state, the Balfour Declaration had a great impact on both Jewish objectives for Palestine and Arab designs on the territory. Once it became apparent to the Arabs that British commitments would not be honored and Arab self-determination was undercut, the declaration came to be seen as an abandonment of this pledge in favor of Jewish aspirations for a homeland. For the Zionist movement, the declaration encouraged steep Jewish immigration to Palestine following World War I that would significantly alter the area's demographics and lead to hardened Arab opinion and intensified confrontation.

3 January 1919: The Faisal–Weizmann Agreement, signed by Emir Feisal, the son of the king of Hejaz (Hussein bin Ali), and Chaim Weizmann, the eventual president of the World Zionist Organization, at the Paris Peace Conference, was a fleeting agreement following World War I for Arab–Jewish cooperation on the development of a Jewish homeland in Palestine and an Arab nation in the Middle East.

4 April 1920: Arab riots broke out in Jerusalem's Old City and were followed in May 1921 by riots in Jaffa. Believing that the British had failed to protect their community, the Jews responded by creating the Haganah, an armed self-defense organization.

24 April 1920: Following the end of World War I, the Allied Supreme Council held the San Remo Conference, which determined the allocation of Class "A" League of Nations mandates for administering the former Ottoman-ruled lands of the Middle East. The British were allotted Iraq and Palestine, defined as an area encompassing present-day Israel and Jordan. The mandate incorporated the Balfour Declaration's support for establishing a Jewish "national home" in Palestine. The League of Nations formally approved the British Mandate for Palestine in 1922.

May 1936–March 1939: This period in Palestine during the British Mandate was marked by dissidence and violence known as the Arab Revolt. Growing antagonism against British rule and outright hostility towards the *Yishuv* induced by immigration, land disputes, and fear of a Jewish state led to Arab strikes, political protests, and, ultimately, armed insurrection. British armed forces, with the support of the Haganah, met violence with violence to suppress the uprising. While the Arabs suffered greatly in terms of loss of life and economics, the revolt brought about a sense of Palestinian identity.

7 August 1936: The Palestine Royal Commission, which became known as the Peel Commission after its chairman Lord Robert Peel, was tasked by the British to determine the causes of the Arab revolt. Its report, issued in 1937, recommended for the first time a partition of Palestine into Arab and Jewish states, as well as population transfers and a cap on Jewish immigration. While the plan was ultimately abandoned, the British government initially endorsed the partition solution for Palestine, which was rejected by Arab leaders and met by division within the Zionist movement.

17 May 1939: The British government issued a White Paper calling for the creation of one independent, shared state for Jews and Arabs, as well as the imposition of severe limitations on Jewish immigration and restrictions on Jews acquiring land. This was considered a betrayal of the Balfour Declaration, and the Zionist movement responded by organizing illegal migration which the British countered by blockading Palestine. With the outbreak of war in September 1939, the head of the Jewish Agency for Palestine, David Ben-Gurion, famously declared: "We will fight the White Paper as if there is no war, and fight the war as if there is no White Paper."

22 July 1946: The King David Hotel in Jerusalem, headquarters of the British authority in Palestine, was bombed by members of the Irgun, a militant Jewish organization that had previously split from the Haganah, and ninety-one people were killed. It was the deadliest terrorist attack against the British during the Mandate period. The commander of the Irgun at the time was Menachem Begin, who later (1977) became prime minister of Israel.

29 November 1947: The partition plan. The UN General Assembly adopted Resolution 181, by a vote of thirty-three to thirteen, calling for the partition of Palestine into two states – one Jewish and one Palestinian – with Jerusalem designated as under international control. The British, weary of the continued violence and unceasing intransigence of the Jews and Arabs, had sought an exit strategy. The UN Special Committee on Palestine was formed, and a majority opinion coalesced around a two-state proposal, with each composed of three noncontiguous sections. The plan attempted to incorporate as many Jews as possible in the Jewish state and provide less populated areas to accommodate additional immigration; however, demographics guaranteed a sizeable Arab minority in the Jewish state. While Jewish leaders declared their support for the partition plan, Palestinian leaders and the Arab League rejected it, refusing to accept a Jewish state in Palestine, and arguing that the rights of the majority population had been overlooked.

9 April 1948: Deir Yassin massacre. Under the pretext of securing a significant roadway to Jerusalem, members of the Irgun and the Lehi (Stern Gang), the smallest and most radical Jewish paramilitary organization, attacked the village of Deir Yassin, killing more than 100 Palestinians. The massacre took on symbolic meaning for Arabs as an event defining Jewish aggression and efforts to depopulate the area of Palestinians.

14 May 1948: Establishment of the State of Israel. A civil war had been raging in Palestine between the Arab and Jewish communities following UN approval of Resolution 181. With the British Mandate set to expire the following day, Jewish leaders declared independence. It was a moment marked by joy and celebration for Jews as the dream of resurrecting a Jewish state in the Holy Land was realized. For the Arabs, the day is known as *al-Nakba*, or the Catastrophe, and brought with it emotions of anger and loss. Lasting and conflicting narratives would develop, as Israel was immediately forced to defend its newly founded state from invading Arab forces from Egypt, Syria, Jordan, Lebanon, and Iraq. For the Israelis, the War of Independence is considered a heroic struggle to survive against the Arabs who rejected their state's legitimacy. From the perspective of the Arabs, their land was stolen and Palestinians were forcibly expelled from their homes and turned into refugees. The boundary lines that were demarcated by the 1949 armistice agreements at the end of the war became the effective boundaries of Israel as well as the basis for future territorial negotiations.

29 October 1956: Suez crisis. Following Egyptian President Nasser's decision in July 1956 to nationalize the Suez Canal Company, Israel, with the support of the British and French, invaded and occupied the Sinai peninsula and the Gaza Strip.

10 October 1959: The founding of Fatah. Yasser Arafat and other Palestinian activists secretly met in Kuwait and founded Fatah, with the vision of defeating Israel by force and completely liberating Palestine. Fatah would grow to become the leading faction of the Palestine Liberation Organization (PLO).

28 May 1964: Creation of the PLO. The first Palestinian National Conference was held in East Jerusalem with more than 400 Palestinian leaders. The conference established the Palestine Liberation Organization and adopted a Charter that called for the liberation of Palestine and declared the establishment of Israel as illegal and null and void.

5 June 1967: Six Day/June War. Israel launched a devastating preemptive military strike against Egypt, Jordan, and Syria to begin the Six Day or June War, which would end in a decisive victory for Israel and the capturing of the West Bank and the Old City from Jordan; the Sinai peninsula and the Gaza Strip from Egypt; and the Golan Heights from Syria. The war was a signature event that would redefine the Israeli–Palestinian conflict. Territorial issues involving the land seized by Israel would become the centerpiece of negotiations, with the development of Jewish settlements built in the West Bank and Gaza generating yet another complexity to the conflict and flash points for future violence. For Israelis, the "liberation" of Jerusalem and the West Bank meant they gained access to significant religious sites. The war also triggered another wave of Palestinian refugees to bordering Arab states. While many fled, the majority remained, and approximately 2 million Palestinians in East Jerusalem, the West Bank, and Gaza came under Israeli military rule.

28 June 1967: Extension of Israeli law over East Jerusalem. Before the 1967 war, Jerusalem was divided into two, with Israel controlling West Jerusalem and Jordan in control of East Jerusalem. Following Israel's military victory, the Knesset decreed that "the law, jurisdiction and administration of the state" of Israel "shall extend to any area of Eretz Israel [the Land of Israel] designated by the Government by order." Using this statute, Israeli law was extended to an area including East Jerusalem and flanking territory in the West Bank.

1 September 1967: Khartoum Declaration. Arab leaders gathered for a summit in Khartoum, Sudan, and issued a defiant resolution declaring "no peace with Israel, no recognition of Israel, no negotiations with the Jewish state."

22 November 1967: The UN Security Council adopted Resolution 242, which called for Israel's withdrawal from territory in return for the Arab world's recognition of its right to exist and respect for its sovereignty. By calling for "withdrawal of Israeli armed forces from territories occupied in recent conflict," and not withdrawal from "the" or "all of the" occupied territories, the resolution is ambiguously worded. The Palestinians insist on a complete Israeli withdrawal from territory gained through the 1967 war and a return to the 1949 armistice lines. In contrast, the Israelis contend the resolution does not detail the extent of the withdrawal, leaving the issue of final borders to be negotiated. The resolution has become the basis of all subsequent negotiations between Israel and the Arabs.

2 February 1969: Yasser Arafat appointed chairman of the PLO.

17 September 1970: Black September. Civil war broke out in Jordan between King Hussein's forces and PLO guerrillas. The PLO was driven from Jordan and relocated its base of operation to Lebanon.

5 September 1972: Members of Black September, a Palestinian terrorist organization, killed eleven Israeli athletes at the summer Olympic Games in Munich, West Germany.

6 October 1973: Yom Kippur/October War. Egyptian and Syrian forces attacked on the Jewish Day of Atonement (Yom Kippur), taking Israel by surprise. After the initial success of the Egyptian and Syrian military, the Israelis counterattacked, recapturing nearly all of the territory they had lost, crossing the Suez Canal, and driving deep into Egypt. Despite their victory, the war was humbling for Israel, exposing its flawed reliance solely on military might. The Arab community heaped praise on Egyptian leader Anwar Sadat for initiating action against Israel and for demonstrating that Israel's borders were not impregnable and their military not invincible.

22 October 1973: The UN Security Council approved Resolution 338, calling for a ceasefire and implementation of UN Security Council Resolution 242.

28 October 1974: The seventh Arab League summit held in Rabat unanimously declared, for the first time, the PLO to be the "sole legitimate representative of the Palestinian people."

March 1974: Foundation of the Gush Emunim, or Bloc of the Faithful, as a movement of religious Zionists favoring the long-term retention of the West Bank, the Gaza Strip, and the Golan Heights by Israel. The movement was based on a religious ideology which viewed the whole of the Land of Israel, as described in the biblical texts, as having been promised to the Jewish people by God and not to be relinquished voluntarily to any form of non-Jewish (Arab) rule. While the movement as such ceased to exist in the 1980s, it spearheaded the growth of Israeli settlement-building in the West Bank and Gaza and gave birth to a large number of settlement, political, and ideological organizations which continue to implement the basic ideology laid out by the movement's founders – focusing, above all else, on the "Greater Land of Israel" ideology.

22 November 1974: The UN General Assembly granted observer status to the PLO.

17 May 1977: In a colossal shift in Israeli politics, a coalition of right-wing parties, led by the Likud Party, won control of the Knesset, effectively ending the thirty-year domination of political power in Israel by Mapai (the Labour Party). Menachem Begin, leader of Likud, was sworn in as prime minister on 20 June.

21 April 1978: In response to a congressional inquiry, a legal advisor to the US Department of State issued an opinion that Israeli settlements in the Occupied Territories are "inconsistent with international law."

5 September 1978: Camp David summit. At the invitation of President Jimmy Carter, Israeli Prime Minister Menachem Begin and Egyptian President Anwar Sadat participated in the historic Camp David summit that would lead to the first formal peace agreement between an Arab state and Israel. The Camp David Accords comprised two parts – the first involving Israel's withdrawal from the Sinai peninsula in exchange for the peace treaty with Egypt (signed on 26 March 1979) and the second establishing a framework to address the dispute over the West Bank and Gaza, including the setting up there of an autonomous regime – with Israel successfully insisting that the first not be contingent on the second. Negotiations over the West Bank/Gaza issue broke down when it became clear that Israel had no intention of withdrawing and the Jordanians and Palestinians had no desire to participate. The Accords drove a wedge between the Arab states, with many feeling betrayed by Egypt's willingness to sign a separate peace treaty with Israel and its failure to prevail on the Palestinian issue.

6 June 1982: Lebanon War. In the early 1980s, violence and Palestinian political protests were on a rise in the Occupied Territories, as was support for the PLO. This period also witnessed an increase in direct conflict between the PLO and Israel, with Israeli aerial strikes in southern Lebanon and Beirut and the PLO shelling cities in northern Israel. The attempted assassination of Israel's ambassador to Britain, Shlomo Argov, served as a pretext for Israel to invade southern Lebanon with the goal of destroying the PLO's military capability and political viability. While Israel succeeded in defeating the PLO and forcing the organization to relocate its headquarters to Tunisia, there was significant fallout and criticism both at home and abroad of its military operation. Israeli troops remained in Lebanon for the next eighteen years, finally withdrawing in May 2000.

9 December 1987: The Palestinian *Intifada*. A grassroots uprising of Palestinians exhausted by Israeli occupation and settlement-building and a failure of the PLO leadership to respond to their plight was sparked by the death of four Palestinians in a traffic accident in Gaza. The following day thousands of Palestinians took to the streets in Gaza to protest, and demonstrations quickly spread to the West Bank and East Jerusalem. As the demonstrations intensified and became militant, Israeli efforts to suppress them were largely unsuccessful and drew criticism both internationally and domestically. The *intifada* had major implications, with the unrest in the Occupied Territories illustrating the limitations of Israel's military prowess and leading many Israelis to question their continued presence there.

December 1987: The founding of Hamas, a Palestinian offshoot of the Muslim Brotherhood, following the eruption of the *intifada*. Committed in its original Charter to the destruction of Israel, the organization perpetrated numerous terrorist attacks, including suicide bombings, against Israeli military and civilian targets.

31 July 1988: King Hussein officially conceded any Jordanian claims to representation of the Palestinian issue and severed administrative and political ties with the West Bank.

15 November 1988: The Algiers Declaration. The Palestinian National Council issued a landmark declaration of independence that implied tacit acceptance of the existence of the State of Israel alongside a Palestinian state. This declaration was recognized by nearly 100 states and further anchored the PLO's position as the sole legitimate representative of the Palestinian people.

30 October 1991: The Madrid conference. Following the Gulf War, President George H. W. Bush seized the opportunity and, in an address to Congress, highlighted Arab–Israeli peace as one of his objectives for the Middle East. His administration worked to orchestrate the Madrid conference, jointly sponsored by the United States and the Soviet Union, which involved Israel, Egypt, Syria, Lebanon, and a combined Jordanian–Palestinian delegation. The conference is considered the starting point in the peace process and, while no agreements were achieved, had two important outcomes. The first was symbolic, with the Israelis and Palestinians at the table engaged in the peace process for the first time. A two-track negotiating framework was established comprising bilateral talks between Israel and individual Arab states and the Palestinians and a set of multilateral negotiations involving issues of a regional nature.

13 September 1993: Signing of the Declaration of Principles (the Oslo Accords), a historic agreement between Israel and the PLO. This was the culmination of several months of secret negotiations held in Oslo, Norway, that provided a framework for negotiations leading to a final settlement of the Israeli–Palestinian conflict and the resolution of issues such as borders, the status of Jerusalem, the future of settlements in the Occupied Territories, water, the rights of Palestinian refugees, and Palestinian self-determination. While the Accords were initially celebrated with great fanfare in the Occupied Territories and had strong support among the Israeli public, optimism eventually turned to renewed mistrust and unmet expectations for each side, as reality on the ground overtook the process, with the expansion of Israeli settlement-building and Palestinian violence and terrorism.

25 February 1994: During Ramadan, Baruch Goldstein, an Israeli settler, opened fire in the Ibrahimi Mosque in Hebron, killing twenty-nine Muslim worshippers. The Hebron massacre set off riots throughout the West Bank.

4 May 1994: The Cairo Agreement (Gaza–Jericho Agreement), signed by Israeli Prime Minister Yitzhak Rabin and Yasser Arafat, established the Palestinian Authority (PA), to which administrative authority of Gaza and Jericho would be transferred, with Israel's subsequent withdrawal from those areas.

1 July 1994: After twenty-seven years in exile, PLO chairman Arafat returned triumphantly to Gaza.

26 October 1994: Israel–Jordan Peace Treaty signed by King Hussein of Jordan and Israeli Prime Minister Yitzhak Rabin, making the Hashemite Kingdom of Jordan the second Arab nation to normalize relations with Israel.

28 September 1995: The Oslo II Accord. The Israeli–Palestinian Interim Agreement on the West Bank and the Gaza Strip, known as "Oslo II," called for further Israeli troop redeployments beyond the Gaza and Jericho areas. Under the agreement, Israel was scheduled to redeploy first from the major Palestinian towns and population centers in the West Bank and later from all rural areas, with the exception of Israeli settlements and the Israeli-designated military areas.

4 November 1995: Israeli Prime Minister Yitzhak Rabin was assassinated at a rally in support of the Oslo Accords by Yigal Amir, who was fiercely opposed to the peace plan and the prospects of Israeli withdrawal from the West Bank.

20 January 1996: The first-ever Palestinian elections were held in the Occupied Territories to select the president of the Palestinian National Authority (PNA) and members of the Palestinian Legislative Council. With Hamas refusing to participate in the electoral process, Fatah dominated and Yasser Arafat was elected as president.

13 March 1996: The Summit of the Peacemakers was convened in Sharm el Sheikh, Egypt, with President Clinton, Egyptian President Hosni Mubarak, Israeli Prime Minister Shimon Peres, and PNA President Arafat participating. It was intended to get the peace process back on track following a wave of suicide bombings in Israel.

17 January 1997: In accordance with the Oslo II agreement, the Hebron Protocol was concluded between Israeli Prime Minister Binyamin Netanyahu and PLO Chairman Arafat for the redeployment of Israeli Defense Forces in Hebron.

6 October 1997: Sheikh Ahmed Yassin, co-founder and spiritual leader of Hamas, returned to a hero's welcome in Gaza after his release by Israel in exchange for two Mossad agents, who had been arrested by the Jordanian authorities in a failed assassination attempt in Amman of Khaled Mishaal, one of the leaders of Hamas.

23 October 1998: The Wye River Memorandum was signed by Israeli Prime Minister Netanyahu and PLO Chairman Arafat to implement the earlier interim agreement known as Oslo II on technical land, security, and economic issues, as well as a pledge to renew talks on permanent-status issues. The Netanyahu government fell in a vote of no confidence shortly afterwards. The eruption of the Second *Intifada* in 2000 would leave the goals set forth in this agreement unfilled.

11 July 2000: Camp David summit. After weeks of secret talks between Israeli and Palestinian negotiators, President Bill Clinton invited Prime Minister Ehud Barak and Chairman Yasser Arafat to Camp David for a summit in the hopes of achieving a comprehensive solution to the conflict. The four primary issues that were to be considered were borders and settlements, security, Jerusalem, and refugees. The summit ended with no agreement and intensified mistrust and stridently divergent opinions as to why the talks had failed. On his return to Israel, Ehud Barak contended that Israel had made unprecedented offers in terms of land which the Palestinians had rejected. President Clinton also praised Barak for his courageous efforts at the summit and laid the blame for the failure of the summit on Arafat.

28 September 2000: Al-Aqsa *Intifada*. Likud Party Chairman Ariel Sharon visited the Temple Mount/Haram al-Sharif in Jerusalem on 28 September in a provocative display of asserting Israel's claim to sovereignty over the site. Palestinians cite Sharon's visit as the spark that ignited the Second *Intifada*, known as the Al-Aqsa *Intifada*, while others fault Arafat for either planning or at least failing to contain the violence. The unrest quickly escalated, with acts of terrorism and violence committed against Israeli military targets, settlers, and civilians, and Israeli forces responding by destroying terrorist targets and targeting Palestinian leaders for assassination. In contrast to the First *Intifada*, this uprising involved coordinated attacks by terrorist groups and a level of violence targeted at civilians not witnessed previously. The Second *Intifada* marked the end of the Oslo peace process and a breakdown in trust between Israeli and Palestinian civil society.

12 October 2000: Two Israeli soldiers mistakenly entered Ramallah and, after being detained by PA security forces, were lynched by a mob. The image of one rioter celebrating and displaying his blood-stained hands became an iconic symbol of the Second *Intifada*.

23 December 2000: The Clinton Parameters. With Bill Clinton's presidency coming to an end, Israeli and Palestinian negotiators returned to Washington, DC, for separate talks with the Americans. President Clinton presented both sides with his parameters for a final-status agreement.

21 January 2001: The Taba talks. Israeli and Palestinian negotiators met at the Egyptian resort of Taba in a last-ditch effort to reach a peace agreement. Significant progress was made and, though significant gaps remained at the end of summit, the meeting concluded with both sides declaring that they had "never been closer to reaching an agreement." Negotiations were to resume after the Israeli elections; however, Ariel Sharon's election as prime minister on 6 February 2001 meant there would be no continuation of the talks.

28 March 2002: The Arab Peace Initiative. The Arab League met in Beirut, Lebanon, and adopted the Saudi-inspired Arab Peace Initiative, which called for Israel to withdraw from all territory acquired after 1967 and the creation of a Palestinian state. In exchange, the Arab nations would normalize relations and make peace with Israel.

29 March 2002: Operative Defensive Shield. Following a wave of suicide bombings, Israel launched Operative Defensive Shield, its largest operation in the West Bank since 1967. It reoccupied most of the territory and surrounded Arafat's compound in Ramallah in an effort to quell the Second *Intifada* and weaken the Palestinian Authority.

2 April 2002: The battle for Jenin. Israel targeted the Jenin refugee camp, where many suicide bombers originated, in a military operation. The Israelis encountered stiff resistance and, when confronted with a web of booby traps throughout streets and buildings, turned to using bulldozers to demolish suspect homes. With the camp sealed off during the battle, rumors of a massacre spread, but were later proven erroneous.

June 2002: Construction of the Israeli separation fence. In response to a wave of suicide bombings, Israel began the construction of a security barrier to thwart terrorist attacks originating in the West Bank. The route of the barrier coincides largely with the Green Line – the 1949 armistice line – but also cuts into the West Bank to incorporate Israeli settlements. The creation and route of the barrier – a high wall in some places and a series of barbed fences and trenches in others – created great controversy. The Palestinians view the separation wall as a unilateral confiscation of their territory that causes great hardship by dividing families and cutting them off from their jobs and farms. For the Israelis, the barrier is a security measure that has succeeded in reducing suicide bombings. The fence/wall has become a *de facto* border that adds a further complicating dimension to any future negotiations over the borders of a Palestinian state.

24 June 2002: President George W. Bush became the first US president publicly to support the creation of an independent Palestinian state existing side by side with Israel.

30 April 2003: The Road Map. The plan commonly known as the Road Map, designed to achieve a comprehensive resolution to the Israeli–Palestinian conflict through a two-state solution, was released by the Quartet – the United States, Russia, the European Union, and the United Nations. The Road Map consisted of three phases, requiring the Palestinian Authority to abandon violence and make democratic reforms in exchange for a state. In parallel, Israel was to freeze settlement expansion in the West Bank and Gaza and accept the emergence of a reformed Palestinian government which was to curtail terrorist activity.

18 December 2003: Gaza disengagement plan. Prime Minister Ariel Sharon announced his disengagement plan, which asserted a willingness to act unilaterally if the PA failed to restrain terrorist acts. His plan called for Israel to disengage from Gaza and the northern parts of the West Bank by withdrawing IDF forces and removing all Israeli settlements and settlers in those areas. Sharon, once a staunch proponent of settlement expansion, believed it was in Israel's best strategic interests to pull back for security and diplomatic reasons. Critics believed the plan validated the success of the Second *Intifada* and would encourage future violence. Sharon's action not only rippled through the Israeli–Palestinian conflict but also ruptured domestic politics in Israel by splitting the right.

22 March 2004: Hamas leader Sheikh Ahmed Yassin was assassinated by Israeli forces, an act that was strongly condemned by many Arab nations, as well as UN Secretary General Kofi Annan.

9 July 2004: The International Court of Justice ruled that Israel's construction of a security barrier in the Occupied Territories is contrary international law. It determined that Israel had an obligation both to end the violation of its international commitments and to make reparation for the damage caused to those Palestinians affected by the construction of the barrier.

11 November 2004: The long-time Chairman of the PLO, Yasser Arafat, died. Mahmoud Abbas, also known as Abu Mazen, was selected to replace him.

9 January 2005: Mahmoud Abbas (Abu Mazen) elected president of the Palestinian National Authority.

15 August 2005: Israel began the evacuation of settlements in Gaza. Withdrawal of its military force was completed and control of Gaza handed over to the Palestinian Authority on 12 September 2005.

25 January 2006: Hamas won a large majority in the elections to the Palestinian Legislative Council, defeating its rival, Fatah. This signaled a significant political shift with major repercussions for domestic Palestinian politics. Ismail Haniyya was sworn in as prime minister on 29 March 2006. Interpretations of Hamas's victory range from a desire among Palestinians to end PA corruption to support for Hamas's violent opposition to Israeli occupation.

30 January 2006: The Quartet principles. Following Hamas's electoral success, the Quartet declared that that all members of a future Palestinian government must be committed to non-violence, recognition of Israel, and acceptance of previous agreements and obligations, including the Road Map. The Quartet has refused to speak with Hamas until it accepts these three principles.

25 June 2006: IDF soldier Gilad Shalit was abducted in a cross-border raid by Hamas.

8 February 2007: Fatah and Hamas signed the Mecca Agreement to stop the factional violence between them, and a Palestinian national unity government was formed on 17 March.

7–15 June 2007: Fighting raged in Gaza in what amounted to a Palestinian civil war between Fatah and Hamas. On 14 June, President Abbas dissolved the Hamas-led Palestinian unity government, and the following day Hamas took over control of Gaza.

27 November 2007: President George W. Bush convened the Annapolis conference with Israeli Prime Minister Ehud Olmert and Palestinian President Abbas in an attempt to develop a pathway to implement the Road Map for Peace that would lead to the eventual creation of a Palestinian state. The conference marked the first time Israel and the Palestinians had met since the collapse of the Oslo process at the end of 2000.

27 December 2008: Operation Cast Lead. With an Egyptian-brokered six-month ceasefire coming to an end, Hamas and Israel were unable to reach an agreement to renew it, as Hamas militants returned to firing rockets into southern Israel. Israel launched Operation Cast Lead, a massive aerial attack on hundreds of targets in Gaza followed by a land assault. Israel's twenty-two-day military (re)invasion left over 1,400 Palestinians dead and was succeeded by an economic blockade of Gaza. While Israel clearly won a military victory and inflicted significant losses on Hamas, an outcry charging the use of disproportionate force by Israel led to an investigation by the UN.

4 June 2009: In a speech given in Cairo, President Barack Obama vowed personally to pursue a peaceful outcome to the Israeli–Palestinian conflict, including fulfilling aspirations for a Palestinian state. Proclaiming that Israeli settlements undermine efforts to achieve peace, Obama called for their construction to cease.

25 August 2009: Salam Fayyad, prime minister of the Palestinian Authority, unveiled an initiative to build the apparatus of a Palestinian state within two years, regardless of progress in peace talks with Israel.

15 September 2009: Goldstone report. The UN's Goldstone Commission investigating Israel's latest military offensive against Hamas in Gaza issued its controversial report alleging Israeli war crimes and concluding that Israel's operation was directed at the people of Gaza as a whole with the aim of punishing the civilian population. Israel countered that the report was politically motivated and one-sided and that it failed to account for Hamas's strategy of operating in densely populated civilian areas and Israel's efforts to mitigate civilian causalities.

31 May 2010: The Gaza flotilla raid was a military operation by Israel against six ships of the "Gaza Freedom Flotilla" in international waters of the Mediterranean Sea. The flotilla was carrying humanitarian aid and construction materials with the intention of breaking Israel's economic blockade of Gaza. On the passenger ship MV *Mavi Marmara*, clashes broke out after activists resisted, reportedly attacking the Israelis with baseball bats and steel bars, and allegedly with live fire. Israeli commandos used both non-lethal weaponry and live fire to suppress the resistance, allegedly in self-defense. Nine activists were killed, and dozens of activists and seven Israeli commandos were wounded.

26 September 2010: A six-month moratorium on building new Israeli settlements in the West Bank expired. President Abbas refused to continue peace talks without an extension of the moratorium. President Obama encouraged Prime Minister Netanyahu to extend the settlement freeze, but to no avail.

4 May 2011: Fatah and Hamas signed a reconciliation agreement in Cairo ending a bitter four-year-old rift. Under the accord, the two factions agreed to form a transitional government that would prepare for parliamentary and presidential elections within a year and manage the reconstruction of the Gaza Strip. The agreement also provides for elections to the Palestine National Council, the broadest decision-making body of the Palestine Liberation Organization, and for Hamas's entry into the PLO.

23 September 2011: In a speech to the United Nations General Assembly, Palestinian President Mahmoud Abbas presented a request that the State of Palestine be admitted as a full member of the United Nations. This request was forwarded to the Security Council's standing committee on admitting new members, which includes all fifteen council members, but failed to secure the nine votes required. On 31 October, the General Council of UNESCO voted to admit Palestine as a new member. The vote was carried by 107 votes in favour of admission and fourteen votes against, with fifty-two abstentions.

Key documents

The Balfour Declaration

Foreign Office
November 2nd, 1917

Dear Lord Rothschild,

I have much pleasure in conveying to you, on behalf of His Majesty's Government, the following declaration of sympathy with Jewish Zionist aspirations which has been submitted to, and approved by, the Cabinet.

"His Majesty's Government view with favour the establishment in Palestine of a national home for the Jewish people, and will use their best endeavours to facilitate the achievement of this object, it being clearly understood that nothing shall be done which may prejudice the civil and religious rights of existing non-Jewish communities in Palestine, or the rights and political status enjoyed by Jews in any other country."

I should be grateful if you would bring this declaration to the knowledge of the Zionist Federation.

Yours sincerely,
Arthur James Balfour

Source:
www.mfa.gov.il/MFA/Peace%20Process/Guide%20to%20the%20Peace%
20Process/The%20Balfour%20Declaration

United Nations General Assembly: Resolution on the Future Government of Palestine (Partition Resolution – Resolution 181), 29 November 1947

The General Assembly,

Having met in special session at the request of the mandatory Power to constitute and instruct a Special Committee to prepare for the consideration of the question of the future Government of Palestine at the second regular session;

Having constituted a Special Committee and instructed it to investigate all questions and issues relevant to the problem of Palestine, and to prepare proposals for the solution of the problem, and

Having received and examined the report of the Special Committee (document A/364)(1) including a number of unanimous recommendations and a plan of partition with economic union approved by the majority of the Special Committee.

Considers that the present situation in Palestine is one which is likely to impair the general welfare and friendly relations among nations;

Takes note of the declaration by the mandatory Power that it plans to complete its evacuation of Palestine by 1 August 1948:

Recommends to the United Kingdom, as the mandatory Power for Palestine, and to all other Members of the United Nations the adoption and implementation, with regard to the future Government of Palestine, of the Plan of Partition with Economic Union set out below;

Requests that

(a) The Security Council take the necessary measures as provided for in the plan for its implementation;

(b) The Security Council consider, if circumstances during the transitional period require such consideration, whether the situation in Palestine constitutes a threat to the peace. If it decides that such a threat exists, and in order to maintain international peace and security, the Security Council should supplement the authorization of the General Assembly by taking measures, under Articles 39 and 41 of the Charter, to empower the United Nations Commission, as provided in this resolution, to exercise in Palestine the functions which are assigned to it by this resolution;

(c)   The Security Council determine as a threat to the peace, breach of the peace or act of aggression, in accordance with Article 39 of the Charter, any attempt to alter by force the settlement envisaged by this resolution;

(d)   The Trusteeship Council be informed of the responsibilities envisaged for it in this plan;

Calls upon the inhabitants of Palestine to take such steps as may be necessary on their part to put this plan into effect;

Appeals to all Governments and all peoples to refrain from taking any action which might hamper or delay the carrying out of these recommendations, and

Authorizes the Secretary-General to reimburse travel and subsistence expenses of the members of the Commission referred to in Part 1, Section B, Paragraph I below, on such basis and in such form as he may determine most appropriate in the circumstances, and to provide the Commission with the necessary staff to assist in carrying out the functions assigned to the Commission by the General Assembly.

PLAN OF PARTITION WITH ECONOMIC UNION

Part I. – Future Constitution and Government of Palestine

A. TERMINATION OF MANDATE, PARTITION AND INDEPENDENCE

1.   The Mandate for Palestine shall terminate as soon as possible but in any case not later than 1 August 1948.

2.   The armed forces of the mandatory Power shall be progressively withdrawn from Palestine, the withdrawal to be completed as soon as possible but in any case not later than 1 August 1948.

The mandatory Power shall advise the Commission, as far in advance as possible, of its intention to terminate the mandate and to evacuate each area.

The mandatory Power shall use its best endeavours to ensure that an area situated in the territory of the Jewish State, including a seaport and hinterland adequate to provide facilities for a substantial immigration, shall be evacuated at the earliest possible date and in any event not later than 1 February 1948.

3.   Independent Arab and Jewish States and the Special International Regime for the City of Jerusalem, set forth in Part III of this Plan, shall come into existence in Palestine two

months after the evacuation of the armed forces of the mandatory Power has been completed but in any case not later than 1 October 1948. The boundaries of the Arab State, the Jewish State, and the City of Jerusalem shall be as described in Parts II and III below.

4. The period between the adoption by the General Assembly of its recommendation on the question of Palestine and the establishment of the independence of the Arab and Jewish States shall be a transitional period.

B. STEPS PREPARATORY TO INDEPENDENCE

1. A Commission shall be set up consisting of one representative of each of five Member States. The Members represented on the Commission shall be elected by the General Assembly on as broad a basis, geographically and otherwise, as possible.

2. The administration of Palestine shall, as the mandatory Power withdraws its armed forces, be progressively turned over to the Commission, which shall act in conformity with the recommendations of the General Assembly, under the guidance of the Security Council. The mandatory Power shall to the fullest possible extent coordinate its plans for withdrawal with the plans of the Commission to take over and administer areas which have been evacuated.

    In the discharge of this administrative responsibility the Commission shall have authority to issue necessary regulations and take other measures as required.

    The mandatory Power shall not take any action to prevent, obstruct or delay the implementation by the Commission of the measures recommended by the General Assembly.

3. On its arrival in Palestine the Commission shall proceed to carry out measures for the establishment of the frontiers of the Arab and Jewish States and the City of Jerusalem in accordance with the general lines of the recommendations of the General Assembly on the partition of Palestine. Nevertheless, the boundaries as described in Part II of this Plan are to be modified in such a way that village areas as a rule will not be divided by state boundaries unless pressing reasons make that necessary.

4. The Commission, after consultation with the democratic parties and other public organizations of the Arab and Jewish States, shall select and establish in each State as rapidly as possible a Provisional Council of Government. The activities of both the Arab and Jewish Provisional Councils of Government shall be carried out under the general direction of the Commission.

    If by 1 April 1948 a Provisional Council of Government cannot be selected for either of the States, or, if selected, cannot carry out its functions, the Commission shall communicate that fact to the Security Council for such action with respect to that State as the Security Council may deem proper, and to the Secretary-General for communication to the Members of the United Nations.

5. Subject to the provisions of these recommendations, during the transitional period the Provisional Councils of Government, acting under the Commission, shall have full

authority in the areas under their control including authority over matters of immigration and land regulation.

6. The Provisional Council of Government of each State, acting under the Commission, shall progressively receive from the Commission full responsibility for the administration of that State in the period between the termination of the Mandate and the establishment of the State's independence.

7. The Commission shall instruct the Provisional Councils of Government of both the Arab and Jewish States, after their formation, to proceed to the establishment of administrative organs of government, central and local.

8. The Provisional Council of Government of each State shall, within the shortest time possible, recruit an armed militia from the residents of that State, sufficient in number to maintain internal order and to prevent frontier clashes.

This armed militia in each State shall, for operational purposes, be under the command of Jewish or Arab officers resident in that State, but general political and military control, including the choice of the militia's High Command, shall be exercised by the Commission.

9. The Provisional Council of Government of each State shall, not later than two months after the withdrawal of the armed forces of the mandatory Power, hold elections to the Constituent Assembly which shall be conducted on democratic lines.

The election regulations in each State shall be drawn up by the Provisional Council of Government and approved by the Commission. Qualified voters for each State for this election shall be persons over eighteen years of age who are (a) Palestinian citizens residing in that State; and (b) Arabs and Jews residing in the State, although not Palestinian citizens, who, before voting, have signed a notice of intention to become citizens of such State.

Arabs and Jews residing in the City of Jerusalem who have signed a notice of intention to become citizens, the Arabs of the Arab State and the Jews of the Jewish State, shall be entitled to vote in the Arab and Jewish States respectively.

Women may vote and be elected to the Constituent Assemblies.

During the transitional period no Jew shall be permitted to establish residence in the area of the proposed Arab State, and no Arab shall be permitted to establish residence in the area of the proposed Jewish State, except by special leave of the Commission.

10. The Constituent Assembly of each State shall draft a democratic constitution for its State and choose a provisional government to succeed the Provisional Council of Government appointed by the Commission. The Constitutions of the States shall embody Chapters 1 and 2 of the Declaration provided for in section C below and include, inter alia, provisions for:

(a) Establishing in each State a legislative body elected by universal suffrage and by secret ballot on the basis of proportional representation, and an executive body responsible to the legislature;

(b) Settling all international disputes in which the State may be involved by peaceful means in such a manner that international peace and security, and justice, are not endangered;

(c) Accepting the obligation of the State to refrain in its international relations from the threat or use of force against the territorial integrity or political independence of any State, or in any other manner inconsistent with the purpose of the United Nations;

(d) Guaranteeing to all persons equal and non-discriminatory rights in civil, political, economic and religious matters and the enjoyment of human rights and fundamental freedoms, including freedom of religion, language, speech and publication, education, assembly and association;

(e) Preserving freedom of transit and visit for all residents and citizens of the other State in Palestine and the City of Jerusalem, subject to considerations of national security, provided that each State shall control residence within its borders.

11. The Commission shall appoint a preparatory economic commission of three members to make whatever arrangements are possible for economic co-operation, with a view to establishing, as soon as practicable, the Economic Union and the Joint Economic Board, as provided in section D below.

12. During the period between the adoption of the recommendations on the question of Palestine by the General Assembly and the termination of the Mandate, the mandatory Power in Palestine shall maintain full responsibility for administration in areas from which it has not withdrawn its armed forces. The Commission shall assist the mandatory Power in the carrying out of these functions. Similarly the mandatory Power shall co-operate with the Commission in the execution of its functions.

13. With a view to ensuring that there shall be continuity in the functioning of administrative services and that, on the withdrawal of the armed forces of the mandatory Power, the whole administration shall be in the charge of the Provisional Councils and the Joint Economic Board, respectively, acting under the Commission, there shall be a progressive transfer, from the mandatory Power to the Commission, of responsibility for all the functions of government, including that of maintaining law and order in the areas from which the forces of the mandatory Power have been withdrawn.

14. The Commission shall be guided in its activities by the recommendations of the General Assembly and by such instructions as the Security Council may consider necessary to issue.

The measures taken by the Commission, within the recommendations of the General Assembly, shall become immediately effective unless the Commission has previously received contrary instructions from the Security Council.

The Commission shall render periodic monthly progress reports, or more frequently if desirable, to the Security Council.

15. The Commission shall make its final report to the next regular session of the General Assembly and to the Security Council simultaneously.

C. DECLARATION

A declaration shall be made to the United Nations by the Provisional Government of each proposed State before independence. It shall contain, inter alia, the following clauses:

General Provision

The stipulations contained in the Declaration are recognized as fundamental laws of the State and no law, regulation or official action shall conflict or interfere with these stipulations, nor shall any law, regulation or official action prevail over them.

Chapter 1:
Holy Places, Religious Buildings and Sites

1. Existing rights in respect of Holy Places and religious buildings or sites shall not be denied or impaired.

2. In so far as Holy Places are concerned, the liberty of access, visit, and transit shall be guaranteed, in conformity with existing rights, to all residents and citizen of the other State and of the City of Jerusalem, as well as to aliens, without distinction as to nationality, subject to requirements of national security, public order and decorum.

Similarly, freedom of worship shall be guaranteed in conformity with existing rights, subject to the maintenance of public order and decorum.

3. Holy Places and religious buildings or sites shall be preserved. No act shall be permitted which may in any way impair their sacred character. If at any time it appears to the Government that any particular Holy Place, religious, building or site is in need of urgent repair, the Government may call upon the community or communities concerned to carry out such repair. The Government may carry it out itself at the expense of the community or community concerned if no action is taken within a reasonable time.

4. No taxation shall be levied in respect of any Holy Place, religious building or site which was exempt from taxation on the date of the creation of the State.

No change in the incidence of such taxation shall be made which would either discriminate between the owners or occupiers of Holy Places, religious buildings or sites, or would place such owners or occupiers in a position less favourable in relation to the general incidence of taxation than existed at the time of the adoption of the Assembly's recommendations.

5. The Governor of the City of Jerusalem shall have the right to determine whether the provisions of the Constitution of the State in relation to Holy Places, religious buildings and sites within the borders of the State and the religious rights appertaining thereto, are being properly applied and respected, and to make decisions on the basis of existing rights in cases of disputes which may arise between the different religious communities

or the rites of a religious community with respect to such places, buildings and sites. He shall receive full co-operation and such privileges and immunities as are necessary for the exercise of his functions in the State.

Chapter 2:
Religious and Minority Rights

1. Freedom of conscience and the free exercise of all forms of worship, subject only to the maintenance of public order and morals, shall be ensured to all.

2. No discrimination of any kind shall be made between the inhabitants on the ground of race, religion, language or sex.

3. All persons within the jurisdiction of the State shall be entitled to equal protection of the laws.

4. The family law and personal status of the various minorities and their religious interests, including endowments, shall be respected.

5. Except as may be required for the maintenance of public order and good government, no measure shall be taken to obstruct or interfere with the enterprise of religious or charitable bodies of all faiths or to discriminate against any representative or member of these bodies on the ground of his religion or nationality.

6. The State shall ensure adequate primary and secondary education for the Arab and Jewish minority, respectively, in its own language and its cultural traditions.

The right of each community to maintain its own schools for the education of its own members in its own language, while conforming to such educational requirements of a general nature as the State may impose, shall not be denied or impaired. Foreign educational establishments shall continue their activity on the basis of their existing rights.

7. No restriction shall be imposed on the free use by any citizen of the State of any language in private intercourse, in commerce, in religion, in the Press or in publications of any kind, or at public meetings.(3)

8. No expropriation of land owned by an Arab in the Jewish State (by a Jew in the Arab State)(4) shall be allowed except for public purposes. In all cases of expropriation full compensation as fixed by the Supreme Court shall be said previous to dispossession.

Chapter 3:
Citizenship, International Conventions and Financial Obligations

1. *Citizenship.* Palestinian citizens residing in Palestine outside the City of Jerusalem, as well as Arabs and Jews who, not holding Palestinian citizenship, reside in Palestine outside the City of Jerusalem shall, upon the recognition of independence, become citizens of the State in which they are resident and enjoy full civil and political rights. Persons over the age of eighteen years may opt, within one year from the date of recognition of independence of the State in which they reside, for citizenship of the other

State, providing that no Arab residing in the area of the proposed Arab State shall have the right to opt for citizenship in the proposed Jewish State and no Jew residing in the proposed Jewish State shall have the right to opt for citizenship in the proposed Arab State. The exercise of this right of option will be taken to include the wives and children under eighteen years of age of persons so opting.

Arabs residing in the area of the proposed Jewish State and Jews residing in the area of the proposed Arab State who have signed a notice of intention to opt for citizenship of the other State shall be eligible to vote in the elections to the Constituent Assembly of that State, but not in the elections to the Constituent Assembly of the State in which they reside.

2. *International conventions. (a)* The State shall be bound by all the international agreements and conventions, both general and special, to which Palestine has become a party. Subject to any right of denunciation provided for therein, such agreements and conventions shall be respected by the State throughout the period for which they were concluded.

   (b) Any dispute about the applicability and continued validity of international conventions or treaties signed or adhered to by the mandatory Power on behalf of Palestine shall be referred to the International Court of Justice in accordance with the provisions of the Statute of the Court.

3. *Financial obligations. (a)* The State shall respect and fulfil all financial obligations of whatever nature assumed on behalf of Palestine by the mandatory Power during the exercise of the Mandate and recognized by the State. This provision includes the right of public servants to pensions, compensation or gratuities.

   (b) These obligations shall be fulfilled through participation in the Joint Economic Board in respect of those obligations applicable to Palestine as a whole, and individually in respect of those applicable to, and fairly apportionable between, the States.

   (c) A Court of Claims, affiliated with the Joint Economic Board, and composed of one member appointed by the United Nations, one representative of the United Kingdom and one representative of the State concerned, should be established. Any dispute between the United Kingdom and the State respecting claims not recognized by the latter should be referred to that Court.

   (d) Commercial concessions granted in respect of any part of Palestine prior to the adoption of the resolution by the General Assembly shall continue to be valid according to their terms, unless modified by agreement between the concession-holders and the State.

Chapter 4:
Miscellaneous Provisions

1. The provisions of chapters 1 and 2 of the declaration shall be under the guarantee of the United Nations, and no modifications shall be made in them without the assent of the

General Assembly of the United Nations. Any Member of the United Nations shall have the right to bring to the attention of the General Assembly any infraction or danger of infraction of any of these stipulations, and the General Assembly may thereupon make such recommendations as it may deem proper in the circumstances.

2. Any dispute relating to the application or interpretation of this declaration shall be referred, at the request of either party, to the International Court of Justice, unless the parties agree to another mode of settlement.

{Section D (Economic Union and Transit) has been omitted. Part II of the Resolution deals with the borders and Part III deals with "Capitulations".}

Adopted at the 128th plenary meeting:
In favour (33): Australia, Belgium, Bolivia, Brazil, Byelorussian S.S.R., Canada, Costa Rica, Czechoslovakia, Denmark, Dominican Republic, Ecuador, France, Guatemala, Haiti, Iceland, Liberia, Luxemburg, Netherlands, New Zealand, Nicaragua, Norway, Panama, Paraguay, Peru, Philippines, Poland, Sweden, Ukrainian S.S.R., Union of South Africa, U.S.A., U.S.S.R., Uruguay, Venezuela.

Against (13): Afghanistan, Cuba, Egypt, Greece, India, Iran, Iraq, Lebanon, Pakistan, Saudi Arabia, Syria, Turkey, Yemen.

Abstained (10): Argentina, Chile, China, Colombia, El Salvador, Ethiopia, Honduras, Mexico, United Kingdom, Yugoslavia.

----

(1) See Official Records of the General Assembly, Second Session Supplement No. 11, Volumes I–IV.

* At its hundred and twenty-eighth plenary meeting on 29 November 1947 the General Assembly, in accordance with the terms of the above resolution, elected the following members of the United Nations Commission on Palestine: Bolivia, Czechoslovakia, Denmark, Panama, and Philippines.

(2) This resolution was adopted without reference to a Committee.

(3) The following stipulation shall be added to the declaration concerning the Jewish State: "In the Jewish State adequate facilities shall be given to Arabic-speaking citizens for the use of their language, either orally or in writing, in the legislature, before the Courts and in the administration."

(4) In the declaration concerning the Arab State, the words "by an Arab in the Jewish State" should be replaced by the words "by a Jew in the Arab State."

(5) On the question of the internationalization of Jerusalem, see also General Assembly resolutions 185 (S-2) of 26 April 1948; 187 (S-2) of 6 May 1948, 303 (IV) of 9 December 1949, and resolutions of the Trusteeship Council (Section IV).

Source: www.yale.edu/lawweb/avalon/un/res181.htm#note1

United Nations General Assembly Resolution 194, 11 December 1948

The General Assembly,

Having considered further the situation in Palestine,

1. *Expresses* its deep appreciation of the progress achieved through the good offices of the late United Nations Mediator in promoting a peaceful adjustment of the future situation of Palestine, for which cause he sacrificed his life; and

Extends its thanks to the Acting Mediator and his staff for their continued efforts and devotion to duty in Palestine;

2. *Establishes* a Conciliation Commission consisting of three States Members of the United Nations which shall have the following functions:

(a) To assume, in so far as it considers necessary in existing circumstances, the functions given to the United Nations Mediator on Palestine by resolution 182 (S-2) of the General Assembly of 14 May 1948;

(b) To carry out the specific functions and directives given to it by the present resolution and such additional functions and directives as may be given to it by the General Assembly or by the Security Council;

(c) To undertake, upon the request of the Security Council, any of the functions now assigned to the United Nations Mediator on Palestine or to the United Nations Truce Commission by resolutions of the Security Council; upon such request to the Conciliation Commission by the Security Council with respect to all the remaining functions of the United Nations Mediator on Palestine under Security Council resolutions, the office of the Mediator shall be terminated;

3. *Decides* that a Committee of the Assembly, consisting of China, France, the Union of Soviet Socialist Republics, the United Kingdom and the United States of America, shall present, before the end of the first part of the present session of the General Assembly, for the approval

of the Assembly, a proposal concerning the names of the three States which will constitute the Conciliation Commission;

4. *Requests* the Commission to begin its functions at once, with a view to the establishment of contact between the parties themselves and the Commission at the earliest possible date;

5. *Calls upon* the Governments and authorities concerned to extend the scope of the negotiations provided for in the Security Council's resolution of 16 November 1948 and to seek agreement by negotiations conducted either with the Conciliation Commission or directly, with a view to the final settlement of all questions outstanding between them;

6. *Instructs* the Conciliation Commission to take steps to assist the Governments and authorities concerned to achieve a final settlement of all questions outstanding between them;

7. *Resolves* that the Holy Places – including Nazareth – religious buildings and sites in Palestine should be protected and free access to them assured, in accordance with existing rights and historical practice; that arrangements to this end should be under effective United Nations supervision; that the United Nations Conciliation Commission, in presenting to the fourth regular session of the General Assembly its detailed proposals for a permanent international régime for the territory of Jerusalem, should include recommendations concerning the Holy Places in that territory, that with regard to the Holy Places in the rest of Palestine the Commission should call upon the political authorities of the areas concerned to give appropriate formal guarantees as to the protection of the Holy Places and access to them, and that these undertakings should be presented to the General Assembly for approval;

8. *Resolves* that, in view of its association with three world religions, the Jerusalem area, including the present municipality of Jerusalem plus the surrounding villages and towns, the most eastern of which shall be Abu Dis; the most southern, Bethlehem, the most western, Ein Karim (including also the built-up area of Motsa); and the most northern, Shu'fat, should be accorded special and separate treatment from the rest of Palestine and should be placed under effective United Nations control;

Requests the Security Council to take further steps to ensure the demilitarization of Jerusalem at the earliest possible date;

Instructs the Commission to present to the fourth regular session of the General Assembly detailed proposals for a permanent international régime for the Jerusalem area which will provide for the maximum local autonomy for distinctive groups consistent with the special international status of the Jerusalem area;

The Conciliation Commission is authorized to appoint a United Nations representative, who shall co-operate with the local authorities with respect to the interim administration of the Jerusalem area;

9. *Resolves* that, pending agreement on more detailed arrangements among the Governments and authorities concerned, the freest possible access to Jerusalem by road, rail or air should be accorded to all inhabitants of Palestine;

Instructs the Conciliation Commission to report immediately to the Security Council, for appropriate action by that organ, any attempt by any party to impede such access;

10. *Instructs* the Conciliation Commission to seek arrangements among the Governments and authorities concerned which will facilitate the economic development of the area, including arrangements for access to ports and airfields and the use of transportation and communication facilities;

11. *Resolves* that the refugees wishing to return to their homes and live at peace with their neighbours should be permitted to do so at the earliest practicable date, and that compensation should be paid for the property of those choosing not to return and for loss of or damage to property which, under principles of international law or in equity, should be made good by the Governments or authorities responsible;

Instructs the Conciliation Commission to facilitate the repatriation, resettlement and economic and social rehabilitation of the refugees and the payment of compensation, and to maintain close relations with the Director of the United Nations Relief for Palestine Refugees and, through him, with the appropriate organs and agencies of the United Nations;

12. *Authorizes* the Conciliation Commission to appoint such subsidiary bodies and to employ such technical experts, acting under its authority, as it may find necessary for the effective discharge of its functions and responsibilities under the present resolution;

The Conciliation Commission will have its official headquarters at Jerusalem. The authorities responsible for maintaining order in Jerusalem will be responsible for taking all measures necessary to ensure the security of the Commission. The Secretary-General will provide a limited number of guards for the protection of the staff and premises of the Commission;

13. *Instructs* the Conciliation Commission to render progress reports periodically to the Secretary-General for transmission to the Security Council and to the Members of the United Nations;

14. *Calls upon* all Governments and authorities concerned to co-operate with the Conciliation Commission and to take all possible steps to assist in the implementation of the present resolution;

15. *Requests* the Secretary-General to provide the necessary staff and facilities and to make appropriate arrangements to provide the necessary funds required in carrying out the terms of the present resolution.

Hundred and eighty-sixth plenary meeting, 11 December 1948.

Source:
http://unispal.un.org/UNISPAL.NSF/0/C758572B78D1CD0085256BCF0077E51A

Palestine National Charter of 1964

(*Al-Mithaq al-Kawmee al-Philisteeni*)*

INTRODUCTION

We, the Palestinian Arab people, who waged fierce and continuous battles to safeguard its homeland, to defend its dignity and honor, and who offered all through the years continuous caravans of immortal martyrs, and who wrote the noblest pages of sacrifice, offering and giving,

We, the Palestinian Arab people, who faced the forces of evil, injustice and aggression, against whom the forces of international Zionism and colonialism conspire and worked to displace it, dispossess it from its homeland and property, abused what is holy in it and who in spite of all this refused to weaken or submit,

We, the Palestinian Arab people, who believe in its Arabism and in its right to regain its homeland, to realize its freedom and dignity, and who have determined to amass its forces and mobilize its efforts and capabilities in order to continue its struggle and to move forward on the path of holy war (al-jihad) until complete and final victory has been attained,

We, the Palestinian Arab people, based on our right of self-defense and the complete restoration of our lost homeland- a right that has been recognized by international covenants and common practices including the Charter of the United Nations-and in implementation of the principles of human rights, and comprehending the international political relations, with its various ramifications and dimensions, and considering the past experiences in all that pertains to the causes of the catastrophe, and the means to face it,

And embarking from the Palestinian Arab reality, and for the sake of the honor of the Palestinian individual and his right to free and dignified life,

And realizing the national grave responsibility placed upon our shoulders, for the sake of all this,

We, the Palestinian Arab people, dictate and declare this Palestinian National Charter and swear to realize it.

Article 1: Palestine is an Arab homeland bound by strong Arab national ties to the rest of the Arab Countries and which together form the great Arab homeland.

Article 2: Palestine, with its boundaries at the time of the British Mandate, is an indivisible territorial unit.

Article 3: The Palestinian Arab people has the legitimate right to its homeland and is an inseparable part of the Arab Nation. It shares the sufferings and aspirations of the Arab Nation and its struggle for freedom, sovereignty, progress and unity.

Article 4: The people of Palestine determine its destiny when it completes the liberation of its homeland in accordance with its own wishes and free will and choice.

Article 5: The Palestinian personality is a permanent and genuine characteristic that does not disappear. It is transferred from fathers to sons.

Article 6: The Palestinians are those Arab citizens who were living normally in Palestine up to 1947, whether they remained or were expelled. Every child who was born to a Palestinian Arab father after this date, whether in Palestine or outside, is a Palestinian.

Article 7: Jews of Palestinian origin are considered Palestinians if they are willing to live peacefully and loyally in Palestine.

Article 8: Bringing up Palestinian youth in an Arab and nationalist manner is a fundamental national duty. All means of guidance, education and enlightenment should be utilized to introduce the youth to its homeland in a deep spiritual way that will constantly and firmly bind them together.

Article 9: Ideological doctrines, whether political, social, or economic, shall not distract the people of Palestine from the primary duty of liberating their homeland. All Palestinian constitute one national front and work with all their feelings and material potentialities to free their homeland.

Article 10: Palestinians have three mottos: National Unity, National Mobilization, and Liberation. Once liberation is completed, the people of Palestine shall choose for its public life whatever political, economic, or social system they want.

Article 11: The Palestinian people firmly believe in Arab unity, and in order to play its role in realizing this goal, it must, at this stage of its struggle, preserve its Palestinian personality and all its constituents. It must strengthen the consciousness of its existence and stance and stand against any attempt or plan that may weaken or disintegrate its personality.

Article 12: Arab unity and the liberation of Palestine are two complementary goals; each prepares for the attainment of the other. Arab unity leads to the liberation of Palestine, and the liberation of Palestine leads to Arab unity. Working for both must go side by side.

Article 13: The destiny of the Arab Nation and even the essence of Arab existence are firmly tied to the destiny of the Palestine question. From this firm bond stems the effort and struggle of the Arab Nation to liberate Palestine. The people of Palestine assume a vanguard role in achieving this sacred national goal.

Article 14: The liberation of Palestine, from an Arab viewpoint, is a national duty. Its responsibilities fall upon the entire Arab nation, governments and peoples, the Palestinian peoples being in the forefront. For this purpose, the Arab nation must mobilize its military, spiritual and material potentialities; specifically, it must give to the Palestinian Arab people all possible support and backing and place at its disposal all opportunities and means to enable them to perform their role in liberating their homeland.

Article 15: The liberation of Palestine, from a spiritual viewpoint, prepares for the Holy Land an atmosphere of tranquility and peace, in which all the Holy Places will be safeguarded, and the freedom to worship and to visit will be guaranteed for all, without any discrimination of race, color, language, or religion. For all this, the Palestinian people look forward to the support of all the spiritual forces in the world.

Article 16: The liberation of Palestine, from an international viewpoint, is a defensive act necessitated by the demands of self-defense as stated in the Charter of the United Nations. For that, the people of Palestine, desiring to befriend all nations which love freedom, justice, and peace, look forward to their support in restoring the legitimate situation to Palestine, establishing peace and security in its territory, and enabling its people to exercise national sovereignty and freedom.

Article 17: The partitioning of Palestine, which took place in 1947, and the establishment of Israel are illegal and null and void, regardless of the loss of time, because they were contrary to the will of the Palestinian people and its natural right to its homeland, and were in violation of the basic principles embodied in the Charter of the United Nations, foremost among which is the right to self-determination.

Article 18: The Balfour Declaration, the Palestine Mandate System, and all that has been based on them are considered null and void. The claims of historic and spiritual ties between Jews and Palestine are not in agreement with the facts of history or with the true basis of sound statehood. Judaism, because it is a divine religion, is not a nationality with independent existence. Furthermore, the Jews are not one people with an independent personality because they are citizens to their states.

Article 19: Zionism is a colonialist movement in its inception, aggressive and expansionist in its goal, racist in its configurations, and fascist in its means and aims. Israel, in its capacity as the spearhead of this destructive movement and as the pillar of colonialism, is a permanent source of tension and turmoil in the Middle East, in particular, and to the international community in general. Because of this, the people of Palestine are worthy of the support and sustenance of the community of nations.

Article 20: The causes of peace and security and the requirements of right and justice demand from all nations, in order to safeguard true relationships among peoples and to maintain the loyalty of citizens to their homeland, that they consider Zionism an illegal movement and outlaw its presence and activities.

Article 21: The Palestinian people believes in the principles of justice, freedom, sovereignty, self-determination, human dignity, and the right of peoples to practice these principles. It also supports all international efforts to bring about peace on the basis of justice and free international cooperation.

Article 22: The Palestinian people believe in peaceful co-existence on the basis of legal existence, for there can be no coexistence with aggression, nor can there be peace with occupation and colonialism.

Article 23: In realizing the goals and principles of this Convent, the Palestine Liberation Organization carries out its full role to liberate Palestine in accordance with the basic law of this Organization.

Article 24: This Organization does not exercise any territorial sovereignty over the West Bank in the Hashemite Kingdom of Jordan, on the Gaza Strip or in the Himmah Area. Its activities will be on the national popular level in the liberational, organizational, political and financial fields.

Article 25: This Organization is in charge of the movement of the Palestinian people in its struggle to liberate its homeland in all liberational, organizational, and financial matters, and in all other needs of the Palestine Question in the Arab and international spheres.

Article 26: The Liberation Organization cooperates with all Arab governments, each according to its ability, and does not interfere in the internal affairs of any Arab states.

Article 27: This Organization shall have its flag, oath and a national anthem. All this shall be resolved in accordance with special regulations.

Article 28: The basic law for the Palestine Liberation Organization is attached to this Charter. This law defines the manner of establishing the Organization, its organs, institutions, the specialties of each one of them, and all the needed duties thrust upon it in accordance with this Charter.

Article 29: This Charter cannot be amended except by two-thirds majority of the members of the National Council of the Palestine Liberation Organization in a special session called for this purpose.

Adopted in 1964 by the 1st Palestinian Conference

Note: *"Al-Kawmee" has no exact equivalent in English but reflects the notion of pan-Arabism.

Source:
www.un.int/wcm/content/site/palestine/cache/offonce/pid/12363;jsessionid=61E5
BE4EC31CD290B9EFE1FCA4B889AB

United Nations Security Council Resolution 242, 22 November 1967

The Security Council,

Expressing its continuing concern with the grave situation in the Middle East,

Emphasizing the inadmissibility of the acquisition of territory by war and the need to work for a just and lasting peace in which every State in the area can live in security,

Emphasizing further that all Member States in their acceptance of the Charter of the United Nations have undertaken a commitment to act in accordance with Article 2 of the Charter,

1. *Affirms* that the fulfillment of Charter principles requires the establishment of a just and lasting peace in the Middle East which should include the application of both the following principles:

   (i) Withdrawal of Israeli armed forces from territories occupied in the recent conflict;

   (ii) Termination of all claims or states of belligerency and respect for and acknowledgement of the sovereignty, territorial integrity and political independence of every State in the area and their right to live in peace within secure and recognized boundaries free from threats or acts of force;

2. *Affirms further* the necessity

   (a) For guaranteeing freedom of navigation through international waterways in the area;

   (b) For achieving a just settlement of the refugee problem;

   (c) For guaranteeing the territorial inviolability and political independence of every State in the area, through measures including the establishment of demilitarized zones;

3. *Requests* the Secretary-General to designate a Special Representative to proceed to the Middle East to establish and maintain contacts with the States concerned in order to promote agreement and assist efforts to achieve a peaceful and accepted settlement in accordance with the provisions and principles in this resolution;

4. *Requests* the Secretary-General to report to the Security Council on the progress of the efforts of the Special Representative as soon as possible.

Source: www.yale.edu/lawweb/avalon/un/un242.htm

The Covenant of the Islamic Resistance Movement (Hamas Charter), 18 August 1988

Selected Articles: The following have not been included: Article 5 (Time and Place Extent of the Islamic Resistance Movement); articles 16–19 (The Education of the Generations, The Role of the Moslem Woman, The Role of Islamic Art in the Battle of Liberation); articles 22–6 (attitudes to Islamic Movements and Nationalist Movements in the Palestinian Arena); and articles 29–35 (attitudes to Nationalist and Religious Groupings, Institutions, Intellectuals, The Arab and Islamic World, Followers of Other Religions, The Islamic Resistance Movement Is a Humanistic Movement, The Attempt to Isolate the Palestinian People, and the Testimony of History).

In The Name Of The Most Merciful Allah

"Ye are the best nation that hath been raised up unto mankind: ye command that which is just, and ye forbid that which is unjust, and ye believe in Allah. And if they who have received the scriptures had believed, it had surely been the better for them: there are believers among them, but the greater part of them are transgressors. They shall not hurt you, unless with a slight hurt; and if they fight against you, they shall turn their backs to you, and they shall not be helped. They are smitten with vileness wheresoever they are found; unless they obtain security by entering into a treaty with Allah, and a treaty with men; and they draw on themselves indignation from Allah, and they are afflicted with poverty. This they suffer, because they disbelieved the signs of Allah, and slew the prophets unjustly; this, because they were rebellious, and transgressed." (Al-Imran – verses 109–111).

"Israel will exist and will continue to exist until Islam will obliterate it, just as it obliterated others before it." (The Martyr, Imam Hassan al-Banna, of blessed memory).

"The Islamic world is on fire. Each of us should pour some water, no matter how little, to extinguish whatever one can without waiting for the others." (Sheikh Amjad al-Zahawi, of blessed memory).

In The Name Of The Most Merciful Allah

Introduction

Praise be unto Allah, to whom we resort for help, and whose forgiveness, guidance and support we seek; Allah bless the Prophet and grant him salvation, his companions and supporters, and to those who carried out his message and adopted his laws – everlasting prayers and salvation as long as the earth and heaven will last. Hereafter:

O People:

Out of the midst of troubles and the sea of suffering, out of the palpitations of faithful hearts and cleansed arms; out of the sense of duty, and in response to Allah's command, the call has gone out rallying people together and making them follow the ways of Allah, leading them to have determined will in order to fulfill their role in life, to overcome all obstacles, and surmount the difficulties on the way. Constant preparation has continued and so has the readiness to sacrifice life and all that is precious for the sake of Allah.

Thus it was that the nucleus (of the movement) was formed and started to pave its way through the tempestuous sea of hopes and expectations, of wishes and yearnings, of troubles and obstacles, of pain and challenges, both inside and outside.

When the idea was ripe, the seed grew and the plant struck root in the soil of reality, away from passing emotions, and hateful haste. The Islamic Resistance Movement emerged to carry out its role through striving for the sake of its Creator, its arms intertwined with those of all the fighters for the liberation of Palestine. The spirits of its fighters meet with the spirits of all the fighters who have sacrificed their lives on the soil of Palestine, ever since it was conquered by the companions of the Prophet, Allah bless him and grant him salvation, and until this day.

This Covenant of the Islamic Resistance Movement (HAMAS), clarifies its picture, reveals its identity, outlines its stand, explains its aims, speaks about its hopes, and calls for its support, adoption and joining its ranks. Our struggle against the Jews is very great and very serious. It needs all sincere efforts. It is a step that inevitably should be followed by other steps. The Movement is but one squadron that should be supported by more and more squadrons from this vast Arab and Islamic world, until the enemy is vanquished and Allah's victory is realised.

Thus we see them coming on the horizon "and you shall learn about it hereafter." "Allah hath written, Verily I will prevail, and my apostles: for Allah is strong and mighty." (The Dispute – verse 21).

"Say to them, This is my way: I invite you to Allah, by an evident demonstration; both I and he who followeth me; and, praise be unto Allah! I am not an idolator." (Joseph – verse 107).

Definition of the Movement

Ideological Starting-Points

Article One:

The Islamic Resistance Movement: The Movement's programme is Islam. From it, it draws its ideas, ways of thinking and understanding of the universe, life and man. It resorts to it for judgement in all its conduct, and it is inspired by it for guidance of its steps.

The Islamic Resistance Movement's Relation With the Moslem Brotherhood Group:

Article Two:

The Islamic Resistance Movement is one of the wings of Moslem Brotherhood in Palestine. Moslem Brotherhood Movement is a universal organization which constitutes the largest Islamic movement in modern times. It is characterised by its deep understanding, accurate comprehension and its complete embrace of all Islamic concepts of all aspects of life, culture, creed, politics, economics, education, society, justice and judgement, the spreading of Islam, education, art, information, science of the occult and conversion to Islam.

Structure and Formation

Article Three:

The basic structure of the Islamic Resistance Movement consists of Moslems who have given their allegiance to Allah whom they truly worship, – "I have created the jinn and humans only for the purpose of worshipping" – who know their duty towards themselves, their families and country. In all that, they fear Allah and raise the banner of Jihad in the face of the oppressors, so that they would rid the land and the people of their uncleanliness, vileness and evils.

> "But we will oppose truth to vanity, and it shall confound the same; and behold, it shall vanish away." (Prophets – verse 18).

Article Four:

The Islamic Resistance Movement welcomes every Moslem who embraces its faith, ideology, follows its programme, keeps its secrets, and wants to belong to its ranks and carry out the duty. Allah will certainly reward such one.

Characteristics and Independence:

Article Six:

The Islamic Resistance Movement is a distinguished Palestinian movement, whose allegiance is to Allah, and whose way of life is Islam. It strives to raise the banner of Allah over every inch of Palestine, for under the wing of Islam followers of all religions can coexist in security and safety where their lives, possessions and rights are concerned. In the absence of Islam, strife will be rife, oppression spreads, evil prevails and schisms and wars will break out.

How excellent was the Moslem poet, Mohamed Ikbal, when he wrote:

> "If faith is lost, there is no security and there is no life for him who does not adhere to religion. He who accepts life without religion, has taken annihilation as his companion for life."

The Universality of the Islamic Resistance Movement:

Article Seven:

As a result of the fact that those Moslems who adhere to the ways of the Islamic Resistance Movement spread all over the world, rally support for it and its stands, strive towards enhancing its struggle, the Movement is a universal one. It is well-equipped for that because of the clarity of its ideology, the nobility of its aim and the loftiness of its objectives.

On this basis, the Movement should be viewed and evaluated, and its role be recognised. He who denies its right, evades supporting it and turns a blind eye to facts, whether intentionally or unintentionally, would awaken to see that events have overtaken him and with no logic to justify his attitude. One should certainly learn from past examples.

The injustice of next-of-kin is harder to bear than the smite of the Indian sword.

"We have also sent down unto thee the book of the Koran with truth, confirming that scripture which was revealed before it; and preserving the same safe from corruption. Judge therefore between them according to that which Allah hath revealed; and follow not their desires, by swerving from the truth which hath come unto thee. Unto every of you have we given a law, and an open path; and if Allah had pleased, he had surely made you one people; but he hath thought it fit to give you different laws, that he might try you in that which he hath given you respectively. Therefore strive to excel each other in good works; unto Allah shall ye all return, and then will he declare unto you that concerning which ye have disagreed." (The Table – verse 48).

The Islamic Resistance Movement is one of the links in the chain of the struggle against the Zionist invaders. It goes back to 1939, to the emergence of the martyr Izz al-Din al Kissam and his brethren the fighters, members of Moslem Brotherhood. It goes on to reach out and become one with another chain that includes the struggle of the Palestinians and Moslem Brotherhood in the 1948 war and the Jihad operations of the Moslem Brotherhood in 1968 and after.

Moreover, if the links have been distant from each other and if obstacles, placed by those who are the lackeys of Zionism in the way of the fighters obstructed the continuation of the struggle, the Islamic Resistance Movement aspires to the realisation of Allah's promise, no matter how long that should take. The Prophet, Allah bless him and grant him salvation, has said:

"The Day of Judgement will not come about until Moslems fight the Jews (killing the Jews), when the Jew will hide behind stones and trees. The stones and trees will say O Moslems, O Abdulla, there is a Jew behind me, come and kill him. Only the Gharkad tree, (evidently a certain kind of tree) would not do that because it is one of the trees of the Jews." (related by al-Bukhari and Moslem).

The Slogan of the Islamic Resistance Movement:

Article Eight:
Allah is its target, the Prophet is its model, the Koran its constitution: Jihad is its path and death for the sake of Allah is the loftiest of its wishes.

Objectives

Incentives and Objectives:

Article Nine:
The Islamic Resistance Movement found itself at a time when Islam has disappeared from life. Thus rules shook, concepts were upset, values changed and evil people took control, oppression and darkness prevailed, cowards became like tigers: homelands were usurped, people were

scattered and were caused to wander all over the world, the state of justice disappeared and the state of falsehood replaced it. Nothing remained in its right place. Thus, when Islam is absent from the arena, everything changes. From this state of affairs the incentives are drawn.

As for the objectives: They are the fighting against the false, defeating it and vanquishing it so that justice could prevail, homelands be retrieved and from its mosques would the voice of the mu'azen emerge declaring the establishment of the state of Islam, so that people and things would return each to their right places and Allah is our helper.

"...and if Allah had not prevented men, the one by the other, verily the earth had been corrupted: but Allah is beneficient towards his creatures." (The Cow – verse 251).

Article Ten:
As the Islamic Resistance Movement paves its way, it will back the oppressed and support the wronged with all its might. It will spare no effort to bring about justice and defeat injustice, in word and deed, in this place and everywhere it can reach and have influence therein.

Strategies and Methods

Strategies of the Islamic Resistance Movement: Palestine Is Islamic Waqf:

Article Eleven:
The Islamic Resistance Movement believes that the land of Palestine is an Islamic Waqf consecrated for future Moslem generations until Judgement Day. It, or any part of it, should not be squandered: it, or any part of it, should not be given up. Neither a single Arab country nor all Arab countries, neither any king or president, nor all the kings and presidents, neither any organization nor all of them, be they Palestinian or Arab, possess the right to do that. Palestine is an Islamic Waqf land consecrated for Moslem generations until Judgement Day. This being so, who could claim to have the right to represent Moslem generations till Judgement Day?

This is the law governing the land of Palestine in the Islamic Sharia (law) and the same goes for any land the Moslems have conquered by force, because during the times of (Islamic) conquests, the Moslems consecrated these lands to Moslem generations till the Day of Judgement.

It happened like this: When the leaders of the Islamic armies conquered Syria and Iraq, they sent to the Caliph of the Moslems, Umar bin-el-Khatab, asking for his advice concerning the conquered land – whether they should divide it among the soldiers, or leave it for its owners, or what? After consultations and discussions between the Caliph of the Moslems, Omar bin-el-Khatab and companions of the Prophet, Allah bless him and grant him salvation, it was decided that the land should be left with its owners who could benefit by its fruit. As for the real ownership of the land and the land itself, it should be consecrated for Moslem generations till Judgement Day. Those who are on the land, are there only to benefit from its fruit. This Waqf remains as long as earth and heaven remain. Any procedure in contradiction to Islamic Sharia, where Palestine is concerned, is null and void.

"Verily, this is a certain truth. Wherefore praise the name of thy Lord, the great Allah." (The Inevitable – verse 95).

Homeland and Nationalism from the Point of View of the Islamic Resistance Movement in Palestine:

Article Twelve:

Nationalism, from the point of view of the Islamic Resistance Movement, is part of the religious creed. Nothing in nationalism is more significant or deeper than in the case when an enemy should tread Moslem land. Resisting and quelling the enemy become the individual duty of every Moslem, male or female. A woman can go out to fight the enemy without her husband's permission, and so does the slave: without his master's permission.

Nothing of the sort is to be found in any other regime. This is an undisputed fact. If other nationalist movements are connected with materialistic, human or regional causes, nationalism of the Islamic Resistance Movement has all these elements as well as the more important elements that give it soul and life. It is connected to the source of spirit and the granter of life, hoisting in the sky of the homeland the heavenly banner that joins earth and heaven with a strong bond.

If Moses comes and throws his staff, both witch and magic are annulled.

"Now is the right direction manifestly distinguished from deceit: whoever therefore shall deny Tagut, and believe in Allah, he shall surely take hold with a strong handle, which shall not be broken; Allah is he who heareth and seeth." (The Cow – verse 256).

Peaceful Solutions, Initiatives and International Conferences:

Article Thirteen:

Initiatives, and so-called peaceful solutions and international conferences, are in contradiction to the principles of the Islamic Resistance Movement. Abusing any part of Palestine is abuse directed against part of religion. Nationalism of the Islamic Resistance Movement is part of its religion. Its members have been fed on that. For the sake of hoisting the banner of Allah over their homeland they fight. "Allah will be prominent, but most people do not know."

Now and then the call goes out for the convening of an international conference to look for ways of solving the (Palestinian) question. Some accept, others reject the idea, for this or other reason, with one stipulation or more for consent to convening the conference and participating in it. Knowing the parties constituting the conference, their past and present attitudes towards Moslem problems, the Islamic Resistance Movement does not consider these conferences capable of realising the demands, restoring the rights or doing justice to the oppressed. These conferences are only ways of setting the infidels in the land of the Moslems as arbitrators. When did the infidels do justice to the believers?

"But the Jews will not be pleased with thee, neither the Christians, until thou follow their religion; say, The direction of Allah is the true direction. And verily if thou follow their desires, after the knowledge which hath been given thee, thou shalt find no patron or protector against Allah." (The Cow – verse 120).

There is no solution for the Palestinian question except through Jihad. Initiatives, proposals and international conferences are all a waste of time and vain endeavors. The Palestinian people know better than to consent to having their future, rights and fate toyed with. As is said in the honourable Hadith:

> "The people of Syria are Allah's lash in His land. He wreaks His vengeance through them against whomsoever He wishes among His slaves. It is unthinkable that those who are double-faced among them should prosper over the faithful. They will certainly die out of grief and desperation."

The Three Circles:

Article Fourteen:
The question of the liberation of Palestine is bound to three circles: the Palestinian circle, the Arab circle and the Islamic circle. Each of these circles has its role in the struggle against Zionism. Each has its duties, and it is a horrible mistake and a sign of deep ignorance to over-look any of these circles. Palestine is an Islamic land which has the first of the two kiblahs (direction to which Moslems turn in praying), the third of the holy (Islamic) sanctuaries, and the point of departure for Mohamed's midnight journey to the seven heavens (i.e. Jerusalem).

> "Praise be unto him who transported his servant by night, from the sacred temple of Mecca to the farther temple of Jerusalem, the circuit of which we have blessed, that we might show him some of our signs; for Allah is he who heareth, and seeth." (The Night-Journey – verse 1).

Since this is the case, liberation of Palestine is then an individual duty for very Moslem wher-ever he may be. On this basis, the problem should be viewed. This should be realised by every Moslem.

The day the problem is dealt with on this basis, when the three circles mobilize their capa-bilities, the present state of affairs will change and the day of liberation will come nearer.

> "Verily ye are stronger than they, by reason of the terror cast into their breasts from Allah. This, because they are not people of prudence." (The Emigration – verse 13).

The Jihad for the Liberation of Palestine is an Individual Duty:

Article Fifteen:
The day that enemies usurp part of Moslem land, Jihad becomes the individual duty of every Moslem. In face of the Jews' usurpation of Palestine, it is compulsory that the banner of Jihad be raised. To do this requires the diffusion of Islamic consciousness among the masses, both on the regional, Arab and Islamic levels. It is necessary to instill the spirit of Jihad in the heart of the nation so that they would confront the enemies and join the ranks of the fighters.

It is necessary that scientists, educators and teachers, information and media people, as well as the educated masses, especially the youth and sheikhs of the Islamic movements, should take part in the operation of awakening (the masses). It is important that basic changes be made in the school curriculum, to cleanse it of the traces of ideological invasion that affected it as a result of the orientalists and missionaries who infiltrated the region following the defeat of the Crusaders at the hands of Salah el-Din (Saladin). The Crusaders realised that it was impossible to defeat the Moslems without first having ideological invasion pave the way by upsetting their thoughts, disfiguring their heritage and violating their ideals. Only then could they invade with soldiers. This, in its turn, paved the way for the imperialistic invasion that made Allenby declare on entering Jerusalem: "Only now have the Crusades ended." General Guru stood at Salah el-Din's grave and said: "We have returned, O Salah el-Din." Imperialism has helped towards the strengthening of ideological invasion, deepening, and still does, its roots. All this has paved the way towards the loss of Palestine.

It is necessary to instill in the minds of the Moslem generations that the Palestinian problem is a religious problem, and should be dealt with on this basis. Palestine contains Islamic holy sites. In it there is al-Aqsa Mosque which is bound to the great Mosque in Mecca in an inseparable bond as long as heaven and earth speak of Isra (Mohammed's midnight journey to the seven heavens) and Mi'raj (Mohammed's ascension to the seven heavens from Jerusalem).

> "The bond of one day for the sake of Allah is better than the world and whatever there is on it. The place of one's whip in Paradise is far better than the world and whatever there is on it. A worshipper's going and coming in the service of Allah is better than the world and whatever there is on it." (As related by al-Bukhari, Moslem, al-Tarmdhi and Ibn Maja).

> "I swear by the holder of Mohammed's soul that I would like to invade and be killed for the sake of Allah, then invade and be killed, and then invade again and be killed." (As related by al-Bukhari and Moslem).

Social Mutual Responsibility:

Article Twenty:

Moslem society is a mutually responsible society. The Prophet, prayers and greetings be unto him, said: "Blessed are the generous, whether they were in town or on a journey, who have collected all that they had and shared it equally among themselves."

The Islamic spirit is what should prevail in every Moslem society. The society that confronts a vicious enemy which acts in a way similar to Nazism, making no differentiation between man and woman, between children and old people – such a society is entitled to this Islamic spirit. Our enemy relies on the methods of collective punishment. He has deprived people of their homeland and properties, pursued them in their places of exile and gathering, breaking bones, shooting at women, children and old people, with or without a reason. The enemy has opened detention camps where thousands and thousands of people are thrown and kept under sub-human conditions. Added to this, are the demolition of houses, rendering children orphans, meting cruel sentences against thousands of young people, and causing them to spend the best years of their lives in the dungeons of prisons.

In their Nazi treatment, the Jews made no exception for women or children. Their policy of striking fear in the heart is meant for all. They attack people where their breadwinning is concerned, extorting their money and threatening their honour. They deal with people as if they were the worst war criminals. Deportation from the homeland is a kind of murder.

To counter these deeds, it is necessary that social mutual responsibility should prevail among the people. The enemy should be faced by the people as a single body which if one member of it should complain, the rest of the body would respond by feeling the same pains.

Article Twenty-One:

Mutual social responsibility means extending assistance, financial or moral, to all those who are in need and joining in the execution of some of the work. Members of the Islamic Resistance Movement should consider the interests of the masses as their own personal interests. They must spare no effort in achieving and preserving them. They must prevent any foul play with the future of the upcoming generations and anything that could cause loss to society. The masses are part of them and they are part of the masses. Their strength is theirs, and their future is theirs. Members of the Islamic Resistance Movement should share the people's joy and grief, adopt the demands of the public and whatever means by which they could be realised. The day that such a spirit prevails, brotherliness would deepen, cooperation, sympathy and unity will be enhanced and the ranks will be solidified to confront the enemies.

Supportive Forces Behind the Enemy:

C. The Palestinian Liberation Organization:

Article Twenty-Seven:

The Palestinian Liberation Organization is the closest to the heart of the Islamic Resistance Movement. It contains the father and the brother, the next of kin and the friend. The Moslem does not estrange himself from his father, brother, next of kin or friend. Our homeland is one, our situation is one, our fate is one and the enemy is a joint enemy to all of us.

Because of the situations surrounding the formation of the Organization, of the ideological confusion prevailing in the Arab world as a result of the ideological invasion under whose influence the Arab world has fallen since the defeat of the Crusaders and which was, and still is, intensified through orientalists, missionaries and imperialists, the Organization adopted the idea of the secular state. And that it how we view it.

Secularism completely contradicts religious ideology. Attitudes, conduct and decisions stem from ideologies.

That is why, with all our appreciation for The Palestinian Liberation Organization – and what it can develop into – and without belittling its role in the Arab–Israeli conflict, we are unable to exchange the present or future Islamic Palestine with the secular idea. The Islamic nature of Palestine is part of our religion and whoever takes his religion lightly is a loser.

"Who will be adverse to the religion of Abraham, but he whose mind is infatuated?" (The Cow – verse 130).

The day The Palestinian Liberation Organization adopts Islam as its way of life, we will become its soldiers, and fuel for its fire that will burn the enemies.

Until such a day, and we pray to Allah that it will be soon, the Islamic Resistance Movement's stand towards the PLO is that of the son towards his father, the brother towards his brother, and the relative to relative, suffers his pain and supports him in confronting the enemies, wishing him to be wise and well-guided.

"Stand by your brother, for he who is brotherless is like the fighter who goes to battle without arms. One's cousin is the wing one flies with – could the bird fly without wings?"

D. Arab and Islamic Countries:

Article Twenty-Eight:

The Zionist invasion is a vicious invasion. It does not refrain from resorting to all methods, using all evil and contemptible ways to achieve its end. It relies greatly in its infiltration and espionage operations on the secret organizations it gave rise to, such as the Freemasons, The Rotary and Lions clubs, and other sabotage groups. All these organizations, whether secret or open, work in the interest of Zionism and according to its instructions. They aim at undermining societies, destroying values, corrupting consciences, deteriorating character and annihilating Islam. It is behind the drug trade and alcoholism in all its kinds so as to facilitate its control and expansion.

Arab countries surrounding Israel are asked to open their borders before the fighters from among the Arab and Islamic nations so that they could consolidate their efforts with those of their Moslem brethren in Palestine.

As for the other Arab and Islamic countries, they are asked to facilitate the movement of the fighters from and to it, and this is the least thing they could do.

We should not forget to remind every Moslem that when the Jews conquered the Holy City in 1967, they stood on the threshold of the Aqsa Mosque and proclaimed that "Mohammed is dead, and his descendants are all women."

Israel, Judaism and Jews challenge Islam and the Moslem people. "May the cowards never sleep."

The Islamic Resistance Movement is Composed of Soldiers:

Article Thirty-Six:

While paving its way, the Islamic Resistance Movement, emphasizes time and again to all the sons of our people, to the Arab and Islamic nations, that it does not seek personal fame, material gain, or social prominence. It does not aim to compete against any one from among our people, or take his place. Nothing of the sort at all. It will not act against any of the sons of Moslems or those who are peaceful towards it from among non-Moslems, be they here or anywhere else. It will only serve as a support for all groupings and organizations operating against the Zionist enemy and its lackeys.

The Islamic Resistance Movement adopts Islam as its way of life. Islam is its creed and religion. Whoever takes Islam as his way of life, be it an organization, a grouping, a country or any other body, the Islamic Resistance Movement considers itself as their soldiers and nothing more.

We ask Allah to show us the right course, to make us an example to others and to judge between us and our people with truth. "O Lord, do thou judge between us and our nation with truth; for thou art the best judge." (Al Araf – verse 89).

The last of our prayers will be praise to Allah, the Master of the Universe.

Source: http://avalon.law.yale.edu/20th_century/hamas.asp

Palestine National Council: The Palestinian Declaration of Independence (Algiers Declaration), 15 November 1988

Algiers, Algeria
15 November 1988

In the name of God, the Compassionate, the Merciful

Palestine, the land of the three monotheistic faiths, is where the Palestinian Arab people was born, on which it grew, developed and excelled. The Palestinian people was never separated from or diminished in its integral bonds with Palestine. Thus the Palestinian Arab people ensured for itself an everlasting union between itself, its land, and its history.

Resolute throughout that history, the Palestinian Arab people forged its national identity, rising even to unimagined levels in its defense, as invasion, the design of others, and the appeal special to Palestine's ancient and luminous place on the eminence where powers and civilizations are joined. All this intervened thereby to deprive the people of its political independence. Yet the undying connection between Palestine and its people secured for the Land its character, and for the people its national genius.

Nourished by an unfolding series of civilizations and cultures, inspired by a heritage rich in variety and kind, the Palestinian Arab people added to its stature by consolidating a union between itself and its patrimonial Land. The call went out from Temple, Church, and Mosque that to praise the Creator, to celebrate compassion and peace was indeed the message of Palestine. And in generation after generation, the Palestinian Arab people gave of itself unsparingly in the valiant battle for liberation and homeland. For what has been the unbroken chain of our people's rebellions but the heroic embodiment of our will for national independence? And so the people was sustained in the struggle to stay and to prevail.

When in the course of modern times a new order of values was declared with norms and values fair for all, it was the Palestinian Arab people that had been excluded from the destiny of all other peoples by a hostile array of local and foreign powers. Yet again had unaided justice been revealed as insufficient to drive the world's history along its preferred course.

And it was the Palestinian people, already wounded in its body, that was submitted to yet another type of occupation over which floated the falsehood that "Palestine was a land without people." This notion was foisted upon some in the world, whereas in Article 22 of the Covenant of the League of Nations (1919) and in the Treaty of Lausanne (1923), the community of nations had recognized that all the Arab territories, including Palestine, of the formerly Ottoman provinces, were to have granted to them their freedom as provisionally independent nations.

Despite the historical injustice inflicted on the Palestinian Arab people resulting in their dispersion and depriving them of their right to self-determination, following upon U.N. General Assembly Resolution 181 (1947), which partitioned Palestine into two states, one Arab, one Jewish, yet it is this Resolution that still provides those conditions of international legitimacy that ensure the right of the Palestinian Arab people to sovereignty.

By stages, the occupation of Palestine and parts of other Arab territories by Israeli forces, the willed dispossession and expulsion from their ancestral homes of the majority of Palestine's civilian inhabitants, was achieved by organized terror; those Palestinians who remained, as a vestige subjugated in its homeland, were persecuted and forced to endure the destruction of their national life.

Thus were principles of international legitimacy violated. Thus were the Charter of the United Nations and its Resolutions disfigured, for they had recognized the Palestinian Arab people's national rights, including the right of Return, the right to independence, the right to sovereignty over territory and homeland.

In Palestine and on its perimeters, in exile distant and near, the Palestinian Arab people never faltered and never abandoned its conviction in its rights of Return and independence. Occupation, massacres and dispersion achieved no gain in the unabated Palestinian consciousness of self and political identity, as Palestinians went forward with their destiny, undeterred and unbowed. And from out of the long years of trial in ever-mounting struggle, the Palestinian political identity emerged further consolidated and confirmed. And the collective Palestinian national will forged for itself a political embodiment, the Palestine Liberation Organization, its sole, legitimate representative recognized by the world community as a whole, as well as by related regional and international institutions. Standing on the very rock of conviction in the Palestinian people's inalienable rights, and on the ground of Arab national consensus and of international legitimacy, the PLO led the campaigns of its great people, molded into unity and powerful resolve, one and indivisible in its triumphs, even as it suffered massacres and confinement within and without its home. And so Palestinian resistance was clarified and raised into the forefront of Arab and world awareness, as the struggle of the Palestinian Arab people achieved unique prominence among the world's liberation movements in the modern era.

The massive national uprising, the Intifada, now intensifying in cumulative scope and power on occupied Palestinian territories, as well as the unflinching resistance of the refugee camps outside the homeland, have elevated awareness of the Palestinian truth and right into still higher realms of comprehension and actuality. Now at last the curtain has been dropped around a whole epoch of prevarication and negation. The Intifada has set siege to the mind of official Israel, which has for too long relied exclusively upon myth and terror to deny Palestinian existence altogether. Because of the Intifada and its revolutionary irreversible impulse, the history of Palestine has therefore arrived at a decisive juncture.

Whereas the Palestinian people reaffirms most definitively its inalienable rights in the land of its patrimony:

Now by virtue of natural, historical and legal rights, and the sacrifices of successive generations who gave of themselves in defense of the freedom and independence of their homeland; In pursuance of Resolutions adopted by Arab Summit Conferences and relying on the authority bestowed by international legitimacy as embodied in the Resolutions of the United Nations Organization since 1947; And in exercise by the Palestinian Arab people of its rights to self-determination, political independence and sovereignty over its territory;

The Palestine National Council, in the name of God, and in the name of the Palestinian Arab people, hereby proclaims the establishment of the State of Palestine on our Palestinian territory with its capital Jerusalem (Al-Quds Ash-Sharif).

The State of Palestine is the state of Palestinians wherever they may be. The state is for them to enjoy in it their collective national and cultural identity, theirs to pursue in it a complete equality of rights. In it will be safeguarded their political and religious convictions and their human dignity by means of a parliamentary democratic system of governance, itself based on freedom of expression and the freedom to form parties. The rights of minorities will duly be respected by the majority, as minorities must abide by decisions of the majority. Governance will be based on principles of social justice, equality and non-discrimination in public rights of men or women, on grounds of race, religion, color or sex, under the aegis of a constitution which ensures the rule of law and an independent judiciary. Thus shall these principles allow no departure from Palestine's age-old spiritual and civilizational heritage of tolerance and religious coexistence.

The State of Palestine is an Arab state, an integral and indivisible part of the Arab nation, at one with that nation in heritage and civilization, with it also in its aspiration for liberation, progress, democracy and unity. The State of Palestine affirms its obligation to abide by the Charter of the League of Arab States, whereby the coordination of the Arab states with each other shall be strengthened. It calls upon Arab compatriots to consolidate and enhance the emergence in reality of our state, to mobilize potential, and to intensify efforts whose goal is to end Israeli occupation.

The State of Palestine proclaims its commitment to the principles and purposes of the United Nations, and to the Universal Declaration of Human Rights. It proclaims its commitment as well to the principles and policies of the Non-Aligned Movement.

It further announces itself to be a peace-loving State, in adherence to the principles of peaceful coexistence. It will join with all states and peoples in order to assure a permanent peace based upon justice and the respect of rights so that humanity's potential for well-being may be assured, an earnest competition for excellence may be maintained, and in which confidence in the future will eliminate fear for those who are just and for whom justice is the only recourse.

In the context of its struggle for peace in the land of Love and Peace, the State of Palestine calls upon the United Nations to bear special responsibility for the Palestinian Arab people and its homeland. It calls upon all peace- and freedom-loving peoples and states to assist it in the attainment of its objectives, to provide it with security, to alleviate the tragedy of its people, and to help it terminate Israel's occupation of the Palestinian territories.

The State of Palestine herewith declares that it believes in the settlement of regional and international disputes by peaceful means, in accordance with the U.N. Charter and resolutions. With prejudice to its natural right to defend its territorial integrity and independence, it therefore rejects the threat or use of force, violence and terrorism against its territorial integrity or political independence, as it also rejects their use against the territorial integrity of other states.

Therefore, on this day unlike all others, November 15, 1988, as we stand at the threshold of a new dawn, in all honor and modesty we humbly bow to the sacred spirits of our fallen ones, Palestinian and Arab, by the purity of whose sacrifice for the homeland our sky has been illuminated and our land given life. Our hearts are lifted up and irradiated by the light emanating from the much blessed Intifada, from those who have endured and have fought the fight of the camps, of dispersion, of exile, from those who have borne the standard for freedom, our children, our aged, our youth, our prisoners, detainees and wounded, all those whose ties to our sacred soil are confirmed in camp, village, and town. We render special tribute to that brave Palestinian woman, guardian of sustenance and life, keeper of our people's perennial flame. To the souls of our sainted martyrs, the whole of our Palestinian Arab people, to all free and honorable peoples everywhere, we pledge that our struggle shall be continued until the occupation ends, and the foundation of our sovereignty and independence shall be fortified accordingly.

Therefore, we call upon our great people to rally to the banner of Palestine, to cherish and defend it, so that it may forever be the symbol of our freedom and dignity in that homeland, which is a homeland for the free, now and always.

In the name of God, the Compassionate, the Merciful:

"Say: O God, Master of the Kingdom,
Thou givest the Kingdom to whom Thou wilt,
and seizest the Kingdom from whom Thou wilt,
Thou exaltest whom Thou wilt, and Thou
abasest whom Thou wilt; in Thy hand
is the good; Thou are powerful over everything."

Source: www.jmcc.org/documents/Palestinian_Declaration_of_Independence.pdf

Israel and the PLO: Declaration of Principles on Interim Self-Government Arrangements (Oslo Accords), 13 September 1993

The Government of the State of Israel and the P.L.O. team (in the Jordanian–Palestinian delegation to the Middle East Peace Conference) (the "Palestinian Delegation"), representing the Palestinian people, agree that it is time to put an end to decades of confrontation and conflict, recognize their mutual legitimate and political rights, and strive to live in peaceful coexistence and mutual dignity and security and achieve a just, lasting and comprehensive peace settlement and historic reconciliation through the agreed political process. Accordingly, the two sides agree to the following principles:

Article I: Aim of the Negotiations

The aim of the Israeli–Palestinian negotiations within the current Middle East peace process is, among other things, to establish a Palestinian Interim Self-Government Authority, the elected Council (the "Council"), for the Palestinian people in the West Bank and the Gaza Strip, for a transitional period not exceeding five years, leading to a permanent settlement based on Security Council Resolutions 242 and 338.

It is understood that the interim arrangements are an integral part of the whole peace process and that the negotiations on the permanent status will lead to the implementation of Security Council Resolutions 242 and 338.

Article II: Framework for the Interim Period

The agreed framework for the interim period is set forth in this Declaration of Principles.

Article III: Elections

1. In order that the Palestinian people in the West Bank and Gaza Strip may govern themselves according to democratic principles, direct, free and general political elections will be held for the Council under agreed supervision and international observation, while the Palestinian police will ensure public order.

2. An agreement will be concluded on the exact mode and conditions of the elections in accordance with the protocol attached as Annex I, with the goal of holding the elections not later than nine months after the entry into force of this Declaration of Principles.

3. These elections will constitute a significant interim preparatory step toward the realization of the legitimate rights of the Palestinian people and their just requirements.

Article IV: Jurisdiction

Jurisdiction of the Council will cover West Bank and Gaza Strip territory, except for issues that will be negotiated in the permanent status negotiations. The two sides view the West Bank and the Gaza Strip as a single territorial unit, whose integrity will be preserved during the interim period.

Article V: Transitional Period and Permanent Status Negotiations

1. The five-year transitional period will begin upon the withdrawal from the Gaza Strip and Jericho area.

2. Permanent status negotiations will commence as soon as possible, but not later than the beginning of the third year of the interim period, between the Government of Israel and the Palestinian people representatives.

3. It is understood that these negotiations shall cover remaining issues, including: Jerusalem, refugees, settlements, security arrangements, borders, relations and cooperation with other neighbors, and other issues of common interest.

4. The two parties agree that the outcome of the permanent status negotiations should not be prejudiced or preempted by agreements reached for the interim period.

Article VI: Preparatory Transfer of Powers and Responsibilities

1. Upon the entry into force of this Declaration of Principles and the withdrawal from the Gaza Strip and the Jericho area, a transfer of authority from the Israeli military government and its Civil Administration to the authorised Palestinians for this task, as detailed herein, will commence. This transfer of authority will be of a preparatory nature until the inauguration of the Council.

2. Immediately after the entry into force of this Declaration of Principles and the withdrawal from the Gaza Strip and Jericho area, with the view to promoting economic development in the West Bank and Gaza Strip, authority will be transferred to the Palestinians on the following spheres: education and culture, health, social welfare, direct taxation, and tourism. The Palestinian side will commence in building the Palestinian police force, as agreed upon. Pending the inauguration of the Council, the two parties may negotiate the transfer of additional powers and responsibilities, as agreed upon.

Article VII: Interim Agreement

1. The Israeli and Palestinian delegations will negotiate an agreement on the interim period (the "Interim Agreement")

2. The Interim Agreement shall specify, among other things, the structure of the Council, the number of its members, and the transfer of powers and responsibilities from the Israeli military government and its Civil Administration to the Council. The Interim Agreement shall also specify the Council's executive authority, legislative authority in accordance with Article IX below, and the independent Palestinian judicial organs.

3. The Interim Agreement shall include arrangements, to be implemented upon the inauguration of the Council, for the assumption by the Council of all of the powers and responsibilities transferred previously in accordance with Article VI above.

4. In order to enable the Council to promote economic growth, upon its inauguration, the Council will establish, among other things, a Palestinian Electricity Authority, a Gaza Sea Port Authority, a Palestinian Development Bank, a Palestinian Export Promotion Board, a Palestinian Environmental Authority, a Palestinian Land Authority and a Palestinian Water Administration Authority, and any other Authorities agreed upon, in accordance with the Interim Agreement that will specify their powers and responsibilities.

5. After the inauguration of the Council, the Civil Administration will be dissolved, and the Israeli military government will be withdrawn.

Article VIII: Public Order and Security

In order to guarantee public order and internal security for the Palestinians of the West Bank and the Gaza Strip, the Council will establish a strong police force, while Israel will continue to carry the responsibility for defending against external threats, as well as the responsibility for overall security of Israelis for the purpose of safeguarding their internal security and public order.

Article IX: Laws and Military Orders

1. The Council will be empowered to legislate, in accordance with the Interim Agreement, within all authorities transferred to it.

2. Both parties will review jointly laws and military orders presently in force in remaining spheres.

Article X: Joint Israeli–Palestinian Liaison Committee

In order to provide for a smooth implementation of this Declaration of Principles and any subsequent agreements pertaining to the interim period, upon the entry into force of this Declaration of Principles, a Joint Israeli–Palestinian Liaison Committee will be established in order to deal with issues requiring coordination, other issues of common interest, and disputes.

Article XI: Israeli–Palestinian Cooperation in Economic Fields

Recognizing the mutual benefit of cooperation in promoting the development of the West Bank, the Gaza Strip and Israel, upon the entry into force of this Declaration of Principles, an Israeli–Palestinian Economic Cooperation Committee will be established in order to develop and implement in a cooperative manner the programs identified in the protocols attached as Annex III and Annex IV.

Article XII: Liaison and Cooperation with Jordan and Egypt

The two parties will invite the Governments of Jordan and Egypt to participate in establishing further liaison and cooperation arrangements between the Government of Israel and the Palestinian representatives, on the one hand, and the Governments of Jordan and Egypt, on the other hand, to promote cooperation between them. These arrangements will include the constitution of a Continuing Committee that will decide by agreement on the modalities of admission of persons displaced from the West Bank and Gaza Strip in 1967, together with necessary measures to prevent disruption and disorder. Other matters of common concern will be dealt with by this Committee.

Article XIII: Redeployment of Israeli Forces

1. After the entry into force of this Declaration of Principles, and not later than the eve of elections for the Council, a redeployment of Israeli military forces in the West Bank and the Gaza Strip will take place, in addition to withdrawal of Israeli forces carried out in accordance with Article XIV.

2. In redeploying its military forces, Israel will be guided by the principle that its military forces should be redeployed outside populated areas.

3. Further redeployments to specified locations will be gradually implemented commensurate with the assumption of responsibility for public order and internal security by the Palestinian police force pursuant to Article VIII above.

Article XIV: Israeli Withdrawal from the Gaza Strip and Jericho Area

Israel will withdraw from the Gaza Strip and Jericho area, as detailed in the protocol attached as Annex II.

Article XV: Resolution of Disputes

1. Disputes arising out of the application or interpretation of this Declaration of Principles or any subsequent agreements pertaining to the interim period, shall be resolved by negotiations through the Joint Liaison Committee to be established pursuant to Article X above.

2. Disputes which cannot be settled by negotiations may be resolved by a mechanism of conciliation to be agreed upon by the parties.

3. The parties may agree to submit to arbitration disputes relating to the interim period, which cannot be settled through conciliation. To this end, upon the agreement of both parties, the parties will establish an Arbitration Committee.

Article XVI: Israeli–Palestinian Cooperation Concerning Regional Programs

Both parties view the multilateral working groups as an appropriate instrument for promoting a "Marshall Plan", the regional programs and other programs, including special programs for the West Bank and Gaza Strip, as indicated in the protocol attached as Annex IV.

Article XVII: Miscellaneous Provisions

1. This Declaration of Principles will enter into force one month after its signing.

2. All protocols annexed to this Declaration of Principles and Agreed Minutes pertaining thereto shall be regarded as an integral part hereof.

Done at Washington, D.C., this thirteenth day of September, 1993.

For the Government of Israel: For the P.L.O.:

Witnessed By:

The United States of America: The Russian Federation:

Annexes

Annex I: Protocol on the Mode and Conditions of Elections

1. Palestinians of Jerusalem who live there will have the right to participate in the election process, according to an agreement between the two sides.

2. In addition, the election agreement should cover, among other things, the following issues:

   a. the system of elections;
   b. the mode of the agreed supervision and international observation and their personal composition; and
   c. rules and regulations regarding election campaign, including agreed arrangements for the organizing of mass media, and the possibility of licensing a broadcasting and TV station.

3. The future status of displaced Palestinians who were registered on 4th June 1967 will not be prejudiced because they are unable to participate in the election process due to practical reasons.

Annex II: Protocol on Withdrawal of Israeli Forces from the Gaza Strip and Jericho Area

1. The two sides will conclude and sign within two months from the date of entry into force of this Declaration of Principles, an agreement on the withdrawal of Israeli military forces from the Gaza Strip and Jericho area. This agreement will include comprehensive arrangements to apply in the Gaza Strip and the Jericho area subsequent to the Israeli withdrawal.

2. Israel will implement an accelerated and scheduled withdrawal of Israeli military forces from the Gaza Strip and Jericho area, beginning immediately with the signing of the

agreement on the Gaza Strip and Jericho area and to be completed within a period not exceeding four months after the signing of this agreement.

3. The above agreement will include, among other things:

    a. Arrangements for a smooth and peaceful transfer of authority from the Israeli military government and its Civil Administration to the Palestinian representatives.
    b. Structure, powers and responsibilities of the Palestinian authority in these areas, except: external security, settlements, Israelis, foreign relations, and other mutually agreed matters.
    c. Arrangements for the assumption of internal security and public order by the Palestinian police force (consisting of police officers recruited locally and from abroad holding Jordanian passports and Palestinian documents issued by Egypt). Those who will participate in the Palestinian police force coming from abroad should be trained as police and police officers.
    d. A temporary international or foreign presence, as agreed upon.
    e. Establishment of a joint Palestinian–Israeli Coordination and Cooperation Committee for mutual security purposes.
    f. An economic development and stabilization program, including the establishment of an Emergency Fund, to encourage foreign investment, and financial and economic support. Both sides will coordinate and cooperate jointly and unilaterally with regional and international parties to support these aims.
    g. Arrangements for a safe passage for persons and transportation between the Gaza Strip and Jericho area.

4. The above agreement will include arrangements for coordination between both parties regarding passages:

    a. Gaza – Egypt; and
    b. Jericho – Jordan.

5. The offices responsible for carrying out the powers and responsibilities of the Palestinian authority under this Annex II and Article VI of the Declaration of Principles will be located in the Gaza Strip and in the Jericho area pending the inauguration of the Council.
6. Other than these agreed arrangements, the status of the Gaza Strip and Jericho area will continue to be an integral part of the West Bank and Gaza Strip, and will not be changed in the interim period.

Annex III: Protocol on Israeli–Palestinian Cooperation in Economic and Development Programs

The two sides agree to establish an Israeli–Palestinian continuing Committee for Economic Cooperation, focusing, among other things, on the following:

1. Cooperation in the field of water, including a Water Development Program prepared by experts from both sides, which will also specify the mode of cooperation in the management of water resources in the West Bank and Gaza Strip, and will include

proposals for studies and plans on water rights of each party, as well as on the equitable utilization of joint water resources for implementation in and beyond the interim period.

2. Cooperation in the field of electricity, including an Electricity Development Program, which will also specify the mode of cooperation for the production, maintenance, purchase and sale of electricity resources.

3. Cooperation in the field of energy, including an Energy Development Program, which will provide for the exploitation of oil and gas for industrial purposes, particularly in the Gaza Strip and in the Negev, and will encourage further joint exploitation of other energy resources. This Program may also provide for the construction of a Petrochemical industrial complex in the Gaza Strip and the construction of oil and gas pipelines.

4. Cooperation in the field of finance, including a Financial Development and Action Program for the encouragement of international investment in the West Bank and the Gaza Strip, and in Israel, as well as the establishment of a Palestinian Development Bank.

5. Cooperation in the field of transport and communications, including a Program which will define guidelines for the establishment of a Gaza Sea Port Area, and will provide for the establishing of transport and communications lines to and from the West Bank and the Gaza Strip to Israel and to other countries. In addition, this Program will provide for carrying out the necessary construction of roads, railways, communications lines, etc.

6. Cooperation in the field of trade, including studies and Trade Promotion Programs, which will encourage local, regional and inter-regional trade, as well as a feasibility study of creating free trade zones in the Gaza Strip and in Israel, mutual access to these zones, and cooperation in other areas related to trade and commerce.

7. Cooperation in the field of industry, including Industrial Development Programs, which will provide for the establishment of joint Israeli–Palestinian Industrial Research and Development Centers, will promote Palestinian–Israeli joint ventures, and provide guidelines for cooperation in the textile, food, pharmaceutical, electronics, diamonds, computer and science-based industries.

8. A program for cooperation in, and regulation of, labor relations and cooperation in social welfare issues.

9. A Human Resources Development and Cooperation Plan, providing for joint Israeli–Palestinian workshops and seminars, and for the establishment of joint vocational training centers, research institutes and data banks.

10. An Environmental Protection Plan, providing for joint and/or coordinated measures in this sphere.

11. A program for developing coordination and cooperation in the field of communication and media.

12. Any other programs of mutual interest.

Annex IV: Protocol on Israeli–Palestinian Cooperation Concerning Regional Development Programs

1. The two sides will cooperate in the context of the multilateral peace efforts in promoting a Development Program for the region, including the West Bank and the Gaza Strip, to be initiated by the G-7. The parties will request the G-7 to seek the participation in this program of other interested states, such as members of the Organisation for Economic Cooperation and Development, regional Arab states and institutions, as well as members of the private sector.

2. The Development Program will consist of two elements:

   a. an Economic Development Program for the West Bank and the Gaza Strip.
   b. a Regional Economic Development Program:

      A. The Economic Development Program for the West Bank and the Gaza strip will consist of the following elements:

         1. A Social Rehabilitation Program, including a Housing and Construction Program.
         2. A Small and Medium Business Development Plan.
         3. An Infrastructure Development Program (water, electricity, transportation and communications, etc.)
         4. A Human Resources Plan.
         5. Other programs.

      B. The Regional Economic Development Program may consist of the following elements:

         1. The establishment of a Middle East Development Fund, as a first step, and a Middle East Development Bank, as a second step.
         2. The development of a joint Israeli Palestinian–Jordanian Plan for coordinated exploitation of the Dead Sea area.
         3. The Mediterranean Sea (Gaza) – Dead Sea Canal.
         4. Regional Desalinization and other water development projects.
         5. A regional plan for agricultural development, including a coordinated regional effort for the prevention of desertification.
         6. Interconnection of electricity grids.
         7. Regional cooperation for the transfer, distribution and industrial exploitation of gas, oil and other energy resources.
         8. A Regional Tourism, Transportation and Telecommunications Development Plan.
         9. Regional cooperation in other spheres.

3. The two sides will encourage the multilateral working groups, and will coordinate towards their success. The two parties will encourage intersessional activities, as well as pre-feasibility and feasibility studies, within the various multilateral working groups.

Done at Washington, D.C., this thirteenth day of September, 1993.

For the Government of Israel: For the P.L.O.:

Witnessed By:

The United States of America: The Russian Federation:

Source: https://www.knesset.gov.il/process/docs/oslo_eng.htm

Israeli–Palestinian Interim Agreement on the West Bank and the Gaza Strip (Oslo II Accord), Washington, DC, 28 September 1995

The Government of the State of Israel and the Palestine Liberation Organization (hereinafter "the PLO"), the representative of the Palestinian people;

PREAMBLE

WITHIN the framework of the Middle East peace process initiated at Madrid in October 1991;

REAFFIRMING their determination to put an end to decades of confrontation and to live in peaceful coexistence, mutual dignity and security, while recognizing their mutual legitimate and political rights;

REAFFIRMING their desire to achieve a just, lasting and comprehensive peace settlement and historic reconciliation through the agreed political process;

RECOGNIZING that the peace process and the new era that it has created, as well as the new relationship established between the two Parties as described above, are irreversible, and the determination of the two Parties to maintain, sustain and continue the peace process;

RECOGNIZING that the aim of the Israeli–Palestinian negotiations within the current Middle East peace process is, among other things, to establish a Palestinian Interim Self-Government Authority, i.e. the elected Council (hereinafter "the Council" or "the Palestinian Council"), and the elected Ra'ees [leader] of the Executive Authority, for the Palestinian people in the West Bank and the Gaza Strip, for a transitional period not exceeding five years from the date of signing the Agreement on the Gaza Strip and the Jericho Area (hereinafter "the Gaza–Jericho Agreement") on May 4, 1994, leading to a permanent settlement based on Security Council Resolutions 242 and 338;

REAFFIRMING their understanding that the interim self-government arrangements contained in this Agreement are an integral part of the whole peace process, that the negotiations on the permanent status, that will start as soon as possible but not later than May 4, 1996, will lead to the implementation of Security Council Resolutions 242 and 338, and that the Interim Agreement shall settle all the issues of the interim period and that no such issues will be deferred to the agenda of the permanent status negotiations;

REAFFIRMING their adherence to the mutual recognition and commitments expressed in the letters dated September 9, 1993, signed by and exchanged between the Prime Minister of Israel and the Chairman of the PLO;

DESIROUS of putting into effect the Declaration of Principles on Interim Self-Government Arrangements signed at Washington, D.C. on September 13, 1993, and the Agreed Minutes thereto (hereinafter "the DOP") and in particular Article III and Annex I concerning the holding of direct, free and general political elections for the Council and the Ra'ees of the Executive Authority in order that the Palestinian people in the West Bank, Jerusalem and the Gaza Strip may democratically elect accountable representatives;

RECOGNIZING that these elections will constitute a significant interim preparatory step toward the realization of the legitimate rights of the Palestinian people and their just requirements and will provide a democratic basis for the establishment of Palestinian institutions;

REAFFIRMING their mutual commitment to act, in accordance with this Agreement, immediately, efficiently and effectively against acts or threats of terrorism, violence or incitement, whether committed by Palestinians or Israelis;

FOLLOWING the Gaza–Jericho Agreement; the Agreement on Preparatory Transfer of Powers and Responsibilities signed at Erez on August 29, 1994 (hereinafter "the Preparatory Transfer Agreement"); and the Protocol on Further Transfer of Powers and Responsibilities signed at Cairo on August 27, 1995 (hereinafter "the Further Transfer Protocol"); which three agreements will be superseded by this Agreement;

HEREBY AGREE as follows:

CHAPTER I – THE COUNCIL

ARTICLE I: Transfer of Authority

1. Israel shall transfer powers and responsibilities as specified in this Agreement from the Israeli military government and its Civil Administration to the Council in accordance with this Agreement. Israel shall continue to exercise powers and responsibilities not so transferred.

2. Pending the inauguration of the Council, the powers and responsibilities transferred to the Council shall be exercised by the Palestinian Authority established in accordance with the Gaza–Jericho Agreement, which shall also have all the rights, liabilities and obligations to be assumed by the Council in this regard. Accordingly, the term "Council" throughout this Agreement shall, pending the inauguration of the Council, be construed as meaning the Palestinian Authority.

3. The transfer of powers and responsibilities to the police force established by the Palestinian Council in accordance with Article XIV below (hereinafter "the Palestinian Police") shall be

accomplished in a phased manner, as detailed in this Agreement and in the Protocol concerning Redeployment and Security Arrangements attached as Annex I to this Agreement (hereinafter "Annex I").

4. As regards the transfer and assumption of authority in civil spheres, powers and responsibilities shall be transferred and assumed as set out in the Protocol Concerning Civil Affairs attached as Annex III to this Agreement (hereinafter "Annex III").

5. After the inauguration of the Council, the Civil Administration in the West Bank will be dissolved, and the Israeli military government shall be withdrawn. The withdrawal of the military government shall not prevent it from exercising the powers and responsibilities not transferred to the Council.

6. A Joint Civil Affairs Coordination and Cooperation Committee (hereinafter "the CAC"), Joint Regional Civil Affairs Subcommittees, one for the Gaza Strip and the other for the West Bank, and District Civil Liaison Offices in the West Bank shall be established in order to provide for coordination and cooperation in civil affairs between the Council and Israel, as detailed in Annex III.

7. The offices of the Council, and the offices of its Ra'ees and its Executive Authority and other committees, shall be located in areas under Palestinian territorial jurisdiction in the West Bank and the Gaza Strip.

ARTICLE II: Elections

1. In order that the Palestinian people of the West Bank and the Gaza Strip may govern themselves according to democratic principles, direct, free and general political elections will be held for the Council and the Ra'ees of the Executive Authority of the Council in accordance with the provisions set out in the Protocol concerning Elections attached as Annex II to this Agreement (hereinafter "Annex II").

2. These elections will constitute a significant interim preparatory step towards the realization of the legitimate rights of the Palestinian people and their just requirements and will provide a democratic basis for the establishment of Palestinian institutions.

3. Palestinians of Jerusalem who live there may participate in the election process in accordance with the provisions contained in this Article and in Article VI of Annex II (Election Arrangements concerning Jerusalem).

4. The elections shall be called by the Chairman of the Palestinian Authority immediately following the signing of this Agreement to take place at the earliest practicable date following the redeployment of Israeli forces in accordance with Annex I, and consistent with the requirements of the election timetable as provided in Annex II, the Election Law and the Election Regulations, as defined in Article I of Annex II.

ARTICLE III: Structure of the Palestinian Council

1. The Palestinian Council and the Ra'ees of the Executive Authority of the Council constitute the Palestinian Interim Self-Government Authority, which will be elected by the

Palestinian people of the West Bank, Jerusalem and the Gaza Strip for the transitional period agreed in Article I of the DOP.

2. The Council shall possess both legislative power and executive power, in accordance with Articles VII and IX of the DOP. The Council shall carry out and be responsible for all the legislative and executive powers and responsibilities transferred to it under this Agreement. The exercise of legislative powers shall be in accordance with Article XVIII of this Agreement (Legislative Powers of the Council).

3. The Council and the Ra'ees of the Executive Authority of the Council shall be directly and simultaneously elected by the Palestinian people of the West Bank, Jerusalem and the Gaza Strip, in accordance with the provisions of this Agreement and the Election Law and Regulations, which shall not be contrary to the provisions of this Agreement.

4. The Council and the Ra'ees of the Executive Authority of the Council shall be elected for a transitional period not exceeding five years from the signing of the Gaza–Jericho Agreement on May 4, 1994.

5. Immediately upon its inauguration, the Council will elect from among its members a Speaker. The Speaker will preside over the meetings of the Council, administer the Council and its committees, decide on the agenda of each meeting, and lay before the Council proposals for voting and declare their results.

6. The jurisdiction of the Council shall be as determined in Article XVII of this Agreement (Jurisdiction).

7. The organization, structure and functioning of the Council shall be in accordance with this Agreement and the Basic Law for the Palestinian Interim Self-government Authority, which Law shall be adopted by the Council. The Basic Law and any regulations made under it shall not be contrary to the provisions of this Agreement.

8. The Council shall be responsible under its executive powers for the offices, services and departments transferred to it and may establish, within its jurisdiction, ministries and subordinate bodies, as necessary for the fulfillment of its responsibilities.

9. The Speaker will present for the Council's approval proposed internal procedures that will regulate, among other things, the decision-making processes of the Council.

ARTICLE IV: Size of the Council

The Palestinian Council shall be composed of 82 representatives and the Ra'ees of the Executive Authority, who will be directly and simultaneously elected by the Palestinian people of the West Bank, Jerusalem and the Gaza Strip.

ARTICLE V: The Executive Authority of the Council

1. The Council will have a committee that will exercise the executive authority of the Council, formed in accordance with paragraph 4 below (hereinafter "the Executive Authority").

2. The Executive Authority shall be bestowed with the executive authority of the Council and will exercise it on behalf of the Council. It shall determine its own internal procedures and decision-making processes.

3. The Council will publish the names of the members of the Executive Authority immediately upon their initial appointment and subsequent to any changes.

4.   a. The Ra'ees of the Executive Authority shall be an ex officio member of the Executive Authority.

       b. All of the other members of the Executive Authority, except as provided in subparagraph c. below, shall be members of the Council, chosen and proposed to the Council by the Ra'ees of the Executive Authority and approved by the Council.

       c. The Ra'ees of the Executive Authority shall have the right to appoint some persons, in number not exceeding twenty percent of the total membership of the Executive Authority, who are not members of the Council, to exercise executive authority and participate in government tasks. Such appointed members may not vote in meetings of the Council.

       d. Non-elected members of the Executive Authority must have a valid address in an area under the jurisdiction of the Council.

ARTICLE VI: Other Committees of the Council

1. The Council may form small committees to simplify the proceedings of the Council and to assist in controlling the activity of its Executive Authority.

2. Each committee shall establish its own decision-making processes within the general framework of the organization and structure of the Council.

ARTICLE VII: Open Government

1. All meetings of the Council and of its committees, other than the Executive Authority, shall be open to the public, except upon a resolution of the Council or the relevant committee on the grounds of security, or commercial or personal confidentiality.

2. Participation in the deliberations of the Council, its committees and the Executive Authority shall be limited to their respective members only. Experts may be invited to such meetings to address specific issues on an ad hoc basis.

ARTICLE VIII: Judicial Review

Any person or organization affected by any act or decision of the Ra'ees of the Executive Authority of the Council or of any member of the Executive Authority, who believes that such act or decision exceeds the authority of the Ra'ees or of such member, or is otherwise incorrect in law or procedure, may apply to the relevant Palestinian Court of Justice for a review of such activity or decision.

ARTICLE IX: Powers and Responsibilities of the Council

1. Subject to the provisions of this Agreement, the Council will, within its jurisdiction, have legislative powers as set out in Article XVIII of this Agreement, as well as executive powers.

2. The executive power of the Palestinian Council shall extend to all matters within its jurisdiction under this Agreement or any future agreement that may be reached between the two Parties during the interim period. It shall include the power to formulate and conduct Palestinian policies and to supervise their implementation, to issue any rule or regulation under powers given in approved legislation and administrative decisions necessary for the realization of Palestinian self-government, the power to employ staff, sue and be sued and conclude contracts, and the power to keep and administer registers and records of the population, and issue certificates, licenses and documents.

3. The Palestinian Council's executive decisions and acts shall be consistent with the provisions of this Agreement.

4. The Palestinian Council may adopt all necessary measures in order to enforce the law and any of its decisions, and bring proceedings before the Palestinian courts and tribunals.

5.   a. In accordance with the DOP, the Council will not have powers and responsibilities in the sphere of foreign relations, which sphere includes the establishment abroad of embassies, consulates or other types of foreign missions and posts or permitting their establishment in the West Bank or the Gaza Strip, the appointment of or admission of diplomatic and consular staff, and the exercise of diplomatic functions.

      b. Notwithstanding the provisions of this paragraph, the PLO may conduct negotiations and sign agreements with states or international organizations for the benefit of the Council in the following cases only:

      (1) economic agreements, as specifically provided in Annex V of this Agreement:

      (2) agreements with donor countries for the purpose of implementing arrangements for the provision of assistance to the Council,

      (3) agreements for the purpose of implementing the regional development plans detailed in Annex IV of the DOP or in agreements entered into in the framework of the multilateral negotiations, and

      (4) cultural, scientific and educational agreements. Dealings between the Council and representatives of foreign states and international organizations, as well as the establishment in the West Bank and the Gaza Strip of representative offices other than those described in subparagraph 5.a above, for the purpose of implementing the agreements referred to in subparagraph 5.b above, shall not be considered foreign relations.

6. Subject to the provisions of this Agreement, the Council shall, within its jurisdiction, have an independent judicial system composed of independent Palestinian courts and tribunals.

CHAPTER 2 – REDEPLOYMENT AND SECURITY ARRANGEMENTS

ARTICLE X: Redeployment of Israeli Military Forces

1. The first phase of the Israeli military forces redeployment will cover populated areas in the West Bank – cities, towns, villages, refugee camps and hamlets – as set out in Annex I, and will be completed prior to the eve of the Palestinian elections, i.e., 22 days before the day of the elections.

2. Further redeployments of Israeli military forces to specified military locations will commence after the inauguration of the Council and will be gradually implemented commensurate with the assumption of responsibility for public order and internal security by the Palestinian Police, to be completed within 18 months from the date of the inauguration of the Council as detailed in Articles XI (Land) and XIII (Security), below and in Annex I.

3. The Palestinian Police shall be deployed and shall assume responsibility for public order and internal security for Palestinians in a phased manner in accordance with XIII (Security) below and Annex I.

4. Israel shall continue to carry the responsibility for external security, as well as the responsibility for overall security of Israelis for the purpose of safeguarding their internal security and public order.

5. For the purpose of this Agreement, "Israeli military forces" includes Israel Police and other Israeli security forces.

ARTICLE XI: Land

1. The two sides view the West Bank and the Gaza Strip as a single territorial unit, the integrity and status of which will be preserved during the interim period.

2. The two sides agree that West Bank and Gaza Strip territory, except for issues that will be negotiated in the permanent status negotiations, will come under the jurisdiction of the Palestinian Council in a phased manner, to be completed within 18 months from the date of the inauguration of the Council, as specified below:

    a. Land in populated areas (Areas A and B), including government and Al Waqf land, will come under the jurisdiction of the Council during the first phase of redeployment.

    b. All civil powers and responsibilities, including planning and zoning, in Areas A and B, set out in Annex III, will be transferred to and assumed by the Council during the first phase of redeployment.

    c. In Area C, during the first phase of redeployment Israel will transfer to the Council civil powers and responsibilities not relating to territory, as set out in Annex III.

    d. The further redeployments of Israeli military forces to specified military locations will be gradually implemented in accordance with the DOP in three phases, each to take place after an interval of six months, after the inauguration of the Council, to be completed within 18 months from the date of the inauguration of the Council.

    e. During the further redeployment phases to be completed within 18 months from the date of the inauguration of the Council, powers and responsibilities relating to territory will be transferred gradually to Palestinian jurisdiction that will cover West Bank and Gaza Strip territory, except for the issues that will be negotiated in the permanent status negotiations.

    f. The specified military locations referred to in Article X, paragraph 2 above will be determined in the further redeployment phases, within the specified time-frame ending not later than 18 months from the date of the inauguration of the Council, and will be negotiated in the permanent status negotiations.

3. For the purpose of this Agreement and until the completion of the first phase of the further redeployments:

    a. "Area A" means the populated areas delineated by a red line and shaded in brown on attached map No. 1;

    b. "Area B" means the populated areas delineated by a red line and shaded in yellow on attached map No. 1, and the built-up area of the hamlets listed in Appendix 6 to Annex I, and

    c. "Area C" means areas of the West Bank outside Areas A and B, which, except for the issues that will be negotiated in the permanent status negotiations, will be gradually transferred to Palestinian jurisdiction in accordance with this Agreement.

ARTICLE XII: Arrangements for Security and Public Order

1. In order to guarantee public order and internal security for the Palestinians of the West Bank and the Gaza Strip, the Council shall establish a strong police force as set out in Article XIV below. Israel shall continue to carry the responsibility for defense against external threats, including the responsibility for protecting the Egyptian and Jordanian borders, and for defense against external threats from the sea and from the air, as well as the responsibility for overall security of Israelis and Settlements, for the purpose of safeguarding their internal security and public order, and will have all the powers to take the steps necessary to meet this responsibility.

2. Agreed security arrangements and coordination mechanisms are specified in Annex I.

3. A Joint Coordination and Cooperation Committee for Mutual Security Purposes (hereinafter "the JSC"), as well as Joint Regional Security Committees (hereinafter "RSCs") and Joint District Coordination Offices (hereinafter "DCOs"), are hereby established as provided for in Annex I.

4. The security arrangements provided for in this Agreement and in Annex I may be reviewed at the request of either Party and may be amended by mutual agreement of the Parties. Specific review arrangements are included in Annex I.

5. For the purpose of this Agreement, "the Settlements" means, in the West Bank the settlements in Area C; and in the Gaza Strip the Gush Katif and Erez settlement areas, as well as the other settlements in the Gaza Strip, as shown on attached map No. 2.

ARTICLE XIII: Security

1. The Council will, upon completion of the redeployment of Israeli military forces in each district, as set out in Appendix 1 to Annex I, assume the powers and responsibilities for internal security and public order in Area A in that district.

2.   a. There will be a complete redeployment of Israeli military forces from Area B. Israel will transfer to the Council and the Council will assume responsibility for public order for Palestinians. Israel shall have the overriding responsibility for security for the purpose of protecting Israelis and confronting the threat of terrorism.

b. In Area B the Palestinian Police shall assume the responsibility for public order for Palestinians and shall be deployed in order to accommodate the Palestinian needs and requirements in the following manner:

(1) The Palestinian Police shall establish 25 police stations and posts in towns, villages, and other places listed in Appendix 2 to Annex I and as delineated on map No. 3. The West Bank RSC may agree on the establishment of additional police stations and posts, if required.

(2) The Palestinian Police shall be responsible for handling public order incidents in which only Palestinians are involved.

(3) The Palestinian Police shall operate freely in populated places where police stations and posts are located, as set out in paragraph b(1) above.

(4) While the movement of uniformed Palestinian policemen in Area B outside places where there is a Palestinian police station or post will be carried out after coordination and confirmation through the relevant DCO, three months after the completion of redeployment from Area B, the DCOs may decide that movement of Palestinian policemen from the police stations in Area B to Palestinian towns and villages in Area B on roads that are used only by Palestinian traffic will take place after notifying the DCO.

(5) The coordination of such planned movement prior to confirmation through the relevant DCO shall include a scheduled plan, including the number of policemen, as well as the type and number of weapons and vehicles intended to take part. It shall also include details of arrangements for ensuring continued coordination through appropriate communication links, the exact schedule of movement to the area of the planned operation, including the destination and routes thereto, its proposed duration and the schedule for returning to the police station or post.
The Israeli side of the DCO will provide the Palestinian side with its response, following a request for movement of policemen in accordance with this paragraph, in normal or routine cases within one day and in emergency cases no later than 2 hours.

(6) The Palestinian Police and the Israeli military forces will conduct joint security activities on the main roads as set out in Annex I.

(7) The Palestinian Police will notify the West Bank RSC of the names of the policemen, number plates of police vehicles and serial numbers of weapons, with respect to each police station and post in Area B.

(8) Further redeployments from Area C and transfer of internal security responsibility to the Palestinian Police in Areas B and C will be carried out in three phases, each to take place after an interval of six months, to be completed 18 months after the inauguration of the Council, except for the issues of permanent status negotiations and of Israel's overall responsibility for Israelis and borders.

(9) The procedures detailed in this paragraph will be reviewed within six months of the completion of the first phase of redeployment.

ARTICLE XIV: The Palestinian Police

1. The Council shall establish a strong police force. The duties, functions, structure, deployment and composition of the Palestinian Police, together with provisions regarding its equipment and operation, as well as rules of conduct, are set out in Annex I.

2. The Palestinian police force established under the Gaza–Jericho Agreement will be fully integrated into the Palestinian Police and will be subject to the provisions of this Agreement.

3. Except for the Palestinian Police and the Israeli military forces, no other armed forces shall be established or operate in the West Bank and the Gaza Strip.

4. Except for the arms, ammunition and equipment of the Palestinian Police described in Annex I, and those of the Israeli military forces, no organization, group or individual in the West Bank and the Gaza Strip shall manufacture, sell, acquire, possess, import or otherwise introduce into the West Bank or the Gaza Strip any firearms, ammunition, weapons, explosives, gunpowder or any related equipment, unless otherwise provided for in Annex I.

ARTICLE XV: Prevention of Hostile Acts

1. Both sides shall take all measures necessary in order to prevent acts of terrorism, crime and hostilities directed against each other, against individuals falling under the other's authority and against their property and shall take legal measures against offenders.

2. Specific provisions for the implementation of this Article are set out in Annex I.

ARTICLE XVI: Confidence Building Measures

With a view to fostering a positive and supportive public atmosphere to accompany the implementation of this Agreement, to establish a solid basis of mutual trust and good faith, and in order to facilitate the anticipated cooperation and new relations between the two peoples, both Parties agree to carry out confidence building measures as detailed herewith:

1. Israel will release or turn over to the Palestinian side, Palestinian detainees and prisoners, residents of the West Bank and the Gaza Strip. The first stage of release of these prisoners and detainees will take place on the signing of this Agreement and the second stage will take place prior to the date of the elections. There will be a third stage of release of detainees and prisoners. Detainees and prisoners will be released from among categories detailed in Annex VII (Release of Palestinian Prisoners and Detainees). Those released will be free to return to their homes in the West Bank and the Gaza Strip.

2. Palestinians who have maintained contact with the Israeli authorities will not be subjected to acts of harassment, violence, retribution or prosecution. Appropriate ongoing measures will be taken, in coordination with Israel, in order to ensure their protection.

3. Palestinians from abroad whose entry into the West Bank and the Gaza Strip is approved pursuant to this Agreement, and to whom the provisions of this Article are applicable, will not be prosecuted for offenses committed prior to September 13, 1993.

CHAPTER 3 – LEGAL AFFAIRS

ARTICLE XVII: Jurisdiction

1. In accordance with the DOP, the jurisdiction of the Council will cover West Bank and Gaza Strip territory as a single territorial unit, except for:

    a. issues that will be negotiated in the permanent status negotiations: Jerusalem, settlements, specified military locations, Palestinian refugees, borders, foreign relations and Israelis; and

    b. powers and responsibilities not transferred to the Council.

2. Accordingly, the authority of the Council encompasses all matters that fall within its territorial, functional and personal jurisdiction, as follows:

    a. The territorial jurisdiction of the Council shall encompass Gaza Strip territory, except for the Settlements and the Military Installation Area shown on map No. 2, and West Bank territory, except for Area C which, except for the issues that will be negotiated in the permanent status negotiations, will be gradually transferred to Palestinian jurisdiction in three phases, each to take place after an interval of six months, to be completed 18 months after the inauguration of the Council. At this time, the jurisdiction of the Council will cover West Bank and Gaza Strip territory, except for the issues that will be negotiated in the permanent status negotiations.

Territorial jurisdiction includes land, subsoil and territorial waters, in accordance with the provisions of this Agreement.

    b. The functional jurisdiction of the Council extends to all powers and responsibilities transferred to the Council, as specified in this Agreement or in any future agreements that may be reached between the Parties during the interim period.

    c. The territorial and functional jurisdiction of the Council will apply to all persons, except for Israelis, unless otherwise provided in this Agreement.

    d. Notwithstanding subparagraph a. above, the Council shall have functional jurisdiction in Area C, as detailed in Article IV of Annex III.

3. The Council has, within its authority, legislative, executive and judicial powers and responsibilities, as provided for in this Agreement.

4.   a. Israel, through its military government, has the authority over areas that are not under the territorial jurisdiction of the Council, powers and responsibilities not transferred to the Council and Israelis.

    b. To this end, the Israeli military government shall retain the necessary legislative, judicial and executive powers and responsibilities, in accordance with international law. This provision shall not derogate from Israel's applicable legislation over Israelis in personam.

5. The exercise of authority with regard to the electromagnetic sphere and air space shall be in accordance with the provisions of this Agreement.

6. Without derogating from the provisions of this Article, legal arrangements detailed in the Protocol Concerning Legal Matters attached as Annex IV to this Agreement (hereinafter "Annex IV") shall be observed. Israel and the Council may negotiate further legal arrangements.

7. Israel and the Council shall cooperate on matters of legal assistance in criminal and civil matters through a legal committee (hereinafter "the Legal Committee"), hereby established.

8. The Council's jurisdiction will extend gradually to cover West Bank and Gaza Strip territory, except for the issues to be negotiated in the permanent status negotiations, through a series of redeployments of the Israeli military forces. The first phase of the redeployment of Israeli military forces will cover populated areas in the West Bank – cities, towns, refugee camps and hamlets, as set out in Annex I – and will be completed prior to the eve of the Palestinian elections, i.e. 22 days before the day of the elections. Further redeployments of Israeli military forces to specified military locations will commence immediately upon the inauguration of the Council and will be effected in three phases, each to take place after an interval of six months, to be concluded no later than eighteen months from the date of the inauguration of the Council.

ARTICLE XVIII: Legislative Powers of the Council

1. For the purposes of this Article, legislation shall mean any primary and secondary legislation, including basic laws, laws, regulations and other legislative acts.

2. The Council has the power, within its jurisdiction as defined in Article XVII of this Agreement, to adopt legislation.

3. While the primary legislative power shall lie in the hands of the Council as a whole, the Ra'ees of the Executive Authority of the Council shall have the following legislative powers:

   a. the power to initiate legislation or to present proposed legislation to the Council;

   b. the power to promulgate legislation adopted by the Council; and

   c. the power to issue secondary legislation, including regulations, relating to any matters specified and within the scope laid down in any primary legislation adopted by the Council.

4.   a. Legislation, including legislation which amends or abrogates existing laws or military orders, which exceeds the jurisdiction of the Council or which is otherwise inconsistent with the provisions of the DOP, this Agreement, or of any other agreement that may be reached between the two sides during the interim period, shall have no effect and shall be void ab initio.

   b. The Ra'ees of the Executive Authority of the Council shall not promulgate legislation adopted by the Council if such legislation falls under the provisions of this paragraph.

5. All legislation shall be communicated to the Israeli side of the Legal Committee.

6. Without derogating from the provisions of paragraph 4 above, the Israeli side of the Legal Committee may refer for the attention of the Committee any legislation regarding which Israel considers the provisions of paragraph 4 apply, in order to discuss issues arising from such legislation. The Legal Committee will consider the legislation referred to it at the earliest opportunity.

ARTICLE XIX: Human Rights and the Rule of Law

Israel and the Council shall exercise their powers and responsibilities pursuant to this Agreement with due regard to internationally-accepted norms and principles of human rights and the rule of law.

ARTICLE XX: Rights, Liabilities and Obligations

1.   a. The transfer of powers and responsibilities from the Israeli military government and its civil administration to the Council, as detailed in Annex III, includes all related rights, liabilities and obligations arising with regard to acts or omissions which occurred prior to such transfer. Israel will cease to bear any financial responsibility regarding such acts or omissions and the Council will bear all financial responsibility for these and for its own functioning.

b. Any financial claim made in this regard against Israel will be referred to the Council.

c. Israel shall provide the Council with the information it has regarding pending and anticipated claims brought before any court or tribunal against Israel in this regard.

d. Where legal proceedings are brought in respect of such a claim, Israel will notify the Council and enable it to participate in defending the claim and raise any arguments on its behalf.

e. In the event that an award is made against Israel by any court or tribunal in respect of such a claim, the Council shall immediately reimburse Israel the full amount of the award.

f. Without prejudice to the above, where a court or tribunal hearing such a claim finds that liability rests solely with an employee or agent who acted beyond the scope of the powers assigned to him or her, unlawfully or with willful malfeasance, the Council shall not bear financial responsibility.

2.   a. Notwithstanding the provisions of paragraphs l.d through l.f above, each side may take the necessary measures, including promulgation of legislation, in order to ensure that such claims by Palestinians including pending claims in which the hearing of evidence has not yet begun, are brought only before Palestinian courts or tribunals in the West Bank and the Gaza Strip, and are not brought before or heard by Israeli courts or tribunals.

b. Where a new claim has been brought before a Palestinian court or tribunal subsequent to the dismissal of the claim pursuant to subparagraph a. above, the Council shall defend it and, in accordance with subparagraph l.a above, in the event that an award is made for the plaintiff, shall pay the amount of the award.

c. The Legal Committee shall agree on arrangements for the transfer of all materials and information needed to enable the Palestinian courts or tribunals to hear such claims as referred to in subparagraph b. above, and, when necessary, for the provision of legal assistance by Israel to the Council in defending such claims.

3. The transfer of authority in itself shall not affect rights, liabilities and obligations of any person or legal entity, in existence at the date of signing of this Agreement.

4. The Council, upon its inauguration, will assume all the rights, liabilities and obligations of the Palestinian Authority.

4.   For the purpose of this Agreement, "Israelis" also includes Israeli statutory agencies and corporations registered in Israel.

ARTICLE XXI: Settlement of Differences and Disputes

Any difference relating to the application of this Agreement shall be referred to the appropriate coordination and cooperation mechanism established under this Agreement. The provisions of Article XV of the DOP shall apply to any such difference which is not settled through the appropriate coordination and cooperation mechanism, namely:

1. Disputes arising out of the application or interpretation of this Agreement or any related agreements pertaining to the interim period shall be settled through the Liaison Committee.

2. Disputes which cannot be settled by negotiations may be settled by a mechanism of conciliation to be agreed between the Parties.

4.   The Parties may agree to submit to arbitration disputes relating to the interim period, which cannot be settled through conciliation. To this end, upon the agreement of both Parties, the Parties will establish an Arbitration Committee.

CHAPTER 4 – COOPERATION

ARTICLE XXII: Relations between Israel and the Council

1. Israel and the Council shall seek to foster mutual understanding and tolerance and shall accordingly abstain from incitement, including hostile propaganda, against each other and, without derogating from the principle of freedom of expression, shall take legal measures to prevent such incitement by any organizations, groups or individuals within their jurisdiction.

2. Israel and the Council will ensure that their respective educational systems contribute to the peace between the Israeli and Palestinian peoples and to peace in the entire region, and will refrain from the introduction of any motifs that could adversely affect the process of reconciliation.

3. Without derogating from the other provisions of this Agreement, Israel and the Council shall cooperate in combating criminal activity which may affect both sides, including offenses related to trafficking in illegal drugs and psychotropic substances, smuggling, and offenses against property, including offenses related to vehicles.

ARTICLE XXIII: Cooperation with Regard to Transfer of Powers and Responsibilities

In order to ensure a smooth, peaceful and orderly transfer of powers and responsibilities, the two sides will cooperate with regard to the transfer of security powers and responsibilities in accordance with the provisions of Annex I, and the transfer of civil powers and responsibilities in accordance with the provisions of Annex III.

ARTICLE XXIV: Economic Relations

The economic relations between the two sides are set out in the Protocol on Economic Relations signed in Paris on April 29, 1994, and the Appendices thereto, and the Supplement to the

Protocol on Economic Relations all attached as Annex V, and will be governed by the relevant provisions of this Agreement and its Annexes.

ARTICLE XXV: Cooperation Programs

1. The Parties agree to establish a mechanism to develop programs of cooperation between them. Details of such cooperation are set out in Annex VI.

2. A Standing Cooperation Committee to deal with issues arising in the context of this cooperation is hereby established as provided for in Annex VI.

ARTICLE XXVI: The Joint Israeli–Palestinian Liaison Committee

1. The Liaison Committee established pursuant to Article X of the DOP shall ensure the smooth implementation of this Agreement. It shall deal with issues requiring coordination, other issues of common interest and disputes.

2. The Liaison Committee shall be composed of an equal number of members from each Party. It may add other technicians and experts as necessary.

3. The Liaison Committee shall adopt its rules of procedures, including the frequency and place or places of its meetings.

4. The Liaison Committee shall reach its decisions by agreement.

5. The Liaison Committee shall establish a subcommittee that will monitor and steer the implementation of this Agreement (hereinafter "the Monitoring and Steering Committee"). It will function as follows:

    a. The Monitoring and Steering Committee will, on an ongoing basis, monitor the implementation of this Agreement, with a view to enhancing the cooperation and fostering the peaceful relations between the two sides.

    b. The Monitoring and Steering Committee will steer the activities of the various joint committees established in this Agreement (the JSC, the CAC, the Legal Committee, the Joint Economic Committee and the Standing Cooperation Committee) concerning the ongoing implementation of the Agreement, and will report to the Liaison Committee.

    c. The Monitoring and Steering Committee will be composed of the heads of the various committees mentioned above.

    d. The two heads of the Monitoring and Steering Committee will establish its rules of procedures, including the frequency and places of its meetings.

ARTICLE XXVII: Liaison and Cooperation with Jordan and Egypt

1. Pursuant to Article XII of the DOP, the two Parties have invited the Governments of Jordan and Egypt to participate in establishing further liaison and cooperation arrangements between the Government of Israel and the Palestinian representatives on the one hand, and the

Governments of Jordan and Egypt on the other hand, to promote cooperation between them. As part of these arrangements a Continuing Committee has been constituted and has commenced its deliberations.

2. The Continuing Committee shall decide by agreement on the modalities of admission of persons displaced from the West Bank and the Gaza Strip in 1967, together with necessary measures to prevent disruption and disorder.

3. The Continuing Committee shall also deal with other matters of common concern.

ARTICLE XXVIII: Missing Persons

1. Israel and the Council shall cooperate by providing each other with all necessary assistance in the conduct of searches for missing persons and bodies of persons which have not been recovered, as well as by providing information about missing persons.

2. The PLO undertakes to cooperate with Israel and to assist it in its efforts to locate and to return to Israel Israeli soldiers who are missing in action and the bodies of soldiers which have not been recovered.

CHAPTER 5 – MISCELLANEOUS PROVISIONS

ARTICLE XXIX: Safe Passage between the West Bank and the Gaza Strip

Arrangements for safe passage of persons and transportation between the West Bank and the Gaza Strip are set out in Annex I.

ARTICLE XXX: Passages

Arrangements for coordination between Israel and the Council regarding passage to and from Egypt and Jordan, as well as any other agreed international crossings, are set out in Annex I.

ARTICLE XXXI: Final Clauses

1. This Agreement shall enter into force on the date of its signing.

2. The Gaza–Jericho Agreement, except for Article XX (Confidence-Building Measures), the Preparatory Transfer Agreement and the Further Transfer Protocol will be superseded by this Agreement.

3. The Council, upon its inauguration, shall replace the Palestinian Authority and shall assume all the undertakings and obligations of the Palestinian Authority under the Gaza–Jericho Agreement, the Preparatory Transfer Agreement, and the Further Transfer Protocol.

4. The two sides shall pass all necessary legislation to implement this Agreement.

5. Permanent status negotiations will commence as soon as possible, but not later than May 4, 1996, between the Parties. It is understood that these negotiations shall cover remaining issues, including: Jerusalem, refugees, settlements, security arrangements, borders, relations and cooperation with other neighbors, and other issues of common interest.

6. Nothing in this Agreement shall prejudice or preempt the outcome of the negotiations on the permanent status to be conducted pursuant to the DOP. Neither Party shall be deemed, by virtue of having entered into this Agreement, to have renounced or waived any of its existing rights, claims or positions.

7. Neither side shall initiate or take any step that will change the status of the West Bank and the Gaza Strip pending the outcome of the permanent status negotiations.

8. The two Parties view the West Bank and the Gaza Strip as a single territorial unit, the integrity and status of which will be preserved during the interim period.

9. The PLO undertakes that, within two months of the date of the inauguration of the Council, the Palestinian National Council will convene and formally approve the necessary changes in regard to the Palestinian Covenant, as undertaken in the letters signed by the Chairman of the PLO and addressed to the Prime Minister of Israel, dated September 9, 1993, and May 4, 1994.

10. Pursuant to Annex I, Article IX of this Agreement, Israel confirms that the permanent checkpoints on the roads leading to and from the Jericho Area (except those related to the access road leading from Mousa Alami to the Allenby Bridge) will be removed upon the completion of the first phase of redeployment.

11. Prisoners who, pursuant to the Gaza–Jericho Agreement, were turned over to the Palestinian Authority on the condition that they remain in the Jericho Area for the remainder of their sentence, will be free to return to their homes in the West Bank and the Gaza Strip upon the completion of the first phase of redeployment.

12. As regards relations between Israel and the PLO, and without derogating from the commitments contained in the letters signed by and exchanged between the Prime Minister of Israel and the Chairman of the PLO, dated September 9, 1993, and May 4, 1994, the two sides will apply between them the provisions contained in Article XXII, paragraph 1, with the necessary changes.

13. a. The Preamble to this Agreement, and all Annexes, Appendices and maps attached hereto, shall constitute an integral part hereof.

 b. The Parties agree that the maps attached to the Gaza–Jericho Agreement as:

 a. map No. 1 (The Gaza Strip), an exact copy of which is attached to this Agreement as map No. 2 (in this Agreement "map No. 2");

 b. map No. 4 (Deployment of Palestinian Police in the Gaza Strip), an exact copy of which is attached to this Agreement as map No. 5 (in this Agreement "map No. 5"); and

 c. map No. 6 (Maritime Activity Zones), an exact copy of which is attached to this Agreement as map No. 8 (in this Agreement "map No. 8"; are an integral part hereof and will remain in effect for the duration of this Agreement.

14. While the Jeftlik area will come under the functional and personal jurisdiction of the Council in the first phase of redeployment, the area's transfer to the territorial jurisdiction of the Council will be considered by the Israeli side in the first phase of the further redeployment phases.

Done at Washington DC, this 28th day of September, 1995.

For the Government of
the State of Israel

For the PLO

Witnessed by:

The United States of America

The Russian Federation

The Arab Republic of Egypt

The Hashemite Kingdom of Jordan

The Kingdom of Norway

The European Union

Source: www.mfa.gov.il/MFA/Peace+Process/Guide+to+the+Peace+Process/THE+
ISRAELI-PALESTINIAN+INTERIM+AGREEMENT.htm

For Annexes to the Accord, see the following.

ANNEX I: Protocol Concerning Redeployment and Security Arrangements
www.mfa.gov.il/MFA/Peace+Process/Guide+to+the+Peace+Process/THE+ISRAELI-
PALESTINIAN+INTERIM+AGREEMENT+-+Annex+I.htm

ANNEX II: Protocol Concerning Elections
www.mfa.gov.il/MFA/Peace+Process/Guide+to+the+Peace+Process/THE+ISRAELI-
PALESTINIAN+INTERIM+AGREEMENT+-+Annex+II.htm

ANNEX III: Protocol Concerning Elections
www.mfa.gov.il/MFA/Peace+Process/Guide+to+the+Peace+Process/THE+ISRAELI-
PALESTINIAN+INTERIM+AGREEMENT+-+Annex+III.htm

ANNEX IV: Protocol Concerning Legal Affairs
www.mfa.gov.il/MFA/Peace+Process/Guide+to+the+Peace+Process/THE+ISRAELI-
PALESTINIAN+INTERIM+AGREEMENT+-+Annex+IV.htm

ANNEX V: Protocol on Economic Relations
www.mfa.gov.il/MFA/Peace+Process/Guide+to+the+Peace+Process/THE+ISRAELI-
PALESTINIAN+INTERIM+AGREEMENT+-+Annex+V.htm

ANNEX VI: Protocol Concerning Israeli–Palestinian Cooperation Programs
www.mfa.gov.il/MFA/Peace+Process/Guide+to+the+Peace+Process/THE+ISRAELI-
PALESTINIAN+INTERIM+AGREEMENT+-+Annex+VI.htm

ANNEX VII Release of Palestinian Prisoners and Detainees
www.mfa.gov.il/MFA/Peace+Process/Guide+to+the+Peace+Process/THE+ISRAELI-
PALESTINIAN+INTERIM+AGREEMENT+-+Annex+VII.htm

MAPS:
www.mfa.gov.il/MFA/Peace+Process/Guide+to+the+Peace+Process/Israel-Palestinian+
Interim+Agremeent+Maps.htm

US President Bill Clinton: Proposal on Israeli–Palestinian Peace (The Clinton Parameters)

Meeting with President Clinton
White House, 23 December 2000

Attendance

<u>United States</u>: President Clinton, Secretary Albright, John Podesta, Samuel Berger, Steve Richetti, Bruce Reidel, Dennis Ross, Aaron Miller, Robert Malley, Gamal Hilal

<u>Palestine</u>: Sa'eb Erakat, Mohammad Dahlan, Samih Abed, Ghaith Al-Omari.

<u>Israel</u>: Shlomo Ben-Ami, Gilead Sher, Penny Medan, Shlomo Yanai, Gidi Grinstein

Minutes

<u>President Clinton</u>:

Territory:

Based on what I heard, I believe that the solution should be in the mid-90%'s, between 94–96% of the West Bank territory of the Palestinian State.

The land annexed by Israel should be compensated by a land swap of 1–3% in addition to territorial arrangements such as a permanent safe passage.

The Parties also should consider the swap of leased land to meet their respective needs. There are creative ways of doing this that should address Palestinian and Israeli needs and concerns.

The Parties should develop a map consistent with the following criteria:
* 80% of settlers in blocks.
* Contiguity.

* Minimize annexed areas.
* Minimize the number of Palestinian affected.

Security:

The key lies in an international presence that can only be withdrawn by mutual consent. This presence will also monitor the implementation of the agreement between both sides.

My best judgment is that the Israeli presence would remain in fixed locations in the Jordan Valley under the authority of the International force for another 36 months. This period could be reduced in the event of favorable regional developments that diminish the threats to Israel.

On early warning stations, Israel should maintain three facilities in the West Bank with a Palestinian liaison presence. The stations will be subject to review every 10 years with any changes in the status to be mutually agreed.

Regarding emergency developments, I understand that you will still have to develop a map of the relevant areas and routes. But in defining what is an emergency, I propose the following definition:

Imminent and demonstrable threat to Israel's national security of a military nature that requires the activation of a national state emergency.

Of course, the international forces will need to be notified of any such determination.

On airspace, I suggest that the state of Palestine will have sovereignty over its airspace but that two sides should work out special arrangements for Israeli training and operational needs.

I understand that the Israeli position is that Palestine should be defined as a "demilitarized state" while the Palestinian side proposes "a state with limited arms." As a compromise, I suggest calling it a "non-militarized state."

This will be consistent with the fact that in addition to a strong Palestinian security forces, Palestine will have an international force for border security and deterrent purposes.

Jerusalem and refugees:

I have a sense that the remaining gaps have more to do with formulations than practical realities.

Jerusalem:

The general principle is that Arab areas are Palestinian and Jewish ones are Israeli. This would apply to the Old City as well. I urge the two sides to work on maps to create maximum contiguity for both sides.

Regarding the Haram/Temple Mount, I believe that the gaps are not related to practical administration but to the symbolic issues of sovereignty and to finding a way to accord respect to the religious beliefs of both sides.

I know you have been discussing a number of formulations, and you can agree one of these. I add to these two additional formulations guaranteeing Palestinian effective control over the Haram while respecting the conviction of the Jewish people.

Regarding either one of these two formulations will be international monitoring to provide mutual confidence.

1 – Palestinian sovereignty over the Haram, and Israeli sovereignty over a) the Western Wall and the space sacred to Judaism of which it is a part; b) the Western Wall and the Holy of Holies of which it is a part.
There will be a fine commitment by both not to excavate beneath the Haram or behind the Wall.

2 – Palestinian sovereignty over the Haram and Israeli sovereignty over the Western Wall and shared functional sovereignty over the issue of excavation under the Haram and behind the Wall such that mutual consent would be requested before any excavation can take place.

Refugees:

I sense that the differences are more relating to formulations and less to what will happen on a practical level.

I believe that Israel is prepared to acknowledge the moral and material suffering caused to the Palestinian people as a result of the 1948 war and the need to assist the international community in addressing the problem.

An international commission should be established to implement all the aspects that flow from your agreement: compensation, resettlement, rehabilitation, etc.

The US is prepared to lead an international effort to help the refugees.

The fundamental gap is on how to handle the concept of the right of return. I know the history of the issue and how hard it will be for the Palestinian leadership to appear to be abandoning this principle.

The Israeli side could not accept any reference to a right of return that would imply a right to immigrate to Israel in defiance of Israel's sovereign policies and admission or that would threaten the Jewish character of the state.

Any solution must address both needs.

The solution will have to be consistent with the two-state approach that both sides have accepted as a way to end the Palestinian–Israeli conflict: the state of Palestine as the homeland of the Palestinian people and the state of Israel as the homeland of the Jewish people.

Under the two-state solution, the guiding principle should be that the Palestinian state would be the focal point for Palestinians who choose to return to the area without ruling out that Israel will accept some of these refugees.

I believe that we need to adopt a formulation on the right of return that will make clear that there is no specific right of return to Israel itself but that does not negate the aspiration of the Palestinian people to return to the area.

In light of the above, I propose two alternatives:

1 – Both sides recognize the right of Palestinian refugees to return to historic Palestine, or,

2 – Both sides recognize the right of Palestinian refugees to return to their homeland.

The agreement will define the implementation of this general right in a way that is consistent with the two-state solution. It would list the five possible homes for the refugees:

1 – The state of Palestine.
2 – Areas in Israel being transferred to Palestine in the land swap.
3 – Rehabilitation in host country.
4 – Resettlement in third country.
5 – Admission to Israel.

In listing these options, the agreement will make clear that the return to the West Bank, Gaza Strip, and areas acquired in the land swap would be the right of all Palestinian refugees, while rehabilitation in host countries, resettlement in third countries and absorption into Israel will depend upon the policies of those countries.

Israel could indicate in the agreement that it intends to establish a policy so that some of the refugees would be absorbed into Israel consistent with Israel's sovereign decision.

I believe that priority should be given to the refugee population in Lebanon.

The parties would agree that this implements resolution 194.

The End of Conflict:

I propose that the agreement clearly mark the end of the conflict and its implementation put an end to all claims. This could be implemented through a UN Security Counsel Resolution that notes that Resolutions 242 and 338 have been implemented and through the release of Palestinian prisoners.

Concluding remarks:

I believe that this is the outline of a fair and lasting agreement.

It gives the Palestinian people the ability to determine their future on their own land, a sovereign and viable state recognized by the international community, Al-Quds as its capital, sovereignty over the Haram, and new lives for the refugees.

It gives the people of Israel a genuine end to the conflict, real security, the preservation of sacred religious ties, the incorporation of 80% of the settlers into Israel, and the largest Jewish Jerusalem in history recognized by all as its capital.

This is the best that I can do. Brief your leaders and tell me if they are prepared to come for discussions based on these ideas. If so, I would meet them next week separately. If not, I have taken this as far as I can.

These are my ideas. If they are not accepted, they are not just off the table, they also go with me when I leave office.

> *Note*: After reading the above text to the Israeli and Palestinian delegates in the Roosevelt Room of the White House, President Clinton left the room. His aides went over the text subsequently to ensure that each side had copied the points accurately. No written text was presented. This version is derived from that published in *Haaretz* (English), 1 January 2001, and a slightly more complete version issued by the Jerusalem Media and Communication Center.
> *Source*: www.peacelobby.org/clinton_parameters.htm

A Performance-Based Roadmap to a Permanent Two-State Solution to the Israeli–Palestinian Conflict (The Road Map for Peace), 30 April 2003

The following is a performance-based and goal-driven roadmap, with clear phases, timelines, target dates, and benchmarks aiming at progress through reciprocal steps by the two parties in the political, security, economic, humanitarian, and institution-building fields, under the auspices of the Quartet [the United States, the European Union, the United Nations, and Russia]. The destination is a final and comprehensive settlement of the Israel–Palestinian conflict by 2005, as presented in President Bush's speech of 24 June, and welcomed by the EU, Russia and the UN in the 16 July and 17 September Quartet Ministerial statements.

A two-state solution to the Israeli–Palestinian conflict will only be achieved through an end to violence and terrorism, when the Palestinian people have a leadership acting decisively against terror and willing and able to build a practicing democracy based on tolerance and liberty, and through Israel's readiness to do what is necessary for a democratic Palestinian state to be established, and a clear, unambiguous acceptance by both parties of the goal of a negotiated settlement as described below. The Quartet will assist and facilitate implementation of the plan, starting in Phase I, including direct discussions between the parties as required. The plan establishes a realistic timeline for implementation. However, as a performance-based plan, progress will require and depend upon the good faith efforts of the parties, and their compliance with each of the obligations outlined below. Should the parties perform their obligations rapidly, progress within and through the phases may come sooner than indicated in the plan. Non-compliance with obligations will impede progress.

A settlement, negotiated between the parties, will result in the emergence of an independent, democratic, and viable Palestinian state living side by side in peace and security with Israel and its other neighbors. The settlement will resolve the Israel–Palestinian conflict, and end the occupation that began in 1967, based on the foundations of the Madrid Conference, the principle of land for peace, UNSCRs 242, 338 and 1397, agreements previously reached by the parties, and the initiative of Saudi Crown Prince Abdullah – endorsed by the Beirut Arab League Summit – calling for acceptance of Israel as a neighbor living in peace and security, in the context of a comprehensive settlement. This initiative is a vital element of international efforts to promote a comprehensive peace on all tracks, including the Syrian–Israeli and Lebanese–Israeli tracks.

The Quartet will meet regularly at senior levels to evaluate the parties' performance on implementation of the plan. In each phase, the parties are expected to perform their obligations in parallel, unless otherwise indicated.

Phase I: Ending Terror and Violence, Normalizing Palestinian Life, and Building Palestinian Institutions – Present to May 2003

In Phase I, the Palestinians immediately undertake an unconditional cessation of violence according to the steps outlined below; such action should be accompanied by supportive measures undertaken by Israel. Palestinians and Israelis resume security cooperation based on the Tenet work plan to end violence, terrorism, and incitement through restructured and effective Palestinian security services. Palestinians undertake comprehensive political reform in preparation for statehood, including drafting a Palestinian constitution, and free, fair and open elections upon the basis of those measures. Israel takes all necessary steps to help normalize Palestinian life. Israel withdraws from Palestinian areas occupied from September 28, 2000, and the two sides restore the status quo that existed at that time, as security performance and cooperation progress. Israel also freezes all settlement activity, consistent with the Mitchell report.

At the outset of Phase I:

- Palestinian leadership issues unequivocal statement reiterating Israel's right to exist in peace and security and calling for an immediate and unconditional ceasefire to end armed activity and all acts of violence against Israelis anywhere. All official Palestinian institutions end incitement against Israel.
- Israeli leadership issues unequivocal statement affirming its commitment to the two-state vision of an independent, viable, sovereign Palestinian state living in peace and security alongside Israel, as expressed by President Bush, and calling for an immediate end to violence against Palestinians everywhere. All official Israeli institutions end incitement against Palestinians.

Security

- Palestinians declare an unequivocal end to violence and terrorism and undertake visible efforts on the ground to arrest, disrupt, and restrain individuals and groups conducting and planning violent attacks on Israelis anywhere.
- Rebuilt and refocused Palestinian Authority security apparatus begins sustained, targeted, and effective operations aimed at confronting all those engaged in terror and dismantlement of terrorist capabilities and infrastructure. This includes commencing confiscation of illegal weapons and consolidation of security authority, free of association with terror and corruption.
- GOI takes no actions undermining trust, including deportations, attacks on civilians; confiscation and/or demolition of Palestinian homes and property, as a punitive measure or to facilitate Israeli construction; destruction of Palestinian institutions and infrastructure; and other measures specified in the Tenet work plan.
- Relying on existing mechanisms and on-the-ground resources, Quartet representatives begin informal monitoring and consult with the parties on establishment of a formal monitoring mechanism and its implementation.

- Implementation, as previously agreed, of U.S. rebuilding, training and resumed security cooperation plan in collaboration with outside oversight board (U.S.–Egypt–Jordan). Quartet support for efforts to achieve a lasting, comprehensive cease-fire.
  - All Palestinian security organizations are consolidated into three services reporting to an empowered Interior Minister.
  - Restructured/retrained Palestinian security forces and IDF counterparts progressively resume security cooperation and other undertakings in implementation of the Tenet work plan, including regular senior-level meetings, with the participation of U.S. security officials.
- Arab states cut off public and private funding and all other forms of support for groups supporting and engaging in violence and terror.
- All donors providing budgetary support for the Palestinians channel these funds through the Palestinian Ministry of Finance's Single Treasury Account.
- As comprehensive security performance moves forward, IDF withdraws progressively from areas occupied since September 28, 2000, and the two sides restore the status quo that existed prior to September 28, 2000. Palestinian security forces redeploy to areas vacated by IDF.

Palestinian Institution-Building

- Immediate action on credible process to produce draft constitution for Palestinian statehood. As rapidly as possible, constitutional committee circulates draft Palestinian constitution, based on strong parliamentary democracy and cabinet with empowered prime minister, for public comment/debate. Constitutional committee proposes draft document for submission after elections for approval by appropriate Palestinian institutions.
- Appointment of interim prime minister or cabinet with empowered executive authority/decision-making body.
- GOI fully facilitates travel of Palestinian officials for PLC and Cabinet sessions, internationally supervised security retraining, electoral and other reform activity, and other supportive measures related to the reform efforts.
- Continued appointment of Palestinian ministers empowered to undertake fundamental reform. Completion of further steps to achieve genuine separation of powers, including any necessary Palestinian legal reforms for this purpose.
- Establishment of independent Palestinian election commission. PLC reviews and revises election law.
- Palestinian performance on judicial, administrative, and economic benchmarks, as established by the International Task Force on Palestinian Reform.
- As early as possible, and based upon the above measures and in the context of open debate and transparent candidate selection/electoral campaign based on a free, multi-party process, Palestinians hold free, open, and fair elections.
- GOI facilitates Task Force election assistance, registration of voters, movement of candidates and voting officials. Support for NGOs involved in the election process.
- GOI reopens Palestinian Chamber of Commerce and other closed Palestinian institutions in East Jerusalem based on a commitment that these institutions operate strictly in accordance with prior agreements between the parties.

Humanitarian Response

- Israel takes measures to improve the humanitarian situation. Israel and Palestinians implement in full all recommendations of the Bertini report to improve humanitarian conditions, lifting curfews and easing restrictions on movement of persons and goods, and allowing full, safe, and unfettered access of international and humanitarian personnel.
- AHLC reviews the humanitarian situation and prospects for economic development in the West Bank and Gaza and launches a major donor assistance effort, including to the reform effort.
- GOI and PA continue revenue clearance process and transfer of funds, including arrears, in accordance with agreed, transparent monitoring mechanism.

Civil Society

- Continued donor support, including increased funding through PVOs/NGOs, for people to people programs, private sector development and civil society initiatives.

Settlements

- GOI immediately dismantles settlement outposts erected since March 2001.
- Consistent with the Mitchell Report, GOI freezes all settlement activity (including natural growth of settlements).

Phase II: Transition – June 2003–December 2003

In the second phase, efforts are focused on the option of creating an independent Palestinian state with provisional borders and attributes of sovereignty, based on the new constitution, as a way station to a permanent status settlement. As has been noted, this goal can be achieved when the Palestinian people have a leadership acting decisively against terror, willing and able to build a practicing democracy based on tolerance and liberty. With such a leadership, reformed civil institutions and security structures, the Palestinians will have the active support of the Quartet and the broader international community in establishing an independent, viable state.

Progress into Phase II will be based upon the consensus judgment of the Quartet of whether conditions are appropriate to proceed, taking into account performance of both parties. Furthering and sustaining efforts to normalize Palestinian lives and build Palestinian institutions, Phase II starts after Palestinian elections and ends with possible creation of an independent Palestinian state with provisional borders in 2003. Its primary goals are continued comprehensive security performance and effective security cooperation, continued normalization of Palestinian life and institution-building, further building on and sustaining of the goals outlined in Phase I, ratification of a democratic Palestinian constitution, formal establishment of office of prime minister, consolidation of political reform, and the creation of a Palestinian state with provisional borders.

- **International Conference**: Convened by the Quartet, in consultation with the parties, immediately after the successful conclusion of Palestinian elections, to support

Palestinian economic recovery and launch a process, leading to establishment of an independent Palestinian state with provisional borders.

- Such a meeting would be inclusive, based on the goal of a comprehensive Middle East peace (including between Israel and Syria, and Israel and Lebanon), and based on the principles described in the preamble to this document.
- Arab states restore pre-intifada links to Israel (trade offices, etc.).
- Revival of multilateral engagement on issues including regional water resources, environment, economic development, refugees, and arms control issues.
- New constitution for democratic, independent Palestinian state is finalized and approved by appropriate Palestinian institutions. Further elections, if required, should follow approval of the new constitution.
- Empowered reform cabinet with office of prime minister formally established, consistent with draft constitution.
- Continued comprehensive security performance, including effective security cooperation on the bases laid out in Phase I.
- Creation of an independent Palestinian state with provisional borders through a process of Israeli–Palestinian engagement, launched by the international conference. As part of this process, implementation of prior agreements, to enhance maximum territorial contiguity, including further action on settlements in conjunction with establishment of a Palestinian state with provisional borders.
- Enhanced international role in monitoring transition, with the active, sustained, and operational support of the Quartet.
- Quartet members promote international recognition of Palestinian state, including possible UN membership.

Phase III: Permanent Status Agreement and End of the Israeli–Palestinian Conflict – 2004–2005

Progress into Phase III, based on consensus judgment of Quartet, and taking into account actions of both parties and Quartet monitoring. Phase III objectives are consolidation of reform and stabilization of Palestinian institutions, sustained, effective Palestinian security performance, and Israeli–Palestinian negotiations aimed at a permanent status agreement in 2005.

- **Second International Conference**: Convened by Quartet, in consultation with the parties, at beginning of 2004 to endorse agreement reached on an independent Palestinian state with provisional borders and formally to launch a process with the active, sustained, and operational support of the Quartet, leading to a final, permanent status resolution in 2005, including on borders, Jerusalem, refugees, settlements; and, to support progress toward a comprehensive Middle East settlement between Israel and Lebanon and Israel and Syria, to be achieved as soon as possible.
- Continued comprehensive, effective progress on the reform agenda laid out by the Task Force in preparation for final status agreement.
- Continued sustained and effective security performance, and sustained, effective security cooperation on the bases laid out in Phase I.
- International efforts to facilitate reform and stabilize Palestinian institutions and the Palestinian economy, in preparation for final status agreement.

- Parties reach final and comprehensive permanent status agreement that ends the Israel–Palestinian conflict in 2005, through a settlement negotiated between the parties based on UNSCR 242, 338, and 1397, that ends the occupation that began in 1967, and includes an agreed, just, fair, and realistic solution to the refugee issue, and a negotiated resolution on the status of Jerusalem that takes into account the political and religious concerns of both sides, and protects the religious interests of Jews, Christians, and Muslims worldwide, and fulfills the vision of two states, Israel and sovereign, independent, democratic and viable Palestine, living side-by-side in peace and security.
- Arab state acceptance of full normal relations with Israel and security for all the states of the region in the context of a comprehensive Arab–Israeli peace.

Source: www.mfa.gov.il/MFA/Peace+Process/Guide+to+the+Peace+Process/
A+Performance-Based+Roadmap+to+a+Permanent+Two-Sta.htm

Statement by the Middle East Quartet (Quartet Principles), 30 January 2006

The following statement was issued today by the Middle East Quartet (United Nations, European Union, Russian Federation, United States):

Representatives of the Quartet – United Nations Secretary-General Kofi Annan, Russian Foreign Minister Sergei Lavrov, Austrian Foreign Minister Ursula Plassnik, United States Secretary of State Condoleezza Rice, High Representative for European Common Foreign and Security Policy Javier Solana, and European Commissioner for External Relations Benita Ferrero-Waldner – met today in London to discuss the situation in the Middle East.

The Quartet congratulated the Palestinian people on an electoral process that was free, fair and secure. The Quartet believes that the Palestinian people have the right to expect that a new Government will address their aspirations for peace and Statehood, and it welcomed President Abbas' affirmation that the Palestinian Authority is committed to the Road Map, previous agreements and obligations between the parties, and a negotiated two-State solution to the Israeli–Palestinian conflict. It is the view of the Quartet that all members of a future Palestinian Government must be committed to non-violence, recognition of Israel, and acceptance of previous agreements and obligations, including the Road Map. We urge both parties to respect their existing agreements, including on movement and access.

The Quartet received updates from Quartet Special Envoy James Wolfensohn and United States Security Coordinator Lieutenant General Keith Dayton at today's meeting. We also had the good fortune of hearing from former President Carter, who helped supervise elections a few days ago. The Quartet called on the Palestinian Authority to ensure law and order, prevent terrorist attacks and dismantle the infrastructure of terror. The Quartet acknowledged the positive role of the Palestinian Authority security forces in helping maintain order during the recent elections. It expressed its view that progress on further consolidation, accountability and reform remains an important task.

Mindful of the needs of the Palestinian people, the Quartet discussed the issue of assistance to the Palestinian Authority. First, the Quartet expressed its concern over the fiscal situation of the Palestinian Authority, and urged measures to facilitate the work of the caretaker Government to stabilize public finances, taking into consideration established fiscal accountability and reform benchmarks. Second, the Quartet concluded that it was inevitable that future assistance to any new Government would be reviewed by donors against that Government's commitment to the principles of non-violence, recognition of Israel, and acceptance of previous agreements and obligations, including the Road Map. The Quartet calls upon the newly elected Palestinian Legislative Council (PLC) to support the formation of a Government committed to these principles, as well as the rule of law, tolerance, reform and sound fiscal management.

Both parties are reminded of their obligations under the Road Map to avoid unilateral actions which prejudice final status issues. The Quartet reiterated its view that settlement expansion must stop, reiterated its concern regarding the route of the barrier, and noted Acting Prime Minister Olmert's recent statements that Israel will continue the process of removing unauthorized outposts.

The Quartet expressed its concern for the health of Prime Minister Sharon and its hope for his rapid recovery.

Finally, the Quartet reiterated its commitment to the principles outlined in the Road Map and previous statements, and reaffirmed its commitment to a just, comprehensive and lasting settlement to the Arab–Israeli conflict, based upon United Nations Security Council resolutions 242 and 338. The Quartet will remain seized of the matter and will engage key regional actors.

Source: http://unispal.un.org/UNISPAL.NSF/0/354568CCE5E38E5585257106007A0834

Fatah and Hamas Reconciliation Agreement, 4 May 2011

Under the auspices of Egypt, delegations from the Fatah and Hamas movements met in Cairo on April 27, 2011, to discuss the issues concerning ending the political division and the achievement of national unity. On top of the issues were some reservations related to the Palestinian National Unity Accord made in 2009.

Both political parties mutually agreed that the basis of understanding made during the meeting are committing to both parties in the implementation of the Palestinian National Reconciliation Agreement. The basis of understanding agreed upon by Fatah and Hamas are as follows:

1. Elections

A. Election Committee:
Both Fatah and Hamas agree to identify the names of the members of the Central Election Commission in agreement with the Palestinian factions. This list will then be submitted to the Palestinian President who will issue a decree of the reformation of the committee.

B. Electoral Court:
Both Fatah and Hamas agree on the nomination of no more than twelve judges to be members of the Electoral Court. This list will then be submitted to the Palestinian President in order to take the necessary legal actions to form the Electoral Court in agreement with the Palestinian factions.

C. Timing of Elections:
The Legislative, Presidential, and the Palestinian National Council elections will be conducted at the same time exactly one year after the signing of the Palestinian National Reconciliation Agreement.

2. Palestine Liberation Organization
The political parties of both Fatah and Hamas agree that the tasks and decisions of the provisional interim leadership cannot be hindered or obstructed, but in a manner that is not conflicting with the authorities of the Executive Committee of the Palestine Liberation Organization.

3. Security
It was emphasized that the formation of the Higher Security Committee which will be formed by a decree of the Palestinian President and will consist of professional officers in consensus.

4. Government
A. Formation of the Government:

Both Fatah and Hamas agree to form a Palestinian government and to appoint the Prime Minister and Ministers in consensus between them.

B. Functions of the Government:
1. Preparation of necessary condition for the conduction of Presidential, Legislative and the Palestinian National Council elections.

2. Supervising and addressing the prevalent issues regarding the internal Palestinian reconciliation resulting from the state of division.

3. Follow-up of the reconstruction operations in the Gaza Strip and the efforts to end the siege and blockade that is imposed on it.

4. Continuation of the implementation of the provisions of the Palestinian National Accord.

5. To resolve the civil and administrative problems that resulted from the division.

6. Unification of the Palestinian National Authority institutions in the West Bank, Gaza Strip and Jerusalem.

7. To fix the status of the associations, Non-Governmental Organizations and charities.

5. Legislative Council:

Both Fatah and Hamas agree to reactivate the Palestinian Legislative Council in accordance to the Basic Law.

Source: www.jmcc.org/Documentsandmaps.aspx?id=828

Selected maps

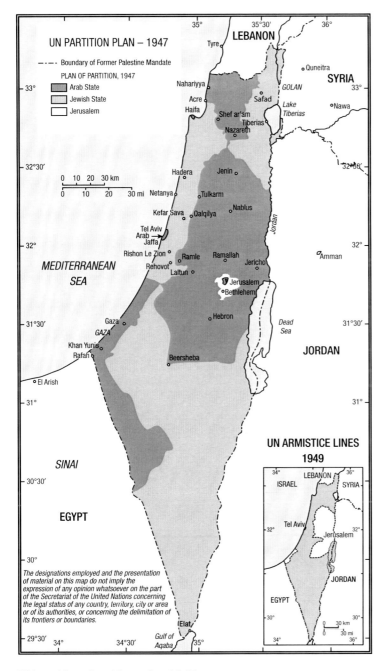

UN PARTITION PLAN – 1947

– – – Boundary of Former Palestine Mandate

PLAN OF PARTITION, 1947

- Arab State
- Jewish State
- Jerusalem

LEBANON

Tyre

Quneitra

SYRIA

GOLAN

Nahariyya

Acre

Safad

Haifa

Lake Tiberias

Nawa

Shef ar'am

Tiberias

Nazareth

33°

Hadera

Jenin

0 10 20 30 km

0 10 20 30 mi

Netanya

Tulkarm

Nablus

Kefar Sava

Qalqilya

Tel Aviv

Arab →

Jaffa

Jordan

Rishon Le Zion

Ramle

Ramallah

Jericho

Amman

Rehovot

Laltun

Jerusalem

Bethlehem

MEDITERRANEAN SEA

Hebron

Dead Sea

JORDAN

Gaza

GAZA

Khan Yunis

Rafah

Beersheba

El Arish

SINAI

EGYPT

The designations employed and the presentation of material on this map do not imply the expression of any opinion whatsoever on the part of the Secretariat of the United Nations concerning the legal status of any country, territory, city or area or of its authorities, or concerning the delimitation of its frontiers or boundaries.

Elat

Gulf of Aqaba

UN ARMISTICE LINES 1949

LEBANON

ISRAEL

SYRIA

Tel Aviv

Jerusalem

JORDAN

EGYPT

0 30 km

0 30 mi

UN partition plan, November 1947

455

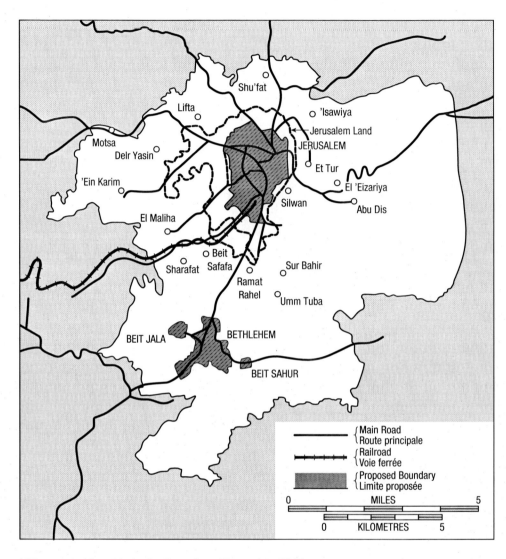

UN proposed boundaries for Jerusalem, November 1947

456

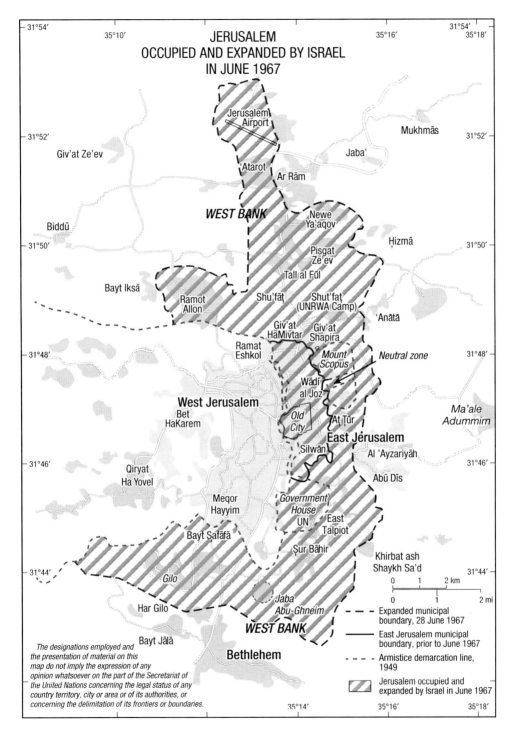

Boundaries of Jerusalem, post 1967

457

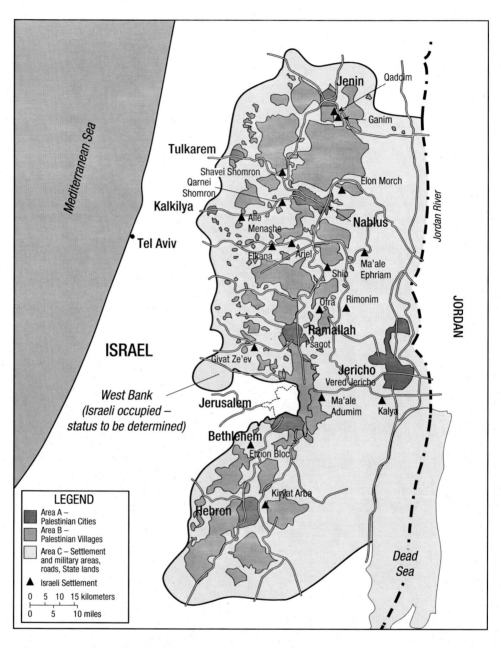

Oslo II Accord, phased deployment (Areas A, B, and C)

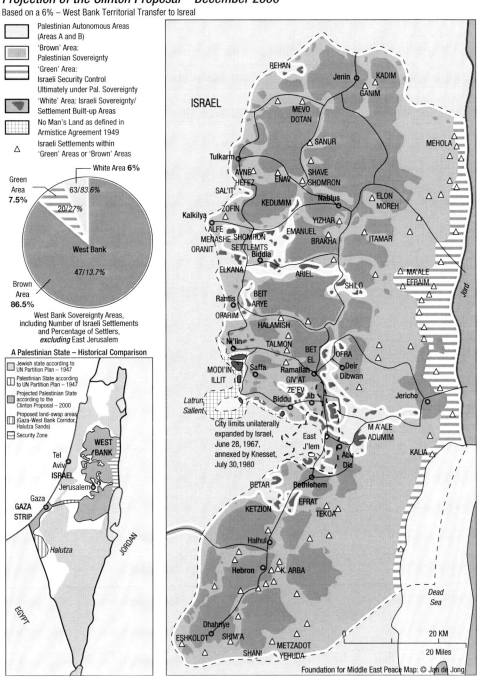

Projection of the Clinton Proposal – December 2000
Based on a 6% – West Bank Territorial Transfer to Isreal

Palestinian Autonomous Areas
(Areas A and B)

'Brown' Area:
Palestinian Sovereignty

'Green' Area:
Israeli Security Control
Ultimately under Pal. Sovereignty

'White' Area: Israeli Sovereignty/
Settlement Built-up Areas

No Man's Land as defined in
Armistice Agreement 1949

△ Israeli Settlements within
'Green' Areas or 'Brown' Areas

White Area **6%**

Green
Area
7.5%

63/83.6%

20/27%

West Bank

47/13.7%

Brown
Area
86.5%

West Bank Sovereignty Areas,
including Number of Israeli Settlements
and Percentage of Settlers,
excluding East Jerusalem

A Palestinian State – Historical Comparison

Jewish state according to
UN Partition Plan – 1947

Palestinian State according
to UN Partition Plan – 1947

Projected Palestinian State
according to the
Clinton Proposal – 2000

Proposed land-swap areas
(Gaza-West Bank Corridor,
Halutza Sands)

Security Zone

ISRAEL

City limits unilaterally
expanded by Israel,
June 28, 1967,
annexed by Knesset,
July 30,1980

Foundation for Middle East Peace Map: © Jan de Jong

Projection of the Clinton Parameters, December 2000

459

Final Status Map Presented by Israel – Taba, January 2001
Based on a 5% – West Bank Territorial Transfer to Isreal

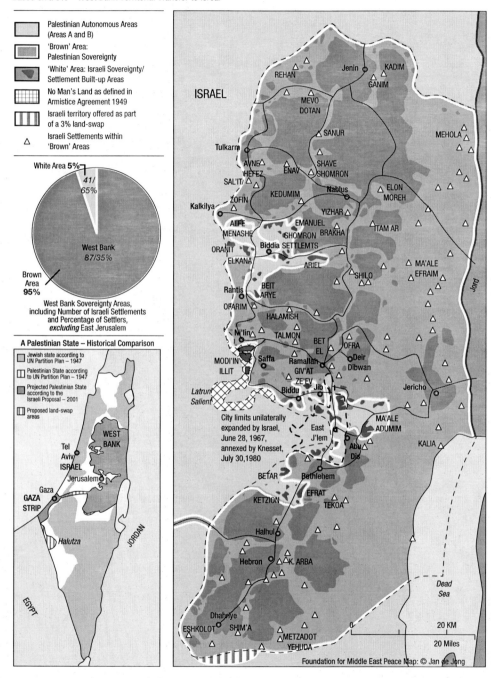

Legend:

- Palestinian Autonomous Areas (Areas A and B)
- 'Brown' Area: Palestinian Sovereignty
- 'White' Area: Israeli Sovereignty/ Settlement Built-up Areas
- No Man's Land as defined in Armistice Agreement 1949
- Israeli territory offered as part of a 3% land-swap
- △ Israeli Settlements within 'Brown' Areas

White Area **5%**
41/ 65%

West Bank
87/35%

Brown Area **95%**

West Bank Sovereignty Areas, including Number of Israeli Settlements and Percentage of Settlers, *excluding* East Jerusalem

A Palestinian State – Historical Comparison

- Jewish state according to UN Partition Plan – 1947
- Palestinian State according to UN Partition Plan – 1947
- Projected Palestinian State according to the Israeli Proposal – 2001
- Proposed land-swap areas

City limits unilaterally expanded by Israel, June 28, 1967, annexed by Knesset, July 30,1980

Foundation for Middle East Peace Map: © Jan de Jong

Final-status map presented by Israel at the Taba talks, January 2001

460

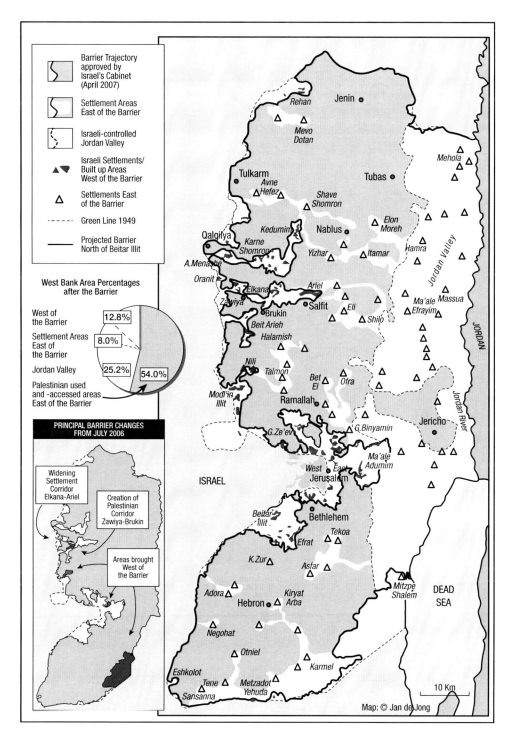

West Bank separation barrier, April 2007

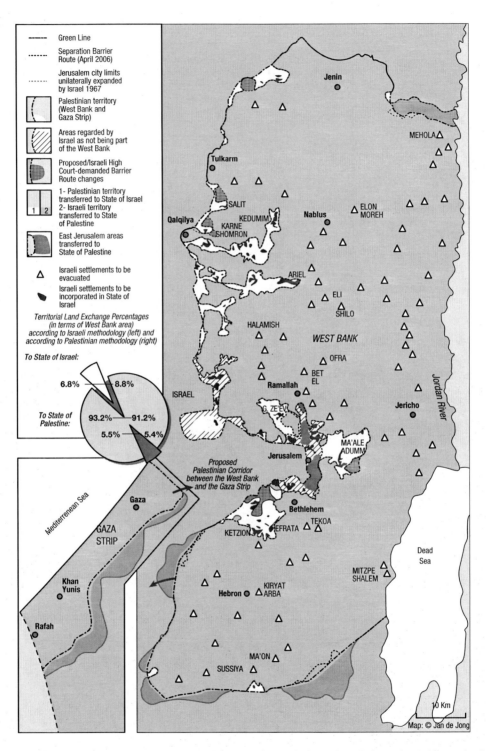

Legend:

- Green Line
- Separation Barrier Route (April 2006)
- Jerusalem city limits unilaterally expanded by Israel 1967
- Palestinian territory (West Bank and Gaza Strip)
- Areas regarded by Israel as not being part of the West Bank
- Proposed/Israeli High Court-demanded Barrier Route changes
- 1- Palestinian territory transferred to State of Israel
  2- Israeli territory transferred to State of Palestine
- East Jerusalem areas transferred to State of Palestine
- △ Israeli settlements to be evacuated
- Israeli settlements to be incorporated in State of Israel

Territorial Land Exchange Percentages (in terms of West Bank area) according to Israeli methodology (left) and according to Palestinian methodology (right)

To State of Israel:

6.8% — 8.8%

To State of Palestine:

93.2% — 91.2%

5.5% — 5.4%

Jenin

MEHOLA △

Tulkarm

SALIT

Qalqilya

KEDUMIM

KARNE SHOMRON

Nablus

ELON MOREH

ARIEL

ELI

SHILO

HALAMISH

WEST BANK

OFRA

Ramallah

BET EL

ISRAEL

G. ZE'EV

Jericho

MA'ALE ADUMM

Jerusalem

Proposed Palestinian Corridor between the West Bank and the Gaza Strip

Mediterranean Sea

Gaza

GAZA STRIP

Bethlehem

TEKOA

EFRATA

KETZION

Dead Sea

Khan Yunis

MITZPE SHALEM

Hebron

KIRYAT ARBA

Rafah

MA'ON

SUSSIYA

Jordan River

10 Km

Map: © Jan de Jong

Projection of Prime Minister Olmert's final-status map of Israel and the Palestinian territories, October 2008

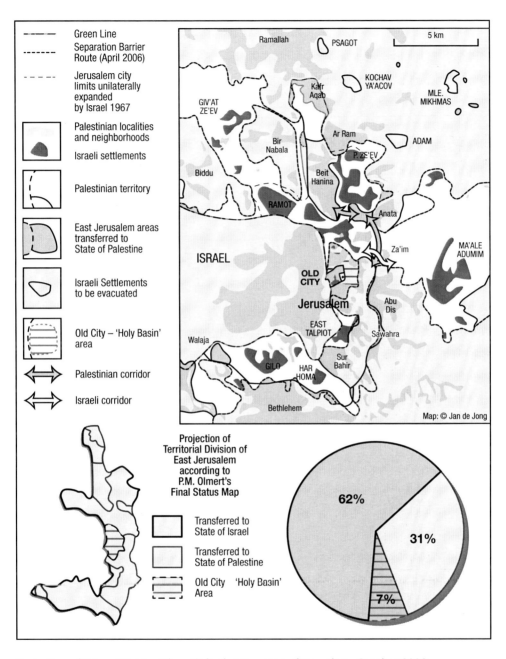

Legend

- Green Line
- Separation Barrier Route (April 2006)
- Jerusalem city limits unilaterally expanded by Israel 1967
- Palestinian localities and neighborhoods
- Israeli settlements
- Palestinian territory
- East Jerusalem areas transferred to State of Palestine
- Israeli Settlements to be evacuated
- Old City – 'Holy Basin' area
- Palestinian corridor
- Israeli corridor

Ramallah   PSAGOT   5 km

Kafr Aqab   KOCHAV YA'ACOV   MLE. MIKHMAS

GIV'AT ZE'EV

Bir Nabala   Ar Ram   ADAM

Biddu   P. ZE'EV   Beit Hanina

RAMOT   Anata

ISRAEL   Za'im   MA'ALE ADUMIM

OLD CITY

Jerusalem   Abu Dis

EAST TALPIOT   Sawahra

Walaja

GILO   Sur Bahir

HAR HOMA

Bethlehem   Map: © Jan de Jong

Projection of Territorial Division of East Jerusalem according to P.M. Olmert's Final Status Map

- Transferred to State of Israel
- Transferred to State of Palestine
- Old City 'Holy Basin' Area

62%

31%

7%

Projection of Prime Minister Olmert's final-status map of Jerusalem, October 2008

463

Index

Note: *Italic* page numbers indicate tables; **bold** indicate figures.